The Making
of Jazz

The Making
of Jazz

A Comprehensive History

JAMES LINCOLN COLLIER

Delta

A DELTA BOOK

Published by
Dell Publishing
a division of
Bantam Doubleday Publishing Group, Inc.
666 Fifth Avenue
New York, New York 10103

ISBN: 0-385-28668-6

Printed in the United States of America

Reprinted by arrangement with Houghton Mifflin Company

August 1979
10 9 8
BG

For my brother

Preface

I have in this book, referred to jazz as an art. Some people will object, and possibly they are correct. Perhaps jazz is not sufficiently universal or informing to warrant the term. It seems to me, however, that it is not a question worth much argument. Art or not, jazz has captured the attention of millions of people across the face of the world. For many of these people, both musicians and listeners, it is a central fact of their existences, one of the main ingredients of their emotional lives. The jazz enthusiast will travel hundreds of miles to spend three hours listening to a favorite performer. He will spend large amounts of money in support of his interest, and he will devote half his spare time, often to the despair of his family, to his music. It is a music, furthermore, that is now attracting its fourth generation of players, young men and women who hope to spend their lives working in it. And it seems to me that any medium that has inspired so much love over so much of the world for so many generations is worth writing about seriously.

A book like this cannot, of course, be the work of one man alone. In a sense I am only the architect. The bricks were made by hundreds of dedicated jazz scholars and record collectors who over the past fifty years or so have devoted countless thousands of hours to rescuing important records from junk piles, sorting out what at times must have seemed a hopeless tangle of personnels, and tracking down details of the lives of several thousand jazz musicians, many of whom lived and died in the obscurity of the Delta country or the big city ghettos. Without their work this book would have been impossible. My own contribution has been merely to pull into what I hope is comprehensible form the vast body of information on jazz and its players that these people have created.

Unfortunately, that work is as yet unfinished. There are great gaps in the record. We have only the sketchiest details on the lives of such major figures as Lester Young, Coleman Hawkins, Ornette Coleman, and James P. Johnson, and about a good many other important players we know almost nothing. The gaps are being closed: in the past few years we have seen first-rate biographies of Bix Beiderbecke, Charlie Parker, Bessie Smith, and three or four others, but there is still a vast way to go. Unhappily, the majority of the books listed in my bibliography, all of which I have recently read in their entirety, are rife with errors, and many are simply useless as source material. As a consequence, too often I have had to work by inference or from educated guess, and it is to be hoped that future scholars will be able to improve the record.

Because this book is intended for students and the lay public, I have not burdened it with citations of my sources. I have tried, however, to credit major sources in the body of the text, and the reader will easily be able to determine which ones I have found most useful. Where other sources have been lacking, I have depended on Leonard Feather's *The New Encyclopedia of Jazz* and John Chilton's *Who's Who of Jazz* for biographical data. I have also relied on Brian Rust's monumental *Jazz Records 1897–1942* for discographic data.

But, inevitably, my main sources have been the records themselves. I have listened intensively, usually in more or less chronological order, to the central corpus of recorded jazz. I have by no means listened to all jazz records. That would have been impossible for a single man to do. I have, however, listened to the bulk of the recordings of all the major figures in the music, representative samplings from the work of lesser figures, and a great deal of peripheral material that I thought might shed light on various currents in the music. I have, for example, made it a rule to listen to any record I could find made before 1925 that could remotely be described as jazz. I have also found it instructive to study the early ragtime records, some of which date back nearly to the turn of the century. It has been an interesting experience. Many of the judgments I made many years ago as a young jazz fan have been confirmed; many others have been overturned. Time and time again I have heard things I had never noticed on records I may have listened to a hundred times before. In the some three years I have been engaged on this project I have never been bored. My appreciation for this marvelous music has only deepened, and I hope I can bring some of that feeling to the reader.

Even in a book of this size I have not been able to cover in any detail all of the interesting players in jazz. I have concentrated on the major figures and the broad movements, and I would like to apologize in advance to the many fine jazz players and their admirers whom I have treated only cursorily or not at all. I would like also to thank, for their many helpful suggestions, emendations, and corrections, the following jazz scholars, record collectors, and musicians, who read portions of the manuscript: Edward Bonoff, Geoffrey L. Collier, William B. Dunham, Robert S. Greene, William Kroll, Arthur Lohman, Lee Lorenz, Robert Andrew Parker, and William A. Robbins. For help in gathering material about jazz in Europe I am indebted to John Chilton, Maurice Cullaz, Charles Delaunay, Lemnart Forss, Pierre Lafargue, Carlo Loffredo, and Malcolm Macdonald, who gave generously of their time. I would especially like to thank John L. Fell, of San Francisco State University, who read the manuscript in its entirety and offered many valuable suggestions on matters of interpretation and criticism. I am grateful for his generous gift of time at a moment when he was finishing a manuscript of his own. Judgments made on players and styles are, of course, my responsibility.

Contents

IV / The Modern Age

Illustrations

PART I

The Precursors

The African Roots

In a time when technology has made it possible for mankind to move information around the world as easily as wind blows leaves down a lawn, and to move himself with almost the same ease, it is hardly surprising to see the ideas and artifacts of one culture appear in other, quite disparate, cultures across the earth. China lives under an ideology formulated in Germany; Islam comes to Chicago from the East via the tribal states of West Africa; the ideas of a Chinese political leader become dogma for millions of young Europeans. But few of these cultural transferences have been quite as astonishing as the worldwide spread, in some sixty or seventy years, of that unique musical form which we call jazz. At the time of World War I it was a folk music indigenous to New Orleans and its environs, played by at most a few hundred musicians, with an audience of perhaps fifty thousand people, most of them the poor black working people of the Delta country. By 1920 it was widely known and badly imitated throughout the United States. Ten years later it had developed not only an audience but players in most of the major cities of Europe. By 1940 it was known throughout the world, and by 1960 it was accepted as an important musical form, perhaps even an art, everywhere in the world.

I do not want to suggest that jazz is, or ever has been, a "popular" music, not even in the United States. To be sure, from time to time variant forms of jazz emerge as popular music. This was the case with the "jazzy" music of the 1920s, the "swing" of 1935–1945, the rhythm and blues of today. But true jazz — what the musicians themselves recognize as their music — rarely achieves more than a modest popularity. Some of the greatest of all jazz musicians are unknown to the general public. How many Americans could identify Joe Oliver, Lester Young, Bud Powell, or Cecil Taylor, all of whom played major roles in shaping the music? A jazz record that sells fifty thousand copies, as opposed to the hundreds of thousands an ordinary popular hit will sell, has done exceedingly well.

Yet if jazz is not really a popular music, it has demonstrated a staying power that popular music lacks. Except for forays into nostalgia, nobody today buys the records of Art Hickman, Ted Lewis, Kay Kyser, all well-known band leaders in their time; and the records of popular music luminaries like Paul Whiteman and Tommy Dorsey stay in print principally for the presence on them of jazz musicians whom the public hardly knew at the time the records were made. But where Whiteman and the rest have faded, jazz musicians like Oliver and Johnny Dodds and Jelly Roll Morton, whose fame during their lifetime was limited to the black ghettos, today not only have worldwide audiences but are the subject of scholarly investigations into the minutiae of their lives and their work.

Furthermore, jazz continues to shape all the music around it. Rock, funk, soul, show music, movie music, television music, and a good deal of modern concert music are filled with elements drawn from jazz. Indeed, it is almost fair to say that jazz is the foundation on which modern popular music has been built. There is, clearly, something terribly compelling about this remarkable music to the human being in the twentieth century.

To discover what that is has never been easy. Jazz likes to consider itself a mystery. When Louis Armstrong was asked what the music was, he is reported to have responded, "If you gotta ask, you'll never know." Fats Waller, in a similar circumstance, is supposed to have replied, "If you don't know, don't mess with it." These stories may be apocryphal, but they reflect an attitude universal to jazz musicians, critics, and listeners: at the heart of the music lies some inexplicable something that can be felt but not explained. Especially the peculiar rhythmic pulse of jazz, which is usually termed "swing," has been assumed to be beyond explication.

But jazz, like any music, is a physical artifact and as such is susceptible to measurement. The truth is that the professional jazz musician has a much clearer idea of what he is doing and why than he is often willing or able to say. It is too much to state that jazz musicians are by nature inarticulate; some are capable analyzers of their art. But the fact is that the caricature of the mumbling jazz player speaking solely in the argot of his trade has more than a little truth in it. The ordinary jazz musician often finds it difficult to make clear even to a knowledgeable layman what he is doing; many are made embarrassed and restless by the questions. As a consequence they tend to fall back on the mindless clichés about "swinging" and "cooking" and "high energy" and "telling your story."

Compounding the difficulty we have had in understanding quite how new and indeed remarkable is jazz is the fact that many of its best analyzers have been raised in the European musical tradition. Some, of course, have informed themselves about African music, but it is inevitable that a Westerner, steeped in notions of chords, keys, and time signatures, will hear as European music things that, although they sound a good deal like the music of Bach and Jerome Kern, are driven by quite different conceptions. We must understand that jazz is a thing of itself. It cannot be analyzed with the tools of Western musical theory any more than poetry can be grasped by the rules of prose. For example, in European music a standard timbre is aimed for — that is, there is an ideal trumpet or violin sound that the player, within narrow limits, aims for. In jazz, timbre is highly personal and varies not only from player to player but from moment to moment in a given passage for expressive purposes, just as European players swell or diminish a note to add feeling. In European music, each note has a fixed pitch (some slight variation is permitted the leading tone) that can be measured by a machine. In jazz, pitch is flexible to a considerable degree, and in fact in some types of jazz certain notes are invariably and deliberately played "out of tune" by European standards. European music, at least in its standard form, is built on the distinction between major and minor modes. The blues, a major building block in jazz, is neither major nor minor; it exists in a different mode altogether. In European music the ground beat is implicit in the melody itself; you can easily "tap your foot to the beat." In jazz the ground beat is deliberately avoided in the melody and must be established by some sort of separate rhythm section. Obviously, jazz operates on principles of its own; it simply cannot be understood from a European vantage point.

I think I can make my meaning clearer by describing the first four bars of a famous solo by the New Orleans jazz pioneer Joseph "King" Oliver. The solo is on "Dippermouth Blues." Over these opening four bars Oliver plays only six notes, and if these were forced into European notation they would make up a banal and inconsequential scrap of melody. There must be more to it than that, however, for the solo was vastly admired and widely copied by jazz musicians of the time, and it is still played today by musicians whose fathers were not born when Oliver recorded it. What is important — crucially important, in fact — is how Oliver inflects the notes.

In the first place, the two most important of the notes are blue notes, having nothing to do whatever with our standard diatonic do-re-mi scale. Nor are their pitches fixed; they shift as they are played. Second, the timbre — the actual sound of the notes — also changes throughout their course, through Oliver's use of mutes and the production of throat tones. Third, the notes themselves do not begin or end on beats, or even in between beats as is the practice in European syncopation, but are dislocated from the time scheme, as if the beat were irrelevant. And as if this were not sufficient complexity, the solo is being fashioned against a complicated syncopated figure that would be quite enough to throw off many trained musicians. It is some indication of both Oliver's skill and what a jazz player is concerned with as he is improvising that he keeps his place exactly despite the difficult syncopation and his own placement of the melody outside the time frame of the ground beat. You can learn to pat your head and rub your stomach at the same time, but try doing so to different tempos, especially when somebody is beating a drum at yet a third tempo.

What we have to understand is that the specific notes Oliver plays are only a canvas on which he paints his picture. The important matters are the shifting timbre, the playing with pitch, and most particularly the disjunction between ground beat and melody. In European music the notes — in this case blue D's and B♭'s — would be the heart of the matter, and any changes of dynamics, simple coloration. But for Oliver, the notes are merely pegs on which to hang his jazz. This distinction is absolutely central. To the jazz players the most important matter is not *which* notes or chords are played, but *how* they are played. Perfectly marvelous jazz can be made on one or two notes, which is not the case in European music. As the old song goes, "It ain't what you do, it's the way that you do it."

The differences between jazz and European music that I have been talking about are technical, but there is a social difference, too, which is harder to pin down. Most jazz musicians like to work in front of a live audience, especially a dancing audience. They get something back from an audience that is reacting, that is involved with them in the music.

This social element comes into jazz through its African heritage. But despite its African elements, however fashionable it may be to say so, jazz is not an African music. Too much of it descends from European music to justify that claim. Its instrumentation, basic principles of harmony, and formal structures are derived from Europe rather than Africa. As a matter of fact, many of the most important jazz pioneers were not members of the black subculture but were the half-caste black Creoles who came from a subculture that was more European than black. African tribesmen who have not been previously exposed to the music find it as incomprehensible as jazz musicians find African music at first listening. Jazz is a true fusion, combining principles and elements drawn from both European and African music. Just as green is something of itself, not merely a variation of the yellow or blue of which it is compounded, so is jazz neither a variety of European nor African music; it is sui generis. Most especially, the rhythmic pulse of jazz, as we shall see in more detail, is not some modification of African or European time schemes but something quite different from, and a good deal less rigid than, either.

But if jazz is not African music, it is nonetheless mainly the creation of American blacks — at first those of the plantations, turpentine camps, and riverboats who made the roux, and then the blacks of the big city ghettos — first New Orleans, then New York, St. Louis, Chicago, Memphis, Detroit, and others, who completed the sauce. It will not do to write off the white jazz players as mere imitators of black music. White musicians were playing jazz almost from the beginning and made important contributions to the music as it developed. But the principal makers of jazz were black. And for the black, the beginning was Africa.

Africa is a continent four times the size of the United States, containing a wide diversity of environments and cultures. But despite this diversity, there are certain common characteristics that underlie most African cultures. One of these is a social intensity, often found in tribal societies, which most of us in our Western, or Europe-based, culture find difficult to grasp. Much of our lives, especially in America where individual freedom has been so emphasized, is built around ourselves. We find the essence of ourselves in our "private" lives. The African, on the other hand, is much less likely to distinguish his private life from his public one. A lot of activities, such as birth, death, marriage, even sex, which we see as "private" or "family" matters, are for the African more a concern of the entire group. The birth, the puberty rite, the wedding, are celebrated by the community as a whole. John Storm Roberts, in his book *Black Music of Two Worlds,* says:

> The Malwaian Dunduza Chisiza, writing on the question of an "African personality" in the *Journal of Modern African Studies* in 1963, contended that there are common features found in most African communities. He noted that Africans are not inclined to meditativeness like Eastern peoples, nor "inquisitive searchers" like Europeans, but primarily "penetrating observers," relying more on intuition than on the process of reasoning, and "excelling in personal relations." Chisiza also found them to be in pursuit of happiness rather than "truth" or "beauty." The ideal African life is communal, he wrote, based on strong and loving family relations shading into a general compassion (the Swahili expression for "my house" translates as "our house"). All activities, from hunting and harvesting to leisure pursuits, are communal. Generosity and forgiveness are encouraged, malice and revenge abhorred. Moreover, Africans are renowned for their sense of humor and dislike of melancholy.

The African feels strongly bonded to the group. He identifies with his tribe the way a boy will identify with a particular athletic team: its triumphs and defeats are personally *felt.* For the African, what concerns the tribe concerns him; what concerns him concerns the tribe.

This sense of oneness with the group is expressed in Africa, as in most cultures, in ritual. There is a ritual for marriage, for burial, for the hunt, for the harvest; but there is also ritual for much more commonplace activities, like prayer and even the butchering of meat.

Besides ritual, the African has another device for affirming his bond with the group: music. His music is woven as thickly through his life as a rose vine through a trellis. To be sure, there is plenty of music in our own lives, but we have nothing like the constant, deep preoccupation with music that the African has. Music is a social glue; it is a way for him to act out many of his feelings for his tribe, his family, the people around him. There is in Africa a certain amount of music intended for aesthetic pleasure only, but it is relatively rare. Most African music has a ritual or social function. That is to say, it is meant to provide a framework for, or add intensity to, some other activity. It serves, often, as a means for expressing the emotions that activity conjures up.

Given this, it is not surprising that African music comes in a wide variety of forms, each appropriate to a certain activity. There are ritual songs, which are sung or played at births, puberty rites, deaths, and such. There are occasional songs, used to inspire courage in hunters or warriors, to mourn those fallen in battle, or to celebrate a victory. There are songs for all sorts of minor events as well; some tribes, for example, have a song to celebrate the loss of a child's tooth. There are work songs, each tailored to a given task — the drawing-in of fishing nets, the flailing of grain, the hoeing of the field, the chopping of trees. There are praise songs sung by professionals for a fee, and songs of insult that can be used to revenge a slight. There is a great deal of music belonging to special groups. Because of the social nature of the African, his societies are honeycombed with subgroups: clubs, fraternal organizations, burial societies, hunting associations, and a great many others. These organizations usually have their own special songs and dances to accompany their activities: special funeral dirges for a deceased member, music for hunting rituals, songs and dances to celebrate admission of the initiates into full membership.

Music, in African society, plays something akin to the role speech plays in ours. Ernest Borneman, one of the first ethnomusicologists to write about jazz, has said of Africans, "Language and music were not strictly divided." In many African languages the actual pitch of the syllables in a word contributes to its meaning. For example, the Yoruba word öko means "husband" if both syllables are pitched the same, "hoe" if the first syllable is lower than the second, "canoe" if the second is lower, and "spear" if both are low. This relationship of meaning to pitch explains how those famous talking drums work. It is a question not of the drummer's tapping out some kind of Morse code, but of sounding the pitch of actual words. Ulli Beier, an authority on Yoruba talking drums, says, "The nature of the language then explains why the drum can talk. Just as a Semitic language is intelligible if represented by the consonants only, so the many African languages are intelligible if represented by the tones alone." Speech and music thus tend to overlap or merge. A person describing something that happened to him may switch into song at the dramatic or moving parts. Litigants sometimes sing portions of their cases. Songs themselves at times revert to speech; there is a great deal of what we would call recitative in African singing.

What, then, is this music like? Its most common characteristic is that it involves the human body. Running like a thread throughout it is hand-clapping, foot-stamping, and, most important, singing. African music is, more than anything, a vocal music. Not all Africans can drum or play other instruments, but all Africans sing — as soloists, in groups like work groups, or in response to a leader. In the main, African singing is done in unison, with little true harmony.

But though vocal music dominates in Africa, there is no shortage of instrumental music. The drum, as every schoolchild knows, predominates, ranging from tiny hand drums to the big four- and five-footers, which the drummer sits astride when he plays. Besides the drums is a raft of clappers, scrappers, bells, rattles — so-called ideophones, which are used essentially as rhythm-makers. In contrast, instruments on which melody can be played are less highly developed. They consist mainly of a few types of simple reed instruments of limited range; horns of conch, elephant tusk, and the like, which usually can play only one or two notes; and a variety of stringed instruments, xylophones and similar instruments, which also are likely to be limited in range to half a dozen notes (although some large xylophones may range over two or three octaves).

The reason for this paucity of melodic instruments, in contrast to the battery of horns, strings, and keyboard instruments we possess, is quite simple: African music is at bottom rhythmic.

It will be hard for the nonmusician to grasp how complex and difficult — for us at least — African rhythm really is. Perhaps the best way to get the idea is to try tapping your foot twice at the same time as you beat with your hand three times. This is something a trained musician can do easily; an ordinary high school player ought to be able to handle these triplets. But now, while keeping the rhythm of the foot steady, try dividing each of the hand beats in two or three, or dividing some into two and some into three, or syncopating them. This sort of maneuver is something even a highly skilled professional would have trouble with. But the African does it with ease, and he does it not against one beat but against several, some of them to our ears completely unrelated to the rest.

This playing with "cross-rhythm" is at the heart of African music. A. M. Jones, one of the leading researchers into African music, says, "This is of the very essence of African music: this is what the African is after. He wants to enjoy a conflict of rhythms." Not all African music is of this type; some of it is in free time — that is, without a strict beat — especially dirges and some ceremonial incantations. But the bulk of African music is deeply committed to rhythmic interplay. Invariably, there is a basic, or ground, beat. This may be laid down by a drummer, but it can be expressed by the feet of a dancer or by hand claps of an audience. Indeed, it may even be silent — not played, but understood by audience and players, just as we can

A Lakkas tribal orchestra. Note the array of drums and the xylophones with gourd resonators slung beneath the tone bars.

feel the beat of a song without actually tapping it out with a foot. On top of this basic beat is laid one or more other rhythmic lines by drummers, dancers, vocalists, or other instrumentalists, according to the formula for each particular type of music. In the main, these rhythmic patterns, each taken by itself, are relatively simple figures that any well-schooled Western musician can handle, though some of them do pose problems of tricky syncopations. The difficulty lies in keeping your own part straight while around you other rhythms are going on, some of them only slightly different from yours, others only distantly related. It is the old problem of patting the head while rubbing the stomach.

These patterns are not, for the most part, improvised. Rather, they are repeated, often for considerable lengths of time, until the master drummer, dancer, or somebody else signals for a shift to another set of patterns. The beauty of the music lies in the way all the lines interlock, meshing and unmeshing, now running counter to each other, now joining together. Close concentration by the listener can produce a feeling of displacement, a little like the effect you experience when sitting in one train while another train begins to pull out of the station. For a moment you are suspended in a relativity limbo, uncertain as to whether it is you, the other train, or the station itself that is moving. In African music, says the noted musicologist

Richard A. Waterman, "the off-beat phrasing of accents, then, must threaten, but never quite destroy, the orientation of the listener's subjective metronome."

One of the central cross-rhythmic patterns in African music is the contrast between duple and triple meters, between patterns of two, four, or eight beats per time unit juxtaposed with patterns of three and six beats. Many rhythmic lines are built around hemiola, where what we would conceive of as measures of triple and duple meter alternate. In other cases the two meters will run along simultaneously, providing tension and contrast. This particular type of cross-rhythm is not the only one in use; the rhythmic contrasts can be extraordinarily complex, as I have said. But the two-over-three cross-rhythm is ubiquitous to the music, found in all the music throughout sub-Saharan Africa.

It is hardly surprising, in view of the African's sense of the group, that the music associated with any activity is part and parcel of it, not merely accompaniment. The movements of the dancers, the hand claps of the audience, the beating of the flails on the earth are an integral part of a whole, which combines movement, music, and other sounds into a unit. The hand claps, the sound of the flails, even the silent movements of the dancer's body are felt as another cross-rhythm, or set of cross-rhythms, as important to the piece as what the drums are playing. If an African musician wishes to demonstrate a work song to an ethnomusicologist, he will always substitute something for the sound of the missing ax, flail, or paddle.

Although rhythm is at the heart of African music, melody is a part of it, too. And this brings us to the thorny matter of African scales, over which ethnomusicologists have been arguing for decades.

A scale, of course, is a set of notes arranged in order of pitch. In European music there are two basic scales, major and minor; the minor comes in three varieties. Each of these scales is based on a tonic, or "home tone" — the C of the C scale, the D of the D scale, and so forth — to which melodies are drawn. These scales are "diatonic" — that is, they are made up of combinations of half steps, each of which is the distance between two adjacent keys on the piano, and whole steps, each the distance between alternate keys.

There are, however, in use in European music, especially in folk music, other scales. One group is made up of what are called "pentatonic scales" because they employ only five notes. There are many types of pentatonic scales. Pentatonic scales are exceedingly common, found in a wide variety of cultures. Of all the possible types, the most common is one made up of the diatonic scale with the fourth and seventh omitted; for example, in the key of C the pentatonic would consist of C, D, E, G, A. This scale is not only very common in African music but is the basic one in use in Scottish and Irish folk music, among the American Indians, in the popular musics of China, Japan, Siam, the lost civilizations of Mexico and Peru as well as other places. From its presence on ancient instruments it can be dated back to at least 2800 B.C. (Surprisingly, one pentatonic scale comprises the black keys of the ordinary piano; wander around among them and you can produce melodies based on this particular pentatonic.) So widespread is its use that we begin to suspect that there is something fundamental about it.

And in fact there is. Music is not arbitrary. Many of its principles are derived from the physics of sound. This is true, for technical reasons, of this pentatonic scale. In a sense it springs from nature just as surely as a painter's colors do. One interesting thing about this scale is that it eliminates the half steps normally found in the diatonic scale, and consists only of intervals of a whole step or more. The exact significance of this fact is difficult to assess, but one gets the very clear feeling that the pentatonic scale in such wide use in so many cultures is at some earlier level of development than other scales, such as the diatonic scale of European music or the modes of India.

Whatever the reason, it is clear in any case that African music, especially music from West Africa, where most of the slaves came from, goes to great lengths to avoid the half steps that are so much a part of European music. My analysis of ten songs, mainly West African, transcribed by A. M. Jones, shows exceedingly few half-step movements. In nine of the ten songs there are no half-step movements whatever; and in the tenth a figure employing a movement from B to C appears some six times. But even this limited half-step movement is illusory, for, according to Jones, when the half steps appear in this music, one or another of the notes is shifted out of place so that the interval is enlarged — either the upper note is sharped slightly, or the lower note is flatted, resulting in an interval of, say, three quarters of a step.

Jones has discovered another scale in wide use in Africa; he calls it the "equi-heptatonic" scale. Like our diatonic scale, this scale has seven notes, but instead of being half tones or whole tones, they are evenly spaced so that, again, they are intervals of something more than a half tone but less than a whole tone. (To Western ears it sounds, of course, excruciatingly out of tune.) Here again we have the avoidance of the half step, which I am prepared to suggest is a principle not only of African tribal music but of much of the music of mankind everywhere.

There are certain other characteristics of African music that made themselves felt later on in the United States. One is the habitual use of call-and-answer patterns, in which one instrument or singer responds to another. In a common instance, the lead singer offers a line or two, to which the audience then responds, as in the following example:

LEADER: Give flesh to the hyenas at daybreak,
CHORUS: Oh, the broad spears.
LEADER: The spear of the sultan is the broadest,
CHORUS: Oh, the broad spears.
LEADER: I behold thee now — I desire to see none other,
CHORUS: Oh, the broad spears.
LEADER: My horse is as tall as a high wall,
CHORUS: Oh, the broad spears.

Obviously, this sort of responsive singing can be worked out in many different ways. In part, the response may have been intended to allow the singer a brief respite in order to think of his next line, but undoubtedly its major function was to let the group participate in the song.

Another important characteristic of the music is the feeling for a coarseness of timbre — what in jazz came to be called a "dirty" tone. In singing, Africans do not strive for some sort of pure, or ideal, tone, as we do. They do not compliment one another on a sweet voice. Instead they employ a variety of techniques for thickening the texture of sound. They will use vocal buzzes or rasps; at times the singing becomes a shout or cry. Falsetto, or near-falsetto, singing is standard practice in some groups, and there is a tendency to sing in recitative. Ernest Borneman has written, "When we want to stress a word, we raise our voice — that is to say, we go up in pitch. But in those African languages where a change of pitch on any given syllable may alter the meaning of the entire word, you are left with only one device to emphasize your point: *timbre.* You can alter the *tone color,* the *voice production,* the *vibrato* of the syllable you wish to stress." Once again, music and speech, for the African, conjoin.

Instruments, too, use devices for coarsening timbre. The hand piano, which consists of several bars fixed into a resonating box shaped to produce a tone, may have bits of metal attached that vibrate with each pitch. A drum may have beads or shells attached to it that rattle when it is struck. Coupled with this avoidance of a pure tone is the use of off-pitch notes, or notes that waver in pitch. In general, the African is not nearly so much a stickler for exactness of pitch as we who are trained in European music. Characteristically, he will slur up into the note that begins a phrase, and let the pitch fall off a note that ends it. He will let it waver slightly so that it seems out of tune to Western ears.

One other characteristic of African music that had a bearing on jazz is a tendency to let a section of a song repeat for a considerable length of time, until the leader or master drummer decides that it has gone on long enough and shifts to another section or pattern. Coupled with this is the use of the last note of a repeated section as the first note of the repeat, after the fashion of a snake swallowing its tail. This open-endedness has a particular importance beyond its musical significance. In most African cultures the trance or possession state is an important feature of religious ceremonies. This state is generally brought on through dancing, possibly for several hours, to an endless stream of music. The entranced was presumed to be "possessed" by a god or holy spirit and was thereby sanctified. Exactly how this state is produced, and how conscious the possessed person remains, is debatable. In any case, there is little doubt that lengthy and repetitive music is essential to producing this particular state.

European art music is generally built in some architectural or dramatic form, from sections of four, eight, sixteen measures, and so forth. Small units make up bigger ones, the bigger ones make up larger ones still. Parts are recapitulated, and the work moves forward in a series of tensions and resolutions, all pointing to a climax or rounding off. This sort of music, with its constant shifting of degrees of tension, would be useless in producing trance states; for this, what is needed is a musical structure that can be added to without disturbing changes in mood.

The relationship between African music and possession states, like pentatonic scales and shifts in timbre, has been carried over into jazz. It hardly takes a percipient observer to note that one of the most visible characteristics of any of the musics derived from Africa — jazz, rock, gospel music, big band swing — has been at least some tendency toward abandonment in the music, usually coupled with repetitive and often athletic dancing.

This is hardly the only practice that African music shares with Western music. The pentatonic scale is not entirely different from our diatonic one, and was in fact being used, especially in Scottish and Irish folk music, right into this century. Contrasting rhythms, though on a much more rudimentary level, have existed in European music for centuries; some of the polyrhythms of the Netherlands school of Ockeghem and Obrecht are quite complex, as anyone who has tried to play them will know. And Europeans do sing special songs for special occasions — in our churches, our football stadiums, at birthday parties, alumni reunions, and Christmas and New Year's Eve. But the differences between African and European music are there, and they are significant. The question that remains is how these differences were adjudicated to produce this astonishing new music we call jazz.

The American Transplantation

When the black man reached the New World he had with him nothing but the clothes on his back and what he carried in his head. A few slaves brought musical instruments; the death rate during the so-called middle passage from Africa was appalling, and many slavers felt that music helped to keep the black man from drifting into fatal despair. But by and large the black man came to America empty-handed.

What he contained in his head, however, could not be so easily stripped from him as his physical possessions. He had his language, his traditions, his ways of doing things; and it was a question of how, and to what extent, they would have to be modified to fit new circumstances.

This pattern applied to music as well as language, religion, or anything else. What could survive did; what couldn't was modified, often beyond recognition. There has been, over the years, considerable debate over the African residuals in black-American music. Some writers see the whole of jazz, the blues, spirituals, and the rest as essentially African. Others insist that the Africanisms have been drowned by the European music of the dominant culture. The debate misses the point. What we have to understand is that black-American slaves developed a culture of their own that departed in many ways from the white culture in which it was embedded. This point has been made by Herbert G. Gutman in his crucial study, *The Black Family in Slavery and Freedom.* Gutman explains, for example, that where marriage with cousins was common among whites, it was virtually nonexistent among blacks. Blacks had, in this case, developed a sexual ethic that was not derived from the white culture but was created out of the conditions they found themselves in. Just as the black slaves developed a sexual morality that differed from the white one, so they developed a musical practice of their own, which, while partaking of the white man's music, was different in important respects. It is essential that this concept be grasped. We have tended to see this early black music piecemeal — that is, we discover that the black man had work songs, he had spirituals, he had "field hollars," street cries, and so on. What we have not understood is that all of these various musical forms were built on the same set of principles. The black man created a musical practice or procedure with which to produce whatever types of music he needed. This is, of course, exactly what the white man had done over the centuries. A Beethoven sonata, a Richard Rodgers show tune, a fraternity drinking song, are very different in emotional content, but all use the same scales, the same concept of tonality, the same set of meters.

We need a term for this music. Unfortunately, the best term, "black-American music," has been usurped to cover everything from spirituals to avant-garde jazz. It was called by the early commentators "slave music," but this will hardly do for music of the post–Civil War period, and I think we shall have to use the term "black-American folk music," despite its shortcomings.

It came into existence only gradually. At first the blacks continued, as much as possible, to practice their own African music. In the South drums and loud horns were generally banned, because the slave owners feared that they might be used for signaling. (The musicologist Dena J. Epstein believes that the banjo, the only modern instrument directly descended from Africa, came forward when drums and horns were banned.) But in the North, where there was not so large a body of slaves as to present a formidable threat of revolt, blacks were allowed to put on music and dance "festivals," which were very much like their African precursors.

The most famous of these were the "Pinkster" festivals, a term derived from the church celebration of the Pentecost. A Pinkster festival might last for several days, or even a week. Hundreds of blacks would gather at some open ground set aside for the purpose. Those who could do so attired themselves in fancy dress — perhaps a British army uniform, or a mélange of finery gathered from wherever. There would be drums, much like the standard African ones, a variety of ideophones made from bones, shells, or wood, which again were copies of their African models, and possibly some European instruments, like flutes or fiddles. There might be speeches; a king or leader would be chosen; and the dancing would go on day after day, often leading to possession states. These festivals, clearly, were almost entirely African in nature, modified only slightly to suit conditions here. Despite the ban on drums, festivals did take place in the South, especially in New Orleans, where they were carried on every Sunday at the famous Congo Square at least until 1855. Here celebrations were permitted, and they kept the old African musical tradition alive for blacks of the New Orleans area.

But most of the festivals did not last much beyond the eighteenth century, and in any case the vast majority of blacks, those working on the plantations of the South, were not permitted them. With no formal

ritual in which to contain African music, the old system began to lose
its force. Through the seventeenth and eighteenth centuries many if not
most blacks were exposed to much European music. Those blacks who
went to church learned to sing in the European manner. Others learned
to perform European music on homemade instruments by emulating the
whites around them. As time passed, European musical practices began
to color the old African system; the two forms began to fuse, and thus
was born black-American folk music.

For blacks, the major music was the work song. It is a curious fact that
Europeans have never had a strong tradition of the work song. Sea chanteys,
meant as rhythmic aids to sailors heaving lines or turning the capstan, were
common enough, but the monotonous reaping, hoeing, shearing, sweeping,
and washing that Europeans did in common with most people everywhere
has gone unaccompanied by music. As a result, in this area the black had
no local cultural tradition to come up against, and he was free to use his
own music. The white overlords generally approved; for them, a singing
black was a happy black, one less likely to stir up trouble. But blacks
themselves insisted that song made the constant, backbreaking drudgery go
easier; the music gave them strength. As a consequence, the work song
became the principal carrier of the black musical tradition down even to the
early part of this century, when body labor began to give way to the
machine.

Work songs were endlessly varied in function, style, and content. The
songs used, for example, at the great corn-shucking bees, were simply
distractions, to take the mind off the work. One description of a corn-
shucking bee has been given by a nineteenth-century observer, Lewis Paine:

> A farmer will haul up from his field a pile of corn from ten to twenty
> rods long, from ten to twenty feet wide, and ten feet high . . . It is so
> arranged that this can be on a moonlight evening. The farmer then
> gives a general "invite" to all the young ladies and gentlemen of the
> neighborhood, to come and bring their slaves; for it takes no small
> number to shuck such a pile of corn . . . The guests begin to arrive about
> dark, and in a short time, they can be heard in all directions, singing
> the plantation songs, as they come to the scene of action. When all have
> arrived, the Host makes the following propositions to the company,
> "You can shuck the pile, or work till eleven o'clock, or divide the pile
> and the hands and have a race." The last offer is generally accepted.
> Each party selects two of the shrewdest and best singers among the
> slaves, to mount the pile and sing, while all join in the chorus.

In such cases, the songs were simply part of the general good times and
an encouragement to the workers. But more frequently the rhythm of the
songs was tied into the pattern of the work itself. A typical boat song, timed

to the movement of the oars, was this one, called "Sold Off to Georgy." It was recorded by a young Baltimorean, James Hungerford, in 1832:

SOLO:	Farewell, fellow servants
CHORUS:	Oho, oho
SOLO:	I'm gwine way to leabe you
CHORUS:	Oho, oho
SOLO:	I'm gwine to leabe de ole country
CHORUS:	Oho, oho
SOLO:	I'm sold off to Georgy
CHORUS:	Oho, oho.

The words of a work song did not necessarily have anything to do with the work itself. They might be about rowing or husking corn, but they were more likely to be whatever the singer felt like speaking about: the hardships of life, his religion, old massa, or whatever. A frequent text was the insult song, or the song of derision, taken directly from the African tradition. Hungerford was surprised to hear the black boatman make fun of the white family he was transporting, teasing the young girls about their beaux or exposing their personal foibles.

The primacy of the work song in slave music is due to the simple fact that the slave spent vastly more time at work than he did at anything else. But it was another type of slave song that has gotten the bulk of the attention, and that is the so-called spiritual. In the colonial period blacks, if they had worshiped at all, worshiped in white churches. The music performed in these early churches was quite rough. The ordinary seventeenth-century churchgoer could not read words well, and he certainly could not read musical notes. It was customary for the minister or some other official to "line out" the hymns; that is, to throw the congregation each line as it came along. Hymnals did not ordinarily contain written music, and the hymns were set to whatever tunes the congregation might know. This system was hardly conducive to mellifluous sounds, and the singing of those early congregations was often wretched — out of tune, toneless, and ragged. However painful the singing, the blacks took part in it, at least in the North.

But the attempt to create a new nation brought to the fore the schism between North and South on the slave question. In the South, the reaction to the threat of the national abolition of slavery was a defensive tightening of the noose. The concept of the black freedman began to die out. There was a push toward segregation, and in part this took the form of driving the black out of the churches. Blacks in their turn were often glad to go, tired of being second-class citizens in the house of God, and around the beginning of the nineteenth century separate black churches began to spring up. These churches, of course, needed music. At first the new black congregations adopted wholesale the white gospel hymns, especially the Methodist hymns of John Wesley. But as time passed and the influence of the white culture dwindled, the musical system developing principally in the work songs began to creep into the hymns. It is difficult to date this change with any precision, but it probably began early in the nineteenth century, not long after the black churches were established, and would certainly have been completed by 1850. In this way, church music picked up the procedures of black-American folk practice.

At the same moment there was developing in white religion a revivalist movement known as "the Second Awakening." This movement was based on the notion of a return to a more emotional religious experience than the rather formal approach to worship practiced in the eighteenth century. A feature of the Second Awakening was the revival meeting. These extraordinary conclaves ran for several days, usually taking place in open fields or in the woods. Here tent cities would be constructed. At night the scene would be dotted by fires as far as the eye could see. Hundreds upon hundreds of worshipers would gather before an improvised pulpit for hours at a time, often all through the night, to listen to impassioned preaching and sing fervent hymns. At the heart of these ceremonies was the emotional breakthrough, which suddenly drove a member of the congregation, weeping or shouting, to be saved and accepted into the church. Trance or possession states often occurred, and sometimes there was speaking in tongues.

These revival meetings were an obvious cultural parallel to African religious ritual, and it is hardly surprising that blacks were swiftly drawn to them. In the beginning, blacks often shared the white meetings, their own encampments set up alongside the white ones. When this tradition of the emotionally charged religious ceremony with possession began to dwindle in white churches, it maintained a hold on blacks, many of whom, in the early part of the nineteenth century, could remember such ceremonies from their childhood in Africa.

It is not my purpose here to discuss the varieties of black religious experience; but we should know about one important feature of the church ceremonies, the ring shout, a form of dance that accompanied the spiritual. A famous description of one appeared in the *Nation:*

> The benches are pushed back to the wall when the formal meeting is over, and old and young, men and women, sprucely dressed young men, grotesquely half-clad field hands — the women generally with gay handkerchiefs twisted about their head and with short skirts, boys with tattered shirts and men's trousers — young girls bare-footed — all stand up in the middle of the floor, and when the "sperichil" is

struck up, begin first walking and by-and-by shuffling around, one after the other, in a ring. The foot is hardly taken from the floor, and the progression is mainly due to a jerking, hitching motion, which agitates the entire shouter, and soon brings out streams of perspiration. Sometimes he dances silently, sometimes he shuffles as he sings the chorus of the spiritual, and sometimes the song itself is also sung by the dancers. But more frequently a band, composed of some of the best singers and of tired shouters, stand at the side of the room to "base" the others, singing the body of the song and clapping their hands together or on the knees.

The spiritual song, which was part and parcel of the ceremony, is familiar to most of us in the watered-down versions that eventually became a part of the national song bag. In the original version, it was often sung in call-and-answer fashion. Words were generally related to some Biblical story or to the black experience of slavery. A typical one is this:

> I know moon-rise, I know star-rise
> Lay dis body down.
> I walk in de moonlight, I walk in de starlight
> To lay dis body down.
> I'll walk in de graveyard, I'll walk through de graveyard
> To lay dis body down.
> I'll lie in de grave and stretch out my arms;
> Lay dis body down . . .

Church songs and work songs constituted the largest part of slave music, but they were by no means all of it. The black, according to his tradition, brought music into his life wherever he could. One musical form often commented on was the field cry or field hollar:

> Suddenly one [a slave] raised such a sound as I had never heard before, a long, loud musical shout, rising and falling, and breaking into falsetto, his voice ringing through the woods in the clear frosty night air, like a bugle call. As he finished the melody was caught up by another, and then another, and by several in chorus.

What the exact function of the field hollar was is not clear. Some commentators say that it helped the slaves "relieve their feelings," but that is saying very little. In the description there is a clear call-and-answer effect, suggesting that the cry was meant to assure the worker that he was not alone; but other descriptions of field hollars indicate that at times they were tossed out by a lone worker, with no following response. Possibly they were signals, meant to warn that an overseer was coming or that white people

were in the neighborhood. We simply do not know. Musically, the field
hollar consisted of a series of notes of fairly indeterminate pitch, and it
appears to have been in free rhythm.

There were also the street vendors' cries. Singing is easier on the throat
than shouting, and I have heard white street vendors crying in the streets
of New York City as recently as the 1950s. One strawberry vendor, quoted
by Eileen Southern in her exemplary book, *The Music of Black Americans,*
hawked her wares thus:

> I live four miles out of town,
> I am going to glory;
> My strawberries are sweet and sound,
> I am going to glory;
> I fotched them four miles on my head,
> I am going to glory . . .

Still the list continues. There were play songs for both children and
adults, such as variations on Musical Chairs or Drop the Handkerchief.
After the Civil War, when blacks were punished by civil authorities rather
than by individual slave holders, there developed a whole range of prison
songs, most of them in the work song tradition. There was a variety of
satiric songs, as we have seen. There were songs about "pattyrollers"
— the patrollers who were supposed to keep blacks in order — and songs
about escaping to freedom usually couched in the religious metaphors of the
Biblical Jews escaping from their Egyptian bondage.

It should be clear at this juncture that the music of the nineteenth-century
American blacks, like the tribal music of their homeland, was essentially
functional. Some of it was made for simple pleasure, to be sure; but most
of it was associated with some other activity — work, worship, dancing.
Even the field hollar, in which a black was apparently giving vent to strong
emotion, reminds us of the African practice of sliding from speech into song
when feelings are high. Furthermore, as in Africa, the subjects of these
songs were primarily matters of immediate concern to the singers: work, old
massa, the day of jubilee, the overseer, loneliness, death. Lyrics were not
necessarily appropriate to the occasion: songs with religious content were
used with work, or were sung by black soldiers around a campfire. The main
function of the lyrics was to express an attitude toward some aspect of black
life.

As it happens, we know more about the lyrics of black nineteenth-century
music than about the music. Words could be written down, but, as nineteenth-century investigators began to discover, the music could not be.

By the time of the Civil War a handful of whites, mainly Northerners
brought into contact with Southern blacks by the war and the events that

followed it, were beginning to study black music. The most important collections of black songs to emerge were *Slave Songs of the United States,* by William Francis Allen, Charles Pickard Ware, and Lucy McKim Garrison, published in 1867; and *Slave Songs of the Georgia Sea Islands,* collected by Lydia Parrish over several decades beginning in 1909. As these commentators and others have been at pains to point out, it was always exceedingly hard to force black folk music into European notation. Lucy McKim Garrison says:

> It is difficult to express the entire character of these Negro ballads by mere musical notes and signs. The odd turns made in the throat and the curious rhythmic effect produced by single voices chiming in at different irregular intervals seem almost as impossible to place on the score as the singing of birds or the tones of an aeolian harp.

Thomas P. Fenner, in *Cabin and Plantation Songs* (1873), says, "Tones are frequently employed which we have no musical characters to represent." And Lydia Parrish says, "Unfortunately our system of notation is inadequate to interpret the Negro's traditional music."

The problem, basically, was that there remained in black-American singing a good deal of the old African approach. Pitches were less exact than in European singing, and there was much slurring from one note to the next. The musical line tended to be colored by sudden leaps into the falsetto, coarsening of the sound by use of throat tones, and the addition of patches of fast quavering notes at crucial points in the melody, akin to what is called melisma. In support of these witnesses, who were, for the most part, amateurs, we have a study called *Phonophotography in Folk Music,* a comparison of black singing with European singing by Milton Metfessel, published in 1928. Metfessel and his colleagues were working with a piece of equipment that "photographed" sound, allowing them to make a very subtle examination of individual notes. Metfessel says, "The Negro will in a fair percentage of his tones go out of his way to get a running start from below . . . The Negro . . . is interested in the more obvious embellishments and rhythmical devices . . ." He finds as well that vibratos tend to be wide and fast, and that at ends of phrases, where the singer is breathing, the intonation falls off, perhaps dropping to a note below.

All of these things — the slurs, the falsetto leaps, the patches of melisma — were African devices that had been passed down the generations, and they remained in black vocalizing to one degree or another into the twentieth century, especially in isolated areas like Lydia Parrish's Georgia Sea Islands. But as I have said, it is important for us to understand that these were not simply African devices pasted onto a European music that blacks had acquired in the United States. This black music was a true fusion of

African and European systems. Not only were devices and practices from both used side by side, but *principles* drawn from both were reinterpreted in new ways.

This black-American folk music has three main features. The first is an approach to time that involved an attempt to reproduce in the European system implications of the old cross-rhythms of Africa. One contemporary report says, "One noticeable thing about their boat-songs was that they seemed often to be sung just a trifle behind time; in 'Rainfall,' for instance, 'Believer cry holy' would seem to occupy more than its share of the stroke, the 'holy' being prolonged until the very beginning of the next stroke; indeed, I think Jerry often hung on his oar a little just there before dipping it in again." Other witnesses have remarked on melodies being "out of time." But because we have no accurate transcriptions, we are at a loss to know exactly what these singers were doing with time. We do have recordings of black-American folk music taken in the twentieth century, many of them made in the 1930s and 1940s by John and Alan Lomax, to whom we owe a debt of gratitude, and from these records, the reports of Garrison, Parrish, and others, and what we know of jazz today, it is possible to make good inferences about rhythms in this black music. It seems clear enough that the singers were, at least in portions of their melodies, breaking away from the time framework of the ground beat to produce lines that were essentially rhythmically free. A phrase would not necessarily begin on a beat, or halfway between two beats as in European syncopation, but at some odd point irrelevant to the time scheme, and the remaining notes of the phrase would be equally unleashed from ground beats and meter. The old game of sidewalk cracks and squares comes to mind: in European music the singer steps firmly in the center of the squares, or syncopates by stepping on the cracks; but in this early black music the singer was skipping helter-skelter down the sidewalk, as if cracks and squares did not exist.

Take the following example, a transcription of a well-known piece called "Rock Me Julie":

It is a rhythmic jumble, a mishmash, and I would suggest that it is the transcriber's attempt to notate a melody line that in fact was arrhythmic —unrelated to the time scheme at all.

It is probable that in many cases these arrhythmic patches of melody were cast in the rough shape of the three-over-two pattern so common to African music. There is in the Library of Congress Archive of Folk Song a remarkable game song called "Old Uncle Rabbit," in which one child is singing in three over an answering voice in two, something that no child raised in the European tradition could do without training. It is equally probable that these three-over-two figures were not played exactly, but were varied so that the middle note of the three was given extra weight. We are going to see, as jazz develops, such a figure cropping up again and again:

or

It is central to African music, to ragtime, and to jazz; and inevitably we find it in transcriptions of black-American folk music. Lydia Parrish, for example, has a Georgia Sea Island song called "Rockah Mh Moomba," which she got from a man who got it from Dublin Scribbin, who was African-born. The song has mainly African words, and it uses as the main figure in eight out of twelve measures the classic figure given above, or two variations on it:

and

Another song of Parrish's, a funeral dirge called "Moonlight, Starlight," has as its characteristic figure

which would be difficult for any but a well-schooled musician to reproduce without practice.

These variations on three-over-two figures are abundant in transcriptions of black-American music. They obviously are drawn from African music, where they were a commonplace. But whether variations on the three over two or not, it seems clear enough from what the transcribers have said, and from the recordings we have, that these melodies, if only in part, were arrhythmic — that is to say, set free of the time scheme laid out by hand claps, foot beats, or sounds of the oars, the axes, the hammers of the workers. And here we see the fusion. The black-American singers had not re-created in America the system of cross-rhythms found in African drum bands. But they had taken the *principle* of the cross-rhythm, and found a new way to express it by standing a melody line apart from the ground beat that ostensibly supported it. This principle became central to jazz. Again and again, as one style succeeds another, we shall see players finding ways to set their melodic lines apart from something established beneath them. Arrhythmic melodies have been in the music from the start. Later on, the bebop players began making metric shifts, so that melodies were set on second and fourth beats in contrast to rhythm sections playing on first and third. Further, they broke up the meter, phrasing in segments of three and five measures, or portions of measures, against the normal four-square cut of the tune. Even later, John Coltrane and his followers began to set modal melodies against a contrasting chord or pedal point in the bass, and in general making a practice of departing, at frequent intervals, from the set harmony of the piece. Whether done harmonically, rhythmically, or metrically, this practice of setting melody free of some explicitly stated undergirding has been at the center of jazz throughout its existence, and it was originally developed by American blacks in an attempt to reproduce something of the feel of the cross-rhythms in African music.

The second major characteristic of black-American folk music of the nineteenth century is the manner in which scales were used. Here we are on a little surer ground, because pitch is something Europeans know better than Africans do. As might be expected, many of these songs use the pentatonic scale so common in folk music around the world. Others use what appears to be a standard European diatonic scale. Still others use truncated scales of one sort or another: Hungerford's "Sold Off to Georgy" is built on a four-note scale consisting of A, C, D, E, probably a pentatonic scale with G missing.

But there is more to these scales than that. Here again the transcribers testified to the difficulty of putting the music into European notation. Fenner says that he has indicated certain notes "as nearly as possible by the flat seventh in 'Great Camp Meeting,' 'Hard Trials' and others . . . These tones are variable in pitch, ranging through an entire interval on different occasions, according to the inspiration of the singer."

It remained to Henry Edward Krehbiel, an excellent musicologist of the turn of the century, to pin the matter down. He says, "Miss Mildred J. Hill, of Louisville, who gathered for me some of the most striking songs in my collection from the singing of an old woman who had been a slave in Boyle County, Kentucky, was careful to note all deviations from just intonation, and from her songs I came to the conclusion that the negroes were prone to intervallic aberrations, not only in the case of the seventh, but also in the third." Once again, we have support from Metfessel's phonophotography device. He has discovered in one song he studied, "I Got a Muly," that neither major nor minor third is present, but "the intervals group themselves between the key-note minor to major third." He calls the resulting note a "neutral third," and he finds a lot of such notes throughout the music he studied.

It is by slightly flatting precisely these notes, the third and the seventh of the diatonic scale, that you eliminate the half steps that West African music seems to be at such pains to avoid. And once again we see the fusion, the reworking of an African principle to suit the new circumstances. In Africa the half steps were avoided mainly by the use of the pentatonic or other scales, which do not contain them. Black-American singers, of course, worked with pentatonic scales a great deal; but as the European diatonic scale — the do-re-mi scale we all know — came more and more to be used by blacks, they began increasingly to get away from the half steps by slightly flatting the third and seventh. The principle was the same, but the method for gaining the end was one used only infrequently in African music.

The third of the main characteristics of this black-American folk music is the use of those guttural tones, rasps, falsettos, and melismas, which I discussed earlier, to color the melodic line, to give it variety and expressiveness. These effects seem to be more directly African residuals, often little changed from their sources, but as any jazz listener should immediately understand, the principle was in time expanded to cover instrumental music. Finally, as in African music, there was no true harmony. A singer might enter at some interval above or below where the majority were singing, but this was not harmonizing the line in the Western sense.

Blacks, it is clear, managed to hang on to an astonishing amount of the African culture through almost three centuries. Richard A. Waterman says:

> There are two reasons why African musical elements have influenced the musical styles of the American. In the first place, American Negro groups have remained relatively homogeneous with regard to culture patterns, and remarkably so with respect to in-group solidarity. This has almost guaranteed the retention of any values not in conflict with the prevailing Euro-American culture pattern. Second, there is enough similarity between African and European music to permit syncretism. This has put some aspects of African musical style in the category of traditions not destined to be forced out of existence because of their deviation from accepted norms.

As I have said, the foregoing picture of this early black-American music is somewhat speculative, but it is clear enough that blacks had created a new musical tradition. This was not simply European music with a few African embellishments, nor, as many early commentators seemed to think, a music made crude because of the inability of blacks to reproduce European music correctly. It was not nearly so rich a music as either of the two types it developed from; that was hardly possible, given the limited access the black man had to musical instruments and the limited time he had for practice and experimentation. It was nonetheless an expressive music, and it served black people well. And it was from this music that they made their work songs, spirituals, game songs, prison songs.

But blacks could hardly ignore the music of the white culture around them, and some of them were involved with it right from the early days of the country. The first impulse for this involvement came from the dancing that played so important a role in eighteenth-century America. The chief physical and social diversion for all classes of people was dancing. As a consequence there was an enormous demand for musicians of all kinds. Although some of the wealthy owned harpsichords and clavichords, the keyboard instruments of that day were generally too soft in tone to be of much use for dance music. The usual dance band consisted of some combination of drum, fife, flute, horn or bugle, and, most important of all, violin. Often the fiddler stood alone. (The so-called country group of today is a direct descendant of those early dance bands.)

That there was considerable cultural pressure on the black man to learn to play this music is well documented by Eileen Southern. In some cases slave owners bought fiddles and drums for blacks in order to have musicians available for dancing. Many free blacks took up the study of European music, sometimes fashioning their own fiddles and drums out of whatever material they could find, as a good source of income. By the end of the eighteenth century there had developed in the United States a body of black professional musicians, both free and slave, who found in a musical career a God-sent opportunity to escape from the grinding toil of the fields. Southern quotes a dozen ads for runaway slaves or blacks up for sale in which mention is made of their musical abilities. One, from the Virginia *Gazette* for August 6, 1767, reads:

> TO BE SOLD a valuable young handsome Negro Fellow about 18 or 20 years of age; has every qualification of a genteel and sensible serveant and has been in many different parts of the world. He . . . plays on the French horn . . . He lately came from London and has with him two suits of new clothes, and his French horn, which the purchaser may have with him.

We are now dealing with a case where the African tradition was faced with a strong local one. The black work song could contain a heavy strain of African elements because there was no white work song for it to contend with. But there was plenty of white dance music, which blacks learned perforce, and inevitably white forms came to dominate, even in the dance music blacks played for themselves. We have again the benefit of James Hungerford's observations:

> Upon benches placed against the outside wall of the hut upon each side of the door sat several of the older negroes of both sexes from the neighboring quarters. Ike was singing the *words* of a jig in a monotonous tone of voice, beating time meanwhile with his hands alternately against each other and against his body. To his music about a dozen or so negro boys and girls were dancing on the hard beaten ground before
>
> "The old cabin door."

Their idea of excellence in dancing seemed to be that it consisted in a rapid motion of the feet; and some of the dancers absolutely moved their feet so swiftly as to cause them to be indistinct in the moonlight; yet even in this rapid action the blows of the feet kept time and tune with the music and gave it emphasis. The scene was one of hearty glee; all seemed to be enjoying themselves vastly . . .

On the plantation Hungerford was visiting there was a man named Uncle Porringer, a house servant who played the fiddle for both black dances and white, and there is no indication in the report that the style of playing was any different for either. Hungerford describes a white cotillion at which Uncle Porringer and another slave, borrowed from a neighbor, provided the music:

The scene around us at this moment was very stirring. Gentlemen were hurrying about among the groups seeking their partners, mostly no doubt already engaged, for the first cotillion. The boys — who immediately on leaving the dinner table had straggled away in parties along the shores, or through the adjoining woods — were seen returning in all directions. The young girls, too, who were straying through all parts of the grove, were hastening toward the green plot of ground between the table and the creek shore, which was intended for the dancers. The negroes, male and female, who were engaged in waiting upon their masters and mistresses, hung around as near to the dancing ground as a proper respect for the white superiors would allow . . . In the background, separated from the place occupied by the white company by the table, those of the negro servants not employed in attending upon their masters and mistresses also arranged themselves for dancing, and frequent bursts of laughter gave token that they were enjoying themselves greatly . . .

This was, of course, a white dance, which the blacks were imitating and probably to a degree parodying. Out of this practice was born the cakewalk, a dance in which both the display of finery and the strutting and by-play with hats and canes were highly exaggerated. From the point of view of the white, the cakewalk was based on the attempts of the ignorant black to emulate his betters; and while this may have been partially the case, undoubtedly the black man saw the cakewalk as a parody of the way dicty white folks put on airs.

In any case, the ability to play a musical instrument was considered a distinct asset by both blacks and whites, and unquestionably slave owners encouraged talented blacks to play. How they were taught is another question. Southern thinks that they were probably not instructed but had to learn to play on their own. One noteworthy black musician was Newport Gardner, born in 1746. Obviously a man of superior ability, he taught himself to read first English, then music. At the age of forty-five he purchased his freedom, presumably with the money he made as a singing teacher, and established a music school. Another famous black musician of the time was Frank Johnson, born in 1792, who was reputed to be one of the best performers on the bugle and french horn that was in use in his time. He capped his career with a command performance at Buckingham Palace, where he was presented with a silver bugle by Queen Victoria.

The examples of Gardner and Johnson are evidence that blacks were not confined to playing dance music. Elizabeth Taylor Greenfield (1808–1876), who had been born a slave, concertized as a vocalist in the United States and, like Johnson, gave a command performance at Buckingham Palace. Dozens of blacks were composing music, and some became quite celebrated, among them Samuel Snaer (born in 1833), Edmund Dédé, and Richard Lambert. There was in New Orleans a black symphony orchestra, and black concert bands abounded. In New York City there was a black theater called the African Grove, where ballets and plays of various sorts were regularly performed.

Blacks were especially in demand as military bandsmen. The artist Robert Andrew Parker, an authority on military uniforms, noted that from at least the beginning of the eighteenth century many European armies, particularly the Germans, the Austro-Hungarians, and the French, used black musicians. The idea, apparently, had to do with skin color more than any notion that blacks were unusually gifted in music. According to custom, if the troops wore red uniforms with white facings, the musicians would have white uniforms faced with red. Similarly, if the troops wore black bearskins and were mounted on brown horses, the musicians would have white bearskins and white horses. And inevitably it occurred to somebody that if the troopers had white faces, the musicians should have black ones. This tradition was carried over to America; and up through World War I, when there were several famous black-American military bands in France, American regiments often featured black bands. When these trained musicians were mustered out, they frequently formed bands of their own for parade work, concertizing, or for their own pleasure. There has been, thus, a continuous tradition of black parade bands reaching back into the eighteenth century.

By the middle of the nineteenth century, then, we have blacks working in two distinct musical systems: their own folk music and, to a lesser extent, the standard European music they found in the white culture around them. It has been pointed out by Herbert Gutman that blacks in the South had "bi-cultural" rearing; that is, they learned the folkways of both white and black cultures. They were thus doing in music what they were doing in other aspects of their lives. But around 1850 there began to develop yet a third kind of music with black roots — a kind of pseudoslave music, which had important effects on the development of American popular music.

White Americans have, for most of the country's history, been curious about, and at times fascinated by, the black subculture in their midst. This fascination with the black subculture has manifested itself, almost continuously since about 1840 and perhaps before, in an interest in black music. One after another, white Americans have engaged in fads for "coon" songs, plantation melodies, minstrelsy, ragtime, the blues, the pseudojazz of the 1920s, boogie-woogie, and today's "soul" sound.

In the nineteenth century the most important vehicle for these songs was the minstrel show. According to Robert C. Toll in *Blacking Up,* the blackface act goes back to colonial times. However, the minstrel show as a fixed form did not come into being until the 1840s. By the 1850s it was running at flood tide, one of the major forms of popular art. The performers were invariably whites in blackface, and the material consisted of jokes, songs, and sketches that purported to show black life as it existed on the plantation. The black was generally portrayed as an ignoramus devoted to good times and a ludicrous aping of his betters, but in the mixture was a lot of sentimental material involving the separation of loved ones by a cruel master and the death of loyal slaves, all guaranteed to leave the audience wet-faced. As the tension leading to the Civil War grew, the minstrel show, by now playing largely in the North (New York was the center of minstrelsy for a long period), propagandized for the Northern cause, but after the Civil War the comic darky appeared again. The music used in minstrel shows was written mainly by whites. It was supposed to be typical black music, but in fact it was ordinary popular music dressed up with occasional ragged rhythms. The work of Stephen Foster comes directly out of this genre.

The idea that the minstrel show was presenting an "authentic" picture of the black led, reasonably enough, to the arrival of the black minstrel man. Who, after all, was more authentic than an actual black? The first black minstrel troupe was formed in 1855, and black shows came more and more to dominate the field. The material changed little, and in some cases blacks even "blacked up" so as to present the traditional minstrel man's appearance. This wave of black minstrelsy had the important effect of creating a whole profession, that of the black entertainer. Blacks became singers, dancers, comics, actors, in order to work in minstrel shows. Some of them were exceedingly successful, even compared with whites. The black minstrel man James Bland wrote some of the country's best-known songs, including "Carry Me Back to Old Virginny" and "Oh, Dem Golden Slippers." Other performers who came out of minstrelsy are W. C. Handy, Bert Williams, Ernest Hogan, and two of the greatest classic blues singers, Ma Rainey and Bessie Smith. It was not, of course, all pie and glory for black minstrels. They were in general paid worse than their white counterparts; they were sometimes cheated by white entrepreneurs; they found it difficult to get lodgings as they traveled (eventually they took to traveling in private trains,

The Fisk Jubilee Singers near the beginning of their career, probably in the early 1870s. Just as they dressed wholly in the white style of the day, so they Europeanized black church music to make it accessible to white audiences.

where they could live); and on occasion they faced violence from whites. But for most blacks the chance to get into show business was well worth the hardship.

Although the minstrel show still surfaces today, it was moribund as an important entertainment form by the turn of the century. However, out of it had already grown another form, the variety show, or vaudeville. Blacks quickly took to it and continued to play important roles in entertainment; witness Bert Williams, Bill "Bojangles" Robinson, Ethel Waters, Sammy Davis, Jr., and Redd Foxx, all of whom became top stars.

Paralleling the minstrel show on a more genteel plane was the black choral group, purporting to sing authentic black religious music. The first and best known of these groups was the Fisk Jubilee Singers, which in 1871 went on tour to help raise money for Fisk University's building program. The group became enormously successful and was followed by others. The music sung by these black choirs was based on their church music, but it was heavily Europeanized for the benefit of white audiences. This was inevitable: the moment the music was transcribed into European notation so that it could be published, the off-pitch notes and out-of-tempo figures disappeared. Like the songs of Stephen Foster, the spirituals as we know them today have little to do with the black church music from which they were derived.

Between minstrelsy, the spiritual choirs, and other types of popular music, there developed by the latter part of the nineteenth century a variant of black folk music that had best be termed "pseudoblack" music. This music was as much the creation of whites as blacks. Although some composers, like Bland and Richard Milburn, who wrote "Listen to the Mocking Bird," were black, a great many were white. Whatever their race, they were working primarily for white audiences, and the music they produced was basically white, with some inflections of black folk music. These inflections consisted, for reasons I will discuss later, of a tendency toward plagal harmonies, an excessive use, in European terms, of the sixth degree of the scale (A in the key of C), and the use of occasional syncopations, supposed

By post–Civil War times, music had become, to a considerable degree, a black profession. Here a black string band performs for a white function of some sort, possibly a sporting event.

to represent the cross-rhythms implied in black folk music. It is possible that some black performers of this music were sticking closer to the folk tradition. Rupert Hughes, a visitor to New York at the end of the nineteenth century, spoke of Ernest Hogan's "impudent determination to keep out of key and out of time." But for the most part the music, especially as handled by whites, was heavily Europeanized.

This influx of blacks into popular music, coupled with a feeling on the part of middle-class whites that the professional entertainer was only a cut above the prostitute, turned the music business into something of a black profession. It was hardly an exclusively black profession, like Pullman portering, but nonetheless it held disproportionate numbers of blacks. According to figures gathered by Herbert Gutman, out of 5267 blacks living in the San Juan Hill and Tenderloin areas of New York in 1905, 119 were musicians or actors, about one out of twenty adult males. In 1925, of 10,585 adult black males, approximately one in thirty were musicians, as compared with only twice as many waiters or half as many tailors. The 1905 figures show a contrast to a similar group of Italians, who themselves had a strong musical tradition, with only a third as many musicians proportionately, and a group of Jews, which included no musicians at all.

By 1890, then, blacks were engaged in an enormous range of musical activities. There were Harry Burleigh, Will Marion Cook, and others writing classical music in the European tradition. There were Bert Williams, W. C. Handy, and many others playing in the minstrel and variety shows. There were the millions of unknown blacks singing their own music in church. And at some time, out of the mélange, there emerged a new musical form that was still to be profoundly affecting music all over the world nearly a century later. That was the blues.

Out of the Hybrid,
the Blues

The evolution of the blues is a story that will probably never be fully told. The first blues records were not made until the early 1920s, when the form already was fully developed. Where, when, and how it grew there is no report. There is, to my knowledge, no use of the term "the blues" in any of the nineteenth-century writings on black music, and there is no description of any music that really resembles the form. We are once again speculating. (The term may have been derived from the phrase "the blue devils," which dates back to Elizabethan times.)

It has usually been suggested that the blues evolved from the spirituals, because both were "sad." As a matter of fact, spirituals were often joyous, and the blues, if not generally joyous, are sometimes comic and often filled with sexual innuendo. Clearly, the blues evolved not from the spiritual but from the common musical practice that undergirt the work song, the prison song, the street cry, as well as the spiritual.

Of these, the most prevalent was the work song. Characteristically, the work song was cast in call-and-answer form; the song leader would throw out a vocal line, which the men would answer with a short phrase, perhaps no more than a single syllable timed to the pull of the oars or the fall of the hammer. It was built on an extremely slow ground beat: a man swings an ax, pounds a hammer on a railroad spike, pulls an oar, heaves on an anchor line, no faster than once every couple of seconds and usually much slower than that. In the chopping song "Looky, Looky Yonder," as sung by Leadbelly, the simulated ax beats come approximately four seconds apart. The song leader sings his melody at a much faster tempo, fitting each line of the song in between the slow work beats. The words of the song were improvised by the song leader as he went along, and were usually drawn from a common stock of themes: the inequities of the company or the job, the fickleness of lovers, the character of the straw boss or "captain," the foibles of particular men on the job, homesickness and the evils of the traveling life, and so forth. And herein lies one good reason for believing that the blues descended from the work song: the subject matter of the blues had far more in common with that of the work song than with that of the spiritual.

The vocal pattern of the work song was set by the cadences of the work itself; that is, the ax or hammer strokes set the length of each vocal line. It had, thus, a little form of its own, made up of a series of related lines. Sometimes they would be paired, as in a couplet, with the second line rounding off the idea suggested by the first, like this prison work song:

LEADER: I wonder what's the matter.
WORKERS: Oh–o, Lawd.
LEADER: Well, I wonder what's the matter with my long time here.

In other cases the words circle around a common theme, or tell a story, as in this hammer song:

Well, God told Norah [Noah].
You is a-going in the timber.
You argue some Bible.
Well, Norah got worried.
What you want with the timber?
Won't you build me a ark, sir?

In other cases the lyric dealt with the work itself, as in this song for unloading rails:

Walk to the car, steady yourself.
Head high!
Throw it away!
That's just right.
Go back and get another one.

There was a good deal of recitative in these songs, patches where the singing might switch to talking, shouting, or falsetto singing, and the vocal range tended to be limited often to two or three notes. The melody line, however, employed the scales and off-pitch notes required by black folk musical practice.

Many of the men who sang these work songs were living in turpentine camps or tent cities along the railroad lines, where there was little to do in their leisure time. As a matter of course, they would sing in the evenings. We remember that many of the songs blacks sang were put to multiple uses; they were sung in cotton fields as well as in churches, in army camps as well as on the docks. In his leisure hours the work songs were near to the black man's mind, and he sang them. And somehow, somewhere, there began to grow out of this leisure music a new form, one more strict than the work song, whose function was to talk about the things that a working man or woman felt about his or her life.

When this took place we cannot be sure. Some writers have suggested that the blues go well back into the nineteenth century, but it is difficult to see how this could be the case. As I have said there are no descriptions of anything resembling the blues in nineteenth-century writings. The term itself does not appear on a piece of sheet music until 1912, when "Memphis Blues" and "Dallas Blues" were published. Ma Rainey, one of the first great blues singers we know anything about, was born in 1886 and must have heard some rudimentary blues in her childhood. The best we can say is that the blues as a separate form of music probably began to develop from other black folk forms, especially the work song, in the 1880s or 1890s, and was complete as a form by about 1910.

Fortunately, long after the blues reached its finished form some older singers were still working with a more primitive version. Numbers of these men were recorded during the 1920s and even into the 1930s. The music they recorded has come to be called "country blues," and because it is much looser in form than the strict form of the modern blues, we can infer that it reflects an early stage in the development of the blues, a form at some intermediate point between the work song and the classic blues that emerged some time before 1920.

As in the modern blues, these early blues were divided into three equal parts, each containing a single line of verse. Usually, but not invariably, the second line repeated the first, and the third line rounded off the idea, as was often true of the work song:

> If you see me comin', heist your window high;
> If you see me comin', heist your window high.
> If you see me goin', hang your head and cry.

Each of these lines was answered by a short instrumental response, or "fill." The instrument might be the singer's own banjo or guitar, the piano or horn of an accompanist, or, in the case of a modern blues by, say, Basie, the entire orchestra. In the evolved blues, with its strict form, each of these little sections is allotted exactly four measures, with the vocal line getting two or two-and-a-half bars, and the fill the rest. But in the early blues, the singer felt free to stretch the line out as long as he cared to. Most commonly the singer introduced an extra bar at the end of the first section in order to allow himself additional space for his instrumental answer. Less often he added a measure or a few beats at the end of the second section. Finally, he frequently stretched out the last section by the addition of two beats or more.

It is sometimes quite difficult to beat time in the ordinary sense to these early blues performances. The natural beat does not seem to be the ostensible 4/4 ground beat, but a beat half that speed, suggesting a residual beat left over from the slower work song, or possibly a feeling for cross-rhythms. A particularly interesting case is a record by Big Bill Broonzy of a blues standard he calls "Joe Turner No. Two," a song he dates back to 1890. The song, which is surrounded by recitative, is stretched out to sixteen bars because Broonzy takes ample time for his instrumental answers. But more important, the answering guitar figure comes in two beats early, so the whole meter of the music suddenly jumps out of place. This is, needless to say, entirely contrary to European practice, but is basic to African music. It is clear enough, in any case, that these early blues had not yet settled into a firm meter and exact bar pattern, and the implication is that they were moving from a still more loose form, like the work song.

The central characteristic of the blues, however, is its melodic line. Blues melody was taken, from the beginning, from the scales employed in black folk music generally. Crucial to it are those off-pitch notes derived from African practice, which have come to be called the blue notes. There has been a great deal of confusion about the blue notes. It has often been thought that they are minor notes, that is, the ordinary minor third and minor seventh (in the keys of C, E♭, and B♭) that are found in European harmony. W. C. Handy himself thought that they were, and in the 1950s the whole so-called funk movement led by black jazz musicians assumed the same thing. The blue notes, in fact, are exactly those off-pitch notes that Krehbiel remarked on and that are derived directly from Africa. It must be clearly understood that they are neither major (E) nor minor (E♭) but lie somewhere in between. They cannot be played on the piano; they fall in the cracks between the keys. Theoretically they cannot be played on keyed instruments like the trumpet and clarinet, either, or on fretted instruments like the guitar and banjo, all of which have fixed pitches; but as a practical matter they can be produced on any instrument but the keyboards and xylophone types.

Not every note in the scale is blued. In jazz practice it is always permissible to hit a note slightly flat and slide up into it, and it is equally possible, though less often done, to let the pitch of a note fall off at the end. A true blue note, however, is not a simple flatting or sharping of a note from the diatonic scale, but a separate pitch of its own, with its own place in the scale. Specifically, blue notes replace the third and seventh in the ordinary diatonic scale: E and B in the C scale. I want to be clear about this: the early blues singers did not indiscriminately flat notes at whim. They were working from well-defined rules that called for the use of the blue sevenths and the blue thirds in place of the regular diatonic thirds and sevenths. This does not mean that the ordinary major and minor thirds and sevenths were not used, but they were used only sparingly. In general, the blue notes were substituted for the diatonic sevenths and thirds.

There has been among jazz writers some speculation about the existence of a third blue note, the blue fifth. Some authorities have said it exists; some have denied it. In fact, it does exist, but it does not work precisely as the other blue notes do. The blue fifth is often used in place of a diatonic or perfect fifth when employed as a passing tone. The perfect fifth is always used when it is the last, or resolution note, of the phrase. That is, when the fifth appears in the middle of a phrase as a relatively unimportant passing note on to others, it may be blued; when it is the final note of the phrase — an important note toward which the others are leading — it will always be the standard perfect fifth. (The blue fifth has nothing to do with the so-called flatted fifth of the bebop movement. The flatted fifth was a standard chromatic note, which can be played on the piano — G♭ in the key of C — and came into jazz as part of the chromaticism of the bop revolution.)

These blue notes, it should be understood, are not exactly fixed pitches as are our diatonic pitches, but tend to wander, now drifting downward a bit, now sliding upward. Winthrop Sargeant, in *Jazz: Hot and Hybrid,* one of the best early critical essays on jazz, says that the blue seventh is somewhat firmer than the blue third, and I believe he is correct.

What is most interesting about the blue notes is their use in blues melody. Typically, the first of the three phrases of a blues will begin on a long, pronounced blue seventh and then descend either to the fifth or down to the tonic by way of a blue fifth, a blue third, or both. The second phrase will be similar to the first, except that the first note will be the upper tonic. The third phrase can attack the blue seventh, but more generally it will break the mold and begin elsewhere. It, too, will normally end on the tonic. This scheme is widely used, but it is hardly the only one. Another one calls for the first note to be a fifth, with the phrase running down through a blue fifth and a blue third to the tonic, a scheme favored by Bessie Smith. Yet another common phrase, characteristic of the singing of Billie Holiday, begins on the blue third, and slides downward through the blue seventh to resolve on the fifth below.

We have, of course, to be careful of generalizing. The foregoing are not rules but only some characteristic ways by which blues melody is worked out. But some generalizations are fair. For one thing, blues melody usually goes down rather than up. For a second, it very often begins on a blue note. And in part as a result of both of these practices, the phrases begin with strength and tail off at the end. This whole scheme is contrary to European practice, in which melody goes up as well as down, does not employ nondiatonic blue notes, and generally reaches the climax at the end rather than at the beginning of phrases.

Harmonically, the blues is a nullity from the viewpoint of Western music. European music, since the time of Bach, has been built on two so-called modes, the major and the minor. The principal difference between the two, the distinguishing mark, is whether the third is major or minor. The blues, however, uses neither a major nor a minor third; it uses a blue third. The blues is therefore played in neither major nor minor mode but in a mode of its own, the blue mode. A blues singer can and will use the full range of the diatonic scale, even at times using diatonic thirds and sevenths instead of blue thirds and sevenths. But a perfectly adequate blues can be made of just the tonic, blue third, blue fifth, perfect fifth, and blue seventh, and I suggest that this group of notes constitutes the basic blues scale.

One final point I would like to make about these early blues is that they usually ended on a minor seventh note, either as part of a guitar or piano chord, or as the last note of a small concluding tag. This again is entirely contrary to European practice.

Of the men who were playing these primitive country blues, two stand out: Blind Lemon Jefferson and Huddie Ledbetter, the latter known as Leadbelly. Jefferson was born blind in 1897 on a farm near Wortham, Texas, about a hundred miles south of Dallas. Like many blind blacks of his time, he took up music as a way of making a living. Early in adolescence he was working parties and dances in the farms in his area, and by the time he was twenty he was in Dallas, playing in brothels, barrooms, and at private dances and parties. In time, following the path of other black musicians, he began to travel through the South. Eventually he came to the notice of the Paramount Record Company, and between 1926 and 1929 he made some eighty records, which were widely popular among blacks. Jefferson is supposed to have been an oafish, drunken lecher, but Pete Welding, an authority on the blues, questions this reputation, saying that several musicians who knew Jefferson found him a pleasant and cordial man. He died young, in about 1930, in unknown circumstances.

Paradoxically, Leadbelly, Jefferson's most important protégé, was older. He was born in the early 1880s and began playing professionally at about fifteen for fifty cents a night and his liquor. At sixteen he married and became a father, and by about 1910 he was in Dallas, acting as lead man for Blind Lemon. He was apparently a quick-tempered man, living in brutal and violent conditions, for he was three times jailed, twice for murder and once for attacking a woman. The Lomaxes, who knew him well, suggest that he was acting in self-defense in some of these instances, but whatever the case, he spent long periods in jail during the first fifty or so years of his life. He was finally released when he was discovered by John Lomax. Lomax was so taken with Leadbelly's singing that in 1934 he had him perform for both Governor Pat Neff of Texas and Governor O. K. Allen of Louisiana,

A publicity photograph of Blind Lemon Jefferson shows him in much more
formal attire than he presumably wore in his early days as a street
musician.

and the two governors pardoned him. (Or so Lomax's story goes. Frederic
Ramsey, Jr., says he was released at the normal time.) Lomax then took him
to New York, hired him as his chauffeur, and began to record him. He was
natural copy for the newspapers and magazines — a murderer who was also
a master folk singer. He began playing concerts and in nightclubs, and
eventually, in 1949, performed in Paris. When he died, in December 1949,
he was a minor celebrity.

Jefferson and Leadbelly were perhaps the best known of the country blues singers, but their numbers were legion, and dozens of them are available to us today through recordings made in the 1920s and 1930s. The blues they created has proven to be one of the most durable and appealing of musical forms created during this century. Like the sonnet, it is small and perfectly rounded, carrying us through a brief emotional experience each time it spins out its progress. Its harmonic base as finally evolved, the tiny constellation of tonic, subdominant, and dominant, has for centuries been recognized as the center of Western harmony, a triumvirate on which endless music has been built. Its three-part form suggests the three acts of the standard play, or the beginning, middle, and end of the Aristotelian formula for drama. Its mixture of European and African melody supplied it with that haunting quality which so often was taken by early writers for the tormented cry of the black spirit. It is no wonder, given its small perfection, that the jazz musician has gone back to it again and again. For nearly a hundred years it has captivated him, and even today he returns to it again and again to refresh himself.

Scott Joplin

and the Ragtime Craze

The blues was a cornerstone on which jazz was built, and continues to inform the music today. But a second black musical form, developing about the same time as the blues came into being, was equally important in giving jazz its initial shape. This, of course, was ragtime.

Searching out the development of ragtime is no easier than discovering how the blues was made. Fortunately, we have one good source work in *They All Played Ragtime,* written by jazz authority Rudi Blesh and Harriet Janis. The collaborators did their research primarily in the 1940s, when some of the early ragtime players were still alive, and they were able to get firsthand accounts of the period of the ragtime boom. An earlier time, when ragtime was evolving from its predecessors, however, we can see only murkily.

Although ragtime has been played on virtually every instrument that exists, as well as by full-scale bands and orchestras, it is essentially a piano music. Its roots lie in the attempt by American blacks of the eighteenth and nineteenth centuries to replicate in their music something of the cross-rhythms that were at the heart of African music. As we have seen, there is one figure that shows up over and over again in black American folk music:

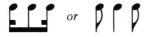

This figure is present everywhere in West African music; it is the basic rhythmic figure in ragtime and the classic figure in jazz. It appeared in popular music as early as 1843 in "Old Dan Tucker" and is familiar to every American as the opening three notes of "Turkey in the Straw." It is, in fact, a variation on that three over two that is so important a principle in West African cross-rhythms. In the European system each of the three notes over the two- or four-beat ground beat is given equal measure. Africans, with their subtler sense of time, do not necessarily give the three notes equal weight. This is what we have here: a three-note figure placed over two (or four) beats in which the middle note is twice the length of the first and third.

In their efforts to understand this and similar figures in their own terms, whites, and blacks educated in the European musical system, saw as syncopation this "ragging" of the melody, as it came to be called. The term "syncopation" is applied to a note or figure that begins between the beats or is arranged so that its principal notes fall between the beats. In the little figure we have been talking about, the syncopation is felt in the middle note, which falls between the beats, although the last note of the figure begins on the second half of a beat as well. Syncopation is a common enough European device: Bach's "Art of the Fugue," for example, is shot through with it. The reader can get something of the feel of syncopation by clapping his hands between his footfalls as he walks.

But syncopation is a European device, not an African one. What looked like syncopation to white transcribers were actually cross-rhythms. The notes were not being set precisely between the beats, but were placed slightly ahead of the beat or behind it. Phrases were stretched out of their natural length; notes were jumped in early. The general effect was a lifting away of the melody from the time scheme, detaching it from the beat so that it seemed to float above it.

Blesh and Janis quote a rag player who was born in 1875, Walter Gould, known as One Leg Shadow, as saying, "Old Man Sam Moore was ragging the quadrilles and schottishes before I was born . . . He was born 'way before the [Civil] war." In any case, it seems certain that by the 1870s, and most probably earlier, players with names like Jess Pickett, Sam Gordon, Sammy Ewell, Jack the Bear, One-Leg Willie Joseph, and dozens of others who have disappeared from the record were working out complete compositions, using ragged figures laid over some sort of ground bass in the left hand.

These men were travelers. Many of them were amateurs or part-timers — the singer or banjo player who entertained his fellow workers on the docks or in the railroad camps in the evenings. But others were professionals. These men, like W. C. Handy, moved back and forth across the country with minstrel and vaudeville shows. Some of them worked the riverboats, the handsome old paddle-wheelers that often carried orchestras for the amusement of the passengers. The elite among them were the piano players, the ivory-tinkling "professors" who moved through the brothels, gambling joints, saloons, and clubs of the big city ghettos, entertaining a clientele that was often racially mixed.

There was a comradeship, a sense of fraternity, among these men. To be sure, they were competitive. Jelly Roll Morton tells the story, quoted by Blesh and Janis, of arriving at a saloon in St. Louis where pianists hung out. He was unknown, but when he admitted that he played, he was invited to sit down for the expected test of his abilities. The resident piano player asked him if he could read. Jelly averred that he could — a claim that was about 30 percent true:

> He had a lot of music lined up on the piano, [Jelly said] and he asked me did I read music and I told him a little bit. Of course he gave me the different difficult numbers, and they were all simple to me because I knew 'em all anyway, and I played everything he had. By that time he started getting in touch with different piano players around that was supposed to be good readers. So they finally start to bringing me different tunes. They brought me all of Scott Joplin's tunes; I knew 'em all by heart anyhow, at that time; so I played 'em all. Finally they brought one, "Poet and Peasant." It seems like in St. Louis if you was able to play "Poet and Peasant" correctly you was really considered the tops. I had known this tune for years and they placed this number in front of me and I started looking at it like I never seen it before — which I had rehearsed it maybe two months before I was able to play it. And I started playing this number, and I had to turn the page over, but it was impossible due to the fact that the passage was so fast. I couldn't turn it over even though I knew the tune, and Mr. Matthews grabbed the tune from in front of me and said, "Hell, don't be messing with that guy, he's a shark."

But the competing was done in a friendly spirit. Underlying it was a sense of community that had been part of the black attitude all along. Musicians encouraged each other; they showed each other their special effects; they taught their friendly rivals their best tunes. In particular, the older, more experienced, or better-trained musicians were expected to help their juniors in age or skill.

It is important to realize that black musicians, even into recent times, did not have the sort of well-defined system of musical training that is standard in the white culture. J. H. Kwabena Nketia, a leading authority on African music, says that in Africa, "traditional instruction is not generally organized on a formal institutional basis, for it is believed that natural endowment and a person's ability to develop on his own are essentially what is needed . . . The principle seems to be that of learning through social experience. Exposure to musical situations and participation are emphasized more than formal teaching." This attitude, brought by the blacks from Africa, continued to shape musical training here. A formally trained musician, as a white usually was, began by learning how to manipulate his instrument so that he could play any music he was handed. The black musician attacked his instrument the other way around: he began by learning to play certain effects or melodies he liked. The black learned only enough technique to enable him to do what he wanted. Where a white trumpet player might, for example, practice scales in all keys, the black would learn a new key only when challenged by a song in that key.

This approach to learning music was of extraordinary significance in the development of jazz. A great deal of what happens in jazz is subtle and cannot be written down or even explained in simple terms. A formal teaching system would not have been able to encompass these crucial details; the only way for a jazz musician to grasp them is to hear them and then try to reproduce them. Had the early jazz pioneers been taught formally, the development of the music would have been far different, and perhaps it would not have occurred at all. For a second matter, this informal way of learning the music encouraged self-expression. The young player did not get into the habit of reproducing whatever material — much of it dreary exercises — was set before him by his teacher. Instead, he chose those sounds, those fragments of melody, those songs he wanted to reproduce, and he developed a technique that was suitable for expressing his choices. He might concentrate on speed, on a broad tone, on a certain type of harmony; but whatever he did, it was a reflection of his own feelings about music.

This system has a serious shortcoming, though, in that it tends to lead the musician into a technical cul de sac from which he cannot escape. Few black jazz musicians until the 1940s were able to play standard European music of any complexity because they had the wrong sort of technique for it. Nevertheless, it was the best system for learning jazz. More often than not the young black musician found himself a mentor, or series of mentors, whose work he admired and attempted to copy, and who, in return for his admiration, would show him how he got his effects and other tricks of the trade.

Many of the early ragtime pianists were spawned in this fashion. The majority of them, probably, could not read much, if any, music. Yet among them, right from the beginning, were some who had had training in European music. A few, in fact, are reported to have attended conservatories. These men began to formalize the ragged way of playing, turning it from a style into a little genre of its own. They not only composed works; they wrote them down and eventually had them published, and in the process they came to Europeanize the music. The blue notes disappeared, discarded by players whose instrument, the piano, could not sound them. The ragged figures in the melodies were converted to formal syncopation, and the melody was tied firmly to the ground beat, with only the rigid syncopation suggesting the African cross-rhythms.

By 1890 a group of men, including Tom Turpin, James Scott, Artie Matthews, Scott Hayden, and Eubie Blake, had begun to create the body of formal rags that has survived until today. Who the first ragtimer was we do not know. The earliest use of the term seems to have been on "Ma

Ragtime Baby," by Fred Stone, published in 1893, but Stone was a popular entertainer, not a ragtimer. In any case, whoever was first, the greatest of them all, by universal critical opinion, was Scott Joplin.

We know Joplin principally through the Blesh-Janis book, although there have been other writings on the subject, the most important an unpublished dissertation by Addison Walker Reed. Joplin was born in 1868 — in Texarkana, a town in the northeastern corner of Texas. His father, a railroad worker, played the violin; his mother sang and played banjo; and not surprisingly the three Joplin boys, Will, Robert, and Scott, were drawn to music. As it happened, there was a piano in a neighboring house — probably a place where Mrs. Joplin worked as a domestic — and Joplin began fooling around with it. It quickly became apparent that he had promise, and his father scraped together the money to buy an old-fashioned square grand piano. It was not as unusual as it might seem for a poor black family to own a piano. The United States underwent something of a piano craze in the last decades of the nineteenth century. Poor black parents with ambitions for their children might buy a piano as poor parents in our time might invest in an encyclopedia. In any case, Joplin began to work at the instrument. Word about the talented black boy started to seep through the neighborhood, and in time he acquired a teacher — according to Blesh and Janis a German who took Joplin on as a scholarship student. Whoever the teacher, we know that Joplin was formally trained in the European tradition and possessed a fairly broad acquaintance with the major European composers of the early nineteenth century and before. Joplin was, from the beginning, a schooled musician with a solid grounding in theory. He certainly knew the black musical tradition, the one of the ring shouts and work songs, for he used some of these forms in his opera *Treemonisha*. But his principal repertory was the Romantic music of nineteenth-century Europe, which has been drummed into hundreds of thousands of American schoolboys and -girls from Joplin's day up to ours.

Joplin's mother was apparently a formidable influence in his life. She seems to have been largely responsible for encouraging him in his music, and probably *Treemonisha,* which is centered on a Joan of Arc figure, was in part a tribute to her. She died in 1882, when Joplin was fourteen, and shortly afterward Joplin left home to become one of those itinerant musicians following their work across America.

But Joplin was not simply another traveling piano player concerned with good times and money to spend. He was never the sort of high-liver some of his peers were. A quiet, reserved, even shy, round-faced man with a dark skin, he was a good and loyal friend, generous in helping others. Underneath this ordinary exterior he possessed a driving ambition to become somebody, to achieve something of significance in what he termed his art.

In this sense he was probably the first American black to conceive of himself as an artist working in a black musical form.

Joplin's wanderings brought him, by about 1885, to St. Louis, which was to remain his base for nearly two decades. He worked throughout the surrounding area, sometimes ranging farther afield, filling whatever engagements came along and eventually developing a reputation through the Midwest and Southwest as one of the leading pianists in his school. For two periods during this time he lived in the town of Sedalia, a railhead in the center of Missouri. How serious he was about his music is made evident by the fact that in the latter part of the 1890s, when he was nearly thirty, he enrolled at George Smith College for Negroes, an institution operated in Sedalia by the Methodist church. What he studied is not known, but the school offered fairly advanced courses in music theory, and it is presumed that he took them. At the same time he was playing cornet in a small brass band, running a dance band, and occasionally touring with a vocal group called the Texas Melody Quartette — it included his two brothers — which he organized and conducted. It is obvious from all this activity that Joplin was, by the age of thirty, a thoroughly schooled musician, teaching, conducting, arranging music, singing, and probably playing a number of instruments, after a fashion, in addition to the piano.

He was also beginning to compose. His first pieces were sentimental songs typical of their time, and no better than thousands of others like them. But by 1897 the ragtime boom was beginning to sound. It was a genuine craze, another one of those popular forms drawn from black folk music and Europeanized. Like similar explosions, such as the jazz boom of the 1920s, the swing band craze of the 1930s, and the soul boom of the 1960s, it was associated with a dance; in this case, the cakewalk. Whites of course got into it quickly, and between about 1900 and 1915 it dominated popular music in America. There were ragtime contests with prizes ranging up to $25,000, schools of ragtime, ragtime instruction books. The movement spread to Europe, and composers began to insert ragtime themes in their work, the most famous of which is Debussy's "Golliwog's Cakewalk."

Joplin was caught up in the boom. In 1899 he showed some rags to a publisher. One of these was "Original Rags," which the publisher took. Among those he turned down was one Joplin had named for the Maple Leaf Club, a Sedalia honky-tonk. Joplin knew better than the publisher. He told a friend, "The 'Maple Leaf' will make me king of the ragtime composers." Shortly after, by chance a small-time sheet-music salesman named John Stillwell Stark heard Joplin play the tune at the Maple Leaf Club. He liked it, offered to publish it, and Joplin accepted the offer. The meeting was crucial in the lives of both men. John Stark, born in 1841, grew up on a farm in Kentucky. First a farmer, then an ice-cream salesman, and next a peddler of cottage organs and pianos around Chillicothe, he eventually landed in Sedalia, where he opened a music store. In the relationship between Stark and Joplin we are for once dealing with something other than the white man exploiting the black one. Stark was a man of honor and principle. He not only paid Joplin an advance of fifty dollars for "Maple Leaf Rag" — a reasonable figure for the time — but he signed a contract giving Joplin regular royalties on sheet-music sales. The song was an instant hit, selling several hundred thousand copies in six months, and on the strength of it Stark moved his business to St. Louis. For the next ten years he remained Joplin's publisher, friend, and confidant.

From this point on Joplin was, if not rich, at least financially secure, and if not celebrated, at least well known. The "Maple Leaf Rag" was the single most popular of all rags, and remains today the best loved by students of the form. Joplin himself was recognized, as he had predicted, as the pre-eminent ragtime composer. Although he always continued to perform in public, the success of "Maple Leaf" allowed Joplin to give up the sporting clubs and to devote himself mainly to composing and teaching. All told,

There are extant only a very few pictures of Scott Joplin. This one, apparently taken from a sheet-music cover or newspaper clipping, around 1911, is the best known. Joplin thought of himself as an artist, not an entertainer; he would never have posed for the vaudevillian-type publicity pictures that were customary for jazz musicians a little later.

Joplin published thirty-three rags, two dozen or so songs, waltzes, solo pieces, and an instruction book; and he left, when he died, another ten pieces, which were not published until recently. These pieces were hardly dashed off. In a good year Joplin might write four rags and perhaps a couple of songs. (Rags themselves were often simplified, fitted out with words, and issued as "songs"; Joplin transformed a number of his rags in this fashion.) He was deadly serious about his music, and he worked hard at it. As the years passed, the texture of his rags grew thicker, and the syncopation began to grow sparser. This was an artistic, not a commercial, choice. The way to make money on rags was to keep them easy enough so that the amateur pianist could get through them without difficulty. Only the really good amateurs attempted Joplin's later work, and skill is required to play properly even "Maple Leaf Rag."

Joplin was scornful of the simplified popular rags — perhaps the most famous was Irving Berlin's "Alexander's Ragtime Band." He decried those ragtime pianists who played the rags faster and faster for showy effect. He would not permit much rhythmic freedom; he insisted that a rag should be played only as written.

This last admonition was important. It suggests that many ragtimers were taking liberties with the melody line — that they were, in fact, continuing to "rag" their rags in the old way. It is difficult to be sure about this, because most of the early piano rags we have were cut as piano rolls rather than records, and we cannot tell how well they reflect the music. However, we do have a few very early records of banjo rags that suggest that the players were taking liberties with strict time. Some of the records of Sylvester "Vess" Ossman, a well-known banjo player of the time, especially his record of "St. Louis Tickle," are played with a looseness that lends an almost jazzlike quality to the rags.

In Joplin's mind, however, a rag was a piece of formally composed music, as carefully worked out as any of Chopin's etudes, and to be taken as seriously. And, indeed, ragtime as we know it today is a very strict form. The left hand sets a steady beat. This may be played as a walking base — that is, a string of single tones or octaves that "walk" up and down the keyboard — or in the so-called stride manner — where the left hand hits a single tone or octave on the first and third beats of the measure, and full chord on the second and fourth beats, producing the "boom-chick, boom-chick" effect so common to popular piano styles. Over this straightforward bass the right hand lays a highly syncopated and, in the classic rags, often quite complex melody line.

Two melodic devices are characteristic. One is repetition — familiar to all lovers of Bach — where a figure is played and then repeated higher or lower, usually at an interval of a second or a third. The second melodic device in ragtime is the familiar call and answer, in which a second figure is played off against the first. Ragtime is usually set in standard time signatures; virtually all of it is in 2/2, 2/4, 3/4, 4/4, and 6/8.

Most ragtime themes are built up from two- and four-bar figures, which are repeated or varied often enough to make up a sixteen- or thirty-two-bar strain. A rag will have three, four, or even five strains, usually repeated or recurring at intervals, in emulation of the rondo form, which a man like Joplin would have been familiar with.

Obviously I am generalizing; many rags depart from this description in one respect or another. But the generalization holds; ragtime is a formal and four-square music, one that none of the Baroque keyboard masters would have had any difficulty comprehending.

Those readers who played in their high school marching bands will immediately recognize something very familiar about the construction of rags. In fact, although ragtime drew on many sources, especially dance forms like the quadrille, lancers, and schottishe, unquestionably it owed more to the march. The marching band has a long history in the United States, and, as we have seen, was important to blacks for decades. The march was a major popular musical form, one utterly familiar to black musicians, and it is hardly surprising that it played a vital role in forming the rag. Indeed, many rags are specifically called marches on the sheet music. Lamb's "Champagne Rag" and Scott's "The Fascinator" were both described as marches.

By the time of America's entry into World War I, the steam was already leaking out of the ragtime boom. Overexposure, the rising popular interest in jazz and the blues, boredom with what was at base a fairly limited form, all combined to deflate it.

But Joplin himself had already turned to other matters. He had left St. Louis about 1907 in part because of emotional turmoil brought on by the death of a baby daughter and the dissolution of his marriage. He moved to New York, where Stark had already established himself, and remarried, this time to a woman who supported him loyally, Lottie Stokes. And he began to give up ragtime in order to concentrate on composing in the European manner. In 1909 he published five rags; in the remaining eight years of his life he was to publish only five more.

He had already, in 1903, written a ragtime opera, *A Guest of Honor,* which was performed once or twice and subsequently disappeared, possibly during the disposition of Joplin's papers after his death. He now began to devote himself to a new opera, *Treemonisha.*

Joplin's concern with this work was obsessive. Stark refused to publish it because he knew it could not make money, so in 1911 Joplin himself arranged to have it published. For years he sought backers in order to have it performed. Nobody would undertake it. To some degree this was owing to musical snobbery in the white musical establishment, which was not willing to admit a black man as an equal. But that was not the whole story. Black musical theater did exist in New York: as early as 1898 *Clorindy,* a musical show written by Will Marion Cook and the black poet Paul-Laurence Dunbar, had appeared in New York and London. The truth was that *Treemonisha* was a flawed work. But Joplin was convinced of its worth, and in 1915 he put on the opera by himself, without scenery and with the music provided by him at the piano. The Harlem audience, mainly black, sat on its hands, and at the end of the evening Joplin's spirit was broken. He was, in any case, already in the grip of an emotional disability brought on by tertiary syphilis. After that year he worked very little, and on April 1, 1917, he died in a mental institution. He was not unmourned, however; his Harlem funeral was impressive and expensive. He may have failed in his great dream, but his rags had made his name.

In working in a longer form taken from the European tradition, Joplin was succumbing to an impulse that has afflicted a number of jazz musicians who came after him. James P. Johnson, Duke Ellington, Bix Beiderbecke, Woody Herman, Stan Kenton, Ornette Coleman, to name just a few, have all written extended pieces in some standard European form — symphony, tone poem, or whatever. The quality of such pieces is usually uneven at best, though there are rare exceptions, and one suspects that ambition to work in a "prestigious" form has more to do with the creation of these works than artistic impulse.

In *Treemonisha* we see all the dangers of a reach exceeded by its grasp. The libretto, which concerns the attempts of a mystical black girl to lead her people out of superstition into education, is a hash of absurdities tied together with a tenuous and incredible plot line. The language of the libretto is embarrassing in its naiveté and lack of nuance. The music ranges from competent to reasonably interesting. As several critics, including Gunther Schuller, who conducted the piece on Broadway, have pointed out, Joplin was using the musical language of the 1830s in the day of Mahler, Schönberg, and Stravinsky. Yet despite its many deficiencies, *Treemonisha* is worth some attention as a minor, if imperfect, composition. Joplin included in it several set pieces drawn from the older tradition of black African music, especially "We're Goin' Around," a ring game, and "A Real Slow Drag," which closes the opera. These pieces are among the most infectious, joyous pieces of music written by any American, and I have no doubt that they will become part of our heritage, to be sung and danced to by school children for generations.

Joplin's death would be a fitting point at which to mark the demise of ragtime, but in fact ragtime was not quite dead. Over the next few decades a handful of enthusiasts kept it alive. They formed clubs, printed newsletters, searched out old manuscripts, and played the music whenever possible. Their devotion was rewarded. In 1971 a musicologist and pianist named

Joshua Rifkin, who had been a jazz fan as an adolescent, became enamored of Joplin's work and recorded an album of his pieces for Nonesuch, a small label, with which he was connected, that specializes in Baroque and Renaissance music. The record, to everybody's surprise, became a hit. A movie producer happened on the small ragtime boom, and used Joplin's "The Entertainer" as background music for a movie called *The Sting.* A ragtime boomlet was on; and it brought with it the production of *Treemonisha,* first in 1972 at Atlanta's Memorial Arts Center and then, in 1975, on Broadway, where it received kind, if not unmixed, notices. Joplin had finally made it.

But in truth, it is his rags that will give him his enduring fame. Ragtime has found a permanent place for itself as a music of real value — not a great music perhaps, but one that at its best has a graceful and translucent charm and a distinction of its own.

PART II

New Orleans

THE BURGEONING
OF THE CLASSIC STYLE

The First Notes Sound

The standard legend about jazz is that it was born in New Orleans, and moved up the Mississippi River to Memphis, St. Louis, and finally Chicago by way of the paddle-wheel boats. This legend has been seriously questioned by recent jazz historians, particularly Ross Russell, who, in his carefully researched study, *Jazz Style in Kansas City and the Southwest,* follows the development of early jazz in Kansas, Arkansas, and Texas. It is more fashionable today to insist that jazz emerged more generally from the black subculture in a number of places, especially New York, Kansas City, Chicago, and St. Louis.

Yet, in truth, the old legend is almost certainly correct. Jazz was indeed created in New Orleans and its environs, and did in fact move out from there, although not necessarily via the riverboats, to the rest of the country. There are several reasons for believing this version of the story. The first is the testimony of the older musicians. The ones alive at the time jazz was emerging from the ghettos invariably say that New Orleans musicians were playing a different kind of music, which other musicians were quick to copy. A Memphis clarinet player, Buster Bailey, says that in his town musicians began to improvise only after they heard the jazz records by New Orleans players, and that the word "jazz" was never used by them until that time. Another clarinet player, Garvin Bushell, in an account published in *Jazz Panorama,* a collection of pieces edited by Martin Williams, offers similar evidence, claiming that Northern blacks learned jazz from the New Orleans players. And the bassist George "Pops" Foster, who has left a fine, out-spoken autobiography, written in collaboration with Tom Stoddard, says, "After the guys from New Orleans got around, guys from the East and West, all of them tried to play like the guys from New Orleans."

Then, too, the evidence of the records is all on the side of New Orleans as the birthplace of jazz. Without exception, all jazz records made before 1924, and perhaps 1925, by both blacks and whites were made by people from New Orleans, or those who were frankly imitating the New Orleans style of playing. An excellent case in point is the early records of Bennie Moten, the leading black band leader in the Southwest throughout the 1920s and into the 1930s. On Moten's earliest records, such as "Elephant Wobble," made in 1923, one hears a band that was playing what was essentially ragtime with some few blues inflections in the cornet. Clarinetist Woody Walder was imitating the white New Orleans player Larry Shields, whose work on the records of the Original Dixieland Jazz Band was widely influential. By 1925, with "18th Street Strut," the Moten group had turned into a New Orleans–style band patterned on Oliver's Creole Jazz Band, which began recording in 1923. Walder was playing more in the manner of Oliver's clarinetist, Johnny Dodds; and cornetist Lammar Wright had acquired the fast terminal vibrato that was a hallmark of New Orleans playing.

If further proof of the right of New Orleans to the title of Birthplace of Jazz is needed, it comes from the records of the white bands from that city. In the early 1920s some of these bands were playing better jazz than all but the best black bands from New Orleans. The New Orleans Rhythm Kings, whom I shall discuss in detail later, was playing in 1922, when it made its first records, better jazz than the black Duke Ellington and Fletcher Henderson bands in New York and the Bennie Moten band in Kansas City, all of which were to make significant marks on jazz. Another group, which recorded under the names of the Original Crescent City Jazzers and the Arcadian Serenaders in 1924, was almost as good. This group, today remembered only by specialists in early jazz history, included a fine clarinetist in Cliff Holman, and two excellent cornetists in Wingy Manone and Sterling Bose, both of whom went on to become well-regarded jazz players of the 1930s and forties. The fact that whites from New Orleans were learning jazz before blacks elsewhere surely makes it plain that the music started there.

Probably the most persuasive evidence that New Orleans was the birthplace of jazz lies in the character of the city itself. New Orleans was an anomaly in the United States. Founded in 1718 by Jean-Baptiste le Moyne, Sieur de Bienville, from its inception it faced south, a member of the Franco-Spanish culture of the Caribbean rather than of the Anglo-Saxon world to the north. Its spiritual homeland was France. There was a libertarian spirit in the city, which manifested itself in the indulgent attitude toward pleasure that was the mark of the French court. The town saw itself as a sort of Paris-sur-Mississippi and attempted to act the part.

Henry A. Kmen, in a carefully researched study called *Music in New Orleans,* draws a picture of a city that for nearly two centuries was drenched in music and dancing. One Northerner who visited the city said that dancing was carried to an "incredible excess. Neither the severity of the cold nor the oppression of the heat ever restrains [the people] from this amusement." Nor was music confined to the dance. At times there were as many as three opera companies playing in the city, astonishing for a town of fewer than fifty thousand people, and there were always symphony orchestras in abundance, including, in the 1830s, the Negro Philharmonic Society.

What is most interesting about this teeming musical activity is the extent to which it was biracial. Dance orchestras, which might run to fifteen pieces, were more often than not black at both black and white dances. (They may even have been mixed; the Negro Philharmonic Society, when short-handed, occasionally filled out with white players.) Upper-class whites frequented the so-called Quadroon Balls, and later were joined in self-defense by white women, who needed dancing partners. Undoubtedly these balls were at times openly sexual in character; one newspaper of the time described them as "inter-racial orgies."

We should not be deluded into thinking that the black was in any sense considered the social equal of the white, or that the largest part of the black population was not condemned to a life of heavy toil. New Orleans was still the South. But for nearly a century and a half, from the city's founding until the Civil War, music and dancing provided occasions when whites and blacks did mix, if not as social equals, at least on a social basis.

New Orleans, thus, was different from other American cities in a number of respects. It was tolerant of pleasure, it was rich with music — undoubtedly it was the most musical American city — and it offered the black man a little more room for expression than was generally true of the South. Perhaps more important, from the standpoint of the jazz historian, it possessed a unique subculture, the black Creoles.

The Creole culture is not well understood. There are people in New Orleans today who will insist that there are no black Creoles, and there are many jazz writers who seem to be unaware that not all Creoles were black. The black Creoles themselves strenuously insisted that they were not Negroes until very recently, when the black-is-beautiful movement made being black more acceptable. One New Orleans writer, M. H. Herrin, says, in *The Creole Aristocracy,* that the name "Creole" is not supposed to be used for people of mixed blood, and Herrin was writing in 1952. The Creoles were people of French or Spanish descent who were born in the New World, as opposed to those who immigrated. The term came to mean those people in New Orleans and elsewhere around the Caribbean who were descended from the original settlers. This was, of course, a point of pride. But after the Louisiana Purchase, in 1803, "Americans," as they were called, began to come into the city and its environs, and gradually they assumed the major positions of power and influence. The Creoles saw themselves more and more as a threatened class. They drew in tighter and made great efforts to maintain their European culture. They continued to speak a French patois, they aped French culture, and those who could afford it sent their children to Paris to study.

One French habit the men maintained was the keeping of mistresses. There developed a custom among many of the Creole men of choosing for their mistresses light-skinned girls of mixed blood, who were in abundant supply in the South. In many cases the men negotiated for the girls with their mothers, as they might have for a bride. They set them up in little houses in the French Quarter, which became for them second households. Through this particular custom there emerged a subclass of "black" Creoles, who were in fact of varying skin colors. They spoke French, took pride in possessing a smattering of culture, and, above all, insisted that they were not Negroes. They were living, after all, in a society in which blacks were not merely at the bottom of the heap but were slaves. Those who had light skins were tempted to pass over into white Creole society, and many of them did.

During the first half of the nineteenth century, and into the second half, the black Creoles were able to keep themselves perched in a precarious social niche of their own, well away from the black mass. But after the Civil War the Southern white instituted oppressive Jim Crow laws designed to drive the black man back into the slavery from which he had so recently been released.

For the black Creoles the new laws were devastating. Louisiana Legislative Code III stated that anybody with any African blood was a Negro. The black Creoles, who had hitherto seen themselves as more white than black, suddenly discovered that they had been anathematized. Driven out of whatever positions of influence they had held, out of affluence, out, eventually, of their jobs, they managed in the end to save only shards of the old Creole culture. Willy-nilly, they were pushed into closer and closer association with the blacks, until by 1890 they were only marginally better off. Still, they continued to struggle against being declassed. They lived "downtown," in the French Quarter, while blacks lived "uptown," across Canal Street. They kept up the French patois; they maintained strong family ties; and they raised their children in a shabby gentility that attempted to hold to a strict morality after the manner of the French bourgeoisie.

One aspect of their culture to which they clung was music. To be able to sing or play a piano or other instrument was a mark of cultivation, and Creole youngsters were encouraged to study music. As with white parents, however, the object was not to turn the young people into professionals. In nineteenth-century America, the professional musician was classed with the actor, only a cut above the prostitute. The black Creole wanted his child to be musical; but that meant attending the opera, playing the piano in the parlor for friends, or playing, as an amateur, in some sort of concertizing ensemble. Given this attitude, it was inevitable that black Creoles refused to have anything to do with black folk music. The Creoles were mainly, although not entirely, urban people. They had no tradition of the work song and the field hollars; and, as Catholics, they did not attend the sanctified church, with its African-influenced spirituals and ring shouts. The black Creole was what was called a "legitimate" musician. He could read music; he did not improvise; and he was familiar with the standard repertory of arias, popular songs, and marches that would have been contained in any white musician's song bag. The point is important: the Creole musician was entirely European in tradition, generally scornful of the blacks from across the tracks who could not read music and who played those "low-down" blues. Alice Zeno, mother of the early New Orleans clarinetist George Lewis, says that in 1878 at black Creole dances people danced the waltz, the mazurka, the polka, and the quadrille. "But I certainly never danced the Slow Drag . . . My, but those Creole dances were elegant."

The blacks of New Orleans had, of course, their own music. Despite the city's sophisticated urban culture, the African tradition had hung on in New Orleans. The African dancing at Congo Square continued until 1855, and went on under cover for a considerably longer period, so it is possible, and indeed probable, that some of the early black jazz musicians had firsthand experience with this neo-African music. New Orleans blacks probably had less experience than other blacks with the field hollar, although some of them came and went between town and the plantations; but they knew the work song from labor on the docks and levees, and they made a specialty of the street vendor's cry. And, of course, there were always the churches. The New Orleans black, thus, partook of the black folk tradition, almost certainly in more variety than did the plantation worker. And numbers of black musicians were at home in the world of white popular music. The black, unlike the Creole or the white, had no compunction about becoming a professional; playing music was an easier way to make a living than sweating in the hold of a banana boat. Even if he did it only part-time, it brought him prestige, good times, and a little extra cash.

By 1890 New Orleans was a city filled with a rich diversity of musical forms. There were the operas and symphonies, the chamber music groups, of both whites and Creoles. There were a number of well-known black Creole concertizing orchestras, like John Robichaux's Lyre Club Symphony Orchestra, a twenty-five-piece ensemble that played the standard classical repertory, or the Excelsior Brass Band, which lasted from about 1890 to the Depression. There were numberless semiorganized or pickup groups, drawn from a pool of black and black Creole musicians, that played marches for parades, dirges for funerals, and popular songs and rags for picnics and parties. There were the pianists working in the cabarets, honkytonks, and brothels. Music was everywhere.

New Orleans was also a city of clubs, or "organizations," as they were termed. Whites, blacks, and Creoles all had their professional, sporting, social, and fraternal clubs, which had various purposes. Among blacks and Creoles, many of these clubs served as "burying societies," a tradition that comes directly from Africa, where, in many cultures, almost everybody belonged to a group that would provide funds and ceremony for a decent burial. Whatever their purpose, these clubs could hardly make a move without music. A dance, a fraternal outing, a parade in celebration of some event or other, a funeral, all required music, a practice at once typical of West Africa and New Orleans. Indeed, on many occasions parades were put on mainly for the purpose of having a parade; it was an opportunity to show off the uniforms, enjoy the music, and eat and drink richly. Pops Foster says in his reminiscences:

> After I turned professional I spent a lot of time at Lake Pontchartrain. Sunday was your big day at the lake. Out at the lakefront and Milneburg there'd be thirty-five or forty bands out there. The clubs would all have a picnic and have their own band or hire one. All day you would eat chicken gumbo, red beans and rice, barbeque, and drink beer and claret wines. The people would dance to the bands, or listen to them, swim, go boat riding or walking on the piers.

Danny Barker, quoted in Shapiro and Hentoff's exemplary source work, *Hear Me Talkin' to Ya,* in a lovely passage says:

> One of my pleasantest memories as a kid growing up in New Orleans was how a bunch of us kids, playing, would suddenly hear sounds. It was like a phenomenon, like the Aurora Borealis — maybe. The sounds of men playing would be so clear, but we wouldn't be sure where they were coming from. So we'd start trotting, start running — "It's this way! It's that way!" And sometimes, after running for awhile you'd find you'd be nowhere near that music. But that music could come on you any time like that. The city was full of the sounds of music.

For the jazz historian, one of the critical movements of the years before the turn of the century was the emergence of the blues as an instrumental, rather than a vocal, music. We are once again working by inference. The most frustrating aspect of studying jazz is that we have no way of knowing for sure what early jazz sounded like. There are no records; and the reports of contemporaries are contradictory and confused, in part at least because few of the men who played the music had enough musicological background to describe the specifics of their practice. Not until 1923 was there a sufficient body of jazz records to give us a sense that we are listening to the mainstream and not to an isolated or atypical example. Again, many of the New

Orleans pioneers never recorded at all. Nonetheless, a substantial number of contemporary reports make it clear that by at least 1900 some black instrumentalists, indeed small bands, were playing blues on horns, primarily, it seems, for sex-inflected "slow drag" dancing in the honky-tonks. These instrumental blues probably, but hardly certainly, grew out of the attempt on the part of wind players, especially brass players, to imitate the sound of the human voice on their horns. Through use of throat tones, lip vibrato, and an endless variety of mutes, brass players were able to "bend" tones to produce blue notes and the coarse sounds characteristic of blues singing. By at least 1900 the blues band playing instrumental blues was a standard feature of honky-tonks and dance halls.

Concomitant with the arrival of the instrumental blues was that other important musical movement of the day, the ragtime boom. Just as in the 1960s a musician had to be able to play rock-and-roll if he was to work regularly, so in 1900 a musician had to have some ragtime in his repertory. For those groups that could read, the playing of rags for their audiences presented no problems. For those that couldn't — and this would have included most blacks — it would have been a fairly formidable task to acquire by ear the whole of a complex rag, with its interlocking bass and treble lines and its many strains. What probably happened, in fact, was that the lead player would learn the melody line of the best-known strain or two from a given rag, and the other players would supply some approximation of the bass and harmony parts.

What we are seeing, then, in the years from, let us say, 1895 to 1910 is the development of a cadre of New Orleans musicians who were at home in a variety of musics — the blues, rags, marches, popular songs, in many cases themes from overtures and operas, and specialty numbers. Armstrong, for example, continued to interpolate fragments from operas into his playing for years. In general, the black Creoles shied away from the blues in favor of more formal music, while the blacks, usually unable to read, inclined toward rougher forms, inflected with the ragged rhythms of the black folk tradition. The streams were converging; march, ragtime, work song, blues, overtures — Europeanized African music, Africanized European music — began to blend together, and one day there came into being a music that had never existed before, a music that, in three decades, was to move out of the honky-tonks, the picnic grounds, the brothels, the streets of New Orleans, and capture the entire world.

According to Jelly Roll Morton this epochal event occurred in 1902. As unlikely as it seems that so specific a date can be given for the creation of jazz, there were things happening in New Orleans that suggest that jazz did indeed emerge from the music around it between 1900 and 1905. One important fact is that with the conclusion of the Spanish-American War in 1898 there came onto the market a flood of used band instruments sold off by the army when the troops were broken up. New Orleans was one of the American ports nearest to Cuba, and many units were broken up there. Thus, from about 1900, the secondhand shops of the city contained a plethora of clarinets, trombones, drums, and cornets, which even a very poor black could afford to buy. In the decades after the Civil War, when the ordinary Southern black lived in the kind of poverty we find difficult to grasp today, the acquisition of a real musical instrument was by no means easy, especially for a child. Louis Armstrong never owned a real musical instrument until he was given one in the Waifs' Home at the age of fourteen, and as recently as 1944 Ornette Coleman's family had to scrape to buy him a battered saxophone. Most musical blacks of the South made their instruments: guitars of cigar boxes and wire, drums of canisters, basses of washtubs and broom handles. The flood of surplus army instruments that came into the city around 1900 thus made it possible for increasing numbers of black children to begin experimenting with cornets and trombones.

Another thing that fertilized the new music was New Orleans' large brothel district. The city already had a history of being a good-time town. As the only major city in that part of the country for a long time in the eighteenth and nineteenth centuries, it was a magnet for trappers, loggers, and rivermen, who came there to sell their goods and go on a spree. From the other direction came the sailors of the seagoing ships that used the city as a port, and eventually there was a United States naval base there. All these men looking for a good time generated a thriving business in prostitution, liquor, gambling, and drugs. In 1897, in order to control the traffic in sin, the town fathers established the brothel district, which was quickly named Storyville, after Joseph Story, the alderman who sponsored the legislation that created it. (Actually, local musicians invariably called it "the District.") The role of Storyville in the birth of jazz has been overplayed by the early writers. Both Bechet and Morton say that it was mainly the pianists who worked the brothels; the bandsmen might play occasional gigs in Storyville and at times some of them held down regular jobs in the biggest of the cabarets, but most of the playing done by the jazz pioneers was at parades, picnics, private parties, funerals, and the like. Yet Storyville did provide employment for musicians, and it gave those who worked there an opportunity to develop their skills and refine the music itself.

But both the opening of Storyville and the freshet of musical instruments pouring into the city were secondary forces in the creation of jazz. The main event was the coming together of the blacks and the black Creoles. The blacks had the black-American musical tradition, specifically the blues. The Creoles had the instruments, the formal training, and the European musical tradition. Prior to 1900, though there unquestionably existed black bands playing the standard band repertory, in all probability most of the music made by blacks in New Orleans was vocal or played on homemade instruments. It was the Creole bands that held sway on the streets, in the dance halls, at the picnic grounds. But as the Creoles were driven into ever-closer alliance with the blacks, the two groups began to mix in both the bands and the audiences. At that point it remained only for the diverse musical practices of these two peoples to fuse.

The fusion involved two basic processes. To begin with, the musical forms that were transformed to make jazz were ones with explicitly stated ground beats, something that much European music does not have. The rags had the "stride" bass; the marches had the drumbeats; the dances the sound of feet on the floor. This was hardly accidental: blacks, with their tradition of cross-rhythms, would be drawn to music with an explicit ground beat. As black musicians came into closer contact with the Creoles, they began to acquire the Creole repertory of marches, rags, dances. A few black musicians had, of course, always played this repertory; but now, as band instruments became more available, it came to be familiar to most black players. Inevitably, black musicians raised in the black-American folk music tradition, would, without even thinking about it, lift their melodies away from the ground beat in at least some spots, thus bringing with them that black-American folk music principle of setting the melody at variance to the ground beat. At the same time, young black Creole musicians, despite the objections of their parents, were hearing the blues being played in black honky-tonks, and they were beginning to inflect their music with blue notes and those implications of cross-rhythms so much a part of black music. The two groups were thus moving onto common ground. Which group got there first is an open question. A very considerable percentage of the jazz pioneers were black Creoles, and from the evidence of the records the first really great jazz players, like Morton and Bechet, were in the main black Creoles. But some of the early pioneers were blacks.

The second process involved in the development of jazz was the undergirding of two-beat musical forms with four-beat ground basses. A word of explanation may be in order. Music, in general, carries with it an underlying beat that we can clap our hands to, tap out with our feet, or, obviously, dance to. These beats, however, do not usually come along regularly, one after another, like ticks of a clock, but are organized into measures of two, three, four, or other numbers of beats. Within these measures are hierarchies of strong and weak beats: in a two-beat measure the first is strong, the second weak; in the three-beat measure the first is strong, the second two weak; in the four-beat measure the first and third are strong, the second and fourth weak; and so on. In most standard European music these meters are not spelled out by a drummer or other rhythm player but are implied by the melody lines. Important notes come on strong beats, lesser ones on weak beats, still less important ones between the beats. Accents, beginnings and endings of phrases, harmonic shifts, changes in instrumentation, and the shape of the melody line itself are cut to conform to the basic meter of the piece. To be sure, the composer will sometimes surprise us by putting an important note on a weak beat or by accenting contrary to the basic meter, but if he does too much of this sort of thing we will make a mental shift and begin hearing as weak beats what had been strong beats.

The marches that were so important a part of the New Orleans repertory were played in two, out of respect for the fact that a marching man has only two legs. Rags were ostensibly in a number of meters, but in fact most of them are subjectively felt as if they were in two-beat time. This effect has to do more with the way the melody line was phrased rather than what was going on in the bass. Now, at some point around the turn of the century New Orleans players began supporting their music with a four-beat ground beat; that is, instead of playing two slow beats per measure, they would play four at twice the speed. Jelly Roll Morton said explicitly that he was the first to play in four instead of two — in his case he was tapping the beat out with his foot — presumably in 1902, and it is probably on the basis of this assertion that he claimed to be the inventor of jazz.

But this movement from two beats to four beats was imperfect. Basses continued to enunciate only the first and third beats of the measure, in the main. Banjoists usually stroked down and up on alternate beats, so the sound of the first and third beats was different from that of the second and fourth. The drummers did something similar.

The standard ragtime bass consists of alternating types of sounds. In the classic one, a single note or an octave is alternated with a chord or part of a chord, to produce the familiar "boom-chick, boom-chick" sound of what came to be called "stride piano." The effect was not of successive strong and weak beats in a four-beat measure, but of two sets of two-beat meters alternating. It seemed natural for the early drummers in the ragtime or incipient jazz bands to attempt to produce the same effect by playing a single stroke on the first and third beats and two quick strokes on the second and fourth beats — or, to put it in the terms I have been using, to intermesh two-beat meters of quarter notes with meters of pairs of eighth notes:

$$\text{♩ ♫ ♩ ♫}$$

It is difficult to know precisely how the early New Orleans drummers played. Because the drums threatened to jiggle the recording apparatus, drummers were often placed at some distance from the machine, or made to work solely with woodblocks, and as a consequence are usually inaudible on the early records. The two best-known drummers from the period are

Warren "Baby" Dodds, brother of the clarinetist Johnny Dodds, and Zutty Singleton. Dodds was the drummer with Oliver's Creole Jazz Band, and both he and Singleton recorded with Armstrong and many other important players around Chicago during the 1920s. Fortunately, we can hear Dodds quite clearly on some of the Oliver sides. On the famous "Dippermouth Blues," he plays woodblocks, but we can assume that he was stroking much as he would have done on drums had he been playing somewhere other than the studio. He plays a great many almost even pairs of notes to a beat, to produce at times what is called a "shuffle beat." Generally, though, he uses the more standard system, alternating single strokes with pairs of strokes to a beat. His playing is very busy, compared with the simpler playing that was to come during the swing period.

The New Orleans rhythm sections thus had their feet in both camps. They were enunciating four beats to a measure, rather than two, all with more or less the same weight. They were, however, playing the first and third beats differently from the way they played second and fourth. It was a compromise between 2/4 and 4/4, and the effect was a back-and-forth rocking motion that came to be one of the most exciting parts of the music.

These processes were not, of course, all of a piece. Many Creoles refused to adopt black techniques; the much-admired Lorenzo Tio continued into the 1920s to play with a smooth, precise style that had little if any jazz inflection. But this fusing of black and European musical practices, begun about 1900, had gone far enough by 1910 or so for the musicians to recognize that here was something new. They did not call it jazz; they still called it "ragtime," or "playing hot." It was probably not until the next decade that the term "jazzing it up," certainly a phrase with sexual implications, came into use.

This early jazz was built primarily around three forms: rags, marches, and the blues. A few dance forms were brought in: "Tiger Rag" descended from a well-known quadrille. But the basic forms were the blues and the rags and marches, which, as we have seen, are similar in shape. Zutty Singleton, born in 1898, says, "In my times they had the blues and ragtime. They played the blues about once or twice a night. A special number, kind of set off by itself." Pops Foster says, "What's called jazz today was called ragtime back then . . . From about 1900 on, there were three types of bands around New Orleans. You had bands that played ragtime, ones that played sweet music and the ones that played nothin' but blues."

Because so much early jazz was played out of doors, at picnic grounds and in the streets, the predominance of the marching band is understandable. Had jazz been born in New England, where it is possible to perform outdoors for only five months of the year, it might have taken a radically different shape. In the South, the marching band form prevailed. Marching bands could be quite large, comprising scores of players in some cases, but the bands of the blacks and Creoles around New Orleans were much smaller. Generally they included cornet, trombone, one or two other brasses like alto or baritone horn, clarinet or piccolo. The rhythm section consisted of a snare drum, a bass, and a tuba. Saxophones were not used. John Joseph, born in 1877, claims that he brought the first saxophone into New Orleans in 1914. When the group played inside, or in a pavillion, a violin might be added, as well as a banjo and possibly piano, with string bass substituted for tuba.

The players of this early jazz were not improvising in the modern sense of the word, where a musician invents a wholly new melodic line within a given harmonic framework. They were, rather, embellishers. A trombone player, for example, would have a basic part worked out for the tunes in his repertory, which he would vary slightly each time to suit what another player was doing, or out of the simple spirit of the moment.

More important than the notes they were playing, however, was what they were doing with those notes. They were doing exactly what you would expect. In the first place, they were syncopating heavily in order to give the

Buddie Petit was considered by his peers to be one of the best of the pioneer jazz cornetists. This picture, taken around 1920, shows his band not in a Storyville brothel, but at some outdoor function, perhaps a picnic, the sort of occasion at which much early jazz was played. Note the string bass, which the early players bowed as a melody voice as well as plucking for rhythm. The clarinetist is a young Edmond Hall. George Hoefer Collection

music the effect of ragtime, the most popular music of the day. Next, they were, at whatever points they deemed appropriate, coarsening their tones either mechanically by means of mutes, or through the use of lip trills and throat tones. Third, they were employing to a considerable degree blue thirds and sevenths, instead of diatonic ones — probably not every time, but when the thirds and sevenths came at climactic or emotionally charged points in the music. Fourth, they adopted a device that became characteristic of New Orleans playing and was eventually carried into all of jazz. This was the terminal vibrato. In classical playing the general rule for wind players is to avoid vibrato. The New Orleans players, especially the cornetists, added to their notes at the end a vibrato that was particularly fast, and it, too, became a hallmark of the New Orleans sound. And finally, of course, they were phasing away from the ground beat. In sum, they were swinging.

Many of the early jazz players did not swing very much, especially the older Creoles. But others did swing, and the best known of them was Buddy Bolden. He has often been referred to as the first jazz musician; some writers have even credited him with inventing jazz. Many of the pioneer jazz players have said that Bolden was the leading player among the black musicians of his period. He was born Charles Bolden in 1868. He grew up to be a swashbuckler, who drank and womanized in a fashion suitable for legend-making. According to various writers, he was a barber by trade and published a scandal sheet called *The Cricket*. He began to have fits of insanity in the earliest years of the century and was committed to East Louisiana State Hospital in 1907, where he died in 1931.

This at least is the legend, but the whole story is called into question by Samuel B. Charters, an authority on early New Orleans musicians. Charters says that in the first place there were a number of musicians named Bolden around New Orleans at the time, and that in the second place, there is extant a picture of a cornet player named Charles Bolden playing with a minstrel show in New York in 1908, a year after Bolden was supposed to have been hospitalized. In any case, Charters says, "Few musicians from his early period remember him as being a jazz musician in the modern sense of the term. He seems to have attracted attention by being the first of the younger men to play the new styles, the raggy cakewalks and walk arounds, while the downtown [Creole] musicians were playing genteel quadrilles."

Bolden and the men around him were probably blues players who filled out their repertories with popular songs and strains from marches and rags. He was, almost certainly, playing, in the years on either side of 1900, a transitional type of music that stood at some indeterminate point between ragtime and jazz, between the black folk music of his musical forefathers and the jazz to come. But what sort of music it was we do not know; and, sadly, we probably never shall.

Because this fusion of black and European musics to make jazz contains

The only known picture of Buddy Bolden (standing, with cornet), made in about 1895. The trombonist is Willie Cornish; the seated clarinetist, Frank Lewis. Note the presence of two clarinetists and the string bass, which, contrary to general belief, was widely used as both rhythm and solo instrument in the earliest days of jazz. Willie Cornish Collection

so many diverse streams, it is worth taking a moment to recapitulate. We begin with the assembling by black slaves of elements from both musics to create what I have termed black-American folk music, the music of the work song, the field hollar, the ring shout, out of which the blues evolved. Paralleling this movement was a similar one made by whites and eventually blacks, in which elements from black-American music were fused with European popular music to create the Europeanized version of black folk music — the spirituals, the minstrel songs, and various vaudeville forms. A third parallel movement, this one made by blacks, was the creation of ragtime again by combining elements of black folk music with European piano forms. We thus have by 1890 *three separate and distinct fusings* of African and European music: ragtime and black-American folk music, represented by the blues, both created by blacks, and the popularized version of black folk music, made principally by whites.

In the years between 1890 and 1910 these three streams converged. There were many pressures forcing this convergence, but a major one was the movement of the black Creole, whose culture was more European than black, into the general black subculture. And even as the fusion was being completed in the music called jazz, it began to spread outward, first through the black world and then very quickly into the white, until in the 1920s it burst into the consciousness of the American public and gave its name to an age.

The Diaspora
from New Orleans

On February 26, 1917, five white New Orleans musicians went into the Victor studios in New York City and made the first jazz record. It was the single most significant event in the history of jazz. Before this record was issued jazz was an obscure folk music played mainly by a few hundred blacks and a handful of whites in New Orleans, and rarely heard elsewhere. Within weeks after this record was issued, on March 7, "jazz" was a national craze and the five white musicians were famous. They called their band the Original Dixieland Jass Band, and the songs they cut that day were "Livery Stable Blues," which featured a whinnying cornet and a mooing trombone, and "Dixieland Jass Band One-Step," today usually called "Original Dixieland One-Step." (This early spelling of the word "jazz" was quickly dropped. It is customary today to use the modern spelling when referring to the band. As an example of the way myths persist in jazz, in every discussion of this record it has been stated that no bass drum was used because of its tendency to make the recording needle jump. H. O. Brunn, the band's biographer, says so, and so does the normally astute Rudi Blesh in the liner notes for the RCA LP reissue of the record. Nonetheless, a perfectly audible bass drum booms away throughout the record.)

For decades, jazz writers have been exasperated by the fact that the honor of making the first jazz record went to this particular group rather than to a black band. Like many other things in jazz, it was largely a matter of chance. The commonly accepted story is that Freddie Keppard turned down the chance to record previously because he didn't want anyone to "steal his stuff," although one source says he did record in 1916 but that the record was never issued.

The band was theoretically a cooperative group, but in fact it was dominated by cornetist Nick LaRocca, who not only provided much of the musical leadership but acted as its business manager as well. LaRocca was born on April 11, 1889, the son of an immigrant Italian shoemaker who played a little amateur cornet.

He began playing around New Orleans and surrounding towns with the juvenile "kid" bands that were abundant in the city, mostly for food and drink or insignificant amounts of money. During his adolescence he belonged to a loose fraternity of white musicians playing hot music, which paralleled the larger group of black musicians. Among his comrades were Larry Shields, later to be clarinetist with the Original Dixieland Jazz Band, Leon Rappolo, an influential clarinetist who recorded early with the New Orleans Rhythm Kings, and the Brunies brothers, who also made early records. In time LaRocca began to work with Jack Laine, a prominent New Orleans leader. Self-taught, LaRocca could not read music, but his musicianship was reasonably good, and because of his natural strength as a leader, Laine used him to front bands.

Then, in December 1915, according to Brunn, a Chicago nightclub owner named Harry James, who was in New Orleans to witness a prize fight, happened to hear a hot band, led by drummer Johnny Stein, that included LaRocca. (Stein's version is that the discoverer was an actor named Gus Chandler and that the year was 1916.) The Stein band was booked into a Chicago nightclub early in 1916. It was not the first hot band to come north. Another white group, Tom Brown's Ragtime Band, had been in Chicago two years before, and black bands had begun to fan out from New Orleans as early as 1912. But Stein's band caught on, partly because the club was a hangout for show business people, who helped to spread the word about this novel music. The band stayed in Chicago for several months. Stein was eventually forced out in a salary dispute, the name was changed to the Original Dixieland Jazz Band, and then, early in 1917, it was booked into an important New York restaurant and dance palace, Reisenweber's, located at Fifty-eighth Street and Eighth Avenue.

Within two or three weeks the group was the sensation of New York. Its fee soared to a thousand dollars a week. There were bookings everywhere, and, because of the fame, those first records. At this point the personnel consisted of LaRocca, trombonist Eddie "Daddy" Edwards, Larry Shields, Henry Ragas on piano, and Tony Sbarbaro. The first record sold over a million copies, an extraordinary accomplishment for those days. At least part of the reason for the popularity was the barnyard noises on "Livery Stable Blues." In the next few years the band issued about a dozen records, toured England, grew more and more commercial, and fell apart in the mid-1920s, due to personality conflicts and, finally, the emotional disintegration of LaRocca. The band was successfully revived in 1936, but it had no particular impact and shortly collapsed, once again beset by internal feuding.

Today the Original Dixieland Jazz Band is of interest primarily to historians. Most contemporary listeners find the music either dull or bewildering. Yet its influence in its day was enormous. For a period of two or three years, before other jazz bands began to record, it had the only game in town. Anybody in America who had even the slightest interest in popular music was familiar with the records. Young musicians, especially but not exclusively white, studied the new music bar by bar, playing and replaying the records until they had learned by heart the parts for their own instruments. Established bands found themselves caught up in a tide they could not resist, and everywhere orchestras were putting out imitation jazz with some sort of spurious ragged rhythm. The influence of the Original Dixieland Jazz Band was, of course, stronger on whites than on blacks because there was no countervailing force; for whites it filled a cultural void. But the black clarinetist Buster Bailey has said that even in Memphis, where there was some familiarity with New Orleans music, those first records of the Original Dixieland Jazz Band had an important effect.

The one bothersome question that remains is how well the music of this band reflected the music of New Orleans blacks, or for that matter, other whites. This music is not quite the same as that recorded in 1923 and thereabouts by black New Orleans players like Oliver's Creole Jazz Band, or the whites in the New Orleans Rhythm Kings. It is probably best to categorize it as some kind of advanced ragtime. LaRocca and his biographer, Brunn, have insisted that the group's music was not derived from the black tradition but was invented by the group. Undoubtedly these men and others like them thought they were playing ragtime, or some variant of it, and did not recognize the role of blacks in the making of ragtime. Despite LaRocca's denials, the black tradition was there, all right; but it was more a reflection of the New Orleans ambience than a specific aping of black ways. As a result of this orientation, the European elements are the most noticeable. The melodic line is heavily syncopated but is tied firmly to the beat, as in ragtime, with the implied counter-rhythm only occasionally creeping in, especially in the playing of LaRocca. Sbarbaro's drumming is particularly leaden, and the blue notes are entirely absent.

But it would not be correct to deny that in some respects it was a jazz band. For one thing, the instrumentation was the classic New Orleans one, taken from the march band, of cornet, clarinet, and trombone front line supported by a rhythm section. For another, although various members of the group, especially LaRocca, claimed authorship of the featured tunes, in fact they were mainly pastiches of themes from marches, rags, and traditional tunes that were part of the known New Orleans repertory, much of it developed by blacks. And, finally, if the band does not really swing in the true jazz fashion, at times it comes very close. Pops Foster has said of the LaRocca group, "Their band was one of the hottest white bands around

The Original Dixieland Jazz Band, the group that made the first jazz record and went on to a brief but enormous celebrity. From left, Tony Sbarbaro (later Spargo), Eddie Edwards, Nick LaRocca, Larry Shields, and Henry Ragas. Culver Pictures

New Orleans." In sum, the music of the Original Dixieland Jazz Band stands at a halfway point between jazz and its precursors, probably more typical of the hot music of 1910 than of the 1920 jazz of Oliver, Morton, and Bechet.

However elusive the music, there is no doubt of its influence. Jazz suddenly was a hot commercial commodity. Within five years after the issuance of "Livery Stable Blues," thousands of aspiring young players, entranced by the new music, had put together hundreds of bands, most of them atrocious from any point of view, that began playing at dances, in nightclubs, and eventually in recording studios. But the sudden jazz boom of the decade that came to be called "the Jazz Age" was fueled not by commercial considerations alone. What set the whole business going was the fortuitous coming together of several unrelated social movements. The first of these was the anti-idealistic philosophy associated with the artistic movement of the so-called Lost Generation. Disillusioned by the war to end all wars, young people rebelled against what they saw as the hypocrisy of the older generation. In life this meant that one was free to "have fun," which usually came down to sex and liquor. In art, it meant experimentation and the overturning of old forms, as Joyce was doing in the novel, Pound in poetry, O'Neill in the theater, Picasso in painting. Jazz fit nicely into both moods: it was fun, sexy, and a new form.

So the generation of the 1920s took up jazz — usually in spurious or watered-down versions, to be sure — and made it their own. Throughout the 1920s and into the thirties, artists and intellectuals in London and Paris, as well as in New York and Chicago, made a point of admiring Duke Ellington and Bessie Smith; they bought the records and, when possible, went to hear the players, especially in Harlem. Carl Van Vechten, a New York–based novelist with connections in both society and the art world, was especially influential in promoting jazz, and by 1930 European intellectuals were writing seriously about the new music.

A second force that helped to bring about the jazz boom was a craze for social dancing that began in the years after 1910. David Ewen, in *The Life and Death of Tin Pan Alley,* says,

> The passion for ragtime that seized America was followed by one for social dancing. This was not a coincidence, it was cause and effect. Before 1910 social dances, such as the polka, the whirling waltz, and the schottische, taxed the endurance and agility of even the young. Rest periods of ten or fifteen minutes were necessary between dances . . . But ragtime changed all that. The 2/4 and 4/4 rhythm encouraged the creation of the simpler kinds of dances. Call it what you will — a turkey trot, or a grizzly bear, or a bunny hug, or a camel walk, or a lame duck, whether the movements involved rocking, or swaying, or sliding — the new dances brought in by ragtime required little more than walking around the dance floor with a partner in an embrace.

Dancing was what Americans did for entertainment, and dance halls sprang up everywhere. Restaurants discovered that they had to hire bands and permit dancing during meals, something hitherto unheard-of.

Dr. William C. Parker, who was at the University of Indiana during the early 1920s, recalls:

> We used to go out dancing, two, three, times a week. There was usually always a subscription dance any night, it might cost you a quarter or fifty cents. There wasn't so much drinking then. The girls didn't drink at all, and the boys would maybe sneak outside and take a pull at a bottle of fortified dandelion wine. The bands worked for two or three dollars a night. Five dollars was a good night. On the campus we had mostly three or four piece outfits. Bix would come down with maybe a four or five piece outfit. They played by ear — I never saw a sheet of music.

And soon the dance craze produced a demand for musicians that, for a time at least, exceeded the supply. Boyd Bennett, a musician active before 1920, says, "There weren't enough good readers around so a lot of people came into the business who played by ear." All of this played directly into the hands of the improvising jazz musician; it is notable that the jazz pioneers of the 1920s, even when they were unpolished, were able to work steadily.

A third social force important in bringing jazz into the American consciousness was the movement of the black out of his serfdom. To a considerable degree this was brought about by the labor boom occasioned by World War I. In endless numbers blacks began to emigrate from the sharecropper shacks of the South to the industrial cities of the North. In the years of the war and immediately after, a half-million blacks pulled up their roots and moved north to Detroit, Chicago, Philadelphia, and New York. Fifty thousand blacks landed in Chicago's South Side alone. For these people the move north was more than just a change of geography. It meant stepping into a culture vastly different from the one they had been born into.

They came north with a sense of adventure, of a new life, of new possibilities. A great many of them, however, lured by money and tales of the high life, found themselves scared, homesick, and lonely; they reached out for anything that smacked of home: a relative, a familiar face, down-home cooking, the old religion, music. This longing of blacks in the Northern cities for their own music produced a good market for the ragtimers, bluesmen, and incipient jazz players in the South. It pulled them from the South into the Northern cities, where they were heard not only by blacks but by whites willing to adventure into Harlem or the South Side. Among the whites were young players trying to learn the new art. The general public, though, did not experience much of this black music firsthand; it came to them filtered through the dance musicians who were interested in it, and were putting jazz elements into their playing.

Yet one more force that brought jazz out of the New Orleans ghetto was the mechanization of public entertainment, principally by the phonograph record. But the record was not the first mechanical invention to have an impact on the development of jazz. The player piano had been an important factor in the ragtime boom, for it allowed people who were poor players to hear the rags of Joplin, Matthews, Turpin, Lamb, and the rest in their homes. It was, furthermore, an important teaching device for aspiring young players. Many budding ragtime pianists, and, later, stride pianists, learned their styles by following the keys as they were pressed down by the automatic machinery of the player piano. Duke Ellington was one such.

The phonograph, however, was a good deal more versatile than the player piano, and it quickly gained a vital place in the culture of the twentieth century. Its role in the history of jazz should not be underestimated. Because jazz is an improvised music, without recorded sound it could hardly have existed at all. It has always been principally through records that new generations of players have been attracted to the music and have learned to play it themselves. From Beiderbecke in 1919, copying out Nick LaRocca's cornet lines on the Original Dixieland Jazz Band records, to the contemporary student, learning Coltrane's "A Love Supreme," young jazz enthusiasts have found in records their school. And, of course, without records people like Beiderbecke, Bessie Smith, Billie Holiday, Louis Armstrong would be merely romantic legends, existing only in the memories of old men. The new players, if there were any, would never know how the older ones sounded.

The first workable phonograph was designed and built by Edison in 1877, although a Frenchman named Charles Cros appears to have hit on a similar idea about the same time. The machines were generally too expensive for the home, but by 1890 thousands of them were in use in saloons and drugstores, where for a nickel a half-dozen listeners could hear a record by using earphones. The music, by and large, was brass bands, rags, comic monologues, trumpet solos, and the like. By the end of the century the first operatic arias and concert pieces were appearing. In 1902 the machine had been sufficiently improved so that the sound quality was reasonably good, and in that year two companies, Victor and Columbia, pooled their patents and emerged as leaders in the field. Very quickly, prices for the machines dropped.

Then, in the early teen years, came the dance boom. Not only did musicians benefit, but the record companies quickly discovered that people would dance at home to records. On the strength of the dance boom, as well as the rising interest in the new, jazzy music, the record business exploded. In 1914 about 27 million records were sold; in 1921 the figure was 100 million. At the same time, some of the basic patents on sound-recording were expiring, allowing a lot of newcomers to sweep into the field. This upsurge in the record business, of course, created a demand for musicians, and was in large measure responsible for so many of the early jazz players being recorded.

Coming together as they did, these forces created a fad for something that was called jazz. In fact, most of what the public heard was merely ordinary dance music and arrangements of popular tunes dressed up with some jazz inflections. This commercial music, which was played by many blacks as well as whites, had a bouncy beat; the musicians employed mutes to produce growls and buzzes supposedly characteristic of jazz and utilized occasional slurred notes suggested by the blue notes. By playing this kind of music, a number of musicians became famous and, in a few cases, rich. The best known was Paul Whiteman.

Born in 1890, Whiteman was trained as a symphonic violinist and worked with both the Denver and San Francisco symphony orchestras. In 1919 he took over leadership of a dance band to which he belonged, and within two or three years made it the most popular band in the country. As the jazz craze widened, he took for himself the title "King of Jazz." He was no jazz player himself, but he had a good ear for the music, and at one time or another most of the best white jazz musicians of the period worked in his band. The music it featured was heavy, overorchestrated, filled with pretentious passages meant to suggest "serious" music, and almost entirely lacking in any jazz feel. However, the jazz musicians in the band, especially Bix Beiderbecke, occasionally were permitted brief solos.

This was the music that the white public of the period took to be jazz. Its taste, however, was not very discriminating, and, as a consequence, a lot of real jazz was carried along, too. This was important because it meant that the jazz pioneers could work regularly, developing their art, and it meant, too, that their music was being widely recorded. The availability of thousands of records by first-rate jazz players was the base on which the interest in New Orleans music was built.

The diaspora of jazz musicians from New Orleans, begun early in the second decade of the century, was given impetus in 1917, when the Storyville brothel district was closed down under pressure from the United States Navy, who had a naval base in the city. Although the effect on employment for musicians was less drastic than some writers have claimed — the bandsmen were working mainly in other areas, as we have seen — it had a symbolic effect, and this, coupled with the economic suck exerted by the developing black ghettos of the North, eventually pulled most of the leading New Orleans jazz musicians out of the city. Two of these were in time to have marked influences on the history of jazz. They were Joseph "King" Oliver and Sidney Bechet.

Sidney Bechet is an anomalous figure in jazz. Most jazz musicians are cliquish. Bechet was essentially a wanderer, drifting from New Orleans to Chicago to New York to London to Paris and back, playing in whatever musical contexts he found.

His autobiography, called *Treat It Gentle,* is a self-serving and unreliable book, but one is especially struck by the absence of long-term relationships in Bechet's life. One reason for this, certainly, was his prima donna attitude; Bechet attempted to dominate every musical situation he was in, and usually succeeded. This did not, obviously, make him a well-loved figure among his fellow musicians. But he was by no means the cold, aloof figure this makes him sound. Prickly and demanding, he was passionate in his life and in his music. His distance from other players stemmed not so much from reserve as from the feuds he became involved in. He was once deported from London for getting into a fight with a prostitute and then being too outspoken with the magistrate before whom he appeared, and he spent eleven months in a French prison for a gun fight with another musician outside a Paris cabaret. He had a brief but tumultuous love affair with the great blues singer Bessie Smith. Bristly and difficult he may have been; but he responded to the world with passion, and this warmth is evident in his music.

Given his nature, it is not surprising that Bechet proved to be the most individual player in the history of jazz. Duke Ellington, who was deeply affected by Bechet, said of him, "I think he was the most unique man ever to be in this music." Ellington is not alone: Bechet's influence on the early jazz players was all-pervasive.

Sidney Bechet was born in 1897 to a typical black Creole family. His father was dark-skinned, but his mother was light enough to *passeblanc.* They had, like most Creoles, aspirations to gentility. Bechet speaks with pride of his father's having gone to a "pay" school, where he learned to read and write both English and French — that is, the Creole patois. He played a little cornet, but he made his living as a maker of "fine" shoes. The members of the family thought well of themselves. There is a studio photograph of Sidney, taken when he was about three, that shows him in a pinafore with a ribbon in his hair, leaning on a couple of photo albums stacked on a fancy carved chest.

Bechet's older brother, Leonard, later a dentist, played clarinet and trombone. According to Sidney, he learned to play the clarinet by sneaking his brother's instrument out of a bureau drawer and practicing on the sly. He claims to have studied with George Baquet, a Creole who was a schooled musician, not so much a jazz player, and later with Big Eye Louis Nelson and Lorenzo Tio, both among the earliest New Orleans players we know about. Whoever it was he studied with, it is reasonable to assume that he was something of a prodigy, a natural player who from the start played the way he wanted to play to express something personal. By the time he was eleven or twelve he was playing regularly around New Orleans with kid bands and apparently, on occasion, with adult ones as well.

At fourteen or so he began to wander. By 1918 he was in Chicago, where he was heard by Will Marion Cook, the well-known black composer and band leader who had written the music for the all-black show *Clorindy,* in 1898. Cook took Bechet to New York, and then, in 1919, to Europe, with a relatively large group that was not so much a jazz band as a concertizing orchestra that probably played overtures as well as ragtime and popular pieces. Bechet, who was featured as an improvising soloist, proved to be the star. Ernest Ansermet, an important Swiss conductor of the time, said in an oft-quoted passage, "There is in the Southern Syncopated Orchestra an extraordinary clarinet virtuoso who is, so it seems, the first of his race to have composed perfectly formed blues on the clarinet . . . I wish to set down the name of this artist of genius, as for myself, I shall never forget it — it is Sidney Bechet."

If Bechet had not already assumed the demanding tone of the star, comments of this sort were certain to make him do so. He played with Cook's and other groups in London and Paris, and it was in London that he ran across an instrument he had never played before, the soprano saxophone. As we shall see later, saxophones were, in 1920, still novelty instruments, only just beginning to be taken seriously by musicians. There was a large group of them, ranging from the double bass to the soprano. The soprano came in two types: the curved soprano, which looked like an undersized alto, and the straight soprano, which resembled a fat metal clarinet. The instrument Bechet found was a straight soprano. He mastered it very quickly, and thus became the first saxophonist of any importance in jazz. He played the saxophone more and more often — although he never gave up the clarinet entirely — until he made it his own instrument.

Bechet returned to the United States in the early 1920s, after his various problems in London and Paris, and for the next two decades worked mainly in the United States. He snuck into Paris with the Noble Sissle band in 1929, and played in both Germany and Russia in the 1930s in the company of trumpeter Tommy Ladnier, but these were brief excursions. He returned to Paris finally in 1949, for a concert, with some trepidation. The French, to whom he was by now a known figure, welcomed him with open arms. He was, after all, a Frenchman himself. And in 1950 he settled permanently in France, where he died in 1959, full of honors.

Bechet made his first records in 1923, after his return from his first European sojourn, with a group called the Clarence Williams Blue Five. Williams was one of a growing group of black music business professionals who led bands, organized record dates, wrote — or adapted from the black music around them — songs, and published sheet music. Among the men coming to the fore at this moment were W. C. Handy, the former minstrel bandsman who Europeanized folk blues for the white market and eventually became a publisher; his sidekick, Harry Pace, founder of Black Swan, the first black-owned record company; and Perry Bradford, who organized many early record dates featuring major blues singers and jazz musicians. None of these men was a true jazz musician, but because they understood the black taste and knew who the best black singers and players were, they could act as middlemen between the musicians and the white entrepreneurs who, by and large, controlled the music business. Clarence Williams was a pianist who started playing the Storyville clubs and brothels and touring as a minstrel man, and then came to New York to be at the center of the music business. During the 1920s he organized a great many record dates, on most of which he played, either as band pianist or accompanist to blues singers, among them Bessie Smith. He had known Bechet in New Orleans and used him frequently on records.

One of the first of these was "Shreveport Blues," made under the title of the Clarence Williams Blue Five. Bechet stands head and shoulders above his companions on this record. His flowing line moves through the cumbrous brass figures like bright water through rocks. Throughout his life he was noted for his unending inventiveness; he hardly pauses for breath as the ideas flow effortlessly out through his fingers, and this characteristic is evident right from this early record. He is not yet, however, a finished jazz player. At points in his playing there remains the stiff regularity of ragtime, produced by the musician's hitting the beat on the head or dividing it into precisely equal eighth notes. Bechet was, in 1923, still trying to shake off the ragtime chrysalis. And by 1924 he had done so.

The evidence lies in an important recording, made by the Red Onion Jazz Babies, of "Cake Walkin' Babies," which included a friend of Bechet's from down home, the blossoming Louis Armstrong. By the time of this record Bechet is fully formed as a jazz musician; his playing changed remarkably little over the rest of his life. Here is that endless flow, that fat tone with its sharp cutting edge, which sliced through ensembles to dominate the music, the growls and rasps, and, above all, that unfailing swing of the line flying above the ground beat. The arrangement calls for a number of breaks by cornet, trombone, and soprano saxophone. (The break is a common New Orleans device in which the band stops and one instrument plays alone for a short space, generally two measures at or near the end of a passage.) The break Bechet takes in the last chorus is a fine example of how the jazz musician pulls his line away from the ground beat. It is made up of four two-bar segments. In the first of these Bechet plays a repeated triplet figure — three notes over two beats — in which the first of the theoretically equal notes is slightly longer and given some accent. The second two-bar segment employs more strictly played triplets. The third segment combines triplet figures with dotted eighth and sixteenth couplets, and the fourth is largely made up of these last again. There is enormous rhythmic variety in the breaks, one of the hallmarks of the best jazz playing.

The dotted eighth and sixteenth figures are worth a moment's attention, for we are dealing here with something of great importance to jazz. In European music there are three primary ways in which two notes are fitted into one beat: pairs of eighth notes, in which the beat is divided into halves; dotted eighths and sixteenths, in which the dotted eighth is allotted three quarters of the length of the beat and the sixteenth the rest; and, more rare, various notations for splitting the beat into two parts to one part. This system is enforced by the limitations of European notation, which lacks the means of expressing finer shadings of time; they would in any case be difficult to read. But the improvising jazz musician habitually makes more subtle and probably unanalyzable divisions of a beat into two parts. Furthermore, by use of stresses and accents of various kinds, he weights each part differently. He is generally unconscious of doing this; he is simply trying "to swing." But it is easy enough to prove that he is doing this, because if you ask him to play pairs of eighths or dotted eighths and sixteenths as written — that is, as a symphonic musician would play them — the swing will disappear and you will no longer be listening to jazz. Probably two thirds, or three quarters, or perhaps even more, of the notes in jazz are strings of these pairs of notes to a beat. One way that the jazz musicians detach these runs of notes from the ground beat is by dividing them in some incommensurate fashion, and spicing them with accents, so that they do not come along like machine-gun bullets. There is, in fact, a kind of zigzag or back-and-forth quality to runs of notes of this kind, a sort of step-forward, half-a-step-back motion; and it is not surprising that much of the dancing that has been done to jazz involves back-and-forth, or hitch-and-shuffle, movements of the body.

By 1924, with "Cake Walkin' Babies," Bechet had grasped this principle. Despite the strength of Armstrong's playing, Bechet dominates the record. It is safe to say that at this early period he was the best horn player in jazz, equaled in producing the rhythmic feel of jazz possibly by the pianist Jelly Roll Morton and probably nobody else.

Bechet continued to record widely through the 1920s and into the thirties, during which time he made a considerable number of records, with a variety of small groups, for Victor. One of the best of these is "Maple Leaf Rag," cut in 1932 with the group called the New Orleans Feetwarmers. It included Tommy Ladnier and pianist Hank Duncan, with whom Bechet often worked during this period. This is Joplin's classic ragtime number, but Bechet gives Joplin short shrift. He simply swirls over everybody, playing with a fluid, driving intensity rarely matched in jazz. There is a short piano solo in the middle of the number, but for the most part it is all Bechet, especially the last six choruses, which he races through virtually without pausing for breath, leaving his colleagues gasping in the dust.

The late 1930s were bad times for small band jazz. By 1938 Bechet was in retirement, working in a tailor shop for a living. He was eager to play, however, and he tried to get a major record company to let him record the Gershwin classic "Summertime." His company refused, but Alfred Lion, owner of Blue Note, a new, small company specializing in jazz, agreed to record it. It became, so far as a jazz record ever does, a hit. At the same time there was a revival of interest in the now-dated New Orleans jazz style. Bechet benefited from both the recording and the new interest, and became, during the 1940s, a celebrated jazz figure, playing regularly at concerts, on radio programs, and in the Blue Note recording studios.

In 1944 he made for Blue Note a clarinet solo called "Blue Horizon," one of his finest recorded performances. It is simply a blues in E♭, taken at metronome 70, about as slow as jazz is ever played. It is basically an exercise in pitch variation, especially on the blue notes. To this end Bechet fills the

Sidney Bechet during the early days of the New Orleans revival, which
made him an international star. The setting is a New York City jazz club.
Trumpeter is Hot Lips Page; drummer is Freddie Moore, who played with
Morton in the 1920s and was still working steadily in the late 1970s.
William P. Gottlieb/Edward Gottlieb Collection

performance with long notes, some of them held out to four beats, which
at this tempo makes them three or four seconds long. In each case he inflects
the note with a rising or falling pitch. In the third measure of the piece, for
example, there is a heart-rending blue third, which begins as a flat G, rises
gradually up very nearly to a true G, and then suddenly drops off to a
G♭, or lower. The effect is of great, heavy vines, looped over and through
the beat, brooding, solid, and endlessly sad. This, almost twenty years after
the heyday of the New Orleans style, is New Orleans jazz transcendent.

It is difficult to measure Bechet's influence. Nobody ever tried to challenge him on the soprano saxophone, and very few even attempted to
emulate him. But all throughout the twenties and thirties — and even into
the forties — jazz musicians were conscious of his presence. Johnny
Hodges, Ellington's great alto saxophonist, the leading man on his instru-

ment for a long period, built his style on Bechet's; and it seems, on the strength of Armstrong's development between 1923 and 1926, that he learned some useful lessons about jazz phrasing from his New Orleans peer. Bechet had his faults. At times his great fluidity fell into slickness, and the richness of his tone became cloying. But these were faults of too much rather than too little. Sidney Bechet was, without question, one of the seminal figures in jazz, and he left us one of the finest bodies of work in the music.

Bechet was an individualist, a lone wolf, the sharp who blows into town, cleans out the locals, and disappears again. A man who left New Orleans at the same moment, and who came to match him in influence, was just the opposite — a team leader who believed that the whole was greater than the sum of its parts. This was Joseph Oliver, one of a series of New Orleans cornet kings, who, like Bechet, had an all-pervasive influence on the burgeoning art.

Character has as large a role in the history of art as genius. For the jazz musician the problem has always been that, unlike most other artists, he must work in close conjunction with other men, whose temperaments may be quite different from his own, often enough difficult. The trouble is compounded by the fact that his art dwells inside the entertainment industry, the goals of which are usually not his. The problem of maneuvering through this thicket of personalities is something the writer or painter has to worry about only occasionally; for the jazz musician it is a daily concern, and his final reputation may depend as much on his ability to deal with it as with his own talent.

In Oliver we have a man who could cope with his professional environment. He was a big man, and confident. He drank little (he chewed tobacco and kept a spittoon on the stand, which he sometimes used to beat time with). He was reliable and businesslike in his dealings, though later in life, it is said, he became stingy and perhaps a little suspicious of his musicians. Most important, he had a clear conception of how he wanted his band to sound and was able to make his men hew the line.

Oliver's biographer was the late Walter C. Allen, a leading authority on New Orleans jazz, Oliver and Jelly Roll Morton in particular. He gives Oliver's birthplace as Dryades Street in New Orleans and the date as 1885. Oliver's mother died when he was fifteen, and he was raised thereafter by an aunt. Some time in his youth he received an injury to his left eye. In about 1900 he began to play with a neighborhood brass band. During the earliest years of jazz he understudied Bunk Johnson and then went on to play with several of the important black and Creole bands — the Henry Allen Brass Band and the Original Superior Orchestra, among others. By about 1910 he was working in Storyville as well, and at one time or another played with almost the entire roster of New Orleans jazz pioneers. By 1915 or thereabouts he was considered one of the leading jazz musicians in the city.

Then, early in 1918, not long after the Original Dixieland Jazz Band records had had their first impact, New Orleans bassist Bill Johnson was asked to supply a jazz band for a Chicago cabaret called the Royal Gardens. He sent for cornetist Buddie Petit, but Petit didn't want to leave home at the time, so Johnson asked Oliver to join the band. For the next two years he played around Chicago in various bands with shifting personnel. In 1922 they opened at the Lincoln Gardens, which was the old Royal Gardens with a new name. The personnel of the band, called King Oliver's Creole Jazz Band, was now Johnny Dodds on clarinet; his brother, Warren "Baby" Dodds, on drums; Honore Dutrey on trombone; Lil Hardin on piano; and Bill Johnson on bass. For reasons that are not well understood, Oliver decided to add a second cornet to the group. Possibly he was growing lazy; possibly he found himself tiring at the end of the evening; possibly he simply liked the two-cornet combination. In any case, the man he chose to join him was the twenty-two-year-old Louis Armstrong. And in 1923 this band began to make one of the most important series of records in jazz history.

For the records Johnson played banjo, because the heavy thump of the bass made the recording needle skip. At times Oliver added a saxophone, too, probably for its novelty value, for it was musically simply a nuisance. These Creole Jazz Band sides were cut before the advent of the electric recording process. Musicians had to be distributed around the room according to the weight of their sound. The balance is poor, and much of the time one instrument or another is muffled or simply inaudible. Oliver's lead line from time to time disappears in a mudbank of noise, and the sound of the instruments is far from accurately reproduced. Nevertheless, a careful listening will be rewarded. After about a half hour the ear becomes accustomed to the tinny, somewhat muffled sound, and the records can be grasped.

What becomes apparent immediately about the Creole Jazz Band is that this is collective music — polyphony, if you will. The records generally include a solo or two, and they feature many breaks. But for most of each side, all seven musicians are playing more or less continuously, and it was owing to Oliver's genius — or the genius of the New Orleans style — that this worked. Each musician was assigned a role, and Oliver made him stick with it. The leader takes the melody, under which Armstrong weaves an embellishment or, less often, adds a simple harmony part. Dodds supplies the filigree, which cascades through the melody and then rebounds. Dutrey provides either connectives between the passages or, sometimes, a series of whole notes that suggest the harmonic underpinning of the piece. The rhythm section lays out the ground beat.

A second thing that is apparent from the start is that the band is not merely blowing a series of ensemble solos, as was done later by white dixieland bands. The Creole Jazz Band numbers have a tight structure, however simple. "Froggie Moore," a Jelly Roll Morton tune, for example, begins with a four-bar introduction, followed by the A theme, which is sixteen bars long and is repeated. The B theme, also a repeated sixteen measures, though entirely different in character, next appears, and is followed by a return of the A theme. There is then a two-bar interlude, rare in jazz, which was probably introduced to give Armstrong a moment to prepare himself for the solo that follows. It is the high spot of the record, a masterly solo that shows that Armstrong was already, at twenty-three, capable of the kind of playing that made him famous a few years later. Then the band returns with the B theme, and the record ends with a two-bar coda, or tag.

By the standards of structure in European music "Froggie Moore" is still at the kindergarten level. But it shows clearly that we are not dealing with a rough folk music, improvised in the heat of the moment. This is a formal, organized, thought-out piece that is only a step away from justifying the term "composition." And for the most part Oliver's bands were not improvising. Because of the formal framework, because of the necessity of keeping the four horns — five when the saxophone was added in the recording studios — out of the way of each other, the musicians in the Creole Jazz Band had to stick pretty closely to a preset arrangement. Of course there

Joseph "King" Oliver's famous Creole Jazz Band at the time it made its classic recordings. From left, Baby Dodds, Honore Dutrey, Oliver, Louis Armstrong, Bill Johnson, Johnny Dodds, and Lil Hardin, soon to become Mrs. Armstrong.

was always variation, but it was variation within strict limits. Like the members of the Original Dixieland Jazz Band, like most New Orleans players, they were embellishers rather than composers. Armstrong's chorus, however marvelously constructed and expressive, is a variation on the B theme, not a brand-new melody.

"Riverside Blues"* follows more or less the same pattern — the juxtaposition of two quite dissimilar themes — but it is of interest for another reason. It is a simple twelve-bar blues in F, made distinctive by the use of an A major chord in the fourth bar rather than the usual F^7. What is most instructive about this record is a series of straightforward solos by clarinet, trombone, and cornets, based mainly on whole notes. Because these solos are so simple and taken at a slow tempo, it is possible for the listener to hear quite clearly how the players are placing their notes around the beats instead of on them. Dodds strikes his notes just a shade behind the beat — not in every case, but often enough to characterize the chorus. On the other hand, Armstrong, who is customarily thought to play behind the beat, places his notes so far ahead of the beat that they can be heard almost, but not quite, as syncopations. A careful listening to these two solos will reward the jazz student. It is often exceedingly difficult to be sure exactly where a note in jazz falls — whether ahead of the beat, behind it, or as part of some sort of implied counter-rhythm that does not relate directly to the ground beat at all. But in these solos we can hear, with a little effort, how the notes depart from the ground beat.

King Oliver's Creole Jazz Band was by no means a perfect musical instrument. Trombonist Dutrey plays out of tune too much of the time; Dodds's solo breaks are sometimes uncertain; and, despite Oliver's formalizing of the music, four or five lines of polyphony are simply too many. But whatever its faults, it was playing in a consistent way, following an established practice, and in doing so it created many moments of moving music.

Armstrong left the band in 1924, and there were other personnel changes. For a year or two Oliver endured a slack period, and then, in 1926, he went back into the recording studios with a band called the Dixie Syncopators. In general, the Dixie Syncopators used a full saxophone section with three voices. Necessarily this called for greater emphasis on written music. But for the listener unfamiliar with this early music, the Dixie Syncopators is a good place to start. For one thing, the quality of the recordings is much higher; you can usually hear what the band is playing. For a second, with fewer lines moving at once, the music is easier to follow. But this is not simple music, as a hearing of "Sugar Foot Stomp" will make clear. This is a new version of "Dippermouth Blues," made with the Creole Jazz Band, which contains Oliver's classic and much-imitated cornet solo. Here is

*I am here using the Paramount version.

exposed the essence of jazz. There is only a handful of notes here; the whole thing lies in how Oliver shades them. The three choruses are built around the blue third, the pitch of which Oliver constantly varies. The notes are then colored by the gradual opening and closing of a mute. And, finally, they are placed at odds to the beat in such a way that it is very hard, even with repeated listening, to figure out precisely where they lie. In sum, throughout this solo the few notes that Oliver takes as his starting point shift like a kaleidoscope. It is impossible to write out even an approximation of this solo in any system of available notation. Among jazz musicians of the 1920s and thirties it was a landmark; and no wonder, for it contains so much of what is important in jazz.

But however much other musicians owed him, Oliver's heyday was to be short. By 1928 he was having trouble keeping his band together, and in 1930 he ran out of work in Kansas City and was stranded there. The problems were many. The Depression had arrived, ruining the recording business and damaging the cabarets. He was suffering from a bad case of pyorrhea, which eventually cost him his teeth (a brass player uses his teeth to support his lip). And, most important, the classic New Orleans style was beginning to be pushed aside by new currents. During the early years of the 1930s he led obscure dance bands, touring around the small towns of Tennessee and the Kentucky mountains for tiny fees. In 1934, beset by buses that constantly broke down, bookers who withheld fees, and the lack of work, he had eight men defect.

Oliver moved to Savannah in 1936, where he ran a fruitstand and then became janitor in a pool hall. His health was going; he was coughing all the time and his blood pressure was high. But, says Allen, "His spirit never broke; he had enough to subsist on, had some of his teeth replaced, and even started saving in a dime bank toward a ticket for New York." Then, on April 8, 1938, he suffered a cerebral hemorrhage and died. He was buried in Woodlawn Cemetery in the Bronx, in New York City, where his sister lived. Before he died he wrote a series of letters to his sister, printed in *Hear Me Talkin' to Ya,* which is among the most poignant writing in jazz literature. He was working fifteen hours a day in the pool hall for a pittance, yet he can write his sister, "I've started a little dime bank saving. Got $1.60 in it and won't touch it. I am going to try and save myself a ticket to New York." It was a ticket that he never bought. Shortly before he died he wrote that he was having trouble getting treatment for his high blood pressure because of money problems and "red tape." "I may never see New York again in life . . . Don't think I'm afraid because I wrote what I did. I am trying to live near to the Lord than ever before. So I feel like the Good Lord will take care of me. Good night, dear . . ."

In the end, of course, Oliver got his revenge on life. Today his records are listened to everywhere in the world, especially in Europe, where he is better remembered than in the United States. More important, the New Orleans style of which he was one of the prime exponents is the base on which traditional, or "trad," jazz, one of the most widely played jazz forms over the world, was built. Oliver's Creole Jazz Band was the first important jazz group to have its work systematically recorded. As the impact of the Original Dixieland Jazz Band faded, those who had been drawn to this new music began to realize that the heart of the matter lay in the Oliver band. It was never widely popular, but its influence on young jazz musicians of the 1920s was immense. This, they understood by 1925, was jazz.

What is perhaps most significant about the stories of Bechet and Oliver is the indication that somewhere around 1923 a true jazz was about to come into being. Bechet, in 1923, still showed occasional traces of ragtime stiffness. Armstrong, though already a forceful and inventive player, was far from the loose, springy player he was to become. In truth, aside from Bechet, Morton, and some of the men in the Oliver band, there is no jazz player whose work is not heavily marked by the stiffnesses of ragtime, the tied-to-the-beat playing that eventually came to be called "corny." Freddie Keppard, certainly one of the leading New Orleans men, was often extremely stiff. And even those men who were breaking out of the older mold, like Armstrong and Bechet, had spells of clumsiness. But 1923 was the year in which jazz finally came to be widely recorded. The record companies had little idea of what jazz was, but they were discovering that there was a large market among blacks for their own music. Totally without system, they recorded whatever they could find. Now musicians, both black and white, had a stock of examples before them, and very quickly began to study them.

Among the most influential of the players being recorded were two clarinetists from New Orleans, Johnny Dodds and Jimmy Noone.

For many listeners Johnny Dodds's playing epitomizes the New Orleans clarinet style. In the days when the music was first being recorded he seemed to have been everywhere. He was on the influential Oliver Creole Jazz Band cuts, he recorded with Freddie Keppard, Jelly Roll Morton, and innumerable small groups of his own; most important of all, he was Armstrong's clarinetist on the majority of the Hot Five and Hot Seven records, which turned jazz around. Anybody who listens to any significant amount of New Orleans jazz will find the sound of Dodds's clarinet clinging so tightly in the ear that it becomes the model for all such playing. It is not surprising, then, that in the hagiography of early jazz Dodds was for a long time considered its finest exponent on his instrument; according to some writers, superior even to Bechet. Today his reputation has diminished somewhat, but he was a player of great consequence.

Johnny Dodds was born in 1892 and he was thus, with Morton and Oliver, one of the founding fathers of the music. He worked with various bands around New Orleans, toured with Billy Mack's Touring Minstrels, worked a stretch on the riverboats, and finally, in his early twenties, began playing with Kid Ory's band, considered by early players perhaps the finest of the New Orleans jazz bands. He left New Orleans in 1918 and eventually landed in Chicago, where he joined the Oliver band at the Lincoln Gardens. When the band broke up in 1924 Dodds went into a club called Kelly's Stable, where he remained in residence until 1930. He recorded steadily during this period with several groups — Jimmy Blythe's Washboard Bands, the New Orleans Wanderers, the New Orleans Bootblacks, and various groups with his own name. By this time the Depression was on and work increasingly harder to get, but Dodds managed to support himself with his music all through the thirties, playing in obscure clubs around Chicago and recording only infrequently. He died in 1940 of a cerebral hemorrhage, just missing out on the New Orleans revival.

Dodds was a reserved and serious man who, in a hard-drinking profession, was something of an oddity because he was a teetotaler. This is surprising because, more than most New Orleans clarinetists, he was a passionate player. The New Orleans clarinet style as expressed by Jimmy Noone or Morton's favorite clarinetist, Omer Simeon, was easy and controlled, a light liquid warble that flowed, rather than being driven, through the propulsive trumpet line. Dodds did at times use this easy manner, as, for example, in his "Bull Fiddle Blues," with Johnny Dodds's Washboard Band. But more typically, he was a driving player, reaching for the high register on climaxes and bending blue notes. Perhaps what was most significant, in the saw-tooth figures characteristic of New Orleans clarinet playing, he tended to make more unequal divisions of the beat than did players like Noone and Simeon, with the first of the pairs of notes much longer than the second of the pair, and distinctly accented, and it was the "hotness" that resulted from this procedure that made him so admired by early jazz fans.

Unquestionably the best known of Dodds's work are the some four dozen sides he made as a member of Armstrong's Hot Five and Hot Seven recording bands. One of the finest examples of his work is on the tune made as both "Gully Low Blues" and "S.O.L. Blues." The piece opens with an up-tempo passage based on the chord changes of "Sister Kate." Dodds plays a strong driving solo here, and then brings the tempo down for a typically passionate blues chorus. It is a prime example of New Orleans clarinet playing at its best. Dodds, however, was not as technically skilled as others among the early clarinetists. His tone often grew shrill in the upper register, and he frequently fumbled notes in quick passages. But he was, we must remember, one of the inventors of the art.

Although Dodds had the larger reputation among jazz fans at the time, Jimmy Noone had a greater reputation with musicians, and today we are able to see not only that was he as influential, but that he was a better musician. Indeed, most jazz clarinet playing since has flowed from Noone.

He was a Creole, raised in the tradition of legitimate musicianship. He studied with Bechet and the much-admired Lorenzo Tio. Like Dodds, he worked around New Orleans in his youth, and, like Dodds, came to Chicago around 1917 or 1918. He worked and recorded with Oliver, Cook's Dreamland Orchestra, a highly reputed band of the day, and with Tommy Ladnier and Freddie Keppard. By the middle of the decade, however, he was working mainly with groups of his own, most of them small bands that featured as lead his clarinet or an alto saxophone rather than a trumpet. Then, like Dodds, he fell on hard times during the Depression and worked in music only sporadically through the thirties. With the New Orleans revival at the end of the decade, he was again recording, and eventually working on the West Coast with the revived Kid Ory band, which was building a considerable following. And yet once more like Dodds, he did not live to enjoy the fruits of the revival; he died in 1944.

But if Dodds and Noone had similar careers, there were considerable differences in their playing styles. Dodds came from the black folk tradition and was self-taught; Noone was a Creole, respected sound musicianship, and studied as a youth and as an adult. In Chicago his teacher was Franz Schoepp, a symphonic clarinetist who also taught the very young Benny Goodman. As a consequence, in the mid-1920s Noone was not only one of the best-trained clarinetists in jazz; he was among the best-trained players, the stride pianists aside, in the music. His ability to play in tune with speed and flexibility, at a time when these skills were in rare supply, impressed other musicians, and clarinetists especially made a point of listening to him. But Noone was not merely a slick player; his melodic conception was sound, and his treatment of the rhythmic elements in jazz was in advance of that of most of the players around him. Noone was, as early as 1927, phrasing in a manner that stood in a halfway house between the New Orleans style and swing. Thus, because he was a fine technician, an inventive improviser, and a leader of the jazz vanguard, he was widely emulated. From him came a whole school of players, including Morton's Omer Simeon, Ellington's Barney Bigard, the St. Louis player Buster Bailey, and others; and out of this school came the swing clarinetists of the 1930s and 1940s — Goodman, Artie Shaw, Irving Fazola, Peanuts Hucko, Joe Marsala, and a host of others.

Because of his technical proficiency, Noone was able to take advantage of the natural fluidity of the clarinet; he played with an easy grace rare in jazz of any time. In a music where so much playing borders on panic, his is never frantic. Characteristically, he starts a line high on the instrument and works his way easily downward in stages, sometimes in long arpeggios, sometimes in the saw-toothed runs that the clarinet lends itself to. On hard-driving final choruses he rises to the top and comes down in very simple figures, often sequences of quarter notes. His tone is almost always pure; there are few of the rasps and growls omnipresent in the work of Dodds and the blues clarinetists in general. Indeed, in comparing Dodds with Noone we can see most clearly the differences between the purely black tradition and the black Creole tradition: the one hard-driving and replete with blue notes and the coarse tone that descends directly from African practice, the other based on a European conception of tone, pitch, and technical facility. This is not to say that Noone never played blue notes; he of course did. But he seemed to use them in a conscious way, as if he learned them in the course of playing jazz rather than abstracting them from the music he knew from birth.

For a man of his reputation Noone recorded surprisingly infrequently. There are a few sides accompanying blues players, a somewhat larger number with pickup blues bands, and a couple with Oliver. The major body of his work is with a group under his leadership generally called Jimmy Noone and His Apex Club Orchestra, after a club where he worked for a long time. The Apex sides were made with a group consisting of Noone, alto saxophonist Joe "Doc" Poston, and various rhythm sections. The cream of them consists of about a dozen sides made in 1928 (some second masters have been reissued) with Johnny Wells on drums, Bud Scott on banjo, and Earl Hines, who was about to become the most influential pianist in jazz through the next decade. The best known are a hard-swinging "Monday Date," "Apex Blues," and a fast "I Know That You Know," which features a Noone solo that became a test piece for other clarinetists. Here are all the hallmarks of Noone's style: the long, graceful runs descending through Poston's lead, the short, hard figures at points of climax, the clean tone.

"Apex Blues" is especially interesting because we can see in it Noone's rather conscious approach to the blues. His solo is made up of a simple, touching figure filled with blue notes; but, played with ease and a clean tone, it lacks the passion we expect to find in the blues of a player from a more purely black tradition. And yet it is a rewarding record. The obscure Joe Poston makes an excellent foil for Noone. His improvising lacks imagination, but he is technically proficient and his timing is excellent, so his statement of the leads around which Noone winds his runs glides easily through the music. Hines was at the top of his powers. All together, these records constitute one of the most satisfactory small bodies of work in early jazz, and are as fresh today as the day they were made. A student interested in early jazz could do worse than start here.

It was, then, these players — Noone, Dodds, Oliver, and Bechet, along with Morton and Armstrong — who were bringing jazz up out of New Orleans and exposing it to the world. Suddenly musicians all over the United States were hearing the new music, and quickly it became clear to them how jazz was different from what had gone before, especially ragtime. In a word, they were learning to make a distinction between what "swung" and what didn't. Not all of them were able to repeat what they were hearing; even Beiderbecke did not free himself of all of his stiffness until about 1925, and neither the Ellington nor Fletcher Henderson bands, both to become major groups, were playing consistently good jazz until 1927 or so. But if, after 1923, the musicians could not always play it, they were hearing the distinction between jazz and other kinds of popular music. Jazz was no longer a music of New Orleans; it had come to the attention of the world.

The Great
Mr. Jelly Lord

In the world of jazz, where the eccentric is commonplace and individuality a sine qua non, the idiosyncratic character of Ferdinand "Jelly Roll" Morton stands out like a beacon. Hustler, poolshark, gambler, pimp, nightclub manager, entrepreneur, and high-liver, Jelly would be worth telling about had he never played a bar of music. He was proud, he was vain, he was arrogant, sensitive, ebullient, a braggart, suspicious, superstitious — but he was nonetheless the genuine article, a true artist. Morton claimed that he had invented "jazz and stomps," as it said on his publicity, and he endlessly fulminated against imitators and those whom he considered his musical inferiors. But as his admiring but nonplussed and often annoyed peers insisted, "He could back up everything he said."

The basic document on Morton's life is Alan Lomax's *Mister Jelly Roll.* The book was adapted from a series of recordings Lomax made of Morton for the Library of Congress folk archives in 1939, in which Morton talks about New Orleans, his life, and jazz practice, all of which he illustrates with dozens of musical examples played on the piano or sung in his clear, rather sweet voice. The book is marred by Lomax's limited understanding of jazz (he was principally a folklorist), his doctrinaire views on race relations, and his belief that the blacker you are the more "authentic" your playing. But we owe Lomax our gratitude for, first, having the foresight to record Jelly, and, second, for pulling together the material into a satisfactory package. Firsthand accounts of the early days of jazz can be numbered on the fingers of one hand, and this is one of only two or three by a major figure of the period.

Jelly Roll Morton was born Ferdinand La Menthe around 1885, or possibly a year or two later. He shifted the date of his birth as it suited him, and he shifted his name, too. His father was a black Creole named F. P. La Menthe, according to Jelly "one of the outstanding" contractors in the

South, but in view of the place held by black Creoles in the social structure by the 1880s, it is more probable that he was a carpenter or builder in a small way of business. La Menthe, whom Jelly remembers as a trombone player, defected early in Jelly's youth, and his mother married a man named Morton, who, according to Lomax, did portering.

It is painfully evident that Jelly lived out his life feeling declassed. In part this may have been because of the desertion by his father and a subsequent slip down the social scale, but undoubtedly a good deal of it had to do with the anomalous position in the New Orleans social structure of the black Creoles, who struggled constantly to escape being classified as black. Morton was light-skinned, and he attempted to pass for white much of the time. He was scornful toward blacks, whom he referred to on occasion as "niggers," and he said that they were troublemakers. He never admitted, except perhaps in the wee hours of an insomniac's night, that he was not a member of the white majority.

But Jelly was the only person who thought he was white. He certainly was not accepted into white society — even though one of his first records was as pianist with the white New Orleans Rhythm Kings — and the blacks with whom he worked perforce were often angry with him for putting on airs. Jelly thus stood in a social limbo he had made for himself, belonging nowhere, everywhere shut out. Had he grown up with a more accepting view of himself, he might have been able to join the black culture in which he in fact lived. Had he been raised in a society where racial lines were less firm, he might have achieved a social position commensurate with his talents. But he could do neither; and as his life progressed, he increasingly fell under the sway of a megalomania.

Yet despite Morton's insistence that he was the greatest this and the inventor of that, there was a winning side to his nature. There emerges from his long, rambling discussion of his life and work, on the Library of Congress records, a charming and basically decent man. He is perfectly willing to talk about his foolish mistakes, his indiscretions and regrets. Throughout his life he continued to send money home to his sisters, at times on a weekly basis. Just a week before he died in near-poverty in Los Angeles, he sent his sisters ten dollars. And the musicians who worked with him, on records at least, found him an ideal leader — clear in his mind about what he wanted to do, but open to suggestion and willing to allow the others blowing freedom. The recording sessions were all business — Jelly was serious about his art — but they were fun, too.

From the beginning of his career, and for some years afterward, Jelly thought of his music as a sideline to his main vocation, that of the New Orleans sharp dabbling in gambling and pimping. But, needless to say, his interest in music began at an early date. He started drumming on tin pans with chair rounds as a baby; then graduated to the harmonica at five, the jew's-harp, and finally the guitar, on which he took lessons with a "Spanish gentleman in the neighborhood." By seven — he claims — he was "considered among the best guitarists around" and was playing with little string combinations, usually bass, mandolin, and guitar. He continued to experiment with other instruments — violin, drums, and apparently trombone; and his grandmother, with whom he lived after his mother died when he was fourteen, encouraged his interest in music, as a good Creole would. Somewhere along the line Jelly had become fascinated by the piano. At first he rejected it "because the piano was known in our circle as an instrument for a lady . . . I didn't want to be called a sissy. I wanted to marry and raise a family and be known as a man among men when I became of age." But eventually he got over this prejudice and began studying the piano with a series of teachers, the most important of whom, he says, was named Frank Richards.

We cannot be sure just when this was because of Jelly's habit of improvising history. For what it is worth he says, "I was considered one of the best junior pianists in the whole city," but this is only in terms of that time and place. Jelly could, of course, read and write music, but on the testimony of both him and his peers he was not a quick sight-reader. His usual practice was to work over a piece until he had memorized it, before displaying it in public. He had, however, a firm grasp of the basics of European music theory — the principles of chord movement and harmonization, which would be part of a beginning theory course. Probably he did not study his theory formally, but, like many artists, abstracted these concepts from the work he played. The music he played as a youth was not, of course, jazz; it was the usual mixture of popular tunes, rags, waltzes, quadrilles, overtures, and other concert pieces that almost any young pianist of the time would have been taught. It is possible that he knew some blues as well, but he certainly would not have been playing them at home where his grandmother could hear them.

In any event, in his mid-teens he was working in a cooperage and at nights hanging around Storyville — he calls it "the Tenderloin." His description of the area, given in the Lomax book, is worth quoting:

> The streets were crowded with men. Police were always in sight, never less than two together, which guaranteed the safety of all concerned. Lights of all colors were glittering and glaring. Music was pouring into the streets from every house. Women were standing in the doorways, singing or chanting some kind of blues — some very happy, some very sad, some with the desire to end it all by poison, some planning a big outing, a dance, or some other kind of enjoyment. Some were real ladies in spite of their downfall and some were habitual drunkards and some were dope fiends as follows opium, heroin, cocaine, laudanum, morphine, et cetera.

As for the men:

> These guys wouldn't wear anything but a blue coat and some kind of stripe in their trousers and those trousers had to be very, very tight. They'd fit um like a sausage . . . If you wanted to talk to one of those guys, he would find the nearest post, stiffen his arm out and hold himself as far away as possible from that post he's leaning on. That was to keep those fifteen, eighteen dollar trousers of his from losing their press.
> . . . Later on, some of them made arrangements to have some kind of electric light bulb in the toes of their shoes with a battery in their pockets, so when they would get around some jane that was kind of simple and thought they could make her, as they call making um, why they'd press a button in their pocket and light up the little bitty bulb in the toe of their shoes and that jane was claimed.

Morton began working as a pianist in some of the "high-class sporting houses" of the District, places where champagne was the drink, the girls were young and fetching, and the rooms were furnished with crystal chandeliers and the inevitable mirrors. Pianists in such places usually worked as singles, playing and singing requests and their own specialties. They were general entertainers rather than jazz musicians, who mixed patter, off-color songs, sentimental tunes of the day, rags, blues, and dances, according to the tastes of the patrons. Pay was nominal, and the pianists were expected to live on tips from the presumably wealthy customers.

One of the best-remembered of these entertainers was a man named Tony Jackson, who wrote a hit tune called "Pretty Baby," and whom Jelly much admired. (Jackson was an acknowledged homosexual. There has persisted a myth among jazz fans that there has never been a homosexual jazz musician, but in fact there are probably no more or no fewer homosexuals in jazz than elsewhere in society. Sugar Johnny Smith, a pioneer New Orleans cornetist, was openly homosexual or bisexual, and so were Bessie Smith and probably Ma Rainey. There are several homosexuals among living jazz musicians as well.) A good pianist could make twenty dollars a night, and often a great deal more, but it helped to be on good terms with the prostitutes, who, if they liked the piano player, would suggest to the customer that he leave a sizable tip. So it was that the pianists developed working relationships with the girls, and from there it was a short step to pimping.

Jelly was successful and began making money. But he made a mistake. Without thinking, he told his proud and imperious grandmother how much money he was making. She quickly guessed where he was making it. "My grandmother gave me that Frenchman look and said to me in French, 'Your mother is gone and can't help her little girls now [Jelly's half sisters]. She left Amèdé and Mimi to their old grandmother to raise as good girls. A musician is nothing but a bum and a scalawag. I don't want you round your sisters. I reckon you better move.' "

Jelly's mother was dead, his father had abandoned him, and now his grandmother had thrown him out of the house. He walked the streets all night, then broke and ran for Biloxi, where he had a godmother who took him in. Throughout his life Jelly continued to want the love and approval of his family; witness the money he regularly sent home. It is probable that this rejection, coming on top of so many others, contributed to the strong need for ego-bolstering that was so obviously part of his personality.

After the break with his family Jelly became a wanderer. He worked in Biloxi, Meridien, Gulfport, and a string of little towns up and down the Gulf Coast. Thence he moved to Chicago, St. Louis, New York, Houston, and the West Coast, turning up in New Orleans between times. He could always make a living playing the piano, but at this period he seems to have been making a career for himself primarily as a gambler and con man. He claims to have been a masterly pool player and a cardsharp, a tough who carried a gun and would accept any man's challenge. But in fact his attempts to make it as a big-time hustler were beset with failure. His exploits are a litany of misadventure — double-crossing partners, faithless women, men who robbed and assaulted him. Despite his boasting and his desire to play the wheeler-dealer, Morton was fundamentally a decent man, honorable in human relations, open with friends, generous toward his family. He simply lacked the character necessary for the bad man.

Perhaps as a result of his failure to make it as a sharp Jelly began concentrating more and more on his music. By about 1923, when he moved to Chicago — there was a developing audience for hot music in the black ghetto of the South Side as well as in the clubs catering to whites — he was committed to music. He began to publish his songs and band arrangements and, finally, to make records as a soloist and with different groups that he led. Between 1923 and 1939 he made about a hundred and seventy-five sides and a handful of piano rolls. Of these some fifty are piano solos; another couple of dozen are accompaniments to vocalists and various ephemera. Aside from the piano solos, which are almost always excellent, the records on which his fame is based are some fifty or so cuts made between 1926 and 1930, mostly under the title of Jelly Roll Morton and His Red Hot Peppers. Victor considered the Red Hot Peppers its number one "hot band." The records made Jelly one of the leading figures in jazz of his time; they brought him the respect and attention he had always considered his due; and, through the exposure they gave him, a good deal of money, both from band dates and from sales of songs. He began to buy Cadillacs and diamonds — hustlers of his time invested in diamonds, which were portable and easy to turn into cash, and occasionally had them set into their teeth. This not only gave them impressive smiles but made the diamonds hard to steal. Jelly had a diamond in a tooth. He was, at last, in the big time on merit.

The first of the piano solos, made in 1923, were of a group of his own compositions, which he was to record again and again. They included "Grandpa's Spell," "Kansas City Stomps," "Milenburg Joys," "Wolverine Blues," and "The Pearls," all of which he eventually worked out as band arrangements for the Hot Peppers. And in these early solos we can once again watch a not-quite-finished jazz emerging from an earlier stage. There are still traces of ragtime in these records, but the music is by no means the purists' ragtime. In a rag, when a beat is split into two eighth notes they are played equally, although many of the early ragtimers were not quite strict about it. In these early piano solos Jelly is still playing his eighth notes more or less equally — I find it hard to determine by ear the exact division — but he is clearly accenting the second of the two eighth notes. He does not do this all the time, however, so there are moments in these records when he is playing very nearly a strict ragtime, and other moments when he is playing jazz. Thus, with Bechet and Oliver, Morton in 1923 was at the front line of jazz. It is not surprising, then, that when he had the opportunity, three years later, to make jazz records on his own terms, they turned out to be landmarks in jazz history.

Jelly — and posterity — was lucky in one important respect. By 1926 he had acquired as his publishers, Walter and Lester Melrose, two young white men who had started in the business as owners of a music store. Apparently more by chance than by design they got involved with the black jazz musicians arriving in Chicago during the early 1920s, and developed the publishing of black music as their specialty. They recognized that Jelly had solid commercial potential, and they worked hard to develop him. For a music publisher in those days, the money lay in building a composer through hit records. The Melroses were never major publishers, but they had contacts with the record companies and they got Jelly a contract with Victor.

In addition, they paid for some rehearsal time in order to give the records the best possible chance. As a consequence, Jelly was able to develop the Red Hot Peppers records in a way he would not have been able to had he not the luxury of working out the material with the men in advance. Few of these players were quick sight-readers, and many of them were only barely adequate. Nor was Jelly a fluent writer. A lot of this music, therefore, was worked out on an I-want-you-to-do-thus-and-so-here basis. This meant working the music over and memorizing it, which required rehearsal time, especially if several tunes were to be cut on a single day, as was often the case. Whatever else the Melrose brothers felt about Jelly — they were on bitter terms with him eventually — they respected his talent and let Jelly

choose the musicians he wanted and do things his own way. It was characteristic of Jelly that he took the recordings seriously. The arrangements
were not thrown together but were carefully thought-out and thoroughly
rehearsed. The men played accurately, and their intonation was superior to
most of the jazz being recorded at the time. Moreover, the recordings
themselves were technically excellent, well balanced and clean, and the
modern listener will find them easier going than much early jazz.

The musicians Jelly preferred were not necessarily the most imaginative
improvisers, but they could be counted on for good musicianship; they
played the notes correctly and in tune. Omer Simeon, Jelly's first choice as
clarinetist, a New Orleans Creole born in 1902, possessed a clean, liquid tone
and something of the ease of Noone, without Noone's surer conception.
George Mitchell, trumpeter on many of the best Red Hot Peppers sides, was
only a limited improviser, but he had a warm, full tone, good intonation,
and a more modest terminal vibrato than was customary among New
Orleans musicians. His solo on Morton's "Jungle Blues," an odd piece built
over a pedal point, very likely the first such in jazz, is a fine example of a
simple line inflected with blues feeling. (Mitchell, who was born in 1899, was
still living in Chicago in the 1970s.)

There is no question that Jelly was in total command of the men and the
music on these dates. Simeon has said:

> He was fussy on introductions and endings and he always wanted the
> ensemble his way but he never interfered with the solo work. He'd tell
> us where he wanted the solo or break, but the rest was up to us
> . . . You did what Jelly Roll wanted you to do, no more and no less.
> And his own playing was remarkable and kept us in good spirits. He
> wasn't fussy, but he was positive. He knew what he wanted and he
> would get the men he knew could produce it. But Jelly wasn't a man
> to get angry. I never saw him upset and he didn't raise his voice at any
> time . . .

The care paid off. The records were an artistic and commercial success, and,
by developing his reputation, brought him his diamonds and Cadillacs.

It is generally said that Jelly Roll Morton was the first real jazz "composer." That is to say, he was not just a songwriter or an arranger of other
men's music but combined both functions to create, for each record, a
unified piece of music that had a beginning, middle, and end, in which
themes were set side by side in some sort of complementary or contrasting
relationship, in which there was a logical sequence of keys — in which, in
sum, we can find many of the procedures standard in European concert
music. Jelly understood how to produce climax and how to shift smoothly
from one mood to a contrasting one and then back again. He was, above
all, a master at using the palette of sounds available to him. With the

exception of Duke Ellington, no jazz composer to this day has been able to endow his music with the slashes of color that are typical of the best of the Hot Peppers records. And Jelly did it with an exceedingly limited number of instruments: two to four brasses, one to three woodwinds, and the usual rhythm instruments. He worked with only a few basic colors, and the effect was of Matisse.

The fundamental framework of the Hot Peppers records was the now-classic New Orleans jazz band brought to finished form in Oliver's Creole Jazz Band. The basic instrumentation was the three-horn front line over a rhythm section, playing music built on rags, blues, and marches. On this basis Jelly elaborated a richer, perhaps slightly rococo edifice. He sometimes combined blues, rags, marches, and concert pieces in one composition; he added instruments to make up harmonized choirs; and he brought the rhythm instruments forward to become part of the polyphony instead of remaining simple timekeepers.

Consider "Sidewalk Blues," made in 1926, one of the earliest of the Hot Peppers sides. The record opens with a bit of hokum involving whistles and an automobile horn (a Model T, I think, but as ever my ear has its limitations). Then follows an eight-measure introduction with two bars each given to piano, trombone, cornet, and clarinet. The opening A theme uses the cornet over a stop-time accompaniment by the whole band. The B theme that follows is jammed in ordinary New Orleans ensemble style, and then the A theme returns, this time played by the clarinet over the stop-time background. There is then a brief interlude by the whole band in choir, modulating into the C theme, played in choir until the last eight bars, when the band breaks out and jams again. (There is also a one-bar break for auto horn in this section.) The C theme is then repeated, this time played by a clarinet trio. (Jelly brought two extra clarinet players into the studio just to play these sixteen bars; the rest of the time, according to Omer Simeon, the principal clarinetist on the date, they sat with their instruments in their laps.) Beneath the clarinet trio Jelly plays a strong piano line. Again the last eight bars are jammed by the band; there is a brief coda, or tag, and the record closes with a return to the opening hokum.

In the very short space of three minutes or so Jelly has employed five different tone colors, not counting the introduction, and he has alternated them in seven different ways. Except for the jammed portions, which amount to about a quarter of the record, no tone color is ever repeated. This short piece also contains three major themes as well as introduction, coda, and the modulating interlude, and it uses three keys — the introduction in B♭, themes A and B in E♭, and the last theme in A♭, a very common sequence of keys, especially in marches. Moreover, the three themes are so different that it is obvious that Jelly meant them to be contrasting. The A theme is a rough blues, actually a variation on an old New Orleans tune usually known as "Bucket's Got a Hole in It." The B theme is typical of the raggy marches that made up so much of the early New Orleans material, sprightly and cheerful. The final theme is a funeral march, out of the European repertory, minor in character until it suddenly breaks out into the jolly portion, jammed. In this segment Jelly is copying the New Orleans funeral bands' custom of playing lugubrious music out to the cemetery and then jamming the hymns on the way back. In "Sidewalk Blues" Jelly has employed most of the basics of New Orleans music. His sense of contrast was sure and satisfying, and is aptly illustrated during the clarinet trio's playing of the funeral piece, when he undergirds the mournful melody with a hot piano accompaniment at twice the speed.

These contrasts, this variety, are the hallmark of Jelly's band music. It is simply shot through with it. He constantly makes use of all the devices the new music was producing: stop-time, in which the ground beat behind the soloist is replaced by a regular punctuation falling on, say, every other beat, or every fourth beat; riffs, where the ground beat remains and one or more instruments add a regular rhythmic figure to support the soloist; breaks, where the rhythm is suspended and a soloist plays on his own, often a totally arrhythmic figure. Furthermore, Jelly took control of the rhythm section at places; for example, shifting the bass from two to four to the bar and back to add rhythmic push at climactic points. Or he put together two or even three layers of rhythms, one twice as fast as the first, and the next one twice as fast again.

There is such a passage in "Smokehouse Blues," where the tempo suddenly doubles up for a brief two bars during the clarinet chorus. As Gunther Schuller points out in his book *Early Jazz,* which contains an excellent analysis of Morton's work, Jelly himself at this point is playing sixteenth notes, which has the effect of a second doubling of tempo, giving us momentarily three layers of rhythm. This playing with time appears again in "The Chant," made the same day as "Smokehouse Blues." The composition opens with a long introduction — preamble is probably a better term — employing a variation of the so-called *habanera* beat. This rhythmic figure is worth a moment's attention. Jelly referred to it as "the Spanish tinge," claiming that good jazz needed a touch of it. He was right, but not for the reasons he thinks. The figure is ubiquitous in the black music of Latin America, especially the Caribbean:

It is familiar to North Americans and Europeans through any number of dances imported from Latin America, especially the tango and the samba. It is, in fact, a variation on the classic three-over-two figure so commonly found in African music, black-American folk music, ragtime, and jazz.

The *habanera* beat is a cousin of the figure on which so much jazz is built, and Jelly senses it. In the introduction to "The Chant" he alternates the *habanera* beat with ordinary jazz time. Then, when the main theme comes in boldly, conjoins the two, giving the Spanish tinge to the trumpet and allowing the clarinet to dash through it in pure jazz style.

Besides this rhythmic variation, the introduction to "The Chant" is remarkable for its shifting tonality. Schuller suggests that the first eight bars shift back and forth between D♭ and D, which would be unusual for jazz of the day. There follow eight bars in B♭ and a return to the D♭-D shift before the emergence of the main theme in A♭. Jelly is playing with tonal centers in a relatively sophisticated way for his time and place.

We can see that in his best compositions Morton was using a range of musical devices in an organized and disciplined way. They are not included simply for effect but are parts of a unified whole. Making parts into a whole is one of the things composition is all about. An artist makes relationships; a great artist makes new and surprising ones. Jelly was not an artist of Armstrong's caliber, but he was an exceedingly fine one, and in the Hot Peppers records we can see him relating solos, breaks, riffs, and themes to each other to make up satisfying wholes.

Most of Morton's recorded work consists of either piano solos or pieces built on the New Orleans band. But occasionally he recorded with smaller groups. Cuts worth mentioning are a trio version of "Wolverine Blues," with Johnny and Baby Dodds of the Oliver band; a trio version of "Shreve-port Stomp," with Omer Simeon on clarinet and Tommy Benford on drums; and a quartet playing "Mournful Serenade," with trombonist Geechy Fields added to the "Shreveport Stomp" group. All of Morton's usual devices are evident on these records: the carefully worked-out arrangement of themes, the breaks, the shifting tone colors. "Shreveport Stomp," a fast, hard-driving number, includes a much-admired passage in which the clarinet races through several keys.

These small groups show off Jelly's piano to advantage. We should not forget that Jelly was not only a composer but a pre-eminent jazz soloist. Schuller considers him superior to everybody of his time except Earl Hines, and while that is covering a lot of territory, a good case can be made. For exuberance and sure, easy swing, Jelly was in a class by himself. His piano style was, he often said, modeled after that of a band. He used his left hand as a rhythm section, or to play trombone figures, and his right to set out harmonies as they might be played by a brass section. Trombones and clarinets are everywhere in Morton's piano playing, and in a sense, when he sat down to compose for the Hot Peppers, he was returning the music to the place where he had found it.

Yet we must not make too much of this analogue, even though Morton himself insisted on it. Several of Morton's best band numbers, like "The

Pearls," "Kansas City Stomps," and "Original Jelly Roll Blues," were conceived as piano pieces first. They are full of ragtime figures, evident even when the tunes are transcribed for the band. Morton, we must remember, was a teen-age piano player in New Orleans during the heat of the ragtime craze; it would have been impossible for him to resist the ragtime influence even had he wanted to. He saw jazz as a new music that had eclipsed a fading ragtime, but he recognized how the two were related. He said, "Ragtime is a certain type of syncopation and only certain tunes can be played in that idea. But jazz is a style that can be applied to any type of tune." It was a very perceptive remark for somebody caught up in the transition of one form to the other, and it indicates that Jelly was a *conscious* artist, possibly the first such in jazz. He knew what he was doing and why, and he could demonstrate it on the piano, as he does in the Library of Congress records.

Unhappily, he came upon his opportunity too late. By 1928, when the Hot Peppers appeared to be still ascending in public favor, Louis Armstrong was already making the Hot Five records that would set jazz on another course. At almost the same moment, the Depression struck. Morton, like Oliver, suddenly found himself outmoded. From 1929 on it was all downhill. The Hot Peppers records made in 1929 are not quite as good as the earlier ones, and the 1930 cuts are distinctly inferior — much less varied, much less carefully worked, dependent more on jamming than on Morton's compositional skills.

Morton might have survived, but at the same time the record business collapsed, almost overnight. By 1932 total sales were down to 5 million, just 6 percent of what they had been five years earlier. The causes were three: the Depression, which made money scarce; radio, which was faddish, and free besides; and a general lack of interest in records as somehow out of date or no longer fresh. It was not merely that people stopped just buying records; they began to store them in attics or sell them to secondhand stores, thus making them available to the early-record collectors.

In any case, by the early 1930s Morton was broke and beginning to lose his health. The jazzmen around him scoffed at his boasts about inventing jazz and the superiority of "his" music. He had become that classic American figure of fun, the foolish old-timer insisting that the ancient ways were best; that the young were ignoramuses who ought to have some respect for their elders. In 1939 he made the Library of Congress recordings, which were not, however, issued to the public until a decade later; and as a result of the revival of interest in the New Orleans players, which had made a place for Bechet as a grand old man, there were a few more recording sessions for General Records, mostly for juke box consumption.

But Jelly Roll Morton was ill. In 1940, he heard that his godmother had died in Los Angeles, where she had moved. Bound by sentiment and by the

The great Jelly Roll Morton, prime entertainer, at a recording session in New York near the end of his life. Otto F. Hess Collection, New York Public Library

hope that a warmer climate would help his health, he chained his Cadillac to his Lincoln, filled them with his clothes, and drove out to the West Coast. It was a terrible trip. He went off the road twice in snowstorms and arrived in Los Angeles broke. He managed to hang on for another six months and then, on July 10, 1941, he died, like King Oliver before him, unnoticed and unsung except by a tiny group of musicians and jazz fans who loved his music.

It has generally been thought that the Hot Peppers were the last flowering of the New Orleans style and that Jelly Roll Morton was a man beyond his time. I do not agree. It seems to me that the Hot Peppers records had a profound and pervasive effect on everything that followed. The plain fact is that as of 1926 there is very little truly fine band jazz on record, aside from the Oliver cuts. A number of individuals were coming forward as major soloists, especially Armstrong, Bechet, Beiderbecke, James P. Johnson, and Jelly himself; but in 1926 the bands that were to make a mark on jazz a few years later — I am thinking of Ellington, Moten, and Henderson especially — were still trying to find their methods and manners. The Hot Peppers sides of 1926 swung harder and made more sheer musical sense than anything anybody else was doing by way of band jazz, and it is difficult to believe that the new men were not listening carefully to the Morton sides. The new men disliked Morton. Ellington was in Los Angeles at the time of Jelly's funeral and, in one of the few openly hostile acts of his life, did not attend. Yet it seems quite clear to me that Morton, in the Hot Peppers records, showed Ellington, Henderson, Moten, Basie, Goodman, and the rest a way that jazz could go.

Bessie Smith
and the New Blues

Until recently, most jazz critics assumed that the blues were part of jazz — not merely one of the roots, but a continuing part of the mainstem. Today we see that the blues has a separate tradition, intermingled with that of jazz but not the same. It has its own followers; its own critics and historians, who are not necessarily interested in jazz; and, more important, its own players, like B. B. King, Muddy Waters, and Bo Diddley, who are not jazz players at all.

Nonetheless, the two musics twine together like grape vines. Jazz grew out of the blues, in part; but in later years the child came to have a formative influence over its father. A modern blues performance is quite different from one in the old tradition, and a good deal of the change was worked by jazz musicians.

The early blues, as we have seen, could not be fitted into the European musical system. It employed a mode, or scale, including blue notes, that was nonexistent in European music. It was neither in major or minor but in a mode of its own. Its time scheme was flexible: "Stone Pony Blues," by Charley Patton, a singer born in the 1880s, is impossible to count out in standard 4/4 measures. To suit the convenience of the melodic line Patton not only adds or subtracts beats from measures, but shifts his stresses so that the first beat of a measure suddenly shows up a beat or two early or late, pushing the meter into a different place. The early bluesmen like Patton paid little attention to form; a blues usually contained thirteen-and-a-half to fifteen bars instead of the twelve standard in modern blues. Further, these early blues had little harmonic underpinning, or chord sequences. "The Gone, Dead Train," by a blues singer known only as King Solomon Hill, employs no chord changes whatever.

The early blues, thus, were very much in the tradition of black-American folk music, which, as we have seen, was difficult for whites, trained in European music, either to transcribe or perform themselves. But in the 1910s the blues were being brought out of the black ghettos and off the pine wood farms into the mainline of American show business, and a way had to be found to Europeanize them. This was not the first time such a process took place. Both the spirituals and ragtime were created by the Europeanizing of black musical forms, in one case black church music, in the other black dance music. And by 1915 a number of forces were pressing the blues to do likewise. One of these forces was the commercial possibilities in the blues. In 1912, W. C. Handy had a great hit with "Memphis Blues," and two years later an even greater hit with "St. Louis Blues." Other less well known blacks were publishing the blues at the same time — Handy was the most famous of these men, but not the first — and though blacks did buy this sheet music, the big money was in selling to the white majority. This meant transmuting the blues into a form comprehensible to whites.

A second force mandating the Europeanization of the blues was the sheer impossibility of producing blue notes on the piano and in band arrangements. On top of this, as the blues moved from the turpentine camps and the barrelhouses into the dance halls and theaters, improvising musicians were more and more often required to play them. A group of musicians improvising together must of course work from a common time scheme and chord sequence, and the growing demand for blues forced jazz musicians to find a set framework for the blues.

How were these changes made? The easiest was the freezing of the time scheme into the system of three four-measure segments. Popular music in the United States has almost always been built up of units of two, four, and eight measures. It was natural for the transmuters of the early blues to set each line to four 4/4 measures, and the three-part form was dictated by the repeated line of the blues vocal. The blue notes posed more difficult problems because there was nothing similar in European music. Various solutions were tried. Handy, in the famous "I hate to see . . ." opening line of "St. Louis Blues," simulates what would have been an initial blue third by the use of a slur from minor third to major third, in this case B♭ to B, and this particular device became a cliché, used in the opening to thousands of jazz choruses. Pianists found another solution available to them, which was to strike the major and minor third or seventh together — a solution Gershwin used in "Rhapsody in Blue" — or to play them as a trill.

But perhaps the most common solution was to substitute notes in the diatonic scale for the blue notes. This practice grew out of ignorance. Virtually no white musicians, and few black ones coming to the blues from other musical disciplines, understood exactly what the blue notes were. In trying to reproduce what they were hearing, they put the minor third in place of the blue third. This usage is so common that most jazz musicians today think that the minor third *is* the blue third. But for technical reasons the minor seventh could not be so easily substituted for the blue seventh. Musicians thus sought another substitute for the blue seventh, and the one they lit on was the sixth (correctly, this note is the thirteenth, but jazzmen invariably called it the sixth), an A in the key of C. The process was probably unconscious. In the late 1920s, blues singers began to use it in places where you would normally expect a blue seventh, and by the thirties it was being widely used. A singer like the well-regarded Leroy Carr uses it almost to the exclusion of the blue seventh. Everybody else took it up, so throughout the thirties and up until the bop takeover in the mid-1940s the sixth at climaxes and moments of intensity was a regular feature of jazz and jazz-oriented popular music. There is hardly a swing band arrangement written between 1935 and 1940 that doesn't end on a chord with the added sixth. As far as the blue fifth was concerned, it had always played a lesser part, and it simply disappeared. By the mid-1930s, then, the blue notes had dropped out of jazz altogether, except, of course, in the playing of those who continued to work in the older tradition.

The third shift in the Europeanization of the blues was the establishment of a harmonic underpinning. African music and its derivatives in the New World did not employ harmony in anything like the sense in which it is used in European music. But a pianist or guitar player or band arranger needs harmonies to work with. In fact, harmony is so naturally a part of European music that anybody working in such music would employ it.

But what harmony did the blues call for? For reasons that are obscure, black-American folk music shows a definite preference for plagal harmonies, that is, movement in and out of the subdominant — F in the key of C. Early black church music used it; gospel music of today uses it; and where there is harmony in the early blues it is almost invariably plagal. Black blues musicians would have found this particular cadence a natural one. On the other hand, basic to European music are dominant harmonies: in the key of C, movements in and out of G. However the process worked, as the black pianists and composers of the early part of this century were beginning to play the blues, they combined both traditions by establishing a movement into the subdominant and return at the beginning of the second segment of the blues — where the second line begins — and a similar movement into the dominant and return where the third segment begins. Not surprisingly, the subdominant has remained the stronger of the two cadences. In many blues by, for example, the Basie band, the move into the dominant in bars nine and ten is ignored in the accompanying riff. The same is true of Lester Young's standard blues tune, "Jumpin' with Symphony Sid," where the melody returns to the subdominant in bars nine and ten despite the chords' moving into the dominant as usual. So, as the standard blues evolved, the first segment made no moves at all but remained in the tonic, giving the following chord sequence:

$$\text{CCCC}^7 \mid \text{FFCC} \mid \text{G}^7\text{G}^7\text{CC}$$

In time, variations on this sequence appeared, the most common of them being the substitution of F in bars two and ten, F minor in bar six, and an A^7 in bar eight. But these substitutions all come on the secondary, even-numbered bars, and do not affect the basic structure.

Thus the blues were Europeanized, acquiring a harmony, the diatonic scale, and a regular time scheme, and these are the blues as we know them in jazz today. It was in the course of this development that there arose a group of women blues singers who came to dominate the medium. These women are today known as the "classic" blues singers. Their names alone evoke a whole romance of big, earthy, cigarette-smoking, gin-drinking women with enormous sexual appetites and a *carpe diem* attitude toward life. Ma Rainey, Bessie Smith, Chippie Hill, Ida Cox: they were idolized by black audiences as well as by a number of whites who ventured into the black world; they made, some of them, considerable amounts of money; and their influence on the whole world of black music was profound.

The music sung by the classic blues singers lived halfway between the older country blues of the male singers and the modern blues of the jazz players. These female singers built their melody lines around the blue notes in a way that was typical of the male singers. In "Runaway Blues," for example, Ma Rainey starts on a high tonic, runs down through a fifth, slurs through a blue fifth, thence to a blue third, and lands on a tonic. She repeats this figure, with very nearly no change, on the second line of the chorus, and varies it by using a blue seventh in the third line. This particular melodic line was characteristic of her work and was a very popular one with the male singers. Ida Cox and Bessie Smith both frequently use a phrase revolving around the blue third and the tonic, again a commonplace in the old blues tradition.

But the classic female singers were not so utterly dependent on the blue notes as were the men. Ma Rainey occasionally resolved a blue third upward into an ordinary major third, and Bessie Smith made of this device a trademark. In her marvelous "Cold in Hand Blues," made in 1925 with Louis Armstrong accompanying her on cornet, she repeatedly drops onto a blue third, which she holds out, toying with the pitch, and then resolves upward into the major. It is doubtful that Blind Lemon Jefferson ever sang a major third in his entire career.

Rhythmically, the women strung out their phrases, as was typical of all black folk music; Bessie Smith, in "T'Ain't Nobody's Bizness If I Do," sings virtually *a capella,* her phrases torn completely away from the ground beat in Clarence Williams's piano, which is not always stated. In general, a blues singer's interest was in the words. This tended to force an arrhythmic shape on the melody line, increasing the departure from the ground beat even more. But on the other hand, the classic blues singers, without exception, worked within the framework of strict meter and the twelve-bar form. They also employed the tonic-subdominant-dominant harmonic system that had been recently developed. These classic singers were laying a loosely phrased, blue-note–inflected melody line against the strict time and formal harmonies of jazz practice. They were, thus, in a most explicit way, setting the residue of the African musical system against the European one. In the blues of the older, rural males, the African influence was strong; in the developing blues of the jazz musicians, the European system was coming more and more to the fore. But in the work of the classic singers, the contrast was so sharp it could almost be tasted, and this no doubt is why, during the decade of the 1920s, these women singers dominated the blues world, both artistically and in popularity. It was one of those rare occasions in recent history when an artist could make a lot of money without compromise, and where the best artists, in general, made the most.

Why were these women closer than the men to the European system? The answer is that most of them were not simply blues singers, as the men were, but popular vocalists in the minstrel tradition, who thought of themselves as general entertainers. They worked less in cabarets than in the minstrel and variety shows that provided much of the entertainment for Southern blacks and some whites as well. These shows worked the theaters generally through the Theater Owners Booking Association, known as T.O.B.A. — which the performers said stood for Tough on Black Asses — and was nicknamed Toby Time. They also worked in tent shows, which covered the small towns of the rural South in the fashion of circuses today.

Typically, a singer like Bessie Smith would have in her repertory tunes of the day as well as the blues. Bessie also did stand-up comedy; she danced; and she acted in the coarse comic skits, with sexual or battling-husband-and-wife themes, that have been a feature of black entertainment up until today. A variety singer like Bessie Smith was presented to the public with the usual elaborate fol-de-rol of the star — satin gowns, furs, diamond necklaces, painted backdrops, and the rest — and was sometimes accompanied by a relatively large band. The women were not backwoods blues singers playing for turpentine hands; they were sophisticated entertainers intent on putting on a good show. They were working in a show business tradition that was part white. It was inevitable that black performers working so close to white show business forms would be highly influenced by European music.

Like ragtime and the commercial jazz of the twenties, the blues was a boom-and-bust phenomenon that broke out of the black ghetto to become a national craze among blacks and, to some degree, whites. The trigger was pulled by a record called "Crazy Blues," by Mamie Smith, issued in 1920. Mamie Smith was a handsome, light-skinned woman who had an excellent, powerful voice but was no real blues singer. She had come to New York from Cincinnati with a white vocal group called the Four Mitchells. In New York she attracted the attention of Perry Bradford, one of the emerging black music entrepreneurs. He got Mamie a chance to record at Okeh. Two tunes, "That Thing Called Love" and "You Can't Keep a Good Man Down," were cut in February 1920. They were ordinary pop tunes and did ordinarily well — well enough to encourage Okeh to use Smith again, so in August 1920 she cut "Crazy Blues." Much to everybody's surprise, the record sold enormously. The record companies leaped in to capitalize on it, and suddenly a boom for blues, aimed mainly at black audiences, was on.

The record companies established "race" catalogues for dealers in black areas. Scouts from all the companies fanned out through the South, indiscriminately signing up black singers, many of whom were straight vaudeville performers with no ability for singing the blues. By 1921 at least a half-dozen black singers were on records; by 1923 the number was running to scores. The boom became a craze, a fad, not only among blacks, but among whites, who were once again smitten by a black musical form, no doubt partly for the sexual overtones of the records, which were drenched in double-entendre.

Virtually every black woman who could sing at all was signed up and presented as a blues singer. Many of them, like Sara Martin, who has a solid reputation among early jazz enthusiasts because she once recorded with King Oliver, were plain bad; some were simply atrocious. Out of the whole lot not more than a dozen at the very outside left a body of music sufficient in quantity and quality to interest anyone but a scholar. The list would include Bessie Tucker, a strong singer with a dark voice; Clara Smith, who had a thinner voice but good control of blue notes; Trixie Smith, another with a light voice and a somewhat easier way of phrasing than was common; Ida Cox, a very popular vaudeville singer who also sang excellent blues on occasion; and Bertha "Chippie" Hill, who had a dark voice and was working as late as the 1950s. Among the other better-known names were Victoria Spivey, Sippie Wallace, and Mae Barnes. But without question, the acknowledged leaders were Ma Rainey and Bessie Smith.

Ma Rainey was the first of the classic blues singers about whom we know much of anything. She was born Gertrude Pridgett and grew up to be a short, plump, dark woman with protruding teeth and a high forehead, which she usually covered with a band of beads. To put no fine point on it, she was an ugly woman. What effect this had on her character is hard to know, but Ma was reputedly bisexual. She was born on April 26, 1886, in Columbus, Georgia, a contemporary of Morton and Oliver. How and why she got into show business is not known. One of her grandmothers had been on the stage, but we have no way of telling what influence she had.

Whatever the circumstances, by 1900 the girl was singing in public, and by 1904, when she married an entertainer named Will "Pa" Rainey, she was established on the Southern entertainment circuit. The Raineys worked for a time with the Rabbit Foot Minstrels, one of the leading touring shows, and then with Tolliver's Circus, which was not so much a circus as a variety show, where they were billed as "Rainey and Rainey, The Assassinators of the Blues." Eventually Ma worked primarily with her own shows, always in the South. She came north only to make records, and she made a good deal of money and managed to hang on to some of it. She cut her last record in 1928, retired from active singing in 1935, and thereafter earned her living by running a few small theaters in Georgia. She died in 1939 and is buried in Porterdale Cemetery in Columbus, Georgia.

This thin sketch is about all we know of Ma Rainey's life. But what really matters to us is the records. She made about ninety sides between 1923 and 1928 — a rate of a record every six weeks or so, which gives some indication of her drawing power. Her voice was deeper, darker, and heavier that that of any of the other classic blues singers. She is most effective at slow tempos, which permit her to play with blue notes and to stretch phrases across the bar lines. Ma Rainey can be heard at the top of her form on "Blame It on the Blues" and "Leavin' This Morning," both recorded in 1928 with accompaniment by guitarist Tampa Red and her musical director, Thomas A. "Georgia Tom" Dorsey, who composed hundreds of religious songs as well as blues and other numbers.

"Blame It on the Blues" is built primarily around blue thirds. These she resolves downward to the tonic at the ends of the choruses, but in the middle she often resolves them upward to a major third, thus keeping the melodic line in suspension. "Leavin' This Morning" is unusual in two respects. For one thing, instead of singing one line over each of the standard three parts of a blues, she sings a little four-line verse over the first part and uses the second and third parts as a chorus made up of the song's title sung several times. For another, the opening verse is built around the sixth, but the succeeding "chorus" section uses blue sevenths at the points where strong emotion is expressed. It is rare to find both the sixth and the blue seventh used in the same blues. These are, in any case, classic examples of great blues singing, powerful and haunting expressions of human feeling.

But powerful as Ma Rainey was, by almost universal opinion the greatest of all the classic blues singers was Bessie Smith. She had an ability to move people that made audiences worship her and left her fellow musicians in awe. The New Orleans guitarist Danny Barker says, "She could bring about mass hypnotism. When she was performing you could hear a pin drop." Frank Walker, the Columbia executive who had charge of her recording career, describes her when she first began to record: "She looked about seventeen — tall, fat and scared to death — just awful. But all of this you forgot when you heard her sing, because when Bessie sang the blues she meant it."

Bessie Smith, unlike most jazz musicians, is lucky in having a sensitive and meticulous biographer, the blues scholar Chris Albertson, whose *Bessie* is one of the few first-rate full-dress biographies in jazz. Albertson has managed to rescue the facts of Bessie's life from the miasma of romance and myth with which early writers invested it. According to Albertson, Bessie Smith was born in Chattanooga, Tennessee, in or around 1894. One of seven children, she was raised in the bottomless poverty of the black South, where nickels and dimes were big money. Her father died when Bessie was a baby, and her mother when she was eight or so, leaving her oldest sister, Violet, to raise the young ones.

What kind of music Bessie heard and where, nobody knows. In the Chattanooga of her childhood it would not have been jazz, certainly. No doubt there were early versions of the blues being sung, as well as pop tunes from minstrel shows. Presumably she would have heard the music of the growing ragtime boom. Her father had been associated with the Baptist church in some capacity, and it is likely, though not certain, that she would have gone to church on Sunday and sung gospel music.

Whatever the case, Albertson says that by the age of nine Bessie was singing on street corners for nickels and dimes, and by 1912, when she was in her late teens, she was competent enough for her brother Clarence, who was traveling as dancer and comedian with a vaudeville show, to arrange an audition for her with the owner. She was big and, if not a great beauty, at least reasonably good-looking. The owner took her on as a dancer.

By great good chance, the show also included Ma and Pa Rainey. Bessie stayed with the show briefly and then struck off with the Raineys for another show. She toured with the Raineys for a short time — probably not much more than a year — and then, having established herself as a singer, began working in the 81 Club in Atlanta for ten dollars a week and tips, which may have doubled her salary. For the next few years she was in and out of theaters, sometimes touring with traveling shows, and by the end of World War I, as the jazz boom was just beginning, she was an established star on the T.O.B.A. circuit. She played Northern cities as well as Southern, had a brief marriage, and acquired the habit of hard drinking, which dogged her the rest of her life.

Then, in 1920 came Mamie Smith's "Crazy Blues." Bessie was merely one of many singers the record companies scouted. Edison turned her down, and so, apparently, did at least one other record company. Her real opportunity did not come until 1923. Frank Walker had heard Bessie several years before in the South, and had never forgotten the power of her singing. Columbia, after 1921, was virtually in the hands of the receivers and was desperate for a hit. In 1923 Walker sent Clarence Williams, who had first recorded Sidney Bechet, to the South to find her and bring her north. Her first record was "Down Hearted Blues," backed by "Gulf Coast Blues." "Down Hearted Blues" caught the public fancy, and the record sold 780,000 copies in fewer than six months. And how the good times began to roll. That summer Bessie married a Philadelphia policeman named Jack Gee, who seems to have done nothing but spend her money and cause her trouble, but at least there was plenty of money available. Bessie never made a great deal of money from her records — most of the time her fees were in the neighborhood of $150 for each — but the records brought her the adulation that enabled her to earn as much as $2000 a week for her public appearances.

For the next eight or ten years she alternated between theaters and traveling tent shows. She had a good head for show business, knew how to put together a show and manage it. She dressed like a star, sported jewelry, and traveled on the road in a private railway car, which black shows often used so that the entertainers could avoid the trouble of finding hospitable hotels and restaurants in strange towns. The idea that Bessie was an innocent mulcted by white businessmen is contradicted by the Albertson biography. To be sure, she was badly underpaid for her records, which helped put Columbia on its feet. On the other hand, the flat fee was standard industry practice, and, more important, in Frank Walker she had a sympathetic, sensitive, and admiring director. Bessie's troubles were brought on mostly by herself. There was the booze: like many alcoholics she could go for long periods without drinking, but once she went on a binge she could drink an ocean dry. She was violent and had a quick temper: she would physically attack people, including close friends, when she was drunk. Her sexual choices were at times undiscriminating. She was bisexual and made conquests of several of the girls in her show. Extravagant with money when it came to her family, she was inclined to be stingy toward the people who worked for her. She could be cruel: several times, in fits of pique, she abandoned her own show on the road, leaving the cast stranded.

Yet there was another side to her. She was overgenerous to her family, who often took eagerly without giving much in return. She could be a good and loyal friend. She could be affectionate; she was always ready for some laughs, some fun, and those drinks. Sidney Bechet, who had a brief affair with her, said, "She always drank plenty and she could hold it, but sometimes after she'd been drinking awhile, she'd get like there was no pleasing her. She had this trouble in her, this thing that wouldn't let her rest sometimes, a meanness that came and took her over." But, said Ida Cox, one of the few competitors Bessie could abide, "Bessie Smith was an old, old friend and everybody loved her, which was why they were so shocked when she died in that accident. Of course she *did* have extremes, who don't?

It is indicative of the esteem in which Bessie Smith was held during the height of her fame in the 1920s that she was the only early jazz musician of any race to attract the attention of a serious photographer. In this case it was Carl Van Vechten, the writer and student of black folk arts, who made a series of photographs of Bessie, including this brooding, somewhat troubled portrait of her in the sort of formal attire she customarily performed in. Collection of American Literature, The Beinecke Rare Book and Manuscript Library, Yale University

She was a very high-tempered person and she didn't take anything from anybody. But she was a good girl, on the whole."

The thing that is clearest about her is that she had absolutely no pretenses. She always said what she thought and did what she wanted. She didn't like whites, a fact she usually made clear, and regardless of the money involved she would walk out of an engagement if she felt that she wasn't being given the royal treatment she believed she deserved. Her troubles stemmed from precisely this willingness to act on the spirit of the moment, heedless of the consequences, and unfortunately the demons that drove her were of the sort likely to provoke consequences.

Analyzing people at long distance is a questionable practice, but it is apparent that Bessie Smith was filled with a great deal of unconscious rage, which continually broke through her defenses, especially when she had been drinking. In view of her having been an orphan, raised in extreme poverty, this is hardly surprising; but once she started drinking, sooner or later she would pick a fight, often a physical one. Bessie was an attacker, and I think that it is this quality, this sense of controlled rage, that we respond to in her work. In general I do not like literary interpretations of music. People who hear in music mankind's striving toward the Godhead, or the sorrows of a race, it seems to me, are simply finding in it messages that another auditor may not hear. Music works its effects in musical terms; contrast, climax, movement, stasis, tension, release, are all expressed in the purely abstract form of notes. But an exception must be made for vocal music, which, after all, is in part literal. Furthermore, especially in music like the blues, derived from the African tradition in which song was often a form of speech, the music itself is supposed to convey some of the inflections of speech.

Bessie's voice, at first rich and round, grew thinner and harsher as time passed, through age, gin, cigarettes, and the fumes from the Coleman lanterns that were used as footlights in tent shows. In her later years she more and more employed a gutteral tone, in part, I believe, to help her control her voice. But sometimes the rasp is deliberate. Listen to the rough edge in her voice as she sings "Don't *mess around* with me," in "Beale Street Mamma." The threatening edge is exactly appropriate, restrained and controlled, and it is an example of what I mean by the violence that seems to be forever about to break through in her singing. There is nothing pathetic or self-pitying about Bessie Smith's blues. They dominate; they demand; they are full of passion. But the passion is not essentially sexual. It is the hoarse, angry cry of the wounded; and that is why so many respond to it, because who among us has never been wounded?

Bessie's great days began to draw to a close at the beginning of the 1930s, when show business grew sick and the record business virtually died. And tastes were changing with the times, among black audiences as well as white. The growing population of urban blacks, increasingly out of touch with the rural black folk music that fed the blues, was demanding a faster, slicker music. The jazz bands were taking over, and the younger musicians — and listeners — were drawing away from the older ways of playing, as Morton and Oliver found to their despair.

Admiration for Bessie never diminished; she was classed apart from fad. Nonetheless, work dwindled. When she recorded for the last time in 1933 she was already something of a voice from the past. This session, on which she made some marvelous records, including a roaring "Gimme a Pigfoot" and two powerful, heartbreaking blues, "Down in the Dumps" and "Do Your Duty" (not strictly a blues in form), shows that she was as penetrating a singer as ever, despite the attenuation of her voice. The musicians who accompanied her included Jack Teagarden, Chu Berry, and Benny Goodman, and the session was a musical success.

And, indeed, thereafter things appeared to be looking up. By 1937 the economy was improving and there was a little more confidence that the Depression was waning. There were nightclub jobs, plans for more records, talk of a movie (she had made a short called *St. Louis Blues* earlier). That fall she set out once more on a Southern tour and in the course of it, early on the morning of Sunday, September 26, she was killed in an automobile accident. Not long afterward there arose the tale that she had not been fatally hurt in the accident, but had been turned away from a white hospital because of her color and had bled to death before she could be brought to a hospital that would accept her. The story has been generally believed, and was the basis for a highly regarded play by Edward Albee, *The Death of Bessie Smith*. But according to Albertson and others who have investigated it, the story was a fabrication, apparently put out as propaganda for political purposes. According to a doctor who happened on the accident shortly after it occurred, "The Bessie Smith ambulance would *not* have gone to a white hospital, you can forget that. Down in the Deep South cotton country, no colored ambulance driver, or white ambulance driver, would ever have thought of putting a colored person off in a hospital for white folks." And it is his opinion that Bessie had been so badly hurt in the accident that she had almost no chance of survival, especially in view of the state of medicine in that time and place.

And so it was finished: the boozing, the parties, the sexual adventuring, and, most of all, the singing. But she left her mark. In 1970 Columbia began to reissue all of her records, which have gone on to have a successful sale. Her voice still commands audiences: people who weren't yet born when she died freeze in their seats at the sound.

By the time of Bessie Smith's death, the craze for female blues singers was well over. Some of them managed to continue to work in music, and a very few, like Ethel Waters, found new careers. But most plunged into obscurity, and hardly any of them recorded after 1930. However, there proved to be a continuing market for male blues singers, many of them still working in the older tradition. These men had never had the success that came to the female singers during the boom, but there had always been a demand for their records. This demand, however much it dwindled, continued. Many, like Leadbelly, were working up into the 1940s, keeping alive a tradition for the younger men coming along, so that a John Lee Hooker would continue to work in the old way two decades later, still ignoring bar lines, still rooting melody in the blue notes, still using only minimal harmonies. But most of the younger men were playing in the new tradition of the jazz-oriented blues. Bumble Bee Slim, a product of the older tradition, by 1931 was playing very close to the strict twelve-bar form, using the subdominant properly and at least suggesting the dominant. By the 1930s popular bluesmen like Broonzy, Sonny Terry, and Leroy Carr were firmly in the new tradition. We can see the change clearly in the work of Robert Johnson, a protégé of Charley Patton's partner, Son House. Growing out of the tradition of Patton's "Stone Pony Blues," Johnson was nevertheless playing the blues in the new way.

Out of this new blues style came two men who, although at base blues singers, have generally been thought of as really jazz singers, or, as they were termed, blues "shouters." One of these was Joe Turner, who was born in 1911 and grew up in Kansas City during the later 1920s and the thirties at a time when it was a rip-roaring good-time town full of the cabarets that made it a fine spawning ground for jazz talent. Turner began as a singing bartender in the cabarets, eventually establishing a partnership with Pete Johnson, a boogie-woogie pianist. Turner came into wider notice in 1938, when the boogie-woogie craze brought him to New York for a concert at Carnegie Hall, arranged by John Hammond, and a subsequent stay at Café Society, a club that featured jazz performers. He recorded with a number of major jazz musicians over the next three decades, toured Europe several times, and was still active in the 1970s.

Turner has a strong, shouting voice. Although he occasionally sings slow blues, notably "Wee Baby Blues," with a group under the leadership of Art Tatum, he is best known for fast blues shouted over a strong rhythmic accompaniment — a boogie piano or a riffing band. He builds his line around blue thirds and sevenths, and sometimes uses a repeated tonic that approaches speech rather than song. "Going Away Blues," made in 1938 with Pete Johnson, is interesting in showing the transition from the blue seventh to the sixth. Turner begins each phrase on a high note in this area, from which the melody then descends. Sometimes the note is a sixth; sometimes a blue seventh; sometimes something in between. Turner's style evolved little over the years. Recording in the mid-1970s with a band including Dizzy Gillespie, he sounds much as he did forty years earlier, his voice amazingly full and strong despite his age.

A blues shouter better known than Turner was Jimmy Rushing, who was a featured singer with the Count Basie band from 1935 to 1948. Grossly overweight, Rushing was known as Mr. Five by Five, and had a popular song written about him in the 1940s. Like Turner, he came from the Southwest; he was born in 1903 in Oklahoma City. His family was musical, and he studied various instruments as well as music theory. He worked for a period in California, occasionally with Jelly Roll Morton, and then began working around Kansas City with several of the important bands of the area. One of these was Walter Page's Blue Devils, which was eventually absorbed into Bennie Moten's band, which in turn was transformed into the Count Basie band.

Rushing's style, too, changed little over the years. In 1929, he made "Blue Devil Blues," a takeoff on Armstrong's "Tight Like This." On the record, which included a young Hot Lips Page struggling to capture the Armstrong cadences, Rushing sang as he did at the end of his career. His sound is richer and fuller than Turner's, presumably because he had had legitimate musical training; and probably for the same reason he uses fewer blue notes — virtually no blue thirds and only an occasional blue seventh. But otherwise he is cut from the same mold — possessing a strong "shouting" voice, a liking for working over powerful rhythmic accompaniment. One of his specialties was "How Long Blues," an eight-bar blues that used an abbreviated set of blues changes:

$$C\,|\,E\,|\,F\,|\,Fmin\,|\,C\,|\,G^7\,|\,C\,|\,C$$

Rushing sang more slow blues than Turner did, and because he was a band vocalist in a day when the big bands were at the center of popular music, he sang pop songs as well. But he was a blues singer at heart, and when he sang popular tunes they were inflected with the sound of the blues.

By the end of World War II, blues singers like Chuck Berry, Muddy Waters, B. B. King, and Bo Diddley, who had great influence on the founders of modern rock, had carried the evolution of the blues farther away from the old style. They used jazz-type rhythms, often double-timed, with a boogie-woogie edge to them. Blue notes were fewer and the harmonic system clear and pronounced. The old tradition, if not dead, was moribund. A John Lee Hooker might still record in the old way, and a few young people continued to imitate the music on the old records as best they could. But the culture from which the blues had originally come was gone. The institutions that had fostered the old blues — the plantations, the work camps, the prison gangs — were disappearing. The American black was no longer totally outside the mainstream of American culture. He had his radio, his television set, his access to white theaters and nightclubs. The cup which for many generations had held the African tradition was broken.

As far as the jazz players were concerned, by the 1930s "the blues" movement meant merely a set of chord changes against which a player could improvise. The basic blues elements had either been incorporated into the general jazz system, or they had disappeared. Blue notes occasionally appeared, principally the blue third, but it was as likely to turn up in a chorus of "I Got Rhythm" as in the blues. Jazz players loved the blues and played them endlessly, but to the musicians they were not now a special form; they were simply part of the jazz repertory.

But the blues are a Lazarus. Apparently dying in 1950, they became, by the end of the fifties, a wellspring for a new music about to sweep the world. Like jazz, rock is built on the blues, which thus lives on in its children.

The White Influx

White influence in Jazz

The position of the white man in jazz has always been ambiguous. Because jazz has so universally been thought of as the black man's music, the white jazz player has often been considered an interloper, not only by blacks who resent the intrusion of whites into what they think of as a private family matter, but also by some white critics, a few of whom have insisted that only the black man can play "authentic" jazz. Blacks, especially those associated with the more militant political movements, have accused whites of "stealing" their music, and some have agreed that no white man can really play it. Black musicians know better. Although a few have taken the line that only the black man can play jazz, by far the largest majority have worked with white players, and recognize them as their peers. But they have not necessarily opened their arms to white players, either.

In the early twenties, when the large influx of whites into jazz began, the blacks tended to be flattered by the attention — in some cases, adulation — they received from whites, many of whom had never before had any social commerce with blacks. By the mid-thirties, however, when whites, many of them undeserving, began to become rich and famous during the swing band period, blacks understandably came to resent white musicians who could command larger salaries and get jobs often barred to blacks. Blacks were resentful, and when they had the opportunity to turn the tables, they took it. Today, in a tight jazz market it is the whites who are feeling excluded.

The blacks' proprietary attitude toward jazz has been termed "Crow Jimism" by jazz writers. There is no doubt that jazz was made in the first instance by blacks, that the majority of superior players have been black, and that most of the significant advances have been worked out by blacks. But the fact remains that whites have played important roles in giving jazz its shape.

What is important to see is that during the early days of jazz, whites and blacks developed their music separately, at least to a degree. White players did not think about the music in exactly the same way as the blacks did, and they had somewhat different ideas about how the music should be played. It has to be understood that these early white players did not always realize that jazz was invented by blacks. Some of them did, of course. Paul Mares, one of the early New Orleans white players, says, "We did our best to copy the colored music we'd heard at home. We did the best we could, but naturally we couldn't play real colored style." But many white players in the North were brought into jazz by the Original Dixieland Jazz Band and the other white groups that developed out of it. They saw jazz as a New Orleans music that both whites and blacks played, and played somewhat differently. Whites, it was understood, could not really play the blues; only a black could do that. But jazz, most whites thought, belonged to neither race. As a consequence, it is possible for one veteran white player to say, as late as the 1970s, "Jazz wasn't invented by those colored guys, it was invented by Bix Beiderbecke and the guys in the Jean Goldkette band."

There were, then, social reasons that tended to force white and black playing into separate streams. To be sure, the records of the Original Dixieland Jazz Band and its followers were bought by blacks as well as whites; some white groups, in fact, were given names to suggest that they were black bands. But blacks could not get into theaters, dance halls, or cabarets where whites were playing, and as jazz moved out of New Orleans it was the black players whom they heard, and eventually worked with, almost exclusively.

On the other side of the coin, it took a certain amount of daring for white adolescents to visit the black ghetto. They could always get into cabarets where the best black bands were appearing, if they looked old enough. The top black bands always, from Storyville up until relatively recently, worked for white audiences, because that was where the money was. But few young whites had much real contact with the black culture. Indeed, it is difficult for young people today to realize how isolated whites were from blacks outside the South during the first few decades of this century. Blacks did not go into white restaurants or nightclubs; they did not appear in public on the same bandstand or baseball diamond. You would not normally see blacks in white shops, even the simplest grocery stores. In 1930 few white people in the United States had ever sat down to a meal with a black, or held a conversation with one as a social equal. To a boy like Bix Beiderbecke or George Wettling, growing up in the Midwest, a black was a rare and exotic creature.

This social isolation of blacks from whites inevitably placed limits on the amount of musical cross-fertilizing that went on. After 1920, therefore, whites began to develop a jazz tradition of their own, which, while unquestionably intertwined with the jazz tradition of the blacks, was still distinct.

I do not want to make too much of this distinction: these early white players were listening to black records and, as they grew older, hearing the musicians in person and occasionally playing with them in jam sessions. We cannot start talking about "white jazz" and "black jazz" because the similarities are far greater than the differences, which in any event began to disappear within a decade or two. The differences, however, are there.

The influx of white players into jazz was part of a broader movement of whites into popular music in general. The concept of a "music business" begins at about the turn of the century. Suddenly there was big money in music; and big money always has a way of legitimating the illegitimate. In increasing numbers whites began to see popular music as a career. Tom Whaley, music copyist and general factotum to Duke Ellington for many years, said that for blacks the music business was a nice living, but "after World War I it wasn't so good. There was an avalanche of white musicians and we had to struggle."

These whites coming into music were mainly interested in achieving success by playing popular music, but some of them were attracted to jazz. The first of these were the players of the Original Dixieland Jazz Band and others associated with them. By the time the first jazz records broke on the public, there already existed in New Orleans a cadre of white musicians capable of playing this advanced ragtime, and by 1920 or so some of them were playing excellent jazz. After the furor following the issuance of the Original Dixieland Jazz Band's records, and their subsequent appearance in New York, the imitators swarmed in. The first important ones were a group of New York players who had heard the band firsthand. The best known of these were trumpeter Phil Napoleon, pianist Frank Signorelli, clarinetist Jimmy Lytell, and trombonist Milfred "Miff" Mole. These men set out frankly to learn the new music and capitalize on it. Through the early twenties, with a shifting group of musicians, they made hundreds of records under many names, the most common of which was the Original Memphis Five. (Many of the records were issued under the name Ladd's Black Aces, in order to reach the black market.)

But at the same time a far more important group of white musicians, also entranced by the Original Dixieland Jazz Band records, was coalescing in the Midwest. The group came to be called the Chicago school of jazz because some of its principal members had gone together to Austin High School in Chicago and because a lot of the work for the bands was in and around that city. But in fact these players came from all over the Midwest: Bix Beiderbecke was from Davenport, Iowa; Eddie Condon from Indiana; Frank Teschemacher from Kansas City; George Wettling from Topeka; Pee Wee Russell from St. Louis. Indeed, some came from farther afield: Max Kaminsky was from Brockton, near Boston, and Wingy Manone was from New Orleans. Furthermore, these musicians worked a great deal in St.

* Pee Wee Russel

Louis, Detroit, and other Midwestern cities, and on the whole it is more accurate to speak of a "Midwest school," rather than of the Chicago school.

These young men began as listeners to the Original Dixieland Jazz Band, but very quickly they fell under the influence of another white group from New Orleans, which was playing in Chicago in 1919 or 1920 under the name of the New Orleans Rhythm Kings. The band was led by trumpeter Paul Mares, who had been called to Chicago to form a New Orleans–style band to take advantage of the popularity of the now-departed Original Dixieland Jazz Band. Mares brought to Chicago, among others, Leon Rappolo, a clarinetist, who was institutionalized for mental illness a few years later, and trombonist George Brunis, who died in 1974 after a fifty-year career in jazz. The band worked for a long period — possibly as long as two years — in a cabaret called Friars' Inn, which was supposed to have been frequented by gangsters Al Capone and Dion O'Bannion. As the successor to the Original Dixieland Jazz Band, it attracted the attention of the young Midwestern players who were learning to play jazz. They spent many hours in front of the bandstand, sometimes sitting in; and when the group's records first appeared, they listened to them over and over. Jimmy McPartland, a trumpet player who was part of the Austin High group, says, "What we used to do was put the record on — one of the Rhythm Kings', naturally — play a few bars, and then all get our notes. We'd have to tune our instruments up to the record machine, to the pitch, and go ahead with a few notes. Then stop. A few more bars of the record, each guy would pick out his notes and boom! we would go on and play it."

The New Orleans Rhythm Kings lasted for about five years; it recorded only some thirty sides; and it never developed any widespread following among the general public. Yet it was by any standards a good, swinging, New Orleans band, rhythmically a little stiffer than the Oliver band, but an excellent jazz band nevertheless. A comparison of its first records, made in 1922, with other records made by jazz musicians in that year and after, shows that it is clearly playing better jazz than any other band that recorded, except those containing black musicians from New Orleans.

The New Orleans Rhythm Kings played strictly in the classic manner, mostly ensemble, with the trombone supporting the trumpet line and the clarinet weaving in and around it. The playing is clean and the intonation good — better than the intonation of the Oliver band. Mares plays with a good feeling for the Oliver style, although he less often plays muted, and Rappolo plays an easy, graceful, and technically sound clarinet that is far in advance of the playing of Larry Shields of the Original Dixieland Jazz Band. In fact, it sounds as if he had been listening carefully to Dodds of the Oliver band, and probably to Jimmy Noone, as well.

This band came to be the primary influence on the Midwesterners. To be sure, by 1925 they were also listening to Oliver, Armstrong, Morton, and other black players. Muggsy Spanier followed Oliver all of his life; Manone was drawn to Armstrong; Benny Goodman appears to have listened to Noone for a time; Krupa to Baby Dodds. But the chief influence on these white players was other whites. Among themselves they had their own heroes, their own ways of playing, their own rules and rituals. And they approached the whole business of jazz playing with an entirely different attitude from the blacks'. A black jazz musician was, among his people, a star, a hero, who held a place something like the place held by a basketball star today. But for the young white players, playing jazz meant entering a forbidden world. Popular music was still a profession that most white families, and certainly white middle-class families, considered beyond the pale. Jazz, with its associations of blacks, liquor, and sexuality, was an abomination. In the 1920s no white parent anywhere in the United States would have been happy about a child going into jazz; the parents of many of these young players hated the idea. As a result, these youngsters, most of them teen-agers when they started, came to jazz with the sense that they were a group of elect outsiders who had dedicated themselves to a high truth.

Because of this attitude, they often hired each other for jobs and made records together. Throughout the 1920s, while times were good and the jazz boom was on, they worked regularly, mainly in the Midwest, in a number of venues — in cabarets as jazz bands; in larger organizations, like the Paul Whiteman or Jean Goldkette bands, that played popular music; at college dances and proms with pickup groups. Their records, too, were made casually, with the leader hiring those among them who happened to be available at the moment. For ten years they rode the wave, usually able to pick up some kind of work, so they were often able to thumb their noses at the big leaders who wanted them to play commercial music. And during that time they created a jazz tradition of their own.

How did this music differ from what the blacks were playing? For one thing, the repertory was different. Where the blacks were playing mainly New Orleans standards, blues, and blues-oriented tunes based on a handful of common chord sequences, the whites were playing mostly for dancing, and were playing the popular songs of the time. "Sugar," "I'm Nobody's Sweetheart Now," "Baby Won't You Please Come Home," "Rockin' Chair," "Back Home Again in Indiana" became standards because these players used them. Beiderbecke made some of his finest solos on tunes like "Singin' the Blues," "I'm Comin' Virginia," "From Monday On," and "I'll Be a Friend with Pleasure," all of which would be entirely forgotten today had he not recorded them. Dancers liked to hear their sentimental favorites, and they liked them played at medium tempos with a little bounce suitable for the two-step and bunny-hug, which were fashionable at the time.

Thus whites did not play many blues; they lacked good tempos for dancing. But there was another reason why the blues did not figure largely in the new white tradition: the whites had no very clear grasp of the blue note, so central to the blues. To be sure, it is unlikely that many black players understood blue-note theory, but they knew the notes empirically. Whites did not understand them at all. I cannot think of a single blue note played by a white musician until the late 1920s, when they began to use the blue third. (It is probable that Jack Teagarden used blue notes, but he did not record until the end of the 1920s.)

But compensating for this impoverishment of the musical vocabulary in one direction was its broadening in another. Whites, in general, had a better understanding of European music than most, though not all, of their black peers. Some of them, like Goodman, the Dorseys, Eddie Lang, and Joe Venuti, had studied music in childhood, before they had any interest in jazz. Many of these men brought to jazz so-called legitimate techniques and a grasp, however elementary, of the principles of European harmonization. To be sure, some blacks, especially pianists, were familiar with standard music theory, but most, especially the horn players, were not, and it remained for whites to advance jazz harmony beyond the barbershop-quartet base with which it started out in life.

But if having one foot planted firmly in the European tradition gave whites an advantage harmonically, it handicapped them rhythmically. The young white child studying with the school bandmaster learned that a beat was a beat and a quarter note a quarter note. Each note had an exact length and was attached tightly to a beat. From the beginning the biggest problem the whites were faced with in dealing with jazz was figuring out how that "swing," which they could feel in the music of the New Orleans players, was produced. For most, it took several years to get the hang of it, and in the meantime, as the early records show, their playing suffered from that ragtime stiffness of which the New Orleans players had already divested themselves.

For a long time in the twenties there was a tendency for the white players to keep pounding the beat on the head. For a second thing, they had a tendency to play pairs of notes on a beat with even weight, instead of giving one or the other more length and accent, as was increasingly coming to be done. Some black players did use these strings of even eighth notes, especially the ones who came from the more European Creole tradition, like Jimmy Noone. But in their runs, the black players, and the Creoles, usually accented the second note of a pair. It was not until the mid- or late 1920s that white jazz players generally got the feel of this practice. In sum, the improvising of whites was tied more closely to the beat, in the ragtime manner, than it was among blacks.

Then, too, the white Midwesterners lacked a certain sense of form that was present in the best black jazz. In the New Orleans bands of both blacks and whites, a division of labor was insisted on, with the trombone sticking to the lower register where it would be out of the way of the trumpet, and the clarinet keeping clear of the trumpet notes in the other direction. But the whites, in their ensemble passages, tended merely to play simultaneous solos. This can work up to a point when only two horns are present, but when you have three or four lines related only because they are moving through the same sequence of chord changes, the effect is often chaos. The effect can be heard on the final "ride-out" chorus of "I'm Nobody's Sweetheart Now," by McKenzie and Condon's Chicagoans, an important record of this genre. The trumpet stays in the middle range, the clarinet phrases on his own, the saxophone blurs in the background, and none of them makes any effort to coordinate their figures with either the trumpet or each other.

In sum, the music of the whites of this period was faster, rhythmically stiffer, and harmonically more European than the black music that had come out of New Orleans. What made it popular then, and what is still its greatest attraction, was a reckless spirit, a heedless, headlong drive. At its best it possessed an intensity that black groups did not always attain, and it is not surprising that this should be so, for it was built on that philosophy of rebellion. These whites were rebelling against a highly ordered and emotionally reserved culture. They thus came to see jazz as everything that the atmosphere of their homes was not: untamed, hot, and filled with feeling. Jazz must come from the heart. Some of them refused to learn to read music for fear that it would pollute the springs of their feelings. The idea was to blow the way you felt, and who cared about an occasional mistake? Consequently, this sense that jazz was emotion set free kept them from formalizing their music beyond a necessary minimum, and it left them excessively dependent on free blowing in their ensemble. This formlessness is what gives their music that reckless spirit, but it was at the sacrifice of the little dramas that a worked-out form can produce.

But of course these men were apprentices, learning what the blacks had grown up hearing all around them, and some of them went on to prove to be major figures in jazz. Among the best known were Jimmy McPartland, a trumpet player in the Beiderbecke mold; Bud Freeman, one of the first saxophonists to solve the problems of that instrument, who played in a somewhat lumbering but forceful manner; drummer Gene Krupa, who went on to fame as a star with the Benny Goodman orchestra and the leader of his own band; Adrian Rollini, who was able to make the cumbrous bass saxophone swing; and players like Tommy Dorsey, his brother Jimmy, and Glenn Miller, who, while of little interest as jazz players, became star band leaders during the big band era.

Of all the men associated with this group, however, three clarinetists and a trombonist stand out. The clarinetists are Benny Goodman, who will be discussed later, Pee Wee Russell, and Frank Teschemacher. In later years Russell came to be considered, by some critics, possibly the greatest of all jazz clarinetists; by any standards he is high on the list. But in the 1920s Frank Teschemacher was acclaimed by his comrades as perhaps the finest musician among them, with the exception of Beiderbecke. Russell himself said, "If Tesch had lived he would now be the greatest clarinet player on earth," and Bud Freeman said, "Teschemacher was a great creative artist who had not developed enough before he died to make any great records."

Teschemacher was born in Kansas City in 1906, the son of relatively well-to-do people of German extraction. He studied violin as a boy, as well as mandolin and banjo, and was one of the better-trained jazz musicians of the time. At some point the family moved to Chicago. Tesch went to Austin High School, took up the alto saxophone, and quickly fell in with some other teen-agers in the school who were interested in jazz, chiefly through the records of the New Orleans Rhythm Kings. The group included Jim Lannigan, who became a respected bassist with this group, Dick McPartland, a banjo player, as well as Jimmy McPartland, and Freeman. They struggled to capture the sound of the new music, and before they were out of high school they were beginning to work both together and separately with local dance bands that played some jazz. For the rest of his life, Teschemacher gigged with a variety of leaders, most of whom were playing commercial music. He played jazz when he could, often coming together with other members of the Midwestern group to make records. He was rehearsing with a band led by cornetist Wild Bill Davison (later to make a major name for himself as a dixieland player) when he was killed in an automobile accident. He was twenty-six years old.

What Teschemacher might have become is a moot question. We have to rate him on the basis of the records he left us, and they show a musician, however talented, whose playing suffers from severe technical handicaps. For one, his intonation was insecure; he simply played out of tune a lot. For another, his tone was unpleasantly shrill in the high registers and flaccid in the low. For a third, his conception was at times chaotic, which was characteristic of these white players. Phrases would appear one after another with little relevance to the whole. Finally, Teschemacher more than most of the white players understood the blue notes, but he used them awkwardly and uncertainly, giving them a kind of quaver instead of a controlled rising or falling, so they wobble rather than move securely from one point to the next. The effect is querulous.

Balanced against these defects, however, are Teschemacher's sure sense of rhythm and his individual, however chaotic, conception. He places his notes in interesting spots over the ground beat, and he does so with a firmness that suggests confidence in what he was doing, imparting at times an easy swing to his music. A typical example of his work is his solo on

"Friars Point Shuffle," with a group of Midwesterners under the title of the Jungle Kings. Teschemacher basically uses two types of figures. One is a series of eighth notes that moves rapidly back and forth in a saw-toothed pattern, usually with accents thrown on the off-beats, a device he probably learned from Dodds or possibly Jimmy Noone. The other, oddly, is a tendency to employ trumpet figurations — cadenzalike passages of long notes separated from the beat after the manner of Armstrong, or staccato eighth-note groups reminiscent of Beiderbecke. On "Wailin' Blues," recorded by a band called the Cellar Boys, under the leadership of Wingy Manone, Teschemacher uses in his brief solo a half-dozen figures straight from the Armstrong canon. Teschemacher, more than most, was a staccato player, and in this solo he attacks the notes sharply. He is at his best here, simpler and better organized than usual, his notes firmly placed.

Although Teschemacher was extravagantly admired by his white colleagues, Charles Ellsworth "Pee Wee" Russell in the long run gained a more durable reputation. Russell was born in 1906 in the St. Louis area of middle-class parents, like Teschemacher. As a boy he studied violin, piano, and drums, and eventually clarinet. He was drawn to jazz at first through the playing of Alcide "Yellow" Nunez, a New Orleans Creole who recorded with a group called the Louisiana Five, which was recording in 1919 on the heels of the Original Dixieland Jazz Band. He was gigging around the Southwest, at one point on an Arkansas River riverboat, before he was out of high school, with dance and pseudojazz bands of the time, and was thus playing jazz while the music was still brand-new. By 1925 he had begun to acquire a reputation among the white Midwesterners and went on to work with many of the best of them, including the Frankie Trumbauer and Jean Goldkette bands, both of which included Beiderbecke when Russell joined them. In 1927 he emigrated to New York, where he worked for several years, principally with the band of Red Nichols, a Beiderbecke-style cornetist, who was commercially successful in leading bands that played dance music heavily spiced with jazz solos, often by musicians of the first caliber.

During the early years of the Depression Russell worked with a series of obscure and usually second-rate dance orchestras, playing various saxophones and the bass clarinet, as well as his regular instrument. Then, in about 1937, there began to coalesce around the figure of Eddie Condon, a banjoist and eventually a guitarist associated with this school, a group of players who were to found what became known as the dixieland movement. Russell became a principal figure with this group, and from that time until his death in 1969 he worked primarily as a jazz musician. The records he made with various Condon groups during the late 1930s and early forties secured him his place in the history of jazz.

In his younger days Russell played in a style that closely matched Teschemacher's; there were the blue notes, the saw-toothed figures, the staccato attack. It was not so much a question of either man influencing the other, but of both sharing a tradition derived from the playing of Shields and Rappolo, Dodds and Noone — that is, the New Orleans tradition of clarinet playing filtered through the white consciousness. Russell, however, did not suffer from the technical failings that beset Teschemacher. His intonation was good and his tone full when he wanted it to be. He employed a terminal vibrato that sounded a little petulant, but he was also master of a growl, which he would sometimes use for an entire chorus.

Russell's early playing is displayed to advantage on a series of records he made with a band generally known as the Billy Banks Rhythm Makers, a pickup group backing the leader's vocalizing. The group featured the black New Orleans trumpeter Henry "Red" Allen, who was to have a long and important jazz career. On these records, made when Pee Wee was in his mid-twenties, the growl and the twisted tempoless figures that characterized his later work are mainly absent. He plays a less "tortured" line, to employ that romantic term, and it is possible to observe the intelligent and economic way he supports Allen's sometimes hectic lead, particularly on "Oh Peter" (the Banner 32462 version) and "Spider Crawl." But the tortured style was also in evidence during this time; witness Russell's chorus on "The Eel," a showcase for Bud Freeman. As he grew older, these tendencies increased. He became more economical, more prone to letting his figure depart widely from the beat, more filled with the twists and turns.

One of the records he made during the Condon period was "Sobbin' Blues." Russell opens his short solo with a blue third nearly four measures long, surely one of the longest notes of its kind in jazz, during which he works the note over with growls and large shifts of pitch. The remainder of the solo is made up of contrasting, simple, candid figures, which he then caps with a rising and falling note built around a blue seventh, flexible of pitch and so dark in color that it might better be called a sound than a note. The tortured phrasing in Pee Wee's work sometimes obscured the fact that he was an excellent melodist. Possibly one of his best solos is on "It's Right Here for You," a brilliant example of the economy of his conception. The solo covers only the last ten measures of the tune and consists almost entirely of quarter notes. The line is simple and logical, dressed out with a slight hoarseness, and the placement of the notes at various distances from the beat is exquisite. This is jazz at its finest.

Despite an extreme addiction to alcohol, Pee Wee Russell lived into his sixties. As he aged, his playing grew mellower, and the tortured phrasing began to disappear. He started to escape from the dixieland style, which, because of the highly individual way he inflected his notes, he had always found confining; and through the last two decades of his life he worked in a variety of venues, including some modern ones. A good example of his

Pee Wee Russell had the sort of face photographers loved; it seemed to reflect the tortured style of his playing. William P. Gottlieb/Edward Gottlieb Collection

last work is on an LP called "Ask Me Now," organized by Marshall Brown. Brown has omitted a piano in order to give Pee Wee more harmonic room, and the tunes include ones by the modernists Thelonious Monk, Ornette Coleman, and John Coltrane. Pee Wee's playing is spare and at times crystal clear, but if the growls are missing, the blue notes are there, and so is the delicate placement of notes around the beat. This aspect of Russell's playing has not occasioned much comment, but it may in time prove to be a most important one. Few jazz musicians have added anything of consequence to their work after the age of thirty-five or so, but Pee Wee Russell may have done so in his fifties.

In many ways the career of Pee Wee Russell is paralleled by that of Jack Teagarden. Teagarden was born a year before Russell. Both gigged around the Southwest as teen-agers — in fact, they were in the same band for a brief period. Both developed highly individual styles, which, while enormously admired, were difficult to emulate. And both lived long enough to develop their talents fully and leave us impressive bodies of records.

Teagarden was born Weldon Leo Teagarden in Vernon, Texas, a small cotton and oil center, which had seen an increasing inflow of blacks from the time of the Emancipation on, who were migrating out of the Deep South in search of work. As was not so for the other white Midwesterners, contact with blacks was normal for Teagarden. He said, "The spirituals I heard — the first ones I remember — were in Vernon, Texas, from a little colored revival under a tent in a vacant lot next door to our house. They called 'em 'Holy Rollers' in those days . . . I'd sit out there on the picket fence we had and listen to it. And [the music] seemed just as natural to me as anything . . . I could hum along with 'em with no trouble at all." A fellow musician says that when he knew Teagarden at sixteen in 1921, "one of the unusual things about [him] at that time was that when we would get through at night he would want me to go with him to hear one of the colored orchestras playing. He strove constantly to improve his style of playing."

Teagarden's mother was a trained pianist who gave lessons and at times played accompaniment for the silent movies, and his father played a little cornet. Teagarden began playing baritone horn at five and switched to the trombone, which has the same mouthpiece, at eight. (A great deal has been written to the effect that because Teagarden could not reach the longer positions on the trombone at this early age, he worked out a set of "false" positions in order to play all the notes. This is simple nonsense. Above the midrange on the trombone most notes can be obtained in two or even three slide positions. Use of these alternate — not "false" — positions is standard trombone technique, practiced by every high school player in America. Furthermore, there are no alternate positions for any of the notes in the bottom octave of the instrument. If the trombonist cannot reach them, he cannot play them. As a juvenile Teagarden would either have avoided notes beyond his reach or worked out some sort of device for extending the slide, as innumerable young trombonists have done.)

Teagarden went on the road at fifteen with his mother, and for the next seven years gigged around the Southwest and thereabouts. At one point he spent a year with a group called Peck's Bad Boys, led by a legendary pianist named John Dickson "Peck" Kelley, born in 1898. According to the testimony of Teagarden and others, Kelley was one of the finest jazz pianists of his day. Despite many job offers from big-name band leaders, he resolutely refused to record or leave the Houston–Galveston–San Antonio area, where he spent his professional life. Eventually a popular song was written about him, "Beat Me Daddy, Eight to the Bar," which opens with the lines "In a little honky-tonky village in Texas/There's a guy who plays the best piano by far . . ."

In 1927 Teagarden arrived in New York with an obscure group, the Doc Ross Jazz Bandits. The group could not find work so it split up, and Teagarden, through his contacts with Pee Wee Russell and Wingy Manone, whom he had played with in the South, began to frequent New York jam sessions. He simply astonished his fellow players, and within weeks after his arrival in New York he was commanding the best free-lance jobs in the city. So towering was his reputation that for the rest of his life he was never short of work. From 1928 to 1933 he worked mostly with Ben Pollack, a drummer who had been with the New Orleans Rhythm Kings and who, like Red Nichols, ran a series of commercially successful bands, which played dance music interspersed with solos by some of the leading white jazz players of the time. In 1933 Teagarden signed a five-year contract with Paul Whiteman, at the conclusion of which he formed his own big swing band in hopes of cashing in on the big band fad. His bands were never very successful, and in 1946 he threw in the towel with some relief. For the next five years he worked in an "all-star" band led by Louis Armstrong, and thereafter led a variety of semi-dixieland groups. It was a long and satisfactory career. He appeared on over a thousand records, worked at one time or another with most of the major figures in jazz, and died full of honors.

As a jazz trombonist Teagarden was an anomalous figure. In his time there were three ways of playing jazz trombone: the glissando "slur-and-smear" style, mostly low register, of the New Orleans jazz bands; a bright, fast, highly technical staccato style played by Miff Mole, Tommy Dorsey, and others; and a legato style being developed by Jimmy Harrison, a black, out of the New Orleans style, which was to become the main line of trombone development. Harrison was born in Louisville, Kentucky, in 1900 and raised in Detroit. He taught himself trombone as a teen-ager and gigged around Ohio until about 1923, when he came to New York and began to work with various bands. In 1925 he landed in the Fletcher Henderson band, which was his musical home for most of the rest of his brief life. He died in 1931 of a stomach ailment.

Aside from his solos with the Henderson band, Harrison left few records, and it is difficult to get a clear understanding of his playing. The best of these is a series made with a pickup group under the leadership of Benny Carter, consisting mainly of men from the Henderson band. His best two solos are on "Dee Blues" and "Bugle Call Rag," made with this group. Harrison was trying to escape from the cumbersome playing of the New Orleans musicians, principally by developing a flowing, legato sound, especially in the upper register, which for technical reasons is more difficult on the trombone than on the other horns. He was never wholly successful; on "Bugle Call

Rag" he has moments of trouble. But he was intense and thoughtful, and his influence on black trombonists of the time, and eventually through them, on whites, was immense. Dicky Wells, Claude Jones, and Benny Morton at one time or another played with, or followed, him in the Henderson band; they went on to become the premier black trombonists of the 1930s, and they all owed Harrison a considerable debt.

Harrison and Teagarden were thought by their peers to be quite similar in their playing, and it is true that they did admire each other and did play together occasionally. But, in fact, they were quite different players. Each used a broad terminal vibrato — which Teagarden eventually dropped; each was a legato player; and each employed a slightly hoarse tone. But Harrison never developed the easy fluidity that Teagarden had, a fluidity that few trombone players even today, in an era of high technique, can match.* Furthermore, Harrison's playing was intense, passionate; Teagarden's playing has been accurately described as lazy and filled with arabesques. This lazy style grew out of the way Teagarden played around the beat, or often invented figures that disregarded the ground beat altogether. It is doubtful that any other white jazz musician, or many blacks, were able to free themselves of the beat as thoroughly as Teagarden did.

In addition, Teagarden had a command not only of the blue third, which the Midwestern whites had come to understand by the late 1920s, but of the blue seventh, which few of them ever grasped. It is plain, in sum, that Teagarden was the first white player to understand thoroughly the essence of black jazz playing. He was not, like a Beiderbecke or an Armstrong, a completely coherent player, able to make melodic wholes with a dramatic or architectural purpose, but otherwise his jazz conception is flawless. He never plays strings of eighth notes, but varies his rhythmic figures, and he habitually accents on the off-beat. Consider, for example, his solo on "Knockin' a Jug," a record, made with a pickup group, that includes a marvelous chorus by Armstrong. Teagarden opens his second chorus with a sequence of slow triplets. The first of the dozen or so notes is an upward rip on the beat to a B♭; the remainder of the triplet sets are played on the B♭ an octave below. The ripped high note sets itself off from the following notes with which it is nominally grouped. The remaining notes thus seem to make up a figure of their own — a figure that begins about a third of the way into a beat. The whole figure is thus shifted away from the beat. There

*Teagarden never talked publicly about how he achieved this fluency; it has even been hinted that it was "a secret." My guess is this: harmonic shifts — shifts of lip position — can be made by raising or lowering the tongue, as well as by changing lip tension. I presume that Teagarden carried his tongue closer to the roof of his mouth than is normal, which facilitated its use for shifting harmonics. This system has one drawback: it thins out the tone in the lower range. And this is the major weakness of Teagarden's playing, a thin colorless tone in the bottom octave.

were few players in jazz at that time who could have invented this figure, or made so much out of so little.

Teagarden was only twenty-two when he made "Knockin' a Jug." Within the next two or three years he lost the fast terminal vibrato, his tone grew less hoarse, and his whole manner became somewhat smoother. These changes are audible on a group of records he made with a band called Eddie Lang–Joe Venuti and Their All-Star Orchestra, which included Benny Goodman and one of Teagarden's younger brothers, trumpeter Charlie Teagarden. Here again is the heavy use of triplets — that three over two so essential to black music from Africa on down — and the long, lazy rubato figures, which abandon the beat altogether. It is as if he were determined to take as much time as he wanted getting to his destination, stopping here and there along the way to examine the scene around him.

Teagarden was not much given to using mutes, but there was one famous device he employed that had the same effect. He would remove the bell section of his horn, leaving just the slide, over the now-empty end of which he would place an ordinary water glass. The sound produced by this "half a horn" was muffled and spooky. Teagarden liked to play in a minor key with this device, as for example "Tailspin Blues," with the Mound City Blue Blowers, and his famous "Makin' Friends."

Because Teagarden was so consistent a player it is difficult to single out one record as his finest. My own preference, however, is "Jack Hits the Road," made in 1940 with a pickup band led by Bud Freeman and including Pee Wee Russell. It is a simple blues, on which Teagarden takes the first two choruses and the last one. His playing on this record ignores the ground beat almost entirely; if his solo were separated out from the record it would be impossible to beat time to it. For example, at the opening of the second chorus he repeats a three-note figure three times. Each time he plays it just a little farther behind the beat. The last chorus opens with a long, low-register slur, unusual for Teagarden; and then in bars seven, eight, and nine he plays a long rubato figure — one of those arabesques — totally outside any tempo, which is absolutely breathtaking. It is a tiny gem of surpassing brilliance.

But Teagarden was more than a pre-eminent trombonist. The astonishing fact is that he was the leading, and virtually the only, white male singer in jazz. Why so few whites have tried to sing jazz, and even fewer have succeeded, is a mystery. Surely if whites can play the music, they should be able to sing it. But Teagarden is very nearly alone in doing so. His tone is rough and a bit nasal, and his phrasing, although certainly much simpler than his trombone playing, is characteristically "lazy." Unfortunately, a sentimental streak not present in his playing surfaces in his choice of tunes, which were sometimes mawkish. But his management of the blues is perfectly sound, as witness his vocal on "Beale Street Blues" with the Lang-

Venuti group, or on "Makin' Friends." Had he never played trombone, Teagarden would have earned a place in jazz history for his singing. But of course it is his trombone playing that counts, and so individual was his conception that he had almost no imitators — none among black players, and among whites only Cutty Cutshall, Lou McGarity, and Eddie Hubble were much known. As much as anybody in jazz, Jack Teagarden was sui generis.

With the emergence in the late 1920s of Teagarden, Pee Wee Russell, Benny Goodman, Bix Beiderbecke, and others, there existed for the first time a cadre of white players who could compete on an equal level with the best blacks. Jazz was still dominated by blacks, as it always would be, but the whites had arrived. This is not to say that whites and blacks were mingling easily in the music. The races did meet occasionally in jam sessions, and a few records by mixed bands were issued, among them the Billy Banks series and some oddities like "Knockin' a Jug," and a version of "Rockin' Chair," which included both Bix Beiderbecke and Duke Ellington's growl trumpet specialist, Bubber Miley. But by and large blacks and whites kept to themselves. And this sharply limited the direct influence each group could have on the other.

But the white influence was there, nonetheless. Blacks have always been exceedingly shy of crediting whites with teaching them anything about jazz. There are not very many who will say that they attempted as youngsters to emulate this or that white jazz star. But in fact many did. In particular, blacks were impressed by the technical skills of whites, the ordinary dance musicians as well as the jazz players, so the white influx into jazz had the effect of driving blacks to improve their techniques. For a second matter, the music played by whites, especially the band arrangements, drew the attention of blacks to what were, for jazz, advanced harmonies. Some blacks, like Coleman Hawkins and Don Redman of the Fletcher Henderson band, were already experimenting with new chords by the late 1920s. In general, though, the whites were leading the way.

But undoubtedly the most important effect that the advent of whites had on jazz had nothing to do with the performance of the music at all. What the white players did was to bring jazz into the American mainstream. In their train came the white fans. Young whites could identify with the white jazz musicians, many of whom were their own age and from similar backgrounds, in a way that they could not with blacks. Then, too, the mystique of the new music, with its cult aspects, had an enormous appeal for them, especially college students, who were familiar with the idea of the outcast

Opposite: Jack Teagarden, one of the very few male singers in jazz, at work. Note hand held to ear to focus background music as he sings. William P. Gottlieb/Edward Gottlieb Collection

artist. The young jazz fans had a sense of being inside, of knowing a secret. Caught up in this mystique, they spent endless hours scouring attics, basements, and secondhand shops for the old records of their heroes, thus saving from oblivion much of the early jazz we now possess. They wore out their records with repeated playings; they talked about the music with the fervor of the convert; they began to analyze, classify, discriminate.

Nor was this cult confined to the United States. In Europe, by 1930 or so, especially in London and Paris, there were similar groups of students interested in jazz. It was these students, not Americans, who founded jazz scholarship. The first books on jazz were written by a Belgian, Robert Goffin, and two Frenchmen, Charles Delaunay and Hugues Panassié, whose *Le Jazz Hot* was responsible for explaining the music to a large number of early listeners. This European writing was full of errors, misplaced emphases, and misinterpretations and is mainly of historical interest today. But much of the scholarship was sound and many insights sharp; these men deserve high marks for making a serious study of an art form that most of their contemporaries dismissed as "nigger music."

But although the Europeans did the first important jazz writing, it was the young American enthusiasts who began to discriminate between the bouncy popular music of the time and "real jazz." They developed standards of taste and the first, tentative critical canons. Their enthusiasm was not without its drawbacks. They were often dogmatic and their vision of themselves as keepers of the flame eventually stood in the way of acceptance of new developments in the music. Yet without this missionary fervor it is uncertain how much jazz would have grown. Their passion was invaluable.

The First Genius:

Louis Armstrong

Louis Armstrong was born into poverty, schooled in drudgery, and raised in ignorance. Fortunately for him and us, he happened to be a genius. That particular word has probably been misused more regularly by writers on jazz than by those on any of the other arts, with the exception, of course, of the film. Virtually every jazz musician able to hold his instrument properly has at one time or another been described as a genius; patently, the description is usually unwarranted.

But if the term means anything at all, it describes Armstrong. I take the word to mean somebody whose accomplishments are beyond analysis. To repeat myself, an artist makes relationships; a great artist makes new and surprising ones, showing us how apparently disparate shapes can be fitted together. With the ordinary artist, we can discover in his background and character where he drew his material from; with the genius, we often are unable to determine how he arrived at his startling conclusion. Armstrong's melodic gift was simply astonishing, and there is no explaining where it came from or how it worked its magic. Consider this: Armstrong did not begin to play the cornet until he was fourteen, a relatively late age for a musician to start. Within months, despite the fact that he could not read music, he was leader of his school band. Four years later he was cornetist with the leading jazz band in New Orleans. In another four years, when he was not yet twenty-three, he was acknowledged by his peers to be the best jazz musician alive. And by the time he was twenty-eight he had made a series of records that not only changed the course of jazz history, and therefore the history of Western music as well, but remains one of the greatest achievements in jazz. To be sure, jazz is a young person's art. Beiderbecke was dead at twenty-eight; Charlie Parker at thirty-four. Lester Young did his best work before he was thirty; Billie Holiday hers before she was twenty-five. So it is not unusual for a jazz artist to do great work in his youth. Still, for a young man in his early twenties to tower over his peers as Armstrong did suggests that he possessed an ability of a different order from simple talent.

Louis Armstrong, by one of those fanciful quirks of fate, was born in New Orleans on July 4, 1900. (John Chilton, one of Armstrong's biographers, questions the date, but it is generally accepted.) His grandparents had been slaves. His father, Willie Armstrong, was a day laborer who spent most of his working career in a turpentine plant, where in time he became some sort of straw boss. His mother, Mary Ann, or Mayann as she was called, worked mainly as a domestic for white families, and probably, though not certainly, earned extra money as a part-time or casual prostitute. (It should be remembered that in the Storyville subculture in which Armstrong lived, prostitution was looked on almost as a normal way of making a living. Armstrong's first wife was a prostitute.) Mayann figures largely in Armstrong's emotional life. However much she neglected him at times, her affection for him seems to have been real, and he returned it. He says, "Mayann's funeral in Chicago was probably the only time I ever cried — when they put that cover over her face."

Not long after Armstrong's birth Willie and Mayann separated, and Louis was raised by his paternal grandmother, Josephine Armstrong. He did not move in with his mother until he was already in school. His life with her was typical of the ghetto, harsh by any standards. We must bear in mind, when we think about Armstrong's nature, that he was not merely "poor"; he was deprived both physically and emotionally in a way that it is difficult to credit. Mayann turned over her boyfriends regularly, so there was a constant series of what Armstrong called his "stepfathers" coming and going and sometimes beating his mother in drunken quarrels. He wore their hand-me-down trousers and not much else; his entire wardrobe might consist of a pair of trousers and one or two shirts. He often went barefoot. His diet ran heavily to red beans, rice, okra, and meat scraps. At times he scavenged in garbage pails. His home, much of the time, was in the heart of Storyville, and he was a daily witness to prostitution, abject drunkeness, drug addiction, violence, and sometimes murder. There was garbage; there were rats; there was filth. The one thing there was never enough of was money. Armstrong worked at all kinds of menial tasks from an early age — jobs like selling newspapers or delivering coal. His schooling was haphazard. Going without shoes, without more than two or three shabby pieces of clothing, living at times on scraps from other people's tables, playing in the dust and the mud of the streets when he wasn't working, grubbing along the railroad tracks for pepper grass out of which to make medicine when he was sick — it is not startling that he grew up to become wealthy and celebrated, but that he grew up at all.

What saved him was the affection first of his grandmother, who appears to have provided some security in his early childhood, and then of Mayann.

Armstrong's relationship with his mother was a little unusual. She appears to have regarded Louis as a younger brother rather than as a son — a friend, an ally and helpmate in times of trouble. There were from time to time other people in the household — his half sister, Beatrice, and occasionally some cousins — and the children seemed to have learned to fend for themselves, for Mayann would sometimes disappear for days at a stretch, leaving them to the kindness of others. But if Mayann was irresponsible, she did care for Louis in her own way, which was more than his father did. Armstrong later wrote bitterly, "My father did not have time to teach me anything; he was too busy chasing chippies." But apparently the affection of his mother was enough. He became a healthy, high-spirited boy, strongly motivated to do what people wanted him to do — that is, to be liked.

Like the other pioneer jazz players, Armstrong grew up with music all around him — ragtime, "hot" music, marches, music of all kinds. It was not, of course, possible for him to acquire a real musical instrument, but he became part of a quartet of street urchins that sang on the sidewalks for pennies in the barbershop-quartet fashion popular at the time. Changing personnel and voices forced youngsters in such groups to become familiar with all four harmony voices. This training in part-singing was unquestionably influential in his later musical development.

The pivotal event in his life — and one of the central events in jazz history — occurred on New Year's Day, 1913. New Orleans traditionally celebrated the holiday with noisemakers and fireworks. Armstrong got hold of a .38 caliber pistol belonging to his current stepfather and fired it off in the street. He was spotted by a policeman, arrested, and remanded to the Colored Waifs' Home. This may sound like harsh treatment for so trivial an offense, particularly for a boy barely out of short pants, but the judge may have assumed that he was doing him a kindness by removing him from what must have seemed a desperate environment. Armstrong was initially homesick, but in time he came to like the Waifs' Home.

The school had a brass band and a vocal group of some kind, probably a chorus. Armstrong joined the chorus, and then was asked to join the brass band by the master, Peter Davis. He started on tambourine, and his sense of time impressed Davis, who moved him on to drums. A short time later he switched to the alto horn, a band instrument akin to the cornet, but lower. Armstrong found himself immediately at home on the instrument. He wrote later, "I had been singing for a number of years and my instinct told me that an alto takes a part in a band same as a baritone or tenor in a quartet. I played my part on the alto very well."

It is not clear what kind of music the band played, or whether the boys as a rule read music. Armstrong, as we know, did not. When he says, "I played my part on the alto very well," he means that he was working out a harmony line to the melody by ear as he went along. One important part of Armstrong's genius was his keen grasp of harmony at a time when many jazz musicians had no real understanding of music theory. Any trained musician can do what Armstrong was doing in the Waifs' Home band, but Armstrong was doing it without any training whatever, at the age of fourteen.

His gift, thus, was obvious from the start. Peter Davis, like a number of other men in Armstrong's life, became fond of the boy. He made Armstrong the institution's bugler when an opening came up; then he taught him the cornet, which has the same embouchure as the bugle, and finally made him leader of the band. Davis, Armstrong has testified, taught him the importance of sound production — that is, tone — and the lesson stuck. Altogether, his stay in the Waifs' Home was a good experience for him, and he came to enjoy the life. He wrote, "The place was more like a health center or a boarding school than a boy's jail."

He left after three years owing to the intercession of his father, who was motivated not by kindness, but by the desire to have a baby sitter at home to look after the children of his second marriage while he and his wife worked. Armstrong disliked the arrangement, and when it was ended was glad to return to Mayann to live. He was now about sixteen and considered himself a man. He began earning his living by delivering coal for seventy-five cents a day and playing cornet in bars around Storyville, when he could, for $1.25 a night plus tips. He became the principal support of the household, as he was to be for the rest of his life.

His cornet playing was developing very rapidly. With a few other youngsters he formed a little band, which played now and then at the tonks and parties. At the same time he started hanging around the cabaret where a band led by Kid Ory was playing. This was the band that had Joe Oliver on cornet. Oliver, as so many other older men did, took a liking to Armstrong and taught him some of the tricks of the trade. A great deal has been written about the influence of various New Orleans cornetists on Armstrong, the names usually given being those of Buddy Bolden, Bunk Johnson, and Oliver. Armstrong talks of hearing Bolden, but he was too young when Bolden stopped playing for him to have had much impact. Armstrong himself has denied Johnson's claims of being a major influence on him. The truth is that Armstrong's teacher was himself. Oliver may have showed the young man some things about fingering, embouchure, breath control, and the like, and perhaps he exposed him to the New Orleans repertory, but Armstrong certainly did not take his conception from Oliver. Their styles are almost diametrically opposed — the controlled, narrowly focused playing of Oliver contrasting markedly with the flamboyant lyricism of Armstrong. The real importance of the association was that Oliver occasionally sent Armstrong to substitute for him in the Ory band, and when Oliver went north to Chicago in 1918 Ory hired Armstrong as his replacement. Ory's was considered one of the best jazz bands in New Orleans, which made Armstrong, at eighteen, the leading cornetist in the ghetto.

For the next five years he continued to job around New Orleans, developing his skills. One important training ground for him was the riverboats. These old paddle-wheelers, already slipping into obsolescence as transportation, were run as pleasure boats or, as they came to be called, "showboats." Some of them made day or evening excursions, returning to the home port after an outing of several hours. Others moved on up the river, stopping at different towns along the way each night, where they would put on a show either at the dock or during a short excursion along the river. A carnival atmosphere prevailed, and music was part of the setting. A St. Louis pianist named Fate Marable organized and operated bands for the boats owned by the Streckfus brothers. These were disciplined groups playing clockwork music. Tempos were sometimes set by stopwatches. But they did play some jazz as well, and leaders sometimes kept a few hot players in the band for this purpose. In 1918 Marable hired Armstrong for one excursion, and for the next two or three years he worked sporadically on the riverboats. On these trips a mellophone player named David Jones taught Armstrong the rudiments of reading music, and it is some indication of Armstrong's reputation around New Orleans that Marable hired a musician who couldn't read when there were plenty around who could.

Most of Armstrong's apprenticeship, however, took place in New Orleans. He continued to play around the city, and he married a woman named Daisy, somewhat older than himself, with whom he apparently spent most of the time fighting. Then in 1922 Oliver "sent" for him to come to Chicago. Armstrong came and simply blew everybody out of the city. He worked with Oliver at the Lincoln Gardens, and very shortly after his arrival the band made its first records. His friends and many fellow musicians right from the start urged him to move out on his own. For a period he resisted. He felt he owed Oliver a debt of gratitude, and he didn't want to hurt his feelings. Anyway, it was not in Armstrong's nature to do things that people would find unpleasant.

However, early in 1924 Armstrong married Oliver's pianist, Lillian Hardin, a classically trained woman who, while never a great jazz player, was certainly competent enough. She was ambitious for her husband. She worked on his sight-reading with him, and that summer persuaded him to leave Oliver for a job in the Dreamland Cafe. In the fall, Fletcher Henderson offered Armstrong a job with his orchestra. The Henderson band in 1924 was not really a jazz band; it was a commercial band that played for dances and shows and backed singers on record dates. Henderson, who proved to be the greatest talent scout in jazz history, felt the need for a jazz soloist in the band to provide the punch demanded by listeners of the times.

Armstrong accepted the offer and stayed with the band for almost a year, recording with it a number of solos, the best known of which was "Sugar Foot Stomp," a version of Oliver's "Dippermouth Blues." During his stay with Henderson in New York, he did some free-lance recording, backing up blues singers and recording with various Clarence Williams groups, including the Red Onion Jazz Babies with Bechet.

But after a year he tired of working with the Henderson group. (Like most jazz musicians, Armstrong drank — there is a famous record of his made in the 1930s named "Laughing Louie" on which the whole band seems to be drunk — but he never let the habit get away from him. His dependence, if it was one, was on marijuana, which he used persistently throughout large parts of his life.) So in the fall of 1925 Armstrong returned to the Dreamland Cafe, to work, for seventy-five dollars a week, with a band organized by Lil. The sum was unheard of for a black jazzman at the time. Soon afterward he began doubling with Erskine Tate's Vendome Theatre Orchestra, where he was the featured hot soloist.

Then, on November 12, 1925, he went into the Okeh studios to make the first of a series of some five-dozen cuts, which have come to be known as the Hot Fives and Hot Sevens. They were landmarks in jazz history, causing great excitement among jazz players and fans both in the United States and Europe, and they turned jazz in its course. For the next four years Armstrong worked as featured soloist with the Tate group, with a group led by Carroll Dickerson, and with others under his own name. The Hot Fives and Hot Sevens, which were recorded between 1925 and the end of 1928, were made with pickup bands. At the same time Armstrong began to make the switch from cornet to trumpet. The difference between the two instruments is slight, having to do with the percentage of tubing that is conical as opposed to straight. The cornet gets a tone that is somewhat mellower and less brilliant than the trumpet. The early jazz players almost invariably used cornets because that was the custom in the brass bands on which the jazz bands were founded. The trumpet was an instrument for classical soloists and symphonic players, and some of the early jazz players were scared to try it. Armstrong began playing the trumpet in theaters because its greater brilliance helped it to carry in large spaces, and possibly because of its larger, flashier physical appearance as well. In time he dropped the cornet altogether, and, with that, it began to disappear from jazz, thereafter played mainly by men loyal to the principles of New Orleans music.

In 1929 Armstrong shifted his home base from Chicago to New York. For the next seventeen years he would play as featured soloist before a large band. He was no longer a simple New Orleans jazz player but, in a small way, an international figure, recognized by those who knew about that sort of thing as the leader of a new art form. From this time on his life consisted almost entirely of trumpet playing and the incredibly bone-wearying travel that is part of a busy musician's life. His stamina was astonishing. Where in the Depression days of the 1930s many musicians had trouble finding any kind of work — Sidney Bechet, as we know, worked in a tailor shop for a period — Armstrong could be booked 365 nights a year, and often was.

The quantity of sheer trumpet playing he did over the twenty years or so after he cut the first of the Hot Five sides is incredible. Most of the bands he fronted existed only as backdrops for his playing and singing, and they often contained no soloist of stature besides Armstrong himself. An ordinary featured trumpet player might have one or two big solo spots in an evening; Armstrong was featured on practically every number. On each song he would play, perhaps, an introductory figure; then lead the trumpet section through the opening chorus; then sing a chorus; then play a solo of two or three choruses; and finally lead the band out, often soaring over them in the upper register for two or three choruses more. Some of the bands, particularly the Luis Russell band, which accompanied him for long periods, contained a few good soloists, like altoist Charlie Holmes and trombonist J. C. Higginbotham, and at times they spelled him. But the amount of playing Armstrong did was still enormous, and he developed, as musicians say, "chops like iron." Yet more than the stamina it produced, that much exposed solo playing gave him a matchless opportunity for development. He could experiment; he could take chances. If he failed, it did not matter because he could make it up on the next number five minutes later. Things that other musicians struggled to achieve became second nature for Armstrong simply because he did them so often. He had the chance every night to practice in public.

His life was not trouble-free, however. His marriage with Lil was on the rocks by the time he left for New York, and he went through a brief marriage, in the early 1930s, before he married Lucille Wilson, a show girl, who provided some emotional stability throughout the rest of his life. His business affairs were in some turmoil, too. Armstrong, was, we must remember, a badly educated man from the ghetto with little experience of the world. By 1930 he had, as a matter of course, acquired some wisdom about the entertainment business, but he was still making mistakes. He took on managers who proved to be inept, venal, or both; and finally, in 1933, discouraged and tired, he made an extended visit to Europe.

Both the adulation he received and the respite from playing were good for him, as can be seen after he began recording again in 1935. At about this time he put his affairs in the hands of Joe Glaser, originally a small-time booker and nightclub owner whom Armstrong had worked for in Chicago for a period. The choice was a good one. Glaser dropped his other affairs, took firm control of Armstrong's career, made the major decisions and

many minor ones, which Louis was happy to have him do, and allowed him to concentrate on the music. From 1935 until the war, Armstrong recorded fruitfully, appeared in dozens of movies, and quietly got rich.

The big band period lasted until 1946, when the swing era collapsed in a rush. Armstrong returned to a smaller dixieland format, his singing increasingly coming to the fore. He was now less a jazz musician than a popular singer, but it was no matter. By 1950 Armstrong really had not much left to say on his trumpet; he had already said it all. He continued to appear in public almost to the time of his death, on July 6, 1971. When he died a great many people who loved him for his singing of "Hello, Dolly" and "Mack the Knife" were startled to discover in the obituary notices that he was one of the greatest jazz musicians who had ever lived.

What, then, makes Armstrong's playing so remarkable? First, there is his mastery of his instrument. His tone is warm and full, like honey, in all registers. His attack is one of the strongest and cleanest of any jazz trumpeter. Where many jazz brassmen have a legato style replete with slurs and half-tonguings, Armstrong always introduced a note instantaneously, with a razor-sharp front edge. His vibrato is broad, but slower than the slightly nervous vibrato of Oliver and other New Orleans players. Although his command of the high register would not be considered remarkable today, he was far ahead of his peers in this respect; in fact, Armstrong brought high-register playing into jazz. In sum, there is no other sound in jazz like Armstrong's. It is immediately identifiable — rich and welcoming. (It should also be noted that Armstrong habitually hits held notes just fractionally flat, and pulls up to true pitch, a procedure, we remember, that Milton Metfessel's phonophotography machine showed to be customary with black folk singers.)

But ultimately it is his melodic conception that dazzles us. Melody is one of those things in music that is difficult to talk about. Harmony has its theory, which is based on reasoned assumptions; rhythm can be approached almost mathematically; and form has analogues in architecture, drama, and geometry. Yet why is it that a particular fragment of melody moves us? Jazz musicians have often spoken of a player's "telling his story"; drummer Jo Jones claimed that he could hear actual words and indeed whole sentences in Lester Young's playing. Too, critics of classical music have spoken of the

Opposite: Louis Armstrong as the American public knew him. Jazz musicians knew him as one of the geniuses of the music, but to general audiences he was a gravel-voiced singer who mugged his way through popular songs, and incidentally played the trumpet. A good deal of the rebelliousness of the bop movement was a reaction to this image of the light-hearted black entertainer of the Armstrong-Waller type. William P. Gottlieb/Edward Gottlieb Collection

conversational element in melody. It is difficult to know how much to make
of this, but in the best music we do catch the feeling that the composer or
improvising musician is talking to us, is telling us a story, or making an
important point about something we can almost, but not quite, put into
words. This effect is no doubt created in part by the resemblances that exist
between music and speech. A story or lecture is coherent. It proceeds from
here to there in logical fashion, and if it is to move us it will contain certain
common dramatic devices — that is, it will elaborate on an initial statement; it will contain climaxes, asides and detours, tensions and resolutions;
and it will round off with a final statement. The best music behaves in the
same way, and it may be these formal similarities that give music the effect
of speech.

This conversational element is abundantly present in Louis Armstrong's
music. He had a greater sense of form than any other player in the history
of jazz. Had he been born into a different culture he might have grown up
to become a master architect or dramatist. His solos are not made of
sequences of melodic fragments related only in mood; they consist of parts
contributing to a whole. They have unity, a beginning, middle, and end. Not
all the time, of course; Armstrong, like any player, had his weak moments,
and there were times when he was simply showing off. But in his best work
that dramatic form is always present.

Armstrong relied, it would seem, on two general devices in organizing
his solos. One of them is the so-called correlated chorus, abstracted from
his work by Bix Beiderbecke and a friend, Esten Spurrier. Spurrier, quoted
by Beiderbecke's biographers, Richard M. Sudhalter and Philip R. Evans,
says, "Louis departed greatly from all cornet players in his ability to compose a close-knit individual 32 measures with all phrases compatible with
each other. So Bix and I always credited Louis as being the father of the
correlated chorus: play two measures, then two related, making four measures, on which you played another four measures related to the first four,
and so on ad infinitum to the end of the chorus." I am not sure how
conscious Armstrong was of using this device, if he used it at all, but there
are certainly moments when it fits, as, for example, in his first solo on a
version of "Sugar Foot Strut," made with the Hot Five, and in the opening
measures of his superb solo on "Hotter Than That."

His other practice is easier to define. Armstrong himself explained, "On
the first chorus I plays the melody, on the second chorus I plays the melody
around the melody, and on the third chorus I routines." He was talking
primarily about his final choruses on a tune, and he meant that after
restating the melody of the song he would then play a variation of it and
close with some sort of climax in simple, repeated figures, which at times
degenerated to high-note showboating. This pattern appears relatively
rarely on records, simply because there was usually not enough time to fit

in that many choruses unless the tempo was quite fast, but it was standard for Armstrong before a live audience to play as many as five choruses at the end of a number. A sample of this system can be heard on "Struttin' with Some Barbecue," made with a big band in 1938, in which he plays a penultimate chorus on the melody more or less as written, a last chorus that is a variation of the melody boiled down to its bones, and then "routines" on a short coda. Another example of this system is found on "Swing That Music," also made with a big band in the same period. The first of four final choruses is a straightforward exposition of the melody; the second chorus simplifies it; the third reduces it to its basic elements; and the fourth, one of those excessive high-note displays that Armstrong's willingness to please sometimes led him into, consists of a single note repeated for thirty-two measures.

Another important characteristic of Armstrong's playing was the extent to which he escaped from the ground beat. This characteristic was something that grew steadily from his earliest recordings on, and it is my suspicion that Louis Armstrong was the first jazz musician to recognize the importance of this practice and to develop it consciously as an artistic device. As we have seen, he was, in those first records with Oliver, like "Riverside Blues," pulling his notes a considerable distance from the ground beat. Anyone who doubts that the practice was deliberate can examine "Skid-Dat-De-Dat," made in 1926. There is a passage, consisting of four whole notes, that appears four times early in the record. Armstrong regularly plays the first of the four whole notes slightly behind the beat, the second farther behind the beat, and the last two much closer to the beat, although we cannot always be sure about the fourth because he precedes it with a pickup note the last two times through. By 1927 and 1928, when he was making the greatest of the Hot Five and Hot Seven records, he was taking greater liberties with the time, habitually extending his phrases, as a drawing on a sheet of rubber can be extended if one stretches the rubber. In these figures, where, say, five or six notes appear where we might expect eight, the relationship between the ground beat and the melodic line is tenuous indeed; the melody is free to soar above everything else.

This practice of setting the notes of the melody at odd points in relation to the beat was of course something that every jazz musician practiced. Some, like Sidney Bechet, had carried it out to a considerable degree. But by 1927 Armstrong was not merely setting notes ahead or behind the beat; he was setting whole phrases in time schemes irrelevant to the beat, or in no time schemes at all. Nobody else in jazz had carried the practice nearly that far. It is worth comparing him with Ernest "Kid Punch" Miller, now known mainly to jazz historians but considered in the 1920s one of the leading New Orleans cornetists. Miller had a strong embouchure, a clean attack, and a full tone, and was very much at home with the blues, as his vocal on "She's Cryin' for Me," with Albert Wynn's Gutbucket Five, attests. (Wynn, an excellent, if neglected, trombonist, has a fine solo on this record.) One of his best solos is on "Parkway Stomp," with the Wynn group. It was made in 1928, the year that Armstrong made such master-pieces as "West End Blues" and "Weather Bird." There is, near the end of the record, a stop-time chorus, a device in which the accompanying instruments play only one, or perhaps two, beats in a measure, leaving the soloist on a tempoless plain. The device virtually begs the soloist to take liberties with time, but Miller continues to play as if tied to the beat. Another interesting case in point is Cladys "Jabbo" Smith. Smith was considered by many, at the time, to be second only to Armstrong among jazz trumpet players. He had a strong high register — in some respects it was better than Armstrong's, though lacking a shade in warmth — and a fervent drive. He had a particularly big reputation with European fans during the 1930s, but, like Punch Miller, he was struggling to grasp Armstrong's conception. In "Take Me to the River," an eight-bar blues made in 1929, we can hear him lift whole phrases, both in his vocal and his trumpet choruses, from Armstrong's "West End Blues." In the Armstrong-derived figures he is away from the beat; on those of his own he is much closer to it.

It is necessary only to compare Armstrong's playing over stop-time in "Potato Head Blues," made a year earlier, to recognize how far Armstrong was ahead of his peers in respect to departing from the ground beat. As he developed he went farther and farther in this direction, until by the 1930s he often enunciated no more than a beat a measure. And it was this practice, probably more than anything, that amazed the players around him and drew them to him.

Louis Armstrong's recording career conveniently divides itself into three periods: from the first records with Oliver until 1928, when he made the last records in the New Orleans genre; the big band period, which lasted until 1946; and his final period, when he worked mainly as a vocalist fronting a dixieland band. His career began on March 31, 1923, when Oliver cut five sides for Gennett, one of which was "Chimes Blues," containing Armstrong's first recorded solo. (Gennett was a small record company belonging to the Starr Piano Company. It recorded many of the early jazz players.) Over the next year or so he appeared on about two-dozen recordings with the Oliver band. He solos infrequently, usually staying in the background as second cornet to Oliver, but even from the little we can hear it is clear that he was already a more interesting, more imaginative player than Oliver. Very quickly he was much in demand for recording. Over the next few years he backed, according to Hugues Panassié, twenty-three blues singers, including all the major ones, and made about thirty records with pickup groups under the leadership of Clarence Williams and others. His playing with the blues singers is generally simple and direct. He occasionally uses the plunger, or "wa-wa" mute, a rarity with him otherwise. He has more chance to display himself on the Williams records. "Terrible Blues," along with "Cake Walkin' Babies" one of the best of this group, shows a solo that fits the concept of the correlated chorus, and an extensive use of triplets, which will evolve into the stretched figures. He also was recording with Fletcher Henderson, but his playing was limited to the occasional hot solo Henderson felt the band needed. "Sugar Foot Stomp" was arranged especially for him. It made a big hit with jazz players and fans, but Armstrong simply plays Oliver's famous solo, and it shows little of his own style. "Alabamy Bound" indicates that he was following the New Orleans practice of making his solo a variation on the melody rather than building something entirely new.

The first group of Hot Fives, made between 1925 and 1927, used Johnny Dodds on clarinet, Ory on trombone, Johnny St. Cyr on banjo, and his wife, Lil, on piano. Small as the band was, it played with enormous force and drive. Ory was unquestionably the best of the New Orleans trombonists of the period — unimaginative, to be sure, but he played with a firm touch and he did not suffer from the intonation problems that plagued most of the early jazz trombonists. Dodds was at or near his peak, and Hardin and St. Cyr, whatever their weaknesses as soloists, provided a reliable ground beat. At the beginning the Hot Fives were solidly in the New Orleans vein, with plenty of ensemble work and the breaks typical of the style. Perhaps the most admired of this group were "Cornet Chop Suey," which contains a solo by Armstrong that was widely copied, and "Heebie Jeebies," on which Armstrong sings a "scat" chorus; that is, he uses sounds suggestive of an instrument instead of words. (It is usually given out that Armstrong "invented" scat-singing when he dropped the song sheet in the studio in the middle of the vocal, but according to Panassié he was using the device in theaters, and in any case, the wordless vocal is probably as ancient as language. The song, incidentally, was taken intact from the second strain of Joplin's "Heliotrope Bouquet.")

By 1927 Armstrong was a rising star, and the change was reflected in his recordings. Although the New Orleans ensemble still appeared from time to time, the majority of the space was given over to solos, mainly by the leader, intermixed with semiarranged passages. There are so many remarkable musical moments in these records that it is difficult to single any out. Probably the most highly acclaimed are "Struttin' with Some Barbecue" and "Big Butter and Egg Man." (The latter is discussed at length by André Hodier in *Jazz: Its Evolution and Essence.*)

The masterpiece of this group, however, is "Hotter Than That," possibly because Armstrong dominates the record. It is merely a jammed version of the last strain of "Tiger Rag," always an Armstrong favorite. After a brief introduction, Armstrong races into a perfectly constructed solo that, despite its flawless architecture, is one of the most ebullient passages in recorded jazz. It is composed entirely of four-measure phrases, each complete in itself, yet following with natural ease out of the preceding ones. The opening phrase is particularly fine, and suggests the concept of the correlated chorus. It begins with two small phrases of a measure apiece, each worked out to throw the accent on the third beat of the bar, a characteristic of Armstrong's playing. The second figure appears to be complete, but instead of the period being put, Armstrong rolls out of it a variation of itself before he concludes the four-measure phrase, producing exactly that surprising new relationship that is inexplicable in genius. At the center of the solo there is a two-measure break, which is meant to end on a note placed at the last half beat of the measure. Then to our astonishment a new phrase, which begins the second half of the solo, appears out of this note and becomes the pivot around which the whole chorus swings, at once the last note of the first half of the chorus and the first of the next, a device, incidentally, very common to West African music. Then follows a clarinet solo, and Armstrong returns to scat a chorus, complete with a break that utilizes a figure similar to the one in the cornet break. There is a trombone solo, and then Armstrong takes another astounding break to lead into the last ensemble chorus. Anticipating Ory's last note (not very difficult to do) he steals it from Ory and uses it as a springboard to leap into the last chorus. For the out chorus he "routines" a high-note figure for about seven bars before suddenly sweeping out of it and driving the number to a conclusion. It is a remarkable performance, powerful without loss of poise and balance, all the more so because it is taken somewhat faster than these men usually played.

Armstrong was now reaching a peak in his career. In May of 1927, Peter Briggs, tuba, and Baby Dodds, drums, were added to the band to create the Hot Seven. In a creative outburst this group cut twelve records in eight days. By this time any feeble pretense that this was a New Orleans band had gone by the boards. The records are mainly of strings of solos, principally by Armstrong, with only enough ensemble jamming to keep the franchise. For example, "Wild Man Blues," based on changes better known as "Rock Me, Mamma, with a Steady Roll," consists almost entirely of long solos by Armstrong and Dodds, with only the first eight and the last four bars played ensemble. Aside from "Wild Man," the most renowned of this group of cuts were "Gully Low Blues" and "Potato Head Blues." "Gully Low Blues" opens with a fast ensemble chorus based on "I Wish I Could Shimmy Like My Sister Kate," which Armstrong claimed he wrote, and then drops down in tempo to become a slow blues. The high point is Armstrong's chorus toward the end of the record. It is made up of six two-bar figures, each of which, except the last, consists of a long, held note, followed by a tempoless, stretched figure that plunges downward in stages, like water down steep rapids. These figures all begin on the fifth (a high B♭) and are patterned after the standard downward phrases of the blues singers, except that instead of using three figures over a chorus, Armstrong shortens them and uses six. Each is a little melodic gem, full of surprises, and the solo is a complete unit. Admittedly, the organizational principle is hardly complex, but it was rare in jazz to find this much unity in a solo chorus. "Potato Head Blues," possibly the most famous of this group, was known for Armstrong's stop-time chorus, during which Armstrong phrases a succession of two-measure figures, each of them loose from the ground beat in a way that other players were not as yet up to.

The New Orleans genre had been abandoned, and now the New Orleans players were dropped, too. For the next series of sides Armstrong was backed by a set of what would today be called studio musicians — competent players, but not necessarily jazzmen — whose function was to support the star. The rhythm section, however, included Armstrong's New Orleans sidekick, Zutty Singleton, and a new pianist named Earl Hines. Once again there is a great plenty of brilliant music to choose from, but three records stand out. "Muggles," an unpretentious blues, contains two very basic choruses by Armstrong in which he strips the blues line to its bare bones. The record begins at a slow tempo, and then follows an Armstrong break designed to double the tempo, which is a remarkable achievement for an improvising player. The break begins with three short notes hit more or less on the off-beats of the original tempo. Then Armstrong unfolds a rising figure in the new tempo, and we suddenly perceive that these first three notes were in Armstrong's mind ambiguous, acting both as quarter notes in one tempo and half notes in the other. It is as if Armstrong is attempting to play in both tempos at once.

The second of the major records in this group is "Tight Like This." Despite what is meant to be an erotic spoken commentary in two or three places, the music is suffused with tragedy. Armstrong plays three final solo choruses that perfectly exemplify his methods. Each of the phrases on which the three choruses is based is a rising figure, giving the whole a melodic unity. But because the choruses are set successively higher, the effect is of climax. The conversational effect is extreme; we can almost hear Armstrong talking about death and transfiguration.

Yet it is "West End Blues," made six months earlier, that is generally held to be Armstrong's masterpiece. A good many early writers, in fact, considered it to be the greatest of all jazz records. It opens with a long, bravura cadenza by Armstrong, which of itself would have made the record imperishable. It is replete with the fractional pauses, hesitations, and little rushes that contribute to the sense that a human voice is speaking to us.

Then follows a simple statement of the melody. The mood is all quietness touched with resignation, and the trombone solo that follows, although of no special value, does not break the mood. Then comes a call-and-answer chorus between the clarinet and Armstrong's scat vocal. Armstrong continues to maintain the mood by eschewing the rough, gutteral tones he usually employed in his singing. Next comes a piano solo, and then Armstrong opens the final chorus with a note held for four full measures. Tension mounts; the quiet mood begins to give way, until the tension is broken by a rapidly descending extended figure repeated five times, the only moment of passion on the record. Then there is a soft piano break, and Armstrong concludes with a simple, fading coda that re-establishes the mood of resignation with which the record began. "West End Blues" has a beginning, a middle, and an end, and it leaves the listener with a sense of completeness. It is an utterly satisfying performance.

This group of records was the last Armstrong was to make with a small band for some years. The records he made henceforth were with the big bands he normally fronted on the road. Some of these were groups already in existence, like the bands of Les Hite and Luis Russell, to which Armstrong was simply added out front. Others were rigged up by his managers as needed. They were often quite bad. There is a introduction by a saxophone section on "High Society" that is played so badly it is difficult to credit. It hardly matters, however. It was what Armstrong did that counted. Until relatively recently, it was customary for critics to dismiss his playing of this commercial music as a sellout on Armstrong's part. To be sure, there is the excessive showboating in the upper register especially noticeable during the early 1930s, and there is the overuse of half-valving, in which the player begins a note with the valves slightly depressed, and then by opening them as he makes lip adjustments, creates slurs. Half-valving imparts a somewhat nasal quality to the tone. Used judiciously it can be an effective device, but Armstrong sometimes let it get out of hand. Nevertheless, during this big band period Armstrong continued to move ahead. He made ever-increasing use of the stretched or extended figures, to the point where he might work over eight bars without touching the ground beat. After the hiatuses surrounding his first European trip, during which he did not record, he began to simplify his work, often stripping his lines to great simple slashes over the orchestra. Of the dozens of first-rate records he cut during this period, perhaps the most highly regarded are "Stardust" (1931), of which two takes have been reissued; "Between the Devil and the Deep Blue Sea" (1932), also available in two takes; "Home" (1932) and "Hobo, You Can't Ride This Train" (1932), in which he was backed by the excellent Chick Webb band; "Swing That Music" (1936); and "Jubilee," "Struttin' with Some Barbecue," and "I Double Dare You," all made in 1938 with improved backup bands.

All of the characteristics of his playing during this period can be heard on "Devil and the Deep Blue Sea." He uses a straight mute for the opening section of his solo, downplaying some very fine melodic figures. As the second chorus of the solo approaches, he removes the mute and goes upward. Despite some half-valving, the simplicity of the high-register finale is touching.

When he began recording again in 1935, after the year-and-a-half gap, his playing had become more relaxed, as if he had achieved a new maturity and self-possession. He is often content to stay fairly close to the melody, and he has dropped much of the half-valving and high-note flag-waving that occasionally marred his earlier work. In "Struttin' with Some Barbecue," vastly admired by young trumpet players of the period, the first chorus of his final solo is a straightforward exposition of the melody, but with many of the notes placed far enough behind the beat so that he is able to give the impression of lingering over them. In "Jubilee," a charming Hoagy Carmichael movie tune featuring an unusual, for the time, modulation up a major third, Armstrong again offers a fairly straight exposition of the melody for the penultimate chorus. On the last chorus the band plays the lead line, while Armstrong once again draws long, sweeping curves over it. Particularly fine is the overlooked "I Double Dare You." His long solo at the end is made up of a sequence of completely formed phrases, each four, five, or even six measures in length, and each cut and lapped to fall at unexpected places across the rigid four-bar segments of the song. Many phrases end on the fourth beat of a measure, a practice later to become widespread with the beboppers. And the closing phrase of the first sixteen bars of the chorus suddenly turns out to be the opening phrase of the next sixteen, something we have seen him do before.

Armstrong continued to record for another twenty-five years after the big bands collapsed in 1946, both with his All-Stars and in a variety of commercial settings. He went on making movies, eventually appearing in some fifty, surely a record for a popular musician. All of this late work contains its moments, but by now Armstrong was repeating himself, content to sing and mug his way through his performances, concerned primarily with pleasing his audience. This unashamed descent to ordinary pop music saddened many of his admirers, and, in addition, it brought down on his head complaints by younger, militant blacks that Armstrong was a blatant Uncle Tom, using a watermelon grin to get on with the white folks. And it is perfectly true that he refused to comment on the issue of segregation, the major public question of the 1950s and 1960s, until late in the game. But these charges fail to take into account who Louis Armstrong was and where he came from.

He grew up in a culture where getting on with the white folks was not merely a matter of good policy but a question of food, shelter, and perhaps life itself. Armstrong liked to quote an old New Orleans bouncer he knêw, who told him, as he got ready to go north to join Oliver, "Always keep a white man behind you that'll put his hand on you and say, 'That's my nigger.' " This little homily may appall us today, but we have to remember that at the time it was said, a black rebellion was simply out of the question. Armstrong, in seeking the support of whites, was not Tomming but was realistically choosing the only path open to him.

This reality was responsible for the extent to which he put his affairs in the hands of Joe Glaser. Glaser, it has been said, got rich off Armstrong, and no doubt this was true. But, on the other hand, without the aid of Glaser or somebody like him, Armstrong could hardly have achieved a quarter of what he did, as far as fame and wealth were concerned. Glaser picked the musicians for the band, made the bookings, chose tunes, and in general ran Armstrong's professional career, all of which saved Armstrong from a great deal of tension. There was a strong emotional bond between the two men, and Armstrong trusted Glaser as he did nobody else, with the exception presumably of his wife Lucille.

On the other side of the coin, Glaser had little interest in Armstrong as an artist. He constantly directed him toward popular material, movies in which he played the grinning darky, radio shows where he jived with Bing Crosby, and whatever else was necessary to build Armstrong as a celebrated public figure who could make them both rich. Any artistic growth Armstrong might have achieved during the second half of his life was stunted by Glaser's idea of what sort of musician Armstrong should be, and we are left to wonder what he might have accomplished had he had a Duke Ellington or Gil Evans finding a new musical conception for him to work from.

But Glaser cannot be blamed alone. In the last analysis Armstrong was responsible for himself, and we must again remember where he came from. The image of the artist as a being apart, a personage with special, almost magical, skills, descends to us from the Romantic movement. It is hardly universal to human culture. As recently as the eighteenth century, writers and painters were dogs of the aristocracy, and actors and musicians classed with servants. The Southern black lacked the idea of the artist almost entirely. Armstrong saw himself as an entertainer, not as an artist. When he was with Tate's Vendome Theatre Orchestra he often did a comic-preacher routine, a standard in black vaudeville, and in the cabarets he sometimes did a low-comedy husband-and-wife act, with Zutty Singleton, in drag, playing his wife. We have to see that the man who mugged his way through "Hello, Dolly" was working in a tradition he had been raised in.

But Armstrong's attitudes were not merely a product of his culture. Like anybody of any race, Louis Armstrong had an individual psyche, built by his relationships with his mother, father, and others around him in youth. The things that stand out most clearly are his unremitting desire to be liked and his need for the love and approval of a father figure. The almost complete absence of his father, and the frequent neglect of his mother, often left him dependent on the kindness of strangers. He was starved for affection, and "starved" is the key word. All his life he would be obsessed with food. In his autobiographical writings he constantly refers to meals, and gives the details of a dinner he had eaten thirty years earlier. Instead of signing his letters in the normal fashion he would close with "Red beans and ricely yours." He put on weight when he first left home to go on the riverboats (he was only five feet four inches), and he constantly fought his waistline thereafter.

It hardly takes a professional psychologist to make something of this obsession. And it is no wonder that he spent much of his life trying to be liked, and no wonder that he engaged himself with father substitutes over and over again: Peter Davis at the Waifs' Home; David Jones, the mellophone player on the riverboats; King Oliver; and eventually Joe Glaser. Had he not been able to earn the affection of people like these he might have lived out his life delivering coal through the streets of New Orleans, and the

A publicity photograph of Louis Armstrong in his later years in a characteristic pose. By this time Armstrong was working principally as a popular singer, with his playing taking second place.

history of jazz would have been entirely different. For what Armstrong did single-handedly was to turn jazz from a collective music to a solo art. Before him, there had been notable soloists — clarinetists Lorenzo Tio and Alphonse Picou, cornetists Bolden, Keppard, and the rest — but the solo was at bottom incidental to the ensemble work. Armstrong, by virtue of his genius, swept all that away. The young players coming up could see easily enough that it was the star soloist, not the sound ensemble man, who was going to become celebrated, glamorous, and possibly rich. After Armstrong, for better or worse, jazz was a soloist's art.

Bix:

The Tragic Temperament

Bix Beiderbecke was the first great white jazz musician. Worshiped by his white confreres, admired by blacks, many of whom paid him the ultimate compliment of copying note for note his best solos, he achieved a place in jazz on a par with the black giants. A great jazz musician must have sufficient command of his instrument to allow him to say what he feels; he must have an expressive tone capable of nuance; and he must have an individual conception in which musical ideas are not simply thrown together at random, but are related both to each other and to the larger framework they are building. Of the thousands of jazz musicians who have aspired to the ideal, not more than a dozen or so have measured up to this standard. Beiderbecke was one of them. He was superior to every jazz player of his day except Louis Armstrong and has been matched since by very few.

Like Bessie Smith, Beiderbecke has been fortunate in his biographers. In *Bix, Man & Legend,* Sudhalter and Evans, with William Dean-Myatt, have traced out Beiderbecke's activities almost day by day during his adult years, and they have managed to strip away the myth that began to encase Beiderbecke when he was barely out of adolescence. The truth about Bix is more prosaic than the myth and is most instructive about the character of the artist.

Leon Bix Beiderbecke was born in Davenport, Iowa, on March 10, 1903, second son of a prosperous coal merchant, grandson of a banker. Significant for the formation of his character, the Beiderbeckes adhered to the late-Victorian standard of gentility, a code of behavior so decorous that most people who have grown up since World War II will find it difficult to believe. Open expression of feeling in any but the most minimal terms was frowned on. A girl was not supposed to kiss a man until she was engaged to him, and a boy like Bix was expected to remain a virgin until he was married — this in a day when people of his class married late. In general,

There exist only a relatively few pictures of Bix Beiderbecke. This, the best-known one, shows him as an intense, slightly poetic, and conservative young man, of whom any mother could be proud.

boys in a family like the Beiderbeckes were not supposed to shout and race about the house, but to live out their childhoods engaged in quiet, useful, or educational activities and grow up to be civic leaders and good family men.

In the ordinary course of things Bix would have become a doctor, a lawyer, a minister, a college professor, a merchant. The path he chose was one his parents abhorred. When he came home, sick, near the end of his life he found in a hall closet all of his records that he had proudly sent home

— still wrapped in their mailing envelopes. To the Beiderbeckes, their son was a dirty secret.

I am being hard on them, of course; they were ordinary, good people living the way they had been taught to live. Fortunately, they knew that music was an attribute of the cultivated mind. Several members of the family played musical instruments, and Bix grew up seeing music as a normal activity. He began very young to pick out songs with one finger on the piano, and by the time he was five he could play "Pop Goes the Weasel" and other tunes of that ilk. Over the years of his boyhood he continued to fool with the piano and for a brief period took lessons. But for the most part he resisted instruction. It is worth noting that Bix did not learn to read music until he was already playing professionally, and never became more than barely adequate at it. Learning to read music, especially for a wind instrument, on which one plays only a line at a time, is not a particularly difficult task. It is something that millions of young students do all the time; there are thousands, if not hundreds of thousands, of adolescents in school bands who can read better than Bix ever did. When somebody like Bix, with his overwhelming talent and his inordinate love for music, fails at something as routine as learning to read, it can be due only to internal resistance. Obviously, even at an early age Bix was finding something in music that was his own, and he was determined, on whatever level of consciousness, to preserve it from the controlling hands that were so busy in other parts of his life.

Bix's first contact with jazz was, inevitably, through the records of the Original Dixieland Jazz Band. He was fifteen, exactly the right age to be smitten by this new music, especially the cornet sound of Nick LaRocca, and he began to learn the LaRocca lines, note by painful note. He did not, obviously, ask to take lessons. He developed both his embouchure and his fingering technique by trial and error. But despite the lack of formal instruction — or perhaps because of it — he came, in time, to produce one of the most compelling sounds in all of jazz: flawless in pitch, warm and seductive of tone, biting in attack, and perfectly controlled of vibrato.

As soon as he developed some rudimentary skill on the cornet, Bix began playing with raw high school bands and listening to whatever jazz was available. He heard Leon Rappolo, not yet with the New Orleans Rhythm Kings; a New Orleans cornetist named Emmett Hardy, about whom a number of unsubstantiated legends have clustered; Wingy Manone; and a nineteen-year-old Louis Armstrong, who was playing on the riverboats that stopped at Davenport. But already Beiderbecke was showing evidence of the emotional disability that was to dog him all his life. Even as a youth he demonstrated an incapacity to cope with ordinary situations in anything like an assertive way. He was certainly intelligent, but he was not able to keep up to the minimum standard of work most intelligent school-haters manage in order to quiet their parents. He was unable to get a union card, mainly because of his inability to read music, and he was thus barred from taking jobs that he desperately wanted. But rather than surmount the obstacle, he let matters drift until some of his friends solved the problem for him. He was never able to confront his parents with his intention to make a career in the detested popular music; he simply did what they wanted him to do and then made a hash of it. Eventually they sent him to Lake Forest Academy, a boarding school near Chicago run along military lines. It was a mistake to set him down so close to Chicago. Very quickly Bix fell in with a few boys who loved jazz, and they began sneaking into town at night to hear, and occasionally sit in with, the New Orleans Rhythm Kings. At the same time, he began to develop a liking for liquor. This was Prohibition, and with his complicated feelings about controls, it was inevitable that he would have begun drinking. But it is also clear that he was drinking more than was customary for a high school student of his time. All of this was, in the end, too much for Lake Forest Academy. He was expelled before his first academic year was over. It was 1922; he was nineteen and committed to music.

His advancement to this point had been rapid. He was still far from being a polished musician, but in the four years he had been playing he had developed a reasonably good technique, a fine ear, and a feel for jazz playing. He already knew some of the other young whites coming into jazz, and he began jamming with them and, soon enough, making gigs around the Midwest. Almost immediately he was recognized as the best among them. In 1924 a group of them formed a band called the Wolverines, patterned after the New Orleans Rhythm Kings. It was good enough to get work at colleges and theaters, and an occasional longer engagement in dance halls, mainly in Ohio and Indiana. In February 1924, the Wolverines made the first in a series of records for Gennett. The records were relatively successful commercially, but, more important, they had an impact on jazz musicians, especially whites, like the one made on Bix seven years earlier by the Original Dixieland Jazz Band records. It was, in fact, Bix who had the impact. None of the other musicians in the band made any further contribution to the course of jazz. So, at twenty-one, Bix Beiderbecke was a recognized figure among jazz musicians.

Unfortunately, his drinking problem was growing worse. In the days of Prohibition, drinking was something of a sport, like fox hunting: it was a little risky; it involved a show of daring; and it made you feel good. For the jazz musician, whose working life was spent at parties, dances, and in bars, alcoholism was a real occupational hazard. It is clear that Bix was drinking as much as any of his fellows and more than most. By the time Bix was twenty-two or -three it is probable that he was a confirmed alcoholic, slightly drunk all the time.

But the alcohol did not immediately appear to interfere with his playing. Near the end of 1924 he left the Wolverines and some time later joined a band led by Frankie Trumbauer. Trumbauer played an instrument called the C-melody saxophone, which has since all but disappeared. At a time when the saxophone in general was being played very badly, especially by jazz musicians, Trumbauer was a fine, perhaps superb, player from a technical viewpoint. He was admired by musicians both black and white and was widely imitated. At this distance we recognize that he was a jazz player of only modest ability. According to Sudhalter and Evans he did not improvise in any complete sense, but worked out in advance what he was going to do on a given tune. But in his day he and Bix were considered more or less equals by many musicians, including jazz players. Trumbauer, who was born in 1903 in Carbondale, Illinois, was in and out of music from the late 1930s on, and died in 1956.

Bix and Tram, as Trumbauer was called, became a team, working together in bands for most of the rest of Bix's life. The relationship was good for Bix; Trumbauer was relatively more steady, and his first-rate musicianship rubbed off on Bix. It has been suggested that his style of "telling a little story" may also have influenced Bix. Bix worked in the Trumbauer band, which included Pee Wee Russell, until May of 1926, when Trumbauer took over a band owned by Jean Goldkette, bringing Bix and some of the other players with him.

Jean Goldkette was a Detroit music entrepreneur who led bands, booked them, and operated the Graystone Ballroom, the leading dance hall in the area. He was a shrewd businessman as well as a competent musician, and his bands were commercial dance bands. However, jazz was the vogue, and Goldkette recognized the value of having some good jazz players in the band, to play hot solos and supply punch to the ensemble, and from time to time many of the leading white musicians of the period worked in his band. The particular Goldkette group that featured Bix and Tram was held in exceedingly high regard by other musicians. It was, without question, the premier, and almost the sole, exemplar of the white big band jazz at its time. Some of the men who played with it insist that it cut the black Fletcher Henderson band when it played opposite it at the Roseland Ballroom, a famous dance hall in the Times Square area of New York. The same people also maintain that it was never recorded at its best, because the record companies wanted commercial music rather than the hot arrangements on which it had built its reputation among musicians. Whatever the case, existing records show a band that was capable of playing at or near the level of the Henderson band in top form (this band also made a lot of poor records), but usually did not.

In Bill Challis, later to have an important career with Paul Whiteman, the band had an arranger who was in advance of any jazz writer of the time, including Don Redman with the Henderson band. Challis was aware of movements in modern concert music and used this knowledge in his work for Goldkette. In violinist Joe Venuti, clarinetist Don Murray, and Trumbauer it had three solid jazz musicians, and in Beiderbecke a superlative one. Beiderbecke plays an exceptional solo on "Clementine," and Don Murray — a vastly underrated player — takes an excellent baritone saxophone solo on "I'm Gonna Meet My Sweetie Now" and a fine clarinet solo on "My Pretty Girl." These two records are up to the level of the Henderson band, and it is probably fair to say that on a good night, when the Goldkette band was using its best arrangements, it could have given the Henderson band a good battle. But the Goldkette rhythm section, with the exception of bassist Steve Brown, was weak; and furthermore, where all of the men in the Henderson band were essentially jazz players, some of them among the finest players in jazz, many of the men in the Goldkette band were ordinary dance musicians, who lacked jazz feel. Necessarily, the section work sometimes failed to swing.

The Goldkette band collapsed financially in the fall of 1927, and shortly afterward Bix, Trumbauer, and some of the other musicians joined Paul Whiteman's huge orchestra, in which Bix would spend most of the rest of his life. The Whiteman band has been calumniated; it was certainly no jazz band, and Whiteman was knowingly perpetrating a fraud when he took the title "the King of Jazz." But an interesting point is made by Gunther Schuller, who has another view. He says:

> Excellent intonation, perfect balances, and clean attacks do not necessarily equate with superficiality. There is in the best Whiteman performances a feeling and a personal sound as unique in its way as Ellington's or Basie's. It was just not based on a jazz conception. For this we cannot automatically condemn it.

Paul Whiteman held a position in his time somewhat analogous to the one held by Frank Sinatra or the Beatles in theirs. For Beiderbecke, joining Whiteman was reaching a pinnacle of sorts. It meant that he was at the top of his trade, and it seems clear that he was prouder of being a star soloist with Whiteman than he was of the major position he held in the subground world of jazz.

By the time Bix joined Whiteman, he was spending more and more time at the piano. He had become interested in the work of a group of minor American composers, especially Eastwood Lane and Edward MacDowell, and, through them, in Delius, Debussy, Ravel, and other modernists. Bix's friends were impressed by his absorption in "classical music," but in truth Beiderbecke's understanding of twentieth-century concert music was sketchy. He picked the brains of Bill Challis and others, but the emotional problems that had made him fail at school and caused his difficulty in learning to sight-read also prevented him from studying music in any systematic way. Yet he drew from these composers certain harmonic devices, especially the whole-tone scale that Debussy made such heavy use of, and he wove these together night after night in his ramblings over the keyboard. Eventually he put some of these ideas together in a group of loose compositions — he never played any of them the same way twice — which were published as "Candlelights," "Flashes," "In the Dark," and "In a Mist." These compositions have been recorded by various pianists, including Jess Stacy and, recently, Dill Jones. The only one Bix recorded himself was "In a Mist." It had a vogue in the jazz world during Bix's lifetime and is still much admired by Bix fanciers, but actually it is the sort of pastiche of fashionable musical ideas that any young composition student might have put together. The influence of Eastwood Lane is especially evident. Its jazz content is minimal; it is, in fact, exactly the type of primped-up pseudo-jazz that critics decried when it was produced by Whiteman.

Bix stayed with Whiteman until the fall of 1929. He made dozens of records with the band, mostly as a section man. His solos are few and usually short, but some of them are gems. More important, between 1927 and 1930 he recorded with a variety of pickup groups, mainly under his own name or Trumbauer's. The musicians in these groups were generally drawn from the Whiteman band; some of them had been associated with Bix in the Goldkette band and earlier. Many of them had only modest talent and never were able to give Bix the kind of accompaniment he should have had. The fault was Bix's. There were excellent jazz players around New York, where most of these records were made; men like Benny Goodman, Jack Teagarden, and Pee Wee Russell, to say nothing of numberless fine black players. He chose instead the inferior company of his friends. No doubt this was partly because he was afraid of offending people; but partly it was due to the extreme lack of assertiveness that characterized everything about him but his playing. It is a shame, not merely because of what a record with a front line of Teagarden, Russell, and Beiderbecke might have been, but also because of the musical growth playing regularly in the company of a Coleman Hawkins or Benny Carter might have brought him.

But he didn't make that choice, and by the end of 1929 it was clear that he never would. Robust by birth (he was a relatively big man and loved baseball), his health had been steadily deteriorating from the effects of too much liquor. In the fall of 1929 he had a nervous collapse and was sent back to Davenport by Whiteman. He entered a sanitorium and stopped drinking, but something had gone out of his spirit. He returned to New York and somewhere along the line began drinking again. His physical and emotional decline thereafter was rapid. Early in August, suffering from pneumonia and acute alcoholism accompanied by delirium tremens, he died in pain and horror in a boarding house in Sunnyside, Queens. Already a cult figure, he quickly became a legend: the sensitive artist killed by the insensate crowd.

It is not to disparage Bix to say that the romantic myth is mostly nonsense. Bix's troubles were mainly of his own making. We should not imagine that Bix was driven to drink by the Philistines who failed to appreciate his work. When he collapsed in 1929 he had a bright artistic future before him. He was unknown to the general public, of course; he was mentioned in print only once in his lifetime. But he was adored by his fellow musicians; he was a star soloist with the most important organization in popular music; he was recording under his own name; he was making a salary large enough to allow him to invest in the stock market; and, most important, he had already created a body of work so admirable that neither he nor any knowledgeable person had doubts about his talent. The only thing he lacked was widespread fame, and that would have come. To be sure, he was not doing much in the Whiteman band that called on his artistry, but we must remember that there was no law keeping him there. With his reputation among musicians, he could have managed to do well enough as a free-lance to permit him to pursue his artistic goals; many of his colleagues with a fraction of his talent were doing so. But he chose to remain protected by the money and the security of the Whiteman band. Looked at from this view it is just as well to say that Bix sold out as that he was killed by neglect.

In fact neither was the case. He was simply an unhappy young man struggling with emotional problems he did not begin to understand. The roots lay, of course, in the iron gentility in which he was raised. The human being, like water, is not compressible. Responses to such controlled upbringings, which are hardly confined to this particular culture, range from full compliance to open rebellion. Bix Beiderbecke took neither position; he floundered between the two, unable either to shuck off the rules of his culture or to obey them. Thus we see him studying the piano, but refusing to learn to sight-read. Thus we see him going to Lake Forest Academy, but refusing to study. Thus we see him becoming that hated thing, a jazz musician, but working in the most genteel and respectable milieu for a jazzman, the Paul Whiteman band. It didn't wash. His parents still did not accept his life — only his younger brother showed up when the Whiteman band played near his home — and Bix could not accept it, either. He was a man in a trap; and the anodyne for his frustration was alcohol.

The result of all this was to leave him almost totally ineffectual in the ordinary pursuits of life. Bix was, unhappily, an infantile personality. He was often late for dates, or he showed up drunk, or missed them altogether. As a white man from an upper-middle-class family he had far more access to the levers of power and influence in his society than most of his fellows, especially the black musicians, an access that should have allowed him to carve out a career along lines of his own choosing, as Goodman, Ellington, Basie, Coleman Hawkins, Dizzy Gillespie, and many others did. Instead, he allowed himself to be moved at the whim of others. If somebody got him a recording date he would turn up for it, instead of insisting on the control of musicians, tunes, arrangements, and other professional matters on which he was surely competent to make judgments. His dealings with women, too, were infantile. He seems to have been serious about only two women in his life, and those just for relatively brief periods. He treated Ruth Schaffner, the woman he appears to have cared for the most, with a thoughtlessness that was nothing short of appalling. Despite protestations of love and loyalty, he left her for months at a time, rarely writing, and passing through St. Louis, where she lived, without calling her. He seems not to have made any effort to cope with his drinking until it was about to kill him, and that effort did not last very long. In short, Beiderbecke cannot be seen as a man too sensitive to live, but as somebody hopelessly stunted emotionally by internal conflicts. And I think the point must finally be made that Bix's personality problems, far from giving him his musical nature, prevented him from exploring the artistic possibilities that lay before him. Imagine what Bix, with his almost intuitive grasp of melodic principle, could have done had he had a personality like that of Ellington, or even Morton. Instead, he floundered like a fish on the sand, and then he died. Human beings are capable of functioning under the weight of a great deal of stress, but psychological infirmity is of no more help to the artist than is a broken arm.

Yet in spite of his irresponsibility, and his occasional churlishness when drinking, Bix was, by all reports, endlessly loved by the people who knew him. His friends forgave him anything and everything, no doubt in part because he seemed like a lost child. But the rest of it has to do with his extravagant talent. What was it that thrilled them and still calls forth our admiration?

To begin with, there was that compelling tone. It is always said of a jazz artist that he "never sounded as good on records as he did in person." These assertions can be taken with a grain of salt: most of the people who heard Bix in the wee hours were caught up in a romantic ambience, and were drunk as well. A recording studio may not be as inspiring as a live audience, but there are certain advantages in playing in controlled circumstances, especially if you are rested and sober. It is true, though, that at the time Bix was recording, electrical reproduction of sound was in its infancy; and we can only imagine what was lost from his tone, which contemporaries said was bell-like, as if the notes had been struck off with mallets. His attack was sharp-edged and firm, his intonation impeccable, and his tone warm, but possessed of a certain metallic resonance that can indeed be described as bell-like. His one defect in tone was a slight huskiness, which occasionally appeared at the front edge of his notes. This is a common affliction of brass players, and is caused either by lack of practice or warmup, or by a momentary uncertainty about which note is being aimed for. On the strength of sound production alone, Bix would have earned a place in the history of jazz.

But he had much more than that. His grasp of melodic principle continued to grow through his life. Long before other jazz players, he understood the critical importance in melody of moving from dissonance to consonance; for example in a phrase built around a C chord, approaching the phrase and some of the individual notes with nonchord tones — a D moving to a C, an F# to a G. He was also using higher degrees of the scale — elevenths, thirteenths, and the even more dissonant raised fourths and fifths suggested by the whole-tone scale — and he was using these notes not experimentally or for occasional color, but as an integral part of his work.

Beiderbecke as his friends knew him was far from the formal young gentleman portrayed in the previous picture. Here we see him in a more natural pose at the Gennett studios in Richmond, Indiana, at a recording session of Bix and His Rhythm Jugglers. The date was January 26, 1925, at which time Bix's own tune, "Davenport Blues," was recorded. From left, Don Murray, Howdy Quicksell, Tom Gargano, Paul Mertz, Beiderbecke, and a man later to be one of the most popular of the swing band leaders, Tommy Dorsey.

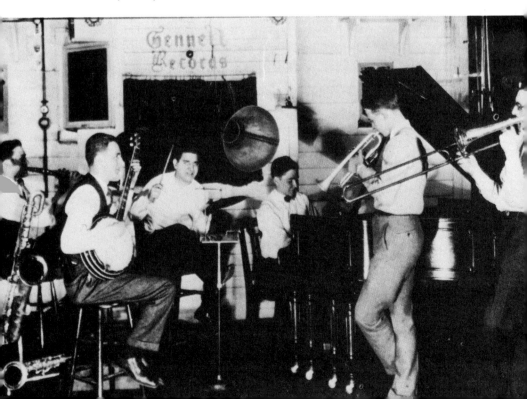

He was a conscious artist; even as he played he would remember to prepare his G with the dissonant F#.

If Bix had one failing, it was in his rhythm. In his earlier work, especially with the Wolverines, he did not entirely escape the white apprentices' habit of banging down hard on the beat, as is clear in his first record, "Fidgety Feet," made early in 1924. But by the fall of that year he had made great progress in eliminating this defect. His solo on "Tia Juana," for example, employs a quarter-note triplet and an eighth-note run beginning on the second half of the first beat of a measure, both of which were to become characteristic of his work. By 1927, when he was at his peak, the corny rhythms were gone. But Bix departed less far from the ground beat than nearly any other major instrumentalist in jazz.

All of these things — rhythmic competence, an expressive tone, rich harmonies — are only part of what it takes to be a great jazz player. A man is a master melodist because of the way he sculpts his musical lines, and at this Beiderbecke had few peers. He used as his theory of composition the correlated chorus he thought he had found in Armstrong's playing: play two measures, play two more related, and follow these four bars with four related, and so on. It was not Armstrong, we should remember, but Beiderbecke who articulated the theory, and in his best work he seems to be following it quite explicitly. Listen, for example, to his "Royal Garden Blues." The entire chorus is of a piece. It opens with a rising and falling, more or less chromatic, line for two bars, which is then recapitulated in the second two bars. This rather quiet, introspective statement is followed by a gradual increase in intensity, rising to a climax with a starker, more forceful figure, both louder and higher, which in turn descends to a slightly quieter dénouement and ends with a little reflective phrase reminiscent of the opening figure. Again, in the ride-out chorus in "Goose Pimples," he repeats one hot, driving figure three times, each time slightly varied. The fourth time, he suddenly twists it into a surprising new shape and stretches it out to double its length. Or yet again listen to "Way Down Yonder in New Orleans." The opening two bars involve a series of quarter notes whose placement is slightly varied against the beat, followed by a variation on this idea. Bars four and six contain an eighth-note figure that is elaborated on in bars seven and eight. In the ninth and tenth bars, where the opening melody of the song returns, Bix goes back to a variation of the quarter-note figure he used in the beginning. Throughout, the choice and placement of notes is as impeccable as it is deliberate: one can almost hear Bix think.

Bix's masterworks are "I'm Comin' Virginia" and, especially, "Singin' the Blues," which was memorized by all the trumpet players of the day and recorded note for note by a number of bands, both black and white. In each of these Bix is paired with Trumbauer; each is taken at a moderate-to-slow tempo; and each exhibits a superior musical intelligence at work, sculpting flawless melodic lines that are logical and filled with surprises. It was the opening measures of Bix's "Singin' the Blues" solo in particular that astonished the musicians of the time. The first bar contains a brief figure that is re-examined in the second bar. Bars three and four amplify this same figure, and the following four measures re-examine the whole. It is one of the best eight-bar constructions in jazz.

Bix Beiderbecke was, more than any of his contemporaries and indeed most jazz musicians since, a conscious artist. There was no question of his simply standing up there and blowing. He knew precisely what he was doing — or attempting, at least. He knew why he was choosing the notes he selected; why he was placing them where he did. He was logical, orderly in his thinking — Germanic, if you will — but always in the manner of Mozart rather than Bach. His placement of notes was exact and delicate. Notice his playing of pairs of eighth notes: the first of the pair is just a shade longer than the second; the second is preceded by a slight hesitation, which gives the listener a sense of Bix's tact. He is always economical, never playing an unnecessary note; but he is not spare. Less is not more, but enough is just exactly enough. There is a humility in his playing, a humbleness toward his art. Always he is saying, I do not wish to intrude, but let me show you this marvel. And marvels they are.

Bix's influence on his contemporaries was both direct and pervasive. Hundreds of white cornetists all over the country attempted to imitate him directly, among them Red Nichols and Sterling Bose, both of whom are sometimes taken for Bix even by knowledgeable listeners. (The case of Bose is especially interesting. He was, we remember, cornetist with the white New Orleans group called the Arcadian Serenaders. In September of 1925 the band played opposite a Trumbauer group that included Bix at the Arcadia Ballroom in St. Louis. One would have guessed that the Midwesterners would have listened to the New Orleanians with interest, but by 1925 the shoe was on the other foot. Both Bose and clarinetist-saxophonist Cliff Holman fell immediately under the influence of Bix and Tram.) Nor was it only whites. Dave Nelson, a nephew of King Oliver's, plays a very Bix-like solo on "Rockin' Chair," even using portions of the arrangement of the "Rockin' Chair" on which Bix appears. Fletcher Henderson took his "Singin' the Blues" note for note from the Bix and Tram record, with the saxophone section playing the opening Trumbauer chorus and Rex Stewart playing the Bix chorus. And there was in the influential Bennie Moten band a trumpet player — I have not been able to determine which of the trumpets in the band it was — who played almost perfect Bix imitations, in, for example, "When I'm Alone," "Mary Lee," and "New Goofy Dust Rag," among others.

But more important than this direct influence on many players was the fact that Bix showed trumpet players of the day that Armstrong's road was not the only way to go. Instead of the bravura, operatic performance that Armstrong favored, it was possible, as Bix proved, to play within a narrower physical and emotional compass, paying close attention to detail — calligraphy rather than great, sweeping strokes; the sonnet rather than the epic. This is hardly surprising. Although Armstrong and Beiderbecke were born only three years apart and both studied the New Orleans idiom intensively, one grew up barefoot, fending for himself in the slums, and the other was raised in one of the most well-ordered societies this country has seen. The playing of each man was as much a product of his childhood circumstances as it was of his own mind.

PART III

The Swing Age

A MUSIC MATURES

Henderson, Goldkette,
and the Making of the Big Band

During the years that Louis Armstrong was making his reputation, there was coming into jazz an interesting group of young black men whose backgrounds were vastly different from those of the New Orleans pioneers — or, indeed, 95 percent of American blacks. These men were from all over: Fletcher Henderson was from Cuthbert, Georgia; Duke Ellington and Claude Hopkins from Washington, D.C.; Don Redman from Piedmont, West Virginia; Luis Russell from Panama; and Jimmie Lunceford from Fulton, Missouri. But despite these disparate birthplaces, these men had astonishingly similar backgrounds. They were born between 1898 and 1903. Ellington's father was a navy printmaker, Henderson's father a high school principal, Hopkins's parents were college teachers. In a day when fewer than a third of all Americans finished high school — and still fewer blacks — these men were all well-educated. Lunceford, Redman, Hopkins, and Henderson had gone to college, and Ellington turned down a scholarship to the Pratt Institute of Art to go into music. Lunceford had studied music under Paul Whiteman's father; Redman had been to conservatories in Boston and Detroit; Russell and Henderson had been trained in European music by musical parents; Hopkins had studied music in college. Only Ellington was primarily self-taught. None of them, at least in the early stages of their lives, was a jazz musician at all. They were unfamiliar not only with New Orleans music but with the entire black folk tradition as well.

These men were, by white standards, middle class, but in terms of the black subculture of the day they were uppercrust — educated young people from comfortable and, in most cases, intact homes. Why did they gravitate toward popular music? In part, no doubt, they were drawn to it as youth will always be drawn to new currents of the time. But the principal reason was that there was no place for them in classical music, which was rigidly segregated and remained so into the 1960s, and little place for them elsewhere in the culture to which their attainments entitled them. They did not move into popular music by design; they drifted into it because it turned out to be a way to make a good living and have a little fun as well. There was room in popular music for the schooled black musician who could accompany black singers, make background arrangements, or organize and rehearse black bands for specific purposes.

The fact that these men had conservatory training, or the equivalent, had formative effects on music. In those days — and indeed today — music education was rooted in the study of voice-leading — that is, the writing of part-harmony. Writing part-harmony came as naturally as breathing to these men (the exception was Ellington, who learned by trial and error), and, inevitably, when they conceived of a band arrangement it was always first in terms of a melody harmonized for a number of voices. Polyrhythms, polyphony, things that are at the heart of jazz, they saw only as embellishments. And as they moved gradually into jazz, they brought with them this approach, rather than the old New Orleans idea. These men, thus, were bound to change the nature of jazz; but they did not do it right away.

The centerpiece of this group was the strange, absent figure of Fletcher Henderson. The Henderson band has always been accounted in jazz history as a crucial one. This being the case, we would expect to find its leader a dominating and original mind, but in fact he was just the opposite. Fletcher Henderson was afflicted with an almost pathological lack of self-assertiveness. He invariably did only what was required of him, and then the minimum of that. Trumpeter Bill Coleman has said, "Fletcher was a very timid guy." He exerted little leadership and, when possible, left the direction of events to themselves. The Henderson band proceeded along its historic course mainly by accident.

Fletcher Henderson was born in 1897. His father, Fletcher Hamilton Henderson, Sr., was principal of the Randolph Training School, an industrial high school for blacks, and his mother, Ozie Henderson, was a pianist and music teacher. Henderson began studying classical piano at six and continued to study throughout most of his youth. He majored in chemistry and math at Atlanta University, and in 1920 came to New York to develop a career as a chemist. The career never began. Henderson no doubt failed to push very hard to open doors, but the main problem was that there were hardly any jobs anywhere for black chemists. To support himself he took a job with the Pace-Handy Music Company, a publishing company that had been brought to New York by W. C. Handy and Harry Pace, a Memphis insurance executive, in 1918. At that period every song publisher kept a house pianist on hand to demonstrate his songs to potential buyers. Henderson became Pace-Handy's song demonstrator. Then, in 1921, Pace left the publishing company to develop Black Swan, the first, and for a time the only, black record company. He took Henderson along as musical factotum.

Henderson made himself useful accompanying singers for the records and putting together little backup bands when necessary, and in this casual fashion he drifted into the role of band leader. He occasionally got extra work for these groups at dances or in cabarets, and by 1923 he had enough work to keep a band organized on a semipermanent basis. That year some members of the group heard about an audition at the Club Alabam, near Times Square. Typically, Henderson was inclined to do nothing about it, but the other men talked him into competing, and they won.

This was at the beginning of the Jazz Age. There was a vogue not merely for Negro music but, among the sophisticated, for Negroes as a race. Modern artists, especially Picasso and Matisse, had discovered African sculpture, in which they saw reflections of cubism. Van Vechten was writing *Nigger Heaven,* about life in Harlem. The better-educated of the white middle class saw an interest in blacks as part of the intellectual stir of the times. The physical separation of the whites, especially middle-class whites, from blacks, left them curious. A middle-class white could envision a black as a stevedore, a boxer, a frenzied singer. What he had trouble imagining was the black family man worried over his children's school work, or taking his family out to Coney Island for a Sunday outing.

Taking advantage of this vogue for blacks were a number of nightclub owners, who, as the Prohibition mentality grew, began opening nightclubs with a black ambience that catered exclusively to whites. These cabarets were given names redolent of the South, like the Kentucky Club or the Cotton Club; they were decorated with motifs suggesting jungle natives; and they were supplied with black singers, dancers, and musicians who put on what came to be called "floor shows" because they took place on the floor open for dancing in front of the bandstand. The late Marshall Stearns, one of the best jazz historians, recalls one show at the Cotton Club in which "a light-skinned and magnificently muscled Negro burst through a papier-mâché jungle onto the dance floor, clad in an aviator's helmet, goggles and shorts. He had obviously been 'forced down in darkest Africa,' and in the center of the floor he came upon a 'white' goddess clad in long golden tresses and being worshipped by a circle of cringing 'blacks.' Producing a bull whip from heaven knows where, the aviator rescued the blonde and they did an erotic dance."

This combination of black exoticness, sex, liquor, and peppy black music proved successful. Clubs flowered in the Times Square area and then in Harlem, where authorities were even less interested in policing the sale of liquor than they were on Broadway. Harlem was not the slum so much of it is today, but a middle- and working-class black enclave. It had, of course, its clubs for blacks, such as the Savoy Ballroom, but the famous ones, like Connie's Inn and Small's Paradise, were run by whites for a white clientele. However degrading the idea was to blacks, these clubs had the salutary effect of providing young black musicians with a livelihood and a place to play where they could train themselves and develop their music. From them came a whole roster of fine jazz musicians.

The band that Henderson took into the Club Alabam in 1923 came quickly to include a number of men who would develop into first-rate jazz players: Coleman Hawkins, Charlie Green, Joe Smith, and arranger Don Redman. The band was not, in the early days, a jazz band or anything like it. It thought of itself as a dance band, which played waltzes as well as fox-trots and accompanied the club's singers.

We forget that in the early 1920s jazz was only beginning to come into public consciousness, and blacks outside New Orleans did not necessarily know much about it. Furthermore, blacks from big cities of the North, especially when they were from middle-class backgrounds, were unlikely to have had much contact with black-American folk music. Ethel Waters has said that Henderson had to learn how to play jazz when it became modish in the twenties. Basically, the Henderson band was playing simulated blues as part of the growing blues vogue, and ordinary pop tunes, such as "Linger Awhile," which it recorded in 1924 with a horrible "doo-wacka, doo-wacka" trumpet duet. Don Redman's clarinet suggests Larry Shields rather than Dodds or Bechet. The solos of Coleman Hawkins, who was to become the premier jazz saxophonist, were inept and fumbling. Joe Smith, who was in and out of the band, possessed a beautiful tone, but his phrasing was stiff. Only Charlie Green demonstrated much jazz feeling. But the band was successful nevertheless, and began to gather a small following. Because of Henderson's contacts in the recording industry, it recorded often, which helped to give the band a wider local exposure.

During this time, Roseland was using the Creole orchestra of Armand J. Piron — no jazz band — as second string to the white band of Sam Lanin. When the Piron bandsmen grew homesick and went back to New Orleans, the Roseland management offered the spot to Henderson. In keeping with his usual behavior, he did nothing about it, but in mid-1924 a row with the Alabam management over a small matter forced Henderson's hand, and the band went to Roseland. The Lanin musicians disliked playing opposite blacks and pulled out, leaving the field clear for Henderson. For the next decade Roseland was to be the band's base between road trips. And over the next two or three years, the group became a jazz band.

The standard theory in jazz criticism is that the arrival of Louis Armstrong in 1924 turned the Henderson band toward jazz, but on the evidence of the records, the change was more gradual. Influences certainly came from many directions. Henderson often used members of the group to back singers on recordings, thus exposing them to the blues. Oliver, Beiderbecke, Morton, and Armstrong were all recording from 1923 on. The Goldkette

The Fletcher Henderson band in 1924, when it was only barely beginning to find its way. Coleman Hawkins is second from left, Armstrong seated just behind him, Henderson sitting behind the bass drum, Buster Bailey behind the tuba, Don Redman at extreme right, and Charlie Green seated next to him. Note the array of saxophones, including Hawkins's mammoth bass saxophone. Culver Pictures

band played opposite Henderson for a brief period in 1926. Pianists like Fats Waller, James P. Johnson, Luckyeth Roberts, and Willie "the Lion" Smith were based in New York during the mid-1920s. The Memphis Five coterie of white players had been recording and working in New York since 1919. What we have, then, was young musicians who, like thousands of others around the United States, were hearing a new music in a variety of legitimate and bastard forms. It was exciting; it was in vogue; it was in demand. So they were caught up in it and began first to try to play it and then to move it in new directions.

According to a reminiscence by Don Redman, which appears in *Jazz Panorama,* he made all of the band's arrangements between 1923 and 1927, except one or two written by Hawkins. Redman, who was born in 1900 three weeks after Armstrong, was a child prodigy who began playing piano at the age of three and was in charge of a school band while still in grade school. He was writing arrangements as a teen-ager, and, given this background and his conservatory training, there is no reason to doubt that Henderson turned the band's writing over to him. How much direction Redman got from Henderson, and how much help he got from other members of the band, we do not know. In any case, the direction in which the music was going was consistent, which suggests the work of a single mind.

At first the arrangements alternated solos and straightforward statements of the melody arranged for reeds or brass in standard harmonies. But quite early, Redman grasped the basic principle that was to animate all big band writing virtually until today, that of dividing the orchestra into saxophone and brass sections and playing them off against each other. (Later, as bands grew larger, the brass section was sometimes subdivided into trumpets and trombones.) Frequently the saxophone players switched to clarinet, adding yet another voice. As we shall see, this development was made possible by the arrival of the saxophone, in the prior decade, as a standard dance band instrument. In the general pattern that developed, one section played the melodic lead, or dominating riff, which the other section either answered during the pauses in the line or punctuated with brief rhythmic figures. Redman began playing the sections off against one another as early as January 1924, in "Darktown Has a Gay White Way." By the end of the year, in a famous record of "Copenhagen," which contains one of Armstrong's earliest solos with the band, Redman had elaborated the principle so markedly, according to an analysis by Gunther Schuller in his *Early Jazz,* that the music moves around from one section or soloist to another no less than twenty-four times in the space of about three minutes. Furthermore, Redman was now writing "solos" for whole sections — that is, variations on the melody in the manner of an improvised chorus harmonized for saxophones or brasses. In regard to rhythm, the band was still stiff, certainly, in comparison with the Armstrong and Oliver records being made in Chicago at this time, but it was beginning to swing.

By 1927–1928, the band reached a peak, its so-called classic period. Henderson was steadily improving the personnel. In 1927 Benny Morton, who would become one of the finest trombonists in jazz, and Jimmy Harrison were in the band. Buster Bailey would prove to be better on clarinet than Redman, who left the band in 1927 to become arranger and musical director of McKinney's Cotton Pickers. Hawkins was coming into his own, and Tommy Ladnier, an excellent trumpeter, was sharing solos with Joe Smith. With first-class players and several years of experience behind it, the band played its ensembles cleanly and in tune, and its soloists were, with the exception of the New Orleans men and two or three of the white Midwesterners, the best in jazz. At times Redman had shown a tendency to overwrite; "Hot Mustard," for example, is chopped into so many breaks and switches that it moves in fits and starts and never really develops much momentum. But on the best sides from these days, such as "Hop Off,"

"Stockholm," "Swamp Blues," the band swings cleanly from start to finish.

But a fall was coming. In the middle of 1927, when Redman left, Henderson scrambled about for new arrangers. He tried several people, but none was really satisfactory. Then in 1928 Henderson hurt his head in an automobile accident. There is some suggestion in reminiscences of people who knew him that he was a changed man thereafter, even more willing than before to let things drift. And then, in 1929, when he should have been riding high, came a final blow.

The story is a little difficult to work out, but as given by Samuel B. Charters and Leonard Kunstadt in their useful *Jazz: A History of the New York Scene,* the band went to Philadelphia to rehearse a revue of which Vincent Youmans, a notable American songwriter, was musical director. The group was augmented by about twenty white musicians, mainly string players. Youmans suggested that, as Henderson had had no revue experience, an outside conductor should be brought in. The implication, of course, was that the white musicians did not want to work under a black conductor, but there is no evidence on that point. Henderson, as was his wont, acquiesced. At the first rehearsal the conductor began either firing Henderson's players or turning their chairs over to the new musicians. Again Henderson was unwilling to assert himself and accepted the firings with a shrug, even when his closest friend in the band, drummer Kaiser Marshall, was let go. The band broke up in bitterness, and most of them never worked for Henderson again.

Henderson then scrambled about, hired a new band, and found new arrangements, but for the next year or so the band recorded little, and that of not much value. Henderson continued to rebuild, however, and by 1931 the band was back on its feet and making celebrated records, such as "House of David Blues," "Radio Rhythm," and the superlative "Just Blues." Hawkins and Jimmy Harrison and possibly Morton remained from the old band. (There is a good deal of confusion about the trombones on some sides.) Trombonist Claude Jones, cut from the Harrison-Morton mold, and cornetist Rex Stewart, later to have an important career with Ellington, had been added. Drummer Walter Johnson made a significant contribution, as we shall see later. Another addition was altoist Benny Carter, a well-schooled musician who went on to become one of the leading men on his instrument and a top-flight arranger.

But although Carter and others were arranging for the band, Henderson at last found himself forced to write some arrangements, too, and it turned out that he was best of them all. "Just Blues" shows what he could do when he wanted to. A showcase for the soloists, it is built around interchanges between the sections and soloists. The arranged figures are simplicity themselves, but so logically worked out and strung together that the piece, which includes a superb trombone solo by Benny Morton, makes a complete whole from beginning to end. Henderson wrote much sparer and simpler arrangements than did Redman; there is no waste to them, no showy passages to impress the crowd, and you guess that plain laziness played a part in this. Whatever the reason, the conception was firm and clear: find a figure for, say, the saxophones, then find another one, but the right one, for the brass to play against it. Mix in solos in good proportion — enough for contrast but not so much that the tune becomes merely a string of solos. Switch tonal elements frequently, but not so frequently that the performance becomes choppy. It is a simple formula, but like any simple formula, it is what you do with it that counts. Henderson used it better than anybody in jazz. His "Down South Camp Meeting" and "Wrappin' It Up," which later helped to make Benny Goodman famous, have a light, airy, unpretentious grace, from which all trace of strain or effort is missing. Dicky Wells, who played trombone with the band for a period, said, "Fletcher had a way of writing so that the notes just seemed to float along casually. You just had to play the notes and the arrangement was swinging. He didn't write too high — there wasn't any screaming — but his music used to make you feel bright inside."

Despite the fact that Henderson had once again managed to put together a band that was in the vanguard, he had become a pathetic figure. According to the stories, he was very much under the thumb of his wife, a trumpet player who occasionally sat in with the band. He could not control his musicians, nor could he command their loyalty; sooner or later they all left for other bands. Too often he let the musical direction of his own group slide into other hands, and in the end it was Benny Goodman, not he, who went on to become rich and famous on the music his groups had in large measure developed. The question is, what was his own contribution?

It was threefold. In the first place, he was perhaps the finest judge of talent to exist in jazz: almost every major black jazz musician of the time passed through his groups. The leading tenor saxophonists of the period were Hawkins, Lester Young, Ben Webster, and Chu Berry; they succeeded one another in the band. The leading trombonists, Teagarden aside, were Wells, Morton, Claude Jones, Sandy Williams, J. C. Higginbotham, and of course Harrison. All played with Henderson, and he had discovered most of them. So too with the other instrumentalists: he found them, made them famous, and they went on to other bands. For a second matter, Henderson was a fine musician. No disciplinarian, he nonetheless managed to instill a respect for musicianship in his players, and they took pride in their ability to play difficult arrangements with accuracy and good intonation. And, finally, there was that tragically underemployed arranging talent. When you look at it, Fletcher Henderson had a combination of skills perfectly designed to make him the top band leader of the swing era. There was only one thing wrong: he couldn't lead.

Henderson continued to have bands off and on throughout the 1930s and even later; but very early in the decade he was being eclipsed by old competitors and new arrivals. In 1935, broke, he sold Benny Goodman a group of his best arrangements, and with this act started the swing band craze. (He also played piano with the band for a time.) Goodman's initial success was built on Henderson's arrangements, and the swing craze followed from that. It was all downhill for Henderson thereafter. He died in 1952, broke and forgotten, except by jazz fans and the old musicians.

In any case, by the late twenties he was being challenged by several competitors. The first of them was the white Goldkette band with Beiderbecke. As we have seen, the band contained some excellent soloists and could, on occasion, give the Henderson band a run for its money. However, it broke up in 1927 for financial reasons, just as the Henderson band was reaching a peak, and there is no way of guessing what it might have done afterward. When it went under, Goldkette, who needed bands for his Graystone Ballroom, decided to back a small, obscure black orchestra led by a man named William McKinney. He was, in part, capitalizing on the vogue for black music; but undoubtedly he was also motivated by the fact that black bands came a lot cheaper than whites. In about 1930 Paul Whiteman, for example, was paying most of his key men between $250 and $350 a week. Whiteman was, of course, the top payer, but, even so, players in black bands considered $75 a good week's pay.

We know little about William McKinney except that he came from Paducah, Kentucky, and was leading small bands in the Midwest in the post–World War I years. He really had little to do with the band that Goldkette called McKinney's Cotton Pickers. In 1927 Goldkette lured Don Redman away from Henderson and put him in charge of the band. Bolstered by good players, some of them from the Henderson band (in a famous session in 1929 Redman recorded nearly the entire disaffected Henderson band as the Cotton Pickers), and by his own arrangements, the band quickly became one of the most popular dance bands of the period. Redman stayed with it until 1931, when he formed the first of a series of bands he was to lead, off and on, through the swing years, though none became well known.

In 1927, one of those middle-class blacks who had come into jazz at the same time as Henderson moved into Harlem's Cotton Club to begin a five-year stand that was to make him famous. Duke Ellington, whom we will consider in detail later, had, by 1931, a band composed of men so well trained that they were capable of challenging Henderson's. And in 1929 there arrived in New York another one of those educated blacks, Luis Russell, who had been touring with King Oliver. Russell, born in Panama in 1902, was the son of a schoolteacher and trained musician, Felix Alexander Russell. In 1919 Luis, in an extraordinary stroke of luck, won $3000 on a lottery. He moved his family to New Orleans, where, with his sound musical background, he was able to find a lot of work, until he joined the exodus to Chicago in 1924. Through his New Orleans contacts he eventually got a job with King Oliver, and then in 1928 or 1929 he took over the Oliver band and moved it into another Harlem night spot, the Saratoga Club, which was to be his home for several years.

The band contained an abundance of fine soloists: altoist Charlie Holmes, capable of challenging Ellington's Johnny Hodges; trombonist J. C. Higginbotham, a fiery player with good technical skills, who played with a broad tone and larded his work with smears and glissandos; and, most important of all, Red Allen.

Allen was, during the first half of the 1930s, second only to Armstrong as the leading black trumpeter in jazz. Born in New Orleans in 1908, the son of a brass musician in the old tradition, he, like Armstrong, gigged around the city, worked with Fate Marable on the riverboats, and then joined King Oliver in Chicago. He developed his style along the same lines as Armstrong's. He had a spectacular high register, a warm, broad tone, and a flamboyant approach to melody. In 1929 Victor decided to build him up as an "answer" to Armstrong. He came to New York, began working with Russell, and recorded frequently, often with men drawn from the Russell band. He had by this time developed a singing style modeled on Armstrong's but still individual. Through the 1930s, he worked with various swing bands, including those of both Henderson and Armstrong. From 1949 on, he worked principally with several small groups, and remained active in jazz until his death in 1967. Some measure of his reputation among musicians may be gathered from the fact that through three jazz eras he worked with the leading bands of the period: the Excelsior Band, Marable, Oliver, Henderson, Armstrong, and, briefly, with Ellington and Benny Goodman. Technically, he was as impressive a player as Armstrong. However, he lacked Armstrong's sure conception and musical logic. Allen was always exciting, but sometimes notes seemed to pour out helter-skelter. Nonetheless, at his best he was a brilliant bravura player, equally adept at high-speed dashes and moving blues. Examples of his best work are "It Should Be You" and "Biff'ly Blues" made with the Russell band under his own name. The debt to Armstrong is clear; Allen stretches phrases and plays showy high-register figures, but these are felt solos. ("It Should Be You" includes excellent solos by altoist Holmes, clarinetist Albert Nicholas, and Higginbotham, reminding us of the high quality of the soloists in the Russell band.) In a quiet, more controlled mood there is his brief solo on Henderson's "Hocus Pocus," a typical simple riff tune arranged by Henderson.

The Luis Russell band has never quite been given its due by jazz writers. The arrangements, mostly by Russell, were not as interesting as those made by Henderson, Redman, or Ellington; for the most part they serve merely to get from one solo to the next. But the soloists were, taken as a group, as good as any similar group of the time, and the rhythm section, driven by the New Orleans bass player Pops Foster, was capable of giving the soloists strong support. The men who played in the band looked back on it later with great fondness. Allen said, "It had brotherly love going. It was also the most swinging band in New York. It put the audiences in an uproar." It can be heard at its best on "Saratoga Shout," based on the familiar chords of "When the Saints Go Marching In," and especially "Panama," a romping flag-waver with typically fine solos, particularly by Higginbotham and the little-known tenor saxophonist Greeley Walton. Also excellent is "Higginbotham Blues," recorded by a small group drawn from the Russell band, in which Foster bows throughout. It, too, contains fine solos, especially by the featured Higginbotham. These players, more impetuous than many of their competitors, did not let musical formalism interfere with the crucial matter of jazz feeling.

And there were more. By 1931 Chick Webb, a hunchbacked drummer who later discovered Ella Fitzgerald, was at the Savoy, Roseland, and the Cotton Club. The Missourians, under the leadership of a popular singer, Cab Calloway, was at the Cotton Club and similar places. These were all black bands, and it is interesting to note that during the early thirties, while there was plenty of work for good black bands, the white players were having trouble finding places in which to play jazz. Once again social attitudes were at work. Blacks were preferred for the nightclubs and show spots, which wanted hot music, but they were not acceptable at the big, expensive, white-only hotel dining and dancing rooms.

As an ironic consequence of this musical segregation, the white bands were forced to play popular tunes and dance music in the saccharine style of the time, tricked up with excruciating novelty effects, even though some of them were capable of playing good jazz. One was the Casa Loma Orchestra, a cooperative group that later became known as Glen Gray's Casa Loma Orchestra. The Casa Loma started out in frank imitation of the Goldkette band. It was highly disciplined and played fairly stiff arrangements of popular tunes, but it could swing on occasion, and it contained one or two players capable of playing good solos, among them clarinetist Clarence Hutchenrider, who was still working in jazz in the 1970s. Besides the Casa Loma band, there were the competing groups led by Red Nichols and Ben Pollack, who employed a lot of the best white players, like Teagarden, Goodman, McPartland, Pee Wee Russell, Bud Freeman, and others, but because they worked mostly in the big hotels and restaurants, they could play little jazz. These bands made numberless records under a lot of different names (many of the Pollack sides were issued as the Whoopee Makers). Most of the material is commercial and often dreadful, but mixed throughout are occasional jazz solos or even an entire jazz performance.

But, at bottom, most of the recording by whites during the early thirties was of little value as jazz. The jazz records were being made by blacks. To be sure, the black bands made plenty of commercial music, too. A considerable number of the records of Henderson, Ellington, and the rest will not bear repeated listening today. But the blacks had the jazz audience, and it was they in the main who developed the big jazz band.

However, the winds of change were blowing. In 1933 Prohibition ended, and drinking lost some of its romantic overtones. The Depression was on, a new seriousness was in the air, and rebellion seemed less important than reform of social institutions. Going out at night to dance and get drunk no longer seemed quite as significant as it had. The cabarets that had supported the jazz bands began to die off. But the stage had been set for the arrival of another vogue — swing.

The years between, say, 1925 and 1935, constituted a period of experimentation and learning. Henderson, Redman, Ellington, Russell, and the rest of the new men had discovered a way to play jazz with a big band, using written music. In doing so they had had to work through two problems. The first was to develop a cadre of players who could sight-read difficult arrangements. And the second, a related problem, was to find a way to play these arrangements with jazz feeling — that is, to make them swing.

The two problems were solved together. Simple experience — and the men in a band like Henderson's, which was working constantly, got plenty of experience — taught the men to read. The solution to the other problem was to have one leader in each section. Usually this was the man who played "first"; that is, he played the melody rather than the harmony parts. It was up to him to establish the way a figure was to be phrased, and up to the other men to follow him as exactly as possible. As the swing bands took form, lead players, especially lead trumpets and alto saxophones, came to be highly valued, for it was they who made the band go. The hot soloists got the celebrity, but among the musicians it was the lead players who were often most admired.

The development of the big jazz band was some ten years in the doing, and it was exceedingly important in bringing jazz to a broader audience, who found the music not quite so unfamiliar as the original New Orleans style. But even as this generation of jazz players was producing the big band, something else was happening that at base was more important to the nature of the music. This was an intangible, almost indefinable, change in the nature of jazz rhythm.

As we have seen, jazz rhythm is subtle and subjective, and therefore difficult to analyze. Furthermore, when we talk about it, we cannot talk about absolutes, but only about "tendencies": it is possible to find in the work of a player from any period figures that belong, rhythmically, to another era. But the change in jazz rhythm that occurred in the late 1920s and early thirties was utterly real to the musicians who were making the change and the jazz fans who listened to it. To the men who came into jazz in the 1930s the music of Morton and Oliver was palpably corny and out of date. They knew, indeed, that the corniness had little to do with the actual notes being played.

The difference lay in the handling of rhythm. The music of the early New Orleans jazz bands was marked by the use of two devices: a detaching of the melody line from the ground beat, and a counterpoising of 4/4 rhythmic feel in the melody line with a modified 2/4 in the ground beat. Now, as I have said, we are dealing only with a tendency; and as jazz began to flower during the 1920s, there developed an ever-stronger habit in the players in the rhythm section to produce a 4/4 feel. In New Orleans procedure, the bass, whether a tuba or string bass, generally played on only every other beat. The banjo stroked up and down, so that alternate strokes had somewhat different sounds. Drummers alternated beats of a single stroke with beats of two quick strokes. The whole effect in the rhythm was of a back-and-forth rocking — the "boom-chick, boom-chick" sound, with each "boom-chick" being felt as a single pulse. That is to say, this system of giving alternate notes in the ground beat a different quality established in the listener or musician's mind a yet more basic pulse built on pairs of beats.

The jazz players of the twenties were not great analysts of their music, and for the most part they assumed that they were playing in 4/4. It seemed natural enough, therefore, for rhythm players to start playing in a more genuinely 4/4 manner. Bass players began to enunciate all the beats instead of alternate ones. (Walter Page, a major bassist with the Count Basie band, early acquired the nickname "Big Four" because of this practice.) Guitarists in rhythm sections came more and more to stroke always downward, to give each beat the same weight. Pianists began to move away from the stride bass, with its "boom-chick" sound, substituting instead patterns of tenths, which walked in even fashion up and down the keyboard. And drummers began to play that "boom da-ta, boom da-ta" somewhat differently. In New Orleans practice, the two short strokes that fell on the second and fourth beats were played almost evenly, as can be heard in the playing of Tony Sbarbaro in the Original Dixieland Jazz Band, or that of Jasper Taylor behind Morton on "Big Fat Ham":

But the swing drummers began to extend the first of this little pair of notes at the expense of the second, to produce something more like:

The effect, eventually, was that the tiny final stroke came to be heard almost as a little pickup or grace note for the succeeding stroke; that is, it seemed to belong to the note after it rather than the note before:

And, in the end, it seemed as if the drummer were stroking equally on each beat, but giving the first and third beats a little "kick" ahead of the actual beat itself.

This was not all, however. As the swing rhythm sections were evening out the beat, they were also lightening it. The guitar replaced the clanging banjo, and the string bass, which played a very short note, took over entirely from the tuba, which sustained its notes longer. Pianists simplified what they were doing — Basie's minimal playing in his rhythm section became classic. And drummers moved the ground beat from the snare to the hi-hat cymbals. Credit for this change has universally been given to Basie's drummer Jo Jones, but in fact it belongs to Walter Johnson, the drummer who played with Fletcher Henderson from 1929 to 1934 and today is almost forgotten. Johnson can be heard playing the so-called ride beat on the hi-hat on Henderson's "Radio Rhythm" and "Low Down on the Bayou," both made in 1931, when Jo Jones was an obscure twenty-year-old working in Lincoln, Nebraska, with Harold Jones's Brownskin Syncopators. It is unlikely that Johnson had heard of Jones at this period, and as the drummer in what was still the most celebrated big band in jazz, Johnson's influence was bound to be formative.

In sum, then, the rocking New Orleans beat was replaced by a more evenly flowing and dryer one. And what did this mean to the horn players? It meant a great deal. The New Orleans soloist was placing his line over a pulse that went, effectively, at half the speed of the one the swing soloist was working against. This meant that he could state that classic three over two in twice the space that the swing soloist was given. That is, the New Orleans musician might play:

The swing player was working in half the space. His three over two had to be done like this:

The syncopations and departures from the ground beat of the New Orleans player were made in larger units. He played a great many quarter notes and not a few half notes. Furthermore, because he was setting his ragged rhythms over two beats instead of one, the way he divided a single beat was not critical. As a consequence, the New Orleans players tended to play eighth notes with fairly equal weight.

But for the swing player the unit was now not the two beats of the "boom-chick" but each single beat. His ragged rhythm had to be worked out against each beat, and for him this meant playing lots of figures in which each beat was divided into two parts. And because the essence of jazz lies in the irregularity of the melody over the ground beat, the division of the ground beat into two parts had to be unequal. This, then, is the essential difference in rhythmic feeling between the New Orleans and swing players. Over an even 4/4 beat the swing players were laying lines of uneven pairs to a beat; over a rocking 2/4 beat the New Orleans players were laying lines of uneven pairs of two beats.

We can see this effect particularly in the work of Coleman Hawkins, a swing player, who gave the first note of each pair three or four times the weight of the second, especially in descending phrases — so much so, in fact, that the second note at times simply disappeared. We know it is supposed to be there from the general shape of the phrase, and we are sure that Hawkins both fingered it and enunciated it, but he enunciated it so briefly and softly that it became inaudible. This is so common a happenstance in the jazz of this period and later that transcribers writing out solos developed a convention for dealing with these inaudible notes: they put them in, but placed them in parentheses.

The swing players, then, were working within the compass of a single beat for their effects, and more and more they searched out ways to accent within the beat itself — to shade the note one way or another as it came by. Not only would the pairs be unequal, but accents would be thrown on certain notes, or groups of notes, as they fled past. Players developed their own particular systems of accentuation. Jess Stacy, the fine pianist who worked for some time with the Benny Goodman orchestra and was noted for his ability to swing the band, habitually followed a strongly stressed note of the pair with one that was almost swallowed up in it surroundings, and a similar tendency can be found in pianists like Mel Powell and Teddy Wilson.

As if all of this were not difficult enough to analyze, the new players were doing something yet more subtle still. This was to imply within the body of a note a secondary pulse. This, in a sense, had always been part of jazz, because a note that begins to any degree ahead of a beat seems to be struck again when the beat actually arrives. But players now had begun to make a general practice of reshaping their longer notes partway through to imply another pulse, or attack. There are three principal ways of doing this. The easiest to hear is the addition of a vibrato to the note at some point after it has been struck. This practice, of course, descends from the use of terminal vibrato by New Orleans players. The clarinetist Edmond Hall, the last black clarinetist of influence in jazz, used this device consistently throughout his playing, slapping a fast, broad vibrato, often colored with a slight rasp, into every note long enough for the purpose shortly after it had begun. To a lesser degree, this added vibrato is present in the playing of most of the new players, and is clearly apparent in the work of two giants, Hawkins and Eldridge. Indeed, some pianists, especially Jess Stacy, reproduced this effect by playing octave tremulos on certain notes, especially those that ended phrases. A second system for creating this secondary impulse inside a beat was to let the pitch suddenly sag, if only fractionally, shortly after the beat began. Benny Goodman often did this. Finally, particularly in the brass players, there is occasionally, again on longer notes or at slower tempos, a tendency actually to hit the note again after the attack with a small rush of air. This practice is difficult to spot, difficult to analyze, difficult to be sure about, but it does seem to occur.

These devices are, all of them, hard to grasp. Players were not necessarily conscious of using them. We must bear in mind that we are talking about tendencies, not universals. But these players were reluctant to let a note go very far without doing something with it rhythmically. They wanted the constant motion, the ever-moving rush toward a nameless goal.

One result of this new approach was that the throwing of large extended or free figures over the beat, in the Armstrong manner, began to dwindle. To be sure, players like Teagarden, Pee Wee Russell, Bechet, Red Allen, and others, as well as Armstrong himself, continued to use these extended figures. But the extended figure began to disappear, replaced by a concern with smaller spaces.

A second effect was that soloists frequently began to start phrases on the third beat of a measure rather than the first, as was typical of the New Orleans style or indeed most ordinary European music. This was possible because the steadily running beats of the swing style made bar lines less evident; the soloists felt less boxed in by the four-square shape of the pattern of the song. This hardly happened all the time; a long phrase running over several bars might not stress any beat. But, as was particularly evident in the work of Roy Eldridge, one of the pre-eminent players in the new style, there was a strong tendency to leave the first beat blank, use the second beat for a couple of brief preparatory pickup notes, with the actual stressed opening note of the phrase coming at — that is, on or around — the third beat.

If this seems complicated, it is. Jazz is not a simple music. It is the necessity for reproducing such effects as the ones I have been describing that makes it so difficult to teach, so difficult to learn. Of the tens of thousands of people who have attempted to play it, not more than a hundred or so have ever done it supremely well. It is a demanding art form indeed.

Fats, Fatha,
and the Stride Piano

The piano has always had a special place in music. Because one can play on it several notes at once, it can be used in substitution for a band as a solo instrument. This quality has attracted composers; there has been far more music written for piano, or the keyboards in general, than for any other instrument. And because a piano can, in effect, accompany itself, it has been for a century the basic instrument for the playing of popular music.

This was especially so during the decades around the turn of the century. In the years before World War I most families felt it important to own a piano, no matter how poor they were, in the same way that poor families today will own television sets and radios. People who could play the piano were welcome visitors, and were generally cajoled into playing the latest popular tunes or accompanying the singing of hymns on Sunday.

But it was not just in the home that the piano flourished. As today, it was the basic entertainment tool in cabarets, clubs, restaurants, brothels, and even in the smaller theaters, which might not necessarily have pit bands. The piano, thus, was central to the social lives of Americans, and in the period between the Civil War and World War I there grew up a considerable industry devoted to it: the pop song business, a huge trade in instructional schools and mail order lessons, the piano roll business, and, of course, the selling of pianos themselves.

Inevitably there grew up a large corps of virtuoso professional piano players of all ethnic groups. These "professors" or "ivory ticklers" were not necessarily trained in European piano practice. Most, although not all, either were self-taught, or studied with older ticklers, who themselves had had little experience with the European practice. Despite the lack of European training, many of these players possessed astonishing techniques, which, if not well suited to a Chopin etude, were exactly right for producing the showy effects with which these professors impressed audiences and competing pianists. Fast arpeggios, octave runs, and other great splashes up and down the keyboard were practiced endlessly. These ticklers, both black and white, were the people who developed and popularized ragtime; it is no accident that the most popular music of the period was a piano form. And, of course, when jazz came into fashion, they were caught up in this new music.

For the jazz musician, the piano offers both advantages and disadvantages. The fact that the player is working with two hands, which can be trained to operate more or less independently of each other, makes the piano a natural instrument for producing with the left hand a ground beat over which the right hand distributes a melody filled with counter-rhythms. It can be, thus, a solo instrument. However, once a key is struck it is very nearly impossible to inflect the resulting tone with shifts of timbre, pitch, or dynamics, so important a practice in jazz. The jazz pianist, then, is working in a somewhat different musical world from the horn players, and he must find different devices for making his effects. As it happened, those devices came from two different places, for jazz piano playing derived from two separate and distinct traditions.

The first of these is the tradition of what has come to be called "stride" or "Harlem stride" piano. It is significant that this tradition did not arise in the South. As ever, the spawning grounds were entertainment centers. In this case it was the cities of the Northeast, which had expanded and grown wealthy in the decades after the Civil War, and the resorts around them. They demanded an enormous amount of music, and responding to the demand were those professors, schooled or self-taught.

Of these piano players, the ones who interest us most are certain blacks who worked around the turn of the century. Most of them have disappeared from the record. The best known today are Eubie Blake, never truly a jazz player, who was born in 1883, James P. Johnson (1891), Luckyeth Roberts (1895), and Willie "the Lion" Smith (1897). These men were not raised as jazzmen. Most were from the North, and, though they had some contact with the black folk tradition through their churches and the working people who were emigrating from the South, they had little experience with the rural music on which the blues was built. Willie Smith has testified that they were not playing the blues until just before World War I, when they were learning them, not from the blues singers like Ma Rainey, but from the sheet music of composers like W. C. Handy. The music these people played in their youth was a mixture of popular and sentimental songs, ragtime, and music for the waltz, schottishe, and the one- and two-steps, demanded by dancers caught up in the dance boom of 1910 and after. Like the New Orleans professors, these men thought of themselves as entertainers and composers. They were broad-based musicians who kept several irons hot in the music business. It is important to realize that when they began to play jazz they already possessed finished styles.

Of all of them, the best and most influential was James P. Johnson. His development was typical of the others and can give us some insight into how the stride style came into being. There is no full-dress biography of Johnson, but fortunately Tom Davin interviewed Johnson extensively shortly before the musician died. The interview was published as a series of articles in the now-defunct *Jazz Review*, and I am drawing my facts from it.

Johnson was born in New Brunswick, New Jersey, and grew up there, in Jersey City, and in New York City. His mother was a Virginian, active in the Methodist church, and a self-taught pianist. She loved country and "set" dances — what we think of today as square dances — and James would see them danced in his home by local people, many of them originally from Georgia and South Carolina. He told Davin, "A lot of my music is based on set, cotillion and other Southern dance steps and rhythms." We do not know what inspired him to become a pianist, but he seems to have had the vocation early. He was presumably started by his mother, but in

James P. Johnson, his customary cigar reposing near at hand, at a fraternity party at Hamilton College in about 1947.

Jersey City he got to know some of the local ticklers, and one, Claude Grew, about whom we now know little else, gave him some instruction. Johnson says, "What they played wasn't ragtime as we know it now. It was mostly popular songs with a strong rhythm and with syncopated vamps."

In the early years of the century, Johnson's family moved to New York. There was a piano in the house, and he continued to work at it. At the same time he was singing with local choral groups. By the time he was fifteen or so, he was working in cellar cabarets. One of them, the Jungle Casino, still had its coal bin, furnace, and heap of ashes. The clientele was made up mainly of Gullah longshoremen, from the outer banks of the Carolinas, who still had Africanisms in their speech. (Lydia Parrish's Georgia Sea Islands were part of this island chain.) Johnson played for them mainly dances, especially waltzes and schottishes. Otherwise he played pop tunes, rags, and piano arrangements of Victor Herbert and Rudolph Friml medleys, novelty songs, music hall hits, and the Indian songs that were in vogue at the time. But even in 1914 or thereabouts "there weren't any jazz bands like they had in New Orleans or on the Mississippi riverboats, but the ragtime piano was played all over in bars, cabarets, sporting houses."

One thing that distinguished the Northeast, particularly New York, from other parts of the country was the presence of a large body of European-trained pianists. As a consequence, Johnson says, New York ragtimers were forced to learn the European system, so they played in a fuller, more orchestral style than was used elsewhere in the country. The effect can be found in Johnson's own work, which is full and rich in texture. Johnson for a time studied with a piano and voice teacher named Bruto Gianinni, and was listening a lot to Luckey Roberts, who, he says, was the "outstanding pianist in New York in 1913." He was also influenced by a friend and pupil of Roberts, whom we know only as Abba Labba, and by Eubie Blake, whom he has called "one of the foremost pianists of all time."

In personality, Johnson reminds us a little of Scott Joplin. He was shy, preferred to let his music speak for itself, but was intensely dedicated to his music. He practiced in the dark to give himself a feeling for the piano, and played complicated exercises through a sheet to improve his dexterity. By World War I he was accepted as one of the leading pianists in his style. He was working regularly at Barron Wilkins's, one of the leading cabarets in Harlem, touring in vaudeville, and writing shows, popular songs, and rags. In 1916 he became one of the first blacks to make a piano roll.

It is important to recognize the role that style played in the lives of these men. In dress, manner, and attitude they felt it necessary to carry themselves like the crown princes they felt themselves, as leading ticklers, to be. The Davin interview has a marvelous passage on style, which is worth quoting at some length:

When a real smart tickler would enter a place, say in winter, he'd leave his overcoat on and keep his hat on too. We used to wear military overcoats or what was called a Peddock Coat, like a coachman's; a blue double-breasted, fitted to the waist, and with long skirts. We'd wear a light pearl-gray Fulton or Homburg hat with three buttons or eyelets on the side, set at a rakish angle over on the side of the head. Then a white silk muffler and a white silk handkerchief in the overcoat's breast pocket. Some carried a gold-headed cane, or if they were wearing a cutaway, a silver-headed cane . . . There was a fellow named Fred Tunstall . . . He was a real dandy. I remember he had a Norfolk coat with eighty-two pleats in the back. When he sat down to the piano, he'd slump a little in a half hunch, and those pleats would fan out real pretty . . . Players would start off by sitting down, wait for the audience to quiet down and then strike their chord, holding it with the pedal to make it ring. Then they'd do a run up and down the piano — a scale or arpeggios — or if they were real good they might play a set of modulations, very offhand, as if there was nothing to it . . . Some ticklers would sit sideways to the piano, cross their legs and go on chatting with friends nearby. It took a lot of practice to play this way, while talking and with your head and body turned . . . Then, without stopping the smart talk or turning back to the piano, he'd *attack* without any warning, smashing right into the regular beat of the piece. That would knock them dead.

Inevitably, this concern with style spilled over in the music. Johnson told Davin,

Sometimes, I would play basses a little lighter than the melody and change harmonics. When playing a heavy stomp I'd soften it right down — then I'd make an abrupt change like I heard Beethoven do in a sonata. Some people thought it was cheap, but it was effective and dramatic. With a solid bass like a metronome I'd use chords with half and quarter changes. Once I used Liszt's "Rigoletto Concert Paraphrase" as an introduction to a stomp. Another time I'd use pianissimo effects in the groove and let the dancer's feet be heard scraping on the floor.

It is obvious from this that Johnson and the players like him were deeply enmeshed in European concert music. Willie "the Lion" Smith — he acquired his nickname in France during World War I, where he was cited for courageous service with an artillery battery — later in life studied the Schillinger system, and his own writing is very European in manner. His "Echoes of Spring," perhaps his best-known piece, could, aside from some jazz inflection, have been written by a pupil of Schubert's. Next to Johnson, Smith was probably the most popular of the Harlem stride players. Like the others, he carried himself with style. He was known by his Homburg and large cigar, and when he walked into a cabaret he would announce grandly, "The Lion is here." He was a strong-minded man who would not play when he didn't like the audience, and he made few concessions to the music business. Despite his personality, his music is prettier and gentler than Johnson's strong, full-textured playing, as witness his "Morning Air" or "Relaxin'."

In one respect we are lucky in dealing with the stride pianists. They came to jazz much later than the New Orleans originators, and we therefore have both piano rolls and records of the transition from ragtime, or prejazz music, to jazz itself. These players, as we have seen, were not very familiar with the black folk music tradition, and they certainly knew nothing of jazz. They learned about it the way the rest of America learned about it, through the playing of the Original Dixieland Jazz Band. It is curious to think of black players, especially such influential ones as James P. Johnson, learning about jazz from whites, but on Johnson's own testimony, that is the case. Johnson was intrigued by the new music. He belonged to that odd black musicians' fraternity, the Clef Club, and he suggested that the members organize a jazz band. In one of the great ironies of jazz, they turned the suggestion down; they did not want their organization associated with that vulgar music, jazz. But jazz had arrived, and there was no avoiding the fact that it was replacing ragtime in the popular fancy.

Johnson and his colleagues never quite gave up their love of ragtime or their sense that it was their special music. Indeed, Eubie Blake, who was active at the age of ninety in the 1970s, was never truly a jazz musician, but a ragtimer. Still, audiences had gone elsewhere, and the pianists, perforce, followed. The earliest examples we have of Johnson's work are piano rolls, which do not carry much subtlety. However, a roll like "After Tonight," one of Johnson's first, made in 1917, is pure ragtime in rhythmic spirit, despite its being listed on the roll as "Fox-Trot Jazz Arrangement." The melody line here is still firmly attached to the ground beat. But in 1921, with "Worried and Lonesome Blues" or "Carolina Shout," his famous set piece, his melody has become much looser, and by the 1927 version of his lovely "Snowy Morning Blues," another of his best-liked works, he is playing jazz, although with occasional rhythmic awkwardnesses.

Despite the jazz approach to rhythm, "Snowy Morning Blues" is in form a rag. We can see plainly enough in the work of Johnson and all these men that the stride style was created simply by the players jazzing or swinging the rags, or pseudoragtime music, they had grown up on — that is, pulling the melody away from the ground beat. They were thus paralleling, a generation later, the process that had gone on in New Orleans to produce jazz in the first place. The various stride basses can be found everywhere in formal ragtime. Moreover, in this early piano jazz the right hand usually is not playing simple melodies, but is laying out involved, very pianistic, figures. There is no question here, as there was later, of the piano player improvising long chains of notes in the manner of a horn. The right hand was playing chords or repeated figures combining chords and single notes; and the players were employing trills, mordents, and other embellishments that were characteristic of the piano, not the horns.

These piano players, it must be remembered, were soloists. They did, at times, work with groups, and they often were required to accompany vocalists, or even shows, but the bulk of their work was done alone, and there was therefore every reason for them to play a strong, full piano, especially where there was noise and dancing. This is particularly evident in their stressing of the importance of a full and powerful left hand, and they were scornful of pianists who were not "two-handed." It is not surprising, then, that their favorite student, a man who was to become, after Armstrong, the best loved by the general public of any jazz musician, possessed a firm left hand. He was a large man with huge appetites and an endless capacity for good times, and his name was Thomas "Fats" Waller.

Waller's family came from Virginia. His father, Edward Martin Waller, was born around 1870. He was a reserved, strong, and somewhat severe man with a religious bent. Waller's mother, by contrast, was lively and warmhearted. The father was determined to raise his children in the North, where they could get a proper education, and around 1888 the Wallers came to New York, where they settled on Waverly Place, in a section of Greenwich Village then populated by blacks. In 1890 came the first of twelve children, of whom six died in infancy. Edward Waller first had a job in a livery stable and then established himself in his own trucking business. The family joined the local black church, and in time Edward Waller became a preacher. Responsible and reliable, he is not the man one would imagine as the father of the wayward piano player who was born in 1904, one of the last of the lot.

By this time, the family had moved to Harlem. The district was only beginning to become a black enclave. Through most of the nineteenth century, it had been a small village, separated from New York City by areas of farmland and, later, by Central Park. Toward the end of the nineteenth century, it got caught up in a real estate boom and began to turn into a sea of brownstones similar to the ones farther south. But the entrepreneurs had overestimated the demand, and, failing to find enough white families to fill the houses, they turned to the black market. The accommodations were a considerable improvement on the area farther south, which bordered on a district of brothels and low "black and tan" drinking clubs. Harlem, by contrast, had broad streets, clean new buildings, and a general atmosphere of prosperity; and gradually it drew to it more and more blacks, a large proportion of them substantial, hard-working people like the Wallers, who were determined to improve their status in life.

Young Fats was a favorite of his mother's, and was spoiled. He was overweight from childhood and acquired his nickname while still a schoolboy. He picked up his interest in music early, too. As good religious people, the family did a lot of hymn-singing, both in church and around home. Like most aspiring families of the time, white or black, they wanted a piano in the home, both to accompany the hymns and, presumably, for the cultural tone it lent to the living room. An arrangement was made with a relative to share the cost, and a piano was bought. A teacher was hired for Fats and one or two of the other children — by this time some of the older children were grown-up — and in time Fats acquired an elementary understanding of the instrument. But he shortly became bored with the lessons and stopped taking them, though he continued to play the piano by ear. Later on, in school, he studied violin and string bass briefly, and by the time he was in high school he was considered one of the best piano players in school, playing regularly at assemblies and other functions.

Like any schoolboy, Fats was principally interested in the popular music of his time, which in this case was ragtime. His father, however, considered it "music from the devil's workshop," and he tried to encourage Fats to become interested in serious music. But Fats was on his course.

By this time, Harlem was changed. The sections around One hundred thirty-third Street had become entirely black, and the population was spreading down toward One hundred twenty-fifth Street, which only a few years later became Harlem's Broadway. There was a flourishing entertainment district around One hundred thirty-third, and other cabarets elsewhere. Particularly important was the institution of the rent party. The parties began as legitimate affairs, intended to raise enough money for the tenant to pay the rent. He would provide cheap liquor, food, and a piano player, and charge something in the order of twenty-five or fifty cents admission. However, as the popularity of these parties grew, they came to be semiprofessional affairs, run on a periodic basis. Out of them grew the so-called buffet flats, apartments that were really run as cabarets, with liquor, music, perhaps gambling, prostitution, and often live pornographic shows. The rent parties formed a substantial source of income for the piano players.

The rent parties were only part of it. During the 1920s there was the ever-expanding cabaret business, catering in part to whites from "downtown." There were little clubs and bars, which used pianists; there were the movie theaters, which used a piano or sometimes an organ to accompany the film; and finally there was always the chance of breaking out of the black community into the larger entertainment world.

Fats moved into this world while he was still an adolescent. The precipitating cause was the death of his mother, a great shock to him; he left home shortly after. It was a world filled with easy women, liquor, marijuana and other drugs, and good times — hardly the sort of thing his father would have liked. But for Fats it was meat and potatoes, and he thrived on it. He got a job playing the organ at the Lincoln Theatre, one of Harlem's best, and picked up whatever else he could on the side. He was, at that time, a good enough pianist for a youngster, but he could not compete with the real lions of the business, James P., Willie Smith, Luckey Roberts, and the rest. But through a mutual acquaintance he came to know Johnson. Johnson was sufficiently impressed with Waller's talents to give him lessons, something he did not ordinarily do. For several years thereafter, Waller became Johnson's shadow, following him around to the cabarets and parties where he was working, occasionally spelling Johnson during the evening, and eventually picking up important work of his own.

Waller made his first piano roll around 1920, and the first of hundreds of records in 1922. He also began to compose songs. Over the years he collaborated with a number of lyricists, but certainly the best was a poet named Andrea Menentania Razafinkeriefo, a nephew of Queen Rànavàlona III of Madagascar. Generally known as Andy Razaf, he wrote the lyrics to some of Waller's most enduring tunes, including "Honeysuckle Rose," "Ain't Misbehavin'," "Black and Blue," and "Keepin' Out of Mischief Now." Fats's fertility was incredible, and Razaf was not far behind. In those days, songwriters often sold their tunes outright. Fats, who was perennially pressed for money, sometimes sold songs for fifty dollars each and occasionally less. It didn't bother him; there was always more in the barrel. At times he and Razaf would take a cab downtown to the office of some music publisher, composing in the cab the songs they were about to sell. Between his playing and his composing, by the mid-1920s, still in his early twenties, Fats was a known figure in the New York show business world.

Unfortunately, he was already showing signs of the personality difficulties that were to cut short his life. It is hard to know how much credence to give to stories of twenty hamburgers or four or five steaks consumed at a sitting, topped off with pie, ice cream, and whiskey. It is clear enough, however, that he was overeating, and it is certain that he was drinking too much. By his mid-twenties he was an alcoholic, drinking almost constantly. He was, in addition, irresponsible in his professional life, partly no doubt owing to drink. He frequently failed to show up for gigs or record dates, and sometimes, when the spirit moved him, would jettison half a tour. Money — and by the 1930s it was big money — went through his hands like melting butter. He made an early marriage, which lasted only two or three years and ended in rancor, and on at least one occasion he found himself in jail for failing to keep up his alimony payments. His second marriage was successful but stormy. In sum, he behaved like a child in most of his relationships.

But a man does not act like this out of simple perversity. Anyone that addicted to drink is suffering from some inner disability, and it was the opinion of Willie Smith that Fats, despite his endless exuberant jiving, both in and out of music, was very insecure. He says in his memoirs:

> Young Waller was really a very shy kid, and I think it was that shyness that eventually turned him into such a heavy drinker . . . Part of it was because he was a mamma's boy, at least when I first knew him, and his life got all jumbled up at the time of her death.

This disorder inside was reflected outside. He lived in turmoil, constantly late for something or other, constantly harassed by money problems, constantly coming or going from one drunken party to the next. Yet to the

A standard publicity shot of Fats Waller, showing the happy-go-lucky demeanor he affected for public display. This was the Fats his large audiences came to see.

outsider he was always the high-spirited, carefree, happy-go-lucky rounder whose primary interest in life was to see that everybody had fun.

This is, of course, not a bad image for an entertainer. In 1932, Waller took on a full-time manager, a man with a broad show business background, named Phil Ponce. Ponce got Waller a two-year contract for a radio show on WLW in Cincinnati, which covered a considerable part of the country. "Fats Waller's Rhythm Club" featured other singers as well as Fats, but it was his playing and singing of popular songs that was the lure, and the show was a hit. From there he went on to WABC in New York. The exposure on these radio programs turned him from a jazzman into a popular entertainer, and after that everything turned to gold. In his peak years, he was making over fifty sides a year, touring as often as his managers could keep him on the road, writing one song after another, and appearing in movies. From 1934 or 1935 until his death he was one of the hottest entertainment properties in the country. Only Louis Armstrong, in jazz, outdistanced him in general popularity, and it took Armstrong thirty years to do it. Had Waller lived he would have become as important a show business figure as Sinatra, Presley, or any other in that league.

He did not, however, live. By the start of World War II, when Waller was in his late thirties, he was beginning to feel the wear and tear of too many parties, too much traveling, too much food, too much liquor. In 1941 he had a physical checkup, and the doctor told him he had to quit drinking if he wished to live. Fats stopped drinking briefly, but then went back to liquor. Willie Smith saw him around this time and reported that he was carrying so much weight that his ankles were painfully swollen. But Fats could not, or would not, slow down. He continued to drag himself through series of one-nighters. Then, in 1943, he went to Hollywood to make a movie. By the time he got on the train for the trip back to New York he was exhausted and sick, although nobody knew how sick. There was a party on the train; it was midnight before Waller got into bed. He slept all the next day and through the night; and at five o'clock of a cold, blowy morning, as the train pulled into the Kansas City station, he died.

His legacy was immense. Fats Waller had careers enough for three men. He was one of the leading show business personalities of his time; he was among America's finest songwriters, the peer of Gershwin, Porter, Kern, and others who made the period so rich in popular music; and he was one of the finest jazz pianists who ever lived. And despite his clowning and the bad songs he often was given to sing, he never once sacrificed jazz feeling to the popular taste. Clown he would — he was after all a showman, and he enjoyed the foolery — but it simply was not in him to play a bar of bad music.

Fats Waller recorded under all sorts of circumstances — as a soloist, as accompanist to singers, as leader of both small groups and a short-lived big band. Between 1922 and 1929 he made at least a hundred sides. There was a period from 1930 through 1933 when he made only a few records, probably because of the collapse of the recording business after the onset of the Depression. Then, in 1934, Phil Ponce got him a lucrative contract with Victor. Over the years between then and his death he recorded more than five hundred sides for Victor, and these are the records he is generally known by. Some of them are piano solos, more are solos with his vocal, and a relatively few were made with his big band. The majority of them, however, were made with the group called Fats Waller and His Rhythm, the setting in which he usually played on tour, and some of these were issued in two versions — with and without a vocal. The personnel of the group shifted, but the most regular members were trumpeter Herman Autrey, reed man Eugene "Honeybear" Cedric, and guitarist Al Casey. Casey was considered one of the best guitarists of the period, and Autrey and Cedric were competent musicians. None of them, however, had significant careers apart from Waller. Fats, with his singing, his clowning, and his piano playing, was the whole show; the other men were essentially spear carriers.

There is some noticeable change in Waller's playing in the two periods, not surprising in view of the changes that were being made in jazz in the late 1920s and early thirties by Armstrong and the swing players. In the earlier decade he is playing jazz ragtime. The melody line is tied fairly closely to the beat, producing some rhythmic stiffness, and his playing tends to be full, with many chords in both hands. By 1935 he is playing farther behind the beat, eliminating the rhythmic stiffness, and he has reduced his playing, especially in the bass, where he often uses lines of single quarter notes.

But the essential spirit of his playing did not change very much. He continued through his life to play music formed on the ragtime system: "Handful of Keys," "Alligator Crawl," Johnson's "Carolina Shout." Indeed, many of his compositions are surprisingly pianistic for popular tunes. For example, the melody of his most famous tune, "Honeysuckle Rose," is arranged to group under the fingers of a pianist's right hand; it does not lie at all naturally for a vocalist or horn player. This sort of lively piano playing with its overtone of good times was what audiences liked, and it is omnipresent on the Victor records cut after 1934. The tunes, except for Waller's own, are usually novelty songs — light love songs with humorous lyrics, pure comic songs, jive versions of concert pieces or folk songs and the like. Among his biggest hits were "I'm Going to Sit Right Down and Write Myself a Letter" (which, contrary to popular opinion, he did not write), "Your Feet's Too Big," and its sequel, "Your Socks Don't Match," "The Joint Is Jumpin'," complete with a mock fight and police sirens, and "Hold Tight (I Want Some Sea Food Mamma)," which had erotic implications missed by most audiences of the time. Waller often opened and closed the tunes with a line or two of comic monologue, and interspersed patter into the lyrics, which he kidded by moving into falsetto at times or by dropping into a deep bass. Tempos were quick, the piano playing merry, and the solos by Autrey and Cedric often somewhat frantic. These were the records that the public bought, the songs they came to hear at the theaters where Waller played.

But, in fact, the merriment was not nearly so spontaneous as it seemed. As a rule the patter was worked out in advance and remained more or less the same night after night. Waller was a show business professional, putting on an act that quite often had little to do with what he was actually feeling at the moment. Many nights what he really felt like playing were tender, reflective, and even melancholy pieces; but audiences would not let him. Gene Cedric has said, "People in the audience would think he was lying down. They'd yell, 'Come on, Fats.' He'd take a swig of gin or something and say resignedly, 'Aw right, here it is.' "

Turning from the stage shows to the records, where he had somewhat more control over what he did, we find a surprisingly large amount of reflective playing. I do not mean the blues. Fats, we must remember, came from the ragtime/stride tradition of the Northeast, where players had little experience with the blues until it became a fad. He recorded few blues; those he did, he played as if they were pop tunes, with little blues feeling. But if he was not a blues player, he was, more than most jazz musicians, a melancholic man. Tender performances of "Waitin' at the End of the Road," "How Can I?," and slow versions of "Rosetta," "Honeysuckle Rose," and other tunes normally given happy treatment are far more frequent in his work than one would expect. He was, furthermore, enamored of the organ, on which he would have played most of the time if it had been feasible. The organ, needless to say, is not an instrument of merriment. It has been said of Fats that the piano was his stomach; the organ, his heart. The truth is that underneath Waller's work is a deep sadness. Although we cannot tell with certainty where it came from, the death of his mother when he was about sixteen left him "all jumbled up," as Willie Smith put it; so jumbled up that he ran away from home and moved in with the parents of a friend. Then, too, he certainly suffered from the same sort of conflict that victimized Bix Beiderbecke, who was just about Waller's age: an expressive nature at war with a strict, almost puritanical upbringing. Out of respect for him as a fellow human, we must remember his reflective pieces as well as the ones full of sparkling merriment, which continue to cheer our lives. If there is really any such thing as the melancholy clown, Fats Waller was one.

The Harlem stride style established by Johnson, Waller, and the others was the dominant school in jazz piano playing during the 1920s and thirties, but it was not the only one. Running parallel to it was a system that came from different roots and grew in another direction. This was the style that has to be called primitive jazz piano. It's practitioners were thousands of self-taught musicians who had worked out ways of coaxing music out of the magical box. Most of them, but not all of them, were black. They played in the evenings for the entertainment of the poor laborer, usually in a barn or shed of some kind that had been turned into a crude cabaret where working people of both sexes could drink and dance. These were the fore-runners of the "jook" joints of the South, from which we get our term "juke box." Here came, of an evening, the pickers of cotton, the hewers of pine, the men from the railroads and the turpentine camps, to blow off steam. The pianists were not full-time entertainers — most of them, in any case — but laborers who could play a little. They worked out their techniques for themselves, finding ways of playing what they wanted to play and nothing more. Few of them could play in more than two or three keys and many of them knew only one, usually F or G. They played hardly any tunes as such, and they certainly could not manage rags or the rag-based stride figures. Their audiences wanted a highly rhythmic music suitable for danc-ing. The music of these people, both audiences and players, grew from black folk music, and by the early part of this century, the pianists among them were working principally with the blues. What they were doing was simply substituting the piano for the guitar or banjo that the early blues singers used to accompany themselves with. The major difference was that their playing was faster and more strongly rhythmic than that of the country blues singers, intended as it was for dancing. Otherwise it was the same. Many of them sang the blues; they stretched out their blues to thirteen or more bars as the rural blues singers did; they ended on the characteristic minor sevenths; and they found ways of imitating the sound of the blue notes by playing major and minor thirds simultaneously or in rapid succes-sion.

Thus, once more we have before us that old tension in jazz, the pull between the European and African elements. On the one hand, we have the stride pianists using European harmonies and European dance and song forms as they were handed down through the formal rags of Joplin and his peers; on the other we have the blues pianists, with only a rudimentary interest in harmony and form, using the piano as if it were a pair of drums. Stride pianists like Smith and especially Johnson knew European concert music years before they ever heard a note of jazz, or even of the blues, and many had ambitions to work in longer European forms. They came to jazz after it had been invented. The primitive players, however, were playing the blues before jazz existed; the music they played was one of the bases on which jazz was built. This piano style was in the black folk music tradition from which jazz sprang, and it probably was being played in much the same way well back into the nineteenth century. As with most dichotomies, it is not so clear-cut in real life as it is on paper. The primitive pianists, of course, varied in regard to level of skill, interest in rags or more complicated raglike figures, feeling for the blues, or the particular audience they were playing for, so some approached, or even at times crossed over, the dividing line into stride playing. But the distinction remains a sound one, reflecting real differences in traditions: one a European one overlaid with African-derived rhythms; the other, at bottom, rhythmic, with only rudimentary harmonic and formal elements taken from European practice.

Because the primitive pianists were more concerned with rhythm than with harmony or melody, their styles were generally formed around what the fingers could be easily taught to do, rather than around some theory of music. Bass lines were often just sequences of notes that walked up and down the keyboard a beat at a time. Most usually consisted of some sort of repeated figure, which the fingers could be trained to carry on without much attention from the player; he just set this pattern in motion at various points on the keyboard to produce a limited set of chord changes. Right hands also ran either to strings of single notes sketching out melodic fragments, or to simple repeated figures that could also be set going at various points on the keyboard as the chord changes dictated. One of the classic and most characteristic of these figures was produced by the player simply drawing his finger through a black key and the white one in front of it once each beat. Done on the proper notes, this produced not only a tension-building repetitive figure but an imitation of the sound of the blue notes.

As pianists will quickly recognize, this music is very much akin to what later came to be called "boogie-woogie." And, in fact, that is precisely what it was. Formal boogie-woogie is a medium-tempo or fast blues employing repeated eighth notes or dotted-eighth and -sixteenth figures in the bass, and repeated figures, sometimes interspersed with single-note runs, in the right hand. The bass figures are traditionally played with more exactitude than is the case in most jazz phrasing; that is, the eighth notes are weighted equally, and the dotted eighths and sixteenths are played closer to the three-to-one division of European music than to the approximately three-to-two division customary in jazz. About the only way boogie-woogie differs from standard primitive blues playing is in the eighth-note basses; an ordinary blues would have quarter notes in the bass. But even this distinction does not always hold, for sometimes, despite a 4/4 bass, the player would suggest the 8/8 feeling in the right hand, as, for example, in Jimmy Yancey's "Big Bear Train."

These piano players were working everywhere in the United States where there were black communities: in the South at first; then in the Northern ghettos when the black migration began. There were probably fewer of them in the Northeast because of the competition of the stride players, but they existed there, too. The names of most of them are lost, but a few of them were recorded in the 1920s and thirties when there was interest in the country blues. Most were never full-time entertainers; they worked at ordinary jobs during the day and performed at night or on weekends. Jimmy Yancey, one of the best known of the group, was a groundskeeper for the Chicago White Sox for some thirty years. Other better-known players in this school were Roosevelt Sykes, Pine Top Smith, Montana Taylor, Cow Cow Davenport, and Rufus Perryman, known as "Speckled Red." Like other blues men, these pioneer players took liberties with the twelve-bar structure and occasionally disregarded chord changes.

By the 1930s, however, the strict blues form was in use, and tempos were speeding up. In the years around 1940, primitive blues playing, as boogie-woogie, became a popular fad. This in part stemmed from John Hammond's interest in the boogie players, especially Meade Lux Lewis, whom he tracked down in Chicago. Hammond arranged for Lewis and some other boogie players to work at Café Society in New York. There were recordings, and a boogie-woogie boom followed. All during the early 1940s adolescent piano players were hammering out boogie at parties, and in time the big swing bands found it necessary to add boogie-woogie instrumentals to their repertories: Tommy Dorsey's "Boogie-Woogie," adapted from one of Pine Top Smith's pieces, was one of the period's biggest hits, and so was Will Bradley's "Beat Me Daddy, Eight to the Bar."

Of the boogie-woogie players who came to prominence during the boogie fad, three stand out: Meade Lux Lewis, Albert Ammons, and Pete Johnson. These three men worked and recorded together, sometimes two in duet and at least once all three as a trio. Occasionally they accompanied blues singers. All three played with accuracy, power, and, within the limits of the form, imagination. Perhaps the best known of their records were "Boogie Woogie Prayer," an extended collaboration by all three, and Albert Ammons's "Shout for Joy." The latter opens with a church bell quotation from a children's song, and offers, on the next-to-last chorus, an unusual bass, which moves around the keyboard in chords without the steady repetition characteristic of boogie-woogie. These men, however, were more polished players than the earlier primitives, like Yancey and Pine Top Smith. The early music was blues — blues at heart, blues in form. And given that almost mystical impulse in jazz to maintain the balance between African and European elements, we are not surprised to find this blues piano style and the stride style merging into what was to become the main line of development of jazz piano playing.

The man in whom this merger is most clearly evidenced was Earl "Fatha" Hines. He was born in Duquesne, Pennsylvania, a little town outside Pittsburgh. His father was a part-time trumpet player who worked with a group called the Eureka Brass Band, and his mother played piano and organ. He also had an aunt, living in Pittsburgh, who was involved in "light opera" — probably the musical theater. Through her, Hines came to meet a number of black musical figures, including Eubie Blake and Noble Sissle, a black band leader of the time. He thus came from a family with roots in European music, and when he began learning piano at about the age of nine, he studied the European composers and worked on his Czerny exercises.

He started to work in clubs around Pittsburgh when he was thirteen or fourteen, and when late hours began to interfere with his schoolwork, he dropped out of school. Around 1918 he met a singer and saxophone player named Lois Deppe — a man, despite the name — who was leading a trio at a Pittsburgh club called the Leaderhouse, or Leiderhouse. Deppe was using a pianist who could play in only a few keys, and he offered a job to Hines and a friend who played drums. The boys were barely out of short pants, but Hines's father made an arrangement for him to live with his Pittsburgh aunt, and he accepted the job. The Deppe band had a good local reputation. Gradually it expanded, began to travel through the Midwest, and, finally, in 1923, cut a few records.

In 1923, Hines landed in Chicago. He began to work as a single in a café that used a small piano on casters; the player would push it from table to table to entertain the customers. His reputation quickly spread, and in the next few years he worked with most of the important black band leaders in Chicago, including Erskine Tate, Carroll Dickerson, Jimmy Noone, and, later, Armstrong. Then, within a few months in 1928, he made a series of records that established him as the leading pianist in jazz. In June of that year he replaced Lil Armstrong in Louis's recording groups, which over the next six months cut some of Armstrong's most enduring sides, including "West End Blues," "Tight Like This," "Muggles," Hines's own tune "Monday Date," and a famous Hines-Armstrong duet called "Weather Bird." During the same stretch of time he made approximately a dozen sides with Jimmy Noone's Apex Club Orchestra, which were widely admired by jazz musicians and early jazz fans. And finally, in December of the same year, he cut eight solo sides for Q.R.S. These sides were an early foray into the recording business by what was basically a piano roll company. The distribution and promotion of the records was badly handled, though, and they did not sell well. But they attracted wide attention in the jazz world, and they have come to be considered among the seminal groups of piano records in jazz.

The effect of all of these records, made within the span of six months, was to make Hines a jazz star. At the end of the year he formed a big band, which went into Chicago's Grand Terrace. For the next twenty years Hines worked in the big band format, traveling and returning to play regular stints at the Grand Terrace. Curiously, in the early 1940s he made a second impact on jazz history when he took a group of young bebop players into his band,

giving this new music its first important exposure. Hines's big bands were always successful, but they never achieved the great fame of Goodman's or Basie's, and he broke up his last band in 1948, as the big band era collapsed. He worked thereafter with Armstrong's All-Stars, a dixieland band of his own, and in various other groups. He was still working in the 1970s, playing in a basically unchanged style, still strong, although inflected with more modern harmonies. His influence, by this point, had diminished, but all around him were players working in a style that he had first put together.

This style was already well formed by the time he made the Deppe records in 1923. He was at bottom a stride pianist of the Johnson-Smith-Waller style, a style he had undoubtedly picked up not only from local pianists — he speaks of players named Jim Fellman and Johnny Watters — but from the piano rolls that were abundantly available during his youth.

But there is something else going on in his work, too, something he did not get from the stride players. From a casual glance at a map Pittsburgh appears to be part of the Northeast. It is, however, at the head of the Ohio River and is the largest inland river port in the United States. It faces south and west, not north. At the time Hines was growing up there, it was filled with black stevedores and riverboat men of one kind or another who worked up and down the Ohio and Mississippi rivers. In addition, during World War I it was flooded with rural blacks coming up from the South to work in the mills. Among these people, certainly, were many part-time piano players in the blues tradition.

Although as members of the black middle class his family would have attempted to shield him from contact with these rough working people, it is clear that Hines was exposed to blues playing. He himself speaks of the influence of Joe Smith, the St. Louis trumpeter who went on to record with Bessie Smith and Fletcher Henderson. Smith appeared in Pittsburgh for a short time in Hines's youth. Hines says, "I followed Joe everywhere in the world he went. I just couldn't believe it, and I wanted to play what he played. It gave me a lot of new ideas."

It is clear that Hines heard pianists moving along the river as well. There is blues feeling in his playing, as, for example, in his solo on "Congaine." It is his own tune, and it is surprisingly close to the main strain of Jelly Roll Morton's "Wolverine Blues," which Morton had recorded not long before. For another matter, as we have seen, Waller rarely played the blues, but when Hines made the Q.R.S. solos, three of the eight were blues. Most

The insouciant Earl Hines at the piano in the early 1940s. Hines, a strong and durable personality, was still leading bands in the 1970s, nearly matching Ellington for longevity. William P. Gottlieb/Edward Gottlieb Collection

striking, however, is the fact that on all of the Deppe records, except one in a minor key, Hines ends with a minor seventh. This convention is an anathema in European practice and was never used by the stride players. But it was characteristic of country blues playing, whether on piano, guitar, or other instrument, and it tells us quite clearly that Hines had been strongly influenced by the primitive blues players.

Hines, then, was playing a modified stride piano, which mingled stride with the primitive blues tradition. It gave him a style that was rhythmically powerful, with a preference for single lines of notes in the right hand, or, characteristically, simple rhythmic figures spelled out with a hard attack in octaves. Hines is a banger at the piano. There is an abrupt, sometimes jagged, quality to his work. Not for him the flowing or rippling right-hand figures of the Harlem stride players. Figures break off in midflight. The melody suddenly jumps into the bass. The bass itself does not run steadily through its course, but is suddenly suspended or changed in character. Frequently the whole progress of the piece comes to a halt while Hines spends a bar or two or four scattering about out-of-tempo figures, with both hands plowing about the piano at high speeds. The whole is filled with cross-rhythms. His playing, in sum, is charged, powerful, rocky, and inventive.

Early critics termed Hines's playing "the trumpet style." By this they meant that his right hand was inventing the same sort of lines that a trumpet player might produce. It was generally thought that he was influenced in this by Armstrong. But, the so-called trumpet style is in evidence in the Deppe records, made when Hines had not yet heard Armstrong. Hines himself disclaims the influence, saying that the trumpet style came from his own abortive efforts to play the trumpet at the age of eight or nine. In general, it seems to me better to say that Hines developed his modified stride style from a broad experience with the older blues tradition, in which lines of melody were emphasized almost to the exclusion of harmony, and in which form played only a minimal role.

The effect of Hines's influence was to drive the older stride style farther and farther out of the mainstream. Waller, of course, remained an important presence on the jazz scene, but by the mid-1930s James P. Johnson and Willie "the Lion" Smith were recording infrequently, working mainly in obscurity. A new line of jazz pianists, stemming from Hines, was coming to the fore. The most important of these were three white players — Jess Stacy, Joe Sullivan, and Mel Powell — and a black one, Teddy Wilson.

Of this group, Wilson was certainly the most influential. He was born in Austin, Texas, in 1912. He studied piano and violin for four years at Tuskegee, and then went on to music theory at Talladega College. He came north in the late 1920s, and in the early thirties worked in Chicago with Armstrong, Noone, Erskine Tate, and others. Given these associations, it was impossible for him to escape the Hines influence, and no doubt in part it was his ability to work in the Hines manner that got him some of these jobs. In New York in 1933 he worked with the Benny Carter band, which gave him exposure to the music world, and especially to John Hammond. Two years later, at a now-famous party, he and Benny Goodman began to play together, accompanied on drums by a young amateur. The collaboration struck everybody as felicitous, and at the urging of Hammond, Goodman formed a trio, using his drummer, Gene Krupa, and Wilson. It is not true that there had never been mixed bands before. A number of light-skinned Creoles had worked as whites in the New Orleans days, and white players had at times sat in with Fletcher Henderson. Indeed, Willie Smith recalls mixed bands playing the Hudson River boats during his youth. But nobody before had attempted obvious racial mixing in major locations where attention would be attracted. Goodman was worried, and so no doubt

Teddy Wilson in 1946. One of the most influential pianists in jazz, Wilson was respected by other jazz players for his musicianship as well as for his piano style. Skippy Adelman, from Culver Pictures

was Wilson; but Hammond was persuasive, and Goodman was willing to take the risk — a rather big one, in view of the fact that his band had only just got established and he might ruin his opportunity to become a star. But apparently the public was better prepared for the experiment than people in the business suspected. There was a little sniping, to be sure, but on the whole the racial mixing was accepted, and the trio, and later other small groups, became an important element in Goodman's success.

Wilson stayed with Goodman until 1939. In the meantime Hammond was using him as musical director for a series of small band jazz records aimed at the black market. Many of these groups were backups for the records that made Billie Holiday famous. These groups included, at one time or another, nearly every important jazz musician of the day, and between them and his exposure with Goodman's trios, which reached a large white audience, Wilson became the best-known jazz pianist of the era. And thus it was he, more than Hines himself, who passed the Hines style along to the next generation of jazz pianists. His manner was much lighter and thinner than Hines's. He eschewed the broken figures and cross-rhythms that were so big an element in Hines's playing, concentrating almost entirely on developing long lines of single notes, with occasional forays into patterns of right-hand octaves. His bass, too, is simpler than Hines's, at times consisting of single notes walked up and down the keyboard.

Later on, he came under the influence of Art Tatum, and began using long right-hand runs, especially downward, in the Tatum manner. Occasionally there are traces of rhythmic stiffness in his work, but he is neither flashy nor sentimental. His is a light, direct style, and it had great appeal for other young pianists.

Oddly enough, two of the other three important pianists in this style were also associated with Benny Goodman. Jess Stacy was born in Cape Girardeau, Missouri, in 1904. He was largely self-taught, and did his first playing on the riverboats. He moved to Chicago in the 1920s at the time of the jazz boom there, and there he met the young white players of the Midwest school: Teschemacher, Pee Wee Russell, and the rest. He went to work for Benny Goodman in 1935, when Goodman was pulling together the band that was to start the swing band era, and stayed with him until 1939. (Wilson worked only in the Goodman small groups.) He subsequently played for other major leaders, including Bob Crosby, who had a dixieland-oriented band, and Tommy Dorsey. After the collapse of the big band era in the late 1940s he worked as a single on the West Coast and played infrequently after the mid-1960s. His playing was even simpler than Wilson's and was harder-swinging. Right-hand octaves, interspersed with single-note runs, predominate almost to the exclusion of chords. The driving force in his work comes particularly from a keen sense of dynamics, which rise and fall constantly as he plays, and a splitting of the beat into distinctly uneven parts so that the second note of the pair is almost swallowed up, in the manner of Coleman Hawkins.

Joe Sullivan was born in Chicago in 1906. He started classical piano lessons when he was five, and went on to the Chicago Conservatory of Music, where he studied until he was seventeen. He began working professionally at the age of twelve, and eventually, like Stacy, came to be part of the white Midwestern group. He worked with nearly all its members at one time or another and was the pianist on many of the most important records produced by this school, including McKenzie and Condon's "China Boy" and "Nobody's Sweetheart." He preceded Stacy in the Bob Crosby band and went on to work with various groups associated with Eddie Condon. Sullivan was a hard-driving player in the Hines line, and used a great many right-hand octave lines, as Hines did. He was, however, strongly influenced by Waller as well, and there is a great deal of the older stride style evident in his work. He spent the 1950s and sixties in and around San Francisco, where he played a twelve-year stand at the Hangover Club. He died in 1971.

The third pianist to make a name for himself in the Goodman band was Mel Powell, almost a generation younger than Stacy and Sullivan. Powell was born in New York City in 1923. He studied classic piano for years as a youth, and entered jazz with one of the best techniques, in the European manner, of any jazz pianist. He began working with the dixielanders associated with Eddie Condon, and then, in 1941, at the age of seventeen, joined the Benny Goodman band. During World War II he played with the famous Glenn Miller Army Air Force Band, and after the war gave up playing to study composition with Hindemith. Although he has since played jazz off and on, most of his life has been spent as a teacher and composer of European concert music, at the Yale School of Music and the California Institute of the Arts. Powell's best-known recording was a blazing fast version of "The World Is Waiting for the Sunrise," done for Commodore Records with Benny Goodman, who was listed as Shoeless John Jackson for contractual reasons. Other good examples of his work are on a series made for Vanguard in the early 1950s under his own leadership, with Ruby Braff on trumpet.

Powell's style contains all the earmarks of the Hines manner — the runs of single notes, the right-hand octaves, the tumbling cross-rhythms — but there are more remnants of the stride style in his work than in that of the other players in the Hines school. This is probably because of his superior technique, which gave him ease with complicated right-hand figures. His European training, in any case, is responsible for the fact that his runs are more evenly played than those of almost any other jazz pianist of the time.

The foregoing are, of course, only a tiny sample of the jazz pianists working before the modern jazz era, yet they are an accurate sample. For two decades, between the late 1920s and the late forties, when the bop style took over, virtually all jazz piano was played in the manner developed principally by Earl Hines from the stride style of Johnson, Smith, Waller, and the others. This was stride piano playing; no doubt of it. But it was stride colored by what Hines and others learned from the blues pianists still working in the older folk tradition. Waller and Johnson did not play the blues very often, but Hines, Wilson, Stacy, and the others did, and it crept everywhere into their playing.

Hawk and Pres:
The Saxophonists Take Over

From the beginnings of jazz, the trumpet or cornet was always the dominant instrument. Jazz "kings" were invariably cornet players: Bolden, Oliver, Keppard, Armstrong, Beiderbecke. But in the early 1930s, there arose a challenger: the saxophone, especially the tenor saxophone.

The saxophone was invented by an ambitious Belgian instrument-maker named Adolphe Sax, who was looking for a clarinet that could overblow an octave — in effect, finger the same in upper and lower registers. In 1840 he achieved this goal with an instrument that not only could finger the same from top to bottom, but could combine — he hoped — the speed of a woodwind with the carrying power of a brasswind. He eventually went on to develop a whole family of saxophones, ranging from the soprano to the double bass, which is so large that it has to be played from a high stool. Yet he did not entirely accomplish what he set out to do. The sax can indeed be played with great speed; it does not, however, sound anything like a brass instrument, but has a sound of its own — not a very good one, according to nineteenth-century musicians. It has never been accepted in symphony orchestras, and was used up until the past fifty years mainly in military bands.

Its movement into the mainstream of popular music was generated in considerable degree by the dance boom that began in 1910. W. C. Handy claims to have had a saxophone quartet in 1902, but this was almost certainly a novelty group got up for a minstrel show. Then, in 1909, he brought saxophones into his dance band — the first saxophones in an orchestra in the United States, he claims. Garvin Bushell says that the first tenor came into Springfield, Ohio, around World War I; the New Orleans player John Joseph claims to have brought the first one into his city in 1914; and Art Hickman, a popular dance band leader, was using the instrument around the same time. The saxophone, thus, was only at the very beginning stages of its development when jazz was moving out of New Orleans.

As this picture indicates, the saxophone first came onto the American musical scene as a novelty instrument played mainly in choirs as part of a vaudeville or variety show. This publicity photograph, made some time after 1910, shows a complete battery of saxophones. From left, baritone, alto, C-melody, soprano, and tenor. There are also sopranino, bass, and double-bass versions of the instrument. This was not, needless to say, a jazz band.

Leaders were drawn to it for its novelty effect — pictures of bands of the time almost always show whole batteries of saxophones of various sizes lined up in front of the orchestra, undoubtedly for show. The leaders very quickly came to see, however, that the saxophone functioned extremely well, especially when used in choirs, for dance music. In good hands — and there were admittedly few in good hands at the time — it could be played more softly and smoothly than could the brass, providing the steady flow of melody dancers wanted, and acting as an effective substitute for strings, which had hitherto been an essential part of the dance orchestra. By the close of World War I, the saxophone was a vogue instrument; people writing about "jazz" at the time constantly referred to the "throbbing" or "wailing" saxophone.

The description was too often apt. The saxophone was for the most part played very badly. It was usually taken up by clarinet players, who already knew the fingering, and in their hands it had a tendency to low. But by the early 1920s, some men were beginning to play it well. By and large these were whites. Blacks came late into the game, mainly because used saxophones were not yet showing up in secondhand stores and pawnshops with much frequency, and few blacks were able to afford new ones.

The fact that whites were ahead of blacks in adopting the saxophone had important long-term effects on jazz. Because the early black saxophonists lacked black models, they imitated the playing of whites on records. In the early 1920s, as we have seen, whites were approaching jazz somewhat differently from blacks. There were fewer of the African elements — the coarsening of tone, the seesawing accents, the departures from the ground beat. On the contrary, the white saxophonists aimed for a smooth, flexible, legato line. The jazz saxophone tradition grew out of a white concept of jazz playing, and it is no accident that the two blacks who came to dominate the instrument, Coleman Hawkins and Lester Young, both hewed closer to the ground beat than was customary among the New Orleans players.

One of the earliest and most influential of the white saxophonists was Adrian Rollini, whose instrument was a curiosity, the bass saxophone. Rollini was born in 1904 in New York. He was a highly schooled musician, who is reported to have given a Chopin recital on the piano at the Waldorf-Astoria at the age of four. By fourteen he was leading his own band, playing both piano and xylophone, another instrument that had novelty appeal at the time. He began playing the saxophone around 1920, when he was working with the California Ramblers, a group popular around the New York area, especially on Long Island, with the college crowd. He played with most of the top white leaders of his time, including Trumbauer, Nichols, and Joe Venuti. He was on a number of good Beiderbecke recordings, including "A Good Man Is Hard to Find," in which he has brief solo passages.

Rollini, because of his considerable musical training, was unquestionably one of the best saxophonists in jazz during the 1920s. His intonation was superior to that of most other saxophonists, who tended to wander all over the lot, and he played his ponderous instrument with surprising ease and lightness. If his conception was somewhat unimaginative, he often achieved a swing feeling that was ahead of that of many of his fellow whites. During the 1930s Rollini led his own bands, the best of them called Adrian Rollini and His Tap Room Gang, but he was mostly playing xylophone and vibraphone by this time. He died in 1956.

A second influential white saxophonist was Jimmy Dorsey. Dorsey played clarinet and alto saxophone. He recorded frequently with Beiderbecke and worked with the Trumbauer and Goldkette bands before teaming up with his brother, trombonist Tommy, to form the Dorsey Brothers' Band, one of the popular white dance bands of the 1930s. Jimmy, who eventually became a star leader during the swing period, was by no means a great jazz improviser, but he, like Rollini, was well equipped technically in comparison with other saxophonists of the time, and he had some reputation among musicians.

Yet another white saxophonist who helped to form the jazz style was Bud Freeman, a leading member of the white Midwestern school. Freeman, who was born in 1906, started on the C-melody sax when his friends at Austin High set about forming a band in imitation of the New Orleans Rhythm Kings. He was well behind the others, who had had some musical training as boys, but eventually he caught up. In 1925 he switched to the tenor sax, which he continued to play into the 1970s. He worked with virtually every white player of importance before the bop era and became one of the principal members of the group of dixieland players around Eddie Condon.

His style is forceful, filled with stubby notes and staccato passages. He often sounds as if he were phrasing like a brass player. His best-known records are "The Eel," a set piece for saxophone, which he wrote, made in 1933; a group of songs played with his own short-lived Summa Cum Laude Orchestra in 1939, which included remakes of a number of tunes cut by Beiderbecke and the Wolverines; and a number of Commodores, including some trios under his own name, which show him off to advantage. He alternates passages of relatively uninflected eighth notes with sudden spurts of those rough, leaping figures, often edged with a rasp. He is not, however, melodically imaginative and as a result there is a sameness to his work.

Of all the white saxophonists, unquestionably the most influential during the formative days of saxophone playing was Beiderbecke's sidekick, Frankie Trumbauer. As we have seen, Trumbauer was by no means a great jazz improviser, but he possessed a technical skill that was superior to that of any other saxophonist of his day. His playing was supple and his tone warm and perhaps too smooth in all registers. As a star soloist with Goldkette, the Beiderbecke groups, and Whiteman, he got a lot of exposure. Musicians will often admire good technicians in a way that the fan will not, because they recognize how difficult it is to do what the player is doing, and many saxophonists of the 1920s took Trumbauer for a model.

In contrast, the few black saxophonists working during the early twenties were, for the most part, bad from any viewpoint. Stump Evans, who recorded frequently in the early 1920s — he worked with Oliver for a period — lacked both skill and character on his instrument. Don Redman and Prince Robinson, who also were recording frequently, were technically somewhat better, but were unable to overcome the instrument's tendency to low. Until Hawkins began to come into his own in 1926, Sidney Bechet was the only black saxophonist of importance, and he was playing the soprano saxophone, which hardly anybody else was using.

In the early days of the saxophone, then, the whites were playing it better than the blacks, and inevitably blacks attracted to the instrument took whites for their models. Hawkins admired Rollini, even going to the point of buying a bass saxophone to play in the Henderson band, and he spoke highly of Freeman as well, though he certainly was playing better than Freeman in 1925. Lester Young modeled himself first after Jimmy Dorsey, and then after Trumbauer. These two men eventually went on to dominate saxophone playing, and carried a white saxophone tradition into jazz.

There is as yet no full-dress biography of either of these important players, and our knowledge of their lives has to be pieced together from the reminiscences of other musicians. Coleman Hawkins was born in St. Joseph, Missouri, in 1904. He began to learn the piano at five, then went on to the cello, and, at about the age of nine, the tenor saxophone, then just coming into vogue. In 1918 he was going to school in Chicago, where he was able to hear some of the early New Orleans players, especially Jimmy Noone. He spent a period of time at Washburn College in Topeka, where he studied theory and composition, and he was working in this area when, around 1922, he was asked to join blues singer Mamie Smith's Jazz Hounds. He was, at this early date, a far better schooled musician than most jazz players, many of whom could not read music, much less understand more than the rudiments of theory. The Smith group brought him to New York, where he came to the attention of Fletcher Henderson, possibly because of his musical training. Henderson began using Hawkins in his recording groups, and when the band opened at the Club Alabam, Hawkins was with it.

A decade later, when he left Henderson, he was the dominant figure on the saxophone, and one of the leading players in jazz, ranked behind Armstrong with only two or three others. In 1934, after some conversations with trumpeter June Cole, Hawkins decided to leave Henderson and go abroad, impelled in considerable part by the greater acceptance of blacks in Europe at the time. He wired a British band leader named Jack Hylton, "I am interested in coming to London," and such was his reputation that Hylton wired back a good offer the next day. A week later Hawkins left on the *Ile de France.* He stayed in Europe for five years, during which time he toured England and the continent repeatedly, and recorded frequently with European and traveling American musicians. In 1939, with war threatening, he returned to the United States.

The saxophonists he had left behind had all been working on their instruments in hopes of filling the void he had left. They were curious about how Hawkins was playing and how he would react to their increased skills. As the story goes, Hawkins spent his first days on his return going around to the New York clubs, listening to his competitors and letting the tension mount. Finally, at three o'clock one morning, carrying his saxophone, he walked into a club where Lester Young was accompanying Billie Holiday. The word went out, the place filled with other saxophonists, and eventually Hawkins walked up onto the stand and played. Whether he cut the rest or not depends on which eyewitness tells the story. Billie Holiday, who was close to Lester Young, says that Young proved superior, but Rex Stewart says no. A third witness, bassist Milt Hinton, says, "I remember the night Hawk came back from Europe. All the fellows came to play for him. He was sitting at a front table. They wanted to see how much he had improved. And finally he got up to play. Hawk was most highly respected. He seemed to be the most creative man of the era. Everybody just thought he was the top man."

The story is no doubt tinted by time, and may well be an amalgamation of several incidents. In any case, shortly afterward Hawkins asserted his dominance with a recording of "Body and Soul," one of the tiny handful of jazz records ever to become a popular hit.

He was now at the top of his powers. For a brief period in 1939 and 1940 he led a big swing band in an attempt to capitalize on the popularity of his "Body and Soul," but he worked for the rest of his life mainly with small groups featuring his own saxophone. In the early 1940s he found himself facing another challenge, this time not from his peers, but from a group of men a generation younger than he, who were turning the jazz world upside down. These were the bop players. Most of the older players, threatened by a new manner of playing they could not handle, reacted to the boppers with venom. Hawkins was one of the few who encouraged the younger men. It is hard to know exactly what his motives were, but two come to mind. For one thing, Hawkins's work had always been distinguished by an interest in harmonies, and he was better equipped than most jazz players to grasp what the boppers were doing. For another, by 1945 he had spent over twenty years in the jazz vanguard, one of the few players who always seemed to be ahead of the pack, and he hated the idea of finding himself left in the ruck.

When the first bop record was made in 1944, it was cut by Hawkins, who used some of the younger players, including Dizzy Gillespie, drummer Max Roach, and saxophonist Leo Parker, on what would otherwise have been an ordinary Hawkins record session.

But try as he might to catch up with the beboppers, Hawkins was by the late 1940s out of the vanguard and into the ruck. He was able to understand what the boppers were doing harmonically, but what they were doing rhythmically eluded him as it eluded every one of the older men. Furthermore, by this time even saxophonists not associated with the bop school, like Stan Getz, were using a light, airy style fashioned on the playing of the man who had emerged as Hawkins's chief competitor, Lester Young. Still, Hawkins continued to play exemplary jazz, mostly in the company of his contemporaries, and his reputation was such, and his following so large, that he could continue to record and to work regularly both in the United States and in Europe. But by the mid-1960s, his work had fallen off badly. He had always been a heavy drinker, and it was apparent to audiences in the last few years of his life that he had become a ruin, however monumental. The walls still stood, but the roof had fallen in. He died in 1969 of liver problems undoubtedly caused by too much Scotch whiskey.

Hawkins's work can be divided conveniently into three periods: the formative years with Henderson, during which he was playing with a coarse tone and a staccato style produced by the "slap-tongue" technique; the middle period, running from about 1930 or so until the boppers took over in 1945, in which he evolved a smoother, suppler style; and the final period, when his tone coarsened again and he began using a lot of harsh, jagged phrases. Hawkins's importance to jazz through the first two periods, when he was in the van, lies in his harmonic approach to improvising. In the pioneer days of jazz in New Orleans and Chicago, players tended to improvise from a melody or set figure. Armstrong, for example, would, while improvising, have the song's melody firmly in mind all along the way, and he would improvise by adding to it notes or phrases that his ear told him were part of the harmonic underpinning of the song at any given moment. To be sure, some of the early jazzmen, especially the pianists, had a better understanding of harmony. But a great many of them had less, which is why so many of the tunes these men played were based on a half-dozen set of chord changes, especially the ones best known as "Ja-Da," "Ballin' the Jack," "Sister Kate," and of course the blues.

Hawkins had another approach. We are not sure what he studied at Washburn College, but we can assume that it included voice-leading and chord movement. He began quite early to use the chords, rather than the melody, as the basis of improvisation. Rex Stewart, in *Jazz Masters of the Thirties,* suggests that Art Tatum may have been responsible for this. Tatum was an extraordinary jazz pianist who had a major influence on jazz playing. He characteristically changed the basic harmonies of the songs he was playing, modulating into distant keys for short periods, inserting passing chords, and using other chord substitions freely. Some time in 1926 or 1927 a group of Henderson's men went to hear Tatum, still only a teen-ager, in a club in Toledo. Stewart says, "The experience was almost traumatic for me, and for a brief spell afterward, I toyed with the idea of returning to school . . . Coleman Hawkins was so taken by Tatum's playing that he immediately started creating another style for himself, based on what he'd heard Tatum play that night — and forever dropped his slap-tongue style."

However Hawkins came by this model, it became the heart of his style. It is too much to say that Hawkins invented playing against the chords; other jazz musicians before him, especially pianists, had done it. But Hawkins explored the chord structure of a song more thoroughly than had most previous improvisers, and he acquired whole schools of followers. Abandoning the melody at the outset, he would think in terms of the implications of each chord as it came along, and of what he could do with it. This freed him of total dependence on his ear and allowed him to add notes to chords or alter them by following standard rules of harmony. It also permitted him to make substitutions, using a slightly different chord from the customary one at a given point, and especially to fit passing chords into the junctures between the one chord and the next.

It will help the reader to understand that a chord can be expressed as a group of notes played simultaneously or played one after another in any sequence. A C⁷ chord moving to an F gives the same effect when played as a melody as when played *en bloc.* There is an elaborate theory saying which notes can be added or omitted from a chord in given circumstances, which chords follow naturally from one another, and which can be used as steppingstones between distant chords. When Hawkins approached a song, he was not essentially trying to make handsome melodies couched in jazz rhythms; he was, rather, setting out to explore the possibilities inherent in this particular set of chord changes: What could he add to each chord? How could he alter any of them? What new chords could he insert into the harmonic framework without doing it damage? He later said, "I had studied music so long and completely — not just the horn — but composition, arranging and all that . . . A lot of people didn't know about flatted fifths and augmented changes and they thought that to go to a D-flat chord you had to go from an A-flat seventh — where I might go from a D-ninth. Of course that sort of thing is extremely common now, but it certainly wasn't before I did 'Body and Soul.' "

This approach explains why Hawkins produced fewer of those little melodic gems we have come to expect of the master improviser than did any other great jazz musician. He was using the notes he played not to make melody, but to express a given chord. It was more important to him that he include all of a certain group of notes in a given measure than it was to turn a striking phrase. The approach is also responsible for Hawkins's endless fertility; that sense, as has been said, that "he just keeps on coming." Hawkins had so much that he wanted to say harmonically that he was always pressed to cram it all in. There are never pauses, open spaces in his solos; he has too much to get done to let time waste, and this sense of hurry, of rush, is one of the important characteristics of his style: his music always seems to be charging forward, strong and muscular.

Hawkins's first records were made with Henderson in 1923, but these were mostly on bass saxophone and are of little jazz interest. But by 1926 the heavy plunging style is already in evidence, in, for example, "Stockholm Stomp" and "Fidgety Feet." His tone is coarse and his playing is filled with power, an express train of melody. But gradually, as he matured, his tone became smoother and a little lighter, although still heavy in comparison with that of anybody else playing his instrument. Characteristically, he was playing descending figures, usually so filled with triplets and out-of-tempo passages that at times he was approaching the extended figure Armstrong made so much of. Typical is his chorus on "Dee Blues," made with a group from the Henderson band called the Chocolate Dandies, under the leadership of Benny Carter. His opening figure on his solo is a big, ponderous phrase, heavy as a breaker crashing on a shore, but the tone itself is smoother than it had been hitherto. These characteristics are evident also in "One Hour," a moody piece made with the Mound City Blue Blowers, an odd pickup group led by a white singer and comb player named Red McKenzie and including Pee Wee Russell and some others of the Midwest school. The sense of power remains, but the percussive hammering of the early records is gone, and his approach is almost entirely legato. Movement is nearly continuous. The record captured the attention of the jazz world not only because of what it suggested about playing off the harmonies, but because Hawkins's busy yet soft-spoken and somewhat breathless conception showed a new approach to the ballad not only for saxophones, but for horns in general.

There remains, however, a major weakness, stemming from Hawkins's overriding concern with harmony, and that is a certain incoherence; there is no sense of dramatic progress in most of his work at this time. But by 1933, when he was about to leave the Henderson band, this problem was disappearing. "Jamaica Shout," made with a small group drawn from the Henderson band, contains a better-organized solo than he usually constructed, and "Lost in a Fog," another moody work on the order of "One Hour," made as a duet with a piano player, shows him constantly returning to the main theme, which helps give the chorus a design.

When Hawkins left for Europe in 1934 he was a leading figure in jazz, and he had no difficulty finding work or setting terms for his records. During the five years he was abroad he recorded with many of the finest European players. Among the best-known records are some sides he cut with Django Reinhardt and collections of French and visiting American players; for example, a pairing of "Honeysuckle Rose" and "Crazy Rhythm" made in 1937 with Reinhardt and two excellent French saxophonists, Alix Combelle and André Ekyan, as well as Benny Carter and drummer Tommy Benford. In "Crazy Rhythm" each of the four saxophonists solos, and it is clear that the Frenchmen are firmly under Hawkins's influence. Hawkins begins his own solo by taking over Combelle's opening riff and repeating it with a fervent swing that was apparently intended to show who was boss.

In 1939, on his return to New York, Hawkins made "Body and Soul," the record that established him in the eyes of the musicians as the most important jazz player of his day. "I'll never know why it became such a classic," he said later. "I was just making the notes all the way and I wasn't making a melody. I just played it like I play everything else."

This was of course true. But "Body and Soul" was exactly the sort of vehicle that suited Hawkins. Its harmony is more varied than most popular songs, with three modulations, including one into a minor key, and this, of course, would have sparked his interest. Hawkins turned it into an exercise in chromatic passing chords. Aside from a brief piano introduction, it is one long saxophone solo lasting two complete choruses of the song. His approach is tender; his tone is warm and relatively smooth; his terminal vibrato a trifle tremulous; and he holds to a narrow dynamic compass, rarely raising his voice, which creates a quiet mood with suggestions of emotion restrained. He opens with about eight bars of a fairly close paraphrase of the melody, and, from this point on, tests the harmonic possibilities of the tune with long sequences of sixteenth notes, which of course imply a doubling of the tempo. Hardly ever does he pause; let him approach a natural resting spot, and he barely touches down before he is off again on his endless explorations. Finally, in the last eight bars, the music peaks in a few harsh, jagged phrases, and then falls again to the quiet mood and closes on a short, subdued coda. It is a marvelous jazz performance, and it is not difficult to understand why it was a popular success. Throughout, Hawkins sustains a mood of restrained emotion that is at once tender and suggestive of pent-up passion. It was ideal for dancing to in a darkened living room.

From 1939 until he began to change his style once more in response to the bop challenge, Hawkins made the body of records on which his reputation will finally stand. Some of these were made with his short-lived big band, but most were made with small pickup groups for a wide variety of labels. To single out any for analysis is difficult. There was a session with Roy Eldridge and Teddy Wilson that includes a superb version of "I Only Have Eyes for You." There were various all-star sessions with Tatum, Buck Clayton, Sid Catlett, and virtually all the major figures in jazz of the time. But two records that stand out are "I Can't Believe That You're in Love with Me" and "The Man I Love." The former is a relatively simple tune, but it has an extremely logical chord structure. Hawkins was fond of it; he recorded it several times. The record consists chiefly of solos by Hawkins, Benny Carter, and Roy Eldridge, one of Eldridge's finest. Hawkins's affection for the tune is apparent. His opening chorus is a fairly straightforward statement of the theme, but played with such force and propulsion that it hardly matters what the notes are. Here Hawkins is playing more long notes than he customarily does, and we can hear an important characteristic of his work, one that is relatively rare in jazz. That is a tendency to phrase close to the bar lines, often attacking a figure at the first beat of a measure — usually fractionally ahead of it — where Eldridge, in his chorus, more frequently leaves the first beat open and begins his figures at the third beat, as had come to be the usual jazz practice. Another characteristic of Hawkins's playing evident in this solo is his system of dividing pairs of notes on a beat into markedly unequal pieces, so that the first pair of notes is considerably longer than the second. Here, too, are those swallowed notes that are barely audible, if they can be heard at all. This effect can be noticed especially in two or three spots in the bridge of his second chorus.

Few jazz musicians divide beats quite as unequally as Hawkins does, and it is this device, perhaps more than anything else, that makes his line seem to press forward so relentlessly. It is abundantly clear on his masterwork, "The Man I Love," made with Shelley Manne on drums, Eddie Heywood on piano, and Oscar Pettiford on bass. The record opens with two choruses of piano solo, shared with the bass, and then Hawkins takes over for the final two choruses. The song was again one to appeal to Hawkins. Its chord structure is logical and a relatively rare one among popular songs, and the bridge modulates into the relative minor. As played in "long meter" by jazz musicians, it is sixty-four bars long, which allows an expansive player like Hawkins room to work out the possibilities. The line keeps moving forward, with a steady rising and falling of the dynamic level. As he often does, he works with sequences of four notes laid over two beats. These are not, of course, simply rows of eighth notes. Hawkins accents the first of the four, again placing it just fractionally ahead of the beat. The third note, also falling at a downbeat, is accented somewhat also, with the second and fourth being played shorter and without accent, and sometimes doing their disappearing act. Less frequently he joins the last two notes into one quarter note, which he accents, so that the first pair acts as a sort of pickup to the quarter note that follows. Here again the second of the three notes is touched only lightly; the pattern is very similar to the ride beat, which became standard practice for drummers. "The Man I Love" is a superb jazz performance and a remarkable demonstration of both Hawkins's harmonic skills and his powerful rhythmic drive. There is that incessant forward movement, that massive sound, and the virtuoso handling of chords. Hawkins's major weakness, the absence of formal structure, of dramatic line, is here, too; but the consistency of his conception makes up for this lack in good measure.

From about this point onward Hawkins's recorded work becomes increasingly characterized by a roughness of texture and, in many instances, elements of disorder. He seems to be pressing under the challenge of the new competition, and his work is no longer of a consistently high order. But he had already accomplished something not more than one or two other jazz musicians have achieved. For two decades he had dominated the jazz world on his instrument, and for four decades he had produced superior jazz, steadily learning and changing all the while. In an art form where so many

Coleman Hawkins, another of jazz's durable figures, managed for fifty years to run at the front of the pack. Even late in life, as a bearded patriarch, he impressed younger players with his force and inventiveness. New York Public Library

people are burned out at thirty and dead at thirty-five, this by itself is remarkable. Hawkins's records stand as one of the great bodies of work in jazz, and an endless source of delight.

When Coleman Hawkins left the Fletcher Henderson band in 1934, Henderson immediately began casting about for a replacement. It is vastly to his credit, and indicative of his perspicacity, that the man he chose to replace his star went on to have as important and influential a career as Hawkins had. This was, of course, Lester Young. But at the time it did not seem as if it would work out that way, for the men in Henderson's band hated the way Young played. Where Hawk's tone was heavy and full, Young's was light, sometimes in the higher registers sounding like a clarinet. Where Hawkins's line was at times Byzantine, Young's was straightforward. Where Hawkins thought harmonically, Young thought melodically. Where Hawkins was powerful, Young was airy and graceful. The men in the band kept urging Young to get heavier reeds, to develop a bigger sound. Leora Henderson, Fletcher's wife, even took Young aside and made him listen to a lot of Hawkins's records. But Young couldn't play like Hawkins, and he finally gave up trying. And in the end Henderson succumbed to the pressure and replaced him, successively, with Chu Berry and Ben Webster, both of whom had formed their styles on Hawkins's.

Lester Willis Young was born in Woodville, Mississippi, in 1909. Shortly after, his family moved to New Orleans, and he spent his early years there at a time when Oliver was the king and Louis Armstrong was emerging as a formidable young player, but he was too young to have heard much of this music. His father, Billy Young, was a barnstorming musician who worked mainly with carnivals and tent shows. Through his adolescence Lester worked with his father, along with his brother, Lee, touring through the South and Midwest. Lester played drums at first and then took up the saxophones, first alto, then tenor, which became his principal instrument, although he occasionally played baritone and clarinet. His influences were Jimmy Dorsey and Frankie Trumbauer. He said years later, "Trumbauer was my idol. When I had just started to play, I used to buy all his records. He played the C-melody saxophone. I tried to get the sound of a C-melody on a tenor. That's why I don't sound like other people. Trumbauer always told a little story. And I liked the way he slurred notes. He'd play the melody first and then after that, he'd play around the melody." It was, of course, this attempt to emulate Trumbauer that produced the sound that made his playing unacceptable to the Henderson men.

Young's musical training was rudimentary. He depended on his excellent ear, and by the time he was eighteen he had become a competent musician. He worked for a while with Walter Page's Blue Devils, one of the sources for what was to become the Basie band, and for another period with King Oliver, in the barnstorming days when Oliver was sliding downhill. Eventually he landed with Basie, who was working out of Kansas City, and from there went on to the disastrous stint with Henderson. In time he returned to the Basie band, and he was playing with it when it was discovered by John Hammond. With Hammond behind it, the band moved out of the Midwest into national attention, just at the moment the swing band era was beginning, and went on to become one of the leading bands of the period. Young, as a consequence, had a showcase in which to display his talents, and very quickly he was recognized as one of Hawkins's principal challengers. Between 1936, when he made his first records, and 1944, when he went into the army, he created one of the three or four most influential bodies of work in jazz.

As in so many other things, Young's recording career was very different from Hawkins's. Hawkins began to record when he was nineteen years old, and he went on making records until he was over sixty. Young made virtually all of his important sides when he was between twenty-seven and thirty-five. By the time he began to record, his style was fully matured. His first records are among his finest, and there is no marked change in his playing until it began to deteriorate in the late 1940s. Those first records were made with a small group drawn from the Basie band, and included Basie, Jo Jones, bassist Walter Page, and the excellent but obscure Carl "Tatti" Smith, who might have had a successful career with Basie had he not left the band, apparently for emotional reasons. He plays an excellent muted solo on "Boogie-Woogie," one of this set of records — controlled, spare, and clean.

Because Basie was under contract elsewhere and could not use his own name, the group was billed as Jones-Smith, Incorporated. It cut four sides. Lester's solo on "Shoe Shine Swing," one of the endless variations on "I Got Rhythm" the Basie band worked from, was one that Young himself considered one of his finest. He was right. It demonstrates the keen sense of melodic form that was among his greatest assets. Most jazz players have trouble constructing a four-bar phrase with any unity of form; Lester opens his solo with an eight-bar figure that is perfectly balanced, without an excess note, and also divides itself neatly into four two-bar segments. The next portion of the solo is made up of four-bar phrases, not so neatly joined as the first eight bars; but the eight bars of the bridge of his second chorus are again all of a piece, and the last eight bars are played in one long, flowing phrase that contains both the surprises and the sense of inevitability that any sound dramatic form has. And so light is the sound that there are points in the solo that could fool the listener into thinking they were being played on a clarinet.

We can see in these cuts as well Lester's habit of playing from scales rather than chords. He tends — and of course this is only a tendency — to use notes that come from the scale of the original key, rather than to emphasize the chords as they come along by playing those notes in them that do not belong to the original scale. Particularly, he uses the ninth and sixth (technically, the thirteenth) where the New Orleans players would have used either the minor or the blue third and seventh. As we have seen, the sixth was at this time coming to replace the blue seventh in jazz, and now the ninth (the "re" of the do-re-mi scale) was replacing the blue third. In a take of "I Want a Little Girl," issued thirty years after the original came out, it is possible to hear in Lester's first chorus a sixth used to lead into the subdominant, where we would normally find the minor seventh. Minor thirds and sevenths are not, of course, in the diatonic major scale, and by substituting sixths and ninths for them, Lester produces a line that is less chromatic than that of most players of his time.

By way of explanation, let us say that the original key of the song is C. When Lester comes to an A chord, he will emphasize the A and E of this chord, which also appear in a C scale, rather than the C#, which doesn't. I do not want to make too much of this; Young, like other jazz musicians of the time, was improvising from the chord changes. But an astonishing quantity of his recorded music was played on the simplest materials

Lester Young in the classic posture, saxophone tipped to one side, eyes half-closed. William P. Gottlieb/Edward Gottlieb Collection

— the blues, variations on the "I Got Rhythm" changes, variations on the "Dickie's Dream" changes, which the Basie men used a lot. These sets of chords lend themselves to staying within a given scale, because they contain no departures into distant keys, as in "Body and Soul," the bridge to "Cherokee," and others of the type that Hawkins was so fond of. This approach prefigured the modal playing that came to prominence twenty years later.

During the second half of the 1930s John Hammond was recording for Columbia small jazz groups for the black juke box market, mostly under the leadership of Teddy Wilson, many of them featuring Billie Holiday. Lester was at this time living with Billie and her mother, apparently on a purely platonic basis. Billie had a great admiration for Lester, whom she nicknamed "Pres," as "president" of the saxophone. He often worked behind her on the Wilson records. He was a perfect foil for Billie, and his playing behind her exposes an important part of his emotional equipment, his great tenderness. He was an erratic and hidden personality, but a gentle one. This quality is evident in all of Young's playing, which is never aggressive, though it can be normally assertive. On Holiday records like "This Year's Kisses," "I'll Never Be the Same," and "If Dreams Come True," on which Young fashions a marvelous opening break, he plays with a melting tenderness that makes an ideal marriage with Holiday's own warm approach.

But though Young made many of his most enduring records with small groups, his professional life during much of this time was with the Basie band. What fame he had in his day he gained primarily as one of the featured soloists with a Basie band famous for its fine players. His solos on swing hits like "Jumpin' at the Woodside" and "Every Tub," which opens with a Lester break and solo that high school saxophonists around the United States tried to copy, gave him his basic reputation. Knowing that there are ways of varying the fingering on certain notes on the saxophone to produce slightly different sounds, Young developed a device players everywhere picked up from him and overused. He would sometimes repeat a note several times, alternating fingerings to change the quality of the note each time. He does this at the beginning of his solo on "Jumpin' at the Woodside." Of all his solos with the big band, one of the most interesting is on "Cherokee," the tune that was to become Charlie Parker's specialty. The bridge of "Cherokee" is long and harmonically more difficult than most of the bridges of the most popular songs. (As originally written, it is polytonal. Few jazzmen of the day understood this concept; most found the bridge puzzling. Eventually, Parker worked out a set of changes for it, built on the "Tea for Two" changes.) After the first two times through, the arrangement drops the bridge, presumably because the soloists were having trouble with it, although it is difficult to believe that Young could not have negotiated it. Pres's solo is therefore short, but it contains everything it needed. Gently played, it is made up of a sequence of four-bar phrases, all following logically one from another. It opens with a descending eighth-note figure. A variation of this figure appears very soon in the second half of the solo, and then is repeated to close the solo. Between the phrases, Lester leaves open spaces, sometimes a measure in length, spaces the impatient Hawkins would have filled. Taken entire, it is a masterpiece of compactness. Nothing has been left out, and there is nothing that could be removed without damage.

Yet despite the excellence of Young's work with the Basie band, his greatest playing was done with small groups. Of a fairly large number of sessions Lester made with small groups, three, in addition to the Jones-Smith sides, stand out: one made for Commodore in September of 1938, which resulted in sides issued as the Kansas City Six; another group made in December of 1943 for Keynote, an excellent short-lived jazz label, which were issued as the Lester Young Quartet; and a superlative group, made in 1940 with an augmented Benny Goodman Sextet, which were not issued until the 1970s. At each of these sessions the quality of Pres's work — and, indeed, that of the other musicians — is so consistently high that it is difficult to choose one to discuss.

On most of the Commodore sides he plays clarinet, and it is surprising how little different he sounds. The tenderness is there, the logical phrasing, and the light sound. Especially well constructed are his solos on "Pagin' the Devil" and "I Want a Little Girl," but the masterpiece of the session is "Way Down Yonder in New Orleans," on which he reverts to the saxophone. In his handling of the tune he departs to a degree from his more typical style. There are fewer open spaces; the phrases are not cut so neatly into two- and four-bar segments; and he shifts away from the bar lines more than is his usual practice. In this solo one phrase rolls out of the other, producing a more continuous line, with shifts of phrase coming at less square-cut points. The first four bars of the bridge, for example, consist of a single phrase, but the figure that closes the second half of the bridge rolls on to become the opening part of the main theme. Another characteristic of Lester's playing apparent in this solo is the constant rising and falling of the line. He runs upward, pauses, then runs down and pauses at the bottom; then he surges upward again, shifting the volume of sound to follow the shape of his line.

By the time of the Keynote session in 1943, Lester was beginning to show the first signs of a change in his playing. His tone had thickened and his lines were no longer so carefully sculpted. The rhythm section is not as good as the one drawn from the Basie band, which he had used in the Commodore session, despite the presence of Sid Catlett, the leading drummer of the period, and there are too many heavy-handed bowed bass solos by Slam

Stewart. But Young's playing is exemplary, especially on "Afternoon of a Basie-ite," where he provides a strong, rich, full-blooded solo.

His best work, though, had been done earlier. It included the curious session made with the Benny Goodman group, which was not issued at the time. The players were Goodman, bassist Artie Bernstein, and Charlie Christian, who was revolutionizing guitar playing, all from the Goodman band; and Young, trumpeter Buck Clayton, drummer Jo Jones, and Basie, from the Basie band. Despite the presence of three other superb soloists, Young dominates. He is at the height of his powers here, playing a degree more forcefully and less tenderly than on the Commodore sides, but still cutting those beautiful lines. His chorus on "I Never Knew" is especially fine. The piece is made up largely, although not wholly, of phrases five to eight bars long, all related. A beautiful opening phrase lasts five bars. It is followed by an open measure, then a two-bar fragment, the only structural lapse in the solo, leading immediately into a seven-bar figure, which, if one counts the open space at the end, covers the second eight measures of the song. The bridge is covered by two figures, divided more or less equally, the second of which rolls out into a brief phrase that is then abruptly recapitulated higher as the beginning of a five-measure phrase running out the song and is capped by a quick coda. It is a masterpiece, perhaps the finest of Lester's solos, and one of the memorable moments in jazz.

If Lester Young reminds us of anybody in jazz it is Bix Beiderbecke. There is the same delicate strength, the same attention to detail, the same concern for structure, the same ability to startle us with twists in the melody line. This should not surprise us: in the course of studying Trumbauer, Young would have heard a great deal of Beiderbecke as well. Unfortunately, Lester also suffered from some of the same emotional disabilities that struck down Beiderbecke. He found it exceedingly difficult to form enduring, responsible relationships with other people, and he became an alcoholic and an obsessive marijuana-smoker, staying high almost constantly. Given his fragile personality, it is not surprising that he began to come apart after his experiences in the army. According to one friend, quoted by Nat Hentoff in *The Jazz Makers,* Lester simply ignored a series of induction notices and was finally taken off the stand one night and drafted into the army. He was accused of possessing drugs and spent a year in the detention barracks.

Being held in any army prison is not a pleasant experience for anybody, but for a man of Young's emotional instability it must have been plain hell. After his discharge his personality had changed. Suspicious and hostile, he was smoking marijuana and drinking more than ever, and his behavior was increasingly eccentric. So was his playing. The smoky flow began to go. The open spaces became simply jagged silences, and the tender melodic line turned harsh and rusty. At times he seemed deliberately perverse, destroying his line in the process of playing it. For whatever reason, the masterly conception was going. The phrases no longer flowed logically one from another, but appeared as unrelated chunks. He still played with the old flow at times through the 1940s, but by the mid-1950s it was gone.

Complicating Lester's problem was the fact that all around him there were tenor players who were playing his style better than he was. Some of them, like Wardell Gray and Paul Quinichette, both of whom filled his spot with Basie, were so close to Young that Lester himself had trouble telling his work apart from theirs. Others, like Stan Getz and a group of white players with the Woody Herman band, were playing his style, if not note for note, at least with his general approach. Young was confused by these imitators and was unable to find a way to respond, as Hawkins did by continuing to beat the rest at his own game. In 1959, feeling ill and worn in a Paris hotel, he gave it all up and came back to New York to die. He was not yet fifty years old, but he left behind him one of the most influential bodies of work in the history of jazz.

Unlike the influence of most seminal jazz players, however, Young's was not felt until after his best playing was done. His followers were, in the main, too young to have heard him in person at his peak, in the years from 1936 to 1940. They came to know him later, through his records. During the 1930s Young was seen generally as merely one of several challengers to Hawkins's crown. The younger men of that time were all modeling themselves after Hawkins. The three most important of these players were Herschel Evans, Chu Berry, and Ben Webster. Evans, an exact contemporary of Young's, was his rival in the Basie band, with which he made most of his important records. His best-known record is "Blue and Sentimental," a slow ballad he used as a showpiece. Two fast Basie numbers, "John's Idea" and "Doggin' Around," show Evans at his best. The full-sized Hawkins tone is there and something of the power, but Evans's melodic conception is weak. The notes come scatter-shot, and there is occasionally the effect of frenzy that a jazz musician sometimes produces when he is striving for excitement but lacks the necessary ideas. Evans died of a heart attack in 1939.

Leon "Chu" Berry was born in 1910. His career parallels Evans's. He worked with a number of the early big bands, particularly the Henderson band, in which he provided the "Hawkins" sound, and spent the last four years of his life as featured soloist with the Cab Calloway orchestra. The group existed mainly to support the singing of Calloway, who had a long and successful career as a jazz-tinged popular black vocalist, but Calloway was sensitive to jazz, and his band usually contained some first-rate men. With Calloway, Berry made a showcase version of "Ghost of a Chance," which gave him some currency with the broader swing band public. During Hawkins's sojourn in Europe, Berry was considered by many critics and fans to be the leading tenor saxophonist in jazz. He won several polls in the late 1930s, and he made a number of small band recordings, some under the title of Chu Berry and His Stompy Stevedores. He was killed in an automobile accident in 1941.

Perhaps those of his records that are best known today are in a series he made for Commodore with Roy Eldridge, Hot Lips Page, a black Armstrong-derived trumpeter who was also a good jazz singer, and others. All the earmarks of the Hawkins style are here: the big tone, the legato flow, the endless cascading notes. But Berry tends to play in the upper register, where his tone thins out, and this tendency, coupled with a fast, nervous, terminal vibrato, gives his sound a somewhat querulous quality. Nor are his rhythmic variations as strong as Hawkins's. He plays pairs of notes more evenly than Hawkins does, and he maintains a relatively even dynamic level, so there is not that rising and falling of sound that is so effective in Hawkins's playing. In general, his musical lines lacked organization; he was, like Evans, sometimes incoherent. Sadly, at the end of his life his tone was becoming thicker and crustier, and the fast terminal vibrato was disappearing. He may well have been on the verge of producing much better work, but he did not live to achieve it. A good sample of his playing is "Sittin' In," made for Commodore; "Jumpin' with the Jive," made with the Calloway orchestra; and "Too Marvelous," with one of the Stompy Stevedores groups.

Of all the followers of Hawkins, the saxophonist who made the greatest mark on jazz of the time was Ben Webster. Born, like Young and Evans, in 1909, he grew up in the Midwest and worked with bands there, eventually coming to New York with Bennie Moten. He was with several of the early big bands, including Henderson's, where he, like Chu Berry, held down the Hawkins desk. In 1935 he began an intermittent association with Duke Ellington, which became permanent in 1939. He played with Ellington until 1943 and again for a short period in 1948. He toured with Jazz at the Philharmonic, a traveling jazz concert run by impressario Norman Granz, and then migrated to Europe, where he spent much of the last two decades of his life. He died in 1973.

Although his stay with Ellington amounted to a relatively small portion of his professional career, he is inextricably associated with the band. In a period when the tenor saxophone was the dominant solo voice in jazz, Ellington had not, before Webster, a strong tenor player. Webster provided that voice, and Ellington gave him a great deal of solo space. He was an important factor in making the Ellington band of the early 1940s the great musical ensemble it was. In up-tempo numbers Webster's tone was often coarse, even gutteral, and filled with trombonelike smears, but he also possessed a warm, silken, legato sound for use on ballads. Like Hawkins, he produced a full sound, and like him he crammed his solo space with notes. However, he less often approached a tune through its chord structure, favoring a more direct melodic approach. His best-known solos were, appropriately, on Ellington's most famous up-tempo numbers: "C-Jam Blues," "Perdido," "Main Stem," and "Cotton Tail," the last one perhaps his most celebrated. "A-Settin' and A-Rockin'," a medium-tempo number with an easy swing, was designed by Ellington as a Webster showcase, and he used him as well on a number of ballads, such as "What Am I Here For?" and "All Too Soon." Outside the Ellington band Webster recorded with many small groups and with Henderson; often, as his reputation grew, under his own name. Because he spent so much time in Europe he developed a large following there and is held in high regard by European jazz writers.

The movement toward the tenor saxophone as the principal jazz instrument continued to grow through the 1930s and into the forties, until saxophonists were legion. Virtually all of them, until the influence of Pres began to be felt in the early forties, were under the sway of Hawkins, playing rough, hard-driving lines made of cascades of notes. Most of them built their names as star soloists with big bands: Don Byas with Basie; Georgie Auld with Berigan, Shaw, and Goodman; Charlie Ventura with Gene Krupa; Gordon "Tex" Benecke and Abraham "Boomie" Richman with Glenn Miller; Eddie Miller with Bob Crosby. Why the saxophone came to dominate jazz playing is undoubtedly the result of a number of forces. One is the simple fact that the tenor saxophone is the easiest of all jazz instruments to learn. The beginner can produce a tone of some sort in an hour, and within a few hours can be playing elementary tunes. Brass players, faced with the difficulty of forming an embouchure, may take weeks to reach the same point, and there is no doubt that a lot of potentially good trumpet players drop out or switch to saxophones. Then, too, there was, in the big band era, more work for saxophones than for other instruments because a swing band used more of them than trumpets or trombones. But finally, I think, the reason why the saxophone so grabbed the attention of both musicians and listeners was that, more than other instruments, it captures the sound of the human voice. Warm, throaty, capable of expressive shifts of dynamics and tone colors, it often sounds like someone speaking. And, as we have seen, this vocal quality, this business of speaking your piece, of telling your story, has always been near the heart of jazz.

Whatever the reason, the trumpet was no longer king. From the arrival into prominence of Coleman Hawkins in the early 1930s until today, the most significant players in jazz have been saxophonists: Hawkins, Young, Charlie Parker, Ornette Coleman, and John Coltrane.

Duke Ellington:
Master Painter

Duke Ellington is the only jazz musician to become a public figure as an artist. To be sure, Armstrong became an international celebrity, many of the swing band leaders were widely known, and the bop players, particularly Dizzy Gillespie, had some momentary notoriety. But Armstrong and the swing band leaders were known to the public as pop musicians, or even entertainers, and the reputation of Gillespie and the beboppers rested on goatees, funny hats, and antic behavior rather than on an appreciation of their music, which was incomprehensible to most of the people who read about it in *Time*. Ellington, however, was seen, even by people who knew little about his music, as a genuine artist. He was nominated for a Pulitzer prize (although it was denied him by the governing board), and he celebrated his seventieth birthday at the White House. Louis Armstrong would never have been nominated for a Pulitzer prize, and Charlie Parker would hardly have been invited to the White House had he lived to see his hundredth birthday. This sort of attention came to Ellington, in part because he was a "composer," and composing is something done by artists, but in good measure because of the kind of man he was.

Edward Kennedy Ellington was born on April 29, 1899, in Washington, D.C. Like many of the other black men who built the big jazz bands, Ellington was a middle-class boy. His father was at first a butler, who occasionally worked at state dinners at the White House, and eventually a print-maker for the U.S. Navy. These were, of course, blue-collar jobs, but they were a measurable cut above the kinds of work most blacks did, and they permitted the Ellingtons a lifestyle that was essentially middle class. Ellington's father appears to have been a confident and easy man, a believer in good food and drink, and plenty of it. Daisy Ellington was more severe — she has been described as prim — a religious woman with strong moral convictions. Duke was raised very much as an only child — his sister, Ruth, was born when he was sixteen — and never wanted attention or material goods. He grew up in a secure and happy home, and from the start was both a talented boy and a natural leader.

Barry Ulanov, in his biography of Ellington, tells a marvelous story about Duke. Coming down in the morning, he would stop at the foot of the stairs and order the adults present to "stand over there." Then he would announce slowly, "This is the great, the grand, the magnificent Duke Ellington." He would bow. "Now applaud, applaud," he would command, and rush off to school. It takes a sure sense that one is loved to play a scene like that, and this confidence remained with Ellington all his life. He took the lead in most situations, and as an adult he became an unabashed hedonist, an eater, drinker, and admirer of women. He was extravagant in dress, always done up in garb that was both showy and debonair. His admiration for women was as great as his love of food and dress. He possessed a rich stock of flowery, even courtly compliments to bestow on pretty girls, and a large number of his compositions were inspired by the presence or memory of women.

Yet despite this assertiveness, there was a quality of aloofness in his relationships with other people. He held himself apart from most of the members of the band. He was not close to his son, Mercer, until relatively late, and as a boy Mercer felt slighted and denied. And he seems not to have formed a solid bond with any woman except his sister. He had a very strong sense that the world inside him was private, not a place to let many people enter. In a brief introduction to a book by Stanley Dance, called *The World of Duke Ellington,* he said, "Stanley is well informed about my activities and those of my associates . . . However, I am sure he has not revealed more than he ought! He and his wife Helen are the kind of people it is good to have in your corner, the kind of people you don't mind knowing your secrets." Needless to say, it is not customary to introduce a book by saying that it will be unrevealing.

Surprisingly, he was devoutly religious all his life. He claimed to have read the Bible through four times, and as he aged the intensity of his religious feeling grew until his religious music became the central concern of his life. Indeed, in later life he became something of an ascetic, giving up liquor and controlling his diet. He was, in sum, a man with a strong sense of himself and of his own value, and he had that faith in his own judgments crucial to the artist; the faith that tells him that if it feels right to him, it is right.

Just as important, he had the presence to handle the people around him. Many of the men in his orchestras became prima donnas, and the music business in which the band swam was filled with sharks, addict personalities, and not a few certifiable loonies. Ellington maintained his aplomb as he moved through this sea, never letting anybody rush him, never getting flustered, never losing his temper, his only weapon a deadpan sardonicism, which his listeners often missed. On the occasion when he was denied the Pulitzer prize he might justifiably have responded angrily, but instead he told the press, "I guess the good Lord didn't want me to become famous too young." (He was in his sixties.)

We must, then, see Ellington as a man concerned with controlling both his feelings and the circumstances of his life, and this attitude set the tone for his art. There is not in his music the high passion of Armstrong or the fervor of Bechet. Much of Ellington's writing was devoted to the exploitation of moods. He once told Richard O. Boyer, a writer for the *New Yorker,* "The memory of things gone is important to a jazz musician. Things like old folks singing in the moonlight in the back yard on a hot night or something someone said long ago." Duke Ellington did not, like most jazz musicians, create from the hot feelings of the moment, but, following Wordsworth's precept, worked from emotion recollected in tranquillity.

His character was evident in boyhood. He acquired the nickname "Duke" for his natty dressing when a youth, and both his talent and instinct for leadership were evident when he was young, too. Like many American boys of his time, he was forced to study the piano, which he did sporadically, under duress. He was more interested in painting. But as he slipped into adolescence he began to realize that there were social advantages to playing the piano and that one could make money at it as well. He began to be more serious about his piano studies, taking both private lessons and a music course at school. He began also to hang around poolrooms and bars, where the adult pianists were to be found. The time was the height of the ragtime boom. The pianists he was interested in were playing rags and popular melodies with raggy inflections. Jazz was still essentially a New Orleans phenomenon, which a youth like Ellington would not have known about. Ellington was particularly influenced by James P. Johnson, whose playing he knew through piano rolls; he learned from the roll to play Johnson's famous "Carolina Shout."

By the time he was in his late teens he was playing occasional professional jobs, sometimes with bands of his own, sometimes under other leaders. When he discovered that the big society bands advertised in the classified section of the telephone book, he took out an advertisement larger than all the rest, and it brought him work. His bands, which at times included some of the men who were with him for years, like drummer Sonny Greer, saxophonist Otto Hardwicke, and trumpeter Arthur Whetsol, usually consisted of piano, drums, one or two horns, and possibly bass or banjo. They

Opposite: Duke Ellington set himself apart from more ordinary folk with an elegant manner, a flowery speaking style, and a sure sense of his own worth. Note the extensive wardrobe, the flashy neckties. William P. Gottlieb/Edward Gottlieb Collection

were still not in any sense jazz bands; they were commercial bands that played pop tunes and rags for dancing and drinking.

In 1919 he graduated from high school, with the offer of a scholarship in art sponsored by the NAACP. But he chose music instead, and began working seriously around the Washington area. He was married in 1918, and a year later his son, Mercer, was born. Then, in 1922, he, Greer, and banjoist Elmer Snowden attacked New York. They failed to get jobs, but Duke was able to meet some of the New York pianists, especially Johnson, Fats Waller, and Willie "the Lion" Smith. They returned to Washington broke, but in 1923 came back to New York and opened at a Broadway speakeasy called the Hollywood Club, soon renamed the Kentucky Club.

Conflicting stories have been told about the organization of the band. Whatever the case, Ellington gradually assumed leadership of the band. His emergence as leader required a considerable amount of diplomacy on his part. There was no particular reason why he should have been leader. He was at this time very much an apprentice musician. His piano playing was barely adequate, and his composing skills rudimentary. The band mainly played head arrangements, which were worked out mutually in rehearsal and memorized. For the first few years in New York Ellington's leadership probably amounted to little more than making announcements and setting tempos. The bandsmen have commented that they felt it was their band, and they were proud of their roles in developing the music, although as time passed it became more and more Ellington's band.

It was still not, in 1924 and 1925, really a jazz band, but a commercial orchestra playing pop tunes and dance numbers for the speakeasy audiences. Ellington and most of the men in the group were from the East, mainly New York, Washington, and Boston. They had little experience with the black folk music tradition. They knew nothing about works songs and field hollars, and the music they heard in church was probably not much different from the hymns being sung in white churches. Indeed, these young men would not even have heard the blues until much before 1923. To be sure, they were undoubtedly closer to the stride piano school of the big-name black pianists than most whites would have been, but in the early 1920s these pianists were still basically playing ragtime, not jazz.

What turned them toward jazz was the arrival in the band of two musicians from the New Orleans tradition. The first of these was James "Bubber" Miley. Miley was born in South Carolina in 1903 and grew up in New York. His father was an amateur guitarist; his three sisters were professional singers who worked as a trio. Miley studied trombone and cornet in school, did a stint in the navy, and then began working clubs around New York. In 1921 he toured with Mamie Smith, and thus had somewhat more experience with jazz than Ellington and the Washington group. Garvin Bushell, an early clarinetist who was still working in jazz in the 1960s, has reported on the impact the New Orleans players had on Miley. He and Bubber were touring with Mamie Smith. In 1921 they heard King Oliver's Creole Jazz Band at the Dreamland Cafe in Chicago. (This was before Armstrong was in the band.) Bushell says, "I was very much impressed with their blues and their sound. The trumpets and clarinets in the East had a better 'legitimate' quality, but their [the Oliver men] sound touched you more. It was less cultivated but more expressive of how the people felt. Bubber and I sat there with our mouths open."

After this experience Miley learned to play the blue notes, and to growl and use mutes after the manner of Oliver. He became, in a word, a jazz player. In 1923 Miley joined the band, and he stayed with it until 1929. He died of tuberculosis in 1932.

Probably more than Ellington himself, it was Miley's "freak" trumpet playing that attracted attention to the records the band made in 1927 and afterward. He contributed a great deal to the band's book. It is the opinion of Gunther Schuller, who has studied Ellington extensively, that Miley was writing far better material than anybody else in the band, including Ellington. More important, it was his jazz playing that showed the band what jazz was. Ellington later said, "Our band changed its character when Bubber came in. He used to growl all night long, playing gutbucket on his horn. That was when we decided to forget all about the sweet music." Miley taught his freak effects to trombonists Charlie Irvis and to Irvis's replacement, Joseph "Tricky Sam" Nanton, and this sound became what Ellington's alter ego, Billy Strayhorn, later called "the Ellington effect."

The second major influence on the band was Sidney Bechet, who entered the band around the same time as Miley. (Ellington gives the date as 1926; Bechet 1924.) He feuded with Miley and some of the other musicians, probably because of his ego, and after a short period he quit. But from him, too, the band learned how jazz was played. Ellington has said, "I consider Bechet the foundation. His things were all soul, all from the inside. It was very, very difficult to find anyone who could really keep up with him." And he added, "Of all musicians Bechet to me was the very epitome of jazz. He presented and executed everything that had to do with the beauty of it all and everything he played in his whole life was completely original . . . He was truly a great man and no one has ever been able to play like him." In 1924 Bechet was possibly the finest jazz player alive, and he could hardly have failed to affect the men he was playing with. Not only did he teach the men something about jazz phrasing, but he had a direct effect on Johnny Hodges, who worked with Bechet in Boston and New York before joining Ellington, and went on to become Ellington's premier soloist and the finest alto saxophonist in jazz before Charlie Parker.

It was, thus, the influence of the New Orleans men — Bechet, and Oliver through Miley — that turned the band toward jazz. By 1926 it was beginning to find itself, and Ellington was emerging as a jazz writer. New York was a good place for a young jazz composer to be. Henderson was at Roseland (Don Redman played with Ellington on a few record sessions), the Oliver band came through from time to time, and there was that parade of stride pianists working around the city. The band was acquiring a sound, and by 1926 it was good enough to impress a music publisher and band booker named Irving Mills, who happened to hear it at the Kentucky Club. Not long afterward, he and Ellington formed a corporation in which each held a 45 percent interest, with the remaining shares in the hands of a lawyer.

A lot of questions have been asked about Mills's role in the life of the band. It has been claimed that the band made Mills rich, and unquestionably it helped to make him a force in the music business. He was not above putting his name on tunes written by Ellington or the group as a whole — he is listed as co-writer of such classics as "The Mooch," "Mood Indigo," and "Rockin' in Rhythm" — but this was a relatively common practice. Ellington finally severed the relationship in 1939, and characteristically he never said publicly what made him decide to do so. If Mills had been taking 45 percent of the band's income, that might have seemed reason enough. But whatever the case, Irving Mills played an important role in getting the band established. As in the case of Joe Glaser and Armstrong, Mills had connections in the white-dominated music business that Ellington lacked. He arranged a good recording contract and in 1927 got the band into the Cotton Club, one of the big Harlem nightclubs catering to whites. Thereupon began a five-year training period that was to turn Ellington from an apprentice into the leading composer in jazz.

At the Cotton Club, besides playing for dancing, the band was expected to accompany the club's dancers and singers and to provide musical backdrops for the shows, most of them those absurd erotic "jungle" sketches. As a consequence, Ellington had to produce a steady stream of arrangements of a wide variety of music although he did not write all of the show music himself. By a lucky accident — or perhaps it was Mills's astuteness — the growl effect, which had already become an important part of the band's sound, lent itself to the jungle motif, and when Miley left the band, Ellington saw to it that his replacement, Cootie Williams, learned his role. As leader of the house band in one of New York's most important nightclubs, Ellington acquired a position in New York's entertainment world, and it may have been this that gained him introductions to two people who were to be important to his development. One of these was Will Vodery, a band leader and schooled musician who, like many blacks of the 1910s and 1920s, was leading showcase bands in important white ballrooms. Vodery showed Ellington some things about voice-leading that improved his ability to handle instrumental choirs. Perhaps a more important influence was Will

Marion Cook, the black composer who had first taken Bechet to Europe.
Ellington said:

> "Will never wore a hat and when people asked him why, he'd say
> because he didn't have the money to buy one. They'd give him five
> dollars and then he and I would get in a taxi and ride around Central
> Park and he'd give me lectures in music. I'd sing a melody in its
> simplest form and he'd stop me and say, "Reverse your figures." He
> was a brief but strong influence. His language had to be pretty straight
> for me to know what he was talking about. Some of the things he used
> to tell me I never got a chance to use until years later, when I wrote
> the tone poem, "Black, Brown, and Beige."

It is apparent that Cook was teaching Ellington some of the fundamentals
of melody-writing, the common devices a conservatory student learns as a
matter of course. These include playing a melody upside down, or backward,
repeating it lower or higher, turning it inside out, and so forth. As we shall see
when we come to consider Ellington's music, he made frequent use of these
devices in adapting to his purposes the themes he found around him.

The Cotton Club was, despite its drawbacks, a marvelous training school
for the band. Regular playing, a lot of rehearsal time to prepare the endless
stream of new pieces, relatively fixed personnel, all helped to weld the band
into a well-coordinated unit. Ellington was now unquestionably the leader.
Compositions still continued to develop from suggestions of the men at
rehearsals, but Ellington was writing a great deal of the basic material
himself. The habit the men had of suggesting changes or additions to
arrangements had led him to the practice of writing for specific members
of the band. That is, Ellington did not simply score a part for a trumpet;
the part was for the specific trumpet player whose sound he wanted at a
given moment. At times he would take a part from one man and give it to
another to get exactly the sound he wanted. And more and more he was
coming to know what he wanted. During the Cotton Club years he recorded
some of his most enduring work: "The Mooch," "Rockin' in Rhythm,"
"Mood Indigo," "It Don't Mean a Thing If It Ain't Got That Swing,"
"Creole Rhapsody," "Flaming Youth," "Creole Love Call" and dozens
more or less well known but equally good.

By 1932, however, Ellington was getting fed up with the music business,
especially with the Cotton Club. So when the opportunity arose in 1933 for
an English tour, he jumped at it. And when he arrived in London he was
startled to discover that he was known there as more than a popular band
leader; he was considered an important composer and a significant figure
in a new music. They regarded "Creole Rhapsody," an extended Ellington
piece that covered both sides of a record, as the first real jazz "composi-

tion," and felt that it was the bellwether, showing the direction jazz would take. Patrick "Spike" Hughes, a composer and critic, and Constant Lambert, a classical composer, were fervent proselytizers for Ellington's music. As Ellington discovered, to his astonishment, these men and people like them were writing pieces about him in slick-paper magazines.

The tour was a success, and, of greater moment, it left Ellington with the sense that his music had importance beyond the Cotton Club. Ellington, of course, had always taken his music seriously in the sense that any professional concerned with his career and the opinion of fellow professionals takes his work seriously. But now he was on notice that it had a broader significance, and he was encouraged to think more carefully about his artistic goals. The result of this new view of himself was a long-term movement toward the writing of longer pieces meant for concert hall presentation. Ironically, the first of these works, "Reminiscing in Tempo," which occupied four sides, was disliked by the very English gents he had thought would most appreciate it. They found it pretentious and somewhat weak in jazz spirit. Ellington did not attempt another extended piece for some time afterward.

He was, in any case, busy in other directions. The swing band era opened in 1935 with the sudden rise in popularity of the Benny Goodman band. The Ellington band never achieved the celebrity of the top white groups, in part because it had some trouble getting booked in the top rooms, in part because it played far fewer pop tunes than the others, and in part because the texture of the music was thicker than what pop fans were accustomed to. Nonetheless, throughout the swing period it remained one of the top dozen or so of the swing bands.

Then, in 1939, came changes that would leave their mark. The partnership with Irving Mills was dissolved; the band left Columbia for RCA-Victor; Ben Webster joined the band to provide the strong tenor saxophone soloist Ellington had lacked; and a bassist who was to prove of major influence, Jimmy Blanton, also joined. Blanton, whom Duke first heard in St. Louis, was so superior to any other jazz bassist of the day that Ellington hired him and for a time carried two basses.

Blanton was born in 1921 and worked around St. Louis until 1939, when Duke hired him. Before him, bassists generally "walked the chords," that is, moved up and down the chords as they came along, one note to a beat. Blanton, however, was playing his instrument as if it were a horn, interpolating fast passages of eighth notes and running scales, or more varied melody lines, behind the band. Furthermore, his tone had a light clarity that few previous bassists got, and his time was impeccable. He turned bass playing around, laying the foundations for what came to be bop bass playing, and he was a chief contributor to the success of the Ellington band of the time. Unhappily, he suffered from tuberculosis. He left Ellington in 1941 and died the next year. His best-known record is Ellington's "Jack the Bear," on which he is featured.

Ellington's band of the 1940s has often been billed as the greatest of his groups, especially in the liner notes on Victor records, which recorded the band during this period. It is a questionable judgment. The music produced by the Cotton Club group in the early 1930s was fresh and imaginative and certainly innovative. Yet the later orchestra possessed a group of soloists superior to any but those of the Basie band, and the addition of Blanton, and, later, of Oscar Pettiford, sharpened considerably Ellington's previously rather dogged rhythm section. Moreover, Ellington, with fifteen years of writing experience behind him, was at the height of his powers.

But this was the peak. In the late forties there began a deterioration in the quality of the band. Hodges, Cootie Williams, and Rex Stewart left; Joe Nanton died; and there followed a series of personnel changes, in which men left the band in the middle of a job or even in the middle of a number. Also, the band had grown larger; at one point Ellington had a brass section of six trumpets and four trombones. Elephantine bands were modish during this period. The justification was that the advanced chords being used required larger sections to play them, which was true. But a large section is inevitably less flexible, less capable of rhythmic subtleties, than a small one.

Ellington himself was growing more and more preoccupied with the concert pieces foreshadowed by "Creole Rhapsody" and "Reminiscing in Tempo." He wrote a number of suites of various sorts, and three full-dress "sacred concerts." These pieces were at least partly out of the jazz tradition, and at times called for "legitimate" rather than jazz playing. Duke answered critics by saying that he was not writing jazz at all, but "black folk music," although in truth the jazz he had always written was closer to the black folk tradition than his concert pieces, which were derivative of European music. Then, at the 1956 Newport Jazz Festival, Paul Gonsalves, tenor soloist with the band, played a long, fervid solo on "Diminuendo and Crescendo in Blue" that left the audiences roaring. Suddenly the band was in the news again: Ellington even made the cover of *Time.* Over the next few years some of the older stars who had helped to establish the band began to return. Hodges came back, then Cootie Williams, and in Quentin Jackson Duke found a trombonist to fill Nanton's chair. It was now, in fact, a band of old gentlemen. By the time of the "Second Sacred Concert" in 1968, Ellington was sixty-eight, Harry Carney was fifty-eight, Hodges was sixty-three, Williams and Russell Procope each was fifty-nine, and Lawrence Brown was sixty-two. But although neither Ellington nor the band as a whole was important in jazz innovation any longer, the band continued to play interesting and swinging jazz. When Ellington died in May of 1974 he went, like Armstrong, full of honors and still active. He stands behind only Armstrong and Charlie Parker in leaving his mark on jazz and, through it, on all of Western music.

What, then, did Ellington's genius consist of? First, right from the beginning he possessed a keen sense of the tone palette. We must remember that Ellington had both talent and training as an artist. He himself said, "I think of music in terms of color and I like to see [coming into Pittsburgh] the flames licking yellow in the dark then push down to a kind of red glow." His instinct from the beginning was to clothe his notes in different sounds. Architecture was something he had to learn, and from the viewpoint of European concert music his forms never progressed to a very interesting level. But in the creation of sheer sound he had few peers in music of any kind. For example, in 1930, when Henderson, Redman, Bill Challis, and the rest were still writing for sections, Ellington took the simplest of melodies and voiced it for muted trumpet, muted trombone, and clarinet to make his classic "Mood Indigo." This is an unusual combination, and the problem becomes which notes to give to which instruments to make the three instruments blend into a distinct, unified sound. How, in other words, do you mix red, yellow, and white to obtain a particular shade of orange? Ellington's ability to solve this sort of problem left fellow arrangers awed.

For a second thing, Ellington had an extraordinary command of dissonance. His management of internal harmonies was such that even extremes of dissonance were never painful but had genuine musical meaning. Behind Harry Carney's bass clarinet solo in "The Saddest Tale," recorded in 1934, muted trumpets play some extremely close harmonies, which never become harsh or irritating.

This harmonic skill, combined with his instinct for the tone palette, gave him a terrible advantage over his contemporaries in writing for an orchestra. But if this were not enough, Ellington was probably the finest writer of short melody in twentieth-century America. I am speaking not just of the numberless formal songs he wrote — "In My Solitude," "I Let a Song Go Out of My Heart," "Don't Get Around Much Anymore," and so many others — but the brief snatches and fragments of melody that bob up everywhere in his compositions. An Ellington piece is afloat with little motifs, some of which are elaborated on, but many of which appear and disappear as coruscations on the surface of the music. The themes from "Jubilee Stomp," "Rockin' in Rhythm," "Blues with a Feeling," "Cotton Tail," "Old Man Blues" are as fresh and bright today as they were when he wrote them two generations ago.

It is in Ellington's mastery of melody that we can see the hand of Will Marion Cook. Cook had shown Duke some of the procedures of melody-writing — reversing the figure, turning it upside down, and so forth — and Ellington made great use of these devices. There is, for example, a

jazz cliché built around a descent from the sixth to the minor third
— that is, in the key of C, from A to E♭. This figure is derived from the
blue notes, with the sixth playing the role of the blue seventh and the minor
third that of the blue third. Ellington's "Main Stem" is built on this figure
played upside down, the motif jumping up instead of down. Or consider one
of Ellington's finest swingers, "Cotton Tail," made in 1940. The chord
sequence is "I've Got Rhythm," one widely used in jazz, and an examination of the melody shows clearly that Ellington created it by rearranging
the Gershwin melody, the outlines of which are visible behind the Duke
line. Again, the major strain of "East St. Louis Toodle-Oo" is a reworking
of "Sister Kate." "Drag," made in the 1960s, is a variation on "Ding Dong
Daddy from Dumas," which itself was a variation of "Ja-Da." "Creole Love
Call" is taken almost entirely from an Oliver number called "Camp Meeting
Blues." (Miley may have been responsible for this adaptation.) Undoubtedly, anybody who wants to can find many more examples of transforma-
tions of themes throughout Ellington's work.

This is not, certainly, to imply that Ellington was a plagiarist. The
practice of transforming melody has a long and honorable history. Ellington's use of themes he found in the music around him is no different from
the use Dvořák and the nationalist composers made of the folk melodies
they found in their cultures. It is what Ellington did with the materials he
found to hand that mattered. Oliver's "Camp Meeting Blues" is forgotten
today, except by Oliver specialists, but "Creole Love Call" is still being
played.

A fourth important aspect of Ellington's work, which was much commented upon by the musically educated people who began to admire him
early, was his effort to break out of the four-square mold of eight-, twelve-,
sixteen-, and thirty-two-bar forms in which virtually all jazz — indeed, all
popular music — was played. "Baby, When You Ain't There," which was
recorded in 1932, is primarily a blues, but it begins and ends with a twenty-
bar segment created by a stretching out of the blues a few bars longer than
is customary. "East St. Louis Toodle-Oo" includes eighteen-bar segments
among the eight- and sixteen-bar pieces. "Birmingham Breakdown" is built
on a twenty-bar theme. The examples are numerous, and so neatly does
Ellington bind the parts together that even few musicians noticed at first
that he was departing from the standard forms, and he had hardly any
imitators in this practice for a decade.

As important as these skills was his ability to find and develop the
instrumentalists who could array his music in the sounds he wanted. He was
always very conscious of the differences in sounds from one trumpet or
saxophone player to the next, differences the audience might not notice; and
rather than bringing into the band men who adhered to a common sound, as
most leaders did, he deliberately sought out men who produced a sound dif-

ferent from what he already had. For example, the trombonists in his classic 1940s band, Joe Nanton, Juan Tizol, and Lawrence Brown, played so differently that they might as well have been using different instruments. Thus, we cannot think about Ellington without considering his players as well.

Five of them stand out: trumpeter Cootie Williams, cornetist Rex Stewart, baritone saxophonist Harry Carney, altoist Johnny Hodges, and clarinetist Barney Bigard. Carney was the first of them to arrive in the band, and he stayed with it for nearly fifty years, dying a few months after Duke died. He was born and raised in Boston, where he knew both Hodges and Charlie Holmes. His parents were not particularly musical, but they had ambitions for their children, and Carney started studying the piano at six and worked at it for another six years or so. This was, of course, classical music; like Ellington and the others, he was not raised in the black folk tradition and had to learn his jazz. His father, he says, liked opera and "the spirituals," but these were almost certainly the Europeanized spirituals of the Fisk Jubilee Singers and other groups; the musical tradition in the Carney home was European. At twelve he began on clarinet, and, probably because of his long piano training, very quickly was able to get work. He added the alto saxophone, and by the time he was seventeen he was working in New York. Shortly afterward he joined Ellington.

His early influences on clarinet were Don Murray and Buster Bailey, not surprisingly the featured clarinetists with the Goldkette and Henderson bands. When, eventually, he made the baritone his principal instrument, he emulated Hawkins, and, for lower-register playing, Adrian Rollini. He cut hundreds of solos with Ellington in a strong, hard, swinging style that was not terribly imaginative, but his main importance to the band lay in the underpinning he gave the saxophone section. It has often been said that "he swung the whole band," and it is certainly true that he provided a drive that might otherwise have been lacking. Carney in time became one of the few men Ellington was close to. He drove the car for Ellington between one-nighters, and he ran the band on the stand in Ellington's absence.

Another Ellington long-termer was clarinetist Barney Bigard, who was in the band from 1927 until 1942. A New Orleans Creole, Bigard was born in 1906 and studied with Lorenzo Tio. He played with various of the better-known New Orleans leaders; then came to Chicago, where he joined Oliver in 1924. He gigged around the Midwest, touring elsewhere intermittently, and then in 1927 went into the Ellington band, one of the New Orleans men who were helping to shape the orchestra. After he left Ellington, he led his own band on Fifty-second Street. Later he worked with Armstrong's All-Stars and various other groups in the dixieland mode. He was still active in the 1970s.

Like that of the other Creole clarinetists, Bigard's style is characterized by a liquid tone and an easy manner. He is particularly fond of long, swooping runs, which reach from top to bottom and then return, something also found in the playing of Creoles like Noone and Simeon. His best-known records, probably, are Ellington's "Mood Indigo," on which he takes a solo that has since become a standard, and "Clarinet Lament," which was written for him by Ellington and recorded in 1936. This was the first jazz piece conceived of as a concerto for a single soloist, and led to similar ones for other members of the orchestra.

Charles "Cootie" Williams, who replaced Bubber Miley in 1929, was, unlike most of the men in the Ellington band, from the South, and had firsthand experience with the black tradition and early jazz. He was born and raised in Mobile, Alabama, about 150 miles from New Orleans, close enough so that the New Orleans influence percolated through. Touring New Orleans musicians, among them Jelly Roll Morton, often played in Mobile. Williams was born in 1910, and during his youth would have been exposed to blues, early jazz playing, ragtime, and church music.

He began on drums at five, then switched to trombone, tuba, and finally trumpet. His father started him studying privately, and pushed him to keep it up. He studied for eight years, developing a sound technique and good reading ability. At fourteen he spent a summer touring with the family band led by Lester Young's father; at sixteen he was working regularly around Mobile; and at eighteen he was in New York, where he became friendly with Armstrong and fell under his influence. He was not, at this point, playing with the mutes and growls that were to become his trademark. He had a strong, clean sound, and a good ability to read, and he became first trumpet in the Henderson band.

Then, in 1929, Bubber left Ellington, and Duke offered the job to Cootie. Williams was torn. Henderson's was the leading band of the time, but Ellington was clearly a comer — and Williams made the decision to go with him. He learned his growl by watching Nanton, who had himself learned it from Miley, and for over a decade provided a good deal of "the Ellington effect," becoming something of a star player. Then, in 1940, much to the horror of Ellington fans, he left Duke to go with the Benny Goodman band. "But that Goodman band — I loved it. It had a beat, and there was something there that I wanted to play with . . . I think I was happier in music the first year I was with him than I ever was." It is particularly in the sextet that Williams got a chance to shine. Probably his best-known record is "Concerto for Cootie," a piece written for him by Ellington in 1940, which was later transformed into a hit song, "Do Nothin' Till You Hear from Me." It shows Williams both as a growl trumpeter and a powerful open player somewhat in the Armstrong vein, but it offers him little chance for extensive improvisation. This record has been analyzed extensively by André Hodier in *Jazz: Its Evolution and Essence.* More typical was his work on "In a Mellotone," in which he not only plays a growl chorus, but holds a fine musical conversation with the saxophones. Among the records made with Goodman, "Breakfast Feud," with the sextet, shows him to good advantage. For a period in the 1940s Williams led a big band and then a series of small groups. He returned to Ellington in 1962, and remained in the band into the 1970s.

The other of Ellington's trumpet players to establish himself as a star was Rex Stewart. Stewart possessed a good open sound, but, even more than Williams, he was a "freak" specialist. Stewart was born in Philadelphia in 1907 and was seven when his family moved to Washington. His father played the violin, his mother the piano, and Stewart was trained on both instruments as a boy. He switched to the cornet and by the age of fourteen was gigging around the Washington area. What he played was not primarily jazz, but dance and novelty music. He reached New York in 1923, worked for Elmer Snowden, the ex-Ellingtonian, and finally got a job with Fletcher

Johnny Hodges, known as Jeep or Rabbit, in a picture made in the 1940s. William P. Gottlieb/Edward Gottlieb Collection

Henderson, where he established himself as an important soloist. For the next few years he worked off and on with Henderson, McKinney's Cotton Pickers, and the Luis Russell band, in the process playing with most of the important black jazz musicians of the time. He landed with Ellington in 1934 and stayed with the band until 1943. Thereafter he spent most of his playing time on casual gigs, mainly with bands of his own, in the United States and Europe. He died in 1967 of a brain hemorrhage.

Stewart was an oddity among musicians in that he had ambitions to write prose. His articles appeared in *Down Beat, Melody Maker,* and other periodicals, and he was the author of *Jazz Masters of the Thirties,* one in a series of books edited by Martin Williams. He acted as disc jockey on small radio stations; he appeared in three movies; and he organized a great many bands of one kind or another.

Stewart had a wider repertory of sounds than any other musician in jazz. He used a straight mute frequently, which gave him a wry, pinched sound, but he also used some of the plunger mutes and growls, which he had learned about from Bubber Miley. He was perhaps best known for his expertise in half-valving. This was not the occasional half-valving that most trumpet players used to inflect notes here and there, but a system in which all of the notes would be half-valved, thus giving the entire solo a unique nasal quality. His best-known record, "Boy Meets Horn," which he made with Ellington in 1937 and later with a small group, features him employing this device. He also developed a system for growling with pedal tones, which he used to produce respectable lion noises in the introduction to "Menelik (the Lion of Judah)." His open playing tends sometimes to short, stubby notes. Good samples of his work are on "Subtle Slough," which he recorded several times with Ellington, and "Linger Awhile," made with a small group, with characteristic half-valved and straight-mute solos. An excellent sample of his open work is on a record made in Paris in 1939, with Django Reinhardt, called at different times "Finesse" and "Night Wind."

Of all of Ellington's men certainly the most celebrated both by the public and his fellow jazz musicians was Johnny Hodges. He was born in Boston in 1906. His mother played a little piano, but his family was not especially interested in music, and Hodges never studied formally. Like the New Orleans players, he was largely self-taught, first on drums and piano, then soprano and finally alto saxophone. When he was thirteen years old he met Bechet, who was working in Boston in a variety show, and he continued to be influenced by Bechet for a long period. He began finding gigs around Boston, and then, when he was about fifteen or sixteen, started traveling to New York on weekends for gigs. In 1924 he ran into Bechet again, and worked with him in a New York club Bechet owned for a brief period. He learned Bechet's style and would play his introductions and choruses when Bechet was absent.

When the Bechet job ended he continued to gig around New York until 1928, when he joined Ellington for a stay that lasted until 1951. Hodges possessed a smooth, flowing sound that contrasted well with the growls and nasal tones in the brass. By the early 1930s Hodges was recognized as pre-eminent on his instrument, and he almost always came in first on his instrument in jazz polls until Charlie Parker and the boppers took the game away. He also continued to play the soprano saxophone off and on until about 1940, both soloing with it, and at times leading the saxophone section with it. He was, after Bechet, the only soprano saxophonist of importance in jazz until the postbop era. But it was the alto that made his name.

He left Ellington in 1951 to form a band of his own. It had some measure of success, especially with a juke box hit called "Castle Rock." But he never achieved real prominence as a leader, and in 1955 he went back into the Ellington band, where he remained for the rest of his life. He died of a heart attack in 1970.

The best known of his records are probably "Never No Lament," a set piece, written for him by Duke, which became a hit as "Don't Get Around Much Anymore," and "Warm Valley," another piece on which Ellington featured him. On slower pieces like these he plays with a sound like poured honey. Nobody in jazz ever played with quite the sensuousness of Hodges, as a listening to "Warm Valley" will prove. The title has erotic overtones, and Hodges's playing, despite the seamless sound, is filled with warmth and sexuality.

On fast numbers the fluidity was still there, but so was an immense swing. One of his best is on "Main Stem," a single chorus of blues over which he throws three looping figures outfitted with the filigree he liked. Hodges tended to let his dynamic level rise and fall with the melody line, making the music come and go, and this characteristic is evident here. He has a tendency, also, to divide beats, as Hawkins does, into distinctly unequal parts, and this is one reason for the endless swing that infects his solos.

Over the years a large number of records were made by small groups drawn from the Ellington band, usually featuring one or another of the Ellington soloists. Hodges was at home in this kind of setting, where his ability to swing is given room. "Rendezvous with Rhythm" contains a marvelous example of this style, sure and firm but always riding easily over the beat. Another record made with a small group is "Jeep's Blues," on which he plays soprano. The influence of Bechet is clear here, especially in the hanging blue thirds in his opening chorus. Another fine soprano solo is on "Dear Old Southland," made in 1933 with the Cotton Club band. The influence of Bechet is pronounced, but there are the long, looping phrases of Hodges, and that management of time that make the piece swing even at a slow tempo.

A sixth member of the Ellington ensemble who played an important role in the later bands was the composer and arranger Billy Strayhorn. He was born in 1915 in Dayton, Ohio, raised in North Carolina, and eventually went to school in Pittsburgh. He was trained as a classical pianist and studied European theory. In 1938 he arranged to meet Ellington in hopes of working with him. He showed Ellington a piece called "Lush Life," and shortly afterward Ellington recorded his "Something to Live For." By 1939 Strayhorn had become a member of Ellington's musical family, filling in at piano with the orchestra occasionally, and helping Ellington with scoring and arranging. The two men established a collaboration so tight that it was difficult even for people who knew the music well to tell their work apart. Strayhorn's best-known pieces were "Take the A-Train," which became the band's theme, and "Chelsea Bridge," a moody, heavily textured piece not entirely in the jazz idiom. In later years he worked with Ellington on some of the concert pieces, including "Such Sweet Thunder" and "A Drum Is a Woman." He recorded little with the Ellington band, but there is an interesting recording of a series of duets he played with Ellington at a private party. It is difficult for the listener to tell who is playing at any given point. After his death in 1967, Ellington wrote a memorial piece for him called "His Mother Called Him Bill."

Despite the contributions made by the musicians, the Ellington band was essentially the creation of the master himself. None of his players ever had significant careers apart from him; it was he who found out what they could do and then made them do it, and his ability to do this was crucial to his accomplishment. In sum, Ellington's genius lay not in a single insight, but in a mastery of many facets of music. Selecting a few records for analysis from the hundreds Ellington made is a fruitless exercise; as Dryden said of Chaucer, ". . . here is God's plenty." But two that had impact when they were issued were the early "Black and Tan Fantasy," recorded in several versions in 1927, and "Ko-Ko," considered by many critics to be his finest accomplishment, made in 1940.

The title "Black and Tan Fantasy" signifies a racial mixture. It may have been chosen inadvertently, but it is eminently suitable because the composition mixes diverse moods. It begins with a dirgelike blues in B♭ minor, played in harmony by muted trumpet and trombone. Then follows a sixteen-bar melody in B♭ major, "pretty" and rather florid, by the alto saxophone. Next are the solos by trumpet and trombone, all muted and growly, carrying out the minor feeling of the opening strain, although this section is in fact an ordinary blues. The minor feeling is produced by a heavy use of the blue third. The importance of the blue notes is made unfortunately apparent when Ellington solos on the piano. Lacking the blue notes, the solo is glaringly out of character with the rest of the piece. The record ends with a brief quote from the famous Chopin "Funeral March."

"Black and Tan Fantasy" is a far from perfect work. The playing is sometimes amateur, the piano solo is a mistake, and the funeral march tagged onto the end is a cliché. But at the time it seemed to listeners that here was something brand-new; here was a piece of music that was true jazz set into the framework of a worked-out composition. I think that Morton's example was important in the making of this piece. Listeners sensed that behind the work was more than a skilled arranger; they were aware of the presence of an imaginative artist who knew exactly what he was about. To be sure, Bubber Miley and others in the band played important roles in forming the piece, but most record buyers did not know that. They were tipped off that members of the Ellington band, whoever they were, were special, and as the other early masterpieces appeared, they were confirmed in their belief.

"Ko-Ko," as it happens, is also a mixture, in this case one of tonalities, not of moods. It is basically a twelve-bar blues in E minor, with an excursion into the relative major — G major — after the trombone passage by Nanton. However, Ellington uses throughout certain chords, at the time advanced for jazz, which produce a good deal of ambiguity about which key is, in fact, intended. According to Edward Bonoff, a musician who has studied the piece carefully, "This piece is shot through with minor eleventh chords, rarely used in jazz in that day. This particular chord is not a true minor chord, but assumes an ambiguous function, suggesting the II minor of another key. The piece as a whole borders on modality, and as such presages a great deal that was to happen in jazz many years later, for example the modal experiments of Miles Davis in 'Kind of Blue.' " The tune itself is a revamping of a simple Kansas City riff, which Ellington quotes explicitly in the chorus played in unison by the saxophones, and appears in yet a third version behind Nanton's trombone chorus. Ellington here is making use of the lessons Will Marion Cook gave him on those taxi rides. The main point, however, is the ambiguous tonality, and this is a superb orchestral solution to the problem of blues playing. The early blues, as we have seen, resided in neither major nor minor, and Ellington has produced the same sort of ambiguity here by different means. This was not an accidental effect. Ellington said that the piece was a musical description of Congo Square, "where jazz was born." Obviously he intended to imply the older music.

But despite the critical significance of "Ko-Ko" and "Black and Tan Fantasy," it was the up-tempo swingers that audiences loved and that will no doubt be the final basis of Ellington's fame: "Take the A-Train," written by Strayhorn, with its lovely theme played in unison by the saxophones; "Things Ain't What They Used to Be," written by Mercer Ellington; "Main Stem," with the superlative Hodges solo and the Eb-A theme over a blues in C; "In a Mellotone," a reworking of "Rose Room," which contains the marvelous conversation between Cootie and the saxophones; "Cotton Tail," with the famous Ben Webster solo and penultimate chorus scored for saxophones, which prefigures Charlie Parker in some of its phrasing. These, and dozens more like them, are the heart of the matter; alive with fire and color, they constitute one of the great works of music created in this century.

This leaves us with the problem of Ellington's concert pieces. After the English journey of 1933, Ellington found himself faced with a conundrum: on the one hand, important critics took his work seriously; but when he tried to write more serious pieces, these same critics took him to task. In the end he decided to ignore the critics, and, as he aged, he turned more and more to longer pieces, most of them only partly in the jazz idiom. The best known are "Reminiscing in Tempo," "Black, Brown, and Beige," "Deep South Suite," "Liberian Suite," and the three sacred concerts. The critics called them pretentious and lacking in jazz feeling. Ellington's response was to insist that they were not jazz, that he was not a jazz composer but simply a composer of music, and that his work should be so judged. Whatever the case, they do not succeed as jazz.

What is perhaps most instructive about the story of Ellington is, once again, the matter of character. Despite his aloofness, and an arrogance that grew as he aged, Ellington was a mature, completed personality. That fact has immense importance, for he was a late starter, an artist who grew slowly, a step at a time. He did not begin to do any important work in jazz until he was twenty-eight, an age at which Armstrong was creating his most enduring masterpieces, and at which Beiderbecke was already finished. If Ellington had died as early as Beiderbecke, he would live in jazz history only as an obscure pianist who had once led a band containing Johnny Hodges. Had he died at the age Charlie Parker did, he would have been remembered as the leader of a fine band in the Henderson mode, as important in jazz history as, say, Luis Russell. Had he died at the age Fats Waller did, his most famous records never would have been made, and he would have gone down as an important jazz composer, but certainly not, as he is considered by some critics, the equal of Armstrong and Parker. But he lived. He did not get involved with drugs; he learned to control his eating and drinking; he managed his business affairs well; he kept order in his band; and he went on studying and learning and letting his art slowly mature. Beiderbecke, Armstrong, Parker, possessed far more raw talent than Ellington. But Ellington had taste, intelligence, and a nature that allowed him to select sound artistic goals and move toward them consistently. There are no long, fallow periods in Ellington's life, and few false starts. In 1926 Bix Beiderbecke was five years younger than Ellington, but nearly ten years ahead in artistry; it is stunning to think what he could have achieved had he had Ellington's character. But it was Ellington who had the character, and it counted for more than talent.

Truckin' on Down:
The Swing Band Boom

From time to time in the modern history of our culture there has grown out of a particular group of artists or manner of working a social philosophy that attracts a large number of adherents, often young. Too pervasive to be called cults, these intellectual waves are built on an antipathy to whatever is established in the social order, and call for changes in moral values, and often in the social structure as well. At bottom emotional, they usually have respectability; and invariably their followers prosyletize for some new artistic trend, often to the exclusion of any other forms.

In the nineteenth century there was, first, a tendency for these movements to coalesce around poets. Intergenerational wars were fought successively by the followers of Wordsworth, Tennyson, and Browning, each of whom began as a rebel against what had gone before but became in time an established figure, as the youthful generation that had cried him up went on to become itself the establishment. The Browning Societies that dotted the nineteenth-century social landscape seem in retrospect to be bastions of gentility, but they began as cells in a literary revolution. In the last decades of the nineteenth century and the first decades of this, the artists around whom these movements formed were often painters. It was Gauguin, Van Gogh, Picasso, and Matisse who were seen as symbols of revolt, and no doubt poor Van Gogh, who sold only two pictures in his lifetime, would be appalled today to see bad reproductions of his sunflowers in hotel rooms in Dubuque.

In more recent decades, with the democratization of "culture" that has occurred in this century, similar sociointellectual movements have grown up around forms of popular music. We have seen how the jazz boom of the 1920s was part of a broad rebellion in art, morality, and social thought. One bought jazzy records the way one read Veblen, Freud, and Hemingway, and it is no accident that the period came to be called the Jazz Age. Associated with it were certain dance forms, modes of dress, and a private language.

A similar coming together of diverse social forces took place in the 1960s, when rock music became the linchpin for a group of ideas expressed in the wearing of long hair, certain dance forms, a oneness with nature, drugs, pacificism, and an earnest dedication to love, all centered on the notion of total freedom for all. I have no doubt that social historians will in time speak of the era as the Rock Age.

These social movements have not been noted for the consistency or the high level of the thought they produced, but they have been significant for the art form involved, because they have provided a large, dedicated, and undiscriminating audience to support it.

Between the jazz boom of the 1920s and rock boom of the 1960s, there occurred a similar movement, which has come to be known as "the swing band era." It too centered on a sociophilosophic view of a popular music; it too had its modes of dress — the zoot suit with the wide lapels and eighteen-inch knees in the trousers; its dance form — the Suzie-Q, Lindy Hop, jitterbugging, trucking; and its slang — hip talk, or, as it was then called, hep talk. Underpinning it all was a revolt against a standard of middle-class "niceness," which for some time had been drifting down into the blue-collar class. In an effort to move out of the ghettos and find places for themselves in the native culture, children of the immigrant flood of 1890–1920 were acceding to a standard of behavior, adopted from the middle class, that they were learning from the mass circulation magazines and movies.

In the 1930s young people were in revolt against this standard of "niceness." The great thing was to be "frank," "open," "honest" — to express your true feelings. This generation, then, was ready for an art form that seemed to them emotional, openly expressive, and perhaps sexual. And in 1934 it found it when an obscure young clarinetist named Benny Goodman began a series of broadcasts with a band dedicated to playing hot music.

Benny Goodman has for a long time been out of favor with jazz writers. The reasons are various. To begin with, Goodman was from a working-class family, unlike many of the other white jazz players of his day, who had come from the middle class. He did not, like many of the young whites he worked with, see himself as a bearer of the holy chalice, but as a professional musician who would rise to the top if he could. Some of the other white players resented this careerism in an art form that they felt one ought to approach as a religion. For a second matter, Goodman was aloof, never much of a drinker or pot-smoker, and he did not fit in well with the clannish whites, who were devoted to a certain camaraderie. For a third matter, Goodman was not charitable; he took as much solo space as he could, in bands run by himself and others. Coupled with this was his demanding and often intolerant attitude toward less skilled players. It was not always fun working for Goodman, because he did not like mistakes and forgave very little. His defenders — and they are many — say that his seeming aloofness was often due to his preoccupation with his music, and that those who knew him well found him warm and generous. But he was seen by most musicians as unbending and cruel. Compounding his problems was the fact that he became a millionaire, a star, and married into the socially prominent Hammond family. The musicians who disliked him brought the jazz writers, who also are likely to see themselves as keepers of the flame, into camp with them, and as a consequence he has been slighted by many of them. But the fact remains that he is one of the finest players in the history of jazz.

Benny Goodman was born in a Chicago ghetto in 1909, the eighth of twelve children. His father, a Russian immigrant, worked in a clothing factory, and the family lived constantly on the verge of penury. The family was not especially musical, but music was seen as something good, and when the opportunity arose for some of the children to join a small band sponsored by a neighborhood synagogue, they took it. Goodman was ten, and he showed signs of talent early, for he moved on from there to music lessons at Hull House, one of the many settlement houses created in big cities to help immigrants adjust to their new surroundings. He was next taken on by Franz Schoepp, a highly reputable Chicago clarinet teacher who also taught Buster Bailey and Jimmy Noone. Schoepp was a classical musician and taught Goodman a legitimate technique, emphasizing reading and good tone production. By the age of twelve Goodman was appearing in public, and by fifteen he was playing professionally around Chicago and elsewhere.

He sometimes played dances at Austin High School, and in time he became acquainted with the Austin High players and through them the New Orleans Rhythm Kings, who were working at the Friars' Inn during this period. He was influenced by the Rhythm Kings' clarinetist Leon Rappolo and by Jimmy Noone, and thus learned at firsthand the New Orleans way of playing. Soon enough he also fell under the influence of Teschemacher and Pee Wee Russell, both only three years older than he, from whom he acquired the occasional rasp that is a feature of his style. He was, at fifteen and sixteen, gigging around Chicago and working from time to time with the other young Midwestern players. He came to New York with the Ben Pollack band in 1928. During the next few years he worked with Pollack and Red Nichols, and free-lanced between times.

Because of his sound musicianship, he was much in demand for record dates. He made his first records under his own name in 1927, and dozens more under various leaders, many of them the Whoopee Makers sides, which had some popularity. As one of the leading free-lance musicians he was working in the radio studios as well as in pit bands, playing with bands in the hotel ballrooms, making records, and earning lots of money at least by Depression standards. But by 1933 he was beginning to chafe under the leadership of other men. He wanted his own band, and the chance arose when John Hammond came up with a contract from English Columbia to produce some sixty jazz sides for England, where the jazz record market was holding up better than it was in the United States.

The importance of John Hammond to jazz history cannot be over-estimated. No other nonmusician, and indeed only the major instrumentalists, has had as broad an effect on the music as he did. He was born in 1910, a descendant of the Vanderbilts. Like many young whites of his time, Hammond had money enough to indulge in his interest, and the connections that gave him entrée to high places. After college, he established an association with Columbia Records. He quickly came to know the major band bookers, managers, and club owners, and in time he made himself a power in the music business, especially the jazz side of it. He was thus able to advance the careers of his favorites. Fortunately, his taste in jazz was impeccable. One after another he brought forward young musicians who turned out to be important players; he recorded them, got them signed to good managers, and found them work. Among the people whose careers he furthered are Bessie Smith (he produced her last record session and paid the musicians out of his own pocket), Billie Holiday, Count Basie, and Charlie Christian.

In Goodman's case he was more than an advocate; he was a musical preceptor. Goodman's idea of a band was one that would make money; but Hammond had the English recording contract, and he asked Goodman to put together a band with a jazz orientation. Through the last quarter of 1933 Goodman, with various players, made a half-dozen or so sides for Hammond, among them "Riffin' the Scotch" and "Your Mother's Son-in-Law," which included Jack Teagarden and was the first of Billie Holiday's recorded performances. These groups were recording bands only.

Then, in March 1934, with his brother Harry, who played tuba and bass, he formed a band to play hot music but with high standards of musicianship. Late in 1934, the band began to appear on a new late-night radio program called "Let's Dance," which featured a Latin band, a sweet band, and a hot band. In the same year, Hammond made a crucially important move. He arranged for Goodman to buy some scores from Fletcher Henderson, who was having financial troubles and needed the money. Some of these were arrangements Henderson had been using with his own band; others were new. Hammond, as quoted by Nat Shapiro in *The Jazz Makers*, has said, "It was at about this time that Benny let Fletcher make arrangements of current pop tunes with a beat and an irreverence he had never dared to employ with his own band. I firmly believe that it was this approach to ballads that gave the Goodman band the style that made it conquer the nation the following year."

Whatever the virtues of the Henderson arrangements, the public was less than enthusiastic. The radio show lasted until spring, and there were jobs in hotel ballrooms and the like. But this was the Depression; those people who had enough money to buy records or go out dancing wanted a music more soothing. But the band attracted enough attention to encourage Goodman and Hammond, and in July 1935 it went on a tour of one-nighters that was to take it to California several weeks later. The audiences along the way were worse than unenthusiastic. They hated the up-tempo swing that Goodman wanted to play and kept demanding syrupy arrangements of popular tunes, which the band was not really prepared to give them. Again and again managers grew irate, and in Denver dancers actually asked for their money back. Goodman later called it "just about the most humiliating experience of [my] life."

The band finally arrived in Oakland, despondent, with some feeling of relief that the tour was almost over. But in Oakland it was greeted by an enthusiastic group. Nonplussed, the band went on to the Palomar Ballroom in Hollywood, the most famous room on the West Coast. When the members arrived in the evening to set up, they found a line from the box office extending all the way around the block. They could hardly believe what they saw, however, and when they went on the stand they continued to play the sweet numbers audiences had been demanding. The crowd in the ballroom was not enthusiastic. Finally Goodman said the hell with it, if the band was going to die they'd go out playing what they wanted to play. He broke out the hot book, and to the band's vast astonishment the crowd went wild. The hot numbers, it turned out, was what people had come to hear.

The story, apparently, was this: the Goodman band had always appeared as the last feature on the "Let's Dance" program, the producer believing that by that time the older audience, which preferred sweet music, would have gone to bed. But in the East, the younger people had also gone to bed. On the West Coast, however, due to the time difference, the Goodman segment of the show had been eagerly listened to by adolescents and people in their early twenties. So the band had a following in California, and it stayed at the Palomar for months.

Thus began the swing band boom. Very quickly other musicians, many of them who had been associated with the Whoopee Makers, like Tommy and Jimmy Dorsey (who already had bands) and Glenn Miller, figured that if Goodman could do it, they could do it too. Swing bands, as they quickly came to be called, sprang up like mushrooms in the spring rain, and already-established bands converted to the new style. Star soloists with one group would find backing and break off to form bands of their own, in turn creating other star soloists who would leave to form bands. Bunny Berigan, Lionel Hampton, Harry James, and Gene Krupa came from the Goodman band; Ray McKinley from Jimmy Dorsey; Sonny Dunham from the Casa Loma Orchestra; Ray Anthony and Billy May from Glenn Miller. By 1937 there were dozens of swing bands of widely varying merit playing to huge crowds across the country, and by 1939 there were hundreds of them.

The importance of radio in building the popularity of the swing bands cannot be underestimated. The younger reader should understand that in 1935 radio was still something of a novelty. It had only just become a standard item in American homes, something that even working families could afford, and it was listened to avidly. The big swing bands entered into a symbiotic relationship with the radio stations. For radio, the bands playing in the restaurants and dance halls were a golden source of free programming; for the bands, radio was an equally golden fountain of free publicity. It became habitual for the radio stations to present two or three hours of swing bands an evening, often in fifteen-minute segments, so that one band would follow another from, say, ten o'clock until midnight. Listeners chose favorites, and when one of these bands showed up in town for a one-nighter, or for a week at the local ballroom, they would pack the hall.

While the swing band movement was just beginning to brew, during the late 1920s and into the thirties, there was occurring in the southwestern part of the United States a local movement in music that was eventually to be swept into the swing band boom. As we have seen, some jazz writers have made a case for the development of jazz in this area in parallel with the New Orleans movement. The case cannot be supported, as I have suggested. The evidence of the early records is that these bands were formed to fill a strong demand for dance music. Blacks, here as elsewhere, were playing for whites as well as their own people. They began to play jazz only under the influence of Oliver, and later Henderson, who frequently played through the area on tours and whose records, in any case, were well known to musicians everywhere. But, in fact, the music that began to form during the 1920s in this section of the country was built on a tradition that was somewhat different from the one in the East.

To begin with, the Southwest, in the early part of this century, was still essentially rural, its wealth based on cattle and cotton rather than on mills and factories. The area had seen a big influx of blacks after the Emancipation. There were black sharecroppers in the countryside, and large black communities in and around the towns and cities. The people were still closely connected to the black folk music tradition through work songs and gospel church music. The area was especially rich in the blues. Leadbelly, Blind Lemon Jefferson, Lightning Hopkins, were all born or raised in Texas; Big Bill Broonzy and Buddy Boy Hawkins were from Arkansas; Joe Turner from Kansas City; Jimmy Rushing from Oklahoma City. They thus were far more inclined to use a blues approach to jazz than were the musicians in the East.

For another thing, the players in this area were less schooled than those from the East. There was not here the wealth of professional teachers, or the access to theater music and concerts in general, that was found in the more sophisticated East. We find few Southwestern players with the schooling of Henderson, Goodman, or Don Redman. As a consequence the Southwestern players tended to think less in terms of complicated written scores, which few of them could write and many could not read, and worked instead from relatively simple head arrangements, which they harmonized by ear and memorized. Much of the material that eventually found its way into band repertories was created in jam sessions. It is a practice in jam sessions for players to back up the soloist with a short riff figure, perhaps changing it with each chorus. There was a large stock of such figures in use, but as often as not the players would create a new one on the spot, one player throwing out a line to which the others would then pick out a harmony. A sample of this practice can be heard on "Ad Lib Blues," a piece cut by men in the studio waiting for Benny Goodman's arrival. Lester Young starts a riff under Basie's piano comping, which Buck Clayton picks up. As the next chorus begins Lester changes the figure and Clayton again picks it up. This was something these players did almost by reflex, and many of these riffs found their way into band arrangements.

It was not, of course, universally true that Southwestern players were badly schooled; the top bands, like the Bennie Moten group, did at times use relatively difficult arrangements. But it is a safe generalization that the Southwestern players were more limited technically than their Eastern competitors. Where Eastern bands were using complex arrangements and rich harmonies, and were working off tunes like "Georgia on My Mind," with its modulation in the bridge, the Kansas City men were improvising mainly from the blues and the simplest sets of chord changes. This explains a good deal about Lester Young's use of basic kinds of harmonies.

The presence of these two factors in the playing of the men in the Southwest — the feeling for the blues and the limited techniques — produced in the area a simpler big band style, utilizing riffs more than worked-out melodies, built on a few basic sets of chord changes, especially the blues and "I've Got Rhythm." The emphasis was on good soloing and the ability to swing. The bands that were developing this music were "territory" bands. Each had a home base — Kansas City, Oklahoma City, Dallas. Its aim was to get a monopoly on the work in its base town and the surrounding area, and then, if possible, encroach on the territories of other bands. If it was very lucky, it might eventually break out to become a nationally known band. Territory bands were not, of course, confined to the Southwest; they blanketed the United States. Lawrence Welk's was a territory band in the Midwest for three decades before it became nationally famous through television. Among the best known of the Southwestern territory bands at the time were the Alphonso Trent, Troy Floyd, Gene Coy, and Terence T. Holder bands from Texas, the Blue Devils from

Oklahoma, and the one that was to make the biggest mark on jazz, the Moten band from Kansas City.

Kansas City was becoming a jazz seedbed. It still had, in the 1920s, something of the character of a frontier town, serving as an entertainment center for the cattlemen, farmers, and railroad men of the surrounding area. Districts of this sort have always been fertile ground for the development of jazz. The honky-tonks of Storyville, the cabarets of Chicago's South Side, the nightclubs of Harlem and New York's Fifty-second Street, have all provided economic sustenance for many musicians, places for them to develop their craft in, and a venue for the exchange of ideas that does not exist for bands on the road.

Kansas City's nightclubs also became such supply houses. They provided work for a lot of musicians, and with so much happening locally, there was less need to look outside for ideas and models. Kansas City musicians were especially addicted to the after-hours jam sessions. Like the New Orleans cutting contests, these sessions were highly competitive: the newcomer did not simply join in; he had, in effect, to challenge the other men on his instrument. Sessions sometimes ran from midnight until noon. There are stories told of musicians going out for dinner and returning to find the band still jamming on the same tune. Under this competitive pressure the Kansas City men, whatever their technical failings, developed into powerful improvisers, especially on the blues and simple changes they preferred. The main thing was to swing.

Bennie Moten was a Kansas City boy, born there in 1894. He studied the piano as a child, and at length began to work around the city. Sometime during the dance boom of the World War I period, he formed his own band, which gradually grew in size and sophistication. The band's first records, made in 1923, show an unpolished group playing jazz rags and blues, with some appalling clarinet effects by Herman "Woody" Walder, probably patterned after the animal sounds of the Original Dixieland Jazz Band.

By 1924 the band had moved toward the New Orleans style. "South," one of the band's big hits, includes duet cornet breaks modeled on the ones Oliver and Armstrong made famous. By 1925 the band was a solid, swinging, New Orleans–style group: trumpeter Lammar Wright, who in 1923 had played almost without vibrato, was using the fast terminal vibrato characteristic of the New Orleans cornetists, and on "18th Street Strut" he used whole phrases taken directly from Oliver. But then, as the records of Henderson, Goldkette, and McKinney's Cotton Pickers percolated west, the band evolved into a big band, influenced by the Eastern bands, but in the simpler, bluesy style that was becoming characteristic of the bands in the area. By the late 1920s the Moten group was acknowledged to be the best band in the Southwest.

But though the Moten group was certainly the Southwest's most prestigious band, it was not considered by everybody to be the hottest band. That title, a good many people felt, belonged to the Blue Devils. The Blue Devils had been organized in Oklahoma City by a local bassist named Walter Page. The group came to include altoist Buster Smith, trombonist and arranger Eddie Durham, trumpeter Hot Lips Page, pianist Bill Basie (not yet known as the Count), and vocalist Jimmy Rushing. All of these men went on to become well-known jazz figures in the 1930s, and it is hardly surprising that their band was a good one. The band made only two records, and it is difficult to know how representative they are. "Squabblin'," an up-tempo number, shows traces of the influence of Henderson or McKinney, coupled with a tendency toward the simple riff. "Blue Devil Blues" is a reworking of Armstrong's "Tight Like This," and contains a fine vocal by Jimmy Rushing. The band plays with fire, and soloing by Lips Page and others is often superior. As reported by Frank Driggs in Hentoff and McCarthy's *Jazz,* in 1928 the Blue Devils cut the Moten band in one of the band battles that were endemic to the area, and Moten, smarting from the defeat, tried to take over the Blue Devils. He did not succeed, but not long afterward the Blue Devils ran into financial difficulties, and Moten lured its stars, one after another, into his band.

The addition of the new men changed the band. It had developed from a dance band and usually played relatively unsophisticated arrangements, hardly up to the level of the Eastern bands. Now, Eddie Durham began writing for the band, and in 1931 Moten bought some arrangements from Benny Carter and Horace Henderson, Fletcher's brother. At about the same time Ben Webster, clarinetist and arranger Eddie Barefield, and Walter Page himself came into the band. Moten now had a collection of first-rate soloists, and Page's strong bass souped up the beat considerably. (Page has been said to have been the first bass player to sound all four beats in the measure instead of just the first and third, but undoubtedly this was a trend that can really be credited to nobody.) But the band had not quite found an identity. On tunes like "Toby," "Blue Room," and "Prince of Wails," the opening portions show fairly complicated writing, especially for the saxophones, whose execution is good. But the closing choruses revert to a simpler mode, built out of brass and saxophone riffs alternating, or sometimes playing simultaneously, as in "Blue Room." In sum, the band was very nearly on a level with the Henderson band, with good writing and some excellent soloing by Lips Page and Ben Webster, playing very much in the Hawkins vein.

What might have become of it we will never know, for in 1934 Moten died, quite suddenly. His death stunned the bandsmen, and the group broke up. Basie found work in Kansas City, and as he developed a following, gradually drew around him many of the men from the Moten band, adding some others from the area, including Lester Young. Eddie Durham gave

Basie important help in creating his book. It might have remained a Midwest territory band indefinitely, but in 1936 John Hammond happened to hear it on late-night radio when he was in Chicago. Hammond was excited by the band, arranged for bookings and a record contract, and eventually saw to it that it got good display in New York. The band did not catch on right away, but in 1938 it went into the Famous Door, a well-known New York jazz club. There were a lot of broadcasts from the club, and these finally gave the band the publicity it needed. Very rapidly it became one of the most popular of the swing bands. Once again, Hammond had played a crucial role in jazz. Other of his discoveries, like Billie Holiday and Goodman, might have made their mark in any case, but without Hammond's involvement it is entirely possible that the Basie band would have lived out the swing years as an obscure territory band working the Midwest. It was through Basie that Lester Young was exposed to the young players; had he not come to widespread attention the course of jazz would have been different.

While the Basie band was struggling to become known, Hammond and others continued to beat the Southwestern bushes for promising bands to record. Of those that were turned up the best known were Andy Kirk's Clouds of Joy, a descendant of Terence Holder's Dallas band, and Harlan Leonard's Rockets, descended from a Kansas territory band originally organized by a pianist named Jesse Stone. Thus, by 1936 or 1937 two streams were feeding the big band movement: one stemming from Henderson and Goldkette, with a concern for interesting scores precisely played; and the other coming from the Southwest, emphasizing riffs and good solo playing. These characteristics did not of course have rigidly defined borders. Southwest bands did use some complex arrangements, and Henderson's band had been using riffs for some time and had excellent soloists; but the differences were there, to be smudged over fairly quickly as the two traditions began to merge into one swing band sound, which used a combination of riffs and more standard orchestral writing, spiced with solos.

The amount of jazz these bands played varied wildly. The most popular and best-paid bands were not those that played a lot of jazz, but the ones that mixed up-tempo riff numbers, featuring one or two jazz solos, with creamy arrangements of sentimental pop tunes, usually featuring a vocalist. The most commercially successful leaders were Tommy Dorsey, Glenn Miller, Harry James, and Jimmy Dorsey, whose bands stuck to this formula. Neither Miller nor either of the Dorseys was more than a modest jazz player, but all of them kept good, and sometimes first-rate, jazz soloists in their orchestras. Miller had trumpeters Billy May and Bobby Hackett in his band; Tommy Dorsey had drummer Buddy Rich and trumpeters Bunny Berigan and Charlie Shavers, among others. Harry James was himself an excellent jazz soloist, but unfortunately he was an example of a talented player willing to sacrifice taste for popularity. He has a number of fine solos with Goodman, for example, "Ride 'Em," and with his own band, such as his hit "Two O'Clock Jump." His playing on a few obscure small band recordings is often exemplary. Particularly fine is his controlled and rather tender playing on "Just a Mood," a lovely two-sided record of a blues with Teddy Wilson on piano and Red Norvo on xylophone. But most of his playing, especially with his own band, is marred by high-note showboating and an insatiable appetite for the half-valved slur that enraptured his fans.

A few of the white bands, however, attempted, within the limits of the taste of the time, to play a lot of jazz. One of the most interesting of these was a band led by saxophonist Charlie Barnet. Barnet was just an ordinary jazz soloist, with not many major players in his band, but he was a great admirer of Ellington, and he generally managed to get arrangements that were more complex and imaginative than those used by most of the swing bands. He had one of the biggest swing hits in "Cherokee," and he made a greater effort than most white band leaders to feature black players with his groups.

Another white band that played a considerable amount of jazz was led by Bob Crosby, younger brother of superstar Bing Crosby, who fronted a group that rose out of the collapse of the Ben Pollack band in the early 1930s. The Crosby band featured "dixieland" arrangements, which to a degree reflected the old New Orleans style. The band included a number of excellent soloists, among them trumpeters Billy Butterfield, Muggsy Spanier, and Yank Lawson; saxophonist Eddie Miller; pianists Joe Sullivan, Jess Stacy, and Bob Zurke; clarinetists Irving Fazola and Matty Matlock; and an unduly neglected trombonist, Warren Smith. Crosby often featured a dixieland group, which he pulled out of the big band. A third excellent white swing band was one led by clarinetist Artie Shaw, a bright, verbal, and somewhat erratic personality who played a fluid, graceful line with the ease of Goodman but without all of Goodman's fire. Shaw's band had big success with popular songs like "Begin the Beguine" and "Stardust," but he played many swing numbers too, and often had first-rate soloists in the band, among them Hot Lips Page and, for a time, Billie Holiday.

But of all the big band leaders, the one who most typified the playing of the day was a bravura trumpeter named Bunny Berigan, who died early of drink and acquired a romantic halo like the one fitted to Beiderbecke on his death. He was born Roland Bernard Berigan, in 1909, in Wisconsin. He played in an orchestra led by his grandfather, then in college dance bands, and then came to New York in time to get in on the beginning of the swing band movement. He was Benny Goodman's principal trumpeter for a few months in 1935, was with Tommy Dorsey in 1937, and then emerged as a band leader in his own right. But his dependence on alcohol and his temperament, one not suited to the rigors of band-leading, kept the group in turmoil, and he abandoned it in 1940 to return to Dorsey. A second attempt at leading proved more than his tangled emotions could handle, and he died in 1942 of pneumonia, brought on by the poor health generally associated with alcoholism. Berigan made a large number of records with small groups of one kind or another, but his sweeping, romantic style demanded more space, and the big band suited him perfectly. He was second only to Armstrong in the warmth and honesty of his tone, and he probably employed the widest range of any trumpet player in jazz: not only was his tone full in the upper register, but he had an excellent command of the lowest notes, which offer such difficulties of pitch and sound production that few trumpet players use them frequently.

His technical skill was important to his style, which was filled with leaps and dashes through the entire range of the instrument. Typically, he leaps into the upper register, whirls his way downward to the bottom, and then races upward again. He uses many of the stretched figures and tempoless phrases of Armstrong, but always in his own personal style. The best known of his solos was "I Can't Get Started," a set-piece showcase for his trumpet playing, on which, unfortunately, he also sings. It opens with a long cadenza, presumably inspired by Armstrong's opening passage on "West End Blues," and Berigan builds the song through a series of long, tempoless phrases to a showy climax in the upper register. Other outstanding Berigan solos are on "The Prisoner's Song," with his own band; "King Porter Stomp" and "Sometimes I'm Happy," with the Goodman band; and two solos with Tommy Dorsey, "Marie" and "The Song of India." Dorsey's "Marie" was one of the biggest hit records of the swing band period, and Berigan's solo was acclaimed by the fans, but the "Song of India" solo is thought out a little more carefully, and is possibly his best. Berigan occasionally used the half-valving and sudden octave rips characteristic of trumpet players of his time, but they are far less offensive in his hands than in those of many other players. Berigan was a genuine romantic, perhaps the purest romantic in jazz, and with him these devices are not mere crowd-pleasers but are thoroughly felt. Exceedingly highly regarded in his time, he has lately been neglected by jazz writers, in part because of the antiromantic movement that has dominated jazz for the past two decades, and in part because he was white. But he certainly was one of the finest trumpet players in the bravura manner jazz has seen, blessed with a fine technique, a rich tone, and a felt imagination.

Yet despite the excellence of Shaw and Berigan as players, and the well-drilled machinery of the Miller and Tommy Dorsey bands, without question the leading white swing band was Goodman's. He always had good soloists in the band, among them Harry James and Ziggy Elman, a trumpeter in the James mold, Lionel Hampton and saxophonist Georgie Auld. And sometimes he had superb ones, including Cootie Williams, Bunny

Next to Armstrong, Benny Goodman acquired more general fame than any other jazz musician. Here he is in the classic posture that earned him the title "the Pied Piper of Swing," afloat above a mob of enthusiasts during the swing heyday. William P. Gottlieb/Edward Gottlieb Collection

Berigan, Charlie Christian, Teddy Wilson, and Goodman himself, all of whom were among the best jazz players of the day. The arrangements were usually above average, and though drummer Gene Krupa was somewhat leaden, the band could swing hard. Yet once again it is the playing of the soloists rather than the ensemble work of the band that matters, and among his soloists Goodman himself was pre-eminent.

As a jazz soloist, Benny Goodman is a paradox. A reserved man, and to some extent a calculating one, who knew how to operate successfully in a difficult business, a man who alienated other musicians by his lack of warmth, Goodman is nonetheless one of the most passionate players in jazz. At times, when he felt the commercial necessities upon him, he could play with a quiet simplicity, but when he was playing what he wanted, he was endlessly hot. We misunderstand Goodman; we tend to see him as one of the major modernists of his time, somebody who had left the old behind and was moving toward the new. Yet, in truth, Goodman's entire manner of playing is filled with the sound of New Orleans. He is, far more than many of the players who have been labeled as being in the old tradition — as, for example, many of Ellington's soloists — a player of the old school. We must bear in mind that he started his apprenticeship young. He was a working musician even before Armstrong, Morton, or Oliver recorded. His earliest influence was Rappolo, a New Orleanian, and his subsequent ones were men who were themselves influenced by Dodds and Noone, with whose work he was himself familiar. The essential elements of Goodman's playing come from the old tradition.

What has fooled us is Goodman's musicianship. Few jazz players of his time, and not many since, are as technically adept as Goodman. His intonation is excellent, his tone warm and full and completely under his control, his lower register rich, and his dexterity quick enough to allow him to play faster than most musicians of his time.

The main characteristic of Goodman's work is that sense of speech, or conversation, that lies in the work of so many of the best jazz players. In Goodman's case this speechlike quality is achieved basically by his management of individual notes or, in the case of quick passages, short phrases. Goodman is always changing inflection. He attacks some notes sharply; lets others slide into existence. He swells some, diminishes others. He often lets the pitch of a long, held note sag briefly, or lets it drop off at the end. He colors his notes with growls and rasps. Most interesting, he uses a terminal vibrato that is almost as fast as the one employed by the New Orleans players, but because it is not as wide as theirs, we fail to notice it. He is also a consummate user of both the blue third and blue seventh at a time when the blue notes have gone out of use. In Goodman's playing we see a man shaping notes as well as lines — or, in some cases, instead of lines.

This sort of thing is exceedingly difficult to analyze because it is subtle and depends on fractional changes in volume, pitch, and timbre. However, the careful listener can find hundreds and perhaps thousands of examples if he wishes to take the time. For example, right after the drum solo in the trio version of "Runnin' Wild," there is a long note, with a distinct pitch sag, and again in the thirteenth bar from the end of the same record another long note with a similar sag. In the thirtieth bar of the trio version of "Sweet Sue," there is a long note that has both dynamic variation and a faint upward curl of the pitch at the end. In the quartet version of "Exactly Like You," the announcing note in the bar before the last eight measures drops off in pitch immediately after Goodman hits it. In the ninth measure of Goodman's solo on "Pick-A-Rib," an oddly constructed tune with ten-bar interludes between pairs of blues choruses, there is a three-beat note in which he changes the whole nature of the sound, as if he were using a plunger mute. In the introduction to "Blues in My Flat," he gets a rather spooky, hollow sound in the low register. He uses a blue seventh, which he pulls up to a tonic, to open his solo after Hampton's vibraphone solo in "Blues in Your Flat," and a blue third in the eighth bar of his sixth chorus in the Carnegie Hall version of "One O'Clock Jump."

Such examples are manifold. There is hardly a chorus of his music in which he does not inflect several notes, or phrases, with something — a variant tonguing, a rasp, a growl, a shift in pitch or dynamics, or some even subtler variation on his tone. And it is this constant shifting of the character of his sound as the line proceeds that is the hallmark of his playing. His weakness is that, like many players, he does not always construct logical lines. At times his ideas, especially when he is at his hottest, are broken off, uncompleted, or do not relate very well one to another. But this is not always so; he is capable at his most thoughtful of executing well-formed lines. The "One O'Clock Jump" mentioned above was made at a concert at Carnegie Hall in 1938 featuring the Goodman band and a few black musicians for small group numbers. Goodman takes six choruses himself down near the end, all of them well played, and in the fourth chorus he shows the sort of construction he can make at times. The chorus is made of three well-separated phrases, each of which seems to pause a little in the middle. The line rises gradually into the second phrase and then falls off. It is a fine construction.

But in general, Goodman's best playing was not with the band. It was with the small groups, which started as trios and gradually grew to sextets and even septets. He saw the big band as, in considerable measure, a commercial operation that must please the dancers, and he often stuck fairly close to the melody in his own playing. The small groups, however, were supposed to play jazz; and although for the earliest trios he usually stayed with safe popular standards and played the melody on first and sometimes last choruses, as his confidence in the acceptability of the music grew, he relaxed and let himself go. It is impossible to select one as superior, because Goodman's playing is always at a high level, but I personally like a chorus he played on "Gone with What Draft," a sextet number with Charlie Christian, based roughly on "Honeysuckle Rose." Both in the opening bars and at the start of the last measure, he throws out a phrase and then elaborates on it through the next several measures. It is superlative jazz playing.

With the arrival of bop and the simultaneous decline of the big band, Goodman found himself, as did so many other men in jazz, suddenly passé. He made a few halfhearted attempts to accommodate himself to the new music, but they were not very successful. He was, in any case, rich. From time to time he revived bands and small groups for special tours or limited engagements, and his playing remained strong. He was still active in the 1970s.

Despite a few bands like Goodman's, the black swing bands as a rule played more jazz than the white ones did, because they tended to play more frequently for black audiences, who were more generally receptive to jazz. But they by no means played only for blacks. Black bands, as had always been the case, were used in white dance halls even in the South. What is more significant, audiences were now beginning to be somewhat mixed. One of the important stands for the swing bands was the big movie house, which often booked a band as a second bill — or often first bill — to a movie. Blacks, who were admitted to theaters in the North, would turn out at times to hear white bands. The dance halls, and especially the hotel ballrooms, remained segregated, although a few white jazz fans would at times visit the Savoy Ballroom in Harlem, with its predominantly black audience.

But whites who booked black bands generally expected a larger portion of jazz in the evening. Among the best of these bands, leaving aside Ellington and Count Basie, was the Chick Webb band. The rhythm section, built around the leader's clean and imaginative drumming, was strong. There was a good trombone soloist of the Harrison school in Sandy Williams and a bravura trumpeter in Taft Jordan. It was a well-schooled band, and as it was the house band at the Savoy, it was able to maintain a clear jazz orientation. It can be heard to advantage on "Clap Hands, Here Comes Charlie" and "Congo," both made in 1937. A second well-known black band was the Jimmie Lunceford group, which usually played light, sometimes gimmicky, arrangements over a rather stiff rhythm section, but occasionally produced powerful racehorse numbers like "White Heat." The band had some competent soloists, and one superior one in altoist Willie Smith. The band's main defect was the air of orderliness that pervades the arrangements; its virtues and defects are apparent on one of its biggest hits, "Organ Grinder Swing," based on the children's song "I Love Coffee, I Love Tea." The Mills Blue Rhythm Band, led by nonplaying Lucky Millinder, who eventually formed a group under his own name, featured rather pedestrian arrangements originally modeled after those of Redman. But Millinder's group often featured superior soloists; Red Allen, J. C. Higginbotham, Buster Bailey, altoist Tab Smith, and Dizzy Gillespie played with Millinder at one time or another. Other good black bands were led by Earl Hines, Don Redman, and Benny Carter, but none of them achieved more than modest fame.

Of all of the swing bands, however, unquestionably the best after Ellington's was the Basie band. It had, for one thing, what was generally accounted the finest rhythm section in the business. Guitarist Freddie Greene, bassist Walter Page, drummer Jo Jones, and Basie himself had developed an ability to play as one, and had a precise, dry sound that perfectly reproduced that even four-beat feel demanded by swing. Basie established himself as a musician in the Kansas City area, but he had been born in New Jersey and had grown up under the influence of the Eastern stride players. He had spent long hours at the Lincoln Theatre listening to Fats Waller, with whom he became friends, and he was capable of playing stride piano in the Waller style. However, during his Kansas City years he developed a simple, very spare manner of playing, which is today instantly recognizable. His choice in both solos and when accompanying the band was to neglect the left hand on the presumption that the other members of the rhythm section would carry the beat; with his right hand he comped sporadically, just throwing in enough precisely timed notes or figures to keep the music going. Properly placed, these fragments helped to spur the band on.

At first the section work was somewhat sloppy and out of tune: many of Basie's men were poor readers and had had little training in ensemble playing. But in time the sections jelled, so the ensemble riffs swung almost as hard as the soloists. But it was the soloists, in the end, who counted. After the band's discovery by Hammond, Buck Clayton was brought in, and, at about the same time, trombonists Dicky Wells and Benny Morton, both of whom had been with Henderson. This was a band that already contained Lester Young and Herschel Evans, and a good altoist in Earle Warren, besides that model rhythm section. In its great years, the band thus contained a half-dozen of the finest players in jazz. Henderson and Ellington bands notwithstanding, there has never been such a concentration of brilliant jazz talent in a single band as in the Basie group from 1936 until about 1940.

Clayton, during this time, was rather overlooked in favor of Ellington's trumpeters Rex Stewart and Cootie Williams, but in retrospect we can see that he was their equal, a player with a fine, if subtle, musical intelligence. Clayton was born in Kansas in 1911, though most of his early musical associations were not with the Kansas group around Moten but with a variety of bands elsewhere, including, for two years, a band led by pianist Teddy Weatherford in Shanghai. He joined Basie on his return to this country, replacing Lips Page, who had formed his own band. Clayton was Basie's chief jazz trumpet soloist during the band's classic period, but he is heard to better advantage on a vast number of recordings cut with small groups made up of men from the Basie band or put together by Teddy Wilson, often to accompany Billie Holiday. In a time when the bravura trumpet style predominated, Clayton chose to work within a small compass. He eschewed the sometimes gauche growls and half-valve effects, which marred the work even of Armstrong, in favor of an unadorned sound, a narrow tessitura, and an almost flat dynamic range. Characteristically, he worked with a cup mute, which reduces the amount of sound considerably and produces a dulcet tone, akin to that of the saxophone.

He was a minimalist and depended for his effects on sculpture. His lines are invariably thoughtful and well constructed. Typically, he produces complete four-measure phrases, often divided into two segments, with the second one a variation of the first. His vibrato is broad and slow, and the secondary pulse is plainly evident in much of his work. You can easily hear him take something off a note after the attack and then hit it again. Good examples of his work with Basie are on "Topsy," "Jumpin' at the Woodside," and "Dickie's Dream." But he is at his best with small groups. His solo on "Way Down Yonder in New Orleans," with the Kansas City Six with Lester Young, is a particularly fine example of an intelligently constructed solo. If Clayton has a failing, it is a rather four-square feeling that his careful constructions sometimes give his work. He left Basie in 1943 to free-lance. In later life his lip failed him, and he turned more and more to arranging. He was still active in the 1970s.

The two trombonists, Wells and Morton, were both influenced by Jimmy Harrison, and although the emotional content of their work is different, they evince a good many similarities in manner and method. Their careers were parallel. Morton was born in New York in 1907; Wells in Tennessee in 1909. Both played with Henderson and other of the early black swing bands; both played with Basie during the classic period; both made many recordings with small groups from the 1930s into the sixties, and both were active into the seventies. In terms of style, both employ a somewhat thick, muted tone, and Wells in particular uses a growl achieved by throat tones. Both are essentially legato players in the Harrison manner, but Morton often attacks his notes fully, instead of using the half-tonguing of legato trombone playing, so he sometimes phrases as a trumpet player would. Wells is fond of glissando sweeps and smears, which are sometimes in bad taste and occasionally noticeably sharp.

Both use a broad, fairly rapid terminal vibrato; much of Morton's emotional effect comes from this device, which can be heard in his solo on Henderson's "Just Blues," made in 1931. The first half of the solo is built on one repeated A ♭. The whole thing depends on the placement of the note and on the rolling terminal vibrato, which supplies intensity. The second half of the solo is given over to rapid passages and is less effective, but it demonstrates how sound a technician Morton was, perhaps the deftest trombone player in jazz at the time except for Teagarden. It is a sign of Morton's restraint that, despite the first-rate technique at his command, in general he reduces his notes to a minimum. It is difficult to think of another jazz player who will use so few notes in the course of a chorus. A good example is "Lady Be Good," made with a small band led by Teddy Wilson in 1940. Here is the throaty, dulcet tone, the quarter and half notes, and the terminal vibrato — the saying of much with little. Again, in an "I Can't Believe That You're in Love with Me," made a few years later with Harry Carney and Edmond Hall, notice especially the last bars, which are played ensemble. Morton plays only a few notes, sketching in the downward chromatic movement that the chord sequence suggests, allowing himself one down slurred note in the third measure. It is his playing that moves the whole ensemble.

Wells is temperamentally a more broadly expressive player. His work, filled as it is with swoops and smears, has been called humorous, but it is a macabre humor. In 1937 Wells came to Europe with the Teddy Hill band, a black swing group that was never more than modestly successful despite some excellent talent. The French critic Hugues Panassié took the opportunity to record Wells, using a local rhythm section, including Django Reinhardt on one session, and various other Americans. Although Wells recorded frequently with Henderson, Basie, and other groups, these records undoubtedly are his finest, in part because they give him space to work in. The best known is "Dicky Wells Blues," one of the very few records that consist entirely of a trombone solo. Wells plays with a big, blowsy sound, which is particularly remarkable in the lower register. Jazz musicians do not invariably attack notes cleanly, in the manner of symphonic players, but often half-tongue them, or start them with little or no tonguing at all. This is especially true of Wells, and it accounts for the blowsiness of his sound in this blues.

Wells's major failing is evident here, too. He has, at times, difficulty in creating a flowing line. Phrases that seem to have logical finishes break off in what appears to be midflight; particularly, Wells has trouble tying sections of a song or choruses together. But he produces what is possibly the finest trombone sound in jazz — rugged, warm, and full. Thus he is often at his best when paraphrasing the line of a song — when he has a melodic sketch to support that gorgeous sound. An example is his opening chorus on "Devil and the Deep Blue Sea" and most especially on "Lady Be Good," both from the Panassié sessions. The latter is without question one of the finest extended trombone solos in jazz, and it is particularly the opening chorus, with its paraphrase of the melody, that strikes the ear. It is perfectly put together, with a beautifully constructed line in the second eight bars that begins with a series of tiny loops rising upward to a climactic note and then falls in larger loops down to the bridge.

As the swing band era moved toward its conclusion after the end of World War II, two other white bands moved to the forefront. These were the groups of Stan Kenton and Woody Herman. We will consider them in more detail later; for the moment we note that they were swollen to twenty or more players at times, and featured symphonic jazz tinged with the new harmonies brought into jazz by the beboppers.

The bands of Kenton and Herman, however influential, proved to be the last gasp of the big band movement. In December 1946, eight of the biggest swing bands, including those of Goodman, James, Dorsey, Teagarden, and Carter, broke up. The causes were several. A wartime 20 percent amusement tax had hurt the entertainment business in general; eventually television began to keep people home; club owners, beset by rising costs, were turning to small groups, which could be had for half the price. Then, too, the swing band vogue, like any vogue, just plain wore out. The big bands could not survive on the support of the jazz fan; they needed the general public, and audiences were turning elsewhere.

But the big band never completely died out. Basie and Ellington got fresh wind in the 1950s, and continued to lead their groups into the seventies. The Dorsey bands carried on in various incarnations into the sixties, and the Glenn Miller band, under one leader or another, into the 1970s. The truth is that many musicians like to play in big bands; they enjoy the feel of good section playing. So they go on starting new bands.

Of the many started in the last two decades, only one has made a considerable mark since the 1960s. This was a group put together by drummer Mel Lewis and trumpeter Thad Jones. The band was formed as a rehearsal group in 1965, and eventually found a home in the Village Vanguard, an important New York jazz club, whose owner, Max Gordon, was willing to let the band have Monday nights for scale. For the first year it did not draw well enough to cover expenses, but gradually a following developed, and in time the band was able to record, to make tours, and even, at intervals, to work at the Village Vanguard for two weeks at a stretch. By the mid-1970s it had become something of an institution, an important showcase for new soloists and arrangers.

But despite the survivors, the big band movement in jazz was essentially over in 1946. What did it leave us? From a musical viewpoint, the remains are slight. Of the thousands of records made during the big band heyday there are, Ellington's and Basie's aside, probably not more than a hundred that will stand comparison with, say, the better records of Morton, Hawkins, Young, or Coltrane, to say nothing of Armstrong or Parker. The best of the big band sides carry an excitement, offer good solos and occasionally interesting orchestral writing; but by far the largest number show weak solos and unimaginative scores undergirt by uninspired rhythm playing. The high points are there, but they are few and far between.

Nevertheless, the swing band movement did make important marks on the history of jazz. For one thing, it brought jazz into the mainstream of American culture. As we have seen, the "jazz" that most people heard in the 1920s was not jazz at all; only a handful of intellectuals and cultists, outside the black community, was listening to real jazz. Again, the early black big bands of Henderson, Luis Russell, and Ellington were, before the big band boom, playing to specialized audiences of nightclub-goers, most of them relatively sophisticated people from the big cities. But the music of the swing bands was the popular music of its time. Glenn Miller, Benny Goodman, and Tommy Dorsey were as celebrated in 1941 as were the

Beatles in the sixties or Bob Dylan today. If you went out to dance, put a nickel in a juke box, turned on a disc jockey, you would hear a swing band. The result was that Americans, over a period of time, heard a great deal of jazz, primarily in the solo work of the best instrumentalists — Goodman, Hodges, Young, Shaw, Lips Page, Clayton, Berigan, and the rest. Neither intellectuals nor sophisticates, these were people from all classes, who just happened to like the music.

Thus, by 1950, when other currents were moving in jazz, there existed an audience to support it — not a large one, perhaps, in terms of the following a major pop musician would attract, but one sufficiently large to buy enough records, enough concert tickets, enough drinks in a club, to make the playing of jazz *for itself,* and not as part of some other vogue, economically feasible. This is an important distinction. Previously, jazz had been supported only accidentally, because it happened to get swept up in some current in the society — an interest in the black culture, a fashion for good times, a vogue for nightclubbing. To be sure, blacks had always supported the music to a degree, though it should be borne in mind that the majority of blacks have never been dedicated jazz fans, but, like whites, followers of one fashion or another in jazz-derived popular musics. For jazz to exist on its own attractions, it must have the support of people from the majority, and that, after the swing band period, it got. From 1950, a big jazz star could expect, with good management, to become rich without compromising, and numbers of lesser ones could expect to make decent livings by playing just what they wanted to play. This had never happened before. Only briefly in the 1920s had a few jazz musicians, carried along by the vogue for hot music, been able to make decent livings. And nobody, except Louis Armstrong, who was in any case seen as a public entertainer, got rich.

A second important effect the swing movement had on jazz was that during its heyday the music began to integrate itself. Earlier, such was the attitude in the United States that it was impossible for blacks and whites to appear together on the same stand. This does not mean that all white Americans objected to racial mixing; but enough did so that nobody was willing to try the experiment. As we have seen, the line was finally broken by Benny Goodman in 1936 when, at the urging of John Hammond, he included Teddy Wilson in his new trio, which first performed at the Congress Hotel in Chicago. After that, there were occasional objections to mixed bands, but no major hostility to the idea, and from that moment on blacks began to edge bit by bit into white bands. There was no flood, surely; the blacks were generally brought in as star soloists, like Cootie Williams with Goodman, Lips Page and Roy Eldridge with Artie Shaw, Peanuts Holland with Charlie Barnet. In general, bands were either predominantly white or black, as indeed they are today. But by 1950 audiences were indifferent to the prospect of a mixed band, except, on occasion, in the

South. Thereafter, bands of any size, although usually mainly black or white, depending on the race of the leader, contained a player or two from the other race. By the late forties Charlie Parker was using a number of whites, including pianist Al Haig and trumpeter Red Rodney, in his groups; conversely, the white dixielanders often worked with Zutty Singleton, Edmond Hall, Joe Thomas, and other blacks. It was by no means a millennium; there still existed in jazz an undercurrent of hostility between the races. But it was an improvement over the situation of a decade or so earlier, when blacks and whites could not appear on the same bandstand. Musically, the big bands were less than satisfactory. But by developing a larger audience for jazz, and by making a beginning toward breaking down the separation of the races, they made an important contribution to the music.

The Dixieland Revival

The swing band movement made jazz popular, and, predictably, there was a reaction. In fact, there were two reactions, one looking back and the other looking forward. The black beboppers began their search for a new way of playing at least in part because of resentment at seeing whites becoming richer and more celebrated at playing jazz than blacks were, and in part because of boredom with what had become, by the early 1940s, a stereotypical music. They wanted something new, something that was their own, and something — some of them hoped — that whites could not play.

Facing in the other direction was a group of jazz writers and older fans who saw the rise of the swing bands as a sellout of the music. For them, only the New Orleans style was authentic jazz. Indeed, Rudi Blesh, the critic, said flatly that only blacks could play the music, preferably blacks from New Orleans. These people considered the swing bands as antijazz, commercial, a heresy. Even Armstrong's playing, after 1930, as a soloist in front of a big band was scorned. This attitude was growing in the late thirties both in the United States and in Europe. Giving it force was the left-wing political movement of the 1930s, which was romanticizing the black as the quintessential working man. The older jazz, arising directly from the heart of the downtrodden, uncontaminated by materialist civilization, was somehow more real than modern musics. By the end of the decade, then, there was in the jazz world a strong feeling against the swing bands and a corresponding desire to see the older jazz revived. This feeling manifested itself in articles in the jazz press and in the first formal American books on jazz, Wilder Hobson's *American Jazz Music,* and Frederic Ramsey, Jr., and Charles Edward Smith's *Jazzmen,* both of which appeared in 1939. *Jazzmen* was particularly influential, because its editors had pulled together a number of firsthand accounts of the early days of the music in New Orleans, and these gave the older music a storybook attraction.

The first consequence was the rediscovery of Jelly Roll Morton and

Sidney Bechet, both of whom began to record again. A second consequence was a small boomlet in reissues of recordings of the older music. The younger reader, familiar with the racks of LPs of Armstrong, Oliver, Morton, and others in the big record shops, should realize that in 1940 all the early jazz records were out of print — all of Bessie Smith, all of Armstrong's Hot Fives, all of Morton's Red Hot Peppers, all of Oliver's Creole Jazz Band, all of Beiderbecke, Teschemacher, even all of Henderson and Ellington except their current releases. In the late thirties this gap began to be filled by reissues, at first by private labels, like that of the Hot Jazz Club of America, and then, timidly, by the big three record companies, Victor, Decca, and Columbia, who had scooped up all the smaller labels in the early days of the Depression and had the old records in their vaults. These early reissue programs began to make available, in album sets, the Hot Fives, the Red Hot Peppers, and the Beiderbecke recordings. At the same time a handful of small record companies started up, dedicated to recording the pure jazz. The most important of these were Commodore, founded by Milton Gabler, and Blue Note, started by Alfred Lion, a German who had emigrated in the 1930s. Both managed to survive in the face of the deluge of swing records, and in time grew healthy. This freshet of records helped to increase the audience for the older, or purer music, as its followers saw it, and by about 1940 or so there were enough people interested in it to make it possible for jazz entrepreneurs to sell it in a few nightclubs and concert halls. Thus began the New Orleans or, as it is now generally called, the dixieland revival.

The dixieland revival appeared as two distinct schools, the members of which, in many cases, had little use for each other. One school was built around older players, many of them the white Midwesterners, who had begun playing jazz in the 1920s and who had been influenced primarily by the Original Dixieland Jazz Band, the New Orleans Rhythm Kings, and Bix and the Wolverines. The second school grew out of a deliberate attempt by young musicians to emulate the playing of the older bands. Their preference was not for Bix or the Original Dixieland Jazz Band, but for the black bands in the New Orleans tradition — Morton, Oliver, and Armstrong of the Hot Fives. This, they felt, was the real jazz. These schools were thus distinguished in two ways: one took white models and the other black; and one group was playing in a tradition it had helped to create and knew firsthand, while the other was attempting to re-create something mainly from study after the fact. Despite these distinctions both were building on the same thing: the traditional New Orleans jazz band, with its front line of cornet, trombone, and clarinet playing polyphonic music over a rhythm section.

The first beneficiaries of the renewed interest in the New Orleans style were those Midwestern whites who had entered jazz in the 1920s to play the music of Oliver and the New Orleans Rhythm Kings. The bell was sounded when a law-student-turned-musician named Nick Rongetti opened a club that featured jazz in Greenwich Village, which he named Nick's. He picked Bobby Hackett to lead the band, and Hackett hired a Midwesterner, Eddie Condon, to play guitar. Condon was never an important musician, but he was an assertive and amusing personality with a flair for publicity. Very quickly he became the central figure of a group of the pioneer white players, including Bud Freeman, Miff Mole, Jimmy McPartland, Pee Wee Russell, Max Kaminsky, and a few blacks, such as Bechet, clarinetist Edmond Hall, and others. Nick's was an idea whose time had come. The writers and fans who admired the old school developed into a following. Very quickly other clubs opened in New York and elsewhere, and the men began to record in various combinations, mostly for Commodore and other small labels. In the

A good proportion of the dixieland cadre of the 1940s seen on the stand at Eddie Condon's Greenwich Village club. From left, Pee Wee Russell, Max Kaminsky, Wild Bill Davison, Jack Lesberg (bass, in rear), George Brunis, Bud Freeman, and Freddie Ohms. William P. Gottlieb/Edward Gottlieb Collection

early forties Condon organized a series of jam sessions at New York's Town Hall, which were broadcast on Saturday afternoons, and these were important in widening the audience for the music. Then, in 1945, Condon found backing and opened his own club, which was immediately successful.

These men were not "revivalists." They had come into jazz to play this sort of music, and they had gone on playing it over the years, whenever possible. To be sure, during the early years of the Depression there had not been much audience for it, and most of them went elsewhere for a living: Brunis spent almost two decades with a novelty band led by Ted Lewis; Bud Freeman, Kaminsky, drummer Dave Tough, and others were in the swing bands. From their point of view the music simply had been out of favor for six or eight years, and now it was modish again. They did not see themselves as reviving an older form so much as continuing to do what they always had done.

The music they were playing, however, was not in a strict sense New Orleans music, nor was it the same thing they had been playing in the 1920s. As the players matured, gaining technical polish and experience with other kinds of forms, the music evolved. In the main, they were using the same approach to rhythm as the swing bands; there were no tubas and banjos in Condon bands, but basses and guitars. The emphasis was on the uninflected four beats to a measure, and hi-hat timekeeping in the drums. Many of the rhythm players worked in swing bands: drummers Wettling and Tough had both been with Shaw and Berigan as well as with other big bands; pianist Stacy with Goodman and Dorsey; Mel Powell with Goodman. For a second matter, although some of these men followed the format of the New Orleans front line, it was by no means true of all of them. Players like Kaminsky, Bobby Hackett, Teagarden, Billy Butterfield, and many others had never really been New Orleans players. They had developed from the solo style that Armstrong had brought to prominence.

But all was not roses in the revival rooms. Some of the writers, particularly Rudi Blesh, were insisting that the dixieland of Condon and similar groups was not the true New Orleans music, an assertion most of the musicians would have agreed with. These writers, and many fans, were demanding something purer, and there were two sets of musicians who were prepared to supply it. One was a group in the San Francisco area led by a hitherto obscure cornet player named Lu Watters. Watters had been operating a big band, but his heart was elsewhere, and he began pulling out of the band a small jazz band, as Goodman, Crosby, and others had begun to do, as a jazz specialty. The group was devoted to the music of Morton and especially Oliver. (The band used two cornets in the Oliver-Armstrong style.) In 1940, under the name of the Yerba Buena Jazz Band, it began to work occasionally at the Dawn Club in San Francisco.

Although Watters himself had played jazz as early as 1926, when he was a fifteen-year-old high school boy, and thus had some slight claim to have been in the early music himself, most of the men around him were younger and had come into jazz after the New Orleans style was moribund. These San Francisco musicians were attempting to restore a mode that was no longer a living part of the musical culture. Audiences had to be fashioned more or less out of whole cloth, and this, as it turned out, could be done. The music was lively; there was a bit of romance attached to it; and it drew not only older jazz buffs who had collected Morton records two decades earlier, but young fans, especially college students, many of whom saw it as good-time beer-drinking music. The Watters band developed a following first on the West Coast, and then nationally, and a spin-off group, led by trombonist Melvin "Turk" Murphy with Bob Scobey, Watters's second cornetist, was even more successful, recording frequently for Columbia in the forties and fifties.

The success of the Watters and Murphy groups encouraged others to start; and in time there existed a considerable number of groups, mostly with local reputations, playing the older music. These bands, sticklers for purity, played mostly the repertory drawn from the Morton and Oliver bands, with some admixture of Hot Five, New Orleans Rhythm Kings, and Original Dixieland Jazz Band tunes. They used tuba and banjo in place of bass and guitar, with tuba playing chiefly on first and third beats of the measure, producing a so-called two-beat feel, although in fact they played, as had Oliver and Morton, in 4/4. The piano playing was heavily inflected with ragtime, and the revivalist groups were important in keeping ragtime alive.

The second set of players prepared to supply genuine New Orleans music was a small group in New Orleans. In 1939 William Russell and Frederic Ramsey, Jr., located the sixty-year-old jazz pioneer Bunk Johnson in a small town near New Orleans. Johnson had given up playing because of problems with his teeth. He was fitted out with a set of dentures, began playing again, and in 1942 made the first of a number of record sessions. He was brought north the next year and began working in jazz clubs, mainly with bands that included other New Orleans jazz old-timers. (Nineteen forty-three was the pivotal year in the history of trad. Not only did Johnson come to public attention that year, but Kid Ory was discovered by Orson Welles and presented on a jazz program Welles had. It was also the year of the founding of the George Webb band in Kent, England, and the Graeme Bell band in Melbourne. The Abadie band in Paris had been formed the year before.)

Johnson was a smash success. Here, audiences felt, was a genuine relic of the past, a piece of the true cross. When so much importance was placed on authenticity, who could be more authentic? The fact that Johnson and his fellows played badly out of tune, muffed notes constantly, and played with little rhythmic ease did not seem to matter. This, surely, was the real

A rare photo of two jazz pioneers, taken during the New Orleans revival of the 1940s. Bunk Johnson and Huddie Ledbetter, better known as Leadbelly, were born in the 1880s, when jazz did not exist, and helped to give it its design. William P. Gottlieb/Edward Gottlieb Collection

thing. For several years, until his retirement in 1948, the year before his death, Johnson was in heavy demand. Unfortunately, he grew progressively more arrogant, drank heavily, and caused endless squabbles within the group. When he finally gave up the leadership of the group, his clarinetist, George Lewis, took over and went on to become even more celebrated than Johnson, especially in Europe.

For the public, the Johnson group and the San Francisco revivalists had a romantic appeal that the Condon groups could not match. Pressure was brought to bear on Condon, both by the writers and the fans, and he bowed to it. In 1947 he let go the swing-oriented dixielanders, like Kaminsky and Dave Tough, and brought in George Brunis, the original trombonist with the New Orleans Rhythm Kings, and Wild Bill Davison, a Midwesterner who had worked in the genre, and began featuring the New Orleans repertory. Regardless of what any of the players might have preferred — Davison was hardly an exclusively New Orleans player — this was the music that audiences liked, and it very quickly came to be called "dixieland." Young people liked it for its strong melody lines, its simple harmonies, and its formal routines. (A typical New Orleans standard has several strains in different keys, often with interludes between them, and various traditional breaks.)

The most influential of the dixielanders were the men around Condon, particularly clarinetists Pee Wee Russell and Edmond Hall, cornetists Davison, Max Kaminsky, and Bobby Hackett, and trombonist Brunis. (The schism between the two groups was quickly patched over.) Of them all, Bill Davison has come to be seen as the primal figure in the dixieland movement. A blunt, outspoken man of the kind who becomes the subject of anecdotes, Davison was born in Defiance, Ohio, in 1906. As a teen-ager he played in local bands, and in 1927 landed in Chicago. Here he met the Austin High group and their confreres, and began to work with them. Unlikely as it seems today, in view of his roughhewn style, Davison was originally a player in the Beiderbecke mold, as can be heard on "Smiling Skies," made in 1928 with the obscure Benny Meroff band. In 1931 he organized his own band, which included some of these men, and began rehearsing it. He was driving Frank Teschemacher home from a rehearsal when the car was struck by a cab, and Teschemacher was thrown out and killed. Teschemacher was much beloved by the other musicians, and, according to at least one story, Davison was ostracized by them after the accident, although it appears not to have been his fault. Whatever the truth, he moved to Milwaukee and worked there from 1933 until 1941, when he came to New York. He became a Condon regular, working at Nick's, Condon's, and various other clubs featuring dixieland. He also began to record frequently, at first mainly for Blue Note and Commodore, and then for a variety of other labels. By the fifties he had developed a considerable personal following and had established himself as the leading star of the dixieland movement. He continued to work in jazz well into the 1970s.

The most influential of Davison's records are certainly a series he made in the early 1940s for Commodore with Pee Wee Russell and trombonist Brunis, especially "That's A-Plenty," "Panama," and "Royal Garden Blues." For abandoned, hard-driving playing, there are few records in jazz to match them. Brunis is not a great trombonist; his tone is colorless and his ideas pedestrian. But he was thoroughly schooled in the New Orleans system, and his ensemble playing is at times flawless, his line complementing Davison's exactly. As an ensemble trombonist Brunis has few peers.

But it is Davison who supplied the fire for these records. He employs a biting attack, one of the most staccato lines in jazz trumpet playing, a wide, fast terminal vibrato, and an assortment of growls and rasps that he uses frequently, even on slow ballads. His notes often come like karate chops. He is impatient, as if he must get down to the end with no time wasted; there is a strong sense of forward push in his music. His besetting weakness is a lack of thought in his line. He has a stock of figures that he rearranges time and again to suit the needs of a given song; some of these he has used unchanged for forty years. But they are not simple clichés for filling blank spaces; they are felt. And whatever else can be said about Davison, he is always a powerful and exciting player.

Davison's major competitors in dixieland were Max Kaminsky and Bobby Hackett. In fact, neither of these men thought of himself as a dixieland player. Both were melodists, influenced by Beiderbecke, and played within small compasses, paying particular attention to producing warm and welcoming sound. Kaminsky was born in Brockton, Massachusetts, in 1908. He worked with various juvenile bands, and by the time he was a teen-ager he was playing with commercial bands in the Boston area. He came under Beiderbecke's influence when the Goldkette band toured New England in 1926, and in 1928 he moved to Chicago, where he met the Midwestern players.

Although Kaminsky spent most of the years of the Depression working in commercial bands and various swing bands, he continued to record from time to time with the white jazz players. Yet his major work, until the late forties, was as a dance musician with larger bands; he never had extensive experience with New Orleans music. The dixieland revival drew him into the music simply because it offered work, and most of the rest of his playing career was with dixieland bands. Well thought-of by fellow musicians, he never developed the public following of a Bill Davison because he lacked a showy approach.

Kaminsky is a minimalist. He rarely uses growls, although he sometimes uses a plunger mute, and he will often play a whole solo within the range of an octave. He frequently does not attack notes, but pushes them out to create a legato effect. He will often use quarter notes where other players would be using eighth notes, and he is not afraid of leaving space between his phrases. In his ensemble playing on, for example, "Rockin' Chair" or "It's Right Here for You," both made for Commodore, he uses the bare minimum of notes, just sketching in the outlines of the melody and letting the other instruments fill it out. His tone is warm but light. Beyond anything, Kaminsky is a melodist; he is, as musicians put it, a "pretty" player.

Bobby Hackett was also, in the musicians' term, a pretty player, perhaps even more so than Kaminsky. A New Englander like Kaminsky, Hackett was born in 1915 in Providence, Rhode Island. His father was a blacksmith, and the family a big one. Hackett started on guitar and violin and learned cornet later. He continued to play guitar, however, and for most of the years of his twenties he worked principally as a guitarist, sometimes playing cornet as a feature or on special gigs.

During the Depression he played with various commercial dance bands, and then, when the swing band era arrived, with several of the big bands. He was no dixieland player. His most important influence was the solo playing of Beiderbecke, not the bands of Oliver and Morton. But like Kaminsky, he was drawn into the dixieland movement because it offered a chance to play jazz. He became associated with Condon, made a number of records for Commodore under Condon's leadership, and worked at Nick's and other clubs that were essentially dixieland houses. In different bands he had in the 1950s and beyond, he tried to escape the dixieland format as much as possible, but he was not always able to do so.

Bobby Hackett's best-known solo is the cornet one he played with the Glenn Miller band, in which he was usually the guitarist, on the Miller hit "String of Pearls." More influential among musicians, however, were records like "Embraceable You," a tune with a good deal of chromatic movement in harmonies. As a guitarist, Hackett was more familiar than many horn players with how chords fit together. He was interested in working with tunes that had subtler harmonies than the dixieland standards, and his ability to sculpt clean lines on these harmonies impressed other players. In time even the bop players found Hackett worth studying. The "Embraceable You" solo is brief but carefully worked out, and it is laved in the spring-water pure tone Hackett likes. Hackett rarely inflects a note; he depends for his effect entirely on the shape of his line, obviously a result of the Beiderbecke influence. Where Kaminsky was a minimalist, playing perhaps only one of the notes of the chord, Hackett very frequently played them all.

His best-known group was one that played at the Henry Hudson Hotel in New York for six months in 1957. The band included pianist Dick Carey, who doubled on E♭ alto horn, a band instrument rare in jazz; a tuba player; and an underrated baritone saxophonist, Ernie Caceres. This was hardly a traditional dixieland line-up, and the group played a lot of sometimes relatively complicated arrangements. But it also played dixieland numbers, no doubt in response to audience demand. Hackett's solo on "Sugar" is typical, filled with lines of eighth notes that move up and down, exploring the chords. Again like Kaminsky, Hackett was better known to musicians than to the larger public, but in the 1950s comedian Jackie Gleason produced a series of lush records filled with strings and overtones of sexuality. Hackett was hired to play trumpet solos over this background, and through these records he developed a wider audience. He died in 1976.

One more major dixieland figure was a black clarinetist, Edmond Hall. Hall is an anomaly; he was one of the few blacks who made a career of playing in the dixieland context, and he was also — as difficult as it is to credit, considering the long tradition of black clarinet playing — the last black clarinetist to make a name in jazz. Hall was born in New Orleans in 1901 and worked around the South in a number of obscure bands until 1929, when he came to New York. He landed a job with the Claude Hopkins band, and worked with Hopkins and the Lucky Millinder big bands until

play at a professional level. Typical is a group surrounding a businessman named Bill Dunham, a stride pianist who did his first playing in a college band at Harvard. Dunham leads a band called the Grove Street Stompers, which has worked regularly on Monday nights at a Greenwich Village club since 1963. He draws from a shifting group of semiprofessional players, and the music they produce is always strongly felt, and often excellent. There are many similar bands in major cities around the country.

In the United States today dixieland is widely derogated as a frivolous, commercialized form of jazz — or, indeed, not even jazz at all. This assessment is often made by people with little sense of jazz history, and it is grossly unfair. Dixieland grew out of a solid jazz tradition, and its virtues are considerable. Nonetheless, a real question is raised about any art form that no longer seems relevant to its time. I do not mean that an art work is no longer valuable when its time passes and it loses its immediacy for the living culture. Quite obviously, the works of Bach and Dickens continue to move us today, and, similarly, the reissues of the dixieland records of the 1940s and fifties, when the music had a real audience, are as interesting as any of the older jazz records. But what would we say of a composer writing oratorios in the Baroque manner, or a novelist turning out books on the order of *Oliver Twist?* The attempt to work in an older form is often made, but the results rarely draw significant audiences. And this, in fact, is what has happened to dixieland. The audience for the music today consists in large measure of its practitioners, the avocational players who are keeping it alive. Even the remaining veterans, like Davison and Kaminsky, both still working in the late 1970s, record infrequently, and their audiences are usually conventioneers who see dixieland as an accompaniment to drinking.

Still, the music has enormous strengths and is surely worth keeping alive. It remains the only jazz form that has really solved the problem of simultaneous improvisation, and as such has escaped the trap most jazz since has fallen into: the routine sequence of unrelated solos fenced in by short, equally unrelated riffs at beginning and end. The alignment of clarinet, trombone, and trumpet, developed by the New Orleans pioneers, is a very workable form. The principal problem with the dixielanders, however, is that they have done little to exploit it. After four decades it ought to have been possible to find something to do with it besides playing "Muskrat Ramble" or "Tin Roof Blues" for the thousandth time, with the same breaks in the same places. But at its best dixieland has a freshness and power that remain compelling. And if it lacks a large audience in the United States, such is not the case elsewhere. In Europe and places in Asia, trad jazz is a highly popular music with serious audiences, which support it, at least to a degree. But that is a story for another chapter.

Roy, Billie,
and the Swing Street Stars

Strangers to New York think of it as a city of skyscrapers, a city where people move through canyons lined with vast stone and glass towers whose tops are not seen from the ground. In fact, the classic New York building is the brownstone, which outnumbers the skyscraper by a factor of perhaps a thousand to one. The brownstone was conceived of as a single-family dwelling by the rising middle class of nineteenth-century New York, itself a rising city. Because real estate was already, in the nineteenth century, expensive, the brownstones were built on plots that were narrow across the front and extended lengthwise halfway through the block.

Often the houses were only one room wide, perhaps no more than ten feet across the front, though usually wider. The main or parlor floor was always set a half-story above ground level. Beneath the parlor floor was a cellar, sunk a half-story into the ground, with a few windows set high up in the walls. Here worked the immigrant help, who sent meals upstairs on a dumbwaiter to diners out of reach of kitchen smells. By 1900 New York was covered with them. In some places in Manhattan they would run on, block after block, a sea of brownstones virtually from river to river.

But as real estate values rose, the brownstones were broken up into apartments. Then, in 1920, it was discovered that the brownstone basement was well suited to another social institution, the speakeasy — the illegal drinking parlors that flourished during Prohibition. The brownstone basement provided a discreet entrance from the street for both patrons and shipments of liquor and an easy exit out the back, just in case. In time, the basements of New York's brownstones became honeycombed with speakeasies, probably numbering in the thousands. Some of them were rough drinking places, but others sported upholstered banquettes and white napery, which lent them a modicum of elegance.

One such speakeasy was run by a former bootlegger named Joe Helbock. Helbock was a good friend of Jimmy Dorsey and hung out with musicians, and when he opened the Onyx on Fifty-second Street in 1927 it was natural for it to become a musicians' hangout. Some of them began to play there on a casual basis, and eventually Helbock started booking musicians regularly, among them Art Tatum, Willie "the Lion" Smith, and a group called the Spirits of Rhythm, which included Teddy Bunn on guitar, scat singer Leo Watson, and Virgil Scroggins playing suitcase with whiskbrooms. With Repeal in 1933 the speakeasies became legal bars. Helbock's Onyx drew well, and other entrepreneurs booking music came onto Fifty-second Street to compete with him. It was the Depression, and people needed a better excuse to go out and spend money than just drink. The swing era was just beginning, so the clubs reached out for the new musical heroes, the men associated with swing. By the late thirties "Swing Street," as its publicists were beginning to call it, contained some half-dozen clubs in one block of West Fifty-second Street, between Fifth and Sixth avenues, offering an extremely high level of jazz — the Three Deuces, Jimmy Ryan's, the Onyx, the Famous Door.

The phenomenon was an old one. We have seen the concentration of jazz places in the honky-tonks of Storyville, Chicago's South Side, the nightclubs of Kansas City, the big show spots of Harlem. Fifty-second Street was another such. It provided economic support for a lot of musicians, a place to practice their trade, and a confluence of musical ideas. It was easy for a man working the street to walk a few doors down on his break and find out what his friends and enemies were doing. Fifty-second Street was not, of course, the only jazz location; there were several clubs in Greenwich Village, others in Harlem, and still others in other cities, notably Chicago. But Fifty-second Street became the symbolic headquarters of jazz, the jazz center of the world. At the time it appeared that the big bands were the major movement in the music, at least to the casual observer; but it was clear to jazz buffs then, and obvious to us today, that the most important developments in the music were taking place on Fifty-second Street and in similar places.

The fact that these clubs were located in brownstones is significant: the very narrowness of them made a mark on jazz. All were laid out along similar lines. On entering, one saw a bar running halfway down the length of one wall. On the rear wall was a small bandstand, big enough to accommodate comfortably at most a half-dozen players, although at times more crowded onto it. The remainder of the room was devoted to tables and minimal decoration.

This layout made the small band the natural form for the clubs. Until this time, most jazz had been played either by the big bands or by New Orleans–derived bands. But owners were discovering that their audiences were drawn by a headliner — a Billie Holiday, a Coleman Hawkins. Why pay for twelve musicians when you could fill the house with a name soloist supported by a house rhythm section? Big bands did occasionally play Fifty-second Street — Basie broke into national prominence as a result of a gig at the Famous Door — but the experiment was rarely tried. Thus, a combination of economics and physical layout began to dictate that the best players — those whose names would draw the jazz fans — would work in small groups. It meant as well that the favored players would be the dominating soloists, men who could work with a three-piece rhythm section rather than as part of a dixieland band. Thus there began to develop a new type of band, built on a rhythm section of two to four men to which one to three horns were added. Today the rhythm section is usually piano, bass, and drums, but in the heyday of Fifty-second Street it was just as likely to include a guitarist, often in place of the bass.

At the same time there began to be some attrition in the types of horns used. The rise of the saxophonists in the 1930s, and especially the dominance of Coleman Hawkins, had put a premium on the playing of rapid lines of notes to express more complex chord sequences. Trombonists especially had difficulty coping with a technical demand for which the instrument was not designed, and fairly quickly the trombone began to lose its place in jazz. The disappearance of the clarinet during these years is more of a puzzle; if anything, it could be played faster than the saxophone. The problem may have been that the clarinet is more difficult to master than the saxophone, which in any case was seen as the premier jazz instrument, so many budding clarinetists became saxophone players. For another, it may also have been that young blacks were identifying the clarinet with whites as a result of the fame of Goodman and Shaw — although there were excellent black clarinetists for models, including Buster Bailey, Barney Bigard, and Edmond Hall. But the fact is that all of the clarinetists to emerge after, say, 1940, were white — Tony Scott, Buddy De Franco, and, later, Jimmy Giuffre. Whatever the reasons, by the mid-1940s the clarinet had very nearly disappeared from jazz, except as it was played by the older players and the dixielanders. The result was to turn the front line, in the main, over to trumpets and saxophones.

With the jazz band cut down to a small group, the problem of form had to be tackled anew. It was not possible, with the new instrumentation, to play anything beyond the simplest sort of arranged passages, and it was not possible to play New Orleans music at all. Something new was needed, and unfortunately, as so often happens in jazz, nobody undertook to find it. The players were content to spend their evenings soloing on their favorite vehicles, and audiences seemed willing to let them. Often a slow tune would be opened by a relatively straightforward statement of the melody for at least eight bars, and perhaps closed the same way. There evolved standard riff patterns that were regularly used to open and close faster tunes. But these were by no means always used, and in many instances, after an eight-bar piano introduction, the piece would consist simply of solos. There was little attempt to relate the solos one to another or give them any sort of emotional unity. The result was a musical Dagwood sandwich in which the parts had little to do with each other or the whole except that they were contained between the same pieces of bread.

Thus there developed the type of jazz band and a system of playing that have existed until today. The bop and neobop bands of the 1950s, the avant-garde bands of Ornette Coleman and John Coltrane, and even the fusion groups of today consist mainly of one to three horns in front of a rhythm section, playing long solos sandwiched between opening and closing arranged passages. Trumpets and saxophones still predominate. This Fifty-second Street style has been called "small band swing," which is as good a title as any. Most of the men had come from the swing bands, and they were playing with the same swing feel that had evolved out of Bechet and Armstrong particularly.

Playing in a small band, however, meant some changes in the rhythm section, particularly by drummers. No longer could they hammer on the snares and tom-toms, for most of the time they were backing a single instrument, often playing quietly. To reduce the sound they played either with brushes on the snare, or in the manner pioneered by Walter Johnson and Jo Jones, with either brushes or sticks on the hi-hat. For the most part they stuck closely to a steady ride beat:

It must be remembered that the two short notes are not played exactly as written above. The first one was generally accented, and the second often swallowed up. The unevenness of the pair of eighth notes was characteristic of swing playing in general and is found in the phrasing of almost all the players of the time.

Four drummers of the period stand out: Sid Catlett, Cozy Cole, Jo Jones, and Dave Tough. All of them worked in more or less the same manner, using the ride beat and accenting on the snare.

It is difficult to talk about drummers, and rhythm players in general, because so much depends on the exactness of timekeeping and subtle placement of accent. A true judgment about a drummer or bass player can be made only by those who have worked with him and can tell by "feel" what he is doing. Horn players have emphatic views on rhythm men, and not always the same ones. For a soloist to relax and let his line flow over the rhythm, the ground beat must be exact; one can hardly place a note fractionally ahead or behind a beat if the beat itself is fractionally out of place. Of the four men named above, Sidney Catlett was considered in his day pre-eminent, in part because of the exactness of his time. He worked with

Benny Carter, McKinney, Henderson, Armstrong, Goodman, Teddy Wilson, and occasionally Duke Ellington, which suggests the esteem in which he was held. He played on dozens of all-star sessions as well, and was voted top on his instrument in fan polls. Catlett worked on the snare drum far more than did the other three men, using brushes to reduce his sound in the context of small groups. He was a master at supplying accents to "kick" a soloist here and there in a chorus. We can hear him using rim shots to drive the soloists into action on "Esquire Blues."

The other men were not far behind, if at all. Cole was with Morton in 1930, played in pit bands and with small groups, and at times with Goodman, Armstrong, Teagarden, and Carter. Jo Jones made his reputation as a member of Basie's great rhythm section, and recorded with a long list of jazz stars, including Holiday, Ellington, and Goodman. Dave Tough, who was white, was part of the Austin High gang in Chicago. He worked with Red Nichols, and, during the swing band era, Tommy Dorsey, Berigan, Goodman, and Shaw, as well as with many small groups, including Condon's. He was best known to the public as the drummer with Woody Herman's Herds. It was these men who led the way in establishing the steady 4/4 swing beat that undergirt both the big bands and the small swing bands.

It should be kept in mind that although the new small swing band format would in time dominate jazz, driving all others out, it was not yet the master of Fifty-second Street. Dixieland bands always held a prominent place on the street, especially at Jimmy Ryan's, which until today continues to give the music a home. Again, by the early 1940s some of the bop players were occasionally working on Fifty-second Street. Indeed, it is probably fair to say that at one time or another every jazz musician of any standing born between 1900 and 1925 played — or at least sat in — on Fifty-second Street. Inevitably there was a mélange of styles represented on Fifty-second Street, sometimes on the same bandstand. The clubs usually offered some sort of second bill, perhaps a solo pianist or a trio to spell the headliner, and these intermission players were not necessarily chosen to match the stars. On Fifty-second Street you could hear almost anything any night. But over the two decades from the late 1930s until the late fifties, when Fifty-second Street was an important jazz center, the new style gradually drove the others out.

From the standpoint of form it was a large step backward; both the big bands in the hands of somebody like an Ellington, or the New Orleans form worked by a Morton or the best of the dixielanders, produced in many respects more satisfactory jazz than the small swing bands. Where there is attention paid to the relating of parts, architecture, and other formal considerations, all does not depend on the brilliance of the soloists. With the small swing bands, when the solos were pedestrian the whole piece failed.

But, in fact, the solos were not often pedestrian, and at times they were superlative.

We know this jazz, of course, from the recordings, and the records do not reflect exactly the actual situation in the clubs. There of course had always been recordings by pickup groups; Armstrong's Hot Five and Hot Seven never existed outside the studios, and Morton's groups were reconstituted for recordings. But the largest amount of recorded jazz was made by groups playing the material they used in clubs, dances, or parties. During the Fifty-second Street era this was no longer the case. Many of the best of the players of the time were working in big bands; others were making up little combinations, or "combos," from whoever happened to be at hand at the time a gig appeared. Few of these small bands existed as permanent units.

Some of this small band swing was recorded by the major companies, usually drawing on name players from the big bands they had under contract. But the bulk of it was recorded by dozens of small, short-lived labels, organized by jazz fans who had a few dollars to spend and liked the idea of producing recording sessions with their heroes. Savoy, Signature, Jump, Dial, Joe Davis — the labels came and went, but they and the big three were responsible for preserving the jazz of the period, and the jazz fan owes their struggling founders a debt. These small companies were, as one would expect, unsystematic, recording whom they could when they could; and the bands that got thrown together in this way often were made up of the more prominent players, regardless of style, who would not necessarily be working together in the clubs.

The leading players in small band swing were the saxophonists, especially the tenor saxophonists — Young, Hawkins, Chu Berry, Webster, and some younger men coming along. They were, however, challenged by several trumpet players who had developed in the big bands and were, by 1940, attempting to set up business on their own with small groups. These players had been caught in something of a historical bind. They had been, at the beginning of their careers, overwhelmed by the figure of Armstrong. But then, as they were coming into their own, the saxophonists were introducing a fast, complex style that posed severe technical difficulties for trumpets — the same sort of difficulties that forced out the trombonists. Their response was to develop a clean, straightforward style that owed something to Armstrong, but that owed a good deal to legitimate systems of trumpet playing, too. Among the best of them were Frankie Newton, who had worked with Charlie Johnson and Teddy Hill; Oran "Hot Lips" Page, who had been with Moten and Basie; Billy Butterfield, with Goodman and Shaw; Bill Coleman, who had played with Charlie Johnson, Lucky Millinder, Benny Carter, and Teddy Hill; Joe Thomas, with Henderson and Carter; Jonah Jones, with Lunceford, Henderson, and Calloway; and Charlie Shavers, who had been with Millinder and Tommy Dorsey. Big band trumpet playing called for power and brilliance, and these men were set in that mold, sometimes at the expense of subtleties to be found in the more enclosed playing of Hackett, Kaminsky, or Clayton.

One among them, however, who was capable of nuance was Joe Thomas, potentially the best of them all. Today nearly forgotten, for a short period he promised to become one of the most important voices in jazz. Born in 1909 in Missouri, he eventually worked with the Fletcher Henderson and Benny Carter bands, and by 1940 or so was recognized by musicians, if not the jazz public, as one of the finest trumpet players working around New York. The extent of his reputation is indicated by the fact that he was often chosen as trumpeter on record dates that included the biggest names in jazz. He recorded with bands including Hawkins, Teagarden, and Tatum, and worked in clubs under such leaders as James P. Johnson, Fats Waller, Teddy Wilson, and, surprisingly, Eddie Condon.

Thomas's playing is pure and simple as mountain water. His tone is full but free of growls and rasps. At times, indeed, you can hear his disdain for freak effects, when he deliberately leaves uninflected a note another player would have bent or rasped. Like Beiderbecke, he is principally interested in exposing the melodic line, which he does gently and without haste. Typically, he alternates quick, delicate phrases in the low or middle register with longer, straightforward notes higher up, though he never rises very high at any time. Like the finest jazz players, at his best he is able to sculpt complete choruses that are unified, the parts assembled into a recognizable whole. In a session made in 1944 with Hawkins and Teagarden, he plays an exquisite solo on "Too Marvelous," which displays these characteristics — a sixteen-measure opening of quiet commentary, followed by a bridge that rises to a stronger, simpler statement, and a closing in the mood of the beginning. But Thomas's masterpiece was made in 1941, with a recording group that was put together to support the blues shouter Joe Turner and included Art Tatum and Edmond Hall. Some of the sides at the session were up-tempo numbers made without the vocalist, and on one of these, "Stompin' at the Savoy," Thomas creates the rarest thing in jazz, a perfect solo chorus. The tempo is moderate, and Thomas's figures characteristically rise and fall between delicate, tender phrases in the lower registers and stronger lines higher up. He opens his chorus a full measure ahead of its beginning, thus immediately throwing the phrasing against the natural flow of the song. But this counter-phrasing is not his normal method, and the rest of the solo is cut more naturally to the song's phrases. The first figure is approximately four bars long and is followed by a related one of the same length. The second eight bars consist of a single phrase, simple and direct, yet full of surprises. At the bridge, changing mood somewhat, he breaks his solo into four two-bar figures, paraphrasing the melody. (The chord sequence of this bridge is so idiosyncratic that it has always forced soloists to conform to its shape.) And he concludes the melody with an absolutely flawless eight-bar figure, as fine as the best work of Beiderbecke or Young in respect to construction. The first two bars mark the solo's peak and are followed by two bars, lower in intensity, that comment on the first figure. The intensity continues to drop as the phrase unrolls to its logical conclusion. Overall, the thirty-two bars of the chorus are bell-shaped — rising gradually to the bridge, where we get a respite, followed by the peak and the final falling away.

Unhappily, Thomas was not recorded often during this, his most fertile period. Through the three decades after World War II he continued to work on the periphery of jazz, almost forgotten.

The leading trumpet player of the period was not Thomas, however, but a hard-driving, fierce little man who was able to solve the technical challenge set by the saxophonists. Roy Eldridge was the dominant trumpet player of the swing period. He strongly influenced all the men who came after him, most particularly Dizzy Gillespie, who at one stage of his career aped Eldridge's manner so successfully that at times it was difficult for listeners to tell them apart.

Eldridge was born in Pittsburgh in 1911. He was largely self-taught, and did not learn to read until after he was working professionally. He was a talented boy, for he played his first job — on drums — at the age of six, and he went on the road with a band when he was sixteen. He was hearing Armstrong, of course, and this influence can be heard as late as 1937 on the last chorus of "Florida Stomp," with his own orchestra. However, he seems to have been more directly affected by Armstrong's competitor, Red Allen: his playing resembles the helter-skelter high-speed fireworks of Allen more than Armstrong's more measured phrasing. Then he came under the influence of Rex Stewart, who was in his brother's band and went on to star with Henderson and Ellington as Eldridge was coming into maturity. Impressed by Stewart's flexibility, Eldridge concentrated on developing his speed. But in the end it was not a trumpet player whom Eldridge took for his model; it was the saxophonists, especially Hawkins and Benny Carter. He learned to play Hawkins's showcase number with Henderson, "Stampede." He has said, "They played so much music, Hawkins and Carter, how could you help not like them if you like music . . . I'd listen to them and be stunned. I didn't know the right names for anything at first, but I knew what knocked me out . . . Changes, man, I dug . . . You see, the saxophones, or some of them, would run changes, would run through all the passing chords and things." Eldridge, thus, based his style on a saxophone conception. It was a while, however, before he had it under control. He said, "I was a young cat, and I was very fast, but I wasn't telling no kind of story."

Yet the saxophone model helped him to develop a technique that was beyond most of his competitors', and by the mid-1930s he was recognized as the coming figure on his instrument. He played as feature soloist with the major Harlem bands: Charlie Johnson, Teddy Hill, McKinney, and eventually Fletcher Henderson. By the time the swing band era was peaking he was so well thought-of that first Gene Krupa and then Artie Shaw risked the color line to take him on as featured soloist. Eldridge, a man of enormous pride, found intolerable the insults he was subjected to as a black man in a white band playing at white dances. He told *Down Beat:*

> We [the Krupa band] arrive in one town and the rest of the band checks in. I can't get into their hotel so I keep my bags and start riding around looking for another place, where someone's supposed to have had a reservation for me. I get there and move all my bags in . . . Then the clerk, when he sees that I'm the Mr. Eldridge the reservation was made for, suddenly discovers that one of their regular tenants just arrived and took the last available room . . . Later on, when I was with Artie Shaw, I went to a place where we were supposed to play a dance, and they wouldn't even let me in the place. "This is a white dance," they said, and there was my name right outside, Roy "Little Jazz" Eldridge, and I told them who I was. When I finally did get in, I played that first set, trying to keep from crying. By the time I got through the set, the tears were rolling down my cheeks. I don't know how I made it. I went to the dressing room and stood in a corner crying and saying to myself, "Why the hell did I come out here again when I knew what would happen?" Artie came in and he was real great. He made the guy apologize to me that wouldn't let me come in and got him fired. Man, when you're on the stage, you're great, but as soon as you come off, you're nothing. It's not worth the glory, not worth the money, not worth anything.

No doubt in part because of experiences like these, Eldridge spent most of his working life after about 1938 playing in small groups in the Fifty-second Street mode. Over a long lifetime of playing, which has lasted until today, he made an enormous number of records in all sorts of contexts, but no matter what his surroundings, his playing is instantly recognizable. The saxophone conception is evident everywhere in his work. He uses a great many downward-plunging figures made of eighth notes weighted on the first of each pair, in the Hawkins manner, and he roughens his tone in places, as Hawkins, Berry, and Webster consistently did, to create intensity and climaxes. His sound otherwise, however, is strictly brass. He attacks cleanly and forcefully, often biting off notes sharply at the end. At other times he employs a relatively fast terminal vibrato, which becomes broader and slower on medium-tempo numbers; so broad at times that it gives the effect of hesitation. His greatest fault, which dogged him through much of his career, was a tendency toward scatter-shot playing, with ideas tumbling one on the heels of the next in a disorderly fashion.

All of these characteristics of his playing are evident on a record, made in 1936 with a small Teddy Wilson group, of a vile pop tune called "Mary Had a Little Lamb," which Roy sings. It is a strong solo and exciting at times, but there is the tendency toward disorder. The opening measures begin with two related figures, and then, at measure six, there appears a figure that starts as if to round off what has gone before but suddenly skyrockets upward into the beginning of something new.

As Eldridge matured, though, he developed better control of his ideas. In 1938 he made with Chu Berry a number called "46 West 52nd Street," in honor of Commodore Records, which had a shop at that address. It is typical of the time. The tune is based on "Sweet Georgia Brown," but the melody is nowhere stated, possibly to save the record company from paying royalties to the composer, a common practice at the time. Roy's playing here is filled with saxophone figures, long skeins of eighth notes, often

Roy "Little Jazz" Eldridge at the peak of his powers, not long before the beboppers overtook him. William P. Gottlieb/Edward Gottlieb Collection

chromatic runs, which fall far more naturally under a saxophonist's fingers than a trumpet player's. By 1940, in the classic version of "I Can't Believe That You're in Love with Me," with Hawkins, Benny Carter, and Catlett, he has a sure and ordered conception. Here is Eldridge at his best — the rasps, the sudden leaps into high places, the headlong plunges — and the organization is sound. Note especially how he begins preparing his second chorus in the twenty-fifth bar, so that the first chorus is felt as a steppingstone to the second one.

This was Eldridge at the pinnacle of his glory, but the seeds of his fall were already being sown. With the emergence of bop in 1945 or 1946, Eldridge found himself, at the height of his powers, in his mid-thirties, passé. For a few years more, on the momentum of the dying swing movement, he continued as a star player, but by the 1950s he was in Europe, suffering from a near–nervous breakdown. He has recorded since then, playing superb jazz, but by the seventies he was working mainly at Jimmy Ryan's, fronting a dixieland band for audiences of conventioneers.

One of the things that can be said about jazz is that it has no elder statesmen: when your day is done you are cast aside like rubbish. What happened to Eldridge was unjust, but it must be remembered that the swing players allowed Morton and Oliver to die in poverty. It is a heavy mark against Armstrong that Oliver died without proper medical attention, saving dimes for a ticket to New York, at a time when Louis was already wealthy.

Yet one more musician of the period who had considerable influence was Benny Carter, an alto saxophonist who also played clarinet, trumpet, and, more rarely, piano and trombone. Early in his career he even sang, although not to much effect. Carter has been held by some critics to be the peer of Johnny Hodges, and certainly he was widely respected by other musicians. In retrospect it seems clear enough that he was not the powerful improviser that Hodges was. The respect he gained from other players had more to do with his musicianship than with his actual playing.

Carter was born in New York, in 1907. He was thus, like most of the Northeastern players from the big cities, largely shut off from the black folk music tradition that fed jazz at its roots. He studied piano with his mother and sister, but he was mainly self-taught. He attended Wilberforce University as a theology student for a brief time, but dropped out to go into the music business. Through the latter part of the 1920s and into the early thirties he worked with many of the important big band leaders, including Fletcher Henderson, Charlie Johnson, Chick Webb, William McKinney, and, for a short time, Duke Ellington. At the same time he was beginning to teach himself arranging. "I used to lay Fletcher's charts out on the floor and study them," he has said.

One of his first efforts at band leading was in 1930, with a recording group called the Chocolate Dandies, drawn from the Henderson band. Carter played alto and clarinet on these records, and sang two vocals. His arrangements were undistinguished, but the records included excellent solos by Coleman Hawkins and Jimmy Harrison, and they were highly regarded by musicians. In 1933 he was chosen by Spike Hughes, the English composer and critic, to organize a group to record a set of Hughes's compositions, which were Ellington-influenced and advanced for their day. Carter was in Europe from 1935 to 1938. On his return he organized a big band to cash in on the swing boom, but the band was never more than a modest success financially, although musically it stood well above the average. From the mid-1940s on, Carter has lived in Hollywood, writing movie and television background music. He continued to play from time to time and was still active on both saxophone and trumpet into the late 1970s.

Carter, like many other saxophonists of his period, was influenced by Frankie Trumbauer. This influence is evident in Carter's purity of tone — he never coarsens his sound with rasps — and in his penchant for a legato line. His strength lies in this flowing line. He is, however, a reserved, quiet man, and this quality manifests itself frequently in a lack of force, of forward propulsion. Among his best-known records are the Chocolate Dandies sides, especially "Bugle Call Rag," on which he plays an excellent alto solo much more in the Hodges manner than is usual with Carter, and a first-rate clarinet solo as well. Another widely known Carter solo is on the "Crazy Rhythm" made in Paris with Django Reinhardt and Coleman Hawkins. Perhaps the best of all his solos is on Commodore Records' version of "I Can't Believe That You're in Love with Me," with Hawkins and Eldridge. Carter uses in this chorus an unusual, long, looping figure played at half-speed over the ground beat. In general, his conception is somewhat florid, his line filled with filigree. But his trumpet playing is direct, simple, and straightforward. Good examples are on records of "Dinah" and "My Buddy," under the leadership of Lionel Hampton. At his best Carter plays with a quiet and appealing grace.

Despite the importance to the swing era of Carter, Hawkins, Eldridge, Young, Goodman, and the rest, in certain respects the presiding genius of the period was not an instrumentalist at all, but a wounded woman singer who became a star, a cult figure, a symbol of the oppression of blacks, and who died in her forties of the aftereffects of alcoholism and drug addiction. But before any of these things happened, Billie Holiday made two or three score of the finest recordings in jazz.

Vocalists pose a peculiar problem for the jazz historian because, the blues singers aside, there are so few of them. This is odd, since singing is basic to African music, at the heart of American popular music, essential to both black and white church music, and a major element in European church music. But Armstrong, Waller, Teagarden, and one or two others are the only males who have successfully managed to capture jazz feeling in a vocal, again excepting the blues shouters, and there are not many more women who have done so, despite the dozens who sang with the big bands. One of the best was a white, Mildred Bailey, a fat woman who had a light voice and excellent jazz phrasing, with her notes lifted away from the beat. A sister of Al Rinker, one of Paul Whiteman's vocalists, she eventually sang with Whiteman and with her husband, Red Norvo. She was recording before Holiday and may possibly have had an influence on her. Others who have made some name for themselves in jazz are the Englishwoman Cleo Laine, Carmen McRae, and Annie Ross. Ross made her reputation in the 1950s with Hendricks, Lambert, and Ross, a vocal group that put words to improvised jazz choruses. And there is the redoubtable Ella Fitzgerald. These women all have good voices, good intonation, and they sing with strength; but at times they all have a tendency to land squarely on the beat, thus interfering with the swing. There have been as well a number of singers associated with the big bands from the 1930s until the present time. Among the best are Lee Wiley; Peggy Lee, who achieved her first fame with the Goodman band; three singers who succeeded each other with Kenton, Anita O'Day, June Christy, and Chris Connor; Maxine Sullivan, who was with John Kirby; and Helen Humes, with Basie. All of these women were capable of singing with jazz cadences, but, again, were presented mainly as popular vocalists, and the amount of true jazz singing they did was often limited. One of the problems may lie in the jazz vocalist's being tied to the melody line to a degree that the instrumentalist is not. The singer must at least approximate the tune to keep the lyric intact, and when the melody line is leaden and immobile there may be no way to give it life.

But Billie Holiday found a way around this problem, and succeeded where so few others have. It is difficult to know exactly what made her stand out, for the facts of her early life are obscure. She produced an autobiography, in collaboration with William Dufty, called *Lady Sings the Blues,* which is one of the most widely circulated books on jazz. Unfortunately, it was written as a quick star biography, and it suffers from the defects traditional to the genre. Self-serving and inaccurate, it concentrates on the sensational parts of Billie's life and tells us little about her music. Fortunately, a corrective has been supplied by British jazz critic John Chilton in *Billie's Blues,* but this book picks up her story only in 1933, when her career was beginning.

Let us see what the facts are. Billie claimed she was born in 1915, and the famous opening line of the Dufty book runs, "Mom and Pop were just a couple of kids when they got married. He was eighteen, she was sixteen, and I was three." According to this, her mother would have been thirteen when Billie was born, which is not impossible, but other evidence suggests that she moved the date up. At one point she says she was thirteen when she came to New York in 1927; at another she is still sixteen in Baltimore; and at another time she is listening to Armstrong's "West End Blues," which was cut in June of 1928, in a Baltimore whorehouse when she was "over sixteen." It is probable, then, that she was born nearer to 1912 than to 1915, and that her parents were correspondingly older.

Her father, Clarence Holiday, was gassed in World War I — at the age of seventeen, if we are to believe Billie's dates — which spoiled his ambition to be a trumpet player. He later took up the guitar and worked with McKinney and Fletcher Henderson, which suggests that he must have had some talent. Her mother, Sadie Fagin, was a quarter Irish and lived with her parents while Billie was a baby. At some point, however, Sadie moved to New York in search of work, and Billie was raised by relatives. The Dufty book is a litany of injustices: relatives beat her; neighbors taunted her; a cousin tried to rape her. Throughout her life Billie made efforts to present herself as unceasingly deprived, and it is therefore hard for the reader to know what to believe. She scrubbed floors for fifteen cents, ran errands for a neighborhood whorehouse, and did other menial tasks to make pin money. Then, probably in 1927, her mother brought her to New York to live. Very quickly she was recruited for a brothel, and within a few weeks landed in jail for four months — framed, she claims, by a customer she rejected.

From this point the details of her life are a little clearer. She began, at some point around 1930, doing a little singing in a small club of some sort in Brooklyn — how often and with whom, we do not know. Then, according to an oft-told tale, came her break. She and her mother were on the point of being evicted from their apartment. Desperate, Billie wandered down One hundred thirty-third Street in Harlem, where there was a group of small clubs, and badgered owners for work. At one place, called Pod and Jerry's, she told the owner, Jerry Preston, that she could dance. He shrugged and told the pianist to play something for her. It became apparent within a minute or two that she was no dancer and Preston told her to stop wasting his time. But the pianist, feeling sorry for her, asked her if she could sing. She said yes, and sang "Trav'lin' All Alone" and then "Body and Soul." The customers sat in silence as if stunned, some of them weeping openly. When she finished they showered her with money, and she went home with a couple of chickens and enough money to pay the rent.

There may be some substance to the story, but it is hard to know how much. Whatever the case, she began working at clubs along One hundred thirty-third Street and developing some reputation among the musicians who worked the area. By 1933 she was in Monette's, and here she was discovered by the omnipresent John Hammond.

Within months, Hammond had recorded her with the incipient Benny Goodman band, she had signed a contract with Joe Glaser, and she began to get good bookings, including the Apollo Theatre, Harlem's first-line showcase, where she worked off and on for a number of years. Most important, Hammond began to use her as vocalist with the little bands under Teddy Wilson's leadership that he was recording for the expanding juke box market. The first of these were made in 1936, and over the next six years, until the recording ban in 1942, she made about seven dozen sides, on which her reputation rests. A few of these were made for Commodore, but the bulk of them were made with small groups put together by Hammond and Wilson. At one time or another virtually every major musician of the day appeared with her on these records: Benny Goodman, Lester Young, Ben Webster, Roy Eldridge, Buck Clayton, Johnny Hodges, Harry Carney, Benny Morton — the list is endless. The records constitute one of the major bodies of work in jazz, and we will return to examine some of them in detail in a moment.

However great the music, her career did not run placidly. Billie Holiday was a temperamental woman who responded to the mood of the moment. She had a strong sense of her rights, and could fight like a cat at an affront, real or fancied. She liked to party, to drink, to smoke marijuana, to make love, and she often did so to the neglect of her profession. At other times she could be moody and depressed, uncertain that she had any talent at all. Her personal life was often chaotic, hardly surprising in view of the way she had spent her early years.

In 1936, when she began to develop a small public following, she was still in her twenties and was enjoying herself. She worked clubs around New York and elsewhere, including the Onyx Club on Fifty-second Street, where she attracted attention; and in March 1937, at the behest of Hammond, she joined the Count Basie band, then still struggling to get to its feet. Because she and Basie were under contract to different record companies, she did not record with the band. (Recently, radio transcriptions of two numbers with Basie have surfaced. They indicate that she was at the top of her form.) In any case, the stay was not a happy one. When Billie did not feel like singing, she gave a cursory performance, and at times she showed up late for work or not at all. In February of 1938 Basie let her go.

By this time her reputation among musicians was secure, and her name with the public growing. She was immediately hired by Artie Shaw, who was willing to buck the color bar. The band was touring the South, and there were countless incidents. Eventually Billie took to waiting in the band bus while the men were at lunch stops, eating a sandwich that somebody brought her. The men in the band supported her, and so did Shaw, but even after they returned to the North there were racial incidents, and finally Shaw and Holiday quarreled. Billie felt that Shaw had not done enough for her; Shaw thought that he had done all he could. They parted on bad terms, though later the break was repaired. It was now 1938, and the swing era was going full throttle. It was time that she had a major breakthrough into public recognition; the question was how to get it. Once again Hammond took charge. He brought her to the attention of Barney Josephson, owner of Café Society, and Josephson booked her.

Josephson's role in the jazz of this time was a considerable one. A shoe clerk from New Jersey, he had in 1938 decided, almost on a whim, to open a nightclub that would be interracial both on the bandstand and at the tables. It will be difficult for the younger reader to understand that as late as 1938 there were almost no nightclubs in the United States, even those featuring black entertainers, that would accept black customers, except for the rare black celebrity. Josephson intended to break this barrier. He opened Café Society in a room on Sheridan Square in Greenwich Village and advertised that blacks were welcome. He was not a particularly knowledgeable jazz fan, but he was introduced to John Hammond, and Hammond, with his persuasive and assertive manner, began directing Josephson to musicians Hammond thought ought to be showcased. The arrangement was a good one: Café Society got the cream of the black players, and Hammond got exposure for the musicians he favored.

Very rapidly the club became successful. Josephson's policies, however, did not please everybody. When the Cold War began in the late 1940s, a few right-wing newspaper columnists began attacking Josephson for his associations with left-wingers. Some of his custom was driven off, and in 1950 he was forced out of the nightclub business.

For Billie Holiday Café Society was an ideal venue. The customers were not only interested in music, but were ready to respond to a woman who had suffered for the color of her skin. Many of them were quite sincere. These people were influential and often well connected in publishing circles, and they took Billie up. The Café Society engagement made her a star — never on the level of Frank Sinatra, Bing Crosby, and the other so-called crooners of the time, but, still, a nationally known singer. It was during this engagement, too, that she was brought the song she became most closely identified with. This was "Strange Fruit," a poem by Lewis Allen which had been set to a lugubrious minor theme — the strange fruit being, of course, "black bodies swinging from the cottonwood trees." However laudable the sentiments, it was a pretentious and overblown song, and Billie sang it in a slow dramatic recitative that only added to the pretentiousness. It sent chills up and down the spines of the Café Society audience, however, and they demanded it time and again. The success of the song turned Billie away from the blues and light pop tunes she had featured to "torch" songs — gloomy recountings of love gone by, dragged along in slow tempos. She had big hits in "Lover Man" and "Gloomy Sunday." For Billie the change in manner was a success; these tales of faithless lovers were what her audiences wanted to hear. From the point of view of jazz it is another matter. In concentrating on the heavy lyrics, she lost a good deal of the

jazz phrasing that had made her the idol of jazz buffs in the first place.

In any case, there were now other factors affecting her music. For one thing, her choice of lovers was getting poor. She had had her affairs in the past, one with Basie's guitarist, Freddie Greene; another with sometime accompanist Bobby Henderson. And she had had some sort of platonic friendship with Lester Young. But now, with her success, she began to attract men who saw her as a useful object, with money and good connections. One of these was a drug addict named Jimmy Monroe, whom she married in 1941. Living in the world she did, Billie had known all about hard drugs for years, but she had avoided them. Sometime in 1942 she started using them, and within five years she was serving a jail sentence. Monroe was followed by Joe Guy, a trumpet player who worked for a time in Coleman Hawkins's big band and was also an addict. Guy was followed by yet another addict, John Levy, who is reported to have framed Billie in a drug bust to save his own skin. Her relationships with these men were, to use a clinical term, exceedingly unhealthy. They mistreated her, sometimes physically; kept her in an emotionally inferior position; took her money; and at times double-crossed her for their own purposes. Billie kept coming back for more. She even returned to Levy after he apparently tossed her to the cops. By 1950, when she broke with Levy for good, she had little to show for her years of work.

Billie never made the millions that the big name singers and band leaders earned, but she made considerably more than most people do in a lifetime, grossing $50,000 or $100,000 or more in some years. She kicked it all away on drugs and the men who used her; she was perennially broke. Furthermore, by the early 1950s her voice was going and her health was beginning to break down. From here on it was a slowly worsening nightmare. There were more drug arrests, more attempts to kick her addiction. Her financial affairs were continually in chaos, and her personality was beginning to disintegrate; displays of temperament frequently disrupted her jobs. Club owners were growing chary of her, both for her notoriety and her temperamental displays.

She continued to record right up until her death, but she was sinking. In 1956 she was arrested on a drug charge once again, and people who knew her said that she never again used hard drugs. To compensate, however, she was drinking a great deal, sometimes appearing on stands so drunk that audiences wondered if she would get through the song, which she usually did. But the jobs were not that frequent. The woman who ten years earlier

Opposite: Billie Holiday at times allowed herself to get fat, and in the later years of her life bore the scars of drug addiction and alcoholism. But in her prime she was a true beauty, and when this stunning woman sang "My man don't love me/Treats me awful mean," she could freeze audiences in their seats. William P. Gottlieb/Edward Gottlieb Collection

was surrounded by men, managers, toadies, admirers, and fans now sat alone in her little apartment on Manhattan's West Side, drinking and watching television night after night. Finally, in May of 1959, she collapsed. She was rushed to the hospital, where she lingered for ten weeks, before dying on July 17.

It is clear from everything we know about Billie Holiday that one of her biggest problems was a staggering lack of self-esteem. This is hardly surprising. She had been rejected by her father, who disappeared when she was still a baby and never was willing to recognize her as his until she was successful; by a mother who, whatever her motives, left her in the care of relatives at an early age; and by the relatives themselves, who, even discounting for the fictionalizing, did not shine on her with much warmth. The sense of rejection caused by this treatment was certainly responsible for the self-pity, which becomes increasingly evident in her work, and also for the angry outbursts, which were often occasioned by some slight, real or imagined, to her exceedingly fragile ego. And no doubt this anguished fear of rejection was what drove her toward men who mistreated her. By the crooked logic of neurosis, it is easier to defend yourself against the lover who threatens to reject you than the one who doesn't. But it is probable that this lack of self-esteem is also responsible for the melting tenderness that infuses her earliest and best work. Love, for Billie Holiday, was momentous: desperately wanted; desperately denied. And love was what she sang about — love lost; love found.

The first of the Teddy Wilson sides, the ones by which she will live, were made in 1936. She has already, with "Did I Remember?," "No Regrets," and "Billie's Blues," discovered the two secrets that were to make her into the greatest jazz singer who ever lived. The first of these was a grasp of that essential matter of lifting the melody away from the beat. According to her own testimony she learned about singing by listening to the records of Louis Armstrong and Bessie Smith, and what she took from them was their phrasing. She said later, "I feel like I am playing a horn. I try to improvise like Les Young, like Louis Armstrong, or someone else I admire." This understanding of a basic jazz principle was crucial to her effectiveness.

But blues shouters like Rushing and Turner also phrased away from the beat and they have never been classed with Holiday. The difference lies in Billie's grasp of yet another principle, this one a general rule of all art. Billie was given to sing many of the best popular songs of the very fertile 1920s and thirties: "The Way You Look Tonight," "Body and Soul," "These Foolish Things," "The Man I Love," "Time on My Hands," "I've Got My Love to Keep Me Warm," "Night and Day," "I Hear Music," and many others. But even at its best, popular song is a minor genre, and Billie understood somewhere in her gut that in art, form and content must be in balance. You cannot use the voice of Shakespeare — the rolling periods, the

elaborate metaphors, the complex speeches — if your subject is the death
of a mouse. The weight of such verse requires the death of kings to bear
it up. What we get when the subject is too small for the form is parody or
satire; for example, Pope's *Rape of the Lock.* Conversely, a large content
requires a large form; where the content overbears the form you have
nonsense or doggerel:

> "The King is dead,"
> He said, he said;
> "The King is dead,"
> Said he . . .

The critical thing is the balance. A small thought can be effective if it is
given minimum presentation, just as a tiny joke can raise a laugh if it is
stripped to bare bones and thrown away. Most singers, unfortunately, when
confronted with the sort of minor theme that informs most popular songs,
try to get more out of it by dressing it up with throat catches, melodic
embellishments, dramatic pauses, and the like. This never works. You can
add to the superstructure of a work of art only if you bolster the underpinning as well. Billie knew this, and she invariably minimized the form to
make the content credible. There is nothing wrong with a light love song
like "No Regrets" if you do not try to make a tragedy of it. When Billie
minimizes a song we are able to take it just as seriously as we ought to take
it, and we are convinced by what she is saying. An example is "What a Little
Moonlight Can Do." The lyric, to put it charitably, is modest:

> Ooh, ooh, ooh,
> What a little moonlight
> Can doo — oo — oo;
> Ooh, ooh, ooh,
> What a little moonlight
> Can do to you.

Billie takes it at a fast clip and throws it off casually, reducing the melody
line as much as possible. The first three notes of the song as written are
D-B-D; Billie sings them all as D's. Again, on "Easy to Love," the first two
notes are C and the F below; both times the figure appears, Billie sings both
notes as C's. "Them There Eyes" begins, on the song sheet, with a series
of quick figures running down a chord; Billie sings most of the first three
bars on a single note. Taking liberties with a song is something that jazz
singers have always done. The tricky thing is to maintain enough conform-
ity to the original melody to avoid distorting the lyrics, so that the listener
thinks he is hearing the song as he knows it. Taking liberties, of course, also
made it easier for her to phrase against the ground beat, which she did to
a greater extent than almost anybody in jazz. Hardly ever does she bring
a note down on a beat. Everything is set in those stretched, extended figures

that Armstrong made so much of, so the entire melody line floats over the ground beat like a cloud drifting across a landscape. The ease with which she manages to keep the melody moving effortlessly forward apart from the beat, and yet coming out where it should at the ends of phrases, bespeaks one of the finest rhythmic senses in all of jazz.

Singling out a record or two for discussion is again difficult because of the generally high quality of her work during her best period. The risk is that one will settle on one's sentimental favorite. Certainly I would not choose "God Bless the Child" ("Mama may have, Papa may have, but God bless the child who's got its own"), a maudlin and self-pitying lyric she wrote herself, which has been vastly admired by her fans. My own preferences are for the earlier cuts, such as "Them There Eyes," "Did I Remember?," a neglected tune that she sings with the insouciant lilt a happy love song calls for, "No Regrets," and "Easy to Love," a superb example of her ability to make the melody float over the beat. But of all her records, I think her greatest is one not typical of her work, a blues called "Fine and Mellow." This was made initially for Commodore, with an arranged backing, not with a Wilson group. Billie was not basically a blues singer but a performer of popular songs. Her mastery of the blues, however, was complete. True, she did not have the powerful voice or the heavy timbre of the classic blues singers like Rainey and Smith, but her grasp of blue notes was as good as theirs, and her sense of phrasing better.

"Fine and Mellow" is, like so many blues, about unrequited love. Billie builds the song around a blue third and the note just below it, the second. Most of the phrases begin on the blue third, slide down to the second, and then resolve to the tonic or the fifth below. It is a classic blues configuration, but what makes it work especially well is that Billie emphasizes the dissonant blue third and second to reflect the yearning in the lyric, touching down on the resolution only lightly before jumping back to the dissonance again. Diana Ross sang this song in the movie made about Holiday. She is not a bad singer, as popular singers go, but she missed the whole point, failing to pull out the dissonance as long as possible, and jumping down on the resolution with both feet, to produce a determined, clunking sound. Billie knew better, possibly because she knew rejection better. Her melody is rich with dissonance, and when Billie sings, "My man don't love me" on those dissonant notes, she can chill the blood. This ability to tell us something real made her not merely the finest of all jazz singers, but one of the finest jazz musicians America has produced.

The Atlantic Crossing

European attitudes toward jazz, almost from the time the music penetrated the Old World, have been undergirt by two myths that have now become so thoroughly a part of the consciousness of jazz that they are simply taken for granted. One is that there is no race prejudice in Europe and that blacks have always been able to live as they like in London or Paris. The second is that Europeans have always been more sensitive and receptive to jazz than Americans — that, as the English writer Benny Green has said, Europeans must explain to Americans the virtues of their own music. As in the case of most myths, there is sufficient truth to these two to give them a surface plausibility. European jazz fans, right from the beginning, have at times showered adulation on visiting American black musicians, in marked contrast with the way they were treated back home. It is easy to imagine the feelings of a black player who had trouble getting his own agent on the phone in New York, on finding himself lionized by a European gentleman — "Look at me, man, I'm talking to a *duke.*"

This is hardly the place for a dissertation on racism in the Old World, but nobody familiar with the situation of the Arabs cooped up in the slums of Belleville in Paris, or the Pakistanis in London ("Paki-bashing" is still a hobby of young English toughs) will believe that racial intolerance is strictly an American product. Louis Armstrong, on his first visit to London, had trouble finding a hotel room, and at least once was refused service in a restaurant.

The second myth, that Europeans have generally been more receptive to jazz than Americans, also has some substance. Europeans wrote about jazz earlier than Americans did, and they have often written about it better since. The European jazz enthusiast is usually more knowledgeable about the background of the music than the American fan, who is likely to be both ignorant and scornful of all kinds of jazz but his own.

Nonetheless there has always existed in the United States a much larger market for the music than in Europe. Even in the days of the Depression, American jazz records could sell in the tens of thousands, where they were selling in the hundreds in Paris or London. Today there are more real jazz clubs — by which I mean clubs that book jazz full-time at adequate fees — in New York City alone than in all of Europe: some twenty-five in New York as compared with two in London, one or two in Paris, two in Stockholm, one in Zürich, one in Rome, two in Munich, and a scattering in Copenhagen, Amsterdam, Hamburg, and the cities of eastern Europe and Russia. The point is that in Europe jazz is treated as an art form, and has about the same sort of audience you expect for, say, the ballet. In the United States, by contrast, jazz has always had a significant place in the general culture, a place more akin to the role played by the novel than by the ballet. Just as any American with the slightest pretension to education knows who Hemingway was and reads a novel occasionally, so these same people will know who Armstrong was, and will occasionally go out to listen to some jazz.

But if jazz plays a larger role in American society than it does in Europe, the fact remains that Europe, and to a lesser degree some of the Asian nations, especially Japan, does have a thriving jazz audience, along with jazz magazines, fans, and scholars. And Europe has produced dozens of first-rate jazz players, and a few superlative ones, who have made some mark on the course of jazz. Europeans have without question made a considerable contribution to the music.

The history of European jazz runs about a decade behind its course in the United States. Recordings of rags became available in about 1905 or so. According to the English pianist Vic Filmer, who was in the music business then, the first ragtime sheet music appeared in London in 1910. Filmer began playing rags at private musicales, usually as novelties sandwiched between contraltos and violin soloists. He achieved a small reputation, and in 1913 began playing rags in the cabarets of Paris, where, he says, he found "a black man" already playing some sort of hot music, presumably standard ragtime. But interest in the music was slow to develop. It was not until American musicians began to arrive in Europe in any numbers that Europeans became conscious of the new music.

As we have seen, the first American black musicians of this period to reach Europe came as military bandsmen accompanying the American Expeditionary Force in the First World War. The best known of these groups were the 369th Infantry Regiment (the Hellfighters) Band, organized and led by James Reese Europe, the kingpin of the Clef Club, which employed the great dancer Bojangles Robinson as drum major; and the Seventy Black Devils of the 350th Field Artillery, directed by Tim Brymm. In February and March of 1918 the Hellfighters band made a six weeks' tour of twenty-five French cities, and in 1919 a group called the Scrap Iron Jazz

Band, probably drawn from the Hellfighters group, made a series of records in Paris. Both of these bands became celebrated in Europe and in the American press. However, neither of these bands was a jazz band. Each mixed a few raggy numbers into its regular repertory of marches and standard concert pieces.

Another black group celebrated at the time was Louis Mitchell's Jazz Kings, which played around Europe, mainly in Paris, from about 1917 until 1925. The group included Cricket Smith, trumpet star from the Clef Club Orchestra. Smith was not a jazzman, and this band, according to the French jazz writer Gérard Conte, *"ne peut pas, sauf en de très rare moments, être considéré comme un ensemble hot,"* although there is some evidence that Bechet sat in with the group and may even have recorded with it.

Bechet's presence in Europe at the time was as a member of yet another black American group, the Southern Syncopated Orchestra, under the direction of Will Marion Cook. The group had been organized in 1918 as the New York Syncopated Orchestra. Cook persuaded Bechet to join it in February 1919, but after a few engagements, Bechet quit to join Brymm's Black Devils, then working as civilians in New York. Cook arranged for a European tour, and at the end of June, according to Jean-Christophe Averty, who has studied the group, Cook kidnaped Bechet and took him along. On November 15, 1919, the conductor Ernest Ansermet, in London to conduct the orchestra for the Ballet Russe, heard the Cook group, and wrote his now-famous celebration of Bechet's virtues. However, the orchestra was beset by conflict, and twice Cook gave up in disgust and returned to the United States. Small groups began to splinter off. One of these was led by drummer Buddy Gilmore. Another, led by Benny Payton, included Bechet. For the next two years or so these groups gigged irregularly around Europe, playing mainly in London, Paris, and Brussels. Finally, in 1922, Bechet was expelled from England for the incident with the prostitute, and a few weeks later a boat carrying the remains of the Southern Syncopated Orchestra across the Irish Sea sank, drowning eight of the bandsmen.

Once again, with the exception of Bechet, few of the men in any of these early touring black bands were jazzmen. The music they were playing was mainly dance music with raggy inflections. Later on, through much of the interwar period, black leaders Noble Sissle and Sam Wooding toured Europe frequently with bands that included men like Tommy Ladnier, Buster Bailey, Juice Wilson, Gene Cedric, and others, but despite the presence of a few good jazz soloists, these bands too were principally dance, or show, orchestras. All of these early black bands were seen as novelties, more than anything else, and had no long-term effect on either European musicians or their audiences in creating a new taste. But Europeans were looking to the United States for new ideas, and inevitably the jazzy new music that was appearing in the twenties struck them as exactly the fresh, direct sort of thing they were seeking. European dance bands began giving their music American touches by the addition of drums, banjos, and, eventually, saxophones. A market for American records developed. Not surprisingly, the records chosen for the European market were the same ones being sold to white American audiences of the day — a great deal of dance music and pseudojazz with some mixture of the real thing. And, of course, the bands were mainly white. It was taken for granted that the rough blues and stomps made by blacks were of interest to black audiences only. Thus it was that the records of Beiderbecke, Goldkette, Red Nichols, the Casa Loma Orchestra, various imitators of the Original Dixieland Jazz Band, Ben Pollack, and various Whoopee Makers groups with Goodman, Teagarden, and others came to Europe. And, again not surprisingly, the first important American jazz band to play in Europe was the Original Dixieland Jazz Band, which visited England in 1919. The group scored a signal success, recorded there, and triggered, especially among English musicians, some interest in the new music. Other white groups followed. Paul Whiteman, billing himself as the King of Jazz, made a highly publicized tour of Europe in the mid-1920s, and he was followed by other groups, like the Ted Lewis Orchestra, a novelty band that included jazzmen George Brunis, Muggsy Spanier, and Jimmy Dorsey. Hal Kemp, primarily a dance band leader, brought in a band with Bunny Berigan around the end of the decade, and in 1928 or 1929 Dave Tough and Mezz Mezzrow, both Chicagoans, had a band around Place Pigalle in Paris. In truth, the emphasis on white players was not entirely accidental. According to John Chilton, "There was a strong color prejudice in England which worked against the black players here."

Whatever the causes, the net result was that the European jazz musicians at first formed their styles on the work of whites. It has long been felt by American writers, including this one, that Europeans, with their sense of history, would have been attracted to the New Orleans pioneers right from the first. In fact, even the most scholarly European jazz lovers had little awareness of Oliver and Morton until the trad revival of the 1940s. European musicians were being influenced entirely by their American contemporaries. Beiderbecke was a major influence: both Philippe Brun and Nat Gonella, respectively the first important French and British jazz trumpeters, began as disciples of Beiderbecke and his shadow, Red Nichols.

Berigan, because of his visit to Europe, also had a major influence. Tommy McQuater, generally considered the leading British trumpet player of the 1930s, and the neglected but excellent French trumpeter Aimé Barelli were both heavily influenced by Berigan. Barelli has a particularly fine solo filled with the marks of Berigan on "Noël Blues," with Noël Chiboust et son Orchestre, made in 1940. Similarly, the major influence on trombonists was Jack Teagarden. Leo Vauchant and George Chisholm, respectively the leading French and English trombonists of the period, were distinctly influenced by Teagarden. Again, the early British saxophonists Don Barrigo, Buddy Featherstonhaugh, and the obscure Reg Dare were influenced as much by Bud Freeman as by Hawkins. Similarly, the big bands found white models. The French group Gregor et ses Gregoriens and the Ray Ventura group, the first big jazz bands outside the United States, were cut along the lines of the Goldkette and the Casa Loma orchestras, rather than the Fletcher Henderson band.

Thus, paradoxically, despite a vogue for black arts among European intellectuals, European jazz was patterned on white models. It had to find its way back to the black bands, and this gives its history a peculiarly convoluted look. The European players knew vaguely that Morton and Oliver had existed, but they had no clear idea of how New Orleans music went, and they were not encouraged to find out by visiting American players, who spoke of the older music as outmoded.

In any case, by the late 1920s European musicians had been exposed, through touring American groups and especially the records, to a good deal of jazz. They had begun to sort out the real thing from the pseudojazz of Whiteman and the rest, and soon began to try their hands at it. In England, it was a Filipino of Spanish descent named Fred Elizalde who fired the opening gun. Elizalde had spent some time in the United States as a musician. In 1928, he persuaded the Savoy Hotel management to let him bring in a jazz band. He imported from America trumpeter Chelsea Qualey, alto saxophonist Bobby Davis, and Adrian Rollini — all white — and filled out the group with a local rhythm section. The band was modeled, more or less, on Red Nichols's Five Pennies. In France, the leaders of the movement were Leo Vauchant, who played a number of instruments besides trombone (and who has spent most of his working career in Hollywood, writing film music under the name of Leo Arnaud), and Philippe Brun, followed rapidly by alto saxophonist André Ekyan. The English musicians had something of an advantage because they spoke the same language as the visiting Americans — the French have always resented the unwillingness of American musicians to learn their tongue — but despite this, the pivotal event in European jazz occurred in Paris. This was the founding, in 1932, of the Hot Club of France.

Various stories have been told of the founding of this, the most celebrated jazz club in history. According to Charles Delaunay, the initial impulse came from two students who had no particular interest in jazz but wanted a place to take girls dancing. They asked Hugues Panassié, who did have a genuine interest in the music, to be president, and Panassié turned the organization into a legitimate jazz club.

Despite its grand name, the club consisted of a few students who met to listen to records. It provided a focus for jazz interest, however, and it started a crusade among the fans to educate the public to what true jazz was all

about. Very quickly it occurred to Panassié and others around him, who
included Delaunay and the poet Pierre Noury, to give a series of concerts.
The first of these, in February of 1933, presented a group of lesser-known
black-American musicians then living in Paris. But by the next year, the
club's leaders were becoming aware of some French musicians who were
learning to play jazz. Among them was a pianist-turned-violinist named
Stéphane Grappelli, and a Gypsy guitarist, Django Reinhardt. Reinhardt
and Grappelli were working in an orchestra led by Louis Vola, a butcher-
turned-musician, who started as an accordionist but did most of his important play as a bassist. (Vola was still working in Paris in the mid-1970s.) The
Vola band was by no means a jazz band — in 1933 it was playing tea dances
at the Hotel Claridge in Paris — but Reinhardt, who was shy when not
among his own people, had fallen into the habit of practicing his jazz during
the band's breaks. Grappelli started joining in, and eventually Vola. Then
guitarists Roger Chaput and Joseph Reinhardt, Django's younger brother,
were added. A third guitarist, Django's cousin Eugène Vées, later replaced
Chaput. It was a jam session group only; but when Panassié and the Hot
Club decided to present Django and Grappelli at a concert, it seemed
sensible to bring the whole group along to support them. In this casual
fashion was born the Quintet of the Hot Club of France. It was the first jazz
group made up of non-Americans to give the Americans real competition,
and it encouraged Europeans to believe that jazz music would, after all,
travel. For the remainder of the thirties much of the most important activity
in the European jazz world revolved around the Quintet of the Hot Club
of France.

But if the Quintet was, by the mid-1930s, the premier European jazz band,
there was probably more actual jazz activity in England than elsewhere in
Europe. The Quintet worked only intermittently, mainly playing tours and
concerts; its members made the bulk of their living playing ordinary popular
music in clubs and hotels. The situation was, in fact, not much better in
England; most of the jazz in London — there was hardly any in other cities
— was played after hours in clubs for beers. But by 1932, at least one British
musician, Nat Gonella, had established himself with the broader public
principally by playing jazz. In September of 1932, he cut solos on "I Can't
Believe That You're in Love with Me" and "I Heard" (the latter a charming
and unusual Don Redman specialty), both of which are executed crisply in
the Beiderbecke mold. But three months earlier Armstrong had been at the
London Palladium, and, presumably as a result, Gonella had begun to
change his style. By November, like a good many Americans, he was in the
Armstrong camp. His "When You're Smiling," made that month, is pure
Armstrong. It is hard to believe that Gonella could have altered his style
so radically in so short a time; probably the process had been going on
longer. His concluding solo on "Rockin' Chair" is the most fascinating

example I know of a style caught in midswitch. The opening sixteen bars or so are plainly in the Beiderbecke mold; but as the solo progresses, he begins to move away from Bix toward Armstrong, until at the end he is playing figures taken directly from an Armstrong solo. Gonella has always been deprecated in England as a mere imitator of Armstrong, and my own feeling is that his Beiderbecke playing was superior. Nonetheless, he was, in 1932, one of the best two or three of the European jazz musicians. His conception shows nothing like the continuity of thought found in Armstrong's work, and his phrasing is, at times, rhythmically weak, but he possesses a rich, full sound in all registers, Armstrong's explosive attack, and an all-around sound technique.

But if Gonella had the larger reputation with the general public, two other players were more admired by musicians. These were two "wild Scotsmen," as they have been described, trombonist George Chisholm and trumpeter Tommy McQuater. The two men played in brass bands together in the north, came down to London, and very quickly became among the most sought-after jazz players in London. It is Chisholm, rather than Gonella, who is accounted the first major English jazz player by English authorities. He possessed a rough, burry sound that owed something to Teagarden, and at times he used some of the arabesques typical of Teagarden's work. In the main, however, his playing was more direct than Teagarden's, simple and forceful. Most important, more than any other British jazz musician before World War II, he understood the necessity of phrasing away from the beat. His sidekick, McQuater, was at first influenced by Berigan, but by the 1940s had developed a more generally polished big band trumpet style, reminiscent of Billy Butterfield's. He displayed a good sense of melody, but his work is marred somewhat by a tendency to hammer down on the beat too often.

Another figure who had an influence on English jazz of this period was a Cambridge graduate, Spike Hughes, who as we have seen was an admirer of Ellington. Hughes, a bass player, had training in classical composition. Through the early years of the 1930s he organized a number of bands for recording sessions and in this way became a figure in English jazz. But the most important of these sessions took place in New York in 1933. Hughes, in the United States on a visit to hear American jazz firsthand, learned of a big band being rehearsed by Benny Carter. He decided to use it to fill out a recording contract he had with an English record company. With the help of John Hammond he augmented the Carter group with Red Allen, Coleman Hawkins, and Chu Berry as major soloists and recorded twelve sides, most of them of his own compositions. Because of his technical background, which was superior to that possessed by most Americans writing jazz at the time, these arrangements were harmonically advanced for the period. However, they owe a debt to Duke Ellington, reflections of whose musical thinking can be heard in many of these pieces, for example, "Nocturne," which features a muted trombone playing an Ellingtonesque theme. In spite of this stiffness, the jazz scorings are advanced for the day and probably had more influence on jazz writing than they have been credited with. Besides writing jazz, Hughes also wrote regularly for the *Melody Maker,* and in this capacity became an important arbiter of musical taste in England.

During the thirties and into the years of the war, England and France — or, more specifically, London and Paris — were the major centers of European jazz. There was, however, a certain amount of jazz activity elsewhere — probably at least some occasional jazz playing in every country in Europe. Sweden and Denmark in particular began to develop home-grown jazz players on the heels of the English and French. Jazz itself was considered vulgar, even dirty, and during the twenties there was little enough of it in Scandinavia. In Stockholm a black ragtime banjo player named Russell Jones was nearly the beginning and end of it. But in the mid-1920s some Swedish musicians working on the Swedish-American Line began hearing the black bands like Henderson, Ellington, and Charlie Johnson in the Harlem cabarets, and by about 1926 they had formed a group called the Paramount Orchestra. This was a six-piece group under the leadership of Folke Andersson, a violinist on the model of Joe Venuti, and included trumpeter Göst Redlig, altoist Steen Westman, and pianist Birger Mattson. Generally better known was trumpeter Gosta Turner, who played a big, full style with dance bands, and in the 1940s began to play dixieland on the order of that played by the Condon bands.

In Denmark, the chief jazz musician of the early period was violinist Svend Asmussen, who, in the late 1930s, teamed up with guitarist Ulrik Neumann to produce a group modeled after Venuti and Eddie Lang, the guitarist. According to at least one man who heard them, "They were greater than Django and Steph." However odd it may seem, if one had to choose the single most important influence on European jazz in general through the 1920s and 1930s it would be the Venuti-Lang combination. In Scandinavia as elsewhere in the early period it was the whites and not the blacks who were the major influence. Armstrong and Hawkins both played concerts in Stockholm in the early thirties, but Bud Freeman and Eddie Miller of the Bob Crosby band were as influential as either.

In Holland the leading, and for a time only, jazz band was the Ramblers, led by Theo Uden Mastman. The group played swing arrangements in the manner of Goodman and Dorsey, toured Europe occasionally, and was regularly broadcast over Dutch radio. It accompanied Coleman Hawkins on a few records during his European stay.

There was even some jazz in Russia. Perhaps the best known of Russian jazz musicians of the prewar period were Adi Rosner, who may have been Polish and who played a bravura style cornet probably under the influence of Armstrong, and pianist Alexander Tsfasman, who essayed a little awkward stride reminiscent of James P. Johnson. Both of these men led their own bands. Another very popular band was led by Leonid Utiosov. The group had a tenor saxophonist influenced by Bud Freeman (or possibly Chu Berry), and featured light riff numbers that could have been played by a second-line American swing band of the period.

The question of jazz in the fascist countries is more problematic. There were ragtime bands recording in Germany as early as 1912, and touring Americans right after World War I. During the Weimar period, with its sense of decadence and *carpe diem* attitude, there was a great deal of "jazzy" music being played, much of it by visiting Americans, among them the German-American Frank Borchard, the New Orleans trombonist Emile Christian, and the Midwesterners Danny Polo and Dave Tough. As elsewhere in Europe, the influence of the white Americans dominated, as for example in the Bixian trumpet of name leader Teddy Kline.

After the rise of Hitler in 1933, jazz was officially anathematized as "non-Aryan," and the foreigners left. However, there continued to exist some swing bands, patterned on the American groups, and jazz went on being played in a few clubs even during the war, when lookouts would warn the bands of approaching police so they could switch from jazz to something else. Emile Mangelsdorff, today a leading German jazz musician, played in such a club. Despite everything, American records filtered into Germany during most of the Hitler years. The predominant influence during the immediate postwar period was not the boppers but the cool school.

The situation in Italy was a little better. Armstrong toured Italy in 1935, and Reinhardt, always an important influence in Europe, played there on occasion. Altoist Pietro Carlini had a band that imitated Ellington's, but without competent soloists, in the early 1930s. Pianist Enzo Ceragioli played in the Teddy Wilson style, and there was a group called Maestri del Ritmo, which based itself on the Fats Waller and His Rhythm groups. It was, in any case, a fairly modest amount of jazz activity, and it grew even more modest when America was drawn into the war. Carlo Loffredo, who as a student was beginning to organize a trad band during the war years says, "Jazz wasn't exactly banned, but it seemed inappropriate to play it when we were at war with the Americans. What the bands would do would be to change the names of American jazz tunes — 'Honeysuckle Rose' became 'Pepe Sulle Rose,' 'Exactly Like You' became 'Ritmando un Ricordo.'"

But despite the existence of at least occasional jazz playing everywhere in Europe, the major centers for the music remained London and Paris. And by the middle of the 1930s, the long-delayed influence of the blacks was finally being felt. For one thing, white musicians like Berigan and Spanier had been extolling the excellence of Armstrong, Hawkins, and the rest to the European players they came in contact with. For another, as the shape of the American record business changed after the 1929 crash, records by the leading black bands, like those of Armstrong, Ellington, and Henderson, moved out of the race category into the mainstream of the business, and were increasingly available in Europe. For a third, there was the Ellington tour of 1933, the Armstrong tours of 1932 and after. This growing interest in black playing, however, had nothing to do with New Orleans music. It was contemporary black music that Europeans were interested in, the music of Hawkins, Ellington, and the rest, and as a consequence European jazz playing through the thirties was mostly of the big band swing school, with a relatively small amount of small band swing being played, mainly in after-hours clubs.

In England, an important factor in the development of jazz was the squabble between English and American musicians' unions, which resulted in the barring of groups from one nation appearing in the other. After 1935, the only American jazz players who could appear in England were soloists, who could be booked as "variety artists." For practical purposes this meant pianists. As a consequence, Fats Waller made several English tours and Art Tatum played for some months in London.

What might have become of European jazz had it not been for the war, nobody can say. In any case, by 1939, when the war broke out, European jazz players were rapidly catching up to the Americans. In many instances they possessed a technical excellence that was superior to the Americans', and as a general rule their intonation was better, no doubt because of their older, stronger tradition of musicality. Their primary failure remained one of rhythm: in 1939 only a tiny handful of non-Americans had grasped the imperious necessity of phrasing away from the beat, which had by this time become nearly second nature to Americans. And among those to grasp it first was the illiterate, childlike, feral Gypsy guitarist, Django Reinhardt.

There have been, since 1930 or so, any number of fine European players, people entirely capable of competing with Americans at their own game. Reinhardt, however, is the only European to become a major influence on the Americans. He is, without question, the single most important guitarist in the history of jazz, and probably would be named on most lists of all-time jazz greats. Despite a crippled left hand, he had a solid technique; his melodic conception was formidable (he composed many songs, some of them still widely popular in Europe); and his ability to swing was immense.

Django Reinhardt was born in 1910 in Liverchies, Belgium. His mother, called "Negros" for her dark good looks, was an acrobat and actor. His father, according to Django's biographer, Charles Delaunay, was probably one Jean Vées, a musician who scraped a living by repairing and selling broken guitars and other stringed instruments. The parents were members of a branch of Gypsies called the Manouche, who apparently originated in the north of Europe, which explains Django's Germanic last name. From the perspective of our complex and highly organized culture, the life of the Gypsies of that time, especially that of the males, appears singularly attractive. They lived in caravans, which they usually parked at the edges of major cities. They made their living by doing odd jobs, street peddling, and stealing. It was generally considered undignified for a man to do any real work: Reinhardt throughout his life referred to ordinary workaday people as "peasants." It was the function of men to gamble, drink wine, play music, and to dress in as much splendor as their estates permitted them. Any necessary work was done by women, who also took pride in seeing that their men were elegantly groomed. Django's wife, in later days, used to carry him on her back across the muddy street where the caravan was parked lest he ruin the shine on his shoes. The Gypsies were outcasts; they lived in poverty, but it was a life none of them would give up.

At birth, Django was named Jean after his father, but was never called anything but Django, a not-very-common nickname for Jean. His mother was stubborn and independent. She never married Vées, and he had little to do with raising his son, although they saw each other on occasion. For most of Django's youth he lived in an area of waste ground on the outskirts of Paris, near Choisy, called "the Zone." Here were small garden plots, dumps, shacks, Gypsy caravans. There is no evidence that, despite this squalor, Django's childhood was anything but happy. He was probably allowed to roam a good deal of the time. He seems to have had no schooling whatever; he never learned to read or write, not even his own name in its entirety. Other people, especially Grappelli, had to take care of his contracts, and at times they signed his autographs for him on the sly.

When and how Reinhardt first became interested in music is unknown. His mother gave him a banjo when he was about twelve. There is no evidence that he took any lessons, however informal, but there were musicians around, including his father, who could have shown him the rudiments of playing. His gift was clear from the beginning. He began playing in cafés with his father within weeks after he got the banjo, and by the age of fourteen was working regularly in the clubs of Paris. Some time during this period he began to shift from the banjo to the more flexible guitar, which was more appropriate to the Gypsy tradition. By the time Django was in his late adolescence he was recognized as one of the leading musicians in the Gypsy community.

Then, quite suddenly, it almost came to nothing. At eighteen he was married to his first wife and living in a caravan near a cemetery. His wife made some spare change selling artificial flowers. Some of the flowers were usually stored in the caravan. One evening Django thought he heard a rat moving somewhere in the caravan. He picked up a candle to investigate, and as he was flashing the candle holder about, the candle dropped out and fell into a pile of the highly inflammable artificial flowers. They instantly burst

into flame, and within seconds the whole caravan was afire. Django grabbed
a blanket and, holding it across his body as best as he was able, pulled his
wife through the flames and out into the night. However, his legs were badly
burned and so was the unprotected left hand with which he was holding the
blanket.

He was rushed to a hospital and gradually he began to heal, his legs first,
and then the arm. But his hand was left a twisted claw, and it seemed likely
that he would never again play the guitar. His love for his music, however,
was too strong for him to give it up. He had the guitar brought to the
hospital as soon as was possible and began working with it. This was, no
doubt, a good sort of physical therapy for him. In time he regained the use
of his thumb and first two fingers, but the two smaller fingers remained
immobile for the rest of his life. He did eventually learn to make some use
of them in his playing. He would lift them onto the guitar's neck and set
them on the two lower strings. By dragging them along behind the rest of
his hand up and down the neck, he was able in this awkward fashion to get
some use out of them in stopping the lower strings. But for most purposes
he was without them. It is the opinion of Stéphane Grappelli, who perhaps
knew him as well as anybody, that the accident was not without its blessing.
"He had to play with economy," Grappelli has said, "which helped to
purify his line, and because he was using his strongest fingers to do all the
fretting, he maintained equal power in the line throughout."

Within months of the accident, Django was playing professionally again.
We are not sure when he was introduced to jazz. By 1928 jazz was something
that an underground of French musicians was investigating, and it would
have come to Django's attention anyway. It is plain that in the years on
either side of 1930, Django was listening to Ellington and Armstrong as well
as to white players like Beiderbecke, Nichols, and, significantly, Eddie
Lang.

The importance of Eddie Lang to jazz history has been often missed. As
the first major jazz guitarist he was founder of the jazz guitar tradition, and
everybody who plays guitar in popular music today owes something to him.
Lang was white, and paradoxically, the jazz guitar — especially solo guitar
— has been dominated by whites. This is particularly odd in view of the fact
that the guitar was the most widely used instrument of the early blues men,
who built such a large part of the foundation of jazz. Probably because so
many of them had only an elementary grasp of European harmony, few of
them were able to evolve into true jazz players. Perhaps they did not care
to do so. The result was that the field was left to whites, and they filled it.
To be sure, there have been excellent black jazz guitarists. Lonnie Johnson
was one blues player who often worked in jazz contexts, recording with
Armstrong, Ellington, and Lang. He said that working with Lang was his
greatest musical experience. Al Casey made a mark with Waller; Charlie

Christian was a major contributor to the bebop movement; Basie's Freddie Greene was considered the finest rhythm section guitarist of his time; and Wes Montgomery made a major reputation in jazz before his early death in the 1960s. But the main line of jazz guitar playing runs from Lang, through Reinhardt and Christian, to the guitarists of the bop movement — Remo Palmieri, Barney Kessel, Tal Farlow, Jim Hall, Kenny Burrell, and others. Of these, only Christian and Burrell were black. And Lang was first.

Eddie Lang was born Salvatore Massaro in Philadelphia in 1904. As an Italian-American he came from a subculture with a strong musical tradition. He studied the violin for eleven years, and played with Joe Venuti, to become his principal musical partner, in his high school orchestra. He switched to banjo some time in late adolescence and moved from there to guitar. For most of his professional life he operated as a free-lance, mainly in and around New York, with occasional stints in commercial dance orchestras, including the Paul Whiteman band. He was very quickly recognized as the leading professional guitarist in America and recorded extensively in all sorts of circumstances. He made a number of records with Bix and Tram, including the classics "Singin' the Blues" and "I'm Comin' Virginia." His best-known records were the many he made with Venuti, under a variety of names, chiefly Joe Venuti's Blue Four, and Joe Venuti and Eddie Lang's Blue Five. One particularly fine set, which includes Benny Goodman and Jack Teagarden, was issued as Joe Venuti–Eddie Lang and Their All-Star Orchestra. By the early thirties Lang was beginning to build a reputation with the general public as well as in the jazz world, but, unhappily, he died in 1933, at the age of twenty-nine, after a tonsillectomy.

The crucial point about Lang was his strong background in European music, especially in standard European harmony. His approach, as a result, was highly European. As a leading musician in the pop music of the time, he played a great deal of ordinary, often quite sentimental music, and this tended to color his jazz approach. He usually played his solos single-string, rather than filling his line with chords, and his melodic sense was good if somewhat four-square. He understood the blue notes and used them frequently, but his management of them was somewhat awkward — the stilted speech of the translator rather than of one born to the language. He was a fine technician, of course, undoubtedly the best of his time on his instrument, and this impressed other players. His influence on Django was considerable; we can find runs in Lang's work that Django adopted. The final effect was that, building on the foundation laid by Lang, the jazz guitarist has always been more European in approach than any other jazz instrumentalist, possibly excepting the jazz pianist. It was Lang and Reinhardt, not the black blues guitarists, who determined the way the guitar would be played.

In 1928, when Django was still an unknown musician laboring, in obscurity, in cafés and musical halls, he met another young musician who was trying to come to terms with jazz. This was Stéphane Grappelli. He was a pianist and violinist playing popular music. They did not play together until 1933, when Louis Vola put together the Hotel Claridge orchestra, out of which grew the Quintet of the Hot Club of France.

The Quintet, as we have seen, was essentially a jam session band; at first it played only the odd concert for little or no money. But Panassié and his associates in the Hot Club were ambitious for jazz, and in December 1934, they arranged with the Ultraphone Record Company to record the group. The first coupling of "Dinah" and "Tiger Rag" had a major impact on the European jazz world, small as it was, and remains one of the most celebrated of all European jazz records. (Panassié and Delaunay were scions of well-off families, though Delaunay's family was not so rich as Panassié's, and both were able to devote a good deal of time to their passion. Delaunay's parents were both well-regarded painters, and, as a youth, Delaunay met many of the great figures of the Paris art world of the interwar period.) After the 1934 recording, the Quintet or variations on it, often including visiting Americans, recorded frequently, generally under the direction of Panassié or Delaunay. It began to develop a modest reputation, and by the late 1930s was able to work often as a unit, especially in concerts, though right up until World War II its members had to depend on more mundane gigs for their living.

Although at first Django and Grappelli appeared to be equally important as musicians — indeed, Grappelli gave the group most of its musical direction — gradually Django emerged as the star. This suited him very well. He was often shy in the company of the artistic and intellectual group represented by Delaunay and Panassié, as well as with the American jazz musicians with whom he played. But he had, as has been said, the heart of a *grand seigneur*. He had the temperament of a star and, despite his shyness, insisted on his prerogatives. Once he noticed that he sat while Grappelli and Vola stood. (In those days guitarists sat, with the right foot hooked into a chair rung so that the knee was cocked up to provide support for the guitar.) Django concluded that, as the star of the group, he should stand, too. He had an elaborate guitar stand concocted, but after a few trials he gave it up and went back to sitting.

Django, despite his eventual elevation into elegant circles, remained a Gypsy all his life. He was forever disappearing from hotel suites to spend a few days at a Gypsy encampment, playing his guitar for nothing while engagements worth thousands of francs had to be canceled. He had no interest in money. He would gamble away a week's take in a night without a qualm. As a Gypsy, the whole point was to be expansive. On one occasion he bought for cash a Rolls-Royce and hired an unfortunate English chauffeur to speed around the countryside while a party went on in the back seat. The driver at last became so unnerved that he plunged the car into a ditch. Django just shrugged and walked away from the wreck without a second thought. Bill Coleman, the black-American trumpet player who worked with Django frequently during this period, has said, "I was in a band with Django in the 1930s, where we were expected to be on hand seven nights a week. Django couldn't stand that kind of discipline. He'd be reliable for a week or two and then he'd disappear for three or four days." On his only trip to the United States, in 1946, he slept through a Carnegie Hall concert he was to play with Duke Ellington.

But there was nothing uncertain about Django's music. He was one of those rare people, even among jazz musicians, who possessed a natural gift. He could not read a note; he did not really even know the keys and chords by name; but his grasp of harmony was complete and his ability to create strong, surprising melodic lines astonishing. Bill Coleman has said, "He had an incredible ear. He could follow you wherever you went."

Django's first known records are "Ma Régulière" and "Griserie," made in 1928, on which he plays banjo in support of an accordion. The records have no jazz value, and neither does his next recording, "Carinosa," with a group led by Louis Vola. Then, in 1933, he made "Si J'aime Suzy" with L'Orchestre du Théâtre Daunou, which contains a brief break by Django that shows clear traces of the influence of Eddie Lang. Finally, in 1934, came the first of the long series of Quintet sides, and we begin to see real development in his playing. In these early records, in 1934 and 1935, his sound is thinner than it was to get, and his melodic conception is still unsure. For example, on a version of "Stardust," made in 1935 with Coleman Hawkins, he plays the melody fairly straight for the first four bars, but then, as he begins to move away from it, stumbles through an ill-collected group of figures, which, when compared with the flowing Hawkins line that follows, seems immature. On "Avalon," he occasionally employs guitaristic "effects," which in fact sound like holdovers from his banjo playing. However, by the time of these records, Reinhardt had thoroughly grasped the essence of jazz rhythm. He is phrasing away from the beat, and he is playing superbly in the rhythm section. On "Avalon" he is overrecorded in the rhythm section, probably deliberately, and it was just as well, because he is driving the whole band. The best of these early solos is probably "China Boy," made with the Quintet. He opens the solo slowly, with simple, abbreviated statements. It begins to build, and then he invents a figure that drops neatly through the end of the first chorus and the beginning of the second one, providing a springboard for a series of driving figures that carries him to the end.

He was developing rapidly, and by an "I Can't Give You Anything But Love," made in 1936 with the Quintet, he is playing with complete confidence. His sound is fuller, and he is using a strong terminal vibrato. On a fairly slow tune, such as this one, he breaks his line with sudden showers of sixteenth notes, a device Charlie Parker was to make use of a few years later, and he uses a great many substitute chords, as in the concluding bars of the bridge on his opening solo on "I Can't Give You Anything But Love" and again at the end of the chorus.

By 1937, he had had wide experience with American players and probably had learned as much as they could teach him. He was now producing one fine solo after another — "Solitude," "Runnin' Wild," "Swing" in 1937; "Billets Doux," "Swing from Paris," "Them There Eyes," "Three Little Words," in 1938; "Montmartre," "Solid Old Man," "Low Cotton," "Finesse" (also issued as "Night Wind"), with Rex Stewart, Barney Bigard, and Billy Taylor from the Duke Ellington band in 1939. By the end of this period he had weeded a lot of guitarisms out of his playing and generally purified his line. He was employing more pauses, more open space. His sound was rich and full, and he had dampened down the terminal vibrato that had appeared in his playing earlier. This was the classic Django: the direct, confident, melodic line, the big tone, the never-ending swing. These records, the ones made from 1936 to the beginning of the war in 1939, are the heart of Reinhardt's recorded work. He was to make superb music later, but there was a subtle change in his playing, and it was these prewar records that astonished other jazz players both in Europe and the United States.

By this time Reinhardt had clearly overshadowed his musical partner, Stéphane Grappelli. Nevertheless, Grappelli was playing first-rate jazz. Inventive and energetic, he was never at a lack for things to say. For example, on "Them There Eyes," he plays the lead on the first chorus, and then, after Django's solo, drives through three more blistering choruses without a pause. This inventiveness is not entirely a blessing. Grappelli's weakness is precisely this willingness to rush headlong through the music. He is at his best when he is a little more thoughtful, and it is a nice curiosity that it is the passionate Gypsy who becomes the more controlled player; the cool European who is heedless in his playing.

A third member of the Quintet who has been unduly slighted is Django's brother, Joseph. Django refused to permit Joseph to solo, and he often spoke to Joseph so cavalierly that Joseph, who after all had the Gypsy pride, too, would quit the group in a fit, and have to be cajoled back by Grappelli or somebody else. He was, however, a strong rhythm player, perhaps as strong as Django himself, and should be given more credit than he has received for the success of the group.

By the opening of the war, relations between Reinhardt and Grappelli were somewhat strained. It is no wonder. The elegant and fastidious Grappelli, who prided himself on his cultivation, contrasted almost totally with

Django Reinhardt, showing clearly the scars on his left hand. The two smallest fingers were paralyzed, but he was able to get some use from them by resting them on the fret board, where they could stop the strings. William P. Gottlieb/Edward Gottlieb Collection

the ill-educated, harum-scarum Django. In many respects Grappelli played the father to Reinhardt, seeing to the business arrangements, chiding Django for his behavior, and at times acting as Django's father confessor. Django undoubtedly resented this aspect of this relationship. He was a star, after all. As it happened, the Quintet was in London at the outbreak of the war. Django and the others departed hurriedly for Paris, but Grappelli, who did not have a family, stayed in London throughout the war.

Throughout Europe, the war provoked a jazz boom. For the French, American jazz was a taste of freedom; it signaled opposition to the Nazi conquerors. Despite official dislike of jazz, the German occupiers of Paris tended to wink at it, and suddenly Django, as the foremost French exponent of the music, was a popular star. He continued to record, and his records sold far better than they had ever done. His new partner was a young reed player, Hubert Rostaing. Rostaing, who was born in 1918, arrived in Paris in 1940 and was immediately taken up by the jazz players there. Influenced by Hawkins on tenor, Johnny Hodges on alto, and Goodman on clarinet, he quickly established himself as one of the leading jazz players in Europe, and he worked with Reinhardt, primarily on clarinet, off and on for much of the rest of Django's career. His clarinet playing is liquid and flowing, and his sound, which comes more directly out of classical style, is purer than that of most jazz players.

These postwar records with Rostaing show something of a return to Django's original Gypsy musical tradition. There is a moody, sometimes sentimental quality to his work. He plays far more in minor keys than is usual in jazz, and many of the pieces are in moderate tempos. Much of his repertory now consisted of tunes he composed himself, and the titles themselves give us something of the attitude behind them: "Manoir de mes Rêves," "Mélodie au Crépuscule," "Nuages," "Songe d'Automne." But the later records should not be neglected, for here we have the master, at the height of his power, slipping into a contemplative mood, the Shakespeare of *The Tempest* rather than of *Henry V.*

The times were, for Django, the best. After the war, as we shall see, the European jazz world was driven into two camps, the traditionalists and the beboppers. The swing players like Django fit into neither category and suddenly found themselves irrelevant. By 1949 or so, Django was bruised in spirit by this neglect, by the disappearance of a once-adoring audience. At times he gave up playing altogether. Then, in 1951, he opened at the Club St. Germain in Paris. He was playing at the top of his form, was warmly received, and for a time made a comeback. But his health was failing. By 1952 he was complaining of stiffness in his fingers. He was suffering from high blood pressure, presumably brought on by too much good living, but he had always been afraid of doctors and refused to get help. He had bought a house on the Seine in Samois, forty miles from Paris, and here he spent a lot of time at his favorite pastime, fishing. And he was fishing on May 15, 1953, when he suffered a final stroke. He was forty-three. But his influence remains immense. Every guitar player in jazz takes him as a source, and even the young players of the rock movement listen to him carefully.

Like Django Reinhardt, before World War II European jazz players were, virtually without exception, swing players. The important visiting players — Hawkins, Ellington, Benny Carter, Dicky Wells, and Bill Coleman — had all been swing players. Astonishingly, the early visit of Sidney Bechet, later to become a French folk hero, had been forgotten. European musicians knew little about New Orleans music and cared less, and throughout the war the swing style remained at the center of European jazz. Reinhardt and Rostaing were the key figures in French jazz, and they quite often recorded with big swing bands patterned on the American ones.

In England the situation was the same. There, too, the war occasioned a jazz boom. At the outbreak of the war, it was decided that the newest of the services, the air force, should have a premier orchestra for morale purposes, and to this end a group of leading players was drafted to form a band eventually called the Squadronaires. The group included Tommy McQuater; George Chisholm, who arranged as well as played trombone; and Andy McDevitt, considered England's leading reed player of the time. The band was patterned on the Bob Crosby Bobcats — again, a white model. Some of the arrangements were taken note for note from Crosby recordings. In intonation and execution it was as good as any American swing band, and better than most; and despite the rhythmic stiffness in the soloing, it could have given the top American groups competition. There was a lot less small band swing; England's cities had never developed a group of jazz clubs to match the ones in Kansas City, Chicago, and on New York's Fifty-second Street. There was, though, some small band jazz, which surfaced after the war in 1947 in the Jazz Club series on the BBC. Once again, these players were taking white models: Freddy Randall, a fine driving trumpeter, built his style on that of Yank Lawson of the Bob Crosby band; clarinetist Bruce Turner imitated Pee Wee Russell; trombonist Geoff Love was a Teagarden follower; pianist Dill Jones followed Jess Stacy. Jones, a Welshman, is one of the finest musicians of the era to come out of the British Isles. He first became interested in jazz when he heard the Waller records. Later, he moved into the swing styles of Wilson and, particularly, that of Stacy. He has spent most of his career working in New York.

But by the end of World War II, although it was not yet apparent, the swing style was finished, not only in England, but throughout the jazz world. In the United States during the late 1940s bop pushed swing out of the mainstream. In Europe bop had its adherents. But in fact the swing movement there was killed not by Parker and Gillespie; it was washed away by a tidal wave of traditional jazz.

What impels an artistic-philosophic current like the trad movement is difficult to pin down. In this case, it was not the musicians especially who were consumed with a passion for the older music. Like working musicians of most times and places, they were interested in contemporary modes. The trad movement was created strictly by the fans. What is surprising is how it seemed to appear all around the world at once. Almost at the same moment traditional bands were being put together in London, Paris, Melbourne, Stockholm, Rome, and San Francisco. They were started by young jazz enthusiasts, for the most part students, although in England there was an admixture of young working men, who had concluded that the swing style was a decadent, or commercialized, form of the true jazz, which was the New Orleans style.

As in the United States, the whole dixieland revival was divided into two streams. The European professionals were, around the beginning years of the war, being attracted to the dixieland of the Condon groups, the Spanier Ragtimers, and especially the Bob Crosby band. In Sweden Gosta Turner had a Condon-type band; in England players like Freddy Randall were involved with the Condon and Crosby styles. But although in the United States the Condon dixielanders were the dominant force in the movement, in Europe the traditional jazz, produced by the amateurs who were inspired by Morton and Oliver, simply took over. How so many different people spread so widely around the world came to the same conclusion at the same time is difficult to understand. One early shot in the battle was the rediscovery in 1939 of the Ernest Ansermet piece on Bechet by a music teacher in Bucharest. He sent it on to Charles Delaunay, who ran it in *Jazz Hot,* possibly the most influential of the jazz journals of the time. At about the same time, George Beal, an American collector, did a piece for the magazine on Morton, and very quickly after this the jazz fans began excavating the whole of the New Orleans school.

Then there was the influence of Panassié, who, outside of the United States, was established as the doyen of jazz critics. Panassié had originally been led to jazz, as most Europeans had, by the whites, and his first book, *Le Jazz Hot,* devoted considerable space to them. By the later 1930s, however, he had concluded that he had been wrong, that the true jazz musicians were the blacks, a point he made at length somewhat later in a revisionist work, *The Real Jazz.* In 1938 he came to New York and organized a curious recording session that included James P. Johnson, Tommy Ladnier, guitarist Teddy Bunn, Bechet, and other of the older black musicians. These records were of exceedingly uneven quality, but they had a considerable impact on jazz fans, especially in Europe, who felt that they were hearing the voices of the true pioneers.

In 1939, a few months after the outbreak of the war, the Spanier Ragtimer records appeared in the United States and found their way to Europe. This was a dixieland band, not a true New Orleans band, but at least, through Spanier's devotion to Oliver, it tipped its hat to the older music. Finally, there were the exhortations in favor of the older jazz by writers like Rudi Blesh, William Russell, and Panassié himself — in particular, the book *Jazzmen.*

The notion of a great art dying in obscurity had a romantic appeal to youth. There is nothing, for a young man, like the sense of sheltering the sacred fire from the rains blowing out of Philistia, especially when Philistia is inhabited by one's parents, and the cult aspect of the traditional jazz movement cannot be discounted. Then, too, it was relatively more easy to play than swing, which required advanced techniques many of the New Orleans pioneers themselves did not possess. But we must not lose sight of the fact that New Orleans jazz was indeed a marvelous music, with a durable appeal that has lasted nearly three quarters of a century. One way or another, thus, the trad movement began. And just as it got started, the war broke out. By 1940, all of western Europe, except England, was under the control of Hitler. A curtain closed, and although occasional American records were smuggled in through neutral Sweden or Switzerland, they were few. The result was that Europeans were thrown back on their own resources just as the trad boom was beginning to sound. Ready for something new after a decade of swing, but cut off from the development of modern jazz in the United States, they turned back toward the older jazz as a yet-unexplored territory. Unaware of the burgeoning trad movement in America, the Europeans had to make their own aesthetic judgments, and as a consequence Europe developed an independent history of its own. The emphasis was on the records of Oliver's Creole Jazz Band and the Armstrong Hot Fives, with less of the interest in Morton found in the United States. The growth of the movement was at first slow; the original trad records were issued almost as vanity press items by tiny companies formed for the purpose. Wartime shortages were, of course, a factor. But when the war ended, the lid came off, and the movement began to grow dramatically.

Giving impetus to the music was the arrival in Europe in the postwar years of three clarinet players who became profoundly influential on European jazz. One of them was George Lewis, who had come into prominence as a member of the revived Bunk Johnson band. After Johnson's retirement and his death in 1949, Lewis emerged as a leader in his own right. He toured Europe extensively, and, an original of originals, a genuine New Orleans pioneer, he attracted a huge European following, far greater than his modest audience in the United States. Like most of the rediscovered New Orleans players around Johnson, he had severe technical deficiencies: his intonation was poor, his execution sloppy. But European audiences felt that the passion in his playing made up for these failings, and he became an important model for European trad clarinetists. A second clarinetist to make a mark on the European scene was Milton "Mezz" Mezzrow. Mezzrow was white, but he felt that there was something special about the black experience, and he made efforts to turn himself into a black man. Possibly because of this, he was the only white to play on the Panassié session of 1938. A member of the Midwestern group, he was considered something of a joke by the others. His intonation was poor, his technical skills were rudimentary, and his conception ordinary. He worked infrequently in the United States, supporting himself by selling marijuana, then very much an underground drug. He settled in Paris in 1948, and because of Panassié's support, quickly became a figure in the trad jazz world and a model for younger players. His autobiography, *Really the Blues,* still available today, is as idiosyncratic as he. Despite his interest in the black conciousness, his principal model was Frank Teschemacher. The third of the clarinet players to have an impact in Europe was Sidney Bechet. Like most Creoles, he had an admiration for things French and thought of himself as a Frenchman. As a result of the proselytizing of Panassié he had developed a considerable following in

Europe, especially in France, and at the end of the war he began to visit
Europe, at first with some trepidation because of the jailing of twenty-five
years earlier, but later settling there, where he died a venerated figure. These
three men, as genuine New Orleans players immediately available to musicians, helped to shape the trad movement in Europe.

One of the first of the trad bands was founded by a French student who
played clarinet, Claude Abadie. Started in 1942 as an oddly assorted group
including violins, it quickly grew into a New Orleans revival band. Its
trumpet player was the poet Boris Vian, today a legend in France. A year
later pianist Graeme Bell started a New Orleans band in Australia. In 1944
pianist George Webb's Dixielanders came into being in England, and at
about the same time Carlo Loffredo and some fellow students were founding
what came to be called the Roman New Orleans Jazz Band. The Dutch
Swing College, under clarinetist Peter Schilperoort, was beginning what
proved to be a long career in the same year. These bands were quickly
followed by others throughout Europe, including Russia and the countries
under its influence. By the 1950s the explosion had turned into a real
cultural phenomenon. Where in the United States trad was hedged in by
other forces in jazz and was never at the center of the music, in Europe it
became, even into the sixties, the basic social music for many young people.
The European demand for trad has today diminished considerably, largely
as a result of the rise of rock, but it continues to have an important place
in popular music. Probably half the jazz clubs in Europe specialize in trad,
and even in such unlikely places as Leningrad it is possible to see people
— older people as well as adolescents — dancing to trad bands playing such
classics as "Panama," in imitation of the New Orleans marching bands of
sixty years ago.

The quality of European trad varied enormously. On the one hand, there
were hundreds of eager amateurs pumping out hopelessly leaden and excruciatingly out-of-tune versions of "Snake Rag" and "Ory's Creole Trombone"; on the other hand, there were a half-dozen or so well-drilled and
disciplined groups playing admirable New Orleans music. On the whole,
European trad bands were producing a better brand of jazz than most of
their American counterparts. For one thing, because of the generally higher
tradition of musicality in Europe, the best of the European trad bands
played more accurately and with better intonation than many of the American bands. For another, by the 1950s Europeans had had a generation's
experience with jazz, and they were more comfortable with jazz rhythms.
They were still rhythmically stiff compared with the American players, but
this mattered less in the New Orleans style, with its less subtle divisions of
a beat, than it did in the swing manner.

Of the lot, perhaps the best known of the European trad bands were those
of Alex Welsh, Humphrey Lyttelton, Ken Colyer, and Chris Barber in

England; the Abadie and Claude Luter bands in France; the Roman New Orleans Jazz Band; and the Dutch Swing College. Of the musicians, two stand out: the French clarinetist Luter and the English trumpeter Lyttelton.

Lyttelton, in fact, was never precisely a trad player, in that his models were not Oliver, Keppard, or George Mitchell, but Armstrong and, more generally, the American dixielanders, whose records were becoming available after the war. The opening figure on Lyttelton's solo on "Maple Leaf Rag" could have been played by Bill Davison — and indeed often has been. But Lyttelton made his first reputation with trad groups, and has to be seen as growing out of the movement. He was born in Windsor in 1921, a member of an established family. He went to Eton, and started in jazz with George Webb's Dixielanders. In 1948 he started his own band, and from then until the mid-1950s he was the leading figure in English trad. Among his sidemen, at one time or another, were Webb himself and Wally Fawkes, possibly the best of the English trad clarinetists, who was very much of the Dodds school. The Lyttelton band had a considerable commercial as well as musical success. There is the ferocious "Snake Rag," recorded in the early fifties, which is a fine example of this genre. Gradually, however, Lyttelton shifted the nature of the band, so that by the late 1950s it was playing a small swing band style, somewhat in the manner of the groups drawn from the Ellington bands. His style is clean, precise, unpretentious, and forceful; and, more than most European players, he attacks behind the beat — not as far from the beat as his mentor, Armstrong, but sufficiently far to make the music swing. Lyttelton is not only a musician; a writer and cartoonist, he has published several books and contributed to the *Melody Maker.* At present he is free-lancing in England and on the Continent.

Claude Luter was born in 1927, and, like many of the early trad musicians, was barely out of adolescence when he started to play. His original influence was Johnny Dodds, and his first band, organized in 1945, was based on the standard New Orleans model. He began working regularly around the Latin Quarter in Paris, especially at Le Club du Lorientais. His big break occurred at the Nice Festival of 1948, where he became a hit. By this time, however, the revival of interest in Sidney Bechet was underway, and Luter came under his influence. Bechet came to Paris in 1949 for a major jazz concert, which also included Charlie Parker. He went back to America after the concert, but returned to Paris that fall to settle there permanently, and he took on the Luter band as his supporting group. He not only increased his influence on Luter, but brought him widespread fame as one of Europe's foremost trad players, and certainly one of the finest players in the Bechet style anywhere, matched perhaps only by Bob Wilber in the United States, a contemporary of Luter's who had studied with Bechet in early adolescence. In 1951 Bechet switched allegiance to a band led by André Rewéliotty, but by that point Luter was firmly established, and went on to be one of the most successful of the European trad players.

Although the trad movement has subsided, it has left a distinctive mark on popular music in general, for the music of the Beatles and similar groups was rooted in trad. The trad revival carried along with it an interest in the blues, especially the country blues of Sonny Terry, Bill Broonzy, Muddy Waters, and the rest. Like New Orleans jazz, the blues was seen as "authentic." The Beatles began as a skiffle band, playing a blues-based music derived from the records of the country blues singers, like Broonzy and Waters. Their earliest jobs in the now-famous Liverpool dance halls were as intermission players to trad bands. "When the Saints Go Marching In" was a part of their repertory. When we consider that the music of Elvis Presley, Fats Domino, Chubby Checkers, and other rock precursors owed a great deal to the jump bands that had been developed by black musicians as a kind of blues-based commercial jazz, we can see how deep the debt of rock to jazz really is.

But if the trad movement dominated European jazz during the years after the war, it did not have the field to itself. Between 1941 and 1945 there was evolving in New York a revolutionary new form of jazz, which came to be called bebop, or bop. In 1945 it broke out into the open, and by 1947 or 1948 it had come to dominate American jazz.

When bop broke on the European scene, it did so with the force of a whirlwind. European audiences, isolated by the war, had almost no idea of what was to come, and the sudden appearance of bop was shocking. The first harbingers were the early records of Charlie Parker and Dizzy Gillespie. Then, in February 1948, Gillespie brought a big band to Europe for a jazz festival at the Théâtre Marigny in Paris. The impact of this group, especially on musicians, was considerable, and when Parker appeared in 1949 with a small group, battle lines formed. The European jazz world split abruptly into two camps. In the United States the emergence of bebop had fragmented the jazz world, but the lines of division were not clear-cut. In addition to bop, there were the swing, trad, cool, and dixieland schools, with overlapping adherents and players at home in two or more schools. But Europeans, with their penchant for philosophic dispute, tended to commit themselves emotionally to one camp or the other. Either you believed that there was only one true jazz and its name was trad, or you carried the banners of the new bebop rebellion. So ferocious was the dispute that Charles Delaunay and Hugues Panassié, colleagues for fifteen years, split, with Panassié, of course, in the New Orleans camp. Panassié took over the Hot Club, Delaunay the magazine *Jazz Hot,* and they never spoke again.

From the point of view of the audiences, trad was the clear victor. Bop at first did not have more than a marginal audience; it grew only slowly through the fifties and into the sixties. But bop did manage to establish itself solidly, and it remains an important thread in the skein of European jazz.

Its best-known practitioners, probably, are two Englishmen, saxophonist Ronnie Scott and reed man Johnny Dankworth; a Frenchman, pianist Martial Solal; and two Swedes, Lars Gullin and Arne Domnerus. Dankworth and Scott were born in 1927, both worked in some of the same bands, and both played in trans-Atlantic ship bands immediately after the war. The ship band experience was important for them, because it brought them to New York frequently at the time when bebop was emerging into daylight, when they themselves were barely out of their teens and susceptible to new movements. They became committed to bop and pursued it through a number of lean years before it became profitable. Both developed sufficient reputations as jazz players to allow them to work in the United States on the strength of their names, Scott touring America in 1955, Dankworth playing at the Newport Jazz Festival and Birdland in 1959. In that year, Scott opened a club in London devoted to modern music. Called Ronnie Scott's, it has become the leading jazz venue in Europe. Dankworth, who is married to the singer Cleo Laine, has established himself as the most important jazz band leader in Europe.

The Swedish bop movement developed from a group called the Royal Swingers, which, like most similar European bands, was working in the swing idiom. Stan Hasselgard, later to make a considerable reputation in the United States as a clarinetist in the Goodman tradition, was associated with this group. Hasselgard, however, died young in an automobile accident, and it was Domnerus and Gullin who went on to dominate in the field. Arne Domnerus was a contemporary of the American beboppers, and like them began with a big band, Owekjell's Band, which also included trumpeter Rolf Eriksson, who gained an international reputation. Lars Gullin was born in 1928. He began as a clarinetist, but played his jazz on the baritone saxophone under the influence of Gerry Mulligan. He very quickly became a leading jazz player and recorded with many visiting Americans, including Stan Getz and Clifford Brown. In 1954 he won the *Down Beat* critics' poll as new star on his instrument, the first non-American to be so honored. He died in 1977.

Solal, an Algerian, was born in 1927. He started on the piano at seven and began playing jazz in adolescence. Settling in Paris after the war, he played occasionally with trad bands, but was primarily committed to the new music. Such was his reputation that he became the pianist of choice for visiting Americans, and worked with many of them. He won a number of awards in Europe and by the 1960s was respected internationally as one of the leading pianists in modern jazz.

Today there is widespread feeling in Europe that in the area of the avant-garde, at least, the European players have caught up with the Americans and may even have surpassed them. The wider experience of Europeans with the advanced music in the classical school has made avant-garde jazz more acceptable to audiences there than in the United States. The Germans in particular have developed a native school of avant-garde jazz. Among its leading figures are trombonist Albert Mangelsdorff and composers Eberhard Weber and Alexander von Schlippenbach. Indeed, Mangelsdorff, who often concertizes as a soloist without rhythm support, is certainly one of the leading players on his instrument anywhere. In England, too, there is an important avant-garde movement, centering around saxophonist John Surman, drummer Tony Oxley, and guitarist Derek Bailey. Even in Russia there is some avant-garde playing: alto saxophonist Gennady Goldstein, who worked with a Basie-type band led by Joseph Weinstein, uses free jazz inflections in a basic bop style. In fact, the country outside of the United States with the largest amount of jazz activity is Japan. Americans concertize there regularly, there is a steadily increasing supply of homegrown players, and record sales are large. However, the history of Japanese jazz is yet to be written.

What finally is to be said about European jazz? The difference between it and the American variety is more a matter of quantity than quality. Since the days of Reinhardt and Grappelli, there have always been at least some Europeans who could compete at the highest levels of American jazz. It was just that there have been a lot fewer of them. For André Ekyan or Humphrey Lyttelton there were a dozen American players as good, and a handful better. This is especially true of rhythm players. Visiting Americans have universally complained about European rhythm sections, and certainly one reason for the international success of the Quintet of the Hot Club of France was the rhythmic strength of the Reinhardt brothers. Second, it seems to me that there is a lack of a certain kind of force generally present in the best American jazz playing. European players tend to be somewhat intellectual about their work; there is less of that insistent, at times hoarse-voice desperation, that driving passion, that sense that the soloist is taking you by the shoulders and shaking you to make his point, that we find in much American playing. The European thinks more, is more conscious of what he is saying, less likely to simply let it rip. But if Europe has not yet found its Armstrong, its Parker or Ellington, it is certain as such things can be that Europeans will play an expanding role in the future of jazz. Jazz is becoming, today, a truly international music.

PART IV

The Modern Age

The Bop Rebellion

Rarely has there been a movement in art that showed so clearly as bop the lineaments of the social forces behind it. Not merely was the philosophy of the players a product of currents in the culture, but the shape of the music itself — the actual length and pitches of the notes — to a large degree was determined by shifts in the structure of society, shifts that are in fact still going on.

Bop, we have to bear in mind, was a wholly black invention. White musicians like Goodman and the Midwesterners had played important roles in the formation of swing music, and they had less important but measurable effects on the development of the jazz of the 1920s. But the pioneer bop players were all blacks, and the whites who came into it early, like Al Haig and Red Rodney, were suppliants who came at first on sufferance.

These young blacks were born around 1920, and they grew up in a different world from the one that formed Louis Armstrong and Jelly Roll Morton. In the period before World War I, most white Americans honestly believed that blacks were mentally and socially inferior to whites; that they were not capable of handling important positions in the society; and that they were relatively content in menial jobs. By the 1920s and thirties, when the bop players were growing up, this attitude had been modified. The interest in black arts, and in jazz itself, that bloomed in the 1920s among intellectuals and artists had carried with it a somewhat greater understanding of the meaning of racial segregation. Left-wing political groups were agitating for black rights.

Furthermore, by the mid-1930s a number of blacks had established themselves not only in the popular arts, as they had always done, but in the high arts, too. Actor Canada Lee, actor-singer Paul Robeson, writer Richard Wright, Singer Marian Anderson, were all seen as real artists. The philosophic and emotional basis for segregation, the idea that blacks were inherently inferior to whites, was becoming harder and harder to justify. Whites were beginning to feel, uneasily, that something would have to be done, and young blacks were concluding, more and more, that it would have to be done now. No longer would a black jazz musician feel, as Armstrong had, that he needed a white man to put his hand on his shoulder and say, "This is my nigger." Blacks were shaking off their sense of inferiority, and as they looked around at the culture with clearer vision, they grew bitter, resentful, and scornful of white society.

For the young black jazz musician the bitterness had immediate causes. In the late 1930s, when the swing band boom was rolling, he could not work with a white band, he was less well paid, and, possibly most galling of all, he could not even invite his friends and family to watch him perform in many of the places where he played. On the road he ate in restaurants in black quarters and lodged with private families, not in hotels. He saw whites around him getting rich on what he conceived of as his music. And despite the fact that whites had helped to make the music, and that most of them did not get rich, the distribution of fame and money was unjust. Thus, by 1940, there existed in jazz a large number of young blacks who, though they might like a few individual whites whom they came into contact with, disliked whites as a class, mistrusted them, and were determined to go their own way, independent of white society as much as possible.

One exception to this rule, probably, was Charlie Christian. In 1939 he was about twenty years old and was playing an odd and almost unknown instrument, the electrically amplified guitar. I say "probably" because we know very little about Christian. What we do know, however, suggests that he was a quiet young man with a sunny disposition who was interested in his music and good times far more than in any philosophic concerns with race problems. Who was first to rig up an amplified guitar is difficult to discover. Credit is usually given to Floyd Smith, who played the Hawaiian guitar, and Eddie Durham, known mostly as trombonist and arranger with Lunceford and Basie. Smith's "Floyd's Guitar Blues," made with Andy Kirk, is thought to be the first important use of the electric guitar on record. Smith was from St. Louis, Durham from Texas, and it is assumed that Christian, who was from the Southwest, learned about the instrument from one of them, probably Smith.

Charlie Christian was born in Dallas, probably in 1919, and grew up in Oklahoma City at a time when it was an important Southwest music center. Growing up, as he did, in that blues-drenched territory it was inevitable that he became a blues player. Even in his more sophisticated playing later on, he frequently used both blue thirds and sevenths.

His father was a blind guitarist, and his four brothers were all musical. Charlie played a little trumpet, bass, and piano as an adolescent, but guitar was his primary instrument, and he played it in the family band. He undoubtedly heard Lonnie Johnson, Blind Lemon Jefferson, and Eddie Lang, all of whom were cutting large numbers of records while Christian was growing up. The influence of Django Reinhardt is more problematic. A very few Reinhardt records, mostly with Hawkins, were issued in the United States as early as 1935, although it is not likely they reached Oklahoma City. But according to Bill Simon, in an essay on Christian in *The Jazz Makers,* by 1939 he apparently could play many of Django's solos, and by the time he was recording with Goodman he was incorporating characteristic Reinhardt figures in his work. A record of "Stardust," cut in a club in Minneapolis in 1940, by which time he would have been well acquainted with Django's records, shows clear signs of the Reinhardt influence. But it seems most likely that Christian was the product of a whole tradition of Southwest guitar playing, rather than of one individual's style.

By 1939 he had developed a considerable reputation in the Southwest and was becoming known to touring jazz musicians. In that year Mary Lou Williams told John Hammond about him. Goodman had been thinking of adding a guitarist to his group. Hammond heard Christian in Oklahoma City. He was strongly impressed, and he persuaded Goodman to add Christian to his quartet. Goodman agreed to hear Christian.

According to Simon, Christian arrived wearing "a ten-gallon hat, pointed yellow shoes, a bright green suit over a purple shirt and for the final, elegant touch — a string bow-tie." The serious and conservative Goodman was put off by this rainbow apparition and listened to Christian only cursorily. But Hammond and some of the members of the band felt that Goodman hadn't given Christian a chance, and that night they sneaked Christian onto the bandstand with his equipment just before the quartet was to go on, when Goodman was on a break. Goodman was not pleased when he returned, but he was reluctant to create a scene, so he called for "Rose Room." And — so the legend is — he was so entranced by Christian's playing that he had the group play "Rose Room" for forty-eight minutes. Shortly after, with Christian and bassist Artie Bernstein turning the quartet into a sextet, the group recorded a selection of numbers, including "Flying Home," which became a hit. Within weeks Christian was a force in the world of jazz.

What immediately captured listeners was the sound of this new-fangled instrument. People were used to a guitar timbre that, in the hands of the untutored people who often played the instrument, was tinny or whiny. Christian's instrument produced a more bell-like sound, which had something of the percussive quality of a keyboard instrument. And it could be played as loudly as any instrument. The guitar could now be used as a horn.

Christian's new instrument attracted the fans, but it was his manner of playing that caught the attention of musicians. His jazz sounded superficially like what the swing players were doing, but somehow it had a tantalizingly different flavor. Both rhythmically and harmonically Christian was edging into something new. Harmonically, the change involved a heavy use of dissonance, especially the so-called higher parts of the chords. A standard chord in European music is made up of alternate notes of a scale — first, third, fifth, and so forth. If you continue this process on up the scale, you eventually reach the ninth, eleventh, and thirteenth notes, which, to simplify, are the second, fourth, and sixth notes in the scale. Jazz musicians had of course been using these notes before, especially the thirteenth (or sixth), which they derived from the blue note. But Christian was using them frequently. He was very fond of the fourth, which he often accented to bring out the dissonant flavor. He was also fond of substituting the diminished seventh chord for the chord normally called for. The diminished seventh chord contains the flatted fifth, the note that was to become the symbol of the bop movement. Used in a normal context, it produces a wry discordance, which Christian enjoyed.

Christian's rhythmic innovations were less obvious than his harmonic ones, but they were in their way more interesting. His solos at times consisted largely of long lines of uninflected eighth notes. Occasionally he bent

One of the relatively rare pictures of Charlie Christian, probably taken backstage during an appearance of the Goodman band in a New York theater in 1940. Drummer is Gene Krupa. William P. Gottlieb/Edward Gottlieb Collection

a blue note, and he accented from time to time; but more than anybody of his era, possibly excepting a pianist like Art Tatum, he was simply laying out the notes for display, flat and uninflected. Even more surprising is the lack of syncopation in his work. Where the ordinary swing player might syncopate half his notes, Christian was capable of playing almost a whole blues chorus without syncopating a single note. He does this in his fourth chorus on "Breakfast Feud," with the Goodman Sextet; only four of forty-eight beats are syncopated. This practice became characteristic of bop.

Christian gets his variety of rhythm by phrasing against the grain of the underlying structure of the tune. Jazz musicians before this time had tended very much to cut their phrases to the two-, four-, and eight-bar patterns of the familiar marches, pop songs, and folk material. Where the phrases were irregular, it was usually a result of simple failure. Christian, however, consistently and deliberately used figures that ran irregular numbers of bars in length and peaked at what seemed, at the time, to be unexpected places. Then, too, jazz players normally ended their figures on the first, or especially third, beat of a measure; Christian habitually ended on the second half of a beat, often the fourth beat, the weakest point in the measure.

A good example of all of these devices is his solo on "Seven Come Eleven," again with the Goodman Sextet. The first phrase begins approximately a half bar early and runs about three measures, peaking at the end, which is the third beat of the third measure of the composition. The next phrase begins at a peak in the middle of the second beat of the fourth measure and runs through the next measure, ending on the fourth beat. The succeeding phrase again begins in the middle of a measure and runs about two-and-a-half bars. Christian has thus fit three phrases over eight measures. In the next eight bars there are four related phrases of different lengths. The peaks in this section fall unexpectedly in the middle of bar nine, across the bar line between bars twelve and thirteen, and in the middle of bar sixteen. It is not so much that the whole shape of the chorus runs counter to the underlying structure of the tune; it ignores it. And it is this irregular phrasing, not a loosening of the melody line from the beat, that makes Christian's work rhythmically effective. It is amazing how often he plunks down his notes heavily on the beat; his playing is tied into the beat more than the playing of any major figure in jazz; and this gives his work a stiffness he might in time have got rid of, had he lived.

In sum, Christian has to be seen as an important innovator, rather than as a superlative jazz improviser. The young guitarists playing jazz today are often puzzled by Christian's reputation; they do not see him as in any way Django Reinhardt's peer. The reason, of course, is that, stripped of the novelty his work had at the time, Christian's playing is sometimes flat-footed and lacking in inventiveness. What seemed fresh then has become established practice today.

In 1940 Charlie Christian was more than a star soloist with one of the most popular musical groups in the Western world; he was being seen by his fellow players as an important innovator. Not Beiderbecke, Holiday, or Goodman himself was so celebrated so young, and it was evident to everybody that Christian had a tremendous future ahead of him. But he was, at bottom, a naive young man from the sticks, newly come to fame and money, and he took up the sweet life. He had suffered from incipient tuberculosis for years, and now late hours and excesses worsened his condition. In 1941 he collapsed and was sent to Seaview Sanitarium on Staten Island. He began to improve, and it seemed that he would make a good recovery. However, according to Simon, musician friends began coming out to the sanitarium with women and liquor to party with Charlie, sometimes even sneaking him out of the hospital. By the time anyone responsible found out about this high living and stopped it, it was too late. Charlie Christian died in February 1942, twenty-two years old, if we can trust the 1919 birth date. From the time he joined Goodman until the time he entered the hospital, there had passed hardly more than twenty months, and his entire professional career was barely seven years long. Yet in those twenty months with Goodman he left an indelible mark on jazz.

In 1939, when Christian was just beginning to make that mark, several young black musicians about his age were moving tentatively in the direction Christian was going. One of the most important of these was a highly talented trumpet player named John Birks Gillespie, called "Dizzy" because of his hijinks on the stands, who was at that moment working in the Cab Calloway orchestra. Gillespie was born on October 21, 1917, in Cheraw, South Carolina, the last of nine children. His father, a bricklayer by trade, led a band as a sideline, and Gillespie was early introduced to music. He experimented with various instruments, and his talent was clear enough that in 1927 he was sent on a scholarship to the Laurinburg Institute, an industrial school for blacks in North Carolina. He started on trombone, shortly switched to trumpet, and was introduced to theory as well.

In 1935 his mother, now a widow, moved to Philadelphia, and Gillespie dropped out of the school to go with her. He began working in local bands there, modeling himself, like other young trumpet players, on Roy Eldridge, then working with the Teddy Hill band. His rise was quick; in 1937, not yet twenty, he took Eldridge's place in the Hill band. Already he was being seen as a wise kid who needed to be put firmly in his place. He was rowdy on the stand. When Hill told him to take his foot off a chair he would respond by putting it on the music stand. At times, when another man was soloing, Gillespie would stand and imitate him. He was, clearly, a smart aleck who was looking for trouble, and the other men in the band tried to persuade Hill to fire him. But Hill wouldn't. Gillespie was already a better musician than most of the men in the band. Solos he cut during this period show a clean, bright style built around a first-class embouchure and a conception that owed a great deal to Eldridge and a little to Armstrong. He was a classic swing band trumpet soloist, at ease both on ballads and hot numbers, and, however unknown, clearly superior to most of his rivals in the business.

In 1939 he left Hill to go with the Calloway band, which included Chu Berry. His unruly behavior continued, and Calloway, who was the leading black male vocalist in popular music, was less patient with him than Hill had been. The climax came in 1941, during a show in Hartford, Connecticut, when a spitball was thrown on the bandstand. It seems to have been trumpeter Jonah Jones who threw it, but Calloway blamed Gillespie. There followed an altercation backstage, during which Calloway was nicked with a knife, and Gillespie's career with the band ended instantly. But Gillespie had been on the way out, anyway. He was beginning to do odd things in his solos, which annoyed many of the men in the band, and which Calloway branded "Chinese music." A man of Dizzy's rebellious temperament would not, obviously, play shadow to Roy Eldridge forever, and as early as 1939 he was beginning to experiment with different approaches to both harmony and phrasing.

At about the same time Gillespie was getting into trouble with Cab Calloway, another young player, a few years Gillespie's senior, was getting into trouble with Gillespie's former boss, Teddy Hill. Drummer Kenny Clarke, a Pittsburgh boy born in 1914, had worked his way up through the ranks of the music business, and by 1940 was in the Hill band. Clarke had evolved a novel way of playing the drums. From the earliest days of jazz, the bass drum had been hit on every beat to establish the ground beat in the simplest and most direct way. The snare was used to provide complementary rhythms or a repeated figure to help establish the ground beat. Walter Johnson and Jo Jones had moved the snare figures onto the hi-hat. Now Clarke was moving the ground beat away from the drum altogether and placing it on the large ride cymbal, which sat in the center of the set. His reasons for doing so, he claims, were simple. He says, in Marshall Stearns's *The Story of Jazz*, "We played so many flag-wavers, man, you know, fast up-tempo numbers like 'The Harlem Twister' that my right foot got paralyzed — so I cut it all out except now and then." That is to say, he would keep the steady beat going on the ride cymbal and use the bass drum only for accents — to drop bombs, as the phrase came to be. But his reasons were not in fact that simple. He is quoted in *Bird Lives!*, Ross Russell's fascinating biography of Charlie Parker, as saying:

> In 1937 I'd got tired of playing like Jo Jones. It was time for jazz drummers to move ahead. I took the main beat away from the bass drum and up to the top cymbal. I found out I could get pitch and timbre variations up there, according to the way the stick struck the

cymbal and a pretty sound. The beat had a better flow. It was lighter and tastier. That left me free to use the bass drum, the tom-toms and snare for accents.

As revolutionary as the change seemed to players at the time, Clarke was in fact only continuing a trend that had been running for decades. The heavy clanging beat of the early jazz bands had been lightened step by step by the replacement of tuba and banjo with bass and guitar, and the shifting of the ground beat away from the drums to the hi-hat. Clarke was following directly in this line, but the shift affronted Hill and his sidemen so much that eventually Hill fired Clarke. It therefore came as something of a surprise to Clarke when, a year or so later, Hill asked him to organize a house band for a club of which he had recently become manager. The club was a seedy box on One hundred eighteenth Street. It was owned by a peripheral musician named Henry Minton, who had been the first black delegate in New York's famous Local 802. Business had been sagging, and Minton had decided some time in 1940 to ask Hill to take the place over. Hill, whose own band had not proved a commercial success, was glad to take the job. He put together a series of "celebrity nights," throwing a free feed for black show business figures. He then went about setting up a house band. Hill apparently lighted on Clarke as leader because he felt that the experimentalists would provide something different and, no doubt, because they would come cheaper than established players. The band was Clarke, Thelonious Monk, bass man Nick Fenton, and Joe Guy on trumpet. Dizzy Gillespie began turning up regularly.

The experiment proved a success. Very quickly word got out that Minton's was a place to sit in, and within weeks after Hill had taken over, most nights the place was crowded with big-name musicians waiting their turns to play. Jazz stars like Hawkins, Eldridge, Ben Webster, Lester Young, and even Benny Goodman, who had moved on to the world of wealth and international celebrity, dropped in from time to time. The music, at first, was primarily mainstream swing, colored, of course, by Clarke's novel approach to drumming and the whimsical, sometimes eccentric, playing of Monk. Charlie Christian, who had already become something of a pet among older musicians, came up to jam after his nightly stint with Goodman, which, confined as it was to the small group, did not offer him much chance to play. And then, in the fall of 1941, Monk and Clarke began hearing about an alto saxophone player who was jamming regularly in an after-hours place called Clark Monroe's Uptown House. This obscure saxophonist, named Charlie Parker, Clarke and Monk were told, had a new and astonishing conception. The Minton's players were skeptical, but they went around to hear Parker. Clarke, quoted in *Bird Lives!,* says, "Bird was playing stuff we'd never heard before. He was into figures I thought I'd

Minton's, the club where bebop first found acceptance, with some of the heroes of the time. From left, Thelonious Monk, Howard McGee, Roy Eldridge, and probably Teddy Hill, manager of the club, who brought the new men in. William P. Gottlieb/Edward Gottlieb Collection

invented for drums. He was twice as fast as Lester Young and into harmony Lester hadn't touched. Bird was running the same way we were, but he was way ahead of us. I don't think he was aware of the changes he had created. It was his way of playing jazz, part of his own experience."

Clarke and Monk made arrangements for Parker to move from Monroe's to Minton's, and the stage was set for a musical revolution. A great deal has been made of the notion that the "new sounds" that were to become bop were developed by these men as a method for keeping inferior musicians off the stand, and Clarke and others have testified that they did in fact introduce odd chord sequences into tunes to discourage the unwanted. But clearly there was a great deal more to it than that. Gillespie and Parker had separately been experimenting with advanced harmonies for at least two

Gillespie, Parker, Clarke, Monk

years; Clarke had been working his new system of drumming since 1937. Much of what happened at Minton's was discussed and worked over among Gillespie, Monk, and other sympathetic young players in casual listening sessions at one another's homes. Gillespie, who was by 1941 a well-schooled musician, seems to have been particularly important in building a theory out of the insights of the group. And, in the end, they changed jazz. The only thing they left intact was the basic small band format they had taken over from the swing players.

The change that was most immediately obvious, and easiest for musicians to grasp, was the new emphasis on what came to be called altered chords — that is, those "wrong" notes that Charlie Christian had begun to use. Over the long history of European music there has been a consistent trend toward increasing the number of permissible notes. In medieval times there were only unisons and octaves; then harmonies in fifths and fourths were added; then chords based on thirds were established; and in the later part of the nineteenth century and the early years of the twentieth, it gradually became permissible to put together virtually any combination of notes. Prior to bop, jazz harmony — and the harmony of popular music, from which jazz harmony was drawn — was about where classical music was in the seventeenth century. The bop players were now demanding acceptance for harmonies using a greater range of notes; they were, in fact, doing what the classical composers did in the nineteenth century.

Where did this idea come from? According to an oft-quoted story, Parker was working at a chili house on Seventh Avenue between One hundred thirty-ninth and One hundred fortieth streets in December 1939 when the idea struck him. "I'd been getting bored with the stereotyped changes that were being used all the time at the time, and I kept thinking there's bound to be something else. I could hear it sometimes, but I couldn't play it. Well that night, I was working over 'Cherokee,' and as I did, I found that by using the higher intervals of a chord as a melody line and backing them with appropriately related changes, I could play the thing I'd been hearing. I came alive."

Today Parker is given the lion's share of the credit for inventing the harmonic changes bop brought to jazz, but on the evidence of the records it seems clear enough that Gillespie was making the same discoveries on his own, possibly in advance of Parker. Ira Gitler, in *Jazz Masters of the Forties*, quotes him as saying:

> When I was with [Edgar] Hayes, Rudy Powell made an arrangement on a tune that was very fascinating. It was something in this arrangement that almost changed my whole playing around. It was like when you go from C-sharp to C . . . Of course Roy had been doing a couple of things like that, but this was really — it had a melody. Just one bar, maybe two bars or something in this arrangement. I used to *like* when

we'd get to that arrangement, and I started playing that same thing in other things — you know, putting it in different places and it evolved around it.

The statement is a little murky, but it is clear that what Gillespie was doing was to slip briefly into a chord containing notes a half step away from the normal one. This procedure came to be a central characteristic of bop. This was probably in 1939, and we can hear him applying the principle regularly soon after.

In May 1940, in a solo on a tune called "Pickin' the Cabbage," which he arranged for Calloway, he deliberately uses major thirds over minor changes at the beginning of the second eight measures. In June 1940, he uses a diminished ninth on "Bye, Bye Blues" at the end of the first sixteen measures as a "turn-around," a cliché today, but at the time something new. By May of 1941, when he was recorded by an amateur at Minton's, he was still playing mostly in the Roy Eldridge manner, but on a tune later called "Kerouac" (based on "Exactly Like You"), he again uses notes a half step away from the normal dominant seventh chord in bars six and fourteen as part of the turn-around.

The ideas of Parker and Gillespie were not so very novel from an academic viewpoint, and would have come into jazz anyway. By the 1940s conservatory-trained musicians were beginning to enter jazz, and they were bringing with them similar ideas worked out by master composers in the previous century. Indeed, it may not be coincidental that Hawkins's "Body and Soul," virtually an exercise in chromatic chord movement, had become, late in 1939, one of the biggest jazz hits of the period. But Parker and Gillespie set about building a whole music around this concept, and, perhaps more important, they had the courage to insist that they were right.

A second change was the regular use of substitute chords by the players working at Minton's. This is hardly a complex idea: you simply replace a chord, or group of chords, in a song with different, but related ones. Hawkins had been doing this sort of thing for a decade, and Tatum even longer. Again, the difference was that the bop players made a regular practice of it.

But as important as these harmonic innovations were in the making of bop, they were in the air, and would have come about anyway. The real revolution in bop was not harmonic, but rhythmic, as change in jazz has always been. The subject is, as always, difficult because we are dealing with almost immeasurable subtleties of accent, time, and divisions of beats. But certain things are clear. To begin with, the swing players had preferred medium tempos, in the range of 100 to 200 beats a minute. The bop players often played at tempos above 300, a speed at which few jazz musicians are able to say very much. On the other hand, when they played ballads they often dropped them to speeds well below 100 — even down to 80, which would be acceptable for a slow blues, but certainly not for ordinary dancing.

In fact, however, these slow tempos are delusory, for their purpose was to allow the soloist to cram in batches of sixteenth and even thirty-second notes. Thus, even at slow tempos the bop players were playing fast. Gillespie, it should be remembered, took as his model Roy Eldridge, who had himself begun trying to be the fastest gun in the West; and Parker at one time emulated alto saxophonist Buster Smith, who liked to introduce patches of double-times notes. Furthermore, the competitive impulse that fed much jazz playing often expressed itself in contests of speed. In the end, the bop players simply became habituated to machine-gun tempos.

These fast tempos were in part responsible for another bop innovation. The swing players tended to divide a beat into two distinctly unequal parts — often so unequal that one of them virtually disappeared, as was the case with Coleman Hawkins. The bop player reversed this tendency and began dividing notes much more evenly, though not perfectly so. At fast tempos it is hard — indeed, almost impossible — to make markedly unequal divisions of a beat, because the short note of the pair becomes in effect a sixteenth, and at a tempo above about 250, sixteenth notes are impossible on a wind instrument. (They could be double-tongued, of course, but then you have equal sixteenths, which was not what you were aiming for.)

This liking for strings of more or less equal notes at fast tempos suggests that the bop players were abandoning the practice of separating their lines from the beat. At times it did happen; at times endless strings of eighth notes became simply endless strings of eighth notes. But in the work of the best players they did not. Parker, in his patches of fast notes, would invariably mix triplet figures with eighths and sixteenths, as well as less-definable figures, in such a way that not just one or two phrases were extended over the ground beat, but the whole patch was set free, like a sudden shower of hailstones on the roof. This, in fact, is the meaning of those fast patches that are a characteristic part of bop playing: they are leaps into the sky that for a moment appear to escape the gravity pull of the ground beat. But in their more regular passages the bop players used the practices standard to jazz. Gillespie consistently played behind the beat, even on fast passages, and Parker used many extended figures. Indeed, Parker played as far away from the beat as anybody in jazz.

It was in yet another aspect of rhythm that the bop players produced the change that troubled the older jazz players of the time. This had to do with a shift in phrasing from first and third to second and fourth beats of the measure — the "on" beat to the "off " beat. As we have seen, in 4/4 time, the first and third beats are strong, the second and fourth beats weak, and music is composed so that phrases in general begin and end on the first and third beats, while the second and fourth beats are left untended. We have seen, too, that jazz players used extended figures that ignore the beats altogether; we have seen that jazz drummers often set up on the second and fourth beats a rhythm running counter to one on the first and third beats; we have seen that jazz players syncopated — that is, began notes between beats so that they were on neither first nor second; we have seen that jazz players accented in odd places. Nonetheless, despite the extent to which jazz improvisers played fast and loose with the beat, prior to the bop revolution jazz fundamentally followed the standard procedure of emphasizing the first and third beats. Jazz phrases began and ended on the first and third beats; peaks came on those beats. Enforcing this system was the fact that — even up until today — chord changes almost invariably came at the beginning of measures, or pairs of measures; and if, as was sometimes the case in slow tunes, there was a chord change within a measure, it would come on the third beat, not the second or the fourth. Thus, harmonic shifts added to the strength of the first and third beats, and, in a broad sense, jazz players responded to the tug by cutting their melodies to the accented beats. They did so because to most Western ears this had been natural.

But by about 1940 Charlie Christian, Dizzy Gillespie, and Charlie Parker were occasionally beginning or ending phrases on the second and fourth beats. Christian frequently ended phrases at the weakest point in a measure, the second half of the fourth beat, and Gillespie, in the fifth bar of his solo on "Hot Mallets," made under the leadership of Lionel Hampton as early as 1939, phrases on the second beat. However, it seems clear that Parker, if not the only creator of this device, was its major user. Jay McShann, quoted in Robert Reisner's *Bird: The Legend of Charlie Parker,* says, "He played everything offbeat; he had it in his head long before he could put it together." He is already applying the principle in the Witchita transcription of "Body and Soul," in 1940. In the second measure of the tune (not counting his introductory figure) he is phrasing very much on two and four. (It is very hard to determine for sure, but it seems to me that he was also at times phrasing a half beat away from the meter. A surprising number of Parker tunes begin on the first beat of a measure, where in the earlier jazz there would have been a pickup note somewhere in the last beat or so of the previous bar; and I have a feeling that these first notes should be heard as pickups, with the true melody beginning at the second half of the first beat. This is true, I think, of "Bloomdido." Furthermore, an astonishing number of his figures end on the second half of the fourth beat of a measure, and again this suggests that he is a half beat away from the meter. We are, however, on exceedingly treacherous ground here.)

By 1941 or 1942, the bop players were making a deliberate practice of this. According to Miles Davis, quoted in Marshall Stearns's *The Story of Jazz:*

> Like we'd be playing the blues and Bird [Parker] would start on the 11th bar, and as the rhythm section stayed where they were and Bird played where he was, it sounded as if the rhythm section was on one

and three instead of two and four. Every time that would happen Max [Roach, the drummer] would scream at Duke [Jordan, the pianist] not to follow Bird, but to stay where he was. Then eventually, it came around as Bird had planned and we were together again.

To be sure, bop players did not push everything over to the second and fourth beats; much of the time they phrased in the standard way, and of course often enough they were playing free patches that did not relate to the beat in any way. But they used this counter-phrasing sufficiently often to give their music a whole different cast. It is no accident that "Salt Peanuts," drawn from Lucky Millinder's "Little John Special," which Gillespie played, came to be one of the earliest bop anthems, for it is phrased around two and four, rather than one and three. And here again we have jazz playing finding new ways of setting melodies against an explicitly stated undergirding. It was this counter-phrasing, rather than the harmonic innovations, that threw the older players off. It was not so difficult, after all, to introduce an F or a G♭ in a run built on a C chord; but the new way of phrasing was contrary to something that had by now become second nature to the players of the old school. Most of them did not even grasp the principle — it was just "crazy music" — and not a single one of them was able to practice it. That sounds like hyperbole, but it is not. Many younger listeners do not find the music of Hawkins and Young much different from that of Parker and Gillespie. I therefore want to make it clear that so profound did the bop revolution appear at the time that not one established swing player ever succeeded in playing bop. And it was mainly this shift in time that caused the trouble.

All of these rhythmic and harmonic departures from earlier jazz practice forced changes on the rhythm section. It became clear very quickly that if the horn player was to be free to introduce altered chords and substitutions, he could not be tied down by the standard piano style, which stated the chords emphatically, beat after beat. Furthermore, at some of the fast tempos a pianist's hands would have become as cramped as Kenny Clarke's foot had become if he attempted to play in stride fashion. As a consequence, pianists began simply to feed the soloist occasional chords as punctuation and/or place marks; say, once or twice a measure. This in turn made the bass the center of the rhythm section. The pianist was no longer playing the ground beat, and the drummer was playing it only on the ride cymbal. The bassist was stating it simply and directly, and he was also outlining the chords as they came along. And, indeed, these changes in piano and drum were made in part to stay out of the bass player's way. In the past the bass had never been seen as essential; there was no bass in Armstrong's Hot Five, in some of the Trumbauer groups with Bix, in the Original Dixieland Jazz Band, in Benny Goodman's trios and quartets, in many of the small Fifty-second Street groups. Piano and drums were considered basic, and the guitar might well be the next addition. But after bop, playing without a bass came to be almost unthinkable. Players who in the past had been used to listening to the piano when they soloed now found it more helpful to focus on the bass. And bass playing itself began to change. For one thing, after the model of Blanton, bassists were playing more lines, rather than stating chords. For another, the bass man now saw himself as a major propulsive force in the band, a role the drummer formerly had. Bass players began to "push" or "play on top of" the beat. By this they meant that they anticipated it, striking it just fractionally before it arrived. This is a risky practice, and soloists unused to it have trouble with it. The bassist seems to be accelerating, and the player who does not realize what is happening can be thrown off.

It is at this point difficult to credit one or another of the players at Minton's with any particular innovation. Parker is today considered the greatest of them all, but this does not say that he was the man with all the new ideas. In 1940 he was no farther along than Gillespie was. Wherever the ideas came from, a process of cross-pollinization was at work, and after that ideas were up for grabs. And by about 1942 it was clear to musicians that here was something more than mere experimentation. Here was a new kind of music.

Unhappily, we cannot pinpoint these developments. In August of 1942, the American Federation of Musicians struck the record companies, and no new records could be made, although of course records continued to be issued from old stock or from cuts made in preparation for the drought. Decca signed with the union in the fall of 1943, and a number of small companies sprang into existence to fill the void, but not until the end of 1944 did Columbia and Victor come to terms with the union. As a result there are few commercial recordings of any of the bop players during the years they were working out their innovations.

What we would particularly like to have is good records of a big band that some of the bop players worked in at this time. It should be remembered that most of the men who played at Minton's went unpaid. They needed other work, and in 1942 Earl Hines, who was leading a swing band, began to hire some of the modernists, among them trombonist Benny Green, drummer Shadow Wilson, and in time both Parker and Gillespie. The band's vocalist was Billy Eckstine, who eventually became a star singer. There were, however, tensions in the Hines band between the new men and the older ones. Gillespie left in mid-1943, played a brief stint with Duke Ellington, and then, with Oscar Pettiford as co-leader, took a group playing the new music into the Onyx. The group included pianist George Wallington, drummer Max Roach, and tenor saxophonist Don Byas, who was one of the few players able to straddle the gap between swing and bop. This stand, which lasted through the winter of 1943–1944, was the first real exposure the new music had. It was, after that, a known quantity, at least to musicians and jazz fans.

Then, in the spring of 1944, Billy Eckstine, Hines's former singer, who was also working on Fifty-second Street, held some conversations with Gillespie about forming a big band that Eckstine would front and that would be built around the new music. With manager Billy Shaw, who was to handle many of the boppers, taking care of the business end, Gillespie was put in charge of the music, and Parker was brought in. Dizzy wrote a number of arrangements for the band. It was not wildly successful, in part because of the strike against the record companies, although it did achieve some popularity due primarily to the presence of Eckstine and his female vocalist, Sarah Vaughan. But musicians were aware of it, and it provided a way of spreading the new ideas. Parker, however, was already exhibiting the personality problems from which he suffered. He missed jobs; slept through others. Fed up with the whole thing, he left the Eckstine band in 1944 to front a rhythm section at the Three Deuces on Fifty-second Street. He prevailed on Gillespie to join him soon after, and very quickly they began to record.

The records generally considered the first bop records were a few made for a small label in 1944 under the leadership of Coleman Hawkins. The group, which included Dizzy Gillespie, Max Roach, and baritone saxophonist Leo Parker, all associated with the new music, is a modified swing band, and the music is essentially in the swing camp, featuring Hawkins's tenor saxophone. However, there are bop tinges in the harmonies, particularly in "Woody 'n' You," which Gillespie wrote, and choruses by Gillespie on that piece and "Disorder at the Border," which are almost fully formed bop. About the same time Parker cut four sides with guitarist-singer Tiny Grimes, which are of little importance except for his own work though they indicate that the new music was becoming accepted even for fairly commercial records. By this time others were getting into the act. Late in 1944 trumpeter Little Benny Harris cut four sides that were distinctly in the bop camp; they have Oscar Pettiford on bass, Denzil Best, an early entry into the new music, on drums, and Clyde Hart on piano. Harris had been in the Hines band and had jammed frequently at Minton's. Hart had started as a Basie-Wilson type of swing player, but began to move very quickly into bop when it surfaced on Fifty-second Street. He was the pianist of choice for bop dates during the early years, but unfortunately he died of tuberculosis before he could develop into a true bop player.

Then, late in 1944, Gillespie was chosen by a board of critics for an *Esquire* magazine poll as the "new star" on trumpet. To be sure, the deck was stacked. Critic Leonard Feather, who selected the board, was already in the bop camp. Nonetheless, the award, although controversial, indicated that bop music was beginning to peep out from underground. And in

Dizzy Gillespie received his nickname because of his penchant for
clowning on the stand, where he sometimes executed a few dance steps
while the band was playing, or burst into song, as he appears to be doing
in this picture. But he was, as has been said, "Dizzy like a fox," and
where Charlie Parker wasted his talent on the pursuit of the moment,
Gillespie managed his career with intelligence and skill, to become in his
later years as close to an elder statesman as jazz has ever had. William P.
Gottlieb/Edward Gottlieb Collection

February and May of 1945, Parker and Gillespie made the first real bop records — records that were to become jazz classics. The first of these sessions used swing players Cozy Cole on drums and Slam Stewart on bass, as well as guitarist Remo Palmieri and Clyde Hart. The second date included Sid Catlett on drums, but it also had bassist Curly Russell and pianist Al Haig, both of them regular members of the Three Deuces group. The tunes were mostly bop originals, built on the chord sequences of standard tunes, among them "Groovin' High," "Salt Peanuts," "Shaw Nuff," and "Hot House."

In November of 1945 came a session with Parker, a very young Miles Davis, Curly Russell, and Max Roach, rapidly becoming the leading bop drummer. Gillespie was under contract to another company and appeared incognito on some tracks as trumpeter and pianist. The tunes again were bop originals, among them "Billie's Bounce," "Now's the Time," and "Koko." It was the sessions of 1945, especially this last one, that exposed the new music to a wide public — not the public of the by-now-moribund big band age, but a public of young jazz enthusiasts, many of them to be the musicians who would set the course of jazz for the next two decades. These sides were the most influential jazz records to be cut since the Hot Fives and Hot Sevens Armstrong had made nearly two decades earlier.

Although Parker today is seen as the consummate bop musician, at the time Gillespie was taken for the bright light of the movement, except by those very close to the scene. All the major characteristics of bop were evident in his playing from the time of these early records. It was certainly he, as much as Parker, who made the shift onto the weak beats of the measure. We have seen him do this as early as 1939 in the "Hot Mallets" chorus, and by 1945 it was an established part of his method. The May 1945 Parker-Gillespie session included a take of "Lover Man," sung by Sarah Vaughan, whom the boppers knew through her work with the Eckstine band. Gillespie plays a brief solo on the bridge, which lasts for eight bars, and in this short space he accents six of the second beats in the eight measures, and three of the fourth beats, demonstrating a definite preference for accenting on these beats. And, as much as Parker, he was using all the new altered chords and previously unacceptable harmonies that he had helped to pioneer.

Yet if we make allowance for the new harmonies and the phrasing against the natural flow of the meter, there remains in Gillespie's playing a considerable amount of the conception he adopted from Roy Eldridge. On "Salt Peanuts," one of the bop classics made during this period, he opens his solo with a break that, except for the bop harmonies, could have been played by Roy. Indeed, throughout the whole solo there is ample evidence of the Eldridge influence — the sudden leaps into the stratosphere; the dashing, tearing, downward runs; the phrases impatiently broken off in midflight to make room for the next one. Prominent in Gillespie's playing is the steady shifting back and forth from rapid runs of evenly played sixteenth notes and passages of uneven eighths, played very much as the swing players would have done. In these slower passages Gillespie plays as far behind the beat as almost anybody in jazz — farther behind than such leaders of the swing movement as Hawkins, Young, or Eldridge himself. At times, in fact, he is as far away from the beat as Armstrong, and it should be remembered that not only did Gillespie's model, Eldridge, owe a great deal to Armstrong, but that when Gillespie was beginning to study music seriously in 1927 Armstrong was the pre-eminent musician in jazz.

These early Gillespie records were made with various pickup groups, but in 1946 Gillespie got a modicum of backing and formed a big band. He was running against the current; by 1946 the big band era was over. Yet he managed to keep the band alive for the next four years, and during that time made a series of records that set the standard for the bebop big band. Perhaps the best known of the records with his group are "Cubana Be" and "Cubana Bop," composed by George Russell in collaboration with Gillespie. Today the use of Latin forms in jazz is a cliché, but at that time it was not. Gillespie was the pioneer. He brought into the band Chano Pozo, a conga drummer widely admired by Latins. Pozo was killed in a knife fight soon after, but Gillespie continued to espouse Latin-influenced jazz, making bongo and conga drums a regular part of the band's instrumentation.

There is beginning, by this time, to be some change in his playing. Some of the Eldridge fire, with its occasional erratic moments, has been smoothed out. He is playing more long lines of fairly even eighth notes than he had done earlier, and the occasional technical failings that had appeared in the 1945 records are gone. By 1950 his control of the horn left other brass players breathless. As fast as he had been earlier, he now seemed able to move anywhere on the horn at any speed, effortlessly and errorlessly. He was now *the* trumpeter in jazz: for the young players, there was no other model.

Gillespie was one of the few of the early beboppers who did not destroy himself. He ran his career with intelligence, and even when later movements in music seemed to make bop obsolete, he continued to work, emerging, in the 1970s, as something as close to an elder statesman as the music has ever seen. Like Hawkins, he kept his standards and continued to play his own way despite shifts in taste, and he continues to reward listeners today.

The most important of his records, from the point of view of influence, are still those 1945 sessions with Parker. With them, the bop revolution was complete. It had all happened very fast. At the beginning of 1941 bop was only a handful of ideas tentatively being tried out by fewer than a half-dozen players. By 1942 it was being played by at least a few men. By 1943 it was circulating through the younger men in jazz; by 1944 it was a recognized, if controversial, movement; and by 1945 it had a public large enough to support it. And it was clear by then that bop was more than just a musical form; it was the core of a set of social ideas as well. Associated with it was an attitude that expressed itself in a habit of language, dress, and behavior. This was what came to be called "cool," and it had important social connotations. The jazz performer of the 1920s and thirties saw himself as, among other things, a public entertainer. There was Armstrong with his mugging and his great, floppy handkerchief; Cab Calloway wearing a white satin suit; the Ellington orchestra in white collar and tie, satin lapels, and a satin stripe down the leg; Billie Holiday with long white gloves and a large gardenia in her hair.

The mode adopted by the bop players and their followers was the obverse of this one. The bop player dressed like an English stockbroker; he spoke as much as possible like a college professor — when he was not using his private slang — and he eschewed anything that smacked of emotionalism. Not for him the grin and widespread arms of Armstrong; instead he coolly bowed to his audience at the end of a number and walked offstage. To be sure, the image was sometimes flawed in the making: Gillespie by nature was a cutup and kidded around on the stand; Monk was given to wearing funny hats; and Parker never had much awareness of clothes one way or another. But the cool intention was quite real, and it had two meanings. On the one hand, it was a deliberate attempt to avoid playing the role of flamboyant black entertainer, which whites had come to expect. On the other hand, it was a send-up of what the blacks saw as the square, restricted world of the whites.

Part of this attitude was the concept of "hip," which can best be defined as a silent knowingness. The hipster — the term "hippie" was a much later formation and had a different meaning — was wise; he knew what was under the surface of things and how the levers were pulled. He said nothing, however, but kept his cool, expressing emotion with a shrug or, when necessary, in his elliptical hip language, made up of a watery vocabulary in which words and phrases were not meant to have specific meanings, but to express an attitude toward the subject. A. B. Spellman, in his excellent study of the period, *Black Music* (it originally had the more salubrious but less commercial title *Four Lives in the Bebop Business*), has this to say: "It was in this era that the idea of hip developed . . . They created a language, a dress, a music, and a high which were closed unto themselves and allowed them to one-up the rest of the world. The bebop era was the first time that the black ego was expressed in America with self-assurance . . ." Certainly, among other things, the black players felt that in bop they were creating a music that "they" couldn't play — an idea that of course proved incorrect.

This attitude, this manner of presenting themselves, had developed from the changes in black thinking that were occurring in the 1920s and thirties.

It was no longer necessary to play up to whites. And if it was, the hell with it. It is hardly surprising, in light of this, that these players changed the music around. Where tempos had been medium, they were now fast or slow. Where the first, third, fifth, and seventh notes of the scale had been stressed, now the second and fourth were played up. Where the first and third beats of a measure had been accentuated, now it was the second and fourth. Where pairs of notes had been played extremely unevenly, now they were played almost equally. Where choirs of instruments had harmonized, now they were played in unison. Bop was, in the exact sense of the word, a musical revolution. These men turned the jazz world upside down and sat on the top, thumbing their noses at their elders falling off the other side.

Social forces, of course, must work through selected personalities, and when we examine the ones who made bop we are surprised not that they brought changes to the music, but that they did not bring more. Gillespie was the archetypical bad boy, and both he and Clarke had lost good jobs in the Depression because they rejected the ordinary discipline of a band. Monk was an eccentric, Christian a naif who died of foolishness, and Charlie Parker, as we shall shortly see, was an egomaniac living in a world that did not extend beyond his own skin. For these black jazz players, their fans and followers, bop was a declaration of independence.

Charlie Parker:
An Erratic Bird in Flight

There have been two authentic geniuses in jazz. One of them, of course, was Louis Armstrong, the much-loved entertainer striving for acceptance. The other was a sociopath named Charlie Parker, who managed in a relatively short time to destroy his career, every relationship important to him, and finally himself. Parker and Armstrong came from fundamentally similar psychic environments, and the contrasts between them are fascinating.

Charlie Parker is one of those rare jazz musicians who have been fortunate in their biographers. Ross Russell's *Bird Lives!,* despite occasional romanticisms, is one of a tiny number of truly first-rate jazz books, and I am depending upon it for the facts of Parker's life. He was born on August 29, 1920, in a suburb of Kansas City. His father, Charles Parker, Sr., was a small-time song-and-dance man who had been stranded in Kansas City and ended up marrying and settling there. When young Charlie was eight or nine the family moved into the central black ghetto, where lay the clubs and cabarets in which Charles, Sr., hoped to get work. This was the Kansas City entertainment district of the Bennie Moten band, of Lester Young and Ben Webster, of the legendary jam sessions. But the Depression was aborning and small-time song-and-dance men were in no great demand. Within a year or two, Charles, Sr., drifted away from the family. Parker's mother, Addie Parker, says, "I became mother, father, everything to Charles. He thought he was Mama's little man. He never worked like the other little boys in the neighborhood. He wanted to carry papers but I wouldn't let him. I thought I could take care of him until he was a man." It is clear enough that Addie Parker was a doting mother, blind to the failings of her son. It is difficult to think of a boy from a broken home growing up in poverty in a ghetto as spoiled, but he was.

Given the time and place, it was inevitable that Parker would get involved with music. Parker attended Lincoln High School, which had a band teacher who had turned out a number of name musicians. He joined the band but was less than enthusiastic about the various brass instruments he was given to play. So his mother bought him, with a hard-saved forty-five dollars, a leaky alto saxophone, and Parker began to learn to play it.

He started with no training, with virtually no understanding of how music was put together or what it was all about. More than any of the leading figures in jazz, Charlie Parker was self-taught. Traditionally, aspiring black musicians have attached themselves to some older player who showed them how things were done, and in time got them jobs or had them join jam sessions. But it is significant that Parker, throughout his life, had difficulty establishing this kind of relationship with a potential mentor. Over and over again he destroyed relationships with older men who were trying to help him. Thus, he did not try to get lessons from any of the scores of saxophone players with whom the neighborhood was saturated, but worked alone in his room, trying to figure out what music was all about. He improved only slowly, but at last he came to grasp the idea that there were twelve keys, each with its own scale and set of chords, and that any tune could be moved from one key to another. He did not know that many of these keys were almost never used by jazz musicians; that, in fact, 75 percent of the jazz of his time was played in four keys: C, F, B♭, E♭. He gave all twelve keys equal attention, and this gave him a facility in moving from key to key that was undoubtedly responsible for some of the chromaticism that came to characterize bop. Nevertheless, working by himself, he was like a blind man trying to put together a picture puzzle, and his progress was slow.

Around the time Parker was fourteen or so Addie Parker took a night job, cleaning the local Western Union office. Parker was now left on his own night after night. He began sneaking out after dark to slip into the cabarets, where he could listen to the local players, especially Lester Young, and watch how they moved their hands over their instruments. By now music had become an obsession. Despite his deficiencies, he was allowed to join a high school dance band called the Deans of Swing, which included bassist Gene Ramey, who was to become a respected jazz musician. He played in schoolboy jam sessions and occasionally at little dances. His class work suffered, and he soon dropped out of school altogether. And flaws in his personality were beginning to show.

He was, at fifteen, an ill-educated high school dropout who was only barely qualified to call himself a musician; an adolescent who had never supported himself. Yet somehow he had come to see himself as the ruling figure in his own world, a little king whose needs always came first, and who expected not only that he could do what he wanted to do, but that others would help him. On at least two occasions, when he knew hardly more than two or three tunes, he insisted on sitting in with some of the leading players of Kansas City and was jeered off the stand. He was still fifteen when he married a woman four years older than he named Rebecca Ruffing, who was soon pregnant. The couple, of course, lived with Addie Parker. He felt that he was the man of the house. The women nagged him to act more responsibly, but they fed him and cared for him even though he did not. It is clear that there was, even at this early age, a piece missing in Parker's understanding. He seemed to feel that if he wanted something, it would instantly be so.

Whatever his personality problems, his improvement as a musician was beginning to accelerate. In the summer of 1936, he was awarded some insurance money after an automobile accident and used it to buy a new saxophone. At about the same time he began working for Tommy Douglas, a conservatory-trained band leader and reed player. Douglas straightened out Parker's saxophone technique and taught him something about chords. He improved, and the next summer he was hired to play at a resort in the Ozarks. The band worked five hours a night, and occasionally in the daytime as well. Parker spent much of his free time copying Lester Young solos from records he had brought with him, and taking harmony lessons from one of the men in the band. The experience of total absorption in music for a whole summer was invaluable, and he came back to Kansas City that fall if not a finished musician, at least a competent one. At about the same time he acquired the nickname "Yardbird," which was soon shortened to "Bird." A number of stories have been told about the genesis of the name. For one, a yardbird is a chicken, and presumably Parker's fondness for fried chicken had something to do with it. He was in addition by this time experimenting with drugs and alcohol.

He also acquired a mentor. This was alto saxophonist Henry Smith, known as "Buster" or "Prof." Smith was reputed to be the best alto saxophonist in the whole territory. He had been a member of the Blue Devils and then of the Basie band when it went east, but he had no faith in the idea and returned to Kansas City, where, in 1938, he was leading his own band. He took Parker on. He says, "He used to call me his dad, I called him my boy. I couldn't get rid of him. He was always up under me. In my band we'd split solos. If I took two, he'd take two. If I'd take three, he'd take three, and so forth. He always wanted me to take the first solo. I guess he thought he'd learn something that way. He did play like me quite a bit, I guess. But after awhile, anything I could make on my horn, he could make too, and make something better out of it." What Parker learned from Smith was conception, not technique. Smith played with a lighter tone than did his contemporaries Hodges, Carter, and Holmes, and he liked to use fast patches of sixteenth notes, both characteristics of Parker's earliest recorded work.

Parker's feeling seems to have been less than sincere. He was by this time shrewd enough to understand that with a bit of flattery — what Russell calls a "pseudo-humble" manner — he could get people like Tommy Douglas and Smith to show him things, but there is no evidence that he felt any loyalty to them or a debt of respect. Two stories are worth telling. One involves a junk dealer who befriended Parker in his early wanderings around the ghetto, and who tried, in an off-hand way, to give Parker a little direction. Parker at one point loaded the old man's coffee with Benzedrine as a prank. The second instance involves Dave Dexter, a white jazz writer based at the time in Kansas City. Dexter wrote for *Down Beat* and other periodicals, and he was in a position to help considerably a young musician whose work he liked. Parker might have buttered him up, as he did Buster Smith; he might have established with Dexter a simple friendship; he might have developed a father-and-son relationship; he might have ignored him. What he did instead was to give Dexter hotfoots, and pick his wallet out of his pocket and then ostentatiously return it. This was not merely prankish, but perverse. Parker had chosen as a target for abuse the one man in Kansas City most able to do him good. He could not be friendly toward him, but he could not leave him alone, either.

By 1938 Charlie went to Chicago, where he played in some jam sessions, impressing musicians, and then on to New York, where Buster Smith was living. He scuffled, picked up odd gigs, including a stint at a taxi dance hall and three months of washing dishes at a restaurant where Art Tatum was playing. It is my sense that this exposure to Tatum was extremely important in forming his style — perhaps the single most important musical influence in his life. Tatum, as we shall see, played at breakneck tempos, habitually substituted new chord changes in a tune for the conventional ones, and frequently jumped abruptly into distant keys and then quickly back again. All of these practices are hallmarks of Parker's work, and although I have no evidence for it other than the music itself, I have a feeling that what Parker was trying to find, and finally discovered that night while playing "Cherokee" at the chili house, were harmonies he had absorbed over three months of listening to Tatum a year or so earlier. In any case, by the end of 1938 he had found a place for himself, however small, in the New York jazz scene. By 1939 he was gigging frequently, sometimes jamming for tips at Clark Monroe's Uptown House. It was during this period that he suddenly had that flash which led him to start playing the upper parts of the chords. In 1939 Parker returned to Kansas City for a period and then was recruited for a new band run by pianist Jay McShann, a typical Kansas City blues group in the Basie mold. In 1940 the band went on the road, and in Wichita it made some transcriptions for a local radio station, the first recordings we have of Parker's work. His tone is very light, even thin, and he plays without that commanding confidence that eventually marked his playing. But his control of his instrument is sure, and he is already employing the jagged phrasing, the fast triplets and sixteenth notes characteristic of his mature style. There are, as well, occasional patches of advanced harmonies. On "Body and Soul" there is a descending figure in the third measure from the end of his chorus that could have come from a solo made ten years later. But he is still essentially a swing player. His solo on "Moten Swing" shows traces of both Hodges and Carter, especially the latter. On "Lady Be Good" he quotes from the Lester Young solo, which he had memorized during the stint in the Ozarks. (McShann also uses Basie's introduction from the same record.)

These transcriptions are fascinating because we can see in Parker's work here a number of influences still in the process of being molded into a unified whole. By 1941, when the McShann band again recorded, Parker's work is more confident and secure. His solos are very typical of what any number of players in the blues-oriented big bands were doing. There are few notes on "Hootie Blues," probably his best solo of this group, that Johnny Hodges would not have played. Parker was twenty-one, as good an alto saxophonist as there was in jazz. He was also, according to the testimony of McShann and Ramey, a pleasant fellow, easy to get along with and well liked in the band. In some ways it must have been the happiest time of his life. He was young, a leading player in a respectable band, a man among men with a place in the jazz world.

In January of 1942 the McShann band opened at the Savoy Ballroom and for the next several months gigged in and around New York. Parker now had the chance to jam regularly at the after-hours spots and to begin exchanging ideas with the young players around the Minton's group. Exactly what kind of music he was playing during this formative period is hard to determine. John Lewis, the pianist who was to become the force behind the Modern Jazz Quartet, heard him on remote broadcasts from the Savoy. He said that Parker was "into a whole new system of sound and time." But a record of "Sepian Blues," made in July of 1942, shows him playing more or less standard blues-inflected swing, albeit, doing so exceptionally well. The most interesting document we have is an amateur recording of "Cherokee." It was found among the effects of a jazz buff named Jerry Newman after his death. Newman owned a portable recorder — this was before the general availability of tape — on which he recorded many of the beboppers at places like Minton's. The record is dated 1940, but it is the conclusion of jazz writer Dan Morgenstern that it was made at Monroe's in the fall of 1942, when Parker was working regularly in the house band there. "Cherokee" had become a specialty of Parker's, and in this case, at least, the version was based on the record Basie had made of the tune in early 1939, with the lovely solo by Lester Young. The riff figure used behind Parker's second chorus is taken intact from the Basie record, and, more important, Parker shows the influence of Pres profoundly. His opening two bars are a loose paraphrase of Young's opening, and in his thirteenth bar he plays a figure identical to one used by Young in his twentieth bar. Because of the ban on commercial recordings in existence at this time, this is about the only example we have of any of the bop players really in transition. This is very nearly bebop as it finally developed, and certainly it was considered odd music indeed by musicians who happened to hear Parker at this stage in his development. Yet the influence of Young is strong; Parker still had a foot in the swing camp.

Parker was by now fed up with the routine swing of the McShann band, and no doubt with band discipline, too. In July of 1942, shortly after "Sepian Blues" was out, he quit the McShann band and began to scuffle around New York, working at Clark Monroe's and Minton's for small sums, and jamming with Gillespie, Monk, Kenny Clarke, and the young experimenters. He was also acquiring the habits that were to destroy him. We do not know when he began to use heroin in a serious fashion, but it was some time during this period, and it is possible to suspect that it might have had something to do with his departure from McShann. He was also drinking heavily, in most cases straight liquor, which acts as an astringent on the mouth, throat, and stomach lining. He was using phenobarbital and presumably other types of pills, eating huge, irregular meals, and womanizing persistently. He was, in a word, indulging every passing appetite with a reckless disregard for long-term concerns. A good deal of this time he was living like a derelict, getting advances or borrowing small sums to get through the day, sleeping wherever he could, dressing in cast-off and often dirty clothing. Nothing mattered except music, food, drugs, and women; and those always now. Whatever he appeared to others, to himself he was still king, subject to no rules, and entitled to have anything he wanted immediately. Ross Russell maintains that Charlie Parker had the constitution of an ox. Parker's regime would have killed most people a lot sooner than it did him.

But if he was not yet suffering physical damage, the cracks in this personality were widening. Hostile and arrogant tendencies apparently held in check while he was with the McShann band, now began to surface. He was a budding star, the leading figure in the avant-garde of his art. He was certain that he was the future, and the more evident this became, the less necessary he found it to consider the opinions of others. There would always be another woman, more drugs, more liquor; always another drummer, another trumpet man; but there was only one Bird. What difference did it make what anybody thought? And he was right, for a time.

Still, it took help from his friends for him to capitalize on his growing reputation. Gillespie and others got him into the Hines band as a tenor player, and from there into the Eckstine band. By 1944 he had come into full command of his artistic powers, and the bop movement, with Gillespie and him at the center of it, was, however controversial, drawing the younger players to it. Parker's undisciplined behavior made life difficult for everybody in the Eckstine band, and in 1944 he made the move into the Three Deuces with a small band. Shortly afterward, Gillespie joined them. Then came the recording sessions in February, May, and November of 1945. From these came the records that stunned musicians and completed the bop revolution.

However, Fifty-second Street was changing. The soldiers and sailors on leave who had crowded it were gone, and times were harder. At the end of 1945, Billy Shaw, who was to become Parker's manager, booked the Parker-Gillespie band into a club in Los Angeles. For Parker, the end of the road that had begun with that forty-five-dollar saxophone some dozen years earlier should have been in sight. The big money was at last arriving, and he was at an artistic peak, considered by the younger players the leading jazz musician in the world. But from now on everything in his life was to go wrong except the music.

There is no point in dwelling at length on his dissolution. The troubles

Because Charlie Parker and Dizzy Gillespie parted company just as they were beginning to reap the publicity whirlwind, there are relatively few pictures of them together. They were not working as a team when this picture, probably taken in a Fifty-second Street club, was made in 1950. The band is Gillespie's, and presumably Parker was sitting in for old times' sake. The picture is all the rarer for the inclusion of a man later to become nearly as influential as Parker himself, John Coltrane, then twenty-four years old. MGM

began in California. The Los Angeles job was a relative success, and in addition, he and Gillespie played, in the early months of 1946, two Jazz at the Philharmonic concerts, which also included at times Lester Young and Coleman Hawkins. These concerts, known as JATP, had begun in 1944 at Philharmonic Hall in Los Angeles. The entrepreneur was a young jazz fan named Norman Granz; the JATP complex, which eventually included record companies and touring groups, had an important impact on the jazz of the late 1940s and through the fifties. The touring concerts drew huge audiences — they were grossing $5 million at times in the 1950s — and Granz was seen by musicians as an ideal employer who paid well, insisted on presenting racially mixed groups, and was reliable in his dealings. Because of all this, he could command nearly any player he wanted.

The music was another question. The players quickly found that audiences burst into cheers at repetitive honking in the saxes, high-note shrieks in the trumpets, and heavy-handed drum solos, so they frequently succumbed to temptation. Granz's interest was in the later swing players, like Eldridge, and the early modernists, and he often featured these musicians. Because of the popularity of the concerts and the live recordings Granz issued by the dozens, JATP was broadly influential in teaching the public what jazz was. Granz, however, cannot be faulted for the limitations of his audiences. No jazz has ever had commercial success without adulteration, and there were, after all, many fine moments in the concerts. From the musicians' viewpoint, they were a blessing.

Parker's playing on the JATP concerts was excellent, but he was beginning to deteriorate both physically and emotionally from the effects of drugs and alcohol. He had trouble sometimes getting through the job, and much of his daylight time was spent trying to obtain drugs. When the other musicians went back to New York early in 1946, Parker stayed behind. During that spring and summer, he cut a group of records for Ross Russell's Dial, one of the small record companies that were springing up everywhere, but did little else except shoot up, drink, jam a little, and figure out ways to get money for heroin. He tried to give up drugs, and finally, his health in ruins, he was arrested on a minor charge and consigned to Camarillo, a state mental institution. Here his health gradually returned. At the end of 1946, he was released, played some gigs, made some superb sides for Dial, and fought off the drug pushers.

But there was no saving Charlie Parker. He came back to New York early in 1947 and, under the guidance of Billy Shaw, put together the Charlie Parker Quintet. Gillespie was by now fed up with Parker and was going his own way, so Parker hired Max Roach and the young Miles Davis, whom he had used on recording dates on the West Coast. The group cut a number of sides for both Dial and Savoy, and it is the opinion of Russell that this was Parker's best year.

Bird, however, was back on drugs and continuing to drink heavily. Moreover, his general demeanor was becoming worse. He was often late for jobs, sometimes failing to show up at all; treated exclusive recording contracts as if they didn't exist; borrowed money shamelessly from anybody he thought had it; was arrogant with club owners; and bullied his musicians. He could, of course, be charming when he wanted to, but he rarely took the trouble. One by one, he was destroying every relationship that meant anything to him. And then one night in 1948, both Max Roach and Miles Davis quit, fed up with Parker's arrogance and irresponsibility. He was not yet thirty, and already the people who admired him most, the musicians, were abandoning him.

Billy Shaw managed to hold things together. With great perseverance, he smoothed over difficulties Parker got himself into with his perverse behavior, and in 1948 Parker won the *Metronome* poll. At the end of the year, a new jazz club, named Birdland, opened. He put together a new quintet, which included pianist Al Haig, who had been on some of the 1945 records, and Red Rodney, a trumpeter from Philadelphia. The group prospered despite Parker's behavior; it commanded high fees and, after 1950, made several tours to Europe.

Meanwhile, his marital arrangements had grown as chaotic as his musical life. His early marriage to Rebecca Ruffing had ended in divorce, and in 1943 Charlie had married a woman named Geraldine Scott. This relationship was brief, and without troubling about a divorce, he took up, in about 1945, with Doris Sydnor, who worked as a waitress and hat-check girl on Fifty-second Street. Doris was a quiet, maternal woman who seemed content to go along after Parker, picking up the pieces. Then, some time around 1950, he became involved with Chan Richardson, a handsome young woman who happened to live on Fifty-second Street and had been hanging around bop musicians since her teens. The relationship with Chan lasted on and off until his death. She bore him two children, and there were periods when Bird at least attempted to lead some semblance of normal family life with her.

Yet, in the end, neither Chan nor Billy Shaw could overcome his perversity. Parker was now struggling with too many problems: drugs, liquor, and the money both required; the demands of his family; and the necessity of making his jobs. The mental confusion he was suffering is evident in a telegram he sent Chan when their tiny daughter, Pree, died in 1954. Parker was working in California at the time. His response to the news was a bizarre series of telegrams, the last of which reads:

> MY DAUGHTER IS DEAD. I KNOW IT. I WILL BE THERE AS QUICK AS I CAN. MY NAME IS BIRD. IT IS VERY NICE TO BE OUT HERE. PEOPLE HAVE BEEN VERY NICE TO ME OUT HERE. I AM COMING IN RIGHT AWAY. TAKE IT EASY. LET ME BE THE FIRST ONE TO APPROACH YOU. I AM YOUR HUSBAND. SINCERELY, CHARLIE PARKER.

This incredible jumble of emotions is not due simply to the shock of the death. One characteristic of the sociopath is an inability to identify with anyone else; Parker recognized that he ought to feel something for Chan, but he was no longer able to distinguish between feelings and obligations, his own needs and others'. Whatever came in from the outside was added, unsorted, to the internal confusion.

It did not much matter. The end was approaching. Grossly overweight, constantly sick with stomach ulcers and other ailments, he was living on stimulants. One night in a fit of temper on the stand at Birdland, he fired the orchestra and walked off. The manager told him he was finished at Birdland. He went home, had a scene with Chan, and attempted suicide by drinking iodine. Saved for the moment, he spent two weeks in Bellevue, trying to straighten out his mental kinks, but it was no use. By the end of the year he was wandering aimlessly around Greenwich Village, still able to play but not able to control the circumstances of his life. There were a few intermittent gigs; nights spent sleeping in tenement rooms with newly scraped friends. Finally, on March 9, 1955, he called at the apartment of Baroness Pannonica de Koenigswarter, an odd figure who made herself a sort of Madame de Staël to the jazzmen of the period. He was clearly very ill. The baroness called a doctor, who tried to get Parker into a hospital, but he refused to go. He hung around the apartment for three days, drinking ice water to cool the flame in his stomach, and then, on March 12, as he sat watching the Dorsey show, his insides fell apart and he died. On the death certificate, the medical examiner listed his age as fifty-three. He was thirty-four.

The life and death of Charlie Parker form one of the tragic dramas in a music that has had no shortage of them. His talent was overwhelming and his dedication to his art was intense. He made fewer concessions to commercial necessity than any major figure in jazz, and he set the highest standards for himself and everybody else, at least when he was able to. But, as we have seen, art is shaped not just by talent; it is cut with the chisel of character as well.

Parker was the victim of what is sometimes known in psychiatry as a character disorder. The term is a catchall to describe people who are not precisely psychotic, but who seem to be unable to fit themselves into the frame of human relationships that we think of as normal in our society — the alcoholic, the drug addict, the habitual criminal, the chronic gambler. For these people, the self is all that exists. Others are seen only as adjuncts to the self, and disappear when they are not present. Such people are capable at times, often for long periods of time, of appearing to be like others, because they learn what is expected behavior and how to carry it out. But this is a mask behind which there hides a closed circle of self. The difficulty with doing anything about them is that they have no desire to change.

Charlie Parker's behavior toward other people was marked by a total lack of concern for their well-being. Despite the sacrifices his mother made for him, in later life Parker made little effort to keep in touch with her. He used women sexually and discarded them like chewing gum. He did little for the four women he putatively married — the legalities of these liaisons made a hash of his estate — and was casually and frequently unfaithful to them. He abandoned his child by Rebecca and did little enough for the children Chan bore him. He bullied the younger musicians around him, especially Red Rodney, who worshiped him; he was contemptuous of fans, who cheered him and paid his wages; he was arrogant with club owners and double-crossed people whom he worked for, like the long-suffering Billy Shaw. In the end, he destroyed every important relationship in his life.

It is habitual with jazz writers, especially European ones, to blame Jim Crow for any evil that attends an American black. There is no doubt that being a black in a segregated society imposes a daily strain and does indeed destroy some people. Had Parker been white he might have been better educated, better watched over by a mother who did not have to work nights to support him — although certainly being white is no guarantee of an escape from poverty. Parker was as angry as any other black at the Jim Crow world in which he lived. But to blame blacks' emotional troubles solely on Jim Crow is simply to say that blacks do not have the strength to accommodate themselves to the strain. In fact, millions do. Parker himself was not an indiscriminate hater of whites. Several of his important collaborators, including Rodney, Al Haig, Stan Levy, Dodo Marmarosa, were white; two of his wives were white, as were many of his other women; and he died in the apartment of a white woman he was friendly with. The truth is that, far from being exploited, Parker was the exploiter. Endlessly taking, he got what he could from people — audiences, friends, lovers, fellow professionals — and then turned his back on them.

What makes a man like that? I find his ragging of the jazz writer Dave Dexter significant. Dexter offered Parker no harm, and the potential of much good, but Parker could neither give him friendship nor leave him alone. This pendulating suggests strong currents of ambivalent feelings about Dexter. He behaved similarly toward Marshall Stearns, at the time probably the leading jazz scholar in America, and toward Billy Shaw, who was trying to make him rich and famous. This teasing, this at times sadistic prankishness, was Parker's way of dealing with important older men in his life.

The parallels between Armstrong and Parker are interesting. Both were abandoned by fathers who were uninterested in them; both were raised by mothers who genuinely cared for them and did their best, within their limits, to take care of them. Armstrong's ultimate response was to put himself under the protection of a succession of father figures. Parker, one guesses, yearned to do the same, but could not bring himself to it, and so instead ragged them. The art produced by such a personality was bound to be difficult and prickly. Not for Parker a luminous sound, the compelling melodies that Armstrong used to please. Instead, he made a music that was deliberately perverse. Whatever Parker's musical models, mentors, or idols said was wrong, he claimed was right. Up was down, left was right, and when he found some men who agreed with him, he led a revolution.

Because of the confusion in Charlie Parker's life, the body of work he left us is smaller than it might have been. Although today various record companies are issuing a haphazard mass of radio broadcasts, amateur recordings made in clubs, and outtakes discarded in the studios, Parker's significant work could probably be included in a half-dozen LPs. It is generally recognized that his peak period was from 1945 — he had hardly recorded before that date — to the end of 1947 or so; but certainly he made many brilliant cuts after that date, including "Parker's Mood" in 1948, "Just Friends," with a string group in 1949, and a concert in Massey Hall in Toronto as late as 1953. It is difficult to single out one or two for special attention, but certainly one of his best-known records is "Koko," made in November of 1945, at one of those early sessions that signaled the arrival of bop. "Koko" is a Parker showcase based on his favorite, "Cherokee," and it simply stunned jazz musicians, particularly the young players who were just discovering bop, with its incredible virtuosity and the astonishing flow of invention in Parker's line. Parker possessed an ability to leap through sequences of keys at machine-gun speeds that left young musicians with their mouths hanging open. Parker thus would have attracted attention on technique alone; but coupled with this technique was a great conception, an ability to produce at a moment's notice a dancing, sinuous line that was constantly full of surprises.

"Koko" exhibits both facets of his playing. The main theme of "Cherokee" is simple enough, but the bridge is long and modulates through four keys. The tempo is above metronome 300, a speed at which few players of the time could play at all. The record opens with a thirty-two-bar introduction, during which Parker and Gillespie take eight-bar breaks. Then Parker sweeps in for the first of two sixty-four-bar choruses. He begins with a brief rising-and-falling opening figure three bars long. This is followed by a contrasting, jagged figure that fills out the eight bars, and he begins the second eight with another three-bar figure that reflects the opening one. This one does not stop, but after the briefest pause cascades onward for another eight bars, making the figure eleven bars in length. Throughout the solo, phrases run, for the most part, in three-, five-, six-, and seven-bar lengths. It was Parker, more than anybody, who led the bop players into working with phrases of odd lengths, instead of the two-, four-, and eight-bar phrases that early jazz players attempted to construct.

One of the classic jazz groups, the Charlie Parker Quintet, in 1947 or 1948, when Parker was making some of his finest recordings. Trumpeter is a twenty-one-year-old Miles Davis, bassist is Tommy Potter, and pianist is presumably Duke Jordan. A corner of the face of drummer Max Roach is visible over Parker's left shoulder. William P. Gottlieb/Edward Gottlieb Collection

A second aspect of Parker's playing that comes clear in "Koko" is his avoidance of long strings of eighth notes. A tendency to runs of this kind, especially chromatic runs, was a weakness of bop playing that even Gillespie manifested. At high tempos, sometimes that was all a player could manage to spit out. But Parker's melodic line is much more varied. Although his phrases tend generally to move downward, there are constant small whirls and eddies out of the main line. Furthermore, far more than other bop players, he interrupts the line with those fast patches of sixteenth notes and triplets. He does not do this much in the "Koko" solo; the speed at which it moves makes faster figures impossible even for Parker. But it is evident in most of his work.

A third aspect of his playing we find in "Koko" is the regular spicing of the line with accents, usually in unexpected places. There is an accent on the next-to-last note of the first figure; the second figure is essentially a play on four accented notes, suggested by the previous figure; there is yet another accent in the fourth measure of the following figure — for a total of six strong accents in some eleven measures, a very short space at this speed.

But his playing with accents is more subtle than this, subtle beyond analysis, for he continually changes the dynamic level of his line, now bringing it up, now letting it fall, now shouting, now whispering, so that the shade shifts constantly like a light show.

Yet one more characteristic of his playing is a marked tendency to quote, at times presumably to cover a momentary failure of inspiration. He does not do this much in "Koko" — inspiration does not fail in this solo — but he begins his second chorus with a figure he used over and over again. It appears so frequently on records that he must have played it every working night of his life. It is, surprisingly, the opening bars to the standard clarinet solo in an old New Orleans number, "High Society," developed by either Alphonse Picou or George Baquet, probably from a piccolo solo. But quotes aside, what matters is his line, which is endlessly filled with surprises, unexpected movements that continually capture the ear. It was this ability to devise unceasingly interesting lines, even at this tempo, that filled his fellow musicians with awe.

A second record worth attention is the LP made at the concert at Massey Hall, in Toronto, in 1953, because the band was an all-star group including the most influential figures in bop at or near the height of their powers: Max Roach on drums, Charlie Mingus on bass, and Bud Powell on piano, as well as Parker and Gillespie. Parker and Gillespie were barely speaking to each other, and Bud Powell, recently released from a sanitarium, was drinking heavily. The audience can be heard laughing as Gillespie clowns around during Parker's solos, especially on "Salt Peanuts," which Parker introduces with heavy irony. Withal, the music was of high quality — hard-driving and exciting, if rough in spots. As it happens, the rhythm section was overrecorded, especially the bass, and the record thus offers a fine opportunity to study a bop rhythm section at its best. Roach stays consistently on the cymbals, producing at fast tempos that famous shimmering sound; Mingus supplies a firm, bass line in which he is "pushing" the beat, that is, anticipating it fractionally, something that is easier to feel as a sense of acceleration than actually to analyze; Powell feeds chords as punctuation. Particularly on the medium-tempo "Perdido" it is possible to hear Roach responding to what the soloists are doing. There are a number of excellent solos, especially one by Gillespie on "Salt Peanuts," and Parker is at top form throughout. His solo on the very fast "Wee" is full of long, descending lines, like "Koko." In contrast, on the slower "Perdido" his line is more broken and jagged, filled with those triplet and sixteenth-note swirls characteristic of his work.

Finally, there is a series of records he made with strings in 1949. The idea was to try to put Parker in a more commercial setting than the standard bop band. The songs are pleasant, but the string arrangements are saccharine and tasteless, and Parker for the most part tends to stay close to the melody. According to Russell, he was awed by the battery of violins. But, for the person unfamiliar with Parker's work, these string records are a good place to begin. Far and away the best of the set is "Just Friends," in which he departs farther from the melody than he does on most of the records in this group.

A word has to be said about Parker's lead lines. These were not compositions in the sense of being worked-out wholes; they were stretches of melody meant to be used as opening and closing lines, usually in unison. Parker did not write them down but would play them over to the musicians in the studio until they learned them. Though they are only fragments, they are spotted with the melodic genius that was Parker's essential strength, and many of them have gone on to become jazz standards. Among the best known are "Confirmation," "Anthropology," "Au Privave," and "Now's the Time," which was turned into a pop hit by somebody else as "The Hucklebuck." ("Donna Lee," "Ornithology," and "Crazyology" are generally assumed to have been written by Benny Harris, although to what extent they were derived from Parker's ideas is difficult to know.) The use of lead lines to open and close tunes was not an original concept; Kansas City players had been doing it for a long time. But previously jazz musicians had done most of their playing on tunes that had been composed as pop tunes. The bop players, by writing lines to be used over standard changes and eventually working out whole tunes meant especially for improvising on, were beginning for the first time in jazz to build a group of tunes expressly designed for jazz playing — tunes with melodies and chord sequences different from the clichés of popular standards.

What, finally, can we say about a man who seemed almost totally incapable of considering the feelings of anyone else, and yet could produce music that drew people like a magnet? How can the art be so gracious, the artist so crabbed? And here lies a truth about art: it often grows out of the artist's attempt to say something he does not want to say. Needing speech, but fearing it, he finds in the symbols of his art a means for speaking in such a way that he does not know he has done so. But he fools himself, because if he is a great artist his audience knows what he is saying despite himself. All of the affection, friendliness, and generosity Charlie Parker refused to admit in himself kept leaking out through his fingers. The inability to bond to other people is normally fatal, and it was so in Parker's case. But who can say that his was a wasted life?

Tatum and Powell
Redesign Jazz Piano

Piano jazz, as we have seen, is in some respects a different music from the jazz played by horns. One important distinction stems from the piano's capacity for sounding several notes at once. Because they can — indeed must — play chords, pianists have always had a deeper concern for harmony than most other jazz musicians. It is therefore not surprising that it was a pianist, himself not a bebopper, who provided much of the foundation on which the new music was based. Art Tatum anticipated by several years many of the harmonic devices the boppers were to bring to jazz. Through his influence on Hawkins, Parker, and jazz players in general, he forced musicians to explore harmonies more thoroughly than they had done. His effect on the music has been all-pervasive.

Unhappily, there is a paucity of biographical material on Tatum, especially on his early life, and much of what we do have is contradictory. He was born in 1910 in Toledo, Ohio. His father was a mechanic who had recently emigrated from North Carolina. Tatum was born with cataracts on both eyes. According to Rex Stewart, a series of operations restored a considerable amount of sight in one eye. He could pick out colors, and he could make out playing cards by holding them close to his face. He apparently worked hard to avoid thinking of himself as blind, but in truth he was.

There are various stories about when he began playing piano. Stewart has him picking out hymns on the family piano at the age of three. He must, in any case, have begun working at the piano when he was fairly young, because by the time he was in his early teens he was playing at rent parties and probably in small cafés, and was already equipped with a good deal of the dazzling technique he stunned other musicians with later on. He was, certainly, discovered early, first by local people and then by the jazz world at large. At about seventeen, he was hired as staff pianist for station WSPD in Toledo. He played a regular fifteen-minute show of his own, and his talent was so evident that the show was put on the network for national broadcast.

Art Tatum, nearly blind, in a cabaret upholstered in the manner typical of the swing street clubs. William P. Gottlieb/Edward Gottlieb Collection

In 1932 he accepted a job as accompanist to Adelaide Hall, a well-known cabaret singer of the time, today best known for her wordless vocal on Ellington's "Creole Love Call."

He took the New York jazz world by storm. People who knew him delighted in taking him around to cabarets and after-hours clubs to spring him on unsuspecting musicians. He simply awed other pianists. Many would not play when Tatum was in the house, and it has been said that others were made so nervous by his presence that they would fumble their own specialties. The esteem in which he was held is indicated by a story told about Fats Waller, who once, discovering that Tatum was in the club where Fats was playing, stood up at the piano and announced, "I play piano, but God is in the house tonight."

Over the next ten years or so, Tatum gradually built a reputation with the general public. He worked occasionally with bands, but most of the time he played as a single. He made his first solo records in 1933, but, considering his reputation, during the 1930s he recorded surprisingly infrequently, with at times hiatuses of a year. But he was in constant demand by clubs everywhere in the United States and in London, where he appeared for a period. With Billie Holiday and Coleman Hawkins, he was the biggest draw on Fifty-second Street during its heyday, and although he was not getting rich, he never had to worry about money. Then in 1943 he formed a trio with bassist Slam Stewart and guitarist Tiny Grimes, later replaced by Everett Barksdale. Grimes and Stewart, both showmen, were leading men on their instruments. The three men interacted musically in a way that attracted audiences, and for a period in the forties Tatum gave promise of becoming a popular star on the order of Waller. But he never made it. The arrival of bop in 1945 or so threw him into obscurity for a time.

By the early fifties he was back again as a major figure, and in four marathon recording sessions, between December 1953 and January 1955, he recorded over a hundred piano solos for Norman Granz, which were issued on eleven LPs. The furor over these records was heightened when André Hodier, in a long review in *Down Beat,* claimed that Tatum's method, basically, was merely to ornament the song's theme with arpeggios and the like, and that these ornaments not only had little musical significance in themselves, but destroyed the rhythmic pulse of the music. A number of musicians protested. One of the important points they made was that Tatum was at his best only at early-morning sessions in after-hours clubs.

The after-hours clubs where he did this sort of playing were an important part of the jazz scene in the 1930s and forties. They arose after the Repeal of Prohibition, when new licensing laws in most cities required clubs and bars to close at a specified hour, usually two or three o'clock in the morning. The after-hours clubs, though illegal, flourished, especially in Harlem, where there were dozens of them. Tatum almost always ended his musical day with a visit to an after-hours club, where, reputedly, he let his hair down. Fortunately, we can test the thesis that he played best in this ambience. There exists a record made by Jerry Newman, the hobbyist who recorded Gillespie and others at Minton's, of Tatum in various informal locales, and if this record is representative, it is clear enough that Tatum did not play much differently in the early-morning spots from the way he did in the recording studios. There is an atmosphere in an after-hours club that makes anything sound better, and besides, usually everybody has been drinking.

However, by the time the Granz records were made, Tatum was seriously ill. What precisely the trouble was is not in the written record, but he had for twenty-five years been drinking and eating heavily. He apparently stopped drinking altogether in 1954, but the damage — if liquor was the agent — had been done, and in November of 1956 he died.

Tatum was an intensely private man; even those who knew him best admit that they did not know him very well. He rarely would criticize another musician, he was cooperative and hard-working, and was liked as well as respected by other musicians. One thing that is obvious was his intense dedication to music. He could play for two days straight with only brief breaks for short snatches of sleep, and incredibly, even as late as the 1950s, he continued to practice scales and exercises for long hours at a stretch to keep his magnificent technique in working order. In all, for Art Tatum, there was little difference between music and life; they were one and the same.

Inevitably, considering the period he was born into, Tatum started as a stride pianist. Tatum himself said, "Fats, man — that's where I come from. Quite a place to come from." The stride style is clearly evident in his earliest records, four solos cut in 1933 for Brunswick. The opening chorus of his "Tea for Two" in this series, except for a fleeting key shift in the twentieth bar, could have been cut by Waller. The remainder of the solo, however, could not have been made by anybody but Tatum. Already he is employing the arpeggios and long runs of various sorts dashing at high speed up and down the keyboard that came to dominate his playing. Here too are the jagged lines — the phrases suddenly interrupted in midflight by an entirely different sort of figure coming from another direction. These broken figures are not so jagged as the ones Hines played. Where Hines would interrupt a figure with a new one and then immediately break into it with yet another, Tatum generally allows the new figure time to finish its flight. It is a reasonable guess, though, that he picked up this mannerism from Hines, of whom he hardly could have been ignorant in his late adolescence.

From this point on Tatum's playing moved steadily in a single direction — away from the stride school into his personal, and at times eccentric, emphasis on runs, arpeggios, and those fleeting leaps into distant keys. This last device was especially interesting to the beboppers. As he matured, Tatum more and more would suddenly shift the whole tune into a key perhaps a half step away from the original key. These shifts sometimes would last only for a bar or less. At other times he might work his way through a whole sequence of modulations, which would take longer, but rarely would he spend more than two bars outside the original key before returning to it.

These little key shifts are idiosyncratic. In formal music, modulations are used to supply contrast by changing the quality of the music for a period. But Tatum's brief modulations are formal irrelevancies; they are meant to add color, to surprise, to twinkle out of the run of the music momentarily and then disappear. Tatum was, moreover, habitually substituting new chords for the standard ones horn players used on a given tune. (It should be understood that in many tunes the chord changes conventionally used by jazz musicians may be somewhat different from the ones that appear on the sheet music.) At times he would run through a whole series of chords that departed completely from the original harmonic structure of the tune, but that would be logical in themselves and would logically return him to the tune in the right place.

In sum, Tatum was not merely improvising against the chords as horn players — and other piano players — were doing; he was reshaping the whole harmonic structure of the song itself. His ability to improvise whole sequences of chords that could be set in place of the standard changes without disturbing the flow of the tune astonished fellow musicians. By 1933, when he made his first records, he clearly had a better grasp of harmonic possibilities than anybody in jazz at the time.

But this harmonic sense was only half of it. At the same time he possessed a piano technique that left other pianists in solemn wonderment. He was able to bring off double runs and complex arpeggios at speeds that nobody else in jazz could approach, and do it with an easy elegance without traces of sweat or strain. His speed, in general, was phenomenal. In that first set of solos there is a "Tiger Rag" taken at about metronome 370, a speed at which few other pianists in jazz could play, and he holds the tempo throughout to within 2 or 3 percent. And at a concert in 1949 he played "I Know That You Know," a fast test piece for clarinet players of the swing period, at an astonishing metronome 450, which means that he was at moments playing at the rate of a thousand notes a minute. Nor were these merely exercises in speed. All of the ordinary marks of his style are present; he is just playing faster.

This description of Tatum's style would suggest that he was not much of a band player. And, indeed, Tatum worked through most of his life primarily as a soloist or with some sort of simple rhythm accompaniment. But he could be, when he chose to, a marvelous band musician. As we have seen in the case of the aforementioned "Tiger Rag," his sense of time was impeccable, surprising in a man who usually worked as a soloist. For another, his studies at the feet of the stride players had taught him the importance of a strong left hand. Tatum did not record often with bands, but as it happens he is present on two of the finest series of small band jazz records made during the swing period, the set with Joe Thomas and Joe Turner that includes "Stompin' at the Savoy," and an *Esquire* magazine all-star set with, among others, Hawkins and Cootie Williams.

It is exceedingly difficult for a critic to judge rhythm players: the only people who really know how effective they are at a given moment are the other musicians in the session. I think, however, that it is no accident that these two sessions with Tatum turned out so well. A clue lies in the spareness of the soloing. We have seen how simple Thomas's "Stompin' at the Savoy" solo is, and if we examine Hawkins's solos on "Esquire Bounce" and "Esquire Blues," we are startled to discover that this man, one of the busiest improvisers in jazz, is content to play a sequence of little riffs. Soloists ordinarily find that when a rhythm section is really swinging they need to play few notes in order to swing themselves, and it is my belief that the spareness of the solos on these records is due to the powerful swing that Tatum could generate. Tatum can be heard driving hard behind Cootie's marvelous short solo on the first bridge of "Esquire Bounce" and again behind Hawkins on "Esquire Blues."

Yet despite the fact that Tatum could swing, the familiar complaint leveled at him by many critics is that too often he was preoccupied by the elaborate runs and arpeggios to swing. And it is perfectly true that by the later years of his career he sometimes supresses the ground beat entirely for substantial periods in a tune. In part, how disturbing these out-of-time passages will be depends on the degree to which the listener is able to keep the ground beat in mind and hear the broken runs and interruptions as cross-rhythms. In any case, however justified the critics may be, pianists have been his defenders, as we can divine from a series of statements gathered from a French radio broadcast on him. From Basie to McCoy Tyner, they have called him the eighth wonder of the world. Hazel Scott, a popular singer and pianist of the 1940s, has said, "One night, Artie Shaw, Vladimir Horowitz and myself went to Café Society Downtown where Tatum worked. Horowitz was bowled over. After 'Tiger Rag' he said, 'It can't be true. I don't believe my eyes and ears.' Two days later Horowitz took along Toscanini, his father-in-law, to hear Tatum, and Toscanini was bowled over too."

What in the end bowled them over was the fireworks. Tatum has to be appreciated not as one listens to a Waller, with his impelling forward motion, but as one watches a Fourth of July display, filled with motion, surprise, astonishment. Tatum never lets you rest for a moment: there is always some fascinating novelty flashing into view only to be pushed aside abruptly by a new trick hung out for view. The term "trick" is not a bad one; Tatum, if nothing else, was a consummate magician.

The pianist who followed Tatum in general influence on jazz is in many respects his mirror image. Where Tatum had the finest technique of any pianist in jazz, Thelonious Monk very rarely displays much technique at all. Where Tatum's style was full and rich, Monk's is spare and dry. Where Tatum often worked at blazing speeds, Monk frequently uses some of the slowest tempos in jazz. Yet despite these marked differences, it seems clear enough that Tatum was an important influence on Monk, and through him on much of modern jazz.

As with Tatum, we know less than we would like to about Monk's early history. He is a private man with neither pretense nor an interest in publicizing himself, and there has been little written about his life. The best information is in Joe Goldberg's *Jazz Masters of the Fifties*. He was born in Rocky

Mount, North Carolina, in 1920. His family brought him to New York when he was an infant, and he grew up there in the neighborhood then called San Juan Hill, where Lincoln Center is now located. He appears to have become interested in the piano when he was about six. Later he studied the instrument more formally, but he must be regarded as essentially self-taught. He played some church organ and toured with an evangelist for a brief period in his teens. By about the age of seventeen he began, like so many other young players, to scuffle for work.

All we know about Monk's playing at this point is what we hear on some of the cuts made in 1941 by Jerry Newman at Minton's. Although it is extremely difficult to hear him on these records, a deciphering of his solo on "Indiana" indicates a hard-swinging style based on Hines with a considerable admixture of Tatum runs. His brief introduction to "Body and Soul," also on the Newman tapes, ends with a run that could have been conceived by Tatum.

He was by this time involved with bebop players like Gillespie, Parker, and Clarke, jamming with them at Minton's and other places, holding late-night conversations with them about music, and occasionally working with them in bands. But it must be remembered that Monk was never essentially a bop player, as the others themselves recognized. He was already, by the mid-1940s, too individualistic a player to fit nicely into any school. When the boppers began to work and record regularly after 1945, they rarely chose Monk for their groups, preferring instead players like Al Haig, George Wallington, and especially Bud Powell. Monk thus had veered away from a movement he had helped to found; or rather, the movement had gone in a direction different from his own.

The major distinction lay not in harmony, but in Monk's approach to phrasing. He was not phrasing primarily on two and four, as the bop players tended to do; he was not at home with the breakneck tempos they preferred; and his phrasing in general was too idiosyncratic to form a predictable ground beat. Nor was his approach to harmony the same as theirs. To be sure, Monk used as many altered chords as the boppers did, but he created them according to a different principle. Where a bop player used these "odd" chromaticisms in the context of a whole chord — that is, incorporating the diminished ninths and flatted fifths into the basic triad either as a chord or in a melodic phrase — Monk tended to leave his chromaticisms naked. To put it another way, the boppers mingled the odd notes throughout their lines, so that their work had harmonic homogeneity — a characteristic flavor. If you slice a section out of a solo by Parker or Bud Powell you will find the approach to harmony roughly the same as in any other section. Monk, however, laid his chromatacisms in like plums in a plum pudding. As you eat the pudding you keep coming across the plums, which are quite different from the context in which they are set. He is particularly

Thelonious Monk in his twenties. Note the standard bopper's outfit, the beret and horn-rimmed glasses, which became symbols of the movement. William P. Gottlieb/Edward Gottlieb Collection

fond of setting off into a phrase, and then using at one or two important points — especially at the end — notes that are a half step away from what the phrase suggests they ought to be. It is this sort of game playing that sometimes gives his work its fey quality; and in the 1940s, it struck many listeners, and musicians as well, as willful and perverse.

By the mid-1940s, then, Monk was sui generis, a man playing in a style of which he was the only practitioner, with very few followers. It is not surprising that he had great difficulty getting work of any sort. And, of course, he got no record contract. He was, however, nothing if not stubborn. He refused to change his manner, work or no work. As it happens he was able to do so in considerable measure because of the willingness of his wife, Nellie Monk, to accept his stand. At various times she worked at menial jobs to support the family, while Monk spent his unemployed hours working at the piano or composing. Eventually, he felt, the world would come to him. In any event, he was not going to go to the world.

One player who supported him was Coleman Hawkins, who had always been open to new voices. In 1944 Hawkins used him in a small group in a Fifty-second Street club, and in October of that year the group recorded. Monk was always grateful and visited Hawkins on his deathbed. Monk has a solo on "Flying Hawk," and we can hear him clearly struggling to disencumber a personal way of playing from the accretion of his past. There are passages here that could have been played by Bud Powell, and Tatum-esque runs (Monk has always been fond of a descending run built on a whole-tone scale); but there are also the spare single-note figures that were to become his mark.

From this point on, his style grew sparer and sparer, until at times he was simply laying out a few notes for exposure, with absolutely no comment. Rather than play the four or five notes of a full chord, he would frequently pick out only two of them to suggest the whole, and he was able to do this with such sensitivity that he was usually successful at implying what he wanted to convey. Adding to the effect of grave simplicity this gave his work was his tendency to play farther and farther behind the beat, and to leave large gaps of space between notes. He was not, however, a sketcher in the sense that John Lewis sometimes is; his line is too firm and positive to give the effect of sketching. He is instead making skeletons. He is indicating shapes not by suggestion, as the sketcher does, but by stripping away the flesh to the bare bones.

It was a unique and personal way of playing, especially as it came out of the orchestral piano tradition reaching back to Johnson, and by the late forties he was beginning to develop a small group of followers, especially among younger musicians. In 1947 he made a series of recordings for the perspicacious Alfred Lion at Blue Note. Some of these records are solos with bass and drums, others of them include various combinations of horns, and a few of them have Milt Jackson as well. Nonetheless, the entire sound of the music is stamped with Monk's initials as firmly as if he had done all the playing himself. This is particularly true of his own compositions, some of the best of which were first recorded in this series, among them "Ruby My Dear," "Straight, No Chaser," and " 'Round About Midnight," certainly his most famous tune.

Monk's compositions are as individual as his piano playing. Jazz musicians often find difficulty playing them the way Monk wants them to be played — that is, giving them the character he himself imparts to them. Consider, for example, "Straight, No Chaser." It is at bottom a twelve-bar blues, but the melody line is laid out in odd-numbered units, so it does not count out in three neat sets of four bars each, as a blues is expected to do. The melody is divided into two six-measure sections. These sections do not break down into ordinary 4/4 measures; the first bit of melody is three beats in length, the second five, and so on. The problem for the soloist is to capture some of the harmonic and formal character of the original melody; it will not do — and Monk does not like it — simply to go off and blow a chorus on the chords of a Monk tune. The result is that the tunes come to dominate the soloist, rather than, as is usual in jazz, the other way around, and this explains why a record under Monk's leadership is so much his own, despite the soloists.

These Blue Note records helped to increase somewhat Monk's following with the jazz public, but work remained hard to come by. Then, in 1951, some narcotics were found in a car Monk was sitting in. It is generally held that the narcotics belonged to a friend of Monk's who was also in the car, but that Monk would not inform on him. The loss of his cabaret card for involvement with narcotics was virtually automatic, and for the next six years he was unable to work in clubs around New York City.

He could, however, record. Between 1952 and 1955 he made a series of records for Prestige. Then in 1955 the contract was taken over by Riverside Records, a small company in the process of making the transition from reissuing jazz of the 1920s to recording the modernists. Riverside recorded him playing a set of Ellington tunes and another set of standards, in order to dispel the myth that Monk could play only his own tunes. The next recording, "Brilliant Corners," cut in 1956, contained only his own compositions. It was a breakthrough for Monk in terms of acceptance, at least in part because of a favorable *Down Beat* review by Nat Hentoff. In 1957 he was able to get back his cabaret card, and he was booked into the Five Spot, a converted derelicts' bar that was becoming a fashionable venue for the presentation of avant-garde music. Monk used the relatively unknown John Coltrane on tenor saxophone — and the now-historic gig was the making of both men.

From the time of the Five Spot gig Monk has been not merely an established figure in jazz, but one of its leading players. Assessing his influence, however, is not easy. Because he is, like Teagarden and Pee Wee Russell, so personal a player, he has had few direct imitators. On the other hand, because he is so much a school to himself, he is held in enormous respect by players of a great many styles. His influence, then, has to be seen as general rather than specific. All jazz players have listened to him, and most have listened to him carefully. What they carry away is often not obvious, but it is there.

The man who had the major direct influence on other piano players of the time was Earl "Bud" Powell. Indeed, Powell had as large an influence on jazz piano players in his day as Earl Hines had had two decades earlier. As with Hines, after Powell all jazz piano playing for nearly a generation was in the style he set.

He was born in New York City in 1924. He had a grandfather who was a musician, and his father was a competent stride pianist who, however, did not work full-time in music. His older brother, William, became a musician, and his younger brother, Richie, was pianist with the Clifford Brown–Max Roach group, a musician of promise if not in Bud's class. Bud's father encouraged him in his music. He began studying the piano seriously at the age of six, and for seven years studied classical piano, acquiring both a knowledge of European music and a legitimate technique. At fifteen he quit high school, already sufficiently accomplished to begin gigging around the city as a professional.

Not long after, the experiments at Minton's began, and Powell fell into the habit of dropping by to listen. Occasionally he sat in. At seventeen he was not yet accepted by many of the beboppers, just a few years older than he, but Thelonious Monk recognized his potential and supported him. His playing at this time, insofar as we can guess, was in the Hines school, especially as filtered through Teddy Wilson and Billy Kyle, a Hines-based pianist of the day who had become prominent through his work with the John Kirby Sextet. It is also clear from his later work that he was much influenced by Tatum, especially in his ballad playing.

The most important influence on him, however, was none of these men. It was Charlie Parker. Working as he was in the single-note "horn" style of Hines and his followers, it was easy enough for him to begin imitating the Parker line in his right hand. Consider for example a version of "Cherokee," Parker's showcase tune, that Powell made in 1949 for Verve. In the statement of the theme he uses a characteristic Parker device, a great many chromatic chord emendations, before leaping into a Parker-like line of eighth notes. Again, in "All God's Chillun Got Rhythm," made for Verve at the same time, his opening figures after the first statement of the theme are pure Parker, both in harmony and phrasing. The piece is taken at about metronome 350, a tempo at the top of Parker's range. The first figure after the theme statement is phrased on the off-beats, and is followed, as Parker was wont to have it, with a fairly lengthy pause. Then comes a brief figure also phrased on two and four, a short pause, and then an extraordinary run approximately nine measures long, a length that Parker could not have sustained because of the sheer necessity for breathing. There is otherwise nothing in this line that Parker could not have played.

At the same time as Powell was developing his Parker line for the right hand, he was reducing the bass to relatively dissonant chords, which were stabbed in once or twice a measure as both place markers and rhythmic accents. There were several reasons for this shift. For one, the bop horn players wanted less harmonic statement in the piano in order to free them to explore by-ways of their own. For another, there was the influence of Monk, who, with his minimalist's approach, often dropped the bass out altogether (although at other times he would emphasize it, even to the point of playing stride passages, as in "Thelonious"). For a third, in concentrating so heavily on his right hand, especially at high speeds, Powell may simply have had trouble operating his left hand. Finally, there was the boppers' need for breaking with the past. The stride style was ineluctably identified with Fats Waller, at his peak of popularity as the bop style was being forged. Waller, however unjustly, represented precisely the sort of stereotypical happy-go-lucky black man that the beboppers had set their faces against. The result was that, for the first time, the pianist no longer played a ground beat.

In creating the bop piano style, Powell — and others — thus applied the harmonic and rhythmic devices of Parker to the Hines right hand. But Powell, as much as he drew from Parker, never moved so far into the bop style, with its emphasizing of the second and fourth beats, as the horn players did. Even when his style was fully matured he phrased more closely to the older system than did Parker, Gillespie, and their followers. Thus, unlike the more idiosyncratic Tatum and Monk, Powell descends in a direct line from the earliest jazz pianists.

This style was already being formed when he got his first major engagement, a stint with the Cootie Williams band. He stayed with Williams from 1943 to 1944, and records made at this time show him well into the bebop style, though the requirements of the job kept him from playing in the new manner more than occasionally.

He was, sadly, already beginning to show signs of the emotional difficulties that were to dog him for the rest of his life. In 1945 Powell, only twenty-one years old, was in Pilgrim State Hospital on Long Island, where he remained for ten months. From that point on, he was in and out of institutions for several years. Finally, in 1949, he seemed to have recovered, if only temporarily, and was able to work at jazz regularly.

He was, however, drinking heavily; it is probable that only drink was able to quiet the internal pain he must have been suffering. By the end of 1951, he was back in the mental institution again, this time for more than a year. Yet in spite of this horror story, during the periods he was able to leave the institutions he worked regularly around Fifty-second Street and made the recordings that transformed jazz piano playing. The most important of these are two series of records, mostly solo piano with rhythm accompaniment, that he cut between 1949 and 1951 for Alfred Lion at Blue Note and for Norman Granz for a label that eventually became Verve. He was also present on some Parker recordings made in 1947, and on one of the finest early bop sessions, a 1949 Sonny Stitt session with J. J. Johnson, Curly Russell, and Max Roach. Later there were more recordings for Verve and other labels, and there has been the posthumous issuance of various concert and radio performances. But it was those early series for Verve and Blue Note that made the great impact on the jazz public.

One characteristic of Powell's style at this period was the marked difference between his playing of ballads and up-tempo tunes. Most jazz players tend to be consistent; their playing on ballads is in large part simply a slower version of what they do on faster numbers. But Powell became quite a different person on ballads, and this may, in fact, be a reflection of his emotional difficulties. The ballad style is heavily influenced by Tatum. Powell liked to play the same sort of standard tune that was basic to Tatum's repertory, and he recorded a number of Tatum's specialties, like "Tea for Two" and "Yesterdays." The latter and "April in Paris," both made for Verve in 1950, are filled with Tatum devices. Here are the supressions of tempo, the long runs and arpeggios, the interruptions of the line, the chord substitutions. In these pieces the bass, kept to a minimum on up-tempo numbers, is full, and at times in "Yesterdays" he uses a pure stride bass, something he seldom does on fast tunes.

His up-tempo style is the one derived from Hines, and it is this manner of playing for which he was celebrated. It is built almost entirely out of long strings of eighth notes. Those long, hard, fast lines of eighth notes, stinging like BB shot, enthralled other musicians. Typical is "Tempus Fugue-it," taken at about metronome 290, for Powell a relatively modest pace. After a brief introduction, and a statement of the theme, itself compounded of lines of eighth notes, Powell flies into those long, breathtaking lines. In this respect, his principal virtue is similar to Parker's. It was the endless surprises in Parker's corruscating lines that fascinated musicians, and the same is true of Powell's work — this leaping, darting line applied with relentless, unremitting force.

His day in the sun was doomed to be brief. By 1953 the ceaseless emotional problems were etching away his skills. He could at times be superb. At the famous session at Massey Hall, he played a set with Mingus and Roach that contains some brilliant playing. Especially fine is a version of "Lullaby at Birdland." Again, on a set made the same year at the Royal Roost (a New York club founded to compete with Birdland) and issued posthumously, he is playing up to his best standard; but on a second set made a week later, his playing is perfunctory. From this point on he was again in and out of institutions. There were lunatic scenes, including a shouting match with Parker, who was also deteriorating, on the bandstand at Birdland. By the mid-1950s he was playing well only sporadically.

Then, in 1959, he appeared to have made a measure of recovery. He

moved to Paris where, he felt, the pressures on him would be fewer than in New York. He worked there frequently, and occasionally played well. There is a record of an excellent session with Art Blakey at a Paris concert. He was still a problem drinker, and his friends had to work hard to keep him away from liquor. His skills came and went. In 1964 he returned to the United States, where he played well at times at an extended stay at Birdland, and embarrassingly badly at a memorial concert for Charlie Parker at Carnegie Hall. It was intended that he go back to Paris after the visit, but he did not, and in the summer of 1966 he died from the effects of alcoholism.

Like most pianists, Powell was a composer as well as a performer, and a few of his tunes, especially "Un Poco Loco" and "Dance of the Infidels," are still sometimes played. He also wrote a few brief pieces in the European manner. The best known of these is "Glass Enclosure." It is similar to other attempts by jazz musicians to work in classical music — a derivative pastiche. What matters about Powell was his extraordinary jazz playing; at his best he may very well have been the most exciting pianist in the music.

Tatum, Monk, and Powell were the men who formed the modern jazz piano style and influenced everything that came after, but, as has often been the case with innovators, others were better known to the general public. In this instance, pianists George Shearing, Erroll Garner, and Oscar Peterson had larger reputations than Tatum, Monk, and Powell. Shearing was the most well known in the early bop era. An Englishman, and blind from birth, he was born in London in 1919. He learned the piano at a school for the blind and began playing jazz after hearing records of Fats Waller and Teddy Wilson. The latter was his major influence. By the time he reached his majority he was recognized as the leading jazz pianist in London and one of the best young jazz players in Europe.

In 1946 he made a visit to the United States, followed by a second one in 1947, and not long after, became a more or less permanent resident there. During these early visits he heard the bop musicians, who were beginning to dominate jazz, and he himself became essentially a bop player. He worked extensively on Fifty-second Street, toured with various combinations, and by the 1950s developed a broad popular following that escaped the confines of the jazz world.

Critics have generally felt that, whatever his talent, Shearing watered

Opposite: This picture, made in August 1953, shows two formidable jazz talents at different points of their careers. Pianist Bud Powell was already suffering from the mental difficulties that shortened his career and eventually his life. His best work was already done. Bassist Charlie Mingus was only beginning to do the composing for which he is known. The scene is the Open Door, a Greenwich Village nightclub that at the time offered Sunday jam sessions, featuring the beboppers. Charlie Parker played here often in his last years. Bob Parent

down his playing, often sticking quite close to the melody, to maintain his commercial success. Yet at times he has played strong, driving jazz in both bop and his earlier swing manner. In the bop style he was particularly noted for his "locked hands" style, in which the two hands move parallel on the keyboard to produce chords in octaves, a style pioneered by Milt Buckner. Shearing is the author of "Lullaby at Birdland," one of the few bop compositions to have a popular success.

Oscar Peterson is a black Canadian, born in Montreal in 1925. He began studying classical piano at the age of six, and by the age of fourteen was working regularly on a local radio show, the result of having won an amateur contest. He developed a local reputation, but for some time refused to leave home. Then in 1949 Norman Granz persuaded him to join his Jazz at the Philharmonic troupe. He was an instant success with the jazz audience, winning the *Down Beat* poll many times during the 1950s, and in time he, like Shearing, developed a somewhat broader popular following. He worked principally in a trio with guitar and bass support. An energetic performer blessed with an excellent technique, he is stylistically an eclectic. At times, especially on ballads, he sounds like Tatum; at other times there are Powell-like runs, the locked hands system of Shearing, traces of Erroll Garner, Teddy Wilson, and even Basie. This eclecticism does not always permit an identifiable personality to come through his playing. He fills his work with riffs and repeated figures, sometimes a single note hammered out relentlessly. This approach offers rhythmic intensity, but from a melodic point of view it often leaves his lines fragmented and somewhat chaotic.

The third member of this group, Erroll Garner, was born in Pittsburgh either in 1921 or 1923; the sources conflict. His father was a pianist, but Garner was more interested in baseball and refused to take lessons. However, he taught himself, and by the time he was eleven or twelve was working professionally around Pittsburgh. He came to New York during World War II and found steady work on Fifty-second Street. He was quickly successful in attracting a wide audience, and by the late fifties he was one of the most popular musicians working in jazz. His song "Misty," written during this period, became a big hit, and has since become a standard. He employed in his playing locked hands and a great many block chords, intermingled with runs of single notes. He tended in the left hand to comp steadily on the beat with close chords, which produces a guitarlike effect. He was an energetic player, at times overbusy and on ballads somewhat florid. He died of a heart attack in 1977.

Shearing, Peterson, and Garner constitute a subschool of modern piano playing. All three were working with established styles before either Monk or Powell recorded. They thus began as swing pianists, influenced by Hines, Wilson, and, inevitably, Tatum, before the beginning of the bop movement.

All of them to one degree or another moved into the new music, but none of them was firmly committed to it, and the swing feeling has always remained an important element in their playing. All of them were rhythmically forceful; all of them concentrated on popular standards instead of originals or the more difficult bop tunes; all of them tended to present the song's original melody frequently in a performance. This combination of straightforward driving rhythm and recognizable tunes in an idiom that owed much to swing made their music a good deal more accessible to a broad public than the music of Monk, Powell, and the beboppers. They all drew wide followings, and, taken together, were the major architects of a light jazz piano style that has become central to modern popular music. All across the United States — indeed, around the world — pianists in thousands of cocktail lounges and nightclubs and on radio broadcasts are playing music derived from the work of these three men.

For jazz itself, this style has its failings. The most important is the players' addiction to repeated figures, which may go on for half a chorus. These figures serve a rhythmic purpose, but melodically they offer little. The problem here is a lack of melodic imagination: we are never suddenly gripped by a line as we are in the work of the greatest jazz musicians. Nonetheless, this is reliable jazz, and because of its accessibility it has helped to broaden the audience for the music. However, it was less well known men like Al Haig, Red Garland, Dodo Marmarosa, Elmo Hope, and Argonne Thorton, most of them born a few years later than Shearing, Peterson, and Garner, who were the inheritors of the bop style Bud Powell was principally responsible for working out.

Yet despite the dominating presence of Powell and his followers during the forties and fifties, the piano player who has had the widest influence in jazz since 1960 or so is not really a bebopper at all. To be sure, the marks of Bud Powell are evident in Bill Evans's work, and he certainly uses the advanced chords typical of bebop, but the whole sense of his phrasing is distinctly different from what the beboppers were doing.

Part of the reason lies in some accidents of biography. Evans was born in Plainfield, New Jersey, in 1929. He studied piano as a boy, as well as violin and flute. His brother had a small band, and when Evans was twelve he was asked to fill in with the group for a missing pianist. "Up to then," he said in an interview in *Jazz Journal,* "I hadn't heard much jazz, I had only read music." This was during the early 1940s, the heyday of the swing band period, and Evans's first influences were the swing pianists. Even as late as the mid-1940s, when bop was surfacing, boys from the white suburbs were likely to know bop more by reading about it than from hearing it. Harlem was *terra incognita,* a place that a musical white adolescent from the suburbs might visit occasionally to hear a band at the Apollo Theatre, or more rarely, one of the well-known clubs along One hundred twenty-fifth Street, but few would have known of the existence of Minton's, or ventured to go there.

After high school, Evans's choice of college was Southeastern Louisiana College, about a hundred miles north of New Orleans. He thus was in a totally different area during the years bop was emerging from the underground. The playing he did was often in rural juke joints, where bebop would have been only a puzzle. After graduation he was drafted into the army — it was the time of the Korean War — and spent another year removed from the new developments in music. So Evans was, during his formative years, having far less direct contact with the bebop movement than were most players of his age.

But because he was already an exceedingly competent musician, when he came to New York he was able to find work with Tony Scott, a highly regarded clarinetist who worked a good deal along Fifty-second Street. Then, in 1956, Mundell Lowe, an excellent guitarist with whom he had worked in college, brought him to the attention of Orin Keepnews and Bill Grauer of Riverside Records. Keepnews and Grauer were impressed, and in 1957 they issued an album of Evans's work. It had very little impact, but musicians were becoming aware of him, and in February of 1958 Miles Davis brought him into his group.

He stayed with the group for only eight months, but it was during his tenure that Miles made "Kind of Blue," one of his most influential records. The record was an early foray into modes. It was felt that Evans's contributions were considerable, not so much in the specific form of the tunes as in helping to shape Davis's thinking in general. Miles has said that Evans taught him a great deal. But despite the fact that Evans was musically at home with the group, he quit it after eight months. He said, "I felt exhausted in every way — physically, mentally, and spiritually." He had been until that time a shy, reserved young man. The Davis band not only pushed him into the spotlight, but caused some emotional shifts in his psyche. He told Nat Hentoff, in an interview published in *Jazz Review,* "One of the things the group did was help me lose my hesitancy and lack of confidence." He needed time to assimilate these changes; so he left New York to visit his parents in Florida, where they had retired — his father was ill — and to spend some time with his brother in Baton Rouge, where there was a piano.

But the stay with Davis, as it had done for so many other young musicians, had brought Evans some renown in the jazz world, and at the end of a brief retirement he recorded again for Riverside. The respite had helped him to consolidate the assertiveness he had developed during the Davis stint. He was now playing stronger, and very quickly, as he began to record on a regular basis with a trio, he gathered an ever-larger audience of both

musicians and jazz fans, until, by the early 1960s he was generally acknowledged to be the most influential pianist working in jazz.

His fame was partly due to the presence in his trio after 1959 of a brilliant
young bassist named Scott La Faro. La Faro had developed an almost
guitarlike facility on the bass, in part by lowering the bridge, which brought
the strings closer to the neck of the instrument. He was also getting away
from strict timekeeping. He had become bored by laying out quarter notes
one beat after the next, and had begun inserting other kinds of figures. He
was not alone in this. There was a feeling in the air that if everybody kept
time in his head, nobody would have to state it explicitly. It is a point that
jazz musicians continue to argue. A good deal of modern drumming is based
on the idea that the drummer can, and should, be free of timekeeping duties
so that he may phrase like a horn, but many players prefer to have somebody — the bassist if not the drummer — state the ground beat explicitly.

In any case, bassists were listening closely to La Faro, and he proved to
be one of the major influences on his instrument until today. Working as
a close-knit team, he, Evans, and drummer Paul Motian produced an
intermeshed music in which each was responding to the others. This was
the group that made Evans famous. Unhappily, La Faro was killed in an
automobile accident in 1961 at the age of twenty-five. Such was the blow that
Evans retired from music for several months. He returned to play with
shifting personnel, which finally settled down to drummer Marty Morell
and another superlative bassist, Eddie Gomez.

The hallmark of Evans's style is a concern with shaping melody, mainly
in single notes. He does not simply let a line run on, as Parker and Powell
did, counting on the twists and turns to allure the listener, but tries to relate
parts of the melody to each other. In general, his line is sectioned into brief
phrases of a bar or two in length, and, as he plays, he is constantly in search
of ways to relate the shorter fragments. He is particularly fond of reiterating
a figure several times, higher or lower. This interest in rational melody is
central to his work. He has said, "Just learning how to manipulate a line,
the science of building a line, if you can call it a science, is enough to occupy
somebody for twelve lifetimes."

A second important aspect of Evans's work is his use of the left hand.
We have seen how Powell and the beboppers usually dropped the older
practice of stating every beat — that is, of establishing a ground beat with
the left hand. Evans carries this trend even further, so that in effect the left
hand no longer has a rhythmic function. Its task, in Evans's playing, is
purely harmonic: the chord in the left hand is there to supply a bottom over
which can be laid a harmonically complementary or contrasting line. That
the left hand has a harmonic rather than rhythmic function is made apparent in the fact that Evans usually sustains the left-hand chord. The bebop-

pers, in contrast, did not, but rather used sharply chopped chords placed
for rhythmic effect.

Evans, then, is less concerned with rhythm than most jazz pianists had
been hitherto, one reason why he most often works with bass and drums.
He is very much a European player, whose approach is thoughtful rather
than directly emotional. He has said that he is not interested in expressing
everyday feelings, but finer, or more exceptional ones. The result is a predi-
lection for pensive moods — the poet at twilight, so to speak. Melancholia
is, of course, a perfectly legitimate mood. If Milton can write "Il Pen-
seroso," surely Bill Evans can produce a "Turn Out the Stars." But Milton
also wrote "L'Allegro," and Evans is not often seen dancing in the cheq-
uer'd shade. This penchant for reflection, often shading into resignation,
gives his work a considerable sameness, which could usefully be broken by
other moods. But despite this weakness, Evans has been, and perhaps
remains, the most influential of modern pianists. Such younger men as
Herbie Hancock, Keith Jarrett, and Chick Corea, who are giving contemporary music much of its present shape, have listened carefully to Evans.

At this point, we should be able to see two things about the history of
jazz pianists. One is that they have been consistently more European in
approach than have other instrumentalists. To be sure, the stride pianists
were highly rhythmic players, but at the same time they were working
mainly with harmonies and figures that claimed as ancestors not the blues
or the black folk tradition, but the European pianists of the early nineteenth
century, and before them the masters of the Baroque. The ragtimers, in
particular Joplin, were familiar with the works of people like Chopin and
Schumann, and deliberately developed their right-hand figures from dance
forms that date back centuries. Joplin's right hand has more in common
with that of Bach than with the guitarists of the Texas backcountry. The
stride pianists grew directly out of the ragtime school, and continued to
employ formal right-hand figures. With Hines and the swing players who
followed him, we have a shift away from Europeanism, with more emphasis
on the African elements in the music. But with the arrival of bop, with its
increasing concern with chromaticism and its devaluation of the ground
beat, the jazz pianist begins again to move in the direction of Europe.

This, then suggests the second thread in jazz piano history, and that is
a steady movement away from the full, two-handed piano of the ragtimers
to the point where, in, say, Evans's duets with the guitarist Jim Hall, he
sometimes goes for long stretches without touching the piano with his left
hand at all, and plays long strings of notes only with the right hand. Some
of these passages could have been played by a clarinet. This gradual thin-
ning out of the piano sound may be in the process of change. Many of the
younger musicians, for example, McCoy Tyner, are playing a fuller piano
style; but it is too early to tell where this trend is going.

Sons of Bird and Diz:
Clifford, Fats, Sonny

One of the most astonishing things about the bop revolution was the speed with which it pushed everything else aside. It did not really break out of the underground until 1944, with the issuance of the first Parker records and the opening of Parker and Gillespie on Fifty-second Street, but by 1948 it had sucked virtually all of the young players into its vortex. To be sure, a handful of young middle-class white musicians were, in the 1940s, caught up in the dixieland revival. But they were a distinct minority. Far and away the largest number of young players very quickly became committed to bop. It was new; it was exciting; it was antiestablishment, revolutionary even. It was heavily involved with drugs, with their heady aura of risk and unmentionable delights. And it was acquiring an overdose of tragic heroes. Here, it seemed, was an adventurous, even dangerous present, and a glorious future. Musical values aside, bop was glamorous, and most young players of ambition wanted to be in on it.

The school in which the earliest adherents to the new style were trained was the band of Earl Hines and the Billy Eckstine band that spun off it. Gillespie and Parker both made a deliberate effort to teach the young men in these bands the rudiments of the new style. "It was like going to school," Benny Green has said. When Eckstine formed his own band, he brought many of the new men with him, and school continued. Alumni of these two bands include a roster of men who made a mark on jazz for a decade: Fats Navarro, Sonny Stitt, Gene Ammons, Dexter Gordon, Lucky Thompson, Tadd Dameron, Wardell Gray, Miles Davis. Through these men the new ideas began to spread in widening circles, so by the time bop reached public consciousness in 1945 or so, there existed a small but growing cadre of musicians who could play it.

At just about the time that bop was taking over, there appeared two technical innovations that were to have significant effects on the new music, and indeed on all jazz thereafter. As early as 1899 a type of "wire" recording, using magnetic principles, had been developed, but it had never proved practical. By the time of World War II, however, there was interest in the device, and it was the Germans, apparently, who first brought it to workable shape. It seemed that here was a system for recording a whole symphony in a piece, but in fact wire, or tape, recording had its drawbacks for home use. The quest for a longer record, however, was on. In 1944 Columbia assigned its highly regarded Peter Goldmark to work on the idea, and in 1948 it was able to spring what it called the Long Playing record, or LP, on the public and its competitors. Victor responded a year later with a 45 rpm record, and for a year the two systems fought it out. But by 1949 it was clear that the Columbia LP was the winner, and Victor capitulated, though the 45 rpm single went on to establish itself in the popular music field.

The LP, of course, permitted the recording of longer cuts. Previously, almost all recorded jazz was tailored to the three-minute length of the ten-inch 78 record, or, rarely, the four-minute-plus length of the twelve-incher. Now players were free to explore a tune for twenty-five minutes if they wanted. Few carried it that far, but the longer solo became customary, and the effects were both good and bad. On the one hand the LP allowed a player room to develop his line at some length; on the other, it also allowed a great deal of sheer aggressive solo-hogging. It is my feeling that very few jazz players have demonstrated an ability to sustain interest in a solo for more than two minutes or so, and most are unable to build a consistent piece of work for as long as a minute. Jazz is, after all, an improvisatory art, which works best in short takes. Why should it be expected that a player can create with intensity for long periods of time? There are exceptions, of course, but they are few. Nonetheless, despite its opening the door to prolixity, the LP did give recorded jazz performances a scope they had lacked before.

It was the young players of the bop school who were to take advantage of it. Perhaps the first of these new men was trumpeter Howard McGee, a contemporary of Gillespie's. McGee was, like Gillespie, a disciple of Roy Eldridge, and during the swing period worked with a number of big bands, principally that of Charlie Barnet, one of the first white leaders to follow Goodman in breaking the color line. McGee, according to Ross Russell, first heard Parker on a radio broadcast of the Jay McShann band, playing Parker's specialty, "Cherokee." He was entranced, and with some other musicians went up to the Savoy Ballroom to hear the band. He requested "Cherokee," and very quickly found out who the saxophonist with the odd style was. Thereafter, although he continued to work with Barnet for some time, he was committed to the new music. He recorded frequently with Parker and with other bop groups, and worked often on Fifty-second Street — at times with Coleman Hawkins — where he became recognized as one of the best of the new men.

But it was another man who was to have the greater influence. This was

trumpeter Fats Navarro, whom Gillespie picked to replace him in the
Eckstine band. He was born in Key West, Florida, of mixed Latin, black,
and Chinese parentage, in 1923. He was a cousin of Charlie Shavers, who
was coming into prominence as soloist with the John Kirby Sextet when
Navarro was a teen-ager. Later, Shavers was known for high-register fireworks displays, but the tone of the Kirby group was quiet and restrained,
and Shavers followed this line, often working with a mute. It is probable
that Navarro took Shavers as his first model. Mainly self-taught, he was a
quick learner and was working professionally by the time he was in his
mid-teens. In 1943 he landed with the Andy Kirk band, then based in New
York. Navarro was quickly caught up in the new music. By the time
Gillespie was ready to leave Eckstine in 1945, Navarro had become a first-
rate bop player. Coming into the Eckstine band as Dizzy's replacement, he
was brought to the attention of other young players, many of whom took
him for a model.

Navarro's approach to the horn, though based on Gillespie's, was different in emotional content. He had acquired the nickname "Fat Girl," and
Gillespie has said, "He was very sweet. He was like a little baby." This
temperament, coupled with the influence of Shavers of the Kirby Sextet,
inevitably made him a restrained player. Gillespie, who had modeled himself on the flamboyant Roy Eldridge, was a headlong player, a risk-taker
who flung phrases about with abandon.

Navarro was more controlled, more deliberate in his playing. His emotional range was smaller than that of Gillespie, Parker, or the other founders of the bop movement. Although he possessed a secure and clean upper
register, he characteristically confined himself to the midrange of his instrument, jumping only occasionally into the upper register and then quickly
returning to midrange again. Nor did he specialize in breakneck tempos, but
played predominantly at medium speeds, even though he possessed the
technique to play fast. His strength was in molding long, flowing lines
composed largely of eighth notes. The line rises and falls easily and calmly,
and there is a constant if subtle play of accent throughout. This accenting
is felt as a withdrawing of force from certain notes in an otherwise even line.
Often in a sequence every other note is lightened, as a sort of negative
accent, giving the listener the sense that the line is moving in and out, of
coming and going. The music seems at times to rustle gently like leaves in
the wind.

This constant play of accentuation through an ostensibly even line is very
typical of bop practice. It is probably not done very consciously, and may
at times be due to vagaries of tonguing methods. In the case of trumpet
players it often is due to double-tonguing. However Navarro achieved it, the
effect shows up clearly in his playing.

Navarro's principal weakness is what appears to be a simple lack of concern for sound. His tone, though sometimes brilliant in the fashion of big band trumpet sound, is usually thin and dry.

Because Navarro was so deliberate and orderly a player, his recorded solos are of consistently good quality, without the highs and lows more typical of jazz performance. A fine example of his work is his solo on "Be Bop Romp," made in 1947. Here is the even, controlled, middle-register playing, the rare excursions into the upper register. The negative accents are particularly evident in this chorus. They can be easily remarked in the third, fifth, and tenth bars of the solo, and are evident other places as well.

However orderly Navarro was in his playing, he allowed his life to take a chaotic turn. Like so many of the other young boppers, he became addicted to heroin after his arrival in New York, when he was still an impressionable youngster. He was unable to break away from the drug, and in 1950 he died of drug-connected tuberculosis.

The role that Navarro played in respect to Gillespie was filled in respect to Parker by Sonny Stitt. His father was a professor of music, and his mother taught piano and organ. Stitt grew up in Saginaw, Michigan, where he studied first piano, then clarinet and the saxophones. Like so many of his fellows, he went on the road with a band as a teen-ager. (During World War II there was a great shortage of musicians; it was hardly rare to find swing bands filled with seventeen-year-olds.)

Two of the men who came into bop early and were to have considerable influence on later players, Fats Navarro and Tadd Dameron, shown here on piano, but known principally for his arranging. William P. Gottlieb/Edward Gottlieb Collection

Stitt has been quoted as saying that he was playing like Parker before he ever heard of Bird, but it is highly unlikely that he arrived independently at Parker's methods. The cause for this remark is undoubtedly Stitt's intense annoyance at forever being referred to, in the early days of bop, as "the new Bird" or some equivalent title. For a time Stitt even abandoned the alto saxophone for the tenor in order to escape the opprobrium of being a mere follower of Parker. Whatever his claims, Stitt became part of the New York bop scene when he barely was out of his teens. Like Parker, he is a strong and passionate player, but it is instructive to note that, like Navarro, his style is characterized by cascading eighth notes, interspersed here and there with the rapid triplets that were Parker's trademark.

One thing that distinguishes this second generation of bop players from the founding fathers was the lack of rhythmic variety in their work. Navarro, Stitt, and the group of young bop players who carried the bop style into the 1950s and beyond were addicted to endless eighth-note runs. Yet a great deal of the force we find in the work of men like Stitt and Navarro stems directly from this relentless outpouring, this cascade, which possesses the attraction of an eddying stream, a wavering flame, a steady snowfall.

We can see it once again in the work of J. J. Johnson, who more than anyone else formed the modern trombone style. The swing trombonists, in the line of development from Jimmy Harrison through Benny Morton and Dicky Wells, were really legato players. In legato playing, there are technical problems posed by the slide as opposed to the keys of the other wind instruments. The tempos at which a good deal of bop was being played made the legato style simply impossible. The solution was a switch to a more staccato style, in which each note is articulated separately. But this in turn presented problems: where a saxophonist can slide from note to note simply by pushing down different buttons, the trombonist must tongue each note if his playing is not to become one long smear, and the faster the tempo, the more difficult it is to tongue clearly. In simple truth, the trombone is not well adapted to high-speed playing.

J. J. Johnson was the first trombonist really to overcome the difficulty. He was born in Indianapolis in 1924, studied piano as a boy, then switched to the trombone. On his graduation from high school he went on the road with a minor swing band, led by Snookum Russell, in which Navarro was playing. He was at this time primarily a swing musician, influenced mainly by Eldridge and Lester Young. He began hearing an obscure trombonist named Fred Beckett, who worked with a number of the Southwest territory bands as well as with Lionel Hampton, and died in military service in 1945. Beckett was playing a fast, linear style quite the opposite of the standard legato style, and Johnson took up the mode. By the end of 1942 he was working with the Benny Carter band, which at one time or another included a number of early bop players, the most important of whom were Freddie

Webster, Max Roach, and Curly Russell, the bassist on many of Parker's early records.

Like most of his generation, Johnson adopted the new music. Unlike most of his fellow trombonists, he had developed the technical skill to play the long, fast strings of eighth notes essential to bop playing. As he moved out of the big bands to work in small groups on Fifty-second Street and elsewhere, and eventually to record, he left other trombonists gasping at this technical skill. Many would not believe that he played slide, but, until they saw him in person, insisted that he was playing a valve trombone, which can be manipulated faster. Johnson was not the first bop trombonist; that distinction probably belongs to Benny Green, who was with Gillespie and Parker in the Hines band. But by the late 1940s, Johnson was the preeminent trombonist in jazz, to whom all others looked, sometimes in awe. Just as Gillespie had set the pattern for trumpet playing for the next twenty years, so Johnson, who was of course molded by Gillespie and Parker, established the trombone style that lasted well beyond the zenith of the bop period.

Typically, Johnson employs a rather muffled sound, sometimes produced by his placing a felt bag over the bell. In general, he avoids almost all the effects that had been characteristic of trombone playing throughout jazz history. There are no glissando smears and slurs. He never toys with pitch; he lands on it four-square and stays there. His terminal vibrato is relatively modest. He attacks most notes distinctly, instead of half-tonguing them, as is customary in legato playing, although his attack is soft rather than the explosive one jazz brass players often employ. In conception, his figures tend to begin high and run downward. His phrasing is rhythmically richer than that of other bop players. He uses far fewer strings of eighth notes than Navarro or Stitt, in part at least because of the difficulty of playing them on the trombone. His line is full of jagged leaps and breaks.

Johnson was well recorded during the 1940s and 1950s, and there is no shortage of samples of his work to choose from. One interesting set is a group he made with Sonny Stitt and an excellent rhythm section in 1949. On "Teapot," taken at a breakneck tempo, he reveals his enormous technical skill, the uninflected notes, and the characteristic jagged line. The set also includes a slow blues called "Blue Mode," and it is interesting to note that even at this slow tempo, when a more trombonistic style of playing would be possible, he still avoids legato playing.

Johnson's greatest celebrity came in the fifties, when he teamed with another trombonist, Kai Winding, a Dane who had come to the United States as a boy with his parents. Winding possessed a somewhat fuller, more legato style than Johnson, as the result of the influence of Bill Harris. He employed a broad terminal vibrato and occasionally the strong secondary impulse that Harris featured, but considerably modified, so at times his work is hard to distinguish from the uninflected playing of Johnson. In 1954 the two men put together a quintet, which had a considerable popular success playing rather smooth and uncomplicated arrangements of standard tunes. The trombone duet sound was novel. The group lasted two years, achieving a prominence in the jazz world of the 1950s that inevitably made Johnson and Winding influential with younger trombonists of the period.

But although the Johnson style changed trombone playing, there is a problem inherent in it that neither Johnson nor his followers ever fully overcame. Jazz feeling, as we have seen, depends a great deal on subtleties of time, accent, and timbre. The notes must be lifted away from the ground beat, and they must be inflected in various ways by means of accent, vibrato, tone color, secondary pulse, and the like. In attempting to cope with tempos that had not been demanded of trombonists before, Johnson and his followers had enough to do just to make the notes; asking them to color their notes one way or another was demanding too much. No doubt there was also a philosophic point involved: bop was new, it was revolutionary, it was kicking away the past. The smears and slurs characteristic of jazz trombone playing from the beginning were now earmarks of a dead time, to be scrupulously avoided at risk of losing one's place in the revolutionary army. As a consequence, there is a flatness to bop trombone playing that is not found in the other instruments. There is not that dash, that electric crackle that characterizes the best bop. And the result has been a continuation in the steady decline of interest in the instrument. After Johnson, no trombonist had a major impact on the line of development of the music, as had Ory, Harrison, Teagarden, and other early players. To be sure, there have been many excellent trombonists in jazz since Johnson emerged in the 1940s: Urbie Green, Jimmy Cleveland, Curtis Fuller, Bobby Brookmeyer, Slide Hampton, and Jimmy Knepper are a few. Of them the most highly regarded today is Knepper. Hardly known outside the jazz world, and not well known inside it, Knepper possesses a superb technique and a conception that does not grow out of the controlled precision of Johnson and his followers, but from the legato school of Wells, Morton, Higginbotham, and especially Bill Harris. Where Johnson plays delicate staccato figures with the notes even and uninflected, Knepper fills his line with swoops and smears. Always in motion, he is capable of high-speed legato playing that amazes fellow trombonists. Why he has not a larger reputation is a mystery; probably it is because he has rarely led his own band or recorded under his own name.

Of all the younger bop players, the one who has had the longest effect, an influence reaching down to today, was Clifford Brown. Considered by his peers a major jazz figure at the time of his early death, his reputation has grown steadily since, until today he is thought almost as important as the master himself, Gillespie. In terms of his character, Brownie was one of the most attractive figures in jazz, and this attribute shines through his musical line.

He was born in 1930 in Wilmington, Delaware. His father, an amateur musician, gave him a trumpet when he was fifteen, making his start one of the latest in jazz. He studied privately in Wilmington, taking lessons in piano, vibraphone, and theory in addition to trumpet. Such was his natural facility that within three years he was playing gigs in Philadelphia with people like Kenny Dorham, Max Roach, J. J. Johnson, and Fats Navarro. Navarro especially encouraged him and became Brown's primary model. After graduation from high school, he entered Maryland State University to study music.

Then, in 1950, his musical career, and indeed his life, was almost cut short by an automobile accident. For a year he was out of music, and then began the hard struggle to work himself back into shape. Gillespie in particular encouraged him to fight his way back. Still only twenty-one, he had acquired a quick reputation among the older bop musicians. There was a feeling that, however inexperienced, he "had something important to say." When he was able to play again, he started working with a rhythm and blues group called Chris Powell and His Blue Flames, with which he made his first two records. He next worked briefly with Tadd Dameron, with whom he also recorded, and finally landed in the Lionel Hampton big band.

The Hampton band made a European tour in the fall of 1953. Brownie had already developed a following in Europe, and he was asked to record with a French rhythm section. The sides he cut with the group are among the few he made with no other horns. He is thus given plenty of room to work in, and it is clear that, at twenty-three, he possessed a sure command of his instrument and an individual conception.

When he returned from Paris he left the Hampton band, and in mid-1954 he was recruited by Max Roach for a group that began working around California. With this group, which became known as the Clifford Brown–Max Roach Quintet, he made a popular breakthrough. He won the *Down Beat* critics' award as New Star on trumpet for that year, and was thereafter a name musician, at least to the degree that any jazz musician becomes a name.

He spent the rest of his life with this group, which included at various times saxophonists Sonny Stitt, Harold Land, and Sonny Rollins, as well as pianist Richie Powell, younger brother of Bud Powell. It was, unfortunately, to be a short life. On June 25, 1956, Brown played an informal gig at a Philadelphia instrument store called Music City. At the conclusion of the gig, Brown, Powell, and Powell's wife, Nancy, left Philadelphia for Chicago, where they were due to play at a cabaret called the Blue Note. Nancy Powell, apparently an inexperienced driver, was at the wheel. In the

Clifford Brown at the Cafe Bohemia, a Greenwich Village jazz club of the 1950s. The picture was taken in 1956, shortly before Brown's tragic death. The saxophonist is Sonny Rollins. Bob Parent

early hours of June 26, the car skidded on a wet stretch of pavement on the Pennsylvania Turnpike and rolled down an eighteen-foot embankment. All three of the people in the car were killed.

Clifford Brown's style derives from Dizzy Gillespie by way of Fats Navarro. Like Navarro, Brown tends to stay in the middle register with brief excursions upward, and he characteristically employs lines of relatively even eighth notes. In "Cherokee," recorded with Roach in February 1955, he plays fourteen measures of uninterrupted eighth notes as he turns the bridge into the last sixteen bars of the first chorus of his solo. (It is worth noting that he quotes Parker's "Koko" near the beginning of his chorus.) The line plunges on and on, rising and falling without a break, very much after the manner of Navarro. However, where Navarro is cool, poised, deliberate, Brown in his work is generally impetuous, rambunctious, full of fire. His solo on "If I Love Again," made at the same time as "Cherokee," is thrown out in a tumbling rush. Brown begins this superb solo with a crisp and well-constructed break in which a brief opening figure is followed by a variation of itself, and resolves into the melody line. A rather delicate paraphrase of the song's theme rapidly gives way to a typically headlong Brown line. The effect is produced in part by the introduction of the high-speed triplet figures Parker so often employed, which here, folded suddenly into the eighth-note strings, give the effect of notes tumbling out in haste, as if Brown had a great deal to say and was eager to get it all in before he ran out of time. This sense of "having a lot to give" was something that musicians commented upon during his lifetime. The listener gets a feeling that Brown is always playing in a passion, that he is never coasting, never idly filling in spaces with remembered ideas, but is working at top capacity and high concentration all the time.

As with Navarro, Brown's lines of eighth notes are less even than they appear at a superficial listening. There are stretches of that in-and-out, coming-and-going quality in which alternate notes are struck stronger and lighter, and again I suspect that Brown was double-tonguing passages even when unnecessary. But despite his debt to Navarro, Brown was far the superior of the two in sound production; indeed, probably the superior in this respect of any trumpet player of his time. His tone is warm and a bit muted. The front edges of his notes crackle and pop as Eldridge's do, and at times there is a breathy quality to them, which adds to the impulsiveness of his line. Over his short musical lifetime, this sound production grew surer and his line crisper and cleaner. On "Gertrude's Bounce," recorded at Basin Street, a New York nightclub, not long before his death, Brown plays a magnificent solo in which each note stands out like a separate drop of paint flung at high speed on a canvas. Here again is evident his willingness to work. The first figure runs unbroken for eight full measures. Then, after the briefest of pauses, Brown repeats the last phrase as a springboard to leap off into another sustained flight of eight bars. Indeed, there are hardly any pauses throughout the whole solo, and those are brief, never lasting for more than a beat or two. Confident, relaxed, and yet filled with that intensity which fellow musicians so much admired, Brown lets one idea flash out of another in an endless display of creative imagination that only the greatest jazz musicians have surpassed.

In his approach to ballads, Brown employs a device that he undoubtedly took from Navarro. This is the grace note. The grace note, which would be difficult to execute at high speeds, in ballads produces the effect of a note struck twice — that secondary pulse found in the work of so many musicians. Brown, like many jazzmen of his time, made a series of standards with strings. His "Smoke Gets in Your Eyes" is replete with grace notes. Characteristically, in this solo there are delays and stretched figures that do not appear in his faster work.

Because Brown's life was so short, we see less development in his work than in that of other major figures. Still, as he matured, he showed, along with the general increase in crispness, more tendency to break out of the middle range into the upper register and a willingness to break his line more frequently. Whether Brown would, in another decade, have gone on to greater triumphs from an already superlative start is a moot question. It is entirely possible that he might have found a new conception for jazz playing and become a leader in pushing jazz into some unknowable direction. Unlike what we feel about Parker or Beiderbecke, we do not sense that Brown had exhausted himself before he died. And it is indeed ironic that when so many of his contemporaries were killing themselves with drugs, Brownie, one of the few bop players who remained "clean," should die in so irrelevant a fashion.

For drugs were, unhappily, relevant to the bop movement. Jazz has never been without the taint of narcotics. Cocaine was sold freely in Storyville, and without question many of the early players sampled it. Marijuana was virtually endemic to jazz from the beginning. And, of course, the entire jazz world, existing so much as it did in nightclubs and parties, has been drenched in alcohol right along. But alcohol usually works its deleterious effects slowly; hard drugs begin to punish very quickly.

Why exactly the bop movement was so saturated with heroin is hard to know. As some musicians have claimed, the Mafia may have deliberately made jazz musicians a target because many of them at times made a lot of money. For another, many musicians may have felt that drugs interfered less with their ability to play than alcohol did. And, of course, there was the example of Parker. Whatever the cause, by 1950, drugs, particularly heroin, had acquired a mystique. Many young musicians felt that the first fix was an intiation; that until you had experienced drugs you were an outsider. So they sampled it, and in the end the carnage was immense. It is probable that 50 to 75 percent of the bop players had some experience with hard drugs, that a quarter to a third were seriously addicted, and that perhaps as many as 20 percent were killed by it.

Many of those whom drugs did not kill simply slid out of music altogether, or, like Red Rodney, who eventually kicked his habit, spent long years playing in commercial bands in order to live. Heroin was a major figure in the bop movement, as significant in shaping the music as Parker himself, because one after another it took away most of the leading figures. Had Parker, Navarro, and Rodney continued to work in the music, they might well have found new roads to explore, supplying the form with a vitality it was to lose a few years after the death of Brown; and surely Miles Davis would not have emerged in the late 1950s as the chief model for young trumpet players.

The Old-World Cool
of Tristano, Mulligan, and Brubeck

The bop revolution left the jazz world a shambles. This time it was divided not into a style in eclipse fighting a rear-guard action against a new style, but into at least four factions, each with its own philosophy, heroes, and villains.

There were, of course, the ever-growing numbers of bop players who were, by 1950, holding the main ground. Poised against them were the swing players, many of them at the height of their powers, who were being pushed into a backwater. For a man like Goodman or Eldridge, each still in his thirties when the bop movement took over, this was a bitter pill. Some of these men, like Teagarden, simply ignored the new music and played as they had always done. Others attempted to make an accommodation with bop. Hawkins was the most successful of the older men in making a place for himself in the new music. He had helped to open the way for the bop players with his "Woody 'n' You" session, and he continued to work with them for a time. But he was never really at home in the music; his playing was essentially swing, with the addition of some advanced harmonics. It is a cruel rule of jazz that only the greatest players learn two musical languages, and most learn only one. That is, the major innovative players as young men develop a second way of playing that grows out of the one they learned as adolescents. Goodman went on from a style based on Teschemacher and the New Orleans players to help form the swing style; Armstrong was originally a New Orleans cornetist in the Oliver mold; both Parker and Gillespie were polished swing players before they developed bop. It is a sad truth that not even the greatest jazz musician has ever learned a third musical language.

But the bop and swing players were not the only groups contending for a place in the music. The dixieland revival was, in 1950, in full bloom. The aging George Lewis was playing to enthusiastic crowds in Northern cities; there were important clubs in most cities devoted to dixieland — the Hangover in San Francisco, the Savoy in Boston, Ryan's, Nick's, and Condon's in New York. Many of the people in this camp insisted that New Orleans jazz, and its derivatives, was the only true jazz, and they simply ignored bop as a fad that would shortly exhaust itself.

Yet one more faction that found itself displaced by the bop musician was a group of younger men who had entered jazz from the big band movement, arguing the merits of Young and Hawkins. These people had been born in the 1920s, and as adolescents had been swept into jazz through the big band boom. They had grown up expecting to make their mark by improving on Eldridge, Young, Goodman, and their confreres, but just as they were coming into their own they found that their models were irrelevant. They reacted in various ways. Some, like Sonny Stitt and Serge Chaloff, the leading baritone saxist of the era, who died in 1957 of cancer, adopted the bop style. Others, like tenor saxophonists Zoot Sims, Stan Getz, and War-dell Gray, continued to play in the swing manner with bop inflections. Still others vacillated. A case in point is Dexter Gordon, a highly regarded player of the late 1940s and fifties. Gordon was associated with the bop school — he recorded with Bud Powell, Max Roach, and other beboppers — but in fact his work was clearly in the swing mode. At times he sounded like Hawkins, especially on ballads like "So Easy" and "I Can't Escape from You." On faster numbers, such as "Blow Mr. Dexter," he was clearly a Young disciple; and on a record like "Dexter Digs In," a riff tune based on "Stompin' at the Savoy," he sounds at times like both.

Yet while the swing players, the dixielanders, and the boppers were contending for the best place in the sun, there quietly arose a fourth mode, which, for a time, threatened to push all of the rest of them into the shade. This mode was controlled, introspective, intellectual, even mannered. It was seen at the time as a reaction to the fevers of other types of jazz, and inevitably the style became known as the "cool" school, as opposed to the hot music around it. But, in fact, the term was not a good one. The cool style was not a reaction to bop, but the continuation of a movement that had been going on in jazz for perhaps a decade.

One pull that has existed in jazz from quite early in its life has been in the direction of the European symphony, and its smaller brother, the chamber group. The concept of "symphonic jazz" is an obvious one, and it was tried out by Scott Joplin, James P. Johnson, Paul Whiteman, and composer George Gershwin, whose "Rhapsody in Blue" and "American in Paris" were attempts to create the jazz symphony. Later, in the 1930s, Benny Goodman had a fugal number called "Bach Goes to Town," and Raymond Scott, not really a jazz musician, had a hit record called "In an Eighteenth-Century Drawing Room," which was based on a theme from Mozart.

Until the 1940s these experiments with symphonic jazz were sporadic and unsystematic. However, during the thirties there was an important change in the schooling of the men coming into jazz. Previously, jazz players had been largely self-taught, developing their own techniques in their rooms and learning the jazz tradition from records and the older players they emulated. This was as true of the whites as of the blacks; Beiderbecke, Russell, Teagarden, Davison, and the rest may have studied their instruments briefly with legitimate teachers, but for the most part they were self-taught. In the thirties, however, there arose in American high schools an accelerating demand for marching bands, generally as an adjunct to the football teams. These bands turned out scores of thousands of players on exactly those instruments in demand in jazz: trumpets, trombones, clarinets, saxophones, drums. By and large these young players were being schooled by teachers who had gone through courses of music education in order to get their teaching certificates. They were for the most part interested in European concert music, and a good many of them were flatly antijazz. What they taught — insofar as they taught anything — was the European tradition. Their students learned symphonic playing techniques; they memorized concertos and other concert pieces; and if they studied any theory, it was the voice-leading procedures of Bach and Mozart. The students who got caught up in music often went on to study it systematically. Especially after World War II, when the U.S. Government was subsidizing students in almost any field they wanted to enter, did musicians enroll for music study. This study was entirely in the European tradition; jazz courses in music schools were almost nonexistent until the 1950s.

It was particularly the whites who were bent toward European music. For one thing, whites were more likely to hear classical music at home than blacks were, because it was the music their mothers and fathers recognized as respectable, and often even liked. For another thing, until the 1950s, American colleges were still sharply segregated; there were fewer music departments open to blacks. Nonetheless, as well as whites many black players were being trained in the European tradition. The result was that by the 1940s a great many musicians who were taking up jazz had had some training in European music. They knew what a fugue was; they knew how to construct a sonata song form, how to move a composition through related keys. And they began wondering why some of these procedures could not be applied to jazz, especially the swing bands most of them were making their living from.

One of the most important of these men was Stan Kenton, a pianist and arranger who has had an oddly pervasive influence on jazz. Born in 1912 in Los Angeles, he began studying piano and composition as a boy, and by sixteen was writing arrangements for local bands. Through the thirties he worked as pianist and arranger with minor dance bands. Finally, in 1941, he put together a band of his own. It made slow progress until 1943, when its record of "Artistry in Rhythm" became a hit and led the band to stardom. "Artistry in Rhythm" was based on a theme from Ravel's "Daphnis and Chloe," and it was tailored very much to European models. It had an introduction, out-of-tempo stretches, and a Chopinesque piano solo. It was very much symphonic jazz. Under the influence of Kenton there was, for a while, a general movement toward more complex arrangements and richer voicing, using increasingly larger bands. By 1946 Kenton had the leading swing band, challenged only by Woody Herman's.

Herman was a reputable swing clarinetist who had made a mark with a band specializing in arrangements of the blues. He was, however, a great admirer of Ellington, and in the mid-1940s he began using more advanced arrangements, many written by an underrated altoist, Dave Matthews, who also worked for Kenton, and a few by Dizzy Gillespie. The band became one of several "Herman Herds," dedicated to playing hard-driving music based on relatively complicated and often difficult arrangements that utilized many devices taken from European practice. It included a number of first-rate soloists, among them trumpeters Sonny Berman and Pete Candoli, saxophonists Zoot Sims, Stan Getz, Serge Chaloff, Flip Phillips, Al Cohn, and trombonist Bill Harris.

Harris particularly marked the band. An eccentric player, he filled his work with smears, gruff staccato passages, and a second pulse so broad that he often appears to halt the note in midpassage before releasing it again. Harris was possibly the latest starter in jazz. Born in 1916 in Philadelphia, he began on the trombone in 1938, when he was twenty-two, although he had played other instruments earlier. He worked with several of the big bands, and was with the Herman band from 1944 to 1946 and again from 1948 to 1950. With Harris, melody is not so much the point as is the inflecting of notes: he attacks some sharply with a crackle, slurs into others, lets others slip out without being tongued at all. At times he cuts notes off abruptly, at other times adds a broad terminal vibrato. His playing is filled with fireworks; there is always something happening. He was featured on most of the important Herman records from this period, including a slow, moody "Everywhere," on which he has the bulk of the space. However, what he is known for is the up-tempo swingers, like "Bijou," "Apple Honey," and "Goosey Gander." As he matured, some of the eccentricities in his style were smoothed out; he has an excellent chorus on "Old Black Magic," with a Benny Carter group in the 1950s, that displays few of the abrupt fragments and broad vibrato of his earlier work. But he remains a highly individual player, and as such has had few followers. The most important is Jimmy Knepper, who shows touches of the Harris style in his work. Harris died in 1973.

Like Kenton, Herman featured a lot of symphonic jazz. Igor Stravinsky wrote a piece for Herman called "Ebony Concerto," which was presented at Carnegie Hall in 1946 with a good deal of fanfare. At the same time Herman introduced an extended work by Ralph Burns called "Summer Sequence," which, though fundamentally a standard big band swing number, employed a European framework. (The last section of this piece, entitled "Early Autumn," contained a tender, erotic solo by Stan Getz, which made him a popular jazz star.)

Both the Kenton and Herman bands were extremely influential during the late 1940s. They were very popular and were respected by musicians, and they could swing hard. They drew young players toward them, especially white players, and this of course served to increase the interest in applying European forms and devices to jazz.

A third band that was moving in the same direction was that of Claude Thornhill. The Thornhill band was never as popular as the Kenton and Herman bands, but it was respected by musicians and eventually had important effects. Thornhill was born in 1909, studied at the Cincinnati Conservatory and then the prestigious Curtis Institute of Music in Philadelphia, which is closely associated with the Philadelphia Symphony Orchestra. During the 1930s he developed a reputation as an arranger, and in 1940 he organized his own band to cash in on the swing boom. It was never especially successful and, like many bands, was hurt during the war, when the draft swept up hundreds of musicians.

In 1946 Thornhill reorganized on more advanced lines. His principal arranger was Gil Evans, a Canadian born in 1912 who had led and arranged for minor bands until 1941, when he began working for Thornhill. The emphasis in the writing was not on hard swinging, as was the case with Herman, or on soloists, although it included at times Red Rodney and Lee Konitz, but on sheer sound. It was one of the first big bands to use french horns and other instruments associated mainly with European concert music. Evans says, "Everything — melody, harmony, rhythm — was moving at minimum speed. Everything was lowered to create a sound, and nothing was to be used to distract from that sound. The sound hung like a cloud." The influence of the impressionist composers was clear. Evans and the men in the band were also aware of the new bop harmonies. John Carisi, arranger and trumpet player with the band, had sat in at Minton's; Rodney was about to become Parker's trumpet player; and in time Evans made arrangements of several Parker compositions, including "Yardbird Suite" and "Anthropology."

Yet one more band that attempted to combine elements of bebop and European concert music was led by saxophonist Boyd Raeburn. Raeburn, who had been leading ordinary dance bands, came to New York in 1944 with a group dedicated to the new musical approach. At times it included boppers Gillespie, Benny Harris, and Dodo Marmarosa. (The band was racially mixed to a greater extent than most of the period.) It included in its book an arrangement of Gillespie's "Night in Tunisia," as well as "Tone Poem" by George Handy, a piece that is difficult to describe as jazz, "Boyd Meets Stravinsky" by Eddie Finckle, and similar material by Johnny Mandel, all three respected jazz composers. Despite the fact that the band had the support of Duke Ellington, audiences found the music too difficult; within two years it was in a decline, and by 1952 Raeburn was virtually out of the music business.

To an ear used to modern harmonies, the records of these bands appear somewhat antique. Herman survives because of the infectious swing he invariably got out of his groups and because of his soloists. Kenton in particular suffers; his complex scorings often seem hollow and pretentious. But the effort of these groups to expand the vocabulary of jazz was laudable, and it continues to echo in jazz playing today. Kenton's mark on the music remains. An articulate man, enthusiastic about jazz — particularly his own type — in the fifties and sixties he ran a series of jazz clinics at high schools and colleges all across the country. These clinics would have been impossible ten years earlier, when music departments were dominated by people trained in European music, but by the 1950s school and college music systems were heavily populated with people who had grown up in the big bands. These people welcomed the Kenton clinics.

Out of this combination of circumstances there grew the "stage band" movement, a term that was chosen to avoid the word "jazz," at which boards of education would look askance. Stage bands today exist in most of the large high schools and colleges. Perhaps the best known are the ones at Indiana University and North Texas State. They are dedicated to playing big band music in the old tradition while reflecting changes in the stream of popular music. The stage bands have been sending into music a steady flow of players accustomed to thinking in terms of arranged music and able to play it. The effect has been felt not so much on jazz as on rock and jazz-rock, which have tended more and more to use horns playing arranged passages.

While Kenton and Herman were making large popular reputations playing a form of jazz heavily indebted to European composers, a blind, eccentric pianist, whom few members of the general public have heard of even today, was attempting a revolution of his own. Lennie Tristano was born in Chicago in 1919 during an epidemic of influenza, which weakened his eyes, and by 1928 he was very nearly blind. He claims to have started "fooling around" with a player piano at the age of two. After studying by himself until he was seven, he took private lessons. He played a variety of instruments as a youth, worked professionally at twelve, and earned a master's degree in composition. By 1943 he was teaching at the Christiansen School of Popular Music and gigging around Chicago on piano and reeds.

He had been attracted to jazz by the records of Armstrong, Beiderbecke, and the Midwesterners, and later he listened to Eldridge, Young, Christian, Tatum, and other swing players. He was, by the mid-1940s, one of the most thoroughly schooled musicians in jazz. He possessed a prodigious piano technique, a thorough grounding in theory and composition, and a solid background in jazz. He had, further, some advanced ideas of his own.

He moved to New York in 1946 and took up teaching, which became his principal source of income. He quickly earned a considerable underground reputation among musicians as a crazy genius who had a lot of ideas about music. Many musicians hated his ideas, and many more found him personally difficult. He was authoritarian and demanding, insisting that the musicians around him hew exactly to the line he set before them. Still, he gathered around him a group of musicians who respected what he was doing and were willing to bow to his authority.

Like Kenton, Gershwin, and others before him, Tristano was conciously trying to weld jazz and classical music. During one relatively rare stay at Birdland, his group would open each evening with a Bach "Invention," in order to get the audience tuned to its philosophy. In 1949 it recorded some records that, though they caused no public stir whatever, were closely listened to by musicians, even those who didn't like them and professed not to understand them. The players included alto saxophonist Lee Konitz, tenor saxophonist Warne Marsh, and guitarist Billy Bauer, as well as a drummer and bassist whose creative roles, as will be clear, were limited.

Tristano was not primarily interested in complicated systems of chord changes — his studies in classical music had thoroughly mined that area for him. His main concern was with creating "pure" melodic lines in shifting meters, or without meter at all. To accomplish this goal, he had his bassist and drummer play absolutely metronomically, without accents, setting forth an endless, uninflected ground beat. Obviously, if the drummer began accenting, he would imply bar lines of his own. Similarly, Tristano insisted that the horns play their notes as evenly as possible so that they too would not inadvertently suggest bar lines.

This was not an invariable practice; his music does contain bar lines, or the suggestion of bar lines. But they mingle measures in different meters, moving from, say, 5/4 to 4/4 to 6/4 in very short spaces of time. The effect can be heard in "Wow" and "Crosscurrent," probably his best-known works. "Wow" opens with what in ordinary 4/4 time would be a three-bar figure. Actually, the opening figure is not really three measures in 4/4, but two in 6/4. The connecting figure appears to be meterless, and the following five-bar figure is in 4/4. The bridge, a virtually uninterrupted line of music, is played at what is probably not double time, but quadruple time — that is, four times as fast as the speed of the main theme. In "Crosscurrent" the same mixing of meters is evident. The theme opens with three measures in 5/4. Then we get a passage in 4/4, and next, after a fairly random segment, some measures in 6/4.

Nor is this all. While Tristano is shifting meters about, he is also rapidly changing from one key to another. Key changes are of course a commonplace in music, but normally they occur some distance apart. In these records Tristano shifts keys as often as every bar, and sometimes at even shorter spans. The opening phrase of "Wow," for example, shifts keys three times in the first nine beats. This is not exactly atonality, in the strict sense of the tone-row school; tonalities do exist, if only temporarily. But the keys shift so rapidly that to most ears the effect is atonal. These records are not all written out; they contain full-dress solos by various of the players, especially Konitz and Marsh. The soloists were expected to approach the music in the spirit of the written passages, with an attempt to use broken meters and to follow the shifting tonalities, and to a considerable degree they did. Despite the obstacles put in their way by Tristano, both men managed to introduce a semblance of swing into their work.

Tristano's experiments did not end here, however. At the conclusion of one recording session in May of 1949, Tristano told the engineers to leave the mike open. He and his musicians thereupon began playing in so singular and incomprehensible a fashion that the record company would not issue the take for some time. When it finally came out, under the title "Intuition," musicians were in the main as puzzled as record company executives had been. (A second take was issued as "Digression," at a later date.) In fact, Tristano and his group were playing free jazz, anticipating by almost a decade the experiments of Ornette Coleman, Archie Shepp, and others in the late 1950s. These pieces were not, like the Coleman experiments, quite timeless; a tempo is implied most of the time, although there is a certain amount of shifting of the pace. But they are free harmonically, with each instrumentalist working in a melodic system that suits him.

Although Tristano was working along lines that other men would follow later on, he was not in the main line of the development of jazz. Few musicians either understood his music or liked it, and even fewer had the technical resources to attempt it themselves. The relatively small group of records Tristano made are as a body of work a thing unto themselves, without predecessors and successors. But they cannot be dismissed as unimportant. At its best Tristano's work has a shimmering, pointillistic quality, lit with pastel tones.

The Europeanization of jazz of this period reached a climax of sorts in 1949, with a series of records that has since come to be called "the birth-of-the-cool" sides. It is rare when a single group of records by itself has a significant impact on jazz. The Armstrong Hot Fives had such an impact, and so did the Parker-Gillespie records of 1945. The birth-of-the-cool sides, although neglected by record buyers, was to have a similar, if somewhat less pervasive, impact on musicians. The star actors in their making were some men who had been associated with the Claude Thornhill band, mainly Gil Evans, baritone saxophonist and arranger Gerry Mulligan, and John Carisi. With pianist John Lewis, these men began meeting informally in 1948 to exchange ideas that, they hoped, would lead to a small band playing music suggested by the work Evans had been doing for Thornhill. Miles Davis, who had recently quit Parker, was brought in as trumpet player, and in ways that none of the principals have specified, he emerged as the nominal leader. Actually, the general concept for the group had come from the Thornhill men; they, along with Lewis, had translated that concept into specific arrangements, and they picked the personnel. Davis's role seems mainly to have been to run rehearsals and front the band, but it was his name that went on the records, no doubt in part because he was the only member of the group whose name was known by the jazz public.

In fact, there was little fronting to do. The band played a brief engagement at the Royal Roost, and that was about it. Fortunately, somebody from Capitol Records heard the group, and arrangements were made to record it in what came to three sessions between January 1949 and March 1950, using somewhat different personnel.

The instrumentation Evans and others had evolved was extremely unusual for jazz of the time, comprising trumpet, trombone, french horn, tuba, alto and baritone saxophones, and a standard rhythm section. But the instrumentation was less novel than the music itself. Four of the arrangements were by Mulligan; the rest by Gil Evans, Carisi, Lewis, and Davis. The writing was heavily influenced by the Thornhill sound. Evans's arrangement of "Moon Dreams" is in fact pure "clouds of sound" in the Thornhill manner, and throughout there is an effort to produce rich sonorities that are derived more from the European impressionists than from men in the jazz tradition, like Ellington or Redman.

The most successful of the cuts are "Jeru," "Boplicity," and "Godchild." All of them evidence the concern for sound that Evans and Mulligan had been schooled in, and all of them are presented in the low-key, undramatic manner that became the trademark of the cool school. The dynamic range is limited: there is no loud playing, no sign of the strong, cutting edge typical of the solos of Parker, Eldridge, Hawkins, Goodman. Tempos, too, are moderate, especially compared with the extremes of fast or slow the bop players favored. In general there is a reaching for tranquillity; the music is introspective, pensive. It was, for jazz, a radical departure in mood. To be sure, ruminative playing had existed in jazz hitherto. Hawkins's "Body and Soul," Lester Young's clarinet playing on the Kansas City Five sessions,

Red Norvo's xylophone on "Just a Mood" are cases in point. But contemplative tranquillity has never been a major mood in jazz, a music generally devoted to more rambunctious passions.

From a technical viewpoint the arrangements are interesting for their departure from the four-square jazz form. Duke Ellington had on occasion departed from the standard eight-, twelve-, and sixteen-bar episodes on which almost all jazz had been based. These records go farther in this direction, characteristically employing phrases of irregular lengths, and sometimes meters other than 4/4. Fats Waller had written a piece in 3/4 called the "Jitterbug Waltz," but there had been few other efforts in this direction; in fact, in 1949 few jazz musicians were capable of improvising in anything but 4/4. But Mulligan's "Jeru" goes into 3/4 at several points in the middle of the first bridge, and again at the opening section of the third chorus, following Davis's trumpet solo. "Godchild," a theme of George Wallington's, was arranged by Mulligan so that two extra beats are tacked onto the first eight bars and four extra beats onto the next sixteen. The bridge, instead of containing the normal eight bars, is cut to seven-and-a-half because the sixth measure is in 2/2 instead of 4/4.

Taken all together, however, these birth-of-the-cool sides are not entirely successful. The arrangements sometimes do not hold together as well as they might, and the playing itself is often tentative or downright weak, especially Davis's trumpet lead, no doubt in part due to the difficulty of some of the material. The solos are not exceptional, either. But these sides are the pioneering work of very young men. Mulligan and Konitz were each twenty-one; Davis was twenty-two.

In the same year that Tristano made "Wow" and "Crosscurrent" and the Davis group cut its first side, there appeared a composition by George Russell called "A Bird in Igor's Yard," played by a group under the leadership of clarinetist Buddy De Franco. The title, with its references to Igor Stravinsky and Yardbird Parker, states explicitly the attempt to combine jazz and European forms. The piece contains passages echoing Prokofiev as well as Stravinsky, interspersed with solos, principally by De Franco, and it is interesting to see how the solos themselves reflect the jazz–classical music fusion. De Franco worked with a sextet modeled after Goodman's as well as with a big band. He became the leading clarinetist in modern jazz, a regular poll winner, in part because he had so little competition. He has a first-rate legitimate technique, can play exceedingly fast, and possesses a clear, liquid tone. He uses very few inflections, and his playing as a result runs to long lines of unvaried eighth notes. "Extrovert," played by the sextet, opens with a fast unison line by clarinet and vibraphone, which suggests Parker in the way the phrases are cut and the Baroque keyboard masters in the general temper of the music. De Franco's solos share this approach, seeming to owe as much to the Baroque and European music in general as to Parker.

By 1949, then, there was a good deal of activity in this area. There began to arise on this foundation a school devoted to the cool, controlled manner that embodied elements drawn from European music. Many of the players had been raised in California or lived there, so they came to be called the West Coast school. By far the best known of them was Dave Brubeck, who had studied theory with Darius Milhaud, at Mills College in Oakland. He joined forces with alto saxophonist Paul Desmond and a bassist and drummer to make a quartet that quickly developed an enormous popular following, especially on college campuses. The Brubeck group was one of the first to work the college concert circuit, and one of the first as well to issue "live" recordings of concerts, today a general practice. However, whether Brubeck's music warranted the acclaim accorded it is another question. Brubeck's playing is often stiff and unyielding. He is addicted to playing long strings of block chords, as, for example, on "Balcony Rock," recorded in 1954 at a concert at Oberlin. A second device he overemploys is long sequences of pairs of evenly played eighth notes, which produce an odd seesawing effect. His extended solo on "Over the Rainbow," cut in 1952 at Storyville, a nightclub in Boston, is replete with such devices and can only barely be classified as jazz.

However much jazz musicians resented the money Brubeck was making and disparaged his playing, they admired Desmond, who died in 1977. An introspective player with a light, airy tone similar to Lee Konitz's, his playing has a reserved quality that is sometimes tentative to the point of diffidence. His forte is in exploring a line of music until he has investigated all its possibilities. It has been said that he often seems to be playing duets with himself, an effect he achieves by reiterating a short figure a number of times at different intervals — that is, playing similar figures somewhat higher or lower. At their best, Brubeck and Desmond worked together to produce, simultaneously, related lines — sometimes paralleling, sometimes contrasting, sometimes in the call-and-answer pattern. A good example of this ability to improvise related lines is found on the last chorus of "Out of Nowhere" and in "Lady Be Good," both from the Storyville session. Toward the end of the latter they consciously begin to play in imitation of a Bach "Invention," and the question arises as to whether we are dealing here with jazz or something else.

But whatever failings the group had, the members were influential as innovators. Particularly important was a tune called "Take Five," which became one of the quartet's most popular numbers. The piece was in 5/4, and it was the basis for one of the earliest attempts by jazz musicians to improvise in a meter other than 4/4. Brubeck has said, "When we first started to play that thing I just pounded out the time to keep us together, and now today it's taken for granted; you see kids improvising in three-and-a-half and things like that."

A second group that achieved almost as much fame and fortune as the Brubeck Quartet was one organized by Gerry Mulligan, which featured trumpeter Chet Baker. This was perhaps the prototypical West Coast group. Baker, who played briefly with Charlie Parker during Parker's disastrous stay on the West Coast in 1946, was an admirer of Miles Davis. He played within one of the smallest physical and emotional compasses in jazz, rarely raising his voice or venturing out of the middle register. His playing is passive, sometimes to the point of self-pity. The group had great popular success with moody, sentimental tunes like "My Funny Valentine" and "Moonlight in Vermont," both of which Baker approached as if he were dusting Venetian glass. In 1953 Mulligan enlarged the group to create a "tentette," which included french horn and tuba, in the manner of the groups that made the 1949 records with Davis.

It must, of course, be remembered that these divisions of jazz into one school or another are to a degree arbitrary devices of more use to the student or critic than to the jazz musician himself. There is always a great deal of overlapping, and there are many musicians who don't fit comfortably into any particular pigeonhole. A good example is Stan Getz. Because of his light tone and sometimes delicate approach, Getz was generally associated in the public mind with the cool school. In fact, he was a swing musician out of the Lester Young mold. Yet he was influenced by what was going on around him. Like most musicians in jazz, he picked up some of the new chordal language created by the bop school, and although basically a straightforward improviser, he did at times, possibly without much forethought, utilize the intertwining lines that came to be a trademark of the cool school. On a set of records made at a concert at the Shrine Auditorium in Los Angeles with valve trombonist Bob Brookmeyer, the two instruments often weave lines together, however unsystematically, and this practice, coupled with his light tone, gives Getz's work something of the mannered and reserved character that defined the cool school.

The Europeanizing movement in jazz, and the West Coast school that grew out of it, did not leave anything like the substantial body of great jazz that the swing players or beboppers did. Despite the presence of some excellent improvisers in Konitz, Desmond, Mulligan, and a few others, and some first-class musical thinkers in Tristano, Evans, Lewis, Mulligan, and Kenton, the music today often seems empty formalism, lacking force. This is not to say that there are not fine moments, for of course there are. But the European elements tended to dominate at the expense of rhythmic propulsion and the personal statement that emerges from the improvisation of a fine jazz musician. Oddly enough, it is the records of Tristano, the most idiosyncratic of them all, that stand up the best. There is force here; the compositions are better constructed and less derivative than most of the work in this school and, despite formidable technical difficulties, are played accurately and with élan.

We must not, however, let the weaknesses of the cool movement obscure its influence. Throughout the 1950s, and indeed up until the present day, jazz musicians have continued to draw on European concert music, especially for formal elements lacking in jazz. Furthermore, two of the most important jazz influences in the decades of the fifties and the sixties grew directly out of the cool school: Miles Davis and the Modern Jazz Quartet.

Miles and the M.J.Q.

The players of the West Coast school were mainly white. Many of them had been raised hearing the quartets of Beethoven and the symphonies of Brahms in their homes, and some of them, like Brubeck and Tristano, had had conservatory training. It is not surprising that they began ransacking the European tradition for elements they could use in jazz. As it happens, however, the man who was most successful in applying European forms to jazz was a black pianist, John Lewis.

Lewis was born in 1920, three months before Charlie Parker, and grew up in Albuquerque. His father was an optometrist; his mother a trained vocalist. Lewis, like Ellington and Henderson, like the whites of the cool school, came from the middle class, and as a middle-class boy was more likely than a child of the working class, especially the black working class, to have some familiarity with European music. He went to the University of New Mexico, where he studied both anthropology and music, eventually concentrating on the latter. He remembers, during this period, hearing on late-night radio an odd and fascinating saxophonist playing at the Savoy with the Jay McShann band. It wasn't until years later that he realized it was Charlie Parker. The tale tells something about the differences in their backgrounds. There was Parker, a homemade musician working at his trade and living a life that was rapidly descending from disorder to chaos; and there was Lewis at the same age, a college boy earnestly working over his studies in the fugue and the sonata song form.

Lewis went into the army during World War II, where he met Kenny Clarke. After his discharge, Clarke brought him to Gillespie, who took him into his big band as pianist and arranger. At the same time he began studying at the Manhattan School of Music, one of the country's leading conservatories, from which he received two degrees. He was, by the early 1950s, a thoroughly schooled musician familiar with European music, especially the music of the Renaissance and the Baroque period, in which he took a particular interest.

The Modern Jazz Quartet was not a deliberate creation, but came together as a matter of chance. Gillespie's band, like most big bands of the period, played arrangements that required a lot of high-register playing by the brass. To give them some rest, Gillespie took to featuring at moments during the evening his vibraphonist, Milt Jackson, supported by the band's rhythm section — Kenny Clarke, bassist Ray Brown, and Lewis. Eventually the group acquired an independent life of its own as the Milt Jackson Quartet. Percy Heath replaced Ray Brown, and as time went on, Lewis began to dominate the group. He was able to do so because he had musical ideas he wanted to put into practice, and the training to work them out.

What he wanted, basically, was to set the improvisations of the group in more interesting forms than had been customary in jazz. He has said, "The audience for our work can be widened if we strengthen our work with structure. If there is more of a reason for what's going on, there'll be more overall sense, and, therefore, more interest in the listener." Formal structure has been at the center of European music for centuries. Large forms like symphonies and operas are built of smaller forms, themselves made up of still smaller ones. Parts contrast with or complement each other; mood is varied through carefully worked-out changes of tempo, key, meter, and instrumentation. Just as we can find the function of every brick, every nail, every board in a well-designed house, so we can discover the function of each note in a piece of European concert music, at least those written prior to this century.

In jazz, form in this sense has never passed beyond a rudimentary level. Only the best players have been able to work out forms in their improvisations. What little structure there is has mainly been taken from the songs on which the improvisations have been based, and these for the most part have been quite simple. Very little attention has ever been paid to moving a piece through changes in tempo or mood. Indeed, few jazz soloists have ever bothered to relate their improvisations to those of a preceding soloist. In taking up these concerns, Lewis was making explorations that were long overdue.

Milt Jackson, by contrast, was the sort of man who was content to go out there and blow, and he was not happy about what Lewis wanted to do with what was, after all, Jackson's group. Three years younger than Lewis, he was raised in Detroit, where he learned several instruments, principally the vibraphone. The vibes, and associated instruments like the xylophone and marimba, pose a severe problem for the jazz player in that once a note is struck it cannot be inflected, except by the addition of vibrato. Indeed, neither the wooden marimba nor the xylophone can produce a vibrato or even sustain their brief notes. (Actually, there is a technique for creating pitch sag on a vibraphone.) Furthermore, because of inherent limitations of

A photograph of the Modern Jazz Quartet taken in 1956 at Music Inn, an institution in the Tanglewood area that specialized in classical music. From left, John Lewis, Percy Heath, Milt Jackson, and Connie Kay. Bob Parent

the mallet technique, these instruments cannot be used, as can the piano, as miniature orchestras, producing rich harmonies or rhythms in the left hand to support melody figures in the right. Perforce, what the vibraphonist does much of the time is to produce lines of single, uninflected notes, and for this reason mallet instruments have never been as widely used in jazz as the horns.

The first important player on a mallet instrument was Red Norvo, who started playing professionally on the xylophone in 1925 and switched to the vibes in 1943. Norvo possesses a delicate and graceful style eminently suited to his instrument. Norvo worked with many major musicians and recorded frequently, mostly with small groups under his own leadership. It was Hampton, however, who made the vibes famous. He began as a drummer with big bands in the late 1920s, added the vibraphone to his repertory in about 1930, and came to the Goodman trio in 1936, making it a quartet. Eventually he started a big band of his own, which existed off and on into the 1970s. In contrast to Norvo and his light graces, Hampton was a hard driver, addicted to riffs, who sometimes let pure activity smother his musical sense.

It would have been expected for Jackson to fall under the influence of these men, but, coming of age in the 1940s, he became instead a bop player. He is, like Hampton, a hard driver, but he manufactures a full, complete line, often inflected with a heavy vibrato, suggesting Parker more than anyone else. Lewis is an almost diametrically opposed musical personality. His own piano playing is exceedingly spare. Indeed, at times he sounds as if he were not really playing, but sketching out how he would like the music to go. Where Jackson is direct and powerful, Lewis is thoughtful and restrained; where Lewis found his models in Venice and Paris, Jackson found his in Minton's and on Fifty-second Street. It is hardly surprising that when Jackson found Lewis was taking over, he grew restive. He said, as quoted in Joe Goldberg's *Jazz Masters of the Fifties,* "It had been my group originally and I'll admit I felt bad for awhile. But John was putting so much time and work into it, more than I would have done. He worked so hard. It was a better idea to be cooperative, and John has been mostly responsible for the way we have gone since." Kenny Clarke was just as restive as Jackson under Lewis's domination, and finally left the group to live in Paris. He was replaced by Connie Kay. The group was thus being tugged in two directions, and this tension was in good measure responsible for its success, both artistically and commercially. Where the West Coast players like Brubeck, Mulligan, and the rest allowed cool European formalism to rule their music, the needs of Jackson would permit Lewis to go only so far in that direction. On the other hand, a Milt Jackson Quartet, devoted mainly to letting Jackson blow, would never have created the impact of the Modern Jazz Quartet, despite the excellence of Jackson's own playing. A balance was achieved; the group had a longevity remarkable in jazz and left an enduring body of work.

It was not always easy to maintain the balance. There were at times demands from an audience to "let Bags [Jackson] blow." Lewis continued to insist that simply blowing was not enough. To be sure, complaints that Lewis was overly concerned with structure at the expense of jazz feeling are sometimes justified; pieces like the fugal "Vendome," however pretty, sometimes lack the emotional substance we expect in jazz. In this particular case Jackson's improvised passages seem crabbed, as if he were unable to shake loose from the framework. Lewis's dedication to earlier European music sometimes seems petty. "Vendome," a piece in a minor key, ends on a major triad, a convention of Renaissance music that has long since disappeared. Again, on "Versailles" — Lewis has a weakness for fancy French names

— another contrapuntal piece, the necessity for producing a line complementary to Lewis forces Jackson into more long strings of eighth notes than he usually chooses to play, giving his line a similar cramped feeling. And a piece like "Fontessa" can hardly be considered jazz at all.

But when the group found the middle road, where form provided a framework for improvisation but did not dominate it, it produced masterly jazz. This is evident in "Django," possibly the group's most admired work. A memorial piece written by Lewis after Reinhardt's death, it opens with a dirge that suggests the sound of a guitar by use of guitarlike arpeggios in piano and vibraphone, and by guitarlike comping by the piano behind Jackson's solo. The dirge is followed by a related theme at a quicker tempo, which is used as a vehicle for improvisation, and the dirge returns to end the piece. The framework is simple but completely effective, and carries precisely the feeling of respectful sorrow that is appropriate to its purpose. The group recorded "Django" several times, and it changed over the years. A later version, cut at a concert in Sweden and issued as an album called "European Concert," has been simplified by the elimination of some of the guitarlike devices of the first version. It was a habit of the group constantly to change pieces. Lewis has said that when a number stopped changing, they dropped it. And it was this flexibility, perhaps, that prevented the Modern Jazz Quartet from falling into the trap that jazz sets for those who attempt to approach it too intellectually. There was always leeway for swinging.

Another case where Lewis has successfully applied European forms to jazz is in his short, four-part suite, "La Ronde." Each part features one member of the group improvising on a simple theme, with appropriate support from other members of the group. Evident in these pieces is a characteristic of the quartet that, if not a drawback, was a limitation. The vibes, combined with Lewis's spare piano style and a considerable amount of cymbal work by Connie Kay, gave the group's overall sound a bright, metallic quality, which at times came dangerously close to tinkling. This sound had the light, dry quality of the early keyboards on which much of the Renaissance and Baroque music Lewis admired was played. But at times the metallic shimmer becomes wearing and makes the ear long for the sound of a horn.

The tension in the group between Jackson and Lewis was bound to snap. After a point the quartet began working only six months of the year, ostensibly so that the members could do other kinds of work, but principally to let Jackson play in other contexts. Finally, in 1974, Jackson quit outright. According to Leonard Feather, in *The Pleasures of Jazz,* "Jackson declared he has little to show for all those years, denounced what he called the overnight rock 'n roll millionaires and implied that he was going out there to make some big bread." Lewis, Feather continued, was crushed. "I think we made quite remarkable livings over the twenty-two years. As for the rock stars who earn the kind of money Milt is talking about, they are people in show business, entertainers. We are musicians." Despite Lewis's bitterness, the breakup was inevitable. All the men in the quartet were in their fifties, or nearly so, and had spent most of their working lives together. It seems unlikely that the group had much more to add. But it left behind one of the significant bodies of work in jazz, a body of work limited in scope, but nonetheless satisfying, and, moreover, unique. Neither Lewis nor Jackson could have achieved it without the other.

The influence of the Modern Jazz Quartet, especially in the 1950s, was a major one. It seemed to many of the players who were coming into jazz with conservatory training that this was the direction in which the music had to go. The straightforward improvised solo, these people felt, was a limited musical form that had been thoroughly explored. It was time to find ways of fitting the music into more spacious frameworks, and during the decade of the fifties a number of composers attempted to combine jazz bands and concert orchestras in various ways. These attempts were heralded by some as the arrival of a "third stream" in music, a term apparently coined by Gunther Schuller. Schuller joined a jazz group with a small orchestra for a piece called "Transformation"; Teo Macero, a well-regarded arranger, wrote a piece that was played by the New York Philharmonic Symphony Orchestra and a jazz group; and Lewis himself joined the Modern Jazz Quartet with a string quartet to perform pieces by Schuller and himself. However inevitable this course seemed, the efforts to form a third stream proved a failure. The problem was the old one of falling between two stools: from the point of view of the jazz audience, if the music lacks jazz feeling, it fails as jazz; if it does swing, the symphony orchestra merely gets in the way.

Yet despite the influence of the Modern Jazz Quartet, the central figure of this period in jazz was Miles Davis, one of the most interesting personalities in jazz, a musician whose career is filled with paradox. The history of jazz is freighted with high talents who failed to make the most of their vast natural abilities. Bix Beiderbecke, Joe Thomas, Bud Powell are just a few who were equipped by nature to do much more than they did. In Miles Davis, we have the reverse, a much rarer case: a man who possessed only a relatively modest natural gift, but who by dint of intelligence and force of personality made himself one of the major figures in jazz. Davis does not have the instinct for melodic line that Beiderbecke and Parker had, the flawless rhythmic sense of Lester Young, or the feeling for drama on which Armstrong built his greatest solos. He is, furthermore, a limited instrumentalist with a poor high register and a tendency to crack more notes than a professional trumpet player should. And yet, with the exception of John Coltrane, since the death of Charlie Parker no jazz musician has been more influential than Miles Davis.

Davis was born in 1926 in Alton, Illinois. Shortly after his birth, his father, a dentist, moved to East St. Louis. Davis was raised not merely comfortably, but amidst affluence. His childhood was, compared with the early years of most jazz musicians, untypically secure.

He played in the high school band, and studied privately with a man who admired both Bobby Hackett and a St. Louis trumpeter named Shorty Baker, later to play with Ellington. Both Hackett and Baker are noted for their tone, and it is likely that Miles picked up from this teacher the concern for sound on which much of his work is based. By sixteen, Miles was playing with a local group called the Blue Devils (not the earlier Walter Page band). Davis came to hear about the experiments of the bop players, and when the Eckstine band came through St. Louis in 1944, Davis pressed Eckstine to let him sit in. This is an important point. Few adolescents would have had the nerve to ask a well-known band leader for that privilege; it wasn't done, especially if your skills were as limited as Davis's were at the time.

As Davis tells the story, he walked into the hall where the band was playing, and Gillespie, seeing the trumpet under his arm, asked him to sit in. But Eckstine, as quoted in a book by Michael James on Davis, says, "He used to ask to sit in with the band. I'd let him so as not to hurt his feelings, because then Miles was awful. He sounded terrible, he couldn't play at all." It is reminiscent of the youthful Charlie Parker pushing himself into jam sessions in Kansas City when he knew only two or three tunes, but Davis was by no means a sociopath. He was simply an ambitious and strong-willed kid who saw no reason to let obstacles stand in his way.

He graduated from high school in 1945 and insisted that he was going to New York to become a musician. His parents objected; they wanted him to go to college. Apparently as a compromise, he enrolled in Juilliard. However, instead of pursuing his studies, he made another overweening move: he tracked Charlie Parker down and moved in with him. How Miles managed this stunt is not known. Parker was by then a charismatic figure and the leading player in jazz; Davis was a kid trumpet player, and not an outstanding one by any means. His aggressiveness, in any case, paid off. He began working with Parker off and on and recorded with him on some of the earliest bop sessions. He played briefly with Benny Carter and with Eckstine's band, taking over the chair that Fats Navarro had inherited from Gillespie.

Then, in 1947, Parker hired him as trumpeter with his own group, in effect replacing Gillespie. It was certainly a triumph for an inexperienced twenty-one-year-old. But it was becoming Parker's habit to use young trumpet players: after Miles there was Red Rodney, who was also twenty-one when he joined Parker, and McKinley "Kenny" Dorham, who was twenty-four. For the next year-and-a-half he worked with Parker, and developed into a reliable musician. He was, in spite of other influences, a bebopper in the

Gillespie mold. As is apparent from the direction he eventually took, the style was not congenial to him, but it was unlikely that he could at that point escape Gillespie's influence.

In 1949 came the break with Parker, and Davis began to look around for something to do on his own. The opportunity came through his involvement with the Thornhill men. He became a part of this group and, as we saw, made himself leader, once again finding a role for himself in a situation where none had existed. What the others thought of Miles's assumption of leadership none has said, but Mulligan has made it clear that though Davis acted as leader and principal soloist, and contributed two arrangements, he did not pick the sidemen or supply the musical ideas, which had been worked out by Mulligan, Evans, Lewis, and the others. Nonetheless the birth-of-the-cool sides that resulted established Davis's reputation with musicians.

He was still far from being a first-rate trumpet player. His solos, such as on "Move" or "Godchild," which resemble the work of Bobby Hackett more than anybody else, are marred by fluffs. Because it seems so improbable that a white cornetist in the Beiderbecke idiom would have anything to say to the beboppers, Hackett has never been credited properly with his role in molding bop trumpet playing. What interested the boppers was his relatively advanced approach to harmony, as, for example, in his "Embraceable You." The Hackett sound is therefore no accident; Hackett was an influence on Davis. But he still had a good deal to learn. While his solos were more than adequate, his lead playing was weak, and the group would have sounded more solid and less insecure on the arranged passages with a strong, professional player in place of Miles. He is, however, beginning to develop the simple style that was to make him famous. His solo on "Venus de Milo," for instance, is much more straightforward and much simpler than Gillespie or Navarro would have played it.

The public was little interested in these records, but the record companies were beginning to see Davis as a potential jazz star. Unfortunately, this was the time of the heroin epidemic. Davis fell victim to the disease, and for the next three years did little recording and indeed stopped playing altogether for a period. But by 1954, by dint of the perseverance that has characterized him, he kicked the habit and began putting together a series of small groups, quintets in the main.

The personnel in those groups changed frequently, and some of the recording sessions were done with musicians scratched together for the occasion, but the overall tone was set by a style of playing that Miles had been developing since the birth-of-the-cool sides. It was a style that contrasted sharply with the bravura trumpet playing of Gillespie and his followers. Where Gillespie poured out cascades of notes, Miles used very few, dropping in little clipped phrases, leaving spaces as long as a bar-and-a-half, even on slow numbers, or holding notes for similar lengths. Where Gillespie used a full, clean sound, developed in big bands, Davis used a soft, more rounded sound, often muted or played with minimum volume into a microphone almost inside the trumpet's bell, and heavily inflected by half-valved pitch sags and downward slurs, which imparted a nasal tone at times. Where Gillespie had a powerful high register and used it often, Davis stayed always in the middle register, sometimes confining his playing to a single octave for measures at a time. Where Gillespie, and the beboppers in general, exposed long rolling lines sometimes lasting ten or eleven bars, Davis played in fragments, dropping short phrases in here and there over the ground beat, sketching, rather than making complete pictures.

The development of this spare style was Davis's major contribution to jazz. Since 1930 or so the music had been dominated by players who spilled out showers of notes, often at high speeds: Hawkins, Goodman, Eldridge, Tatum, Parker, Gillespie. There had, of course, been spare trumpet players before, like Buck Clayton and Max Kaminsky; but the full, headlong players had dominated the music. Davis's approach was something of a novelty at a time when Gillespie, Navarro, and Clifford Brown were throwing off those streams of eighth notes, and he was thus a major factor in freeing jazz from a mold that had confined it for two decades.

What prompted Miles to take this course he has not said. It is generally thought that Davis's basic model was Freddie Webster, a well-regarded trumpet player who worked with a number of big bands and died in 1947 at the age of thirty. However, in the few records of Webster's I have heard there is nothing to suggest that Davis took him for a model. Again, it is reasonable to suppose that the spare style that Thelonious Monk was developing through the late 1940s had an influence on Miles. Further, Davis's technical deficiencies no doubt made him more comfortable with a simple style than with a faster, fuller one. I would suggest, though, that Davis developed his manner deliberately, as a means of finding an independent path for himself. He is intelligent, thoughtful, and ambitious; he has always been quick to grasp new trends in the music and to find ways of applying them. And it is entirely likely that at some point early in his career he simply sat down and figured out that, in the face of the awful competition of Gillespie, he must find a different road to take.

However he developed it, this spare manner of playing was to become enormously influential for the next decade, and it is probably, despite Davis's later experiments with modes and jazz-rock forms, his most important contribution to jazz history. Through the 1950s and well into the sixties there was hardly a trumpet player in jazz who did not owe something to Miles. Indeed, so pervasive did the Miles manner become, that in time it seemed a cliché.

All aspects of Davis's playing are evident on a record called "Walkin'," cut in April of 1954, which had a measurable effect on both musicians and the jazz public. The personnel included pianist Horace Silver, later a leader in the "funk" movement, trombonist J. J. Johnson, who had been on some of the birth-of-the-cool sides, and tenor saxophonist Lucky Thompson, a player in the Hawkins mold who had better luck adapting to the bop era than many swing players. The record, a blues in F, has a simple opening and closing figure in F minor that is meant to suggest something of the "funky" or "soul" sound of the gospel church or the early blues. The record was thus part of the beginnings of the funk movement, which dominated jazz in the second half of the 1950s.

Davis's own solo work exhibits all the earmarks of his style: it is hesitant, tentative, spare. The other soloists maintain the mood. J. J. Johnson cuts his phrases almost exactly as Miles does, and pianist Silver, in contrast to the busyness of, say, Bud Powell, plays thin lines of single notes, supporting them in the left hand at times with only two or three single notes in a measure. Davis's style was now mature, the influences melded into a single, unified, and unique conception. Both musicians and audiences responded to it immediately. Its spareness made it easier to grasp than the experiments of the cool composers or the convoluted embellishments of Parker, and the mood of controlled tenderness appealed to young people, who were about to be called the "Silent Generation." With "Walkin'," and the records that followed, Miles became the model for young trumpet players all over the country.

By 1955, the Davis group had settled down to a more or less fixed personnel: bassist Paul Chambers, pianist Red Garland, Philly Jo Jones, a direct, hard-driving drummer much admired by other musicians, and at various times, Sonny Rollins, John Coltrane, and Cannonball Adderley on saxophones. The group recorded frequently, and Davis's style, if anything, got even sparer. In "Oleo," a Rollins tune recorded in 1954, Davis plays an enormous number of half and whole notes, and his solo on "Tad's Delight," cut a couple of years later, probably contains more half and whole notes than any solo by another major jazz figure. Again, on "Blues by Five," made in 1956 with Coltrane, the first three choruses of Davis's solo use the harmonic language of Armstrong, even including a pair of blue notes.

The men in the quintet were chosen expressly to set off this spare style. Jones is a busy drummer who keeps a steady, sizzling beat on the cymbals and accents frequently on the snare, and Coltrane was a florid, coarse improviser boiling with ideas that he could not always control. Set against this backdrop, Miles's spare line and delicate tone made his notes gleam like jewels. The quintet appeared at the Newport Jazz Festival in 1955 and was the hit of the occasion. Miles had been recording for Blue Note and Prestige, but now Columbia offered him a contract and the publicity buildup a major label can mount.

In general, the Prestige records are more forceful than the Columbia ones. They contain, basically, the repertory the band used in the clubs, and they give us a good idea of how Miles sounded in his day-to-day playing. He is still, from time to time, using fast strings of notes in the bop manner, as for example on "Oleo," but in the main, the spare style prevails. He employs mutes often, and he is playing a lot of very simple pop tunes, not ballads with intricate chord patterns such as the bop players liked, but ones like "S'posin' " and "If I Were a Bell," both of which have quite uncomplicated changes.

His opening chorus on "Bye Bye Blackbird" is a fine example of his musical methods. He plays the simple theme relatively straight; the point of it lies not in the notes themselves, but in their exquisitely subtle placement. It is, in fact, a classic exercise in just this central element in jazz, the lifting of the melody line away from the beat. The simple tune is built around a three-note rhythmic figure that is repeated three times in each four-measure segment. Miles plays this figure differently each time: the first time the three notes are placed with some exactness on the beat; the second time the figure is stretched out to last fractionally longer than it should; and the third time the figure is condensed to take up slightly less than its allotted time. When he comes to the same passage again in bars nine, ten, and eleven, he handles it in much the same way.

This ability to place his notes in unexpected places is Davis's strongest virtue. It colors his work everywhere. His masterwork in this respect is his "Milestones," made for Columbia in 1958. It is made up of the simplest sort of eight-bar melody — little more than a segment of a scale, in fact — which is repeated and then followed by a bridge made of a related eight-bar theme, also repeated. After the bridge the first theme is played once more. The point of it all lies in the bridge, where the rhythm goes into partial suspension. Miles stretches this passage out with the notes falling farther and farther behind their proper places. Indeed, in the reprise of the theme at the end of the record he stretches the bridge so far out that he cannot fit it all in and has to cut it short. During the solos as well, the players make some attempt to play arrhythmically over suspended rhythms, with mixed success. Only Davis seems really to have grasped the principle. His toying with time, in fact, threw the rhythm section off, so the whole piece slows down, despite the rhythm section's excellence. What Davis is doing here, surprisingly enough, is quite rare in jazz. Jazz players, of course, have habitually separated their melody lines from the ground beat, but almost invariably they have done it instinctively, unconsciously; it is simply ingrained. It has seldom been done consciously, according to a pattern, as Miles does here.

There is a second thing to be said about this piece, and that is that it is built not on chord changes but on modes. As the reader will remember, a mode is essentially a collection of notes — a scale, if you will — through which the composer or improviser is free to wander as he wishes. I have suggested that the reader can get the feel of playing in a pentatonic mode by wandering around on the black keys of the piano. Who was responsible for bringing the modes into jazz is difficult to say. Any conservatory student will learn about both the Greek and medieval modes in his "History of Western Music" course, and he may well study the use of modes in the musics of Asia and primitive cultures. By 1951 or 1952, John Coltrane was familiar with Nicholas Slonimsky's *Thesaurus of Scales and Melodic Patterns,* which he had learned about from his theory teacher, Dennis Sandole, who was interested in scalar approaches to music. Perhaps more influential was composer George Russell, who, by 1953, had worked out his "Lydian Concept of Tonal Organization," a complicated modal theory that could be used to justify the employment of almost any note in any context.

The interest in modes developing in jazz during the fifties represented a critical departure, one that was to have permanent effects on the music. The New Orleans pioneers were basically melodists who embellished preset lines, and whose grasp of harmony was for the most part limited and instinctive. After the diaspora from New Orleans, as jazz drew into it musicians with some grasp of music theory, like Hawkins, Henderson, Don Redman, Beiderbecke, Lang, and others, the chord sequence became the basis of improvisation. The player selected his notes to fit with the chords as they came along every bar or two. The use of "the changes" as a basis for improvising was sound, in that it both provided a form for the music and set harmonic guidelines from which a group of musicians playing simultaneously could work. Through the 1930s and especially with the bop revolution of the forties, chordal systems grew steadily more elaborate; the framework was becoming a maze, requiring ever more knowledge of theory on the part of the players, and by the fifties many musicians were finding that the chord sequence, rather than offering a springboard, had become a prison. As knowledge of the modes percolated through the jazz world, it quickly became apparent that here was a basis for improvisation that was simplicity itself: all you need do is stick more or less to the notes of the mode, which might last for four or eight or even sixteen measures at a stretch. To many players the modes seemed a new freedom.

For Davis, who was already making a point of simplicity, they were a perfect vehicle. He was not the first to see what could be done with them, but he was the one who brought the idea to fruition. "Milestones" uses one mode on the main theme, then switches to a second mode for the bridge. The success of the piece encouraged Davis to work further in the same direction. In 1959 he produced an LP called "Kind of Blue," with a group including John Coltrane and Bill Evans. The pieces in "Kind of Blue" were all modal, built on various arrangements of scales that Davis outlined to the

other players in the studio. The playing is spare, controlled, even moody
— very much in the melancholy vein the album title suggests. The record
was seen at the time as a new departure; it was widely influential; and is
considered today a landmark in the development of the jazz-rock movement.

But there were other things happening in jazz. Indeed, 1959 was a year
of considerable ferment. The free-jazz movement was surfacing, bebop was
wearing thin, and rock was beginning to take the play away from jazz
altogether. It was a time of new beginnings. Davis was openly contemptuous of the free-jazz players, but at the same time he could hardly stay put
if he was to maintain his position as a leading figure in contemporary music.
What he did was to move in a direction directly opposite from the one taken
by the free-jazz players. There was still much interest in "the third stream";
jazz players were increasingly studying European music and trying to find
direct applications for it. Miles had been struck by Joaquin Rodrigo's
"Concierto de Aranjuez for Guitar and Orchestra," and he asked Gil Evans
to produce something along the same lines for him. The result was
"Sketches of Spain." The piece had a sizable commercial success, but it is
difficult to describe it as jazz.

In "Kind of Blue," "Sketches of Spain," and subsequent albums, like
"E.S.P.," he has come a long way from "Bye Bye Blackbird." His playing
is thoroughly modal, often interrupted with tempoless stretches. He is
inflecting his line with a lot of half-valving and often intentionally letting
notes fall off pitch, as if he were mocking his own music. He is using the
upper register more. The delicacy and interest in note placement that
characterized his work previously is less in evidence, and at times, as, for
example, in "Iris" on "E.S.P.," his line is filled with vast, empty phrases,
like wind in a ruined cathedral.

But for the next several years Davis had difficulty finding a line for
himself. There were constant personnel shifts and a good deal of uncertainty
about the music. By 1964, however, at least the personnel problem was
straightening itself out. Miles had made a decision to use younger men, who
were more likely to be in tune with new audiences. He brought into the band
drummer Tony Williams, bassist Ron Carter, and pianist Herbie Hancock
— all conservatory-trained players — and added Wayne Shorter, whom he
had wanted for some time, on saxophone. All of these men went on to be
leading figures in jazz and in the fusion musics around it in the 1970s. The
group was to remain intact for four years.

The question of the music still remained. By the mid-1960s rock had
developed into something more than a music, a kind of centerpiece for a
set of philosophic or social ideas. Free jazz was still in its ascendency, and
John Coltrane was emerging as its leading apostle. Miles, however, refused
to take either of these paths, preferring to stick to the course he had been

following for a decade. The most important of the records to come out of
this period were "Nefertiti," recorded in 1967, and "Filles de Kilimanjaro,"
recorded in 1968. The cuts on "Nefertiti" are, typically, filled with open
spaces, jagged lines, and very simple melodic lines, often played in unison
by Davis and Shorter. There is strong drumming from Williams, but often
very little pulse in the horns. There are many rhythm shifts, but at points
no real meter. The piano is used largely as a solo instrument, allowing the
horns a good deal of freedom in their choice of notes. Again, the playing
is scalar. In "Filles de Kilimanjaro" Miles begins to suggest a new direction.
On some of the cuts Chick Corea comes in to play the electric piano. There
is stronger playing from everybody, and a heavier beat at times, and it is
clear enough that Miles was beginning to flirt with rock.

Neither of these records sold more than moderately, and Miles now
recognized that he had lost his place at the cutting edge of new developments in music. He had been urged by Clive Davis, then president of
Columbia Records, to face the rock challenge head-on. "In a Silent Way,"
cut early in 1969, was meant to do that. It used a number of electric
instruments, and included John McLaughlin, a guitarist associated more
with rock than with jazz. There was relatively little of the leader's own
trumpet. But this compromise was still not enough for commercial success,

A recent photo of Miles Davis, perhaps the most important trend-setter in
the history of jazz, taken during his jazz-rock period. Columbia Records

and in 1970 Miles made "Bitches Brew," a rock-oriented record sporting the full regalia of electronic devices. Again McLaughlin was featured. This album turned the trick: "Bitches Brew" sold a half-million copies in its first year, and Miles became a star of the new form called jazz-rock, or, more recently, fusion music.

Who gets credit for first amalgamating jazz and rock is difficult to pin down. Vibraphonist Gary Burton, guitarist Larry Coryell, flutist Jeremy Steig, an English group called the Soft Machine, and others had been toying with the idea from 1967 on. Billy Cobham claims that Dreams, a group he had with Randy and Mike Brecker, had been playing jazz-rock in 1969, ahead of both Davis and Weather Report. It was, in any case, an obvious idea. Young musicians who had started in rock but found it limiting were turning to jazz for new ideas, and the older jazz players were tempted to add rock elements to their work in order to hold the young audience. Many jazz musicians do not feel that this music is jazz. Nonetheless, once again Davis had been a leader, and again we see the marks of character on music.

Miles Davis has a strong personality; he is driven to dominate. Each time changes in music threatened to shove him from his place in the forefront of jazz, he managed to find systems for regaining his perch. From the mid-1950s into the seventies, a period of almost two decades, he ruled jazz, his only real challenger John Coltrane. Not even Armstrong had stood at the top of the hill so long. All through the fifties and sixties, as Davis moved from one phase to the next, he was followed by shoals of imitators, leaving behind him little schools in his passing.

But if his influence was profound, the ultimate value of his work is another matter. Miles Davis is not, in comparison with other men of major influence in jazz, a great improviser. His lines are often composed of un-related fragments and generally lack coherence. His sound is interesting, but too often it is weakened by the petulant whine of his half-valving. He has never produced the melodic lines of a Parker or Beiderbecke, or the dramatic structure of Armstrong or Ellington. And although certainly an adequate instrumentalist — we should not overstress his technical in-adequacies — he is not a great one. Perhaps more important, he has not really been the innovator he is sometimes credited with being. Most of the fresh concepts he incorporated into his music originated with other men, ironically, in view of his black militancy, many of them white. Parker and Gillespie formed bop; the birth-of-the-cool music was worked out by the Thornhill men and John Lewis; the modes had been introduced by George Russell and others; Gil Evans was largely responsible for "Sketches of Spain"; jazz-rock was already in existence when "Bitches Brew" was made. He has to be seen, then, not as an innovator, but as a popularizer of new ideas. His importance lies in the fact that he has been able to find out what ideas are in the wind, which ones have a future, and to understand what can be done with them. Over and over, he gave jazz a new direction, and this is no mean accomplishment.

By the late fifties, cool jazz, as a dominating force in the music, was dead. The experimentalists were taking over. But the cool school had created a larger audience for jazz than had ever existed before. There are issues of *Down Beat* from the 1930s in which just two jazz records — 78s, mind you — are reviewed. To be sure, the swing bands of the period had a national following, but this music was only partly jazz. Cool music was jazz, and it was popular for the simple reason that the European elements in it made it comprehensible to white audiences raised in the European tradition. It gave players like Mulligan and Getz a financial security few jazzmen had had previously, and it made Davis and Brubeck rich. For the white majority before 1950, jazz was a hobby for a handful of eccentrics; by the 1950s, especially on college campuses, it was an accepted part of the cultural scenery, something one knew about in the way that one knew about Freud, Beethoven, and Van Gogh. For jazz, then, before rock swept everything away, the 1950s were a relatively good time.

That Funky Sound:
Better Git It in Your Soul

During the early years of the fight for black rights, much of the energy and leadership came from whites. But after World War II a shift began to take place in the way blacks thought about themselves, their place in American society, and methods for bringing about change. They began to announce that the white way was not necessarily the best; that black folkways were as legitimate as any other. Blacks, who had hitherto imitated white styles in dress and deportment, began to grow Afros and wear dashikis. Hair-straighteners were despised. Soul food — the spare ribs and chitlings that were staples of the Southern black diet — was popularized, with soul food restaurants appearing in black sections of most cities. "Black is beautiful" became a watchword. More important, blacks took over leadership of the civil rights movement, with whites increasingly playing smaller parts, until by the late sixties the black rights organizations were almost entirely black.

Jazz was, of course, considered the major contribution of blacks to American culture, and black musicians were involved with the black pride movement willy-nilly. Numbers of them adopted Islam, many of them taking Muslim names. They began visiting Africa, in some cases studying African music, even playing with tribal drummers. There also began to grow a feeling among many black musicians and the black audience that jazz was black music. Not only was the white contribution denied, but some began to insist that whites could not play it properly. In some cases, black band leaders were excoriated for using white players. Cannonball Adderley, for example, was taken to task for using white pianists, and Ornette Coleman was similarly charged for his association with white bassists. The view that only blacks were authentic jazz players gained some currency, even among young white audiences, and by the 1960s some white players were complaining that they were being discriminated against.

More significant was a change in the music itself that was encouraged by the new respect for black folkways. By the mid-1950s many musicians were turning away from the cool school. Some could not understand the more abstruse experiments of people like Tristano. Still others understood it well enough, but did not like what they considered an overly intellectual approach to the music. Blacks particularly sensed that cool jazz was essentially a white movement. This was white music, European music. Jazz had lost touch with its "roots." If black was beautiful, why not play jazz in a black way? What was needed was a return to the old black culture for renewed strength and vigor.

The musical roots these players were referring to was the black-American folk music tradition out of which the blues, ragtime, and, ultimately, jazz had grown. This music still existed in the gospel churches and honky-tonks where the rural blues were sung. Despite the urbanization of the blacks in the interwar period, many of them had maintained contact with this older music. Black churches had migrated into the big cities along with their parishioners, and blues singers — or at least their records — had moved north with their audiences. Many young blacks in the 1950s had had some acquaintanceship with the old folk tradition, and some of them had grown up participating in it in church every Sunday. This gospel music came in varying degrees of sophistication. At its most primitive, as in the rural South, it was still built on the old black folk scale, with its blue thirds, fifths, and sevenths. As was the case with the early blues themselves, this music often lacks real chord changes, although at times it contains intimations of plagal cadences — fleeting movements into the subdominant. The exhorting preacher breaks into song at points in the sermon, typically using a melody that begins on the fifth and then descends through a blue fifth and blue third to the tonic. This, of course, is a very common melodic pattern in the blues. A good example is a sermon offered by Sin-Killer Griffin at the Darrington State Farm, Sandy Point, Texas, which is available on a Library of Congress recording.

Although this very primitive sort of gospel singing can still be heard in the United States, there had evolved as early as the turn of the century a more sophisticated version, built around what is known as "close" or "barbershop" harmony. Close harmony, which is derived from standard European theory, uses a lot of scalewise movement through patterns of secondary dominants to give the impression of smooth, steady flow. Gospelers in the tradition of the Fisk Jubilee Singers used this type of harmony, and several groups, the most famous of which was the Golden Gate Quartet, went on to become popular entertainers in this style.

During the fifties, black musicians began to add elements drawn from both of these styles to standard bop playing. Lines were simplified; there was a more straightforward approach to rhythm; and there was a measure of retreat from the advanced harmonies the bop players had espoused. Most particularly, the players in this expanding school began to use a lot of minor thirds and sevenths in their work. Ironically, this was due to a misunderstanding of the nature of the blue notes.

As we have seen, black folk music, and the blues and gospel music built on it, employs *blue* thirds, not the *minor* thirds that are the sine qua non of the minor keys in European music. However, most jazz musicians even today are confused on this point, and think that the blue notes are ordinary minor thirds, even when they are unconsciously playing them correctly. There is really no excuse for this mistake. Anyone with an ordinarily good ear can hear the difference, and jazz writers have been quite explicit on the subject for decades. But, unfortunately, few jazz musicians ever study their art systematically; they adopt whatever mode is being played at the time they come into the music, rarely if ever looking backward.

This heavy use of minor, then, was an attempt to recapture the sound of blues and primitive gospel music. The second type of gospel music, the one built on barbershop harmonies, was less frequently used as a base. But it appears in such compositions as "The Preacher," written by pianist Horace Silver, based on a chord sequence that had been used previously as the harmonic underpinning for, among others, "Show Me the Way to Go Home" and "Ole Miss," a college march that became a dixieland standard. "The Preacher" went on to become one of the biggest hits of this school of playing. Significantly, pseudogospel numbers like "The Preacher" did not use blue notes any more than did the attempts that relied on imitations of primitive church sounds based on the use of a minor scale. A case in point is a number called "One Mint Julep," by Freddie Hubbard, a trumpet player of the 1960s and seventies much admired for his prodigious technique. The principal theme of "One Mint Julep" is a modification of an old blues figure found in "Aunt Hagar's Blues." The fourth note of this figure is a minor seventh; an older player would have bent it into a blue seventh. The difference is a small one — a matter of one note out of five being a quarter of a tone higher — but it is crucial, for the character of the blues is changed entirely when minors are used in place of blue notes. This, however, was what was happening. Charlie Parker and the pioneer bop players had used blue notes, and even Miles Davis used them occasionally; but in the 1950s they disappeared totally from jazz.

As this new music developed, it came to be called "funk," or "soul," music. The term "soul," of course, comes from the church. The term "funk" is harder to pin down, but probably originally meant something to do with body smells; it has implications of earthiness. A third term applied to the music, one that may have been technically more sound, was "hard bop." Whatever the title, this new, simplified funky bop, with its overtones of down-home feeling, was a commercial success during the second half of the 1950s. The word "soul" was on half the jazz albums issued during this period, and anybody who could pass for funky had a chance of making money. The result in many cases was a loud, forceful, coarse-toned music that could be exciting but that suffered from a degree of sameness. The trumpeters were invariably building on Gillespie filtered through Navarro with touches of Miles; the saxophonists were finding models in Dexter Gordon, Sonny Stitt, and of course Parker; Bud Powell was the dominant influence on piano; Max Roach on drums. In form the music was in the mold Parker and Gillespie had found ready to hand in the small swing groups of Fifty-second Street. There was always an opening line, either harmonized, or in unison, often set to the chords of a standard tune, followed by a string of solos, with the line then repeated to close out the number. Characteristically, the instrumentation was the bop rhythm section of bass, drums, and piano, with trumpet and saxophone — usually tenor saxophone — out front. This limited instrumentation only added to the sameness of the sound.

One of the leading figures in the funk movement was a drummer, Art Blakey. Born in Pittsburgh in 1919, Blakey was a contemporary of the bop pioneers. He grew up knowing the black folk music at firsthand, and he came of age musically when the swing style was in its ascendancy. He was, thus, more familiar than most of the funk players with the tradition funk grew out of. He studied piano as a boy, but got married at the age of sixteen and was forced to go into the steel mills to support his family. He worked in clubs at night when he could. His switch to drums occurred at that time. He got a major break in 1939 when Fletcher Henderson formed a short-lived band, using young Pittsburgh musicians, and included Blakey. Trumpeter Vernon Smith, who played in the band, said, "It was like going to school. Smack [Henderson] would rehearse us and rehearse us at half-tempo until we could play in all those odd keys he used." After the stint with Henderson, Blakey began working around the East. Then, in 1944, he was asked to join the Billy Eckstine band, which also contained Parker and Gillespie. Eckstine's original choice was the well-regarded Shadow Wilson, but Wilson had been drafted, and Eckstine, who was from Pittsburgh and had known Blakey, gave him the job. (Blakey had a silver plate in his head, the result of a beating by police, which exempted him from the draft.) In the company of the pioneer bop players, Blakey as a matter of course developed a style that owed much to Clarke and Roach but was more direct. He was keeping time on the ride cymbal, often using the hi-hat to mark the second and fourth beats, and punctuated on the snare.

In the late 1940s he became, like a lot of other blacks, interested in his African heritage. He adopted a Muslim name, Abdullah Ibn Buhaina, took up Islam, and made a trip to Africa, where he played with tribal drummers. He continued to work with a variety of leaders, and then, in 1955, he put together the first of his Jazz Messengers. Actually, a group with that title had been organized in 1954 as a recording vehicle for Horace Silver. Blakey adopted the name and organized the group around the musicians who had been on the Silver date: Kenny Dorham, the last of Parker's young trumpet players, saxophonist Hank Mobley, bassist Doug Watkins, and Silver. For the next two decades the Jazz Messengers would continue to work steadily as a stream of musicians flowed through it.

In character, Blakey is a dominating leader and teacher. Musicians who have worked with him say that he views himself as a father to the young players he brings into the group, and who, in many cases, go on to become leaders themselves. Bobby Timmons, a pianist who worked with Blakey for a considerable period around the end of the 1950s, says, as quoted in *Jazz Masters of the Fifties:*

> He's a leader who builds other leaders. Not many men are really leaders, it has to do with more than music. Miles is one and Art's another. You learn decorum with him, and how to be a man. That little speech he gives at the end of his sets, about how jazz is our native cultural contribution to the world. Who else could get away with that speech? . . . He believes that jazz is feeling, the same as I do. But he knows about music. He's the one who taught me to build a solo to a climax.

A second important figure in the funk movement was the pianist Horace Silver, who was born in 1928 in Norwalk, Connecticut. He studied piano with a church organist and gigged around Connecticut on both saxophone and piano as a youth. Stan Getz heard him in Hartford and in 1950 hired him to work with his quintet. He then worked around New York until 1954, when he made the Blue Note recording that first established the Jazz Messengers. He remained with the group under Blakey's leadership until 1956, when he put together the first of a number of groups of his own, most of which were called the Horace Silver Quintet. (Although the name usually stayed the same, the personnel often changed.)

Silver's style is based on Bud Powell's. He employs the left-hand comping and even eighth notes that were typical of Powell and the bop pianists in general. Mixed throughout are figures drawn from the blues players and the early stride pianists. One of his earliest recorded pieces, done as a piano solo with drums and bass, was "Opus de Funk," cut in 1953. The Powell style is there, but the figures in the right hand are taken directly from the boogie-woogie fad of the 1940s. In general, though, he owes more to bop than to boogie; many of his solos are pure Bud Powell. But, like Blakey, he lays the blues figures of the gospel church over the bop cadences. Silver is not a major improviser. His phrasing is often disjointed and repetitious, moving from one unrelated figure to another. But as a widely followed representative of a major mood in jazz, his influence was considerable.

The jazz musician who had the soundest grasp of the older music was, however, neither of these, but an extraordinary character, Charles Mingus, the leading bass player of the bop and postbop period. Mingus reminds one of Jelly Roll Morton. A dominating figure in any company, he is a man of gargantuan appetites, fond of bragging about his sexual exploits, and is often directly emotional.

He was born in 1922 and grew up in Watts, the black ghetto of Los Angeles. He began on trombone at eight, but because of what he claims was bad instruction, dropped it and switched to cello. Again he says he was victimized by bad instruction, but he seems to have mastered the instrument well enough to play in the Los Angeles junior choir. He was at the same time getting a good deal of exposure to the gospel church. "My father went to the Methodist church; my stepmother would take me to the Holiness church. My father didn't dig my mother going there. People went into trances and the congregation's response was wilder and more uninhibited than in the Methodist church. The blues was in the Holiness churches — moaning and riffs and that sort of thing between the audience and the preacher."

It is probable that he also heard the work of many of the blues singers and the New Orleans bands, especially that of Morton, whose records were sold principally in ghettos like Watts. The music he was most drawn to, however, was that of the Ellington band, which he heard in concert as a youth. He switched to bass when he joined a high school dance band, and thereafter studied seriously with Red Callender, a highly respected swing bassist who at one time or another worked with Armstrong, Lester Young, and Hampton. From 1941 to 1943, Mingus worked in the last of Armstrong's big bands, and then spent a period with the New Orleans pioneer Kid Ory in a revival band. He also worked with Alvino Rey, a popular dance band leader who played atrocious Hawaiian guitar music, and then from 1946 to 1948 he worked with Lionel Hampton.

During this period he spent five years studying with a bassist who had been with the New York Philharmonic. Later Mingus worked with Red Norvo in a trio that included Tal Farlow, a guitarist much admired by musicians of the time for his technical skills. Mingus left this band because, he says, he was barred from appearing on a television show with the trio. The producer did not want to present a mixed group. At the same time he was becoming involved with the bop movement; he eventually appeared on the famous Massey Hall date.

After leaving Norvo, bitter and discouraged, he went to work for the post office for several months. But he had by this time acquired what is probably the broadest jazz experience of anybody who ever played the music. Trained primarily as a swing musician, he had had direct exposure to gospel singing and had played for considerable periods with leading figures in every jazz style from New Orleans to bop. Besides his jazz background, he had a good knowledge of European concert music. And his technique was prodigious. He has been quoted as saying, "For awhile I concentrated on speed and technique almost as ends in themselves. I aimed at scaring all the other bass players."

He was by now, with Oscar Pettiford, the leading bass player in jazz. But his major importance to the music is as a composer. He sold his first arrangements, "Mingus Fingers," to Lionel Hampton in 1947, and since that time has produced an impressive number of jazz compositions. Both in method and manner he resembles two earlier jazz composers, Morton and Ellington. At the beginning of his career he wrote out his music in the usual fashion, but very quickly he began using a system of composition that both Ellington and Morton — and indeed many of the early musicians — had used before him. It became his practice to bring to rehearsal only sketches of the final product. He would play on the piano what he wanted each player to do and would discuss with him the emotional effects he wanted to achieve. This was not a common approach. In music what usually stirs us is the working out of relationships. Notes and chords do not come and go at random, but in such a fashion as to make shifting patterns. These patterns often involve what we feel as tension and release, and probably they parallel, or in some way suggest, movements in human life that evoke our passions: separation, wedding, conflict, expectation, departure, tangency, truce, and the like. Music calls up generalized emotions or moods; very little of it is intended to raise specific feelings. For example, the titles of most of Ellington's pieces are meant to suggest moods, but not well-defined ones. "Sophisticated Lady" has a certain elegant sadness to it, but it could just as well be called "Falling Leaves" or "Winter Twilight" or some such.

Mingus, however, expected his pieces to deliver a specific emotional freight. "Fables of Faubus" has as its subject Mingus's feelings during the Little Rock school integration crisis. "Goodbye Pork Pie Hat" is "about" the grief Mingus felt at the death of Lester Young. "Lock 'Em Up" is supposed to tell us what Mingus was feeling when he was in the mental ward of Bellevue, a New York City public hospital. Mingus has said of Charlie Parker that he could make everybody in the room feel what he was feeling, and it is clear that this is what Mingus himself is aiming for. Whether it is actually possible to achieve this effect is another matter. Is one arrangement of musical notes going to affect you as it affects me? It is an exceedingly interesting question, not merely for musicians, but for any artist. Broadly speaking, the answer obviously is no. African tribal music has little to say to most jazzmen, just as jazz has little to say to tribal musicians. But assuming that audience and performers are using a musical language familiar to both, can the musician — or writer or painter or sculptor — reproduce in other people a mood or feeling that results from a specific event? Until we know more about the nature of feeling — is all anger the same, or do different causes make it feel different? — it is an impossible question to answer. And for an audience it leads to another question, which is: Do I really want to feel what Mingus felt in Bellevue?

Yet it was an interesting idea, and Mingus's attempts to put it into practice produced some music that was exciting, along with some that was not. His first forays came in 1953, when he began working with a group of younger men who called themselves the Composers' Workshop. These included vibist Teddy Charles, and Teo Macero and John LaPorta, both of whom became respected jazz writers. (LaPorta, through many years of teaching at the Berklee College of Music in Boston, has been widely influential with the succeeding generation.) Mingus began the custom of bringing in only sketches of his pieces at this time. His reasoning was that to produce jazz feeling a player cannot read notes as written, but must inflect them according to his own musical instincts. What he is feeling at the moment thus takes precedence over what the composer had intended. Mingus's method for achieving this collaboration between composer and the instrumentalists was to give each player a line or a particular scale he wanted him to use. He then explained to the player what feeling he wanted to convey, and the player was expected to use the given musical material to get the emotion across.

By Mingus's own admission, it did not always work. At times soloists simply got caught up in the music and went off in emotional directions of their own. But Mingus was often successful in making the soloists stay with the idea he had laid out, and the effect gave his music an emotional unity that is lacking in a good deal of jazz, especially where strings of soloists are at liberty to tell severally the world what kind of day they have been having. The system did tend to put the improvising musician in something of a strait jacket, though it must have been a challenging experience for the more imaginative. But Mingus was nothing if not stubborn, and he clung to his way.

The record that brought Mingus to public attention was the title tune of the album, "Pithecanthropus Erectus." The work was recorded early in 1956. Mingus said:

> The composition is actually a jazz tone poem because it depicts musically my conception of the modern counterpart of the first man to stand erect — how proud he was, considering himself the "first" to ascend from all fours, pounding his chest and preaching his superiority over the mammals still in the prone position. Overcome with self-esteem, he goes out to rule the world, if not the universe; but both his own failure to realize the inevitable emancipation of those he sought to enslave, and his greed in attempting to stand on a false security, deny him not only the right of our being a man, but finally destroy him completely.

One of the strongest individualists in a music filled with them, Charles Mingus was the pre-eminent bass player in jazz for some two decades. Columbia Records

Mingus has got his paleoanthropology wrong: the first man to stand erect was not *Pithecanthropus* but *Australopithecus,* and there is no evidence that he kept slaves, if that is what Mingus meant. That aside, the piece, which lasts about ten minutes, uses a few simple modal themes, and is remarkable mainly for the cries and "hollars" in the saxophones, and a certain amount of free playing at times, all of which is meant to suggest chest beating, perhaps primordial jungle sounds, and destruction. From the vantage point of today, the use of nonmusical tones seems hardly unusual. But in 1956 Ornette Coleman had not yet put in an appearance, and free jazz was yet to come. For the day it was a startling work, which caused comment and, as a precursor to the free-jazz movement of the 1960s, had an impact on the future course of jazz.

A second record that was widely reviewed was "Haitian Fight Song," issued in 1957 on an album called "Clown." Mingus told Nat Hentoff that it could have been called "Afro-American Fight Song," and added, "I can't play it right unless I'm thinking about prejudice and hate and persecution, and how unfair it is. There's sadness and cries in it, but also determination." This, needless to say, is a very different artistic premise from beginning with the emotion recollected in tranquillity that Wordsworth suggested and Ellington espoused.

The piece, basically a minor blues, begins with a quiet bass solo that rises in volume and then moves into a strong, repeated boogielike figure that does indeed seem to be marching implacably forward, filled with determination. Very quickly the trombone and alto come in with more strong, repeated figures, turning the determination into sheer bellicosity. The intensity rises; there are shouts and cries, and then a crescendo, out of which comes a remarkable trombone solo by Jimmy Knepper, who worked with Mingus off and on through much of the leader's most fruitful period. Openly emotional, he made a perfect foil for Mingus, and in the "Haitian Fight Song" solo he is everything Mingus could want him to be: passionate, angry, and relentless. The remainder of the record is less effective. Piano and saxophone solos, which follow, lack the ferocity of what has gone before, so the final return to the opening repeated figure, with trombone and saxophone rising in intensity as before, does not have the force it might have had had there not been that slackness in the middle. But the record is a remarkable example of Mingus's ability to use music to express specific feelings.

A similar attempt to give his compositions specific subject matter is "Better Git It in Your Soul," issued in 1959 on a record called "Mingus Ah Um," in which Mingus reproduces the atmosphere of the gospel church he worshiped in as a boy. By 1959 this was hardly a novelty; the soul-funk movement as a popular fad was dying, and the musicians themselves had long since become fed up with it. Issuing a record against a dying fad is risky, but Mingus succeeded in making this a hit, at least in jazz terms.

Where many others in the soul-funk movement were really hard boppers, using a few devices to imitate gospel music, Mingus understood its essence. This piece is not in the minor mode, which the soul-funk players used to imitate the gospel or blues sound, but in F major. The gospel cast is supplied by bent notes in the saxophones. Like gospel music, the composition shifts back and forth from tonic to subdominant — the plagal cadences common to gospel music — and there are throughout heavy, repetitive figures in the bass, often simply very rapid sixteenth notes hammered out on the tonic. This is not, however, merely a re-creation of the music Mingus heard in the church of his youth, nor is it one more mechanical soul-funk number. It is jazz used to express the real emotional sense of a gospel meeting, a musical picture of Mingus's church service, and it is wholly successful.

An even more fascinating composition is one called "Conversation," which was recorded in 1957 and issued on an LP called "East Coasting." It is exactly what the title says it is. There is nothing new about using musical instruments to imitate human voices. King Oliver had a famous routine in which he employed mutes to "preach" a sermon; and laughing trombones, crying trumpets, and sobbing clarinets have been standard novelty items in music since the days of vaudeville. But I know of no other jazz record in which an attempt is made to carry out a whole range of human discourse. The piece opens with trumpet, trombone, and saxophone playing a quiet, boppish line at octaves. It sounds uncannily like the rising and falling of a voice — somebody casually describing an event in his day, perhaps, or explaining why something had to be a certain way. This short section is followed by a conversation between saxophone, trumpet, and trombone, at first utilizing very short and often lovely figures. The voices then begin to grow contentious; they argue. Next follows a set of longer individual statements, as if each instrument were being given a chance to state his case without interruption. The statements grow briefer and more insistent as the voices, in their haste to make their points, begin to jump in before the other's are finished, until they are all jabbering away at once. They stop talking. There is a statement by the piano, and then the quiet discourse that opened the record returns to close it. It is again a wholly successful tour de force. Throughout, the musicians maintain the conversational quality, the sound of the human voice, never succumbing to the temptation simply to blow, and it is one of Mingus's major accomplishments that he is able, without the use of written music, to bring off such a composition.

His work, however, is by no means always successful. Often there are turgid passages in which neither the voice of Mingus nor the player's voice comes through. Sometimes the players simply ramble off on their own, forgetting about the particular emotional quality Mingus wants to impart. At times Mingus's ideas just do not work. But considering the difficulty of what he is attempting, Mingus has produced a considerable body of successful work. His writing of melody is individual and fresh; he always reaches for something new, never contenting himself with refashioning a current idea. Interestingly, in many ways Mingus has always remained a swing player. He prefers the simplest blues changes to the more complex substitutions the bop players had brought to them. On a blues made as late as 1972, issued on an LP called "Charles Mingus and Friends in Concert," he plays a bass line that could have been played by Walter Page in 1936.

But Mingus's allegiance to the swing era is apparent in his approach to his music as a whole. He has always preferred the direct, passionate players to the more controlled ones, which the second generation of boppers tended to be — the Jimmy Knepper or Booker Irvin to the J. J. Johnson or Paul Desmond. But Mingus, more than most jazz musicians, is difficult to tie to a given school or period. His work is marked by a rampant individualism that makes it hard to categorize. He has used materials from virtually every time and tide in jazz, often mining them with such great skill that we have difficulty sorting them out.

Mingus's greatest influence was felt from about 1955 to the early 1960s. As the leading bass player in jazz he was accorded respect by both musicians and jazz writers, and his compositional experiments attracted considerable attention. Thereafter he was less often in the center of jazz. His loss of place was due in part to the rising rock stream and the turn to free jazz, but in part it had to do with personal problems. He was at this time going through deep emotional turmoil — at one point he went to Bellevue and insisted upon being admitted. Quick to take offense, he was suspicious of club owners, record company executives, jazz competitors, whites (although he married a white woman and had many white friends), and the power structure in general, and he was marked down in the jazz business as "difficult," not, obviously, without reason. Very much involved, however, was the fact that Mingus, like many other jazz musicians of the time, was wrapped up in the civil rights movement.

Understandably, he and the others wanted to use their music to express their feelings about the struggle against inequities in this country, and they felt that whites in positions of power in the jazz world — the bookers, club owners, record company executives — were trying to stop them from doing so. Undoubtedly they exaggerated the strength of the opposition; many people in the jazz business were sympathetic to the civil rights movement, and many others didn't care one way or another. But just as clearly some people were motivated by simple fear or because they felt it was bad for business. Younger readers may be surprised to learn that, for example, in 1960 it was almost unheard-of for a black model or actor to appear in a magazine or television advertisement.

One may not like it, but one can understand the feelings of a club owner of that time who said, "Why should I book a black activist who's going to make speeches to my customers when I can get somebody just as good who won't?" This was, after all, at the time when rock was beginning to kill the jazz business. How much of this sort of thing went on — and still goes on, for that matter — is difficult to assess. But that many jazz entrepreneurs were leery of the civil rights issue there can be no doubt. At the time of the attempt to integrate the schools in Little Rock, Arkansas, the state's governor, Orval Faubus, made a national spectacle of himself by refusing blacks admission. The lyrics of Mingus's "Fables of Faubus" described the governor as a "fool" and "sick and ridiculous." On the original issue of the record Mingus was asked to leave out the vocal. Similarly, the liner notes in Max Roach's "Freedom Suite" went to great lengths to point out that Roach was talking about freedom in general, when he patently was not. The decline of Mingus's influence, then, resulted from a combination of factors: racial friction, the rise of new musical forms, and his own inner problems. But he has already given us a substantial body of work, and as a man still in his fifties he is surely capable of producing more.

In the end, however, it was not Blakey or Silver or Mingus who had the greatest influence in jazz in the 1950s, but another in the long line of tenor saxophonists who have dominated jazz for some four decades, Sonny Rollins. Rollins had often been seen as an important innovative player. He was not, as we shall see, but he was a jazz soloist of superior skills, undoubtedly the finest jazz saxophonist to emerge in the fifties. His influence stemmed less from any new conception of jazz playing than from his powerful, natural playing, which captured the admiration of so many of his peers.

He was born Theodore Walter Rollins in New York in 1930. A brother and sister both played musical instruments, and he himself studied piano briefly at eight or nine. His interest in music grew slowly. Finally, attracted by the work of altoist Louis Jordan, he took up the alto saxophone. Jordan is worth more than a footnote in contemporary music. There had developed in the late 1930s and early forties a jazz offshoot called the "jump band," a small, modified swing band that featured two or three horns in front of a rhythm section, and played an assortment of riff tunes and blues, usually fitted out with comic or off-color lyrics. This was really commercial jazz aimed at black cabaret audiences, and owed as much to the black vaudeville tradition, with its sexual and husband-and-wife sketches, as to the blues of Basie and the Kansas City school. Jump band music became one of the cornerstones of early rock; the Elvis Presley of "Hound Dog" would have fit into a jump band without difficulty. Today's rhythm and blues is, in fact, simply a modification of this style. Louis Jordan's Tympany Five was the best known of the jump bands of the period and had a wide popular following, which extended beyond the black audience.

So we see Rollins first being influenced by a hard-swinging, blues-oriented type of music, not by any of the bop experiments that were carried out during his adolescence. He came next under the influence of Coleman Hawkins, who happened to live in the same neighborhood. He switched from alto to tenor and began to develop a big, heavy sound of the type Hawkins was using. He also met two other older men who happened to live in the neighborhood, Thelonious Monk and Bud Powell. He became close to both, and they showed him a lot of things about the now-triumphant bop music. He was, of course, deeply affected by the work of Charlie Parker; and it is one of his strengths that he was able, better than any of the other saxophonists of the period, to avoid being overwhelmed by the Parker influence. Hawkins remained an important force in his playing. Rollins is thus an eclectic player with elements of both swing and bop styles in his work.

He graduated from high school in 1947 and began gigging around New York and then elsewhere. He recorded with Fats Navarro and Powell, and, in 1950, found work with a house band in a Harlem nightclub. His reputation spread, and at the end of 1951 Miles Davis, whose own reputation was growing, brought Rollins into his group. Rollins was running against the current of his time. In 1951 the influence of Lester Young was at its height, and most of the best-known saxophonists, like Wardell Gray, Stan Getz, Zoot Sims, and Paul Quinichette (whose work with Basie was so close to Lester's that he was known as the "Vice-pres"), were playing with light, feathery tones and simplified lines. Rollins's influences — Hawkins and Parker — were among the real powerhouses in jazz; they employed coarse tones and sweeping lines built on the fullest possible explorations of the chord changes.

For the next two or three years Rollins recorded with various groups, among them Davis's and occasionally under his own name. The most important of the records made during this period was a set under the leadership of Miles Davis in 1954 with a rhythm section including Percy Heath, Horace Silver, and Kenny Clarke. Several of the pieces were originals by Rollins. The records were well conceived and well performed and included nice work by Miles. Rollins's "Oleo" went on to become a jazz standard. The Hawkins influence, except in a broad way, was dropping away, and he was beginning to employ, particularly on "Oleo," the short, jagged figures, with a lot of open space in between, that were to become characteristic of his playing.

Then, in 1954, Rollins took the first of his highly publicized sabbaticals from jazz. Like many other admirers of Parker, he had become addicted to heroin. He settled in Chicago, put himself in the hands of a doctor, took a variety of jobs as a day laborer — he worked for a time as a janitor and truck loader — and kicked his habit. Within a few months Davis asked him to rejoin the group. Rollins turned down the opportunity; he did not feel ready yet. Davis then turned to an unsung young tenor player who was just beginning to make a reputation in the jazz world, John Coltrane. Although nobody could recognize it at the time, it was an omen. However, by November of 1955, after a year out of jazz, Rollins felt ready to play again. The Clifford Brown–Max Roach Quintet happened to be in Chicago, and when the group's saxophonist, Harold Land, left to return to California, Rollins joined it. Rollins, as quoted by Joe Goldberg in *Jazz Masters of the Fifties,* says, "Clifford was a profound influence on my personal life. He showed me that it was possible to live a good clean life, and still be a good jazz musician."

The record that, more than any other, made Rollins a substantial figure in jazz was not made with the Brown-Roach group, however, but with a pickup band comprising Tommy Flanagan, a consistent and much-admired bop pianist, Doug Watkins on bass, and Max Roach. The album was given the hyperbolic title "Saxophone Colossus," and it was analyzed extensively by Gunther Schuller in the first issue of *Jazz Journal.* Schuller was particularly taken by a minor blues called "Blue Seven." He pointed out that in his solos on this cut Rollins again and again derived ideas from the basic theme, elaborating on it, turning it upside down, and so forth. "What Sonny Rollins has added to the scope of jazz improvisation is the idea of developing and varying a main theme," Schuller said. Whitney Balliett praised the record highly in the *New Yorker,* other jazz writers took up the cry, and Rollins was suddenly cloaked in the mantle of genius.

It seems to me that far too much was made of this particular record. It is true that on "Blue Seven" Rollins returns over and again to a basic figure taken from the simple main theme. He had done this before; for example, on "St. Thomas," another cut on this album, or, as Schuller himself points out, on "Veird Blues," made a couple of years earlier with Davis. But this was hardly an innovation. Oliver's famous "Dippermouth Blues" solo is built around two figures, which keep returning in different forms; Armstrong builds the brief up-tempo section of "Muggles" out of variations on a skeletal figure; Davis, too, liked to play with simple figures.

Rather than seeing Rollins as "developing and varying a main theme," it seems to me better to say that he was simply dotting his line here and there with a repeated idea. Rollins's solos of this time sound as if he had broken a Parker chorus into bits and strung the pieces out in a different order. It is possible to call this a "cubist" approach to the solo. It is also possible, however, to say that Rollins was at times simply incoherent. Rollins himself, in any case, had been unaware that he was "varying a main theme," but he was an avid reader of his reviews, and for some time after he set out to do what Schuller had said he was doing. The effort only left him confused, and in time he dropped the idea and announced that henceforward he would not read anything written about him.

I think it unfortunate that Rollins felt it necessary to experiment as much as he did. When he permitted himself to play straightforward hard bop, he could be a truly magnificent improviser. During this period he made a set with Dizzy Gillespie and Sonny Stitt that contains a fourteen-minute cut called "The Eternal Triangle." The tune is based on "I've Got Rhythm," and it represents a peak of hard-driving ferocity in this style. The saxophonists solo separately, and then exchange fours and eights, rolling on minute after minute in a torrent of musical ideas. Rollins here demonstrates that he is capable of that extraordinary inventiveness, that tumbling outpouring of phrases which characterizes the work of both of his mentors, Hawkins and Parker. Here there is none of the broken, jagged phrasing that he used in "Blue Seven" and other pieces. But the jagged phrasing, which was seen at the time as "sardonic" or "humorous," foreshadowed the experimental jazz of the 1960s, and unquestionably had an impact on John Coltrane, Eric Dolphy, and others of the next decade.

The death of Clifford Brown shortly after "Saxophone Colossus" was issued was a heavy blow to Rollins, and in 1957 he left to go out on his own. He had become a star in the jazz world, and he was in heavy demand for recordings. The sides he made during this time are uneven, and Rollins himself came to regret that he hadn't exerted more control over them. He was increasingly beset by personal problems, one of them alcohol, and in 1959 he took the second of those furloughs from jazz, both to deal with his troubles and to work more formally on his instrument.

This time he was famous. Rumors ran around that he had gone mad, that he was inventing a brand-new kind of jazz, that he was in one sort of trouble or another. Actually, he was living the quiet life of a physical-fitness buff — working out with weights, eating health foods, and neither drinking nor smoking. The one rumor about him that was true was that he was practicing at nights on the Williamsburg Bridge, which runs over New York's East River. He simply liked the sound he got there. When he began to play publicly again in 1961, people were disappointed. They had expected something new, and Rollins was doing only what he had always done, if perhaps with more confidence.

He had, in any case, come back too late. The hard-bop style was exhausted, worn out by overuse. The musical language that Gillespie, Parker, and their colleagues had begun devising twenty years before was boring musicians and boring their audiences. The central problem was a lack of musical intelligence, a failure of the imagination on the part of the players in the style. They were still using the tattered format of strings of unrelated solos sandwiched between opening and closing themes. Blues, "I've Got Rhythm," and other standard tunes still provided many of the chord sequences. This would not have mattered had the boppers extended their range in other directions, by, for example, the employment of greater instrumental diversity or more variety of form. But instead of expanding, they contracted. Instrumentation was reduced to trumpet, tenor saxophone, bass, piano, and drums. Nobody was searching for different ways of doing things. It was simply line up and blow.

As had happened to dixieland a decade earlier, hard bop had come to a dead end. Indeed, by 1960 the aging players of the dixieland school were producing more interesting music than the hard boppers, not because they were necessarily better soloists, but because the dixieland form, with its polyphony, was intrinsically more interesting than the hard-bop formula. This is not to say that nobody played bop after 1960. Like all of the schools of jazz that have gone before, it is still played, still admired, still recorded. Gillespie, Rollins, Stitt, J. J. Johnson, and others continued to be active long after bop stopped being the central form in jazz. Indeed, today there is a major revival of interest in the form by a generation of players who were born around the time that Parker was dying. But in 1959 jazz was ready for something new, and it got it with a vengeance.

Cecil, Ornette,
and the Revolutionaries

All during the decade-and-a-half from the late 1940s until the early sixties, it seemed clear enough that the main line of jazz's development was from New Orleans through swing to bop. Where precisely it was going afterward, nobody was quite sure, but this line of development seemed so obvious that the term "mainstream" was coined to cover it. But jazz, as Whitney Balliett has said, is the sound of surprise, and by 1965 the mainstream had flowed into a quiet millpond.

Jazz was following a course that had hitherto appeared merely as a tributary of the main line. While everybody was watching the beboppers, a group of men who were working — if they were working at all — in obscure nightclubs, the lofts of SoHo (New York's art colony), rehearsal halls, and practice rooms were creating something new. Like the men who had made bop, they were all separately coming upon the same set of ideas; but unlike the bop players, they had no Minton's, no Billy Eckstine band in which they could share these ideas and give each other the emotional support that keeps an experimentalist confident that his work has worth. Cecil Taylor was in Boston, hammering away at a spavined piano in a ruined practice studio littered with broken glass; Ornette Coleman was practicing in a garage in Los Angeles; Steve Lacy, Roswell Rudd, and the still obscure Herbie Nichols were playing in dixieland bands for their living.

These men came from diverse musical and social backgrounds, and their approaches to music were often diametrically opposed. But disparate as their backgrounds were, they were all motivated by one idea: to "free" jazz from what they saw as restrictions of chords, ordinary harmony, bar lines, and even the tempered scale; that is, the ordinary do-re-mi notes on which Western music, including jazz, has largely been based.

This striving against musical barriers did not, of course, come out of nowhere, but was produced, as are most activating principles of this sort, by a confluence of forces. For one thing, the increasing intensity of the black rights movement through the late 1950s and into the sixties had produced a generation of angry young blacks who, not content with demanding reform of the society, wanted to overturn it entirely. Paralleling, and at times overlapping, this movement were two other intellectual currents, especially prevalent among college students. One of these was a broadening interest in Marxism, Maoism, and other shades of left-wing thought. The other was the philosophic idea, one basic to the "hippie" culture of the period, that everybody should be free to "do his own thing." Societal strictures were seen as having no utility, existing only to satisfy the power drives of those in authority.

From these related movements there grew a value system that stressed at once individual freedom and the importance of love, particularly as it manifested itself in communal enterprises in which all were willing to subordinate their personal needs to the interests of the group. That these ideas might be contradictory did not occur to many of their adherents until the system began to founder, and they were accepted as givens by many of the young people entering jazz. Blacks in particular felt a commitment to revolution. If freedom was good, then the musician ought to liberate himself from the tyranny of bar lines, chord progressions, regular tempos, and even the pitches of the tempered scale. Anything was allowed; you played as you felt.

Reinforcing this philosophic penchant for freedom in music was the interest of the conservatory-trained musicians like Taylor in trends in European concert music, dating back to the 1920s, toward the employment of chance elements, microtones, and random sounds, which were not even music at all in the old sense. John Cage and Karlheinz Stockhausen were of particular interest to this group. Finally, there was the simple fact that a lot of young musicians were bored by what they were hearing, especially bop. They were restive; they did not want to play like their musical fathers; they wanted something new.

The first of these young players to make an impact, if only among his fellow musicians, was Cecil Taylor, a pianist. The best material on Taylor is contained in A. B. Spellman's *Black Music.* According to Spellman, Taylor was born in 1933 and grew up in Corona, Long Island, a middle- and lower-middle-class suburb on the edge of New York City. There was a considerable musical tradition in the family. Two of Taylor's uncles played part-time, and a cousin was reputed to have been the first black to play on the radio. His mother, motivated by cultural aspirations for her son, pushed him into piano lessons when he was five. By good fortune there lived across the street a tympanist who was playing with Toscanini. His wife was a piano teacher of high caliber, and Taylor was able to acquire a sound foundation on his instrument from her and to study some percussion with the husband. He says, "Percussion has always been a big influence on my music."

But even as a little boy Taylor had taken an interest in jazz, especially in the leading big swing bands of the 1940s. Living as close to New York as he did, he was able to see many of these bands when they played the big theaters around Times Square, and to hear them on radio. By the end of his closing years in high school he was gigging around the New York area as a professional musician. He studied at the New York College of Music, and then, in about 1951, he began studying at the New England Conservatory. He studied piano there for three years, along with the usual courses in composition and theory. At the same time he continued to gig with bands when he could. He began to mingle with some young Boston musicians, like pianist Jackie Byard; saxophonists Gig Gryce, Charlie Mariano, and Serge Chaloff; and trumpeter Joe Gordon, never widely known to the public but a player who had an excellent reputation among the bop musicians. He became interested in the bop musicians, especially Bud Powell and Horace Silver.

But for a period in his early years in Boston he was especially drawn to the work of Dave Brubeck. He had developed a keen interest in Stravinsky, along with various of the French expressionists, and had begun thinking in terms of using these European influences in his jazz playing. Brubeck had been doing precisely this, and for a period Taylor listened closely to him and to Tristano, on whom the European influence was also marked. But in the end it was another type of piano player, Horace Silver, who affected him most deeply. He says:

> Horace was playing with Getz. Getz was all over the sax and Horace was right with him. Listening to Horace that night I dug that there were two attitudes in jazz, one white and one black. The white idea is valid in that the cats playing it play the way their environment leads them, which is the only way they can play. But Horace is the Negro idea because he was playing the real thing of Bud, with all the physicality of it, with the filth of it, and the movement in the attack.

And it is instructive to note that Taylor, in his own playing, is strong and physical.

By the time Taylor reached his majority he had turned himself into one of the best-prepared young players in jazz. He had begun to evolve an approach to music that, though similar to what a few other young musicians were attempting, was his own. It involved efforts to escape from the standard thirty-two-bar form and, most especially, to break with the chord sequence as the basis for improvising.

As I have pointed out, Western music from the time of Bach and before has been given much of its forward momentum by the shifting back and forth from consonance to dissonance. This system, however, began to break down in the nineteenth century, when composers started to use what had previously been thought of as dissonance so regularly that the older consonant chords virtually disappeared. In time, composers — Debussy is the most well known — began to see chords not as files of men marching across a plain, or as building blocks in a cathedral, but as swatches of color on a tone palette. This group of composers was beginning to see music not so much as story or drama, but as a light show, more concerned with establishing a mood than telling a tale.

In jazz, too, the movement of dissonance to consonance has always been an integral part of the music. The blues was built on the resolution of dissonant blue notes to fifths, tonics, and, rarely, thirds. Later, players like Beiderbecke and Hawkins began deliberately introducing dissonances in order to resolve them, and of course the sections of the big band used chords in the same way as Mozart used them. To be sure, the displacement of melody against the ground beat was more important than chord movement in supplying the propulsion so central to jazz, but the dissonant-consonant alternations had always been part of the music.

By about 1954 Taylor was abandoning this standard system. As the classical impressionists had done, he was using chords as swatches of color, not building blocks. He was back and forth between Boston and New York, playing occasional gigs in both places, and he had begun to develop a small following among the younger, unknown players. One of these was the white soprano saxophonist Steve Lacy, who had begun as a disciple of Sidney Bechet. Lacy started studying with Taylor, and this led to the establishment of a musical partnership. Then, in 1956, Transition, a fledgling record company that led a brief life, offered Taylor a record date. Taylor and Lacy worked for several weeks on the material they were to record. Drummer Dennis Charles and bassist Buell Neidlinger, a conservatory-trained musician long associated with Taylor, were added. The record was far short of a best-seller, but it had an impact on East Coast musicians, especially the younger ones who had some contact with Taylor.

The music on this record exhibits most of the devices — or, rather, antidevices — that became part of the free-jazz canon. A piece called "Song," for example, opens with a section in which a tempo is only vaguely suggested. Essentially a duet between piano and soprano saxophone, it lacks a clear-cut tonality. Further, although the bass and drums mark out fairly well-defined 4/4 measures, both Taylor and Lacy are at pains to shape their phrases so that they do not relate in any simple way to the bar lines. They accomplish this in part by slicing their phrases into odd numbers of beats — as Parker did — and in part by using figures that are completely unrelated to the time scheme.

But, in fact, the departures from standard jazz playing on these records are fewer than one would think on first listening. For the most part the pieces are set in some standard arrangement of measures and chord progressions, no matter how much the player may ignore them at times. "Charge 'Em Blues," for instance, is that most classic of all jazz pieces, a B♭ blues, and even contains a series of drum breaks swapped with the piano. Indeed, at moments the group uncannily suggests the Brubeck Quartet: Lacy's soprano has the same light tone that Desmond got on alto saxophone, and Taylor sometimes hammers out repeated phrases as Brubeck is wont to do. What took listeners aback — and still does, for that matter — was mostly the choice of notes, which were selected not according to any harmonic scheme derived from earlier jazz, but according to principles Taylor had picked up from the European modernists like Stravinsky and Webern. The truth is that a listener who was oriented to modern classical music would have found this music less difficult than it appeared to the jazz world.

Whether Taylor had, by the time he made the first Transition record, heard another pianist who was moving in the same direction is not known. This pianist, Herbie Nichols, is one of the few jazz musicians of whom it can safely be said that he was underrecorded. A sympathetic figure, Nichols died of leukemia in 1963 at the age of forty-four, having been recorded only four or five times, mainly as a soloist with rhythm support. He was West Indian by ancestry, and though raised in San Juan Hill, his parents had separated themselves emotionally from the ghetto life. Nichols grew up as a bookish boy and something of a home-grown intellectual. He was thoroughly trained on the piano in the European tradition, possessed an excellent technique, and was familiar with the Western repertory from the Baroque on down.

After World War II, he began working clubs — many of them strip joints — around New York, and spent the remainder of his short life playing in dixieland bands — he was one of the few black modernists sufficiently well-rounded to play the style — or backing singers in third-rate nightclubs. Fortunately, he was able to persuade Alfred Lion of Blue Note to record him in four sessions in 1955 and 1956. (He later made another solo record for Bethlehem and one with Joe Thomas for Atlantic.) Nichols thought of himself as a composer as much as a pianist. The influence of Monk is clear in his work. There are the odd, angular, somewhat broken lines that Monk favored. His chording is thicker and more dissonant than Monk's, undoubtedly because of his familiarity with European music; it contains a lot of chromatic movement. At times in his playing he sounds a little like Mel Powell. There is the same crisp accuracy and evenness of attack, and it is obvious that some of the resemblance between Powell, Taylor, and Nichols lies in the fact that they all had years of legitimate training.

What Nichols might have accomplished had he been able to work with a group of his own is a matter of speculation. Roswell Rudd, who studied with him informally for a year or so before his death, says that Nichols was always eager to orchestrate his songs for horns. Had he been able to do so it is probable, on the basis of what little we have of his work, that he would have produced some fascinating music, quite different from anything that came out of the avant-garde, and possibly changing the course of jazz. But when the time arrived when doors might have been open to him, he was dead.

It was, in any case, Cecil Taylor and not Nichols who found the open doors. While the Transition record did not sell, it helped to increase Taylor's fame in the jazz world, and in 1957 he got a break. There existed at the time in New York's East Village a neighborhood bar called the Five Spot, which catered mostly to a clientele of the raffish and the down-and-outers. It occasionally attracted some of the avant-garde painters who lived in the area and hung around at the now-famous Cedar Tavern — De Kooning, Kline, Larry Rivers. The place had sawdust on the floor, and a ruin of a piano, which was used from time to time by avocational jazz musicians who wanted a place to play. In 1957 the owners, the Termini brothers, hired a Boston musician named Dick Whitmore to bring in a small group. Whitmore hired Taylor and some associated musicians to provide the rhythm section. Taylor says:

> I had started using my Bud Powell style. But after the first night there we got into our thing, and by the third night — it wasn't even the end of the third night — there we were with all this cat's [Whitmore's] instruments piled on top of the piano, his violins and euphoniums and everything, and he was nowhere to be seen . . . Then Lacy came over and started playing with us, and we played there for about seven weeks.

Some of the painters, many of whom were already celebrated, were jazz fans; Larry Rivers was an amateur saxophonist. And having only recently won their own fight for acceptance of an art that had been characterized by many critics as childish scribbling, they were inclined to sympathize with what Taylor was doing. They began to come regularly to the Five Spot. Naturally, the presence of the artists gave the bar cachet. The press took up the place, and both Taylor and the Terminis benefited. The derelicts were cleared out, and within weeks the Terminis were booking people like Mingus and Thelonious Monk, who came in with John Coltrane for a historic stand.

As a result of the Five Spot gig Taylor became a force, however controversial, in jazz. In the summer of 1957 he was invited to play at the Newport Jazz Festival. Among his detractors were most of the established musicians, who, for one thing, could not understand what Taylor was doing, and, for another, were afraid that they were about to be pushed aside by a new music, just as they themselves had pushed aside a previous generation. But

if Taylor's detractors outnumbered his supporters, he still had some powerful people in his camp. When he played the Great South Bay Festival in
1958 he got an approving review from Nat Hentoff, one of the most influential critics in jazz. He had enough publicity attached to his name to get
another record date, this one with a major label, United Artists, which
resulted in an album called "Love for Sale." Surprisingly, some of the lines
Taylor wrote for this date were very much in the soul style. However, they
tended to wander in and out of odd time signatures, a device introduced into
jazz by Tristano, and common enough in European music. "Motystrophe"
moves into 3/4 in places, and "Little Lees" has measures that contain an
extra half beat, a practice that became widespread in the jazz rock of the
1970s. But Taylor's own playing was growing thicker in texture and even
less readily grasped than it had been on the Transition record. His solo on
"I Love Paris" appears to have little in common with the song, aside from
a rough paraphrase that Taylor uses for an introduction.

But whatever the renown Taylor had gained in the jazz world, he continued to have difficulty finding playing jobs. Most listeners were confused
by his work, finding it too difficult to comprehend. Consequently, Taylor
at times was forced to take day jobs, often menial ones, to support himself.
And still his work became, if anything, more difficult. By the time of "Unit
Structures," one of his best-known records, he had gone all the way into
free jazz. The piece entitled "Unit Structure/As of Now/Section" lacks
regular tempo, bar lines, a chord progression — or indeed anything that
could conventionally be described as chords — and it uses a great many
notes of indefinite pitch.

While Taylor was beginning his studies at the New England Conservatory, another young musician, who was to have an even greater impact on
jazz, was making some first fumbling steps in the direction Taylor was
taking. Ornette Coleman is without doubt the most controversial musician
in the history of jazz. He was resented and hooted at by musicians twenty
years ago, many of whom walked off bandstands when he appeared, and he
is intensely disliked by many musicians today, although he has become an
accepted figure in the world of jazz.

The best source for information on Coleman is the Spellman book. Coleman was born in Fort Worth, Texas, in 1930. His father died when he was
seven, and Ornette has few memories of him. He was reared in poverty and
sorrow, but fortunately in a family where there was common care and
concern. In his early teens a number of his friends joined a local church
band. Ornette wanted to join, too, but there was no money for a horn. He
begged his mother for one, and she told him she'd buy him one if he would
get a job and contribute something to the family income. We are talking,
remember, of a time when a brand-new student's instrument from Sears,
Roebuck might cost seventy-five dollars, and hockshop horns were selling

Cecil Taylor and his group at the Newport Jazz Festival in 1957, as they were making the publicity breakthrough that called attention to the burgeoning avant-garde or free-jazz movement. From left, Buell Neidlinger, Taylor, Steve Lacy, and Dennis Charles. None of the men in the group was over twenty-four. Bob Parent

for twenty-five and often a lot less. Coleman got a job, and one night his mother woke him up and told him to look under the bed. There he found an alto saxophone.

There was, however, no money for lessons, a constant problem faced by many youthful black musicians, and Coleman undertook to teach himself to play. A great deal has been made by writers of the idea that Coleman misunderstood the fact that the alto saxophone, like most wind instruments, is a transposing instrument. As a consequence, alto saxophone music is written in keys that differ from the true keys of the music in order to correct for this discrepancy. Coleman apparently did not understand this. Some writers have felt that this error was somehow responsible for his interest in free music. The theory is a dubious one. The error is one many young musicians have made, and is quickly corrected by a little experience.

Despite his problems, in time Coleman picked up enough grasp of music to begin playing with rhythm-and-blues bands around Fort Worth. He had a cousin named James Jordan, a well-schooled saxophonist, who helped him, and there was a local alto player named Red Connors who had him listen to records of Parker and other boppers. By the time he graduated from high school Coleman had learned enough to go on the road with a traveling variety show. He was playing tenor saxophone in this group, and he got as far as Natchez, where he was fired for trying to interest other players in jazz. One of them told the owner that Ornette was "trying to turn the player into a bebopper."

His next job, in 1949, worked out no better. This one was with a rhythm-and-blues band run by a man named Clarence Samuels. Ornette got as far as Baton Rouge this time, when a group of blacks beat him up and destroyed his saxophone. He had not done anything to deserve this treatment, and it has been suggested that the locals had become angry at seeing traveling musicians steal their girl friends. Possibly Coleman became the target because he had attracted the attention of some women, but probably because of his appearance, and perhaps because of the way he was playing. Still in his teens, Coleman had already adopted the role of the rebel, the outsider who goes his own way.

He landed in New Orleans, and after six months there caught on with another rhythm-and-blues band, this one run by a Fort Worth musician named Pee Wee Crayton. The band was working its way to Los Angeles. Coleman continued to introduce his new ideas into his solos, and by the time the band reached its destination Crayton was paying him not to play. In Los Angeles he was fired. He was to stay in the city for the next nine years, except for a single trip back to Fort Worth. As it turned out, Los Angeles musicians didn't like what he was doing any better than Pee Wee Crayton had. After a few exposures, his attempts to sit in with jazz bands around the city were met with hostility. Sometimes musicians walked off stands when he came on to play. In other cases they would not ask him up until the tag end of the evening, when everybody had gone home. Dexter Gordon once peremptorily ordered him off the stand. The musicians insisted that he didn't know the chord changes and that he played out of tune. It didn't help matters that he had long hair and a beard, and often dressed oddly. The jazz world is filled with eccentrics who wear unusual clothes, pronounce strange mystic philosophies, and insist that they can play when in fact they lack even an elementary knowledge of music. Coleman was taken as another of these and was turned away by other musicians. This hostility wounded him badly. He said, "They said I didn't know the changes and was out of tune, but I knew that wasn't so. But something, I thought, must be wrong. I didn't know what."

What was wrong? Any jazz musician can play out of tune at times, especially if he has been drinking heavily, and he may occasionally miss a chord change or fumble his way through a tune with which he is not familiar. But it is rare for a jazz musician of much experience to fail to hear that he is playing incorrect changes. The simple truth is that most professional jazz players can correctly identify the chord changes of a tune on first hearing, provided that they are not too unusual, and improvise a suitable solo to them. The fact that Coleman could not understand what he was doing wrong tells us something about him.

A musician who hires out to a rhythm-and-blues band and then insists on playing something quite foreign to the music is either being perverse or doesn't know what he is doing. Although Coleman has been self-defeating at times, the feeling persists that part of his trouble was that he really was not entirely sure of what he was doing. He was not hearing the chords, and he did not really know what notes were in them. Learning what notes go into the hundred or so basic chords on which virtually all jazz is played is about as difficult as learning to conjugate twelve regular French verbs. All are built from the basic twelve major triads, according to a few simple rules. Learning to hear chords is harder and takes experience, but it is something that young jazz players do as a matter of course. Why Coleman failed to do so is a puzzle. It is always risky to analyze at long distance, but it seems clear enough that something, somehow, was interfering with Coleman's understanding of some basic musical principles. Long after he had become a major figure in jazz he still did not know how to read or write music correctly. We can also deduce, from the way he was composing, that he did not really understand music theory, even to the modest degree that many improvising musicians know it.

Ornette Coleman, then, must be seen as a primitive artist. I do not mean at all to deprecate him with this term. A primitive artist is one not trained in the standard tradition, who develops his method and manner independent of the main line. The Douanier Rousseau, whose *Sleeping Gypsy* most people are familiar with, was a primitive whose work is now in important museums. Ornette Coleman's lack of standard music theory in no way invalidates his work. But where Coleman Hawkins knew chords inside out and could tell you the precise harmonic function of any note that he played, Ornette has been quoted as saying, "I don't know how it's going to sound before I play it than anyone else does." Coleman Hawkins knew exactly how it was going to sound before he played it, as indeed do most jazz musicians. Charlie Parker was reputed to be able to think so far ahead in his soloing that he might change the line several times in his mind before he got to it.

There seems, thus, to be an element of chance, or randomness, in Coleman's improvising, and at a time when classical composers are deliberately introducing chance elements into their work, we can hardly fault Coleman for this practice, even when it is not always intentional.

Given Coleman's deviant methods, it is hardly surprising that jazzmen did not like his playing. Through most of his nine years in Los Angeles he was forced to work as a day laborer to support himself, a situation that was worsened by a marriage and the birth of a son, Denardo. But through his wife he met a young trumpet player named Don Cherry. Cherry, only nineteen at the time, had begun to make a reputation with the local jazz musicians as a coming trumpeter of the Fats Navarro–Clifford Brown school. He was impressed by Ornette. He began working out with Coleman, and gradually there gathered together a small group of dedicated young musicians who labored in a garage belonging to one of the men. They worked on tunes composed by Coleman, and developed the style of improvising that Coleman was pioneering.

They might have continued to work in obscurity had they not been heard by Red Mitchell, an established bass player with whom Cherry had worked. Mitchell suggested that Coleman bring some of his tunes to Lester Koenig, the owner of a small record company called Contemporary. As the story goes, Coleman and Cherry took the tunes around to Koenig. After struggling to pick them out on the piano for Koenig's benefit, Coleman gave up, and he and Cherry played them on their horns. Koenig was interested. They played him some other tunes, and when they finished Koenig suggested that they themselves record the tunes for him. On February 10 and 22, 1959, Coleman and Cherry, with bassist Don Payne, pianist Walter Norris, and drummer Billy Higgins, cut a record that Koenig issued as "Something Else!!!!" The record did not go anywhere, but it did bring in a little work, and it established for the group a sort of legitimacy. Then Don Payne brought bassist Percy Heath, from the Modern Jazz Quartet, to hear Coleman. Heath says, "I jammed with him. It sounded strange but it felt very good and it felt fresh. I don't say I understood it, but it was exciting and that's one quality jazz has to have. But believe me, those guys were starving then, and musicians were still walking off the stand when Ornette came in."

Heath in turn brought John Lewis to hear Coleman. Lewis was more than impressed; he was highly enthusiastic. He arranged for Coleman and Cherry to attend a summer jazz school that then existed in Lenox, Massachusetts, an institution with which various jazz powers, including Lewis and Gunther Schuller, were connected. Before they left Los Angeles they cut a second record for Contemporary, this one called "Tomorrow Is the Question." Now the balloon went up. Controversy swirled around the two men while they were at Lenox, but they had the support of some of the most prestigious figures in jazz, including Lewis, Schuller, and two of the most respected of jazz critics, Hentoff and Martin Williams, both of whom wrote enthusiastic liner notes for various of Coleman's records. The upshot was an engagement at the Five Spot that November and a new record contract with Atlantic, which shortly issued two more albums, "The Shape of Jazz to Come," and "Change of the Century."

The Five Spot gig threw the jazz world into turmoil. At first few musicians liked the music, or even pretended to understand it, and some were outspoken in their contempt for it. It did not help that Coleman was playing a plastic alto, which produced a particular sound he liked, and that Cherry was using a pocket trumpet, a half-sized instrument that plays normally. It looked as if they were playing on toys. But all musicians, those who liked the music and those who did not, had the uneasy feeling that here indeed might be the future, and that just as Parker and Gillespie had thrown the swing players into obsolescence, so Coleman was about to make them outmoded. Coleman was even chic, and was for a while taken up by members of New York's art and high-fashion circles, the same sort of people who touted novelty painters. For Coleman it must have been an extremely heady time. Only months before he had been an obscure — indeed, despised — out-of-work musician, practicing in a garage. Now he was a lion, befriended by famous people and written up in the magazines.

Looking at Coleman in retrospect, it is hard to see what caused so great a furor. The jazz audience at least had been prepared for his innovations by the work of Tristano and of Mingus especially, who had used in "Pithecanthropus Erectus" many of the off-pitch shouts and cries Coleman and his players were using. Moreover, Coleman's playing was much more a continuation of the mainstream than it seemed at first listening. In the first place, most of the early pieces consisted of solos sandwiched between opening and closing themes, the standard bop formula. In the second place, Coleman and his principal associate, Cherry, had evolved directly out of bop. The marks of Charlie Parker are everywhere in Ornette's playing. He lacks the long, sinuous line that Parker was able to create, but the strong rough-edged quality of Parker's playing is there, as well as many recognizable Parker cadences. (Like Parker, Coleman enjoys quoting. He opens his solo on "Congeniality" with a quotation from "The Flight of the Bumblebee" and later quotes "The Peanut Vendor" and "Tonight We Love," a popular song of 1941 derived from Tchaikovsky's Piano Concerto in B-Flat Minor.) Cherry too was from the same school: his solo on "Alpha" could have been cut by any first-rate bop trumpeter ten years earlier. The blues influence on both players was strong. "Tears Inside," for example, is an old-fashioned swinger with much of the funk feel of the hard boppers.

Finally, Coleman's tunes were almost entirely in the ordinary major-minor system, and except for some interesting switches of meter, would cause no high school musician any difficulty. As even his detractors recognize, Coleman is a superior, perhaps even superb, writer of short melody. Tunes like "The Disguise," "Angel Voice," and "Congeniality" are fresh

and bright, and his dirges, especially "Peace" and the extraordinarily haunting "Lonely Woman," are as fine bits of melody as anything written by a jazz musician. "Congeniality," for example, opens with a four-bar introduction made up of the last bars of the theme. The theme itself begins with three measures in slow 3/4, followed by eight measures of fast 4/4. The entire theme is played four times, both at the opening and closing of the cut, where it is followed by a two-bar coda.

But if the themes are often melodically a little more complex than has been customary in jazz, the chord changes on which the soloing is based are simplicity itself. Most of them are cast in the ordinary thirty-two-bar form and usually are built out of some variation on "I Got Rhythm" or a similar tune. "Chippie" uses the "I Got Rhythm" chords with a somewhat different bridge, and "Angel Voice" is built on a variation of "Honeysuckle Rose." Nor are the improvised solos quite as free as they seemed originally. Coleman often plays long stretches of first-rate, straightforward jazz, with a warm, broad tone, and, curiously enough, occasional phrases that suggest Benny Carter. On "Alpha" he actually plays a fragment of Carter's famous solo on "I Can't Believe That You're in Love with Me." Especially on some of the blues pieces, such as "Tears Inside," and "Giggin'," he plays with great strength and feeling, mainly within the ordinary blues compass. He plays, as on "Giggin'," way behind the beat, and had he chosen to continue working in a more standard vein he would unquestionably have been one of jazz's finest blues players, probably in a style combining aspects of Parker and Young.

What is most interesting to note — and was missed at the time, even by musicians who were listening to them — is that the solos were cut strictly according to standard metric frameworks. That is, if a theme was thirty-two bars in length, the solos would be cast over some multiple of thirty-two bars, in exactly the same fashion as Parker or Armstrong or Teagarden cut their solos to the song. For example, on "Chronology" Cherry plays precisely four thirty-two-bar choruses, and with a little concentration you can hear him quite clearly indicate the eight-bar segments of the tune in the shape of his solo.

But the harmony was another matter. Here freedom was king. The chord changes were ignored, and the player was really free to introduce what often appeared to be foreign elements, some of them simple cries and grunts. Coleman's playing in general tends to stay within a very limited harmonic compass. His solo on "Congeniality" is built almost entirely on a B♭ major chord, with occasional brief excursions into C minor. Similarly, his chorus in "Ramblin' " is principally in D, with some shifts into G — again the

Opposite: Ornette Coleman in the 1970s, the avant-garde player who has never truly been accepted into the jazz establishment. Columbia Records

subdominant, that plagal cadence we have seen so much of. This way of playing is essentially modal and should have caused no problems for musicians of the time. What threw them off was the jagged phrasing, the off-pitch honks and grunts, and the way Coleman had of spilling out broken fragments of melody in what seemed to be random fashion. But once the ear becomes accustomed to the cries, honks, shouts, and grunts, you discover that Coleman is an astonishing improviser. His line is strong, his feelings intense and audible in the music; and the conversational quality so important to the best jazz playing is everywhere evident. Any listener capable of reacting to the work of Parker or Young should quickly find his way into these early pieces of Coleman's. Cherry is not so strong an improviser, and he frequently has intonation problems, but if anything, his playing is more accessible than Coleman's.

But by 1960 Coleman was moving farther afield, and in that year he issued one of the most important records in the avant-garde movement. This was "Free Jazz," by a group Coleman chose to call a double quartet, presumably after the model of the double quartets used by Gabrieli at opposite ends of the nave of San Marco, in Venice. The personnel consisted of bassists Charlie Haden and Scott La Faro, drummers Higgins and Blackwell, trumpeters Cherry and Freddie Hubbard, and clarinetist Eric Dolphy, as well, of course, as the leader. The group is split in two, with one section heard on the right-hand speaker, the other on the left. Beyond this, the resemblance to the double quartets of Gabrieli is slight, to say the least. The piece has no tempo, no bar lines, no chords, no clinging to the strict pitch. Even the long introductory passages contain little real melody. Each soloist is introduced by the playing of a brief theme. These themes are simply series of a dozen or so long notes played by groups of instruments. They are set in what Coleman calls "harmonic unison," which, according to Martin Williams's notes, means that "each horn has its own note to play but they are so spaced that the result will not sound like harmony, but like unison." What precisely this statement means is hard to understand. The passages do not sound anything like unison; they sound like fairly dissonant harmony. These introductory passages are about all the form the work has.

Many early listeners had problems with this kind of music because they kept looking for underlying principles that were guiding the players in their choice of notes when, in fact, there were no underlying principles. All is random. Coleman explained, "We were expressing our minds and emotions as much as could be captured by electronics." The supporting players were supposed to be listening to the soloist and producing phrases that would somehow complement what he was doing, and it seems to have been assumed that they would avoid phrases that might suggest chords or tonalities. These slight limitations aside, the musicians were to play anything they felt like playing. Roswell Rudd, in speaking of his own efforts at free jazz, has said:

> Soloists could play by free associating the melody without reference to the bar lines. Maybe stick with the first three notes or something. One guy would take the lead. If he stayed on the first bar for five minutes everybody would go with him. You could put the chords in any sequence you wanted.

The "Free Jazz" album jacket was illustrated with a reproduction of *White Light,* a famous painting by the abstract expressionist Jackson Pollock. The painting is entirely abstract, lacking anything that could be called a picture of something. Lines and curves of color swirl through each other in a seemingly random fashion, although of course the total effect adds up to considerably more. "Free Jazz" was supposed to be a sort of parallel to this kind of painting. There is the same sort of randomness, the same lack of obvious linkage between the parts; but the total effect, the players hoped, would add up to something more.

There was, however, no general agreement that it did. A lot of clubs would not book Coleman, and he continued to be the center of controversy in the press, with some musicians insisting that he was a genius and others, a fraud. But he was now able to get a reasonable amount of work at respectable fees, and it seems likely that he would at least have been able to support himself by his music. What he did instead was drop out of public sight. The cause, apparently, was a gig he played at the Jazz Gallery, a club opened by the Terminis in Greenwich Village to capitalize on the new jazz wave. Coleman was getting something like $1200 a week for his group, playing to a packed house each time. He discovered that Dave Brubeck was getting something like $4000 a week at the same club and not drawing as well as Coleman had done. (These figures are my estimates, based on a variety of sources.) He had already been embittered by what he had experienced in the big-time jazz scene. He was having drug problems with his sidemen, who kept demanding advances in order to pay their suppliers; he had been vilified by other musicians; and the matter of Brubeck's fee seemed to him the last straw. He thereupon raised his fee into Brubeck's range, and after that nobody would hire him.

The gesture was both naive and self-defeating. Whatever he felt about his drawing power and his importance relative to Brubeck as an artist, the fact remained that Brubeck had an enormous popular following and Coleman was a highly controversial player who had only recently become known to the jazz public.

The nightclub business is hard and often ruthless. It is not entirely governed by the Mafia, as some jazz musicians think, but there has always been a criminal element involved. Nobody in jazz believes that things ought to be this way, or that jazz musicians should have to create in what are often exceedingly depressing circumstances — bars where the cash register rings incessantly, where the length of tunes is tailored to the need to sell drinks during the breaks, where the audience is ignorant of the music and drunks badger the band to play tunes totally outside their métier. Jazz musicians have always spoken bitterly about the nightclub situation, which is why players like Brubeck, Miles Davis, and others who can get away with it concentrate on college dates and theater concerts. Unfortunately, few jazz musicians have taken the trouble to inform themselves about the economics of the nightclub business and are therefore unable to estimate how much money the band is bringing in. There are few clubs in the United States even today that can pay $4000 a week to any but the biggest draws, and most cannot pay that much under any circumstances.

Club owners and bookers simply said they couldn't pay the fee he asked for — which was generally true — and if he wouldn't work for the price they offered, then somebody else would. As a result Coleman was out of jazz from 1962 until 1965, by which time he realized the futility of his gesture and scaled down his salary demands.

By that time free jazz, or "the new thing," as musicians had come to call it, was firmly established in the jazz world. It did not take over entirely, as bop had done. Its audience was too limited for it to be presented at more than a handful of clubs, and while college students sometimes booked some of the new-thing players out of curiosity, rock was the chief musical interest of youth during the period, and an Ornette Coleman or a Cecil Taylor could not count on the highly profitable college tours that Brubeck, Davis, Adderley, and others had been making. But the new music was being played in public; its exponents were being recorded; it was provoking comment in the jazz press; and it was attracting the interest of many young jazz players. By the mid-1960s there were a number of young players at home in the new style, among them saxophonists Archie Shepp, Albert Ayler, Steve Lacy, and a Danish black, John Tchicai; trumpeter Don Ayler; drummers Sunny Murray and Milford Graves; and trombonist Roswell Rudd.

The one who had the widest following after Coleman and Cecil Taylor was Archie Shepp. In Shepp we have the case of a player who appears to have been more concerned with his ideology than his art. A college graduate with a special interest in literature, he made himself a spokesman for the young black avant-garde jazz musicians of his time. He was born in Fort Lauderdale, Florida, in 1937 and grew up in Philadelphia, where his parents moved in search of better jobs. He began to study the piano at ten and eventually the reeds. He began working with a rhythm-and-blues group called Karl Rodgers and His Jolly Ramblers.

He went to college at seventeen, and in 1959, after he graduated, he moved to New York, where he got work playing in a coffee house. Dave Pike, a bassist associated with Cecil Taylor, heard him there and recommended him to Cecil Taylor. He joined Taylor and appeared on his record "The World of Cecil Taylor." But after a week on a gig at the Five Spot, Taylor fired him. Because he found it difficult to get work as a sideman, Shepp formed a group with avant-garde trumpet player Bill Dixon, which recorded for Savoy. In this record the rhythm-and-blues influence is still strong in Shepp's work, but the mark of Ornette Coleman is there.

Then, in 1963, he joined the New York Contemporary Five, with Don Cherry and John Tchicai. This was strictly an avant-garde group, and it worked briefly in Denmark, Tchicai's birthplace, but broke up when it could not find jobs. By this point John Coltrane had taken an interest in Shepp, helping him where he could and getting him a recording contract. Shepp expressed his thanks with an album, under his own leadership, of four Coltrane tunes — "Syeeda's Song Flute," "Mr. Sims," "Cousin Mary," and "Naima" — as well as Shepp's own "Rufus." The album, called "Four for Trane," is by no means entirely free music. The rhythm section of drummer Charles Moffett, who had worked with Coleman, and bassist Reggie Workman, who had worked with Coltrane, for the most part plays a hard-driving beat in 4/4, which would not have been amiss in a bop group. The solos, however, are freer, with patches of jagged diatonic playing as well as cries and moans. There is strong playing by Rudd, who uses a coarse, cutting tone and a style that owes a good deal to Bill Harris, especially the smears and broad terminal vibrato. Shepp shows signs of having been influenced by various saxophonists: Hawkins, Ben Webster, Johnny Hodges; and at times he even sounds like Pete Brown, a bouncy, rhythmic altoist of the swing period. The record sounds far less shocking today than it did when it was issued.

"Four for Trane" proved to be Shepp's most important record, and it established him as a figure in the avant-garde. Over the next few years he was the subject of a number of interviews, especially in *Down Beat,* England's *Melody Maker,* and *Jazz,* a journal strongly supportive of the experimental musicians and the ideology of black rebellion. Shepp was literate, intelligent, and outspoken, and his statements, which sometimes owed more to passion than to reason, made him a lightning rod for the anger of those who disliked the new music. During the late 1960s he was a figure of contention in jazz, and it was sometimes difficult to know whether the quarreling was over his music or his political ideas, so intertwined had the two become in the minds of people on both sides. Shepp's position was that the two were indeed related. He said, "We are not angry men. We are enraged . . . I can't see any separation between my music and my life. I play pretty much race music; it's about what happened to my father, to me, and what can happen to my kids. They can't blow up three children and a church without its somehow reflecting itself in some aspect of your cultural development." His opponents, many of them whites who thought of themselves as political liberals, responded that jazz belonged to whites as well as blacks, that not all whites were bigots, and that music and the black cause should not be confused. Shepp's rebuttal was that liberalism was merely a more subtle scheme for keeping the black man in his place, and the liberal rebuttal was that Shepp had lost sight of reality in his passion for his cause. It was a debate that could have no conclusion, and in the end it expired as the social turmoil of the sixties died away. In any case, Shepp's playing toward the end of the decade became gentler and more accessible.

Next to Shepp, the musician in the second line of the avant-garde who caught the most attention was another saxophonist, Albert Ayler. Ayler occasionally played alto saxophone and at times odder instruments, such as the slide whistle, but his principal instrument was the tenor saxophone. On it he got a distinctive dry sound, which, in the upper registers, where he played a good deal, had some of the shrillness of a primitive flute. He was particularly influenced by Cecil Taylor. He began to have an impact on the jazz public, notably the one that was interested in free jazz, in 1964, when his first records began to appear. His playing was largely free, utilizing nontempered pitches, and was characterized not so much by the abrupt, slashing figures of Coleman as by long, rather ceremonious looping phrases and swoops, based on held notes. Much of his work was tempoless, and he used the upper-register harmonics much employed by saxophonists of the style. He tended to work with small groups — often including only his brother, trumpeter Don Ayler, a bass, and a drum. Typical is the piece called "Saints." The first half consists of a solo by Ayler containing many long notes and slow runs, punctuated at intervals by brief trumpet fragments and supported by minimal drum and bass playing. There is a brief bass interlude, the trumpet constructs a solo of fragments of the tempered scale, and then Ayler joins in for a short finale.

Toward the end of his career Ayler began playing in a much less free fashion. His work took on a strong streak of rhythm-and-blues phrasing; indeed, of gospel playing. Pieces like "New Ghosts" and "Sun Watcher" are really gospel music, employing the typical plagal cadences and using piano figures that could have come straight from a storefront church. Much of this later work was modal, as, for example, "Love Cry," which is built on a two-note figure, or "Universal Indians," in which the trumpet plays again and again a two-note figure on a fourth. When Ayler began playing in this more conservative style he was criticized by many of his followers for selling out. In fact, a valid criticism that can be leveled against Ayler's work is that it is dull. The long, slow phrases that characterize his work have none of the melodic inventiveness of the best of Coleman's work. Nor is there anything approaching the harmonic interest to be found in the playing of Cecil Taylor. Concerning rhythm as well, Ayler has little new to add, and this lack of inventiveness, coupled with his dry sound, the minimal instrumentation, and the spareness of the playing on his records in general, produces a total effect that is often monotonous. An example is "Witches and Devils," a piece that runs on for almost twelve minutes with very little development or movement. Ayler died under mysterious circumstances in 1970.

Another figure in this genre who is sometimes considered a jazz musician is Sun Ra, a pianist who in another incarnation worked briefly with Earl Hines. Ra is leader of what he calls the Intergalactic Arkestra, or Intergalactic Research Arkestra. The music appears to exist not so much for itself but as an adjunct to a complicated religion. I have not investigated it in any depth, but it seems to be a mélange of ancient Egyptian mythology and Christian ideals of brotherhood wrapped in a cosmic mantle. Ra has explained that he came from Saturn as a prophet to make us citizens of the universe. The Arkestra, in any case, consists of a varying number of players, up to as many as twenty-two, and employs different kinds of drums, woodwinds, and strings, as well as electric organs and synthesizers. The members play freely much of the time. There is, of course, nothing unusual in music being at the service of a religion. Bach, Handel, Palestrina, to name just a few, wrote a great deal of music meant primarily to accompany ceremonies of the Christian church. Ra's philosophy of itself need not detract from his music. Nonetheless it is difficult to describe as jazz the music on, say, "It's After the End of the World: Sun Ra and His Intergalactic Research Arkestra Live at the Donaueschingen and Berlin Festivals," and I will therefore leave it to another critic.

Another player who is often grouped with the experimentalists is Rahsaan Roland Kirk, who plays a variety of woodwinds, some of his own invention. Kirk's music is an outgrowth of the hard-bop school. His own writing, in fact, is often so straightforward harmonically that it appears to be rooted in prebop jazz. But his use of odd instruments, like the nose flute and his inventions, the stritch and the manzello, coupled with forays into free playing, has attracted to him some of the same audience that follows "the new thing." Actually his music is usually much more easy to grasp than that of most of the other members of the school. This may have something to do with his steady, however modest, popularity.

It is not surprising that the new music developed a considerable following in Europe — considerable, that is, in terms of jazz audiences. More Europeans than Americans have become familiar with advanced tendencies in classical music, and this has made them more receptive to the experiments of the jazz avant-garde than Americans have been.

There were concerts of free jazz in Berlin in 1965 and in London in 1966.

Coleman, Taylor, and others found that they could play successful concerts and even make tours in Europe at a period when they were having difficulty finding work in the United States, and in the end several of them, including Don Cherry and Steve Lacy, settled there.

Today — and it seems quite astonishing — free jazz is a generation old. Archie Shepp, the angry young man of the movement, has turned forty; Cecil Taylor is in his mid-forties; and Ornette Coleman is nearly fifty. The movement is middle-aged, and it is apparent that whatever mark it was to make on jazz has already been made. One difficulty we have in judging how large a mark that is stems from the belief of many of its adherents that it was more than a musical style; it was a cause. Since the death of Keats, art in the Western world has been afflicted by a rampaging avant-gardism. Critics, audiences, and artists themselves are conscious of the fact that many people scorned in their times or even ignored have often turned out to have been seminal figures. Who has not turned wet-faced from the lines on Keats's headstone in the Protestant cemetery in Rome:

> This grave contains all that was mortal of a young English poet, who, on his deathbed, in the bitterness of his heart, and the malicious power of his enemies, desired these words to be engraven on his tombstone "Here lies one whose name was writ in water."

And Keats was hardly the only one. There was Van Gogh selling only two pictures in his lifetime; Joyce unable to find a publisher for *Ulysses;* Turner scorned by his early admirers when he took up the style on which his lasting fame rests; Stravinsky and the rest hissed at their early performances. The list is endless. Of course critics are today made nervous by the incomprehensible newcomer; each worries lest he should become a footnote to history as a denigrator of the new Joyce or Van Gogh. Artists often convince themselves that the very fact that they are ignored is a sign of their greatness. As a consequence new movements in art often receive more réclame than they deserve, and this is especially true when they are associated with antiestablishment social or political movements.

The free-jazz movement of the 1960s had strong ideological components, mostly based on those contradictory calls for individual expression of feeling and for love, collective activity, shared concerns. These ideas were consciously used as bases for creation by many of the avant-garde players. Archie Shepp said, "When my own dreams sufficed, I disregarded the western musical tradition altogether." For some musicians, the whole point of the music was no longer the reaction of the audience, but the emotional interaction of the musicians themselves. It came to be a sign of success when a musician could say, "There was a lot of love going on up on the stand tonight." Too much soloing, said many of these players, smacked of self-aggrandizement. Collective improvisation was seen as desirable, and it was no accident that the term "collective" had political overtones. For example, the drum was brought forward as a voice in the ensemble, rather than being left as the supporting instrument it had always been, precisely because it was felt that all men were equal and that no one player should be put in a subordinate role.

The unanswered question is whether social theory is a proper base for a working aesthetic. In the past, of course, art has often been put at the service of ideology. We think of the celebration of Christianity in the quattrocento and cinquecento paintings and the oratorios of Bach and Handel, of the underdoggery of Dickens, of the swingeing of the establishment's hypocrisy in Rabelais and Swift, of the antirationalism of the beatnik and hippie writers of the post–World War II era. Works like these are often taken up as much for their ideology as for their aesthetic merits. As the force behind the ideology wanes, they must draw their audiences by their own attractiveness, and those that cannot will fall through the sieve of history.

But there is a difference between using ideology as content and using it as a means for producing that content. The Christian church may have expected the fifteenth-century painters to make pictures of religious scenes, but they did not insist that certain colors were holier than others, or that perspective was an invention of the Devil. Similarly, although a few of the antirationalist writers, William Burroughs, for example, used antiforms to express this viewpoint, most of them used the language of reason to insist on its impotence. But the free-jazz players were using their ideology as a means, a method, indeed a language. Whether this can ever be done is questionable; the social realists used their ideology to shape both form and content, and however useful it may have been politically, it failed as art.

The free-jazz players were further hampered by an ideology that was at cross-purposes with itself, espousing both individualism and collectivism at the same time. Roswell Rudd, in a statement about his own work, has put the matter clearly: "I was trying to get the music out of each guy in a kind of democratic or communal way — so everybody could unload his stuff but with a balanced and coherent form." In jazz we have seen collectivism work in the New Orleans–dixieland form, where players are expected to subordinate their own impulses to the general structure of the piece, and we have seen individualism work in the small swing bands, where the soloist was everything and his rhythm section was there solely to support him. The free-jazz movement was attempting to do both, and it was in the cards that it would fail. One man's dream may be compelling, but the dreams of several men expounded simultaneously are chaos.

And chaos will not make art. We must remember that art, in the broad sense, is relationships. This is especially true of music, which, leaving aside the odd wood note in the flutes or the train boogie in the piano, has no literal content. It is entirely abstract; all that it can be is relationships. That is to say, the *meaning* of a note is its relationship to the notes around it. Is this note higher or lower, longer or shorter than that one? Is this theme a variation of that one, or does it contrast with it? How does this phrase join another to make a building block, and how are those blocks put together to make some larger whole? How are tempo changes, shifts of key or mode, variations in timbre juxtaposed? What common elements give a work its unity? How, finally, how are the parts contained in the tent of shape they themselves create?

These are all questions of relationships, and from the beginning music theory has concerned itself with rules for relating notes and groups of notes. The basic struggle between one generation of musicians and the next has always been over the question of how musical tones are to be organized. The music of the Baroque masters, for example, was highly ordered. It is virtually impossible to make a change in, say, a piece by Scarlatti without causing a noticeable hitch in the flow of the music. On the other hand, the writing of the Romantics is somewhat more arbitrary; it is possible to conceive of alternate phrases or chord movements in a piece by, say, Brahms, that could be substituted without doing damage to the work.

Jazz has always contained a good many arbitrary, chance, or random elements. The horns of a dixieland front line know roughly what each of the others is going to do, but not exactly. As a consequence what is played in any given measure is to a degree arbitrary and may even clash. This chance element is limited, however, because the players are working within a framework of tempo, chord structure, general construction of the tune, and the conventions of that particular type of playing. The question is thus not whether chance, random, or arbitrary elements are permissible in jazz, but to what extent.

The early work of Ornette Coleman, Cecil Taylor, and other of their contemporaries is sometimes jarring and difficult, but it is always at least partially accessible to a listener willing to work at it a little, and it is quite often first-rate jazz. Yet the experiments made by these and others with wholly free jazz have proven, in sum, to be less than successful. The difficulty is that most people find exposure to a random environment anxiety-provoking. To be unable to put the parts of our world together in some rational way, to be unable to understand how the pieces fit together, to be faced with total disorder, is for most of us an intolerable condition. Music in which we cannot find some principle of order, which seems to lack relationships, will make us anxious. We stop concentrating on it; our minds drift away; we become, as we term it, "bored." Most audiences today find that free jazz is too random for them to deal with. (It has been suggested to me that one reason for the rise of free jazz was that it was often listened to by people on marijuana highs, which would have made the randomness more tolerable.) Undoubtedly they are missing some relationships that the musicians are aware of, a figure that one player is making in response to what somebody else has done. Nonetheless, a great deal of free jazz is in fact random, and it is random because the organizing principles, those social ideas of freedom and expressiveness and brotherhood and love, do not have the same concreteness as pitch, chord, meter, time. What the avant-garde sometimes forgot was that the first thing the Lord did was not to pronounce freedom, but to make an ordered universe out of chaos.

The free-jazz player probably will respond that order is not the point; what matters is the free expression of feeling. Writings about avant-garde music are filled with phrases to the effect that the "playing is full of feeling" or "projects direct, raw emotion." I submit that the direct expression of emotion is not the point. A baby's cry, a slap in the face, the thrashing of the body in orgasm — these are direct expressions of emotion. Art, we have always held, is something different: the organizing of symbols in such a way as to call up a response in an audience. It is not the artist's emotion that matters; it is our own. To listen to somebody crying, shouting, grunting, and groaning, whether through a horn or not, may serve an artistic end if it is contributing to some larger meaning, as it does in a play, an opera, or, for that matter, a blues. But the simple spectacle of a human being shrieking, however it might touch or frighten us, is simply the spectacle of a human being shrieking, unless it is connected to other material that makes a point about it. It has been said that there is nothing unnatural in human life but a work of art. The two are not the same. The emotion, the heightened sensibility art affords us does not arise from the mere exposition of nature, but of something said about nature. Anyone who has been overwhelmed by the mighty roar of civilization in the organ music of Bach knows that you can call up passion within the closely ordered world of the Baroque.

It is not the prerogative of any writer to say whether free jazz is a legitimate pursuit. Of course it is; a musician has a perfect right to play as he chooses, and undoubtedly the experiments of Coleman, Taylor, and the rest have been of considerable value in opening pathways for other players. But by the same token listeners are equally free to spend their time listening to something else. No artist, however noble his soul, is owed an audience, and it is a species of artistic fascism for him to demand the world's attention. What many of the youthful experimentalists were not aware of is that over the past quarter of a century jazz audiences have been pelted by one experiment after another by musicians who have felt it necessary to invent new, and often private, musical languages in which to express themselves. It takes a long time for even a dedicated enthusiast to learn a new musical language; it is simply too much to ask him to learn a new one every five years or so. Nonetheless, free jazz has earned an honorable place in the music. It will continue to be performed, in one degree or another, and it will continue to influence the playing around it.

John Coltrane:
A Jazz Messiah

The history of jazz is filled with the names of musicians who have been extravagantly admired. Beiderbecke was openly loved and forgiven all transgressions by the small audience that knew his work. Armstrong was idolized by both his fellow musicians and the critics. Parker was the subject of hero worship as the Babe Ruth of jazz by musicians and listeners who aped his manner and, unfortunately, his morals. But no jazz musician has ever received the extreme adulation visited on John Coltrane.

Not merely loved, not merely idolized, he came to be revered as a saint, a mystic being whose simple presence on earth, some of his worshipers believed, would set the world straight. One writer, Frank Kofsky, wrote his name in for vice president during the 1964 elections. Another placed him in a pantheon along with Muhammad and Jesus. Yet another, Joachim Berendt, claimed that there emanated from him "a hymnic power of love." Even such normally commonsensical writers as Nat Hentoff and Martin Williams began bubbling superlatives when dealing with him. Beiderbecke was mentioned in the public press only twice during his lifetime, and waited until forty years after his death for his biographer; and such major figures as Goodman, Hawkins, and Young have yet to find theirs. But Coltrane was the subject of not one, but three biographies before he was dead a decade. John Coltrane, in sum, was seen — and still is seen by many — not merely as a great jazz musician, but as a spiritual leader on a level with the founders of the world's great religions.

What puzzles the writer is why this should be so. As we shall see, there is little in Coltrane's life or thought — his music aside, of course — that would suggest he was anything other than an ordinary mortal human being; a decent, perplexed man struggling with demons he never quite defeated. Yet he was revered. And he became, without question, one of the most influential jazz musicians who has ever lived. Coltrane directly shaped a whole generation of musicians, not only in jazz, but in rock and the various fusion musics that have appeared in the 1970s.

John Coltrane was born in Hamlet, North Carolina, in 1926, and grew up in another North Carolina town, High Point, today the center of the furniture industry. His maternal grandfather, William Blair, was a preacher highly regarded in the region, something of a charismatic figure. His father ran a tailor shop. The entire family — grandparents and their descendants — were comfortably off by the standards of that time and place. They lived in a two-story frame house in the "good" black district, when many people were living in shacks and sharecroppers' shanties. Coltrane's father, according to writer J. C. Thomas, "convivial and outgoing, was known in the community as a good family man and a genial host," and his paternal grandfather was a respected figure in the black community. Both his father and mother were musical. It was, certainly, a secure and probably a happy home. But even at an early age, according to Cuthbert Simpkins, another Coltrane biographer, John was "a quiet, thinking boy." He did reasonably well in school, and his boyhood was not much different from that of any small town American of the period, once the fact of segregation is allowed for. There was nothing at this point to mark him as special.

Then, when he was twelve, his father died, and shortly after his grandfather the preacher died, too. Undoubtedly these two deaths, coming as they did at the beginning of John's adolescence, made a mark on what was already a somewhat withdrawn personality. His mother, with the help of relatives, managed to hold the family together. After the war began, in 1941, she moved alone to Philadelphia, where there was high-paying war work, and sent money home. John remained with the family in High Point. He joined local church and school bands, starting first on E♭ alto horn, a band instrument analogous to the french horn, then switched to clarinet and finally alto saxophone. He took as his primary model Johnny Hodges, although his biographers say he was influenced by Lester Young as well. His grades in high school were only adequate, but he graduated with a satisfactory record in 1943, and, along with two friends, moved to Philadelphia to find work and wait out the draft. His mother was by this time working in Atlantic City, a short train ride away, and Coltrane was able to see her fairly frequently. At later periods he lived with her; his relationship with her was apparently quite close.

In the fall of 1943 he began to study alto saxophone at the Ornstein School of Music, a good, small private conservatory. According to his teacher, a reed specialist, Coltrane was an eager and disciplined student, who demonstrated an ability to work hard. He stayed at Ornstein for about a year, working in a sugar refinery to support himself. Then, in 1945, he was drafted into the U.S. Navy and was sent to Hawaii, where he played in a navy band, mainly as a clarinetist.

When he was discharged he returned to Philadelphia. The bop revolution was breaking into the open, and as an altoist he naturally kept track of what Charlie Parker was doing. He took up his studies at Ornstein again and began working with rhythm-and-blues bands, which were at the heart of black popular music of the day. He was obviously already a more-than-competent musician, for he was working for some of the better-known leaders in the genre — King Kolax, Big Maybelle, Eddie "Cleanhead" Vinson — all people who could be choosy about whom they hired. The job with Vinson required him to play tenor. He was not really happy about the switch, but he made it, and gradually the tenor came to be his chief instrument. He was influenced at this time by Dexter Gordon.

He was also at this time showing signs of what later became a major and significant personality problem, his oral compulsion. He was addicted to sweets — candy bars, Cokes, and his favorite, sweet-potato pie. He was smoking, and he was beginning to drink heavily as well. It was the sweets that proved to be the most detrimental to his health. The continual eating of sugar began to rot his teeth. Although he suffered from chronic toothache, he refused to see a dentist. We do not know why. At the time dentistry was less sophisticated than it is today, and drilling was somewhat more painful, but most people with aching teeth did seek treatment. Coltrane would never go to the dentist until the pain could no longer be deadened by alcohol. His teeth became so tunneled with cavities that they finally had to be extracted. This was a self-inflicted injury and a painful one; playing the saxophone with a mouthful of aching teeth can be excruciating.

Two other aspects of his character were now well developed. One was his shyness, his reserve. He would often retire to his room and practice rather than go out with his fellows. In groups he was quiet; he did not push himself forward. A corollary to this shyness was his capacity for being liked. Quiet, unobstreperous, agreeable, reluctant to hurt anyone, he was something of a rarity in a business filled with flamboyant personalities, oversized egos, and dog-eat-dog aggressiveness.

Late in 1949 Coltrane joined Dizzy Gillespie's big band, and when the band was reduced to a small group due to financial pressure, Dizzy kept Coltrane, a token of how well thought-of he was among musicians even at this early stage. He played with Gillespie until 1951, when he moved back to Philadelphia. His mother had bought a house there, and Coltrane moved in. He was at this point — if he had not been before — determined to make a significant mark on music. Coltrane, it seems clear enough, was not simply ambitious, like Miles Davis, or intent on being king of the hill, as Hawkins had been, or pleased with the acclaim he received, like Armstrong. He was a driven man, impelled by the same force that pushed Scott Joplin: an intense desire to be a figure of major stature.

He was willing to work hard to achieve his goal. On his return to Philadelphia he entered another small music school, the Granoff School of Music. Here he studied both saxophone and theory, the latter with Dennis Sandole, who was particularly interested in abstruse theories of bitonality and the use of scales as a basis for composition and improvisation, of which there are endless possibilities.

In 1952 Coltrane went to work with Earl Bostic, an alto saxophonist who was leading a small swing-cum-rhythm-and-blues band. Bostic was of the Hodges school, though he favored frantic, disorderly solos. He possessed an excellent technique, especially in the upper register, and Coltrane learned some things from him. He next joined a band led by Johnny Hodges, who had left Ellington shortly before. Again Coltrane had the opportunity to work closely with a major saxophonist.

Unfortunately, some time during this period Coltrane became addicted to heroin, like so many of his peers. He began nodding off during gigs, and in 1954 Hodges had to fire him. He went back to Philadelphia to play whatever pickup gigs he could get, mainly with rhythm-and-blues groups. He was now, at the age of twenty-six, suffering from a number of physical and emotional problems. His mouth continued to trouble him. He was drinking a lot as well as using heroin, and he was putting on weight. The combination of these things and his emotional problems was giving him stomach trouble. It was clear that a crisis was impending, but for the moment he staved it off. In 1954, he met Juanita Grubbs, known as Naima. She was the sister of a friend of his. Later Coltrane named a song for her. John and Naima were married in October of 1955. And the same year he got a call from Miles Davis, which brought him into the main current of jazz.

Davis had apparently wanted Sonny Rollins, but Rollins at that point was in Chicago, kicking his habit, and did not feel ready to play. Coltrane, besides being well schooled, was a muscular player in the Hawkins tradition. Davis has always surrounded himself with strong musicians, partly to supply a contrast to his own delicate playing, and partly to produce the power he lacked. The strong Hawkins-Webster-Gordon-Rollins type of saxophonist was what he needed. Coltrane fit the prescription.

He was, at this time, basically a hard-bop saxophonist, one of the men like Stitt, Rollins, and Dexter Gordon who grew up on Coleman Hawkins but came into their maturity with Parker and played in some combination of the two styles. He did not — or did not choose to — play with the rolling fluidity that characterized the work of Hawkins and Parker and their followers. Instead, he employed a staccato, often choppy, style — possibly under the influence of Sonny Rollins — which was broken into pieces and filled with odd, convoluted little figures that seemed to spring up on their own. His solo "It Could Happen to You," a pop tune of the time played at a medium tempo, is filled with these little often-unrelated swirls, like a bed of mixed flowers. It is tender, but there is a searching quality to it, and this searching is perhaps the most salient characteristic of both his work and his life. There was, for example, his obsessive hunt for the perfect mouthpiece. He bought literally hundreds, and discarded most of them immediately, either giving them away, throwing them out, or tucking them away in boxes. There was his endless rummaging among religions for the final truth, the word that would illuminate the way. There was the constant experimentation with new musical forms, new systems, new theories, in hope of finding — what?

As saxophonist with the Miles Davis group, rapidly becoming the leading group in jazz, Coltrane began to attract a lot of attention, and he might have expected to begin to record on his own. Unfortunately, he continued to be dogged by emotional troubles. He broke his drug habit, only to take it up again, and he continued to drink heavily. Finally, in 1957, he left the Davis band, apparently at Miles's request. It was not the drugs; there was plenty of that in the band. One can only guess that, bedeviled as he was, Coltrane was not doing justice to the music. He went back to his mother's house in Philadelphia and once again began scuffling for work.

Then, some time in 1957, there occurred the pivotal event in his life. He awoke one morning determined to finish with liquor, cigarettes, and drugs. He retired to his room, according to one biographer, and decided that:

> like a prisoner, but a self-sentenced one, he would subsist on water alone. He would fast, not sweat, it out; and he would not walk again among his family until he was clean. From time to time either Naima or John's mother would knock on his door asking him if he was all right. He would either say "Yes," or "May I have some more water?" Naima does not remember how long this period lasted; perhaps three or four days, but not more than a week.

The experiment was successful, although he did continue to smoke tobacco from time to time. It appears to have involved a religious awakening, because thenceforward Coltrane became more and more deeply involved with religion, especially the Eastern religions, which appealed to many blacks at the time. With his emotional life in better order than it had been for years, Coltrane was now ready to make his mark. His opportunity arose when Thelonious Monk was offered an engagement at the Five Spot, the dingy club that had given Cecil Taylor his first exposure and was to launch the free-jazz movement with its booking of Ornette Coleman. Monk brought Coltrane in to play tenor saxophone. The engagement, which ran for months, into the fall, and was a breakthrough for Monk, brought Coltrane before a knowledgeable audience and furthered his musical education. He said, "Working with Monk brought me close to a musical architect of the highest order. I would talk to Monk about musical problems, and he would show me the answers by playing them on the piano. He gave me complete freedom in my playing, and no one ever did that before."

Monk, of course, was an eccentric player, possessed of a spare style with absolutely no fat on it, a marvelous sense of internal harmony, and an approach to rhythm that was unique in jazz — ironic, even comic at times. Coltrane's playing was almost the direct opposite: deadly earnest, based on an effort to cram as many notes as possible into each inch of space. But they shared a fondness for irregularity. Both liked to make jagged, angular lines; both used odd time figures, those little swirls pulled away from the ground beat.

Unhappily, the group went virtually unrecorded, but four takes have been issued. They are all Monk tunes: "Monk's Mood," "Ruby My Dear," "Trinkle, Tinkle," and "Nutty." This last is a typical Monk work, filled with the spirit of play. The basic melody line is deliberately banal, but the dissonant harmonies Monk has set it against, and the way he has made the accents fall in unexpected places, give it a fey charm, reminiscent of the *Mad* magazine character Alfred E. Neuman. This displacement of accent appears especially in a repeated two-note figure that opens and closes each of the parallel four-bar phrases the piece is made of. At the opening of each phrase the two quarter notes are on the first and second beats of the measure; when they reappear at the end of the phrase they skip in early to land on beats three and four. You cannot help smiling.

Coltrane's work on these records exhibits what came to be called his "sheets-of-sound" style, a term coined, probably, by Ira Gitler. By this term he meant that the notes poured out so fast that they could not be heard individually, but only as a continuous line of a given shape. In fact, what Coltrane was doing was not nearly so random as this sounds. As we have seen, jazz from the late 1920s through the bebop period was ever spinning elaborations on chord systems. The Coltrane of this period was the man who brought the complexities to the highest pitch; he was, in this respect, at the end of the road. As one of the second generation of boppers, he had of course learned the new harmonic system the founders had invented. His interest in chords had been fed further by his studies with Dennis Sandole and others, and by the mid-1950s he had become obsessed with them. He had learned that it was possible to substitute two or three or even more chords for any given one in a sequence, something that solo pianists often do as a matter of course to enrich a thin harmonic line. Coltrane began in the late fifties to employ a system in which he regularly used four chords in place of each one in the standard progression.

Obviously, it takes more notes to play four chords than it does one, and, therefore, in order to fit all of his substitutions and additions into a short space he had to play the notes at a blazing speed. As he pointed out himself, to make his method work he at times was compelled to place an odd number of notes over an even number of beats, and this forced him into irregular time patterns that departed widely from the basic beat — those swirls that were appearing in his work with Davis. Sometimes he was playing at speeds approaching a thousand notes a minute, not an impossible speed for a classically trained pianist, but unusual in jazz. Actually, the task Coltrane had set for himself was more than he could cope with. There are places where it all got beyond him, and patches of random playing appear in which there seems to be more simple key-flapping than an orderly progression of chords.

The long stay at the Five Spot with Theolonius Monk made Coltrane more than just a known quantity in jazz; he was a figure of consequence. Now he was being mentioned as Sonny Rollins's equal. When Sonny left Davis, Coltrane was the obvious candidate to succeed him, and when the Five Spot gig ended in the fall of 1957, he returned to the quintet where he had begun to make his name. Earlier in the year he had signed a recording contract with Prestige, and by the next year a number of other record companies were ready to sign him as soon as he became available. He began to turn up on various jazz polls, if only far down the lists. Thus, already in his thirties, an age at which most jazz musicians have done their best work and long since achieved their first fame, Coltrane finally arrived. And in 1960, after a European tour with Davis, he went out on his own.

Because Coltrane's development was slow, his fans were able to follow his career, as it unfolded, much more closely than was possible with other musicians. They divided it into anywhere from three to five stages, of which four seem clear enough: the early days as the hard bopper; the sheets-of-sound period; the modal period; and the free-jazz years before his death. The division is sensible enough if we bear in mind that he did not abandon his older methods when he adopted new ones, but added the new ones to his repertory. Coltrane was, among other things, an excellent ballad player, of the Stan Getz school. He admitted that Getz was an influence, and he continued to do the chord-based kind of improvising through most of his career. Nor did he abandon the modes when he became interested in free jazz; "Naima" and "My Favorite Things," both modal pieces, remained in his repertory until his last illness. So, with this proviso, the foregoing division of Coltrane's career is reasonable enough.

By the time of the Five Spot engagement with Monk, the sheets-of-sound style had begun to predominate, but, curiously enough, the first of his important records was a throwback to the hard-bop style. "Giant Steps," cut in late 1959, was the first album on which Coltrane was able to control the music. He had, of course, previously expressed his highly personal idiom on records with Davis and Monk, but these were records bossed by other leaders. On "Giant Steps" he used all of his own compositions, worked out according to his own musical precepts. The title tune was the one that caused the fuss. It seemed, at the time, to be a novelty, a new departure. It was, in fact, the simplest sort of sixteen-bar tune, repeated to make thirty-two bars. What gave it interest was the chord progression. It was based on alternate movements of up a minor third, and down a fifth, although it departed from this pattern at some points. This was, from the viewpoint of a schooled musician, hardly a novel approach; but compared with the chord sequence of the standard popular tune, wedded as it is to strings of secondary dominants, it had an appealing freshness. The tune itself has a charming lilt, and it is not surprising that it found an audience. For musicians, however, the excitement lay in the fact that the chord changes came along steadily, every two beats. Taken at the tempo Coltrane selected, it was a killing exercise in improvising at a rapid clip to an unusual set of chords. Coltrane succeeds marvelously. He drives through the chords with force and élan, hardly pausing for breath. But the actual structure of the solo is curiously old-fashioned. It is built almost entirely of eighth notes; there are few sixteenths, no sheets of sound. It is hard-bop playing, which, the chord changes and Coltrane's skill at working at high speeds aside, would not have sounded unusual ten years earlier.

But if "Giant Steps" looked backward, there were other cuts on the record that prefigured the future. Coltrane had been aware of modes and other types of scalar playing for some time. His studies with Dennis Sandole had introduced him to Slonimsky's *Thesaurus*, a vast storehouse of modes and scales that could be used as a basis for improvisation. For another thing, Coltrane's interest in Eastern religions had led him to a study of Eastern music, with its heavy reliance on modes. Then, too, he had been on Davis's "Kind of Blue" LP, the first record dedicated to explorations of the modes. Whatever the sources, many of the Coltrane pieces that began to appear around the time he struck off on his own were highly modal in character — "Cousin Mary," "Syeeda's Song Flute," and "Naima," all named for members of his family. The modes had originally been adopted by jazz players as a way of escaping from the thickening web of chords, to allow more concentration on melody. But Coltrane was by nature a searcher, an explorer. Once he had come to terms with the modes, he began looking for something further to do with them, and just as the beboppers had elaborated on the simple chord changes they had inherited, so Coltrane began to elaborate on the modes.

The system he found was polytonality, something that had long been a part of European concert music. To put it simply, polytonality is the use of two keys at once. An obvious example is the playing of a melody in G minor over a chord sequence in B♭ major. The reader can get some idea of the sound by playing three of the black keys on the piano, preferably three that are not adjacent, and then working out against this chord a melody on the white keys. Coltrane's polytonality arose mainly from movement of the melody line in and out of the mode he was, ostensibly, using. This device was something Dizzy Gillespie had suggested in his playing as early as 1940 with those brief excursions into a chord a half step away from the one in the chord sequence. Again, the reader can get some idea of Coltrane's method by working out on the black keys a melody that occasionally jumps onto the white keys for periods.

This interest in polytonality, which Coltrane was responsible for developing and bringing to prominence, has become a major harmonic movement in jazz and the various fusion musics that surround it. Much of what seems difficult in contemporary music is this polytonality, which has been endlessly elaborated on. Students of modern classical music should have little trouble with it, but to those whose ears were trained on standard Western music, it can be mystifying.

The song that seemed to epitomize the modal mood was Coltrane's version of "My Favorite Things," a Rodgers and Hammerstein number from the sentimental show *The Sound of Music*. The song is a waltz. It has very simple chord changes and relatively long passages, during which the chords do not change at all, giving it something of a modal character. The melody is made up of a basic 3/4 rhythmic figure repeated again and again, higher or lower. As Coltrane played it, after the introductory statement of the theme, done in a more or less straightforward fashion, the rhythm section shifted to a purely modal form, with two modes alternating over and over, bar after bar. Against this back-and-forth shifting of the modes, Coltrane improvised without regard to bar lines, but he stuck close to the notes implied by the modes, which were in turn suggested by the melody itself. The result was a highly approachable piece of music, filled with filigrees and sudden bursts of sound characteristic of Coltrane's playing and overlaid with a slightly melancholy air, produced by the minor character of the mode.

"My Favorite Things" represented Coltrane's recording debut on the soprano saxophone. Coltrane had been listening to Sidney Bechet, and through his association with Monk he had become aware of the work of Steve Lacy, who had played soprano with Monk. In 1959 Coltrane acquired a soprano saxophone and began practicing on it, mainly, he said, because he kept hearing higher notes than he could get on the tenor. On the soprano Coltrane produces a smoother, somewhat more dulcet sound than he does on tenor, and this too helped to make his music easier to listen to. "My Favorite Things," issued late in 1960, became a best-selling jazz record. In its first year it sold fifty thousand copies and was widely played on radio stations. With the success of the record, Coltrane became, at last, the most respected figure in jazz. His price for an engagement rose sharply; by the end of 1961 he was one of the highest paid jazz musicians in the country, with an income that eventually rose to $200,000 a year.

Already, by the time of "My Favorite Things," Coltrane's searching nature was manifesting itself in his selection of sidemen. He changed his men repeatedly; none of the first five records he made used the same personnel. But by 1960 it had settled down to Elvin Jones on drums, McCoy Tyner on piano, and Steve Davis on bass, although Jones was often out of the group because of his problems with drugs. Eventually Reggie Workman replaced Davis, and then Jimmy Garrison replaced Workman, to form what came to be the classic Coltrane group. It lasted for several years.

Given Coltrane's character, it was inevitable that he became interested in the free-jazz movement. The appearance of Ornette Coleman's first records and his stint at the Five Spot came at the time Coltrane was beginning to consider leaving Miles and striking out on his own. His followers have often gone to great lengths to deny the influence of Coleman on their hero. The fact is, however, that in mid-1960 Coltrane recorded a Coleman composition, "The Invisible," using two of Coleman's players, Don Cherry and Billy Higgins, as well as Percy Heath, the man who had discovered Coleman in that Los Angeles garage.

It seems clear enough that Coltrane did not find his way into free jazz on his own, but picked it up from the example of others. Coltrane was, we must remember, a driven man, determined to stamp himself with greatness. He was hardly likely to let pass, without comment, a revolutionary current in an art of which he considered himself the leader. "The Invisible" is short, a sort of experimental flight. A fuller attempt to explore free jazz came a year later, with the record "Impressions," which was cut in 1961 but did not appear until two years later. The two long cuts on the record are "India" and the title tune. "Impressions" itself is not really free. It is a modal piece based on simple scales, which Coltrane explores in a series of short, abrupt, jagged figures. "India," however, is more definitely in the Coleman system. Although there is a regular pulse and meter, Coltrane departs from the even-tempered scale at points, reaching out for the shouts and cries typical of the free-jazz players.

Although Coltrane was, at this point, committed to free jazz, he continued to record ballads and to work in modal forms. In fact, the record that was to make him a public figure, insofar as a jazz musician ever becomes one, was by no means free. "A Love Supreme" is built around a very simple four-note figure and consists mainly of repetitions of this figure, interspersed with improvisations, most of them by Coltrane, around a mode. It has a regular pulse, and the piece, which takes both sides of an LP, is divided into four roughly equal parts, each with its own tempo. Harmonically it gets its interest from the use of a pedal point, or drone, in the bass, which produces polytonality as the melody moves over it. Here again, jazz was finding a way to contrast the melody with its underpinning. As the title suggests, "A Love Supreme" is Coltrane's offering to God in gratitude for the conversion that enabled him to escape from his addictions. (According to biographer Bill Cole, Coltrane said that God had spoken to him before he made the record.) Like many similar pieces produced by jazz musicians — Ellington's religious music is a case in point — the music may strike some as dull and pretentious. Despite that, or perhaps because of it, the record sold about 250,000 copies, an extraordinary figure for a jazz record. It meant that Coltrane was reaching beyond the jazz world for a wider audience, a feat achieved by very few jazz players, Armstrong, Waller, Ellington, and Goodman being among those few.

The nature of Coltrane's wider audience is significant. It consisted of young people, mainly members of what came to be thought of as "the Woodstock generation." Many of them were imbued with rather vague religious ideas. A piece called "A Love Supreme" and offered as a gift to God was bound to appeal to them. Moreover, rock music of the time was essentially modal, principally because it was derived from the blues by young, self-taught guitar players. Consequently, the modal sound of the Coltrane record was more familiar to these listeners than to older jazz buffs. They began buying his records and attending his concerts, and in time they made him a genuine, if minor, show business star. It was at this point that he became a cult figure, and ordinary fan adulation began to turn, on the part of many of his followers, to reverence.

Despite the success of "A Love Supreme," Coltrane continued to move, however slowly, into free jazz, until in 1965 he recorded "Ascension," a true free-jazz piece. He used on the record Freddie Hubbard, who had been on Coleman's "Free Jazz," as well as other men associated with the free-jazz movement, including Archie Shepp and John Tchicai. The piece begins with a brief opening statement, marred by faulty intonation in some of the horns, and then proceeds through a number of solos interspersed with ensemble interludes. It is typical free-jazz playing, filled with the groans and growls characteristic of the school. For the rest of his life the main thrust of Coltrane's work was in the direction of free playing, though he never abandoned his interest in the modes. The music he made at his last recording session, which was issued as "Expression," for the most part contains no fixed pulse and no bar lines. He does not depart from the tempered scale altogether, but there are long passages, notably in the title tune, that contain a great deal of bubbling and seething.

Coltrane's drift into free jazz was reflected by the men he chose to surround himself with. One of the most important was Eric Dolphy, a woodwind player who specialized in the bass clarinet. Coltrane had known Dolphy since 1954. Over the years they had carried on many discussions of both music and Eastern philosophy. Dolphy had come to be as close a friend as Coltrane had, and when, in 1961, he decided to add a second horn, he began using Dolphy, first on records and then, in 1961 and 1962, as a member of the group on a part-time basis.

Dolphy, who was born in 1928, began as an alto saxophonist in the Parker mold. He studied a whole range of woodwinds and eventually recorded on flute and alto as well as bass clarinet. He was very much affected by the free-jazz movement, and by 1961, when he began to play with Coltrane, he was using more of the characteristic cries and howls than Coltrane used. But Coltrane, of course, was an influence on his players. By 1962 Dolphy was using some of Coltrane's sheets of sound. Oddly, he recorded with Coltrane very little, appearing on only three of Coltrane's LPs, and not on all tracks of those. By 1963 Dolphy was spending a lot of time in Europe, where he died in 1964.

Dolphy's successor in the group was Pharaoh (Farrell) Sanders, a tenor saxophonist who was even deeper into free playing than Dolphy had been. Sanders plays with a coarse, heavy tone, and his soloing is heavily devoted to exploration of sounds outside the tempered scale. Yet another late addition was drummer Rashied Ali, also of the free-jazz school. There was tension between him and Elvin Jones, which often resulted in noise battles in which the two drummers drowned out the horns in their efforts to overpower each other. Coltrane was aware that the older members of the group were upset by the new men. McCoy Tyner left, then Elvin, saying, "The other drummer had a different sense of time from mine, so it didn't sound right," and finally Jimmy Garrison walked off the stand during a concert on a Japanese tour. Coltrane let him leave, making it clear where he felt his music was going. It was not only musicians who were defecting; his bewildered fans did not understand where Trane was going, either.

He was, in any case, not going much farther. In retrospect those who knew him agree that he had been gravely ill for perhaps a year before he died. He was seriously overweight — J. C. Thomas reports that in the last months of his life he weighed 240 pounds. If this is so, he was some seventy or eighty pounds too heavy. By the spring of 1967 it was clear that something was seriously wrong with him. His wife insisted that he see a doctor, but after the first tests he checked out of the hospital and went home. Did he know he was terminally ill and that there was no point in more tests? If so, why did he bother going to the hospital in the first place? Had he reached the point where he no longer cared to live? Was he simply exhausted by bearing the internal tension he suffered? Coltrane was a secretive man; beyond a point he confided in nobody. In the middle of June 1967 he entered a hospital again, and on July 17 he died.

Any work of art is the product of many forces: the personality of the creator, the nature of the culture he lives in, the prior history of the art itself. In Coltrane's case the foremost element seems to have been the personality of the man. His work owed less to the history of the art than did that of most influential players in jazz; highly idiosyncratic, it seems to have been built on principles that were chosen almost arbitrarily. This is not to say that Coltrane completely escaped the currents of the time. Modes, free jazz, Eastern forms — these were all around him. But in Coltrane's case they were refracted by a particularly resistant personality, which gave them a unique shape. What was that personality?

Coltrane was always seen by his friends and fellow musicians as gentle, quiet, reserved, shy, unwilling to hurt. After his religious conversion and his rejection of drugs, this gentleness came more and more to appear as a species of aloofness, of deliberately controlled calm in the midst of turbulence. Once when Elvin Jones smashed up a car belonging to his leader, Coltrane did not remonstrate, but replied to the effect that he could always get another car, but he could not get another Elvin Jones. He disliked giving orders; when his men asked for direction he often refused to give it, simply telling the player to find his own way.

Nor did he attempt to discipline his sidemen in the ordinary way. At times they argued with him on the stand. As the leading figure in jazz, he could easily have demanded control; but rather than assert himself, he preferred to give way in all directions. When the two drummers began playing so loud that Coltrane himself could not be heard by the audiences who had come to hear him play, he did nothing. The men felt free to walk off the job or not show up at all. Jones in particular was obstreperous, drinking and using drugs heavily, often absent and at times temperamental. Coltrane put up with it all.

But if Coltrane maintained an unruffled surface, beneath the skin there was turmoil. His marriage to Naima began to disintegrate in the early 1960s. In 1963 he started seeing Alice McLeod and, according to J. C. Thomas, another woman, whom the biographer does not identify. Three years later he married Alice, and she became the pianist with his band. His eating problems increased. He was oscillating between Spartan diets of fruit and vegetables and binges of overeating, especially of sweets. He found it necessary to own two sets of clothing — fat suits and thin suits. He ate incessantly — sunflower seeds or Life Savers all day long. The inner disturbance showed itself in other ways, too. There was, for example the compulsive practicing. At times Coltrane would walk around the house all day, playing. Even when people visited he might excuse himself and disappear for an hour or two to practice. He is said to have fallen asleep on many occasions with the saxophone in his hands, and once he awoke with it in his mouth. Most of us have oral cravings: we smoke or snack or drink or chew gum. But in few people are the cravings this severe; the pacifierlike quality of the saxophone is too obvious to miss. Coltrane, clearly, was suffering from a larger load of anxiety than most of us are called upon to bear.

The classic publicity shot of John Coltrane, characteristically moody and introspective. ABC Impulse

Perhaps what is most significant is that Coltrane had, at some point, come to see himself as a special being. We do not know when this idea began to germinate, but few psychologists would allow that it would come late in life. So important a facet of the self-image does not break through in a man's forties unless it has been growing beneath the surface for some time. By the closing years of his life there was ample humus for it. He was surrounded by people who kept informing him that he was a genius, who spoke reverently about his spiritual powers, who treated him, in a word, as if he were Jesus Christ incarnate, which, in fact, some of them could have been convinced he was. Even the best balanced of personalities will have trouble coping with this sort of adulation, and Coltrane was far from a balanced personality. In any case, whatever the cause, by the last years of his life he had begun to identify himself with Albert Einstein, not a surprising choice since Einstein was both a genius in his field and, in his concern for peace, a moral leader.

Not long before his death Coltrane was asked what he hoped to be ten years from that time. He replied that he wanted to be a saint. One presumes that he meant he hoped to have achieved some advanced state of spiritual or moral goodness. This vision of himself was plainly a delusion. There is nothing in any of the interviews he gave to indicate that he had anything more than a normal intelligence. Nor had he evidenced any special qualities of spiritual or moral leadership, other than that calmness which he seems to have cultivated more sedulously as he aged. He did not devote a great amount of time to good works, nor did he contribute large sums to organizations he admired, or play many benefits. In fact, he poured his energies and his time into an obsessive pursuit of his music. The truth is that, far from being a saint, John Coltrane was a tense, driven man trying somehow to maintain his equilibrium in the face of internal and external pressures. That endless searching was a hunt for peace of mind, or, to use a more clinical term, an escape from the ever-present anxiety that he would not allow himself to still with liquor or drugs.

But if we must deny Coltrane his sainthood, we still must see him as a kinder and more honorable man than most. He thought deeply about his moral code, and he made the effort to live up to it. To the people around him he seemed to radiate an uncommon decency, rare enough in the music business. And we must also see that his music was the product of an imaginative, though restless and insecure personality. He lacked Parker's contemptuous self-confidence or Ellington's sure sense that what sounded right was right. In part this was because he had come, by the last years of his life, to see music itself as a moral problem. Alice Coltrane said, "A higher principle is involved here. Some of his latest works aren't musical compositions. I mean they weren't based entirely on music. A lot of it has to do with mathematics, some on rhythmic structure and the power of repetition, some on elementals. He always felt that sound was the first manifestation in creation before music." It was not, for Coltrane, a question of aesthetics so much as of philosophy. He seemed, then, forever to be trying on things to see how they felt, and this, at last, may be the closest we can come to the truth about John Coltrane: his music appears to have become not something that stood apart from him, but a scheme for working out his personal problems. And, unfortunately, it never in the end felt good enough to save him.

But of course the music remains. Where Coltrane will stand finally in the jazz pantheon it is too early to tell. Only when a new generation has stripped the music clear of the politico-philosophic ideas it became encumbered with will we know. But we do know that John Coltrane was, with Parker and Armstrong, one of the great formative influences in jazz.

The Future:
Some Afterthoughts

At this point in a book of this sort it is customary to write on the subject "Whither Jazz?" I am not going to do that, however, because making predictions about jazz is exceedingly risky. In 1927 it seemed obvious that the New Orleans music of Oliver and Morton was coming to fruition and would move out to capture the world. But by 1929 the New Orleans style was moribund, and the big bands, which had been growing in importance almost unnoticed for half a decade, were dominating jazz. Again, in 1945 it seemed clear that the future of jazz lay in "symphonic" compositions drawing heavily on European concert music. But by 1947 the big band was dead and bop was sweeping all before it. Ten years later bop was still ascendant, and it was assumed that any future jazz would be a modification of the bebop style. But by 1960 free jazz was pushing bop aside, and by 1965 the future seemed to belong to Coltrane, Coleman, Shepp, Taylor, and the rest. And yet by the end of the decade free jazz in its turn had been buried under a welter of electronic music, which owed as much to rock as to jazz.

At this moment, the future of jazz is in the hands of a lot of fifteen-year-olds who are being attracted to one or another aspect of the music. What they will have made of it ten years from now depends on what they are bringing to it from other sources — that is, the records they were listening to at ages ten and twelve and fourteen and will be listening to over the next few years. Are they rejecting rock as the square, old-fashioned music of their fathers, as the rock generation rejected the jazz of theirs? Are they listening to some small, obscure group of musicians working in a musical by-way, as the early beboppers listened to the unknown Parker and Gillespie? Has the recent spate of jazz biographies fed their adolescent romanticism, drawing them back to Parker, Bessie Smith, or even Beiderbecke? It is impossible to know, but it will be fascinating to watch.

If we cannot predict where jazz is going, however, we can at least discern certain trends. It seems to me that there are three important ones. The most obvious is the turning to what has been called jazz-rock, rock-jazz, or one of the group of fusion musics. To define it simply, this music is created by combining a rock beat with more advanced jazz harmonies, jazz-type soloing, and some admixture of both free jazz and European concert music. Its best-known practitioners are the pianists Herbie Hancock and Chick Corea; guitarists Larry Coryell and John McLaughlin of the Mahavishnu Orchestra; the current Miles Davis; and a variety of groups like Blood, Sweat, and Tears, the Brecker Brothers, Michael Urbaniak, and Weather Report. Hancock and Corea came from jazz; McLaughlin and Coryell had mixed jazz and rock backgrounds; Blood, Sweat, and Tears came from rock.

Randy and Mike Brecker are a typical case. Their father was an amateur jazz pianist with a light bop orientation, and they grew up with an involvement in that music. In their teens they were both swept up in the rock movement of the 1960s. They studied at Indiana University, where the emphasis was on bop-oriented big band music, and they came into professional music with wide experience in both jazz and rock, as well as rhythm and blues, or funk music, which was shaped by both. It was inevitable that they look for some way to combine the two, and they claim to have made the first efforts to do so with the group called Dreams, which included Billy Cobham. As we have seen, Miles Davis was moving in the same direction at about the same moment, and prior to either Davis or the Breckers there had been an English group called Soft Machine, which had added a great deal of European concert music to the mix. By the mid-1970s, fusion music had developed a sizable audience, not as large a one as was still commanded by rock, but larger than the hard-core jazz audience. Corea and Hancock were making large commercial successes of themselves, and were drawing many other players, especially young ones, into the form. However, whether this fusion music can be classified under the rubric of jazz is an open question. Most committed jazz players do not think so.

A second pattern in jazz at the moment is what has to be called the neo-bop movement. Its adherents are in part the older musicians who have been working in the form all their lives and have gone on playing it through lean times and good, just as the dixielanders clung to their own way of playing through the big band era. These are men like Gillespie, Lee Konitz, Al Haig, Art Blakey, the Thad Jones–Mel Lewis big band, and many others. To them have been added a number of young men just coming into jazz. These young players grew up on rock, but became bored with the music and turned back to bop for inspiration. They have been particularly influenced by Davis and Coltrane, but they have been investigating the earlier beboppers, especially Parker and Bud Powell. They are familiar with Parker lines, and regularly play tunes like "Donna Lee" and "Ornithology," as well as standards the boppers favored, such as "All the Things You Are," and more recent vehicles, like "Green Dolphin Street." This neo-bop is not pure. The people who are playing it, both the young men and the older ones, have of course been influenced to one degree or another by developments in the music since the days of Minton's, but it is, essentially, bebop.

A third line in jazz today is a continuation of free-jazz mode, especially under the influence of Coltrane. Players like Cecil Taylor, Pharaoh Sanders, Elvin Jones, and others who had been associated with Coltrane continue to work with nondiatonic pitches and various shouts and cries, and this form continues to influence the younger people in jazz. Players associated with both neo-bop and fusion music at times make forays into free music; it is probably safe to say that most younger players have worked in free jazz at one time or another.

Finally, there continues to exist in jazz a body of men playing in even older forms. Swing players like Earle Warren, Roy Eldridge, Benny Carter, and Benny Goodman work frequently, and a few of the somewhat younger ones, like Zoot Sims, who has a personal following, make good livings and still record. Alongside them are a few veteran dixielanders, the most active of whom are Max Kaminsky and Wild Bill Davison, who work regularly, mostly in the company of younger men who came into jazz through the dixieland revival of the 1940s. And of course there remain clutches of avocational players, some of them working in the Oliver manner or even playing ragtime, who cannot support themselves with their music, but find modest audiences for it. It is possible, for example, for Bob Greene, a Jelly Roll Morton specialist, to fill Carnegie Hall once a year with a concert of Jelly's music. (Greene, formerly an avocational player, now makes his living playing Morton's music.)

Which of these trends will prove to be the main line in the development of jazz is impossible to tell. It may be that some genius will come along to pull elements from all of them to make something totally new and unexpected, as Armstrong and Parker did. It may, in fact, be that for practical purposes jazz has already ended its history. The jazz authority John L. Fell has said, "Jazz is so shifting into mixtures with other forms that it is unlikely to survive as an autonomous form." Perhaps he is right, but I think even that prediction risky.

However, if I cannot say where jazz is going, I can suggest some directions that I should like to see it take. The first of these is toward a broader understanding of, and corresponding tolerance for, the variety of forms that exist in the music. As we have seen, it is a peculiarity of jazz that its practitioners know very little of the past of their own art. We have seen how the funk players misunderstood the nature of the gospel music they were trying to infuse into their work, even though a number of earlier authors, among them Winthrop Sargeant, had discussed the blue notes in detail. The situation has not improved. Most young people coming into jazz as both players and listeners believe that everything before "now" was bebop. It is doubtful that one in ten has ever heard a record by Earl Hines, Roy Eldridge, or Coleman Hawkins, and even less likely that they have heard Oliver, Morton, Noone, or Beiderbecke. Needless to say, no budding painter would be unfamiliar with the work of Titian or El Greco, no young poet would have neglected to read Shakespeare or Milton, no young composition student would have failed to study intensively the symphonies of Haydn and the oratorios of Bach.

On the other side of the coin, few of the older fans have made any serious effort to come to grips with the work of Cecil Taylor or John Coltrane, despite their obvious importance in the recent history of the music. As I have pointed out, it is not reasonable to expect the older fan to take to his bosom every new turn of the music; but on the other hand, it is not reasonable of him to complain about young people's ignorance of the older music if he does not trouble to examine the newer forms. Whatever his age, no single jazz enthusiast will like equally every player or care to listen to every style. But it seems to me that anybody who cares for the art ought to learn something about it. The musician or listener who does not know, for example, how bop grew out of what went before, does not really know what Charlie Parker is saying. Anybody who cares to can get some understanding of Coltrane or Morton, Taylor or Armstrong, with a few hours of concentrated listening. He will not become an authority on Coltrane or Morton in a few hours, but he can get an idea of what their work is about.

And I think that if young people coming to jazz will take the time to study the music a little, they will be amply rewarded. Indeed, they may even find that they come to enjoy some of the older forms. Perhaps more important, they may well develop a tolerance for forms other than their own special interests.

To be more specific: we have to divest ourselves of the idea that the history of jazz has always been toward better and better. In no art has this ever been the case; all forms have their ups and downs, their changing fashions. As jazz has advanced, it has frequently discarded the valuable as well as the useless. There are things in the older forms worth exploring. As will be clear to the reader at this point, jazz has always been obsessed with the new, with experimentation, and the result has been that it has rarely paused to exploit its discoveries before leaping out to make fresh ones.

Bop is an interesting case in point. Once Parker and Gillespie had worked out the new harmonies and the new way of phrasing, all players picked up the manner and did nothing more with it. There was no attempt to experiment with new instrumentation. Oscar Pettiford, for example, had demonstrated that first-rate jazz could be played on the cello, but nobody, not even he, followed up on this lead. Nothing much has ever been done with the french horn, and the double reeds have been entirely neglected. The boppers, in fact, narrowed jazz instrumentation: the use of trombones and clarinets dwindled, and the violins, tubas, and bass saxophones, which had been used in jazz at least occasionally, disappeared altogether. Further, they made little effort, despite the example of Ellington, to find different ways of using the new material in a big band context; the bop big band was merely a swing band using advanced chords and bop soloing. There was no effort to find systems for collective improvisation or polyphony in general. Why could not a dixieland front line be used for the presentation of bebop? Why could not two bop players improvise simultaneously, as had Noone and Joe Poston or Armstrong and Hines or any number of earlier players? It has not been only the beboppers who failed to exploit fully their special form. Because of the music's constant flight into the new, no jazz form has ever been completely mined.

It should thus be clear that, as a practical matter, knowing what came before can have real value in suggesting solutions to present problems. John Lewis's best-known work stems from his admiration of an earlier player, Django Reinhardt. The variety in the work of Charlie Mingus is undoubtedly due to his great familiarity with all that had happened in jazz. Ornette Coleman built on a foundation of the blues.

I think, then, that jazz can have a future, but I think, paradoxically, that it is in the past. Jazz needs, at the moment, a respite from experiments. It needs time to consolidate the gains, to go back and re-examine what is there. There is enough work left undone to last many lifetimes. But even if nobody takes the challenge, even if the stream of jazz is fated to run out in a larger lake of other forms, it will not have run for nothing. The music remains. And I have no doubt that a hundred years from today, and a hundred years beyond that, the sounds of Armstrong and Parker and Reinhardt and Ellington will still be freezing spines.

Discography
Bibliography
Index

Discography

Where the collector of classical music is generally sure of locating any of the significant works in this field in a well-stocked record store, the jazz fan will never find more than a proportion of the major jazz records in even the best of record stores. Jazz reissue programs have been haphazard in the extreme. Important cuts go in and out of print constantly. Often recordings are bundled together on LPs according to schemes that defy any reasonable explanation. The Goodman Carnegie Hall Concert, for example, has been issued in at least two formats, with the cuts differently arranged on the LPs. Some major records are available in several forms; others not at all. The Tatum-Hawkins "Esquire Bounce" has been reissued in at least three different ways, while the Tatum-Thomas "Stompin' at the Savoy" has not been available in the United States for twenty years.

I have, therefore, felt that it would serve no purpose to give a list of the LP sources of all the records discussed herein; that would amount to a catalogue of records no longer available. The following discography includes only LPs that have been available within the past ten years, and that therefore stand some chance of still existing in record stores and libraries. (It should be noted that most record stores will have in stock many records not listed in *Schwann* as being current.) Most of the major records and many of the minor ones discussed in this book will be found here. In any case, the list constitutes a representative sampling of the history of jazz, despite unavoidable omissions. It should not be thought that relative numbers of records listed for the artists constitute some weighing system: apparent disparities have to do with what happens to have been available, not with the merits of the artists.

Records are generally alphabetized by artist, but in cases where I have felt that a cut was important for more than one artist, I have catalogued it under the name of the leader as given in the text; for example, works by Lester Young will be found either under his name or under the name of

Count Basie. As much as has been possible, I have given the titles of specific cuts mentioned in the text in parenthesis after the LP title.

African Music. *Music of the Mende,* Folkways FE 4322.

African Music. *African Music,* Folkways FW 8852.

Allen, Red. *Red Allen,* RCA LPV-556 (It Should Be You, Biff'ly Blues).

Ammons, Albert. *The Original Boogie Woogie Piano Giants,* Col. KC 32708 (Shout for Joy, Boogie Woogie Prayer).

Armstrong, Louis. *Louis Armstrong with Fletcher Henderson,* BYG 529086 (Alabamy Bound).

Armstrong, Louis. *Young Louis Armstrong,* Riverside RLP 12–101 (Terrible Blues, Cake Walkin' Babies).

Armstrong, Louis. *The Louis Armstrong Story, Vol. 1, The Hot Five,* Col. CL 851 (Skid-Dat-De-Dat, Cornet Chop Suey, Heebie Jeebies, Struttin' with Some Barbecue, Hotter Than That).

Armstrong, Louis. *The Louis Armstrong Story, Vol. 2, The Hot Seven,* Col. CL 852 (Wild Man Blues, Potato Head Blues, Gully Low Blues).

Armstrong, Louis. *Louis Armstrong Story, Vol. 3, with Earl Hines,* Col. CL 853 (Muggles, Tight Like This, West End Blues, Sugar Foot Strut, Weather Bird, Knockin' a Jug).

Armstrong, Louis. *V.S.O.P., Vol. 1,* CSP JEE 22019 (Stardust, Between the Devil and the Deep Blue Sea, Home).

Armstrong, Louis. *A Rare Batch of Satch,* RCA LPM 2322 (High Society, Hobo, You Can't Ride This Train).

Armstrong, Louis. *Rare Items,* Decca DL 0225 (Struttin' with Some Barbecue, Swing That Music, I Double Dare You, Jubilee).

Armstrong, Louis. *Back in N.Y., Vol. 1,* Decca DL 79248.

Armstrong, Louis. *July 4, 1900/July 6, 1971,* RCA VPM 6044.

Armstrong, Louis. *The Greatest of Louis Armstrong,* Tele House (Columbia) CD 2018.

Ayler, Albert. *Reevaluations: The Impulse Years,* Impulse AS 9257 (New Ghosts, Universal Indians, Sun Watcher).

Ayler, Albert. *Witches & Devils,* Arista AL 1018 (Witches and Devils, Spirits).

Banks, Billy. *Billy Banks and His Rhythmakers,* CBS 52732 (Oh Peter, Spider Crawl).

Barnet, Charlie. *Charlie Barnet,* RCA LPV-551 (Cherokee).

Basie, Count. *Super Chief,* Col. G-31224 (Shoe Shine Boy, Boogie-Woogie).

Basie, Count. *The Best of Count Basie,* MCA2-4050 (Jumpin' at the Woodside, Every Tub, Cherokee, Blue and Sentimental, John's Idea, Doggin' Around, Topsy).

Bechet, Sidney. *The Blues New Orleans Style,* BYG 529 068 (Cake Walkin' Babies).

Bechet, Sidney. *Bechet of New Orleans,* RCA LPV 510 (Maple Leaf Rag).

Bechet, Sidney. *Sidney Bechet Jazz Classics, Vols. 1, 2,* Blue Note BLP 1201,2 (Blue Horizon, Summertime).

Beiderbecke, Bix. *Bix Beiderbecke and the Wolverines,* La Storia Del Jazz SM 3087 (Fidgety Feet, Tia Juana).

Beiderbecke, Bix. *Legend, Vol. 3,* Black and White 731.131.

Beiderbecke, Bix. *Story, Vols. 1-3,* Col. CL 844-6 (Singin' the Blues, Riverboat Shuffle, I'm Comin' Virginia, Way Down Yonder in New Orleans, For No Reason at All in C).

Berry, Chu. *The Influence of Five,* Mainstream 56002 (Sittin' In).

Black Folk Music. *The South,* Folkways FJ 2801.

Black Folk Music. *Afro-American Blues and Game Songs,* Library of Congress AFS L4 (Old Uncle Rabbit).

Black Folk Music. *Negro Work Songs and Calls,* Library of Congress AAFS L8.

Black Folk Music. *Negro Religious Songs and Services,* Library of Congress AAFS L10 (Sin-Killer Griffin).

Black Folk Music. *Negro Blues and Hollers,* Library of Congress AFS L59.

Blake, Eubie. *The Eighty-Six Years of Eubie Blake,* Col. C2S 647.

Blakey, Art. *Thermo,* Milestone MSP-47008.

Blue Devils. *Territory Bands Vol. 2,* HLP 26 (Blue Devil Blues, Squabblin').

Blues. *The Story of the Blues,* Col. G 30008 (Stone Pony Blues).

Blues. *The Blues Tradition,* Milestone MLP 2016 (The Gone, Dead Train).

Blues. *Rare Blues,* Historical Records, Vol. 4.

Broonzy, Big Bill. *Big Bill Broonzy,* Disc. D-112 (Joe Turner No. Two).

Brown, Clifford. *Study in Brown,* Emarcy 36037 (Cherokee, If I Love Again).

Brown, Clifford. *Brown & Roach, Inc.,* Trip TLP 5520.

Brown, Clifford. *Clifford Brown and Max Roach at Basin Street,* Trip TLP-5511 (Gertrude's Bounce).

Brown, Clifford. *Clifford Brown in Paris,* Prestige 24020.

Brubeck, Dave. *Fantasy Years,* Atlantic 2–317.

Calloway, Cab. *Classics,* Aimez-vous le Jazz CBS 62950 (Ghost of a Chance).

Carter, Benny. *Coleman Hawkins, 1930–1941,* Aimez-vous le Jazz 68227 (Dee Blues, Bugle Call Rag).

Christian, Charlie. *The Genius of Charlie Christian,* Col. G-30779 (Gone with What Wind, Seven Come Eleven, Breakfast Feud).

Christian, Charlie. *Charlie Christian,* Archive of Folk Music FS-219.

Coleman, Ornette. *Something Else!!!!,* Contemporary S7551 (Invisible, Angel Voice, Alpha).

Coleman, Ornette. *The Shape of Jazz to Come,* Atlantic 1317 (Congeniality).

Coleman, Ornette. *Science Fiction & Skies of America,* Col. CG 33669.

Coleman, Ornette. *The New Music of Ornette Coleman,* Contemporary S7569 (Tears Inside, Giggin').

Coleman, Ornette. *Free Jazz,* Atlantic 1364.

Coltrane, John. *Miles Davis,* Prestige 24001.

Coltrane, John. *More Lasting Than Bronze,* Prestige 24014.

Coltrane, John. *Giant Steps,* Atlantic 1311 (Giant Steps, Cousin Mary, Syeeda's Song Flute).

Coltrane, John. *My Favorite Things,* Atlantic 1361 (My Favorite Things).

Coltrane, John. *Coltrane "Live" at the Village Vanguard,* Impulse 10.

Coltrane, John. *Impressions,* Impulse 42 (Impressions).

Coltrane, John. *A Love Supreme,* Impulse 77.

Coltrane, John. *Ascension,* Impulse 95.

Coltrane, John. *Expression,* Impulse 9120.

Condon, Eddie. *Dixieland–New Orleans,* Mainstream S/6003 (Rockin' Chair).

Condon, Eddie. *Dixieland–Chicago,* Mainstream S/6010 (Sobbin' Blues).

Condon, Eddie. *A Legend,* Mainstream S/6024 (It's Right Here for You, Oh, Lady Be Good).

Crosby, Bob. *Bob Crosby and His Orchestra,* Joker SM 3243.

Davis, Miles. *Miles Ahead,* Prestige 7822.

Davis, Miles. *'Round About Midnight,* Col. CS 8649 (Bye Bye Blackbird).

Davis, Miles. *Birth of the Cool,* Cap. DT 1974 (Move, Godchild).

Davis, Miles. *Walkin',* Prestige 7608.

Davis, Miles. *Kind of Blue,* Columbia PC 8163.

Davis, Miles. *Sketches of Spain,* Col. KCS 8271.

Davis, Miles. *Nefertiti,* Col. PC 9594.

Davis, Miles. *Filles de Kilimanjaro,* Col. KCS 9750.

Davis, Miles. *In a Silent Way,* Col. PC 9875.

Davis, Miles. *Davis,* Prestige 24001.

Davison, Wild Bill. *Dixieland–New Orleans,* Mainstream 56003 (Panama, Royal Garden Blues).

Dodds, Johnny. *Johnny Dodds and Tommy Ladnier,* Biograph BLP-12024.

Dorsey, Thomas. *This Is Tommy Dorsey,* RCA VPM-6038 (Marie, Song of India).

Eldridge, Roy. *Era of the Swing Trumpet,* Mainstream 56017 (I Can't Believe That You're in Love with Me).

Ellington, Duke. *Duke Ellington,* BYG 529.071.

Ellington, Duke. *The Beginning,* Decca DL 79224 (Birmingham Breakdown, East St. Louis Toodle-Oo, Black and Tan Fantasy).

Ellington, Duke. *Hot in Harlem,* Decca DL 79241 (The Mooch).

Ellington, Duke. *Rockin' in Rhythm,* Decca DL 7–9247 (Mood Indigo, Creole Rhapsody).

Ellington, Duke. *Daybreak Express,* RCA LPV-506 (Dear Old Southland).

Ellington, Duke. *The Ellington Era, 1927–1940 Vol. 1* (3-record set), Col. 3CL 27 (East St. Louis Toodle-Oo, Black and Tan Fantasy, The Mooch, Rockin' in Rhythm, Mood Indigo, It Don't Mean a Thing, Clarinet Lament, Blues with a Feeling, Saddest Tale, Jubilee Stomp).

Ellington, Duke. *The Ellington Era, 1927–1940 Vol. 2* (3-record set), Col. 3CL 39 (Creole Love Call, Reminiscin' in Tempo, Flaming Youth, Baby, When You Ain't There).

Ellington, Duke. *In a Mellotone,* RCA LPM-1364 (Take the A Train, Main Stem, In a Mellotone, Cotton Tail, Just A-Settin' and A-Rockin').

Ellington, Duke. *The Indispensable Duke Ellington,* RCA LPM-6009 (Chelsea Bridge, Things Ain't What They Used to Be).

Ellington, Duke. *At His Very Best,* RCA LPM-1715 (Jack the Bear, Black, Brown, and Beige, Ko-Ko, Warm Valley, Concerto for Cootie).

NOTE: Decca, Columbia, and RCA are issuing in complete form their early Ellington files.

English Jazz. *London Trad Scene the 50's,* Ace of Clubs ACL 1154.

Evans, Bill. *At the Montreux Jazz Festival,* Verve V6-8762.

Evans, Bill. *Peace Piece and Other Pieces,* Milestone M 47024.

Evans, Bill. *Bill Evans,* Verve VE 2-2509.

Evans, Bill. *Since We Met,* Fantasy F-9501.

Garner, Erroll. *Play It Again, Erroll!,* Col. PG 33424.

Getz, Stan. *Stan Getz,* Prestige 24019.

Gillespie, Dizzy. *Dizzy Gillespie,* RCA LPV-530.

Gillespie, Dizzy. *The Greatest of Dizzy Gillespie,* RCA LPM-2398 (Cubana Be, Cubana Bop).

Gillespie, Dizzy. *The Development of an American Artist,* Smithsonian Collection R 004.

Gillespie, Dizzy. *In the Beginning,* Prestige P-24030 (Lover Man).

Gillespie, Dizzy. *Big Bands Uptown,* Decca DL 79242 (Little John Special).

Gonella, Nat. *Nat Gonella and His Trumpet,* Ace of Clubs ACL 1241.

Goodman, Benny. *Trio, Quartet, Quintet,* RCA LPM-1226 (Whispering, Opus 1/2, Runnin' Wild, Pick-A-Rib, Sweet Sue).

Goodman, Benny. *The Small Groups,* RCA LPV-521 (Blues in My Flat, Blues in Your Flat, Exactly Like You).

Goodman, Benny. *The Golden Age of Benny Goodman,* RCA LPM 1099 (King Porter Stomp).

Goodman, Benny. *Carnegie Hall Concert,* Col. CL 814/6 (One O'Clock Jump, Sing, Sing, Sing).

NOTE: The RCA recordings of Benny Goodman are currently being reissued on Bluebird and Black and White.

Gordon, Dexter. *Dexter Rides Again,* Savoy MG 12130.

Hall, Edmond. *Celestial Express,* Blue Note B-6505 (Jammin' in Four, Profoundly Blue).

Hampton, Lionel. *Hampton's Best Records, Vol. 3,* Black and White 731.048 (Hot Mallets).

Hawkins, Coleman. *Jazz Pioneers,* Prestige 7647 (Lost in a Fog, Jamaica Shout).

Hawkins, Coleman. *Body and Soul,* RCA LPV 501 (Body and Soul, One Hour).

Hawkins, Coleman. *Classic Tenors,* Flying Dutchman FD 10146 (The Man I Love).

Hawkins, Coleman. *Coleman Hawkins and His Orchestra, 1940,* Alamac QSR 2417.

Hawkins, Coleman. *Coleman Hawkins,* Vogue CMDINT 9863 (Woody 'n' You, Disorder at the Border).

Hawkins, Coleman. *Hollywood Stampede,* Cap. M-11030.

Henderson, Fletcher. *Fletcher Henderson 1923,* BYG 529083 (Darktown Has a Gay White Way, Linger Awhile).

Henderson, Fletcher. *The Immortal Fletcher Henderson,* Milestone MLP 2005 (Swamp Blues, Hop Off).

Henderson, Fletcher. *Fletcher Henderson,* Black and White 730.584 (Hocus Pocus).

Henderson, Fletcher. *First Impressions,* Decca DL 79227 (Copenhagen, Stockholm Stomp, Fidgety Feet, Just Blues, Hop Off, Hot Mustard, Low Down on the Bayou).

Henderson, Fletcher. *Swing's the Thing,* Decca DL 79228 (House of David Blues, Down South Camp Meeting, Wrappin' It Up, Radio Rhythm).

Herman, Woody. *Woody Herman,* Everest Records FS 281 (Bijou).

Hines, Earl. *A Monday Date: 1928,* Milestone MLP 2012 (Congaine).

Hodges, Johnny. *Hodge Podge,* Epic EE 22011 (Rendezvous with Rhythm, Jeep's Blues).

Holiday, Billie. *Lady Day,* Col. CL 637 (Billie's Blues, What a Little Moonlight Can Do).

Holiday, Billie. *The Billie Holiday Story,* Columbia KG-32121-4. (Most titles mentioned are included in this six record set.)

Hubbard, Freddie. *Open Sesame,* Blue Note 4040 (One Mint Julep).

Hughes, Spike. *Spike Hughes and His All-American Orchestra,* London LL 1387 (Nocturne, Arabesque).

Jackson, Milt. *The Atlantic Years,* Atlantic SD 2–319.

Jazz at the Philharmonic. *Bird and Pres: The '46 Concert,* Verve VE 2–2518.

Jefferson, Blind Lemon. *The Immortal Blind Lemon Jefferson,* Milestone MLP 2004.

Johnson, Bunk. *Echoes from New Orleans,* Storyville 670 203 (with George Lewis).

Johnson, J. J. *The Finest of Kai Winding, J. J. Johnson,* Bethlehem BCP-6001.

Johnson, James P. *The Original James P. Johnson,* Folkways FJ 2850 (Snowy Morning Blues).

Johnson, James P. *Father of the Stride Piano,* Col. CL 1780 (Worried and Lonesome Blues, Carolina Shout).

Johnson, James P. *James P. Johnson Ragtime,* Biograph BLP-1009Q (After Tonight).

Johnson, Lonnie. *Lonnie Johnson,* Jazum 2.

Joplin, Scott. *Complete Works for Piano by Dick Hyman,* RCA CRL5-1106.

Joplin, Scott. *Piano Rags by Joshua Rifkin, 3 Vols.,* Nonesuch, H-71248, H-71264, H-71305.

Kenton, Stan. *Stan Kenton's Greatest Hits,* Cap. SM 2327.

Keppard, Freddie. *Freddie Keppard,* Herwin 101.

Kirby, John. *The John Kirby Sextet,* Classic Jazz CJ 22.

Kirk, Rahsaan Roland. *I Talk with the Spirits,* Limelight LS 86008.

Ledbetter, Huddie. *The Legendary Leadbelly,* Olympic 7103.

Lunceford, Jimmie. *Rhythm Is Our Business Vol. 1,* Decca DL 79237.

Lyttelton, Humphrey. *The Best of Humph 1949–56,* EMI PMC7147.

McKinney, William. *McKinney's Cotton Pickers Vol. 4,* Black and White FPM 1 7007.

Mezzrow, Mezz. *The Panassié Sessions,* RCA LPV 542.

Miller, Glenn. *A Memorial 1944–1969,* Victor GM 1 (String of Pearls).

Mingus, Charles. *The Best of Charles Mingus,* Atlantic SD 1555 (Pithecanthropus Erectus, Haitian Fight Song).

Mingus, Charles. *Mingus Ah Um,* Col. CS 8171 (Fables of Faubus, Goodbye Pork Pie Hat, Better Git It in Your Soul).

Mingus, Charles. *The Art of Charles Mingus,* Atlantic SD 2–302.

Modern Jazz Quartet. *Fontessa,* Atlantic 1231.

Modern Jazz Quartet. *The Modern Jazz Quartet,* Prestige 24005.

Modern Jazz Quartet. *First Recordings!,* Prestige 7749 (Vendome, La Ronde, Django).

Modern Jazz Quartet. *European Concert,* Atlantic SD 2–603 (Django).

Monk, Thelonious. *Sweets, Lips & Lots of Jazz,* Xanadu 123 (Indiana).

Monk, Thelonious. *Brilliance,* Milestone M47023 (Brilliant Corners).

Monk, Thelonious. *Monk & Coltrane,* Riverside 490 (Nutty, Trinkle Tinkle).

Monk, Thelonious. *Greatest Hits,* Riverside RLP 421.

Monk, Thelonious. *Genius of Modern Music Vol. 1,* Blue Note BLP 1510 (Ruby My Dear, 'Round About Midnight, Thelonious).

Monk, Thelonious. *Genius of Modern Music Vol. 2,* Blue Note 81511 (Straight, No Chaser).

Morton, Jelly Roll. *The Library of Congress Recordings, Vols. 1–8,* Classic Jazz Masters CJM 2–9.

Morton, Jelly Roll. *The King of New Orleans Jazz: Jelly Roll Morton,* RCA LPM-1649 (Sidewalk Blues, Smokehouse Blues, The Chant).

Morton, Jelly Roll. *Stomps and Joys,* RCA LPV 508 (Shreveport Stomp, Mournful Serenade).

Morton, Jelly Roll. *The Immortal Jelly Roll Morton,* Milestone MLP 2003.

Morton, Jelly Roll. *New Orleans Memories and Last Band Dates,* Atlantic SD2-308.

Moten, Bennie. *Bennie Moten's Kansas City Orchestra,* EMI PMC 7119 (South, 18th Street Strut).

Moten, Bennie. *Count Basie in Kansas City,* RCA LPV 514 (Toby, Blue Room, Prince of Wales).

Mulligan, Gerry. *Gerry Mulligan Tentette,* Cap. M-11029.

Navarro, Fats. *Nostalgia, Vols. 1, 2,* BYG 529 102, 103 (Be Bop Romp).

New Orleans Rhythm Kings. *New Orleans Rhythm Kings,* BYG 529.069.

Nichols, Herbie. *The Third World,* Blue Note BNLA45.

Noone, Jimmy. *At the Apex Club,* Decca DL 79235 (Monday Date, I Know That You Know, Apex Blues).

Oliver, Joseph. *The Immortal King Oliver,* Milestone MLP 2006 (Riverside Blues).

Oliver, Joseph. *King Oliver's Jazz Band,* EMI PMC 7032 (Riverside Blues, Dipper-mouth Blues).

Oliver, Joseph. *King Oliver and His Dixie Syncopators,* Decca DL 79246 (Sugar Foot Stomp).

Original Dixieland Jazz Band. *The Original Dixieland Jazz Band,* RCA LPV-547 (Livery Stable Blues, Tiger Rag).

Original Memphis Five. *The Original Memphis Five,* Black and White 741 115.

Parker, Charlie. *First Recordings!,* Onyx 221 (Body and Soul, Cherokee).

Parker, Charlie. *Jay McShann and His Orchestra,* Coral CP4 (Hootie Blues).

Parker, Charlie. *The Bird on Savoy,* BYG 529 121 (Tiny's Tempo).

Parker, Charlie. *Dizzy Gillespie: In the Beginning,* Prestige P-24030 (Groovin' High, Salt Peanuts, Shaw 'Nuff, Hot House).

Parker, Charlie. *The Complete Charlie Parker,* BYG 529 129 (Koko, Billie's Bounce, Now's the Time).

Parker, Charlie. *Cool Blues,* Saga ERO 8005.

Parker, Charlie. *Bird & Diz,* Saga ERO 8035.

Parker, Charlie. *Bongo Bop,* Saga ERO 8052.

Parker, Charlie. *Get Happy,* Saga ERO 8053 (Night in Tunisia).

Parker, Charlie. *Swedish Schnapps,* Verve V6-8010.

Parker, Charlie. *Jazz at Massey Hall,* Fantasy 86003 (Salt Peanuts, Perdido, Wee).

Parker, Charlie. *The Essential Charlie Parker,* Verve V6-8409 (Just Friends, Au Privave).

NOTE: The complete recordings of Charlie Parker on Dial and Savoy are now being reissued.

Peterson, Oscar. *Return Engagement,* Verve V3 HB 8842.

Pollack, Ben. *Ben Pollack and His Orchestra,* Sunbeam SB 136.

Powell, Bud. *The Jazz Legacy of Bud Powell,* Verve VSP 34 (Tempus Fugue-it).

Powell, Bud. *The Amazing Bud Powell,* Blue Note BST 81598.

Powell, Bud. *The Amazing Bud Powell Vol. 2,* Blue Note BST 81504 (Un Poco Loco, Dance of the Infidels, Glass Enclosure).

Powell, Bud. *Bud Powell,* Verve VE 2-2506.

Powell, Bud. *Bud Powell Trio,* Fantasy 86006.

Ra, Sun. *Live at the Donaueschingen and Berlin Festivals,* BASF 20748.

Raeburn, Boyd. *On the Air,* Hep Records Hep 1 (Boyd Meets Stravinsky, Tone Poem).

Ragtime. *Pastimes & Piano Rags by William Bolcom,* Nonesuch H-71299.

Ragtime. *Heliotrope Bouquet, by William Bolcom,* Nonesuch H-71257.

Ragtime. *Ragtime and Novelty Music Vol. 1,* Black and White Vol. 152.

Ragtime. *The City,* RBF Records RBF 17 (St. Louis Tickle).

Rainey, Ma. *Ma Rainey,* Milestone M 47021 (Blame It on the Blues, Leavin' This Morning).

Redman, Don. *Master of the Big Band,* RCA LPV 520.

Reinhardt, Django. *Django Reinhardt,* EMI 1 C 188–10395/96 (Ma Régulière, Carinosa, Si J'aime Suzy).

Reinhardt, Django. *Djangologie 1,* Pathe C 054–16001 (Griserie, Stardust, I Can't Give You Anything But Love).

Reinhardt, Django. *Django Reinhardt and the American Jazz Giants,* Prestige 7633.

Reinhardt, Django. *The Quintet of the Hot Club of France,* Decca ECM 2051 (Swing from Paris, Billets Doux, Three Little Words, Them There Eyes, China Boy).

Reinhardt, Django. *Django and His American Friends, Vol. 1,* EMI CLP 1890 (Stardust, Honeysuckle Rose, Crazy Rhythm).

Reinhardt, Django. *The Best of Django Reinhardt, Vols. 1, 2,* Cap. T-10457–8 (Solitude, Runnin' Wild).

Reinhardt, Django. *Django and His American Friends, Vol. 11,* EMI CLP 1907 (Montmartre, Low Cotton, Finesse, Solid Old Man).

Reinhardt, Django. *Memorial Vols. 2, 3,* Period SPL 1202–3 (Manoir de mes Rêves, Melodie au Crépuscule, Nuage, Songe d'Automne).

Rollins, Sonny. *Dizzy, Rollins and Stitt,* Verve V-8477 (Eternal Triangle).

Rollins, Sonny. *First Recordings!,* Prestige 7856.

Rollins, Sonny. *Saxophone Colossus,* Prestige 7326 (Blue Seven).

Rollins, Sonny. *Sonny Rollins,* BST 81542.

Russell, Luis. *Luis Russell,* Col. KG 32338 (Saratoga Shout, Panama).

Russell, Pee Wee. *Ask Me Now,* Impulse A-96.

Shearing, George. *Vol. II The Early Years,* Everest FS-236.

Shepp, Archie. *Four for Trane,* Impulse AS 71 (Syeeda's Song Flute, Cousin Mary, Naima, Rufus).

Shepp, Archie. *There's a Trumpet in My Soul,* Arista AL 1016.

Silver, Horace. *Horace Silver,* Blue Note BN-LA402-H2.

Smith, Bessie. NOTE: Columbia has issued the complete works of Bessie Smith in a 10-record set: Col. CG 33, CG 30126, CG 30818, CG 30450, CG 31093.

Smith, Jabbo. *The Ace of Rhythm,* MCA Records 510.139 (Take Me to the River).

Smith, Willie "the Lion". *Memorial,* Vogue DP 20 A.

Spanier, Muggsy. *The Great 16,* RCA LPM-1295.

Squadronaires. *London Jazz Scene: The 40's,* Ace of Clubs ACL 1121.

Stacy, Jess. *Ralph Sutton and Jess Stacy,* Ace of Hearts AH 39.

Stewart, Rex. *Things Ain't What They Used to Be,* RCA LPV-533 (Menelik, Subtle Slough, Linger Awhile).

Sullivan, Joe. *Piano,* Folkways FA 2851.

Tatum, Art. *The Art of Art,* Verve VSP-33.

Tatum, Art. *Solo Piano,* Cap. 5C052 80 800.

Tatum, Art. *Concert,* Aimez-vous le Jazz 62615 (Tea for Two, Tiger Rag, I Know That You Know).

Tatum, Art. *God Is in the House,* Onyx 205.

Taylor, Cecil. *Looking Ahead!,* Contemporary S7562.

Taylor, Cecil. *In Transition,* Blue Note BN-LA458-H2 (Sweet and Lovely, Charge 'Em Blues, Song).

Taylor, Cecil. *Unit Structures,* Blue Note BST 84237.

Teagarden, Jack. *"J.T.",* Ace of Hearts AH 168.

Teagarden, Jack. *Big T's Jazz,* Ace of Hearts AH 28.

Teagarden, Jack. *Jack Teagarden,* RCA LPV-528 (Tailspin Blues).

Teagarden, Jack. *The Golden Horn of Jack Teagarden,* Decca DL 4540 (Beale Street Blues).

Teagarden, Jack. *Bud Freeman and His All-Star Jazz,* Harmony HL 7046 (Jack Hits the Road).

Teschemacher, Frank. *The Chicagoans,* Decca DL 79231 (Wailin' Blues, Nobody's Sweetheart Now, China Boy).

Thomas, Joe. *Art Tatum 3,* MCA 510.105 (Stompin' at the Savoy, Battery Bounce).

Thornhill, Claude. *The Memorable Claude Thornhill,* Col. KG 32906 (Yardbird Suite).

Tristano, Lennie. *Crosscurrents,* Cap. M-11060 (Wow, Crosscurrent, Intuition).

Turner, Joe. *Boss of the Blues,* Atlantic 590.006.

Waller, Fats. *Fats Waller,* Black and White 730.660 (Alligator Crawl, Zonky, Blue Turning Grey).

Waller, Fats. *Ain't Misbehavin',* RCA LPM 1246 (Honeysuckle Rose, Ain't Misbehavin', The Joint Is Jumpin', Your Feet's Too Big, Hold Tight).
NOTE: The complete recordings of Fats Waller are currently being reissued on Black and White.

Watters, Lu. *Lu Watters' Yerba Buena Jazz Band,* Good Time Jazz L-12007.

Webb, Chick. *King of the Savoy,* Decca DL 79223 (Congo, Clap Hands, Here Comes Charlie).

Wells, Dicky. *Dicky Wells in Paris, 1937,* Prestige 7593 (Dicky Wells Blues, Between the Devil and the Deep Blue Sea, Lady Be Good).

Wilson, Teddy. *The Teddy Wilson Piano Solos,* Aimez-vous le Jazz 62876.

Wilson, Teddy. *Teddy Wilson's All-Stars,* Col. KG 31617 (Lady Be Good, Mary Had a Little Lamb, Just a Mood).

Young, Lester. *The Alternative Lester,* Tax m-8000 (Shoe Shine Boy, I Want a Little Girl, alternate masters).

Young, Lester. *Charlie Christian–Lester Young Together Again,* Jazz Archives JA-6 (I Never Knew).

Young, Lester. *Pres at His Very Best,* Trip TLP 5509 (I Never Knew, Afternoon of a Basie-ite).

Young, Lester. *The Lester Young Story,* Col. CG 33502 (Shoe Shine Boy, Lady Be Good).

Bibliography

Albertson, Chris. *Bessie*. New York: Stein and Day, 1972.

Allen, Walter C., and Rust, Brian. *King Joe Oliver*. London: Sidgwick and Jackson.

Allen, William Francis; Ware, Charles Pickard; and Garrison, Lucy McKim. *Slave Songs of the United States*. New York: Peter Smith, 1951.

Armstrong, Louis. *Satchmo: My Life in New Orleans*. New York: New American Library, 1955.

Asch, Moses, and Lomax, Alan, eds. *The Leadbelly Song Book*. New York: Oak Publications.

Balliett, Whitney. *New York Notes*. Boston: Houghton Mifflin, 1976.

Bechet, Sidney. *Treat It Gentle*. New York: Da Capo Press, 1975.

Beier, Ulli. "The Talking Drums of the Yoruba," *Journal of the African Music Society*, Vol. I, 1954.

Berendt, Joachim. *The Jazz Book*. New York: Lawrence Hill, 1975.

Blesh, Rudi. *Eight Lives in Jazz*. New York: Hayden, 1971.

———. *Shining Trumpets*. New York: Da Capo Press, 1975.

Blesh, Rudi, and Janis, Harriet. *They All Played Ragtime*. New York: Oak Publications, 1971.

Brunn, H. O. *The Story of the Original Dixieland Jazz Band*. Baton Rouge: Louisiana State University Press, 1960.

Buerkle, Jack V., and Barker, Danny. *Bourbon Street Black*. New York: Oxford University Press, 1973.

Charters, Samuel Barclay. *Jazz: New Orleans 1885–1963*. New York: Oak Publications, 1963.

———. *The Poetry of the Blues*. New York: Avon, 1970.

Chilton, John. *Billie's Blues*. New York: Stein and Day, 1975.

Cole, Bill. *John Coltrane*. New York: Schirmer Books, 1976.

———. *Miles Davis*. New York: William Morrow, 1974.

Collier, Graham. *Jazz*. London: Cambridge University Press, 1975.

Condon, Eddie, and O'Neal, Hank. *The Eddie Condon Scrapbook of Jazz*. New York: Galahad Books, 1973.

Courlander, Harold. *Negro Folk Music, U.S.A.* New York: Columbia University Press, 1963.

————. *The World of Earl Hines.* New York: Charles Scribner's Sons, 1977.

Dance, Stanley. *The World of Duke Ellington.* New York: Charles Scribner's Sons, 1970.

Delaunay, Charles. *Django Reinhardt.* London: Cassell.

Dexter, Dave, Jr. *The Jazz Story.* Englewood Cliffs: Prentice-Hall, 1964.

Ellington, Duke. *Music Is My Mistress.* New York: Doubleday, 1973.

Epstein, Dena J. "The Folk Banjo: A Documentary History," *Ethnomusicology,* Vol. XIV, Sept. 1975.

Ewen, David. *The Life and Death of Tin Pan Alley.* New York: Funk and Wagnall's, 1964.

Fairbairn, Ann. *Call Him George.* New York: Crown, 1961.

Feather, Leonard. *From Satchmo to Miles.* New York: Stein and Day, 1972.

————. *The Pleasures of Jazz.* New York: Horizon Press, 1976.

Fenner, Thomas P. *Cabin and Plantation Songs,* 1873.

Finkelstein, Sidney. *Jazz: A People's Music.* New York: Da Capo Press, 1975.

Foster, Pops, as told to Stoddard, Tom. *Pops Foster.* Berkeley: University of California Press, 1971.

Fox, Charles. *Fats Waller.* New York: A. S. Barnes, 1961.

————. *Jazz in Perspective.* London: British Broadcasting Corporation, 1969.

Freeman, Bud. *You Don't Look Like a Musician.* Detroit: Balamp Publishing, 1974.

Gammond, Peter. *Scott Joplin and the Ragtime Era.* New York: St. Martin's Press, 1975.

Gelatt, Roland. *The Fabulous Phonograph.* New York: Appleton-Century, 1965.

Gitler, Ira. *Jazz Masters of the Forties.* New York: Collier Books, 1974.

Gleason, Ralph J. *Celebrating the Duke.* New York: Dell Publishing, 1975.

Goffin, Robert. *Jazz: From the Congo to the Metropolitan.* New York: Da Capo Press, 1975.

Goldberg, Joe. *Jazz Masters of the Fifties.* New York: Macmillan, 1965.

Hadlock, Richard. *Jazz Masters of the Twenties.* New York: Collier Books, 1974.

Hammond, John. *John Hammond on Record.* New York: Summit Books, 977.

Handy, W. C. *Father of the Blues.* New York: Collier Books, 1970.

Hare, Maud Curey. *Six Creole Folk Songs.* New York: Carl Fischer, 1921.

Harris, Rex. *Jazz.* Harmondsworth: Penguin Books, 1952.

Hentoff, Nat. *Jazz Is.* New York: Random House, 1976.

————. *The Jazz Life.* New York: Da Capo Press, 1975.

Hentoff, Nat, and McCarthy, Albert J. *Jazz.* New York: Da Capo Press, 1975.

Hobson, Wilder. *American Jazz Music.* New York: W. W. Norton, 1939.

Hodier, André. *Jazz: Its Evolution and Essence.* New York: Grove Press, 1956.

Holiday, Billie, with Dufty, William. *Lady Sings the Blues.* New York: Lancer Books, 1965.

James, Burnett. *Bix Beiderbecke.* New York: A. S. Barnes, 1961.

James, Michael. *Dizzy Gillespie.* New York: A. S. Barnes, 1961.

————. *Miles Davis.* New York: A. S. Barnes, 1961.

Jewell, Derek. *Duke: A Portrait of Duke Ellington.* New York: W. W. Norton, 1977.

Jones, A. M. *Africa and Indonesia: The Evidence of the Xylophone and Other Musical and Cultural Factors.* Leiden: E. J. Brill, 1971.

————. *Studies in African Music.* London: Oxford University Press, 1959.

Jones, LeRoi. *Blues People.* New York: William Morrow, 1963.

Jones, Max, and Chilton, John. *Louis.* Boston: Little, Brown, 1971.

Kaminsky, Max, with Hughes, V. E. *My Life in Jazz.* London: Jazz Book Club, 1965.

Keepnews, Orin, and Grauer, Bill, Jr. *A Pictorial History of Jazz.* New York: Crown, 1955.

Keil, Charles. *Urban Blues.* Chicago: University of Chicago Press, 1969.

Kirkeby, Ed, in collaboration with Schiedt, Duncan P., and Traill, Sinclair. *Ain't Misbehavin',* New York: Da Capo Press, 1975.

Kmen, Henry A. *Music in New Orleans.* Baton Rouge: Louisiana State University Press, 1966.

Kofsky, Frank. *Black Nationalism and the Revolution in Music.* New York: Pathfinder Press, 1970.

Krehbiel, Henry Edward. *Afro-American Folksongs: A Study in Racial and National Music.* New York: G. Schirmer, 1914.

Lambert, G. E. *Duke Ellington.* New York: A. S. Barnes, 1961.

———. *Johnny Dodds.* New York: A. S. Barnes, 1961.

Lomax, Alan. *Mister Jelly Roll.* Berkeley: University of California Press, 1950.

Maultsby, Portia K. "Music of Northern Independent Black Churches During the Ante-Bellum Period," *Ethnomusicology,* Vol. XIX, Sept. 1975.

McCarthy, Albert. *The Dance Band Era.* London: Spring Books, 1971.

———. *Louis Armstrong.* New York: A. S. Barnes, 1961.

———. *Piano Jazz #2.* London: 1945

Meryman, Richard. *Louis Armstrong — A Self-Portrait.* New York: Eakins Press, 1971.

Metfessel, Milton. *Phonophotography in Folk Music.* Chapel Hill: University of North Carolina Press, 1928.

Mezzrow, Milton, and Wolfe, Bernard. *Really the Blues.* New York: Dell Publishing, 1946.

Mingus, Charles, ed. by King, Nel. *Beneath the Underdog.* New York: Alfred A. Knopf, 1971.

Murray, Albert. *Stomping the Blues.* New York: McGraw-Hill, 1976.

Nanry, Charles, ed. *American Music: From Storyville to Woodstock.* New Brunswick: Transaction Books, 1972.

Newton, Francis. *The Jazz Scene.* New York: Da Capo Press, 1975.

Nketia, J. H. Kwabena. *The Music of Africa.* New York: W. W. Norton, 1974.

Oliver, Paul. *Bessie Smith.* New York: A. S. Barnes, 1961.

———. *The Meaning of the Blues.* New York: Collier Books, 1963.

———. *Savannah Syncopators.* New York: Stein and Day, 1970.

Ostransky, Leroy. *Understanding Jazz.* Englewood Cliffs: Prentice-Hall, 1977.

Panassié, Hugues. *Louis Armstrong.* New York: Charles Scribner's Sons, 1971.

———. *The Real Jazz.* New York: Smith and Durrell, 1942.

Parrish, Lydia. *Slave Songs of the Georgia Sea Islands.* New York: Creative Age Press, 1942.

Ramsey, Frederic, Jr., and Smith, Charles Edward, eds. *Jazzmen.* New York: Harcourt, Brace, 1939.

Reed, Addison Walker. "Scott Joplin." Unpublished dissertation.

Reisner, Robert George. *Bird: The Legend of Charlie Parker.* New York: Da Capo Press, 1973.

Rivelli, Pauline, and Levin, Robert. *Black Giants.* New York: World Publishing, 1970.

Roach, Hildred. *Black American Music.* Boston: Crescendo Publishing, 1973.

Roberts, John Storm. *Black Music of Two Worlds.* New York: Praeger, 1972.

Rublowsky, John. *Black Music in America.* New York: Basic Books, 1971.

Russell, Ross. *Bird Lives!* New York: Charterhouse, 1973.

———. *Jazz Style in Kansas City and the Southwest.* Berkeley: University of California Press, 1971.

Sargeant, Winthrop. *Jazz: Hot and Hybrid.* New York: Da Capo Press, 1975.

———. "Types of Quecha Melody," *Musical Quarterly,* April 1934.

Schafer, William J. *Brass Bands & New Orleans Jazz.* Baton Rouge: Louisiana State University Press, 1977.

Schuller, Gunther. *Early Jazz.* New York: Oxford University Press, 1968.

Shapiro, Nat, and Hentoff, Nat. *Hear Me Talkin' to Ya.* New York: Dover, 1966.

———. *The Jazz Makers.* New York: Rinehart, 1957.

Shaw, Arnold. *52nd Street.* New York: Da Capo, 1971.

Simpkins, Cuthbert Ormond. *Coltrane.* New York: Herndon House, 1975.

Smith, Charles Edward, with Ramsey, Frederic, Jr.; Rogers, Charles Payne; and Russell, William. *The Jazz Record Book.* New York: Smith and Durrell, 1942.

Smith, Jay D., and Guttridge, Len. *Jack Teagarden: The Story of a Jazz Maverick.* London: Cassell, 1960.

Smith, Willie the Lion, with Hoefer, George. *Music on My Mind.* New York: Da Capo Press, 1975.

Southern, Eileen. *The Music of Black Americans.* New York: W. W. Norton, 1971.

———. *Readings in Black American Music.* New York: W. W. Norton, 1971.

Spellman, A. B. *Black Music: Four Lives.* New York: Schocken Books, 1970.

Stearns, Marshall W. *The Story of Jazz.* New York: Oxford University Press, 1956.

Stewart, Rex. *Jazz Masters of the Thirties.* New York: Macmillan, 1972.

Stewart-Baxter, Derrick. *Ma Rainey and the Classic Blues Singers.* New York: Stein and Day, 1970.

Sudhalter, Richard M., and Evans, Philip R., with Dean-Myatt, William. *Bix, Man & Legend.* New Rochelle: Arlington House, 1974.

Thomas, J. C. *Chasin' the Trane.* New York: Doubleday, 1975.

Toll, Robert C. *Blacking Up.* New York: Oxford University Press, 1974.

Ulanov, Barry. *Duke Ellington.* New York: Creative Age, 1946.

Vance, Joel. *Fats Waller: His Life and Times.* Chicago: Contemporary Books, 1977.

Walton, Ortiz M. *Music: Black, White and Blue.* New York: William Morrow, 1972.

Waterman, Richard Alan. "African Influence on the Music of the Americas," in *Acculturation in the Americas.* Chicago: University of Chicago Press, 1952.

Wells, Dicky, as told to Dance, Stanley. *The Night People.* Boston: Crescendo Publishing, 1971.

Williams, Martin. *Jazz Masters in Transition, 1957–69.* New York: Macmillan, 1970.

———. *The Jazz Tradition.* New York: Oxford University Press, 1970.

———. *Jelly Roll Morton.* New York: A. S. Barnes, 1963.

———. *King Oliver.* New York: A. S. Barnes, 1961.

Williams, Martin, ed. *Jazz Panorama.* London: Jazz Book Club with Crowell-Collier Press, 1965.

Williams-Jones, Pearl. "Afro-American Gospel Music: A Crystallization of the Black Aesthetic," *Ethnomusicology,* Vol. XIX, Sept. 1975.
Wilmer, Valerie. *Jazz People.* Indianapolis: Bobbs-Merrill, 1970.
Wonk, Dalt. "The Creoles of Color," *New Orleans* magazine, May 1976.
Work, John W. *American Negro Songs.* New York: Howell, Soskin, 1940.

Index